A COMPLETE GUIDE TO PRESSED GLASS

A Complete Guide
to
Pressed Glass

By
BOB H. BATTY

Drawings by John T. Hendricks

A book giving extensive and accurate coverage to three hundred patterns of pressed glass, with titles, description, discussion, and accurate and beautiful pen and ink drawings.

PELICAN PUBLISHING COMPANY GRETNA 1978

In Memoriam

RUTH WEBB LEE   MINNIE WATSON KAMM

SAMUEL T. MILLARD   E. MCCALMY BELKNAP

GEORGE S. MCKEARIN   BESSIE M. LINDSEY

ALICE HULETT METZ

God Bless Them.

Library of Congress Cataloging in Publication Data

Batty, Bob H
  A complete guide to pressed glass.

  Bibliography: p. 254
  1. Pressed glass—United States. 2. Pattern
glass—United States. 3. Glassware—United States—
History—19th century. 4. Batty, Bob H.—Art
collections. I. Title.
NK5203.B37   748.2'913   77-19211
ISBN 0-88289-057-3

Poem "Pitcher Collection" by Ethel Jacobson is reprinted
from *Better Homes and Gardens*, copyright 1952, Meredith
Publishing Company, Des Moines, Iowa.

Manufactured in the United States of America
Published by Pelican Publishing Company, Inc.
630 Burmaster Street, Gretna, Louisiana 70053
Designed by Oscar Richard

Contents

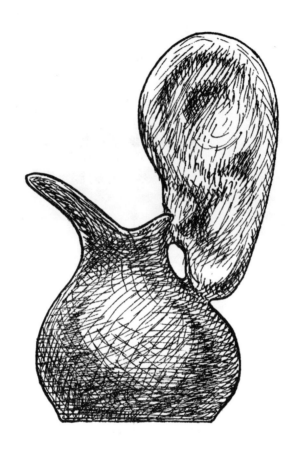

LITTLE PITCHERS HAVE BIG EARS

Pitcher Collection

There are pitchers of tin and pitchers of brass;
Pitchers of luster and cranberry glass;
Hand painted pitchers like kittens and cows
With tails for their handles and garlanded brows.

There are china ones teamed with a plumbingless basin;
Gold ones depicting the exploits of Jason;
Pitchers like Toby, and pitchers that wear
Inscriptions extolling the Danbury Fair.

There are pitchers for cream, there are pitchers for honey,
And pitchers for hiding the grocery money;
But essence of pitcherdom, like it or not:
Some drip a little, the rest drip a lot!

ETHEL JACOBSON

Preface

This is a collector's and dealer's book to aid in correctly identifying three hundred patterns of American pressed glass. It covers three hundred of the author's extensive collection of approximately twenty-one hundred patterns. Each pattern is illustrated with a black and white drawing. Accurate descriptions, measurements, and discussion identify each subject. About one hundred and twenty-five patterns are named, illustrated, and described for the first time.

Some foreign patterns are shown here for purposes of comparison. A few previously named patterns are used to assist the collector and dealer in cases where there is (1) a confusion of multiple titles, (2) difficulty in distinguishing between similar patterns, (3) new information available about reproductions, and (4) new information about date of manufacture, identity of manufacturer, and list of items made in the pattern.

Acknowledgments

I owe a deep debt of gratitude to my teachers on the subject of American pressed glass. Fortune prevented my knowing any of them personally or sitting at their feet. Constant use of their texts has resulted in all their books becoming ragged, frayed, filled with notations and cross references, and coming apart at their seams. They are invaluable, and under no circumstances could they be discarded and replaced by shiny new ones. Through their works I have come to respect these authorities highly, to admire their pioneering accomplishments and cherish a strong inner feeling of friendship for them. They have furnished excellent texts and are due warm praise for their labor and their sacrifice. They are: Ruth Webb Lee; Minnie Watson Kamm, Ph.D.; Samuel T. Millard, M.D.; E. McCalmy Belknap; George S. and Helen McKearin; and Laura Woodside Watkins (see Bibliography).

Until I began this volume, I did not realize how puny my individual efforts would be. There was no question in my mind as to the innate goodness of people, but present experience has shown me how much more friendly, helpful, kind, and good they really are. Most of my help has come from strangers whom I know only through correspondence. They have scoured the countryside to secure source material to make this work possible. They have been untiring in their searching, have given me courage, kindly urging me on or making helpful, constructive suggestions and criticisms. Those I met were wonderful. Those I did not meet were equally so. Charlotte Bolton, Herb and Thelma Bowles, Ken Chapman, Elbert Fielden, Liz Thompson, Mary Bee Schroeder, Joe Lindeman, Dorothy Mostert, Myrtle Burger, Victoria Krumsick, Birdie Crawford, Oskar Rusch, Ellen Guthridge, Vera Gibson, Mrs. Hancock, and Betty Gorman Kaye have been untiring in their efforts.

To the following dealers over the country I wish to say thank you: George Abraham and Gilbert May, Granville, Massachusetts; Mrs. Bennett, St. Louis, Missouri; Charlotte H. Bolton, Georgetown, Massachusetts; Mary Bee and Carl Schroeder, Route 1, Alexander, Arkansas; Nelson Rapp, Martinsville, New Jersey; Herbert H. and Thelma Bowles, Assinippi, Massachusetts; Elizabeth Thompson, Paris, Texas; the late Myrtle G. Burger, Washington, Missouri; G. L. Tilden, Northboro, Massachusetts; J. Alfred Way, Orange, Massachusetts; Elbert H. Fielden, Owensboro, Kentucky; Alice M. Walker, Davenport, Iowa; Maude B. Feld, New York, New York; Mariam Goode, Phillipsburg, Kansas; Oskar Rusch, Mt. Angel, Oregon; Mrs. E. B. Skilton, Downington, Pennsylvania; Victoria Krumsick, Kansas City, Missouri.

Harold Hungerford, Detroit, Michigan; Mrs. Karl W. Kranz, Hamburg, New York; Louise Marvin, Pacific Palisades, California; Kenneth Johnson, Plymouth, Massachusetts; Mrs. T. R. Joseph, Williamson, West Virginia; Bertha M. Shelby, Kirkwood, Missouri; Dorothy K. Dawson, East Milton, Massachusetts; Gladys Cavallero, Davis, California; Mrs. James A. Boehner, Denver, Colorado; Alice M. Bohn, Napoleon, Ohio; Birdie Crawford, Potts Camp, Mississippi; Madeline Clugh, Natick, Massachusetts; Lucile and Paul Emerson, Geneva, New York; Joe Lindeman, Middletown, Ohio.

Bob F. Liffingwell, Rochester, New York; B. E. Neves, Cincinnati, Ohio; Pearl Bradley Henshaw, Buzzards Bay, Massachusetts; Mary White, Wellsburg, West Virginia; Shirley Eileen

Shattuck, Reading, Massachusetts; Grace L. Hogan, Roslindale, Massachusetts; Ann Aslan, Patterson, New Jersey; Mrs. Lyndall Harlow, Lewisburg, West Virginia; Lorene Marshal, Springdale, Pennsylvania; Bill Morgan, Decatur, Illinois; Dorothy Mostert, Arkadelphia, Arkansas, and Houston, Texas; and Kenneth M. Chapman and Garland Kennard, Ripley, Ohio.

When the way seemed darkest, there was the ever-present friend to lend encouragement, give a kindly pat on the back, inflate the ego, and encourage new endeavor. To these I am most grateful: Oliver Kamm, Ph.D., Grosse Pointe, Michigan (widower of Minnie Watson Kamm); Charles A. Jacobus, Little Rock, Arkansas; Young M. Orsburn, North Little Rock, Arkansas; the late Dr. Henry M. Owen, Little Rock, Arkansas; Helen Wycoff, Little Rock, Arkansas; the late Kate Clark Ward, Pascagoula, Mississippi; Louise Otts, North Little Rock, Arkansas; Mr. and Mrs. L. G. Crowe, St. Louis, Missouri, and Monroe, Louisiana; Ellis Doyle Herron, former Director of the Museum of Science and Natural History, Little Rock, Arkansas; Lydia Buchanan, Dallas, Texas; Judge and Mrs. Boland Turner, Washington, D.C.; Francis Ferris Hall, Highland Park, Illinois; Allen J. Hodges, Rockey River, Ohio; Lois B. Brantley, Texarkana, Arkansas; Earl E. Jones and Harry Bullard, Dallas, Texas; Claudie Ambrose, Albuquerque, New Mexico.

Emma B. Sowards, Texarkana, Arkansas; Max L. Herter, Union City, Indiana; Mrs. Clinton A. Sharpe, Knoxville, Illinois; Peg Rhoda, Oconomowoc, Wisconsin; Mr. and Mrs. Woodrow W. Harrelson, Jonesboro, Arkansas; Henry J. Kavanaugh, Mandeville and New Orleans, Louisiana; Marion La Masney, Chattanooga, Tennessee; Aylene Ragland, Fort Smith, Arkansas; Ralph and Martha Templeton, Fullerton, California; Ellen Guthridge, Little Rock, Arkansas; Charles Albright, Little Rock, Arkansas; Ouida Lawson, Little Rock, Arkansas; Eunice Sims, Little Rock, Arkansas; Elizabeth Collins, Little Rock, Arkansas; Elizabeth Urton, Little Rock, Arkansas; Flosada Boyd Huff, Star City, Arkansas; Ercil F. Brown, North Little Rock, Arkansas; Mayselle D. Burchfield, Little Rock, Arkansas; Minnie Lee and Etta Neal Mayhan, Little Rock, Arkansas; Mr. and Mrs. Rufus Crews, North Little Rock, Arkansas; Jean V. Harper, Conway, Arkansas; Jack L. Zelsman, Little Rock, Arkansas; Alton and Mattie Lou Jameson, Little Rock, Arkansas; Mr. and Mrs. Lowell C. Thompson, North Little Rock, Arkansas; Helen K. Hill, Waco, Texas; Loyce Stewart, Little Rock, Arkansas; Louis J. Oberste, North Little Rock, Arkansas; Karl Baresch, Little Rock, Arkansas; W. Stanley McLemore, Little Rock, Arkansas; Mr. and Mrs. Charles B. Righter, Iowa City, Iowa.

Dr. Wayne B. Stone of Little Rock, Arkansas, was more than helpful in the preparation of this volume. He has read and weighed every sentence. He wanted to know the why on syntax, orthography, punctuation, grammar, statement of fact, choice of words, lucidity, verbosity, and any other feature he felt might be improved. He cheerfully spent untold hours in his effort to assist. He can only be repaid with friendship and affection.

Special praise is due Mrs. Stanley W. (Melba) Yates, Mrs. Jesse F. (Sarah Emily) Smith, Mrs. Robert (Betty Louise) Rutledge, and Mrs. Doyle (Peggy Jane) Covington for their assistance in proofreading and correcting the manuscript. Their cheerfulness, patience, and enthusiasm were infectious.

I am deeply indebted to John T. Hendricks, from Little Rock (Geyer Springs), Arkansas, and Amarillo, Texas. This artist, who as a boy was a member of my Boy Scout troop, did all the artwork for this volume. He strove continually to do each drawing exactly as desired, often suggested better methods, and in many ways assisted in getting the work done. He was a most agreeable co-worker. He did all the artwork used here.

Special thanks are due the following for granting permission to me to use certain material and make references to other writings about glass: Mrs. Samuel T. Millard, for granting permission to make numerous references to the three books on glass by Dr. Millard; Helen McKearin, for permission to use lists of items known to have been manufactured and listed in McKearin's *American Glass*; Edwin G. Warman, for permission to use his lists of items known to have been made in a pattern, and for permission to make many references to his works; J. Stanley Brothers, Jr., for permission to make several references to patterns in his *Thumbnail Sketches*; Crown Publishers, for informing me that no permission was necessary for making reference to patterns in *Milk Glass* by E. McCalmy Belknap; *Better Homes and Gardens* (Meredith Publishing Company), for permission to use the poem "Pitcher Collection" by Ethel Jacobson; and *Spinning Wheel, the Magazine for Collectors*, for permission to use material from their publication.

A COMPLETE GUIDE TO PRESSED GLASS

LYRE

The molten flow of lead and sand
 First met within the mold
To bring us priceless beauty; here
 The treasure we behold.

The elements of earth combined
 With skills of men and fire
To fashion first, for all to see,
 The pattern known as "Lyre."

As patriarch of pattern glass,
 The Lyre plays the role
Most fittingly—and brings to man
 Sweet music for his soul!

      —ERCIL F. BROWN

Introduction

Minnie Watson Kamm used a considerable amount of material from my collection of pattern glass creamers in volumes seven and eight of her Pitcher Books. It was her intention to use still other pieces from my collection in *A Ninth Pitcher Book*, but her untimely death prevented its completion. Her husband, Oliver Kamm, made the journey from Grosse Pointe, Michigan, to Little Rock to return my creamers, turn Mrs. Kamm's partially completed notes and drawings over to me, and insist that I complete *A Ninth Pitcher Book*. Circumstances beyond our control, however, prevented my using any of her work in this book.

My reasons for undertaking this project were: (1) it was a challenge; (2) I had information on previously described patterns that should be published; (3) my collection contained many pressed glass patterns still unnamed and unlisted; and (4) the book is needed.

Mrs. Kamm began the introduction to her *Fifth Pitcher Book* with this statement: "No one is more surprised than the writer that this series of small books on pattern glass has now attained the number five, and yet the subject of domestic pattern glass is by no means exhausted. When one firm could ship fifteen carloads of pressed glass in a single day (McKee, 1894) and another, one and one-half million tumblers in a year (Rochester, during the Eighties), the magnitude of the business can be appreciated."

To give some additional indication of the broad scope of the subject, one need only say that Mrs. Kamm found ample material for three additional books after book five. The reader will find many patterns described and illustrated for the first time in this volume. In addition, my collection contains hundreds of other patterns that need to be named and illustrated in still other books, and I have by no means located all of them. The search requires more time and more funds than I possess.

My study of pattern glass tempts me to make a prediction. I fully believe that when the subject of American pressed glass is completely covered, we will have a total of between forty-five hundred and five thousand patterns. Even then, some will probably escape us. Certainly it will give the discriminating collector an extensive field from which to make selections. No apologies are made for using late patterns in this book. What a boon it would be today if some writer of the 1860s had written about the late patterns of that day, or subsequent authors, of the 1870s, 1880s, and 1890s. Today's patterns will be priceless keepsakes in the years to come.

Some patterns that are shown appear unsightly and unworthy. It is not my mission to determine which patterns shall and shall not be collected. That is left to those who feel they have a divine mission to tell their neighbor what they should garner and cherish. Botanists did not refuse to name and describe skunk cabbage because it smelled bad, or poison ivy because it caused skin irritation.

Imitation cut glass is a case in point. Many such patterns are illustrated and described in this book. This was done for three reasons: (1) imitation cut glass patterns are part and parcel of the American pressed glass family; (2) they are loved, cherished, and collected by many cultured and intelligent people; (3) such patterns have been exceedingly popular, as attested by the fact they were made in such a multiplicity of design, by so many glass manufacturers, and in such staggering quantities. Could so many people have been entirely wrong? Personally, I find many to be beautiful, while others—like some of the non-imitation cut glass motifs—I see as abominations. To blanket all imitation cut glass patterns as beyond the pale and beneath the dignity of a discriminating person is ridiculous.

One of our self-acknowledged authorities on American pressed glass derides all imitation cut glass in just such a manner and "expertizes" that no one should even mention such unworthy glass, much less illustrate and describe it. Not being an authority on the subject and certainly no expert (I have heard an expert described as a worn-out fountain), I can describe and illustrate it without a blush. I adore many of them—as our forefathers and early manufacturers did. In fact, I would hitch up the old mule and plow the lower forty on a hot day for any one of five or six of the following imitation cut glass creamers not now in my possession. The list contains such "unworthy" imitation cut glass patterns as these: ARGUS, ASHBURTON, BAKEWELL'S BLOCK, BIGLER, BLAZE, COLONIAL, DIAMOND POINT, DIAMOND THUMBPRINT, ETRUSCAN, EUGENIE, EUREKA, EXCELSIOR, FOUR PETAL, FLUTE, GOTHIC, HAMILTON, HONEYCOMB (St. Louis cut), HUBER, ICICLE, MIRROR, PILLAR, PRESSED BLOCK, PRISM, SANDWICH STAR, SAXON, SAWTOOTH, SUNBURST, THISTLE (very early), THUMBPRINT, VICTORIA, WAFFLE, WAFFLE AND THUMBPRINT, BLOCK AND THUMBPRINT, HOURGLASS, and HINOTO.

Counteracting the late patterns used in this volume are many as old and fine as any in American glass literature.

Articles of rare beauty or great price are likely to be copied or reproduced. Emulating superior quality is commendable. It becomes pernicious when employed to deceive. Not everyone can conceive and create a worthwhile object or one of sheer excellence. If one cannot, then it is probably better to copy a worthwhile example. Take the average man with an ordinary kit of tools, who can fix things or make something similar to what he has seen. Perhaps his wife wants a stool for the living room, something really nice. He sees a magnificent stool in a museum. He makes a sketch, then painstakingly strives to duplicate the original. His wife is delighted. Should he have lugged in a thick flat stone? Or should he have sawed off a short section of a log and used that? The answer is obvious. Most progress and advancement is made by improving on conditions, things, and knowledge. Immeasurable science and know-how had to be available as a basis for developing the atomic bomb.

Reproductions themselves are to be desired. It is only when they border on counterfeits and are produced to deceive or defraud that they become detestable. Much of our reproduced pressed glass of today is marked and sold as reproduction. Unless the mark is of a permanent nature, it can be removed and sold as an antique by the unscrupulous. A permanent pressed date on each piece would thwart such practices. Some present-day manufacturers are parceling out a few pieces here and there with no other object than to make money.

Patterns of pressed glass are not usually reproduced until they become scarce and popular demands drive the price to fantastic heights. Also it is well to bear in mind that when a reproduction of a pattern is made, it is usually a goblet and not a creamer. A collector would want only one creamer, whereas he would buy six, eight, or even twelve goblets. The reproducer is shrewd enough to know that selling twelve items to one collector creates a larger market and returns a better profit.

There are, however, some brighter aspects of the reproduction problem. This becomes apparent when we realize that many more reproductions of pattern glass were made during its heyday from 1865 to 1895 than are being made today. Reproductions made then have attained a place of their own now. For example, I have a soda-lime creamer dating from the 1880s. It was a reproduction of the early flint TULIP AND SAWTOOTH pattern of the 1860s. The minimum price for which the reproduction could be bought today would be about $20. Time may do the same for some present-day reproductions.

It is also comforting to know that probably no more than ten patterns have been reproduced in all items. Some of these are: ROSE IN SNOW ROUND, MOON AND STAR, HEAVY PANELED GRAPE, WILDFLOWER, DAISY AND BUTTON, and DAISY AND BUTTON WITH THUMBPRINT. Also, of the nearly five thousand patterns originally produced, probably no more than fifty to sixty patterns have been reproduced in one item or at most two or three items. That means we have hundreds of patterns that have never been reproduced. If too many of us start collecting a few patterns and begin bidding against each other for scarce pieces, we will create a climate for fakes, and fakers will supply the demand.

Fakes and reproductions present some puzzling questions I cannot answer. Let us suppose that a company purchased molds to make an entire table setting of pressed glass in 1881 and two years later the plant was destroyed by fire, but the molds were saved. Suppose the plant was then rebuilt and the same pattern was again produced in the same molds. Would they be reproductions? If the intervening period were ten years, or even fifty years, at just what date would they cease to be the original items and become reproductions? On the other hand, if no fire occurred and if a pattern were kept in continuous production until the present time, would the present-day item be an original or a reproduction? Who can say?

Much pattern glass is being pressed today in the original molds. One factory owns some 150 such molds and is actively pressing glass in them. Other molds are owned by individuals who lease them to glass factories, thus insuring a steady income. (See Appendix for alphabetical listing of known articles that have been reproduced.)

People often ask how old an item has to be before it becomes antique. This is a relative matter entirely, and there is no fixed rule. For instance, a range of mountains twenty-five thousand years old would be new. A silver teapot, if dropped, can have the dents removed and continue a long and useful life. Probably two hundred years would place it as a genuine antique. An early flint glass creamer, which will not tolerate being dropped and cannot have its dents removed, is relatively as old at eighty-five years as the teapot at two hundred. The writer at three score and twelve is an accepted antique. An unrefrigerated egg becomes an antique after three weeks.

The conception that anything made before 1830 is an antique was adopted by our country to regulate tariffs. It should have been established on a sliding scale so as to advance a year every twelve months. The prevalent practice of accepting 1830 as the demarcation date for classifying antiques is absurd. The 1830 date was adopted in 1930 and thus, at the time, covered articles made at least 100 years earlier. Today articles have to be 148 years old to be considered antiques rather than 100. If the 1830 date is adhered to, think of how few antiques we will have by A.D. 2930.

Suppose nothing made since 1830 is an antique. Then only the Du Ponts, Vanderbilts, Rockefellers, and Mellons could buy one. I have a collection of which I am quite proud, yet only a few of mine were made before 1830. No pressed glass was made prior to 1827. Is my collection worthless? Surely not.

A few years ago a collector sold several hundred flasks that had been made after 1800. He retained only those made prior to that date. Some of the individual flasks brought from eight hundred to fifteen hundred dollars. How many persons could, or would, afford so expensive a hobby? The price of one flask would be more than thousands of collectors could afford to lavish on an entire collection. Are those unable to afford such expensive baubles to be denied the pleasure of collecting something within their reach? I abhor a snob. Nothing in this book will appeal to such a person. May it appeal to just plain people like myself—average middle-class Americans. If they are interested in collecting, then good luck to them in their quest. To each his own, whether the collection be exotic plants, rich husbands, 15-carat diamonds, Sandwich cup plates, matchbook covers, Victorian furniture, coins, Blue Willow Ware, Sheffield plate, bad debts, advanced degrees, stamps, oriental rugs, Meissen figurines, Rembrandts, or pressed glass.

It is well to remember that no pressed glass was made before 1827, the year that the first machine was invented for such a purpose. We should also recollect that very little of the glass produced between 1827 and 1857 is now available to collectors. Most of it has long been in museums and private collections. When a piece does show up in a shop it is usually very expensive. Therefore, when the average collector starts gathering American pressed glass, he is forced to confine his purchases to glass made after the 1860s.

In buying from private individuals, the collector should generally discount the claimed age of a piece. The following example will illustrate the point. A lady called and offered me first chance at some glass she was forced to dispose of. She was giving up an old mansion and moving into a small apartment. Upon arriving at her home, I found her pieces already well picked over. She did, however, have a pressed glass water pitcher which she "knew" was over 200 years old and for which she asked an exorbitant price. (Remember, it could not have been made before 1827.) Her explanation of its extreme age was arrived at as follows: Her grandmother had it all her life and lived to be 90 years old. It was in her mother's possession for her entire lifetime and she also lived to be 90. That made 180 years. Her mother had been dead for 20 years. Altogether this totaled 200 years. This was intriguing, and her grandmother was indeed a remarkable woman. She received the pitcher on the day of her birth, cared for it through infancy and childhood, and died in childbirth at the age of 90 when her mother was born. Her mother likewise cared for the piece through 90 long years, which is also remarkable. As a matter of fact, the water pitcher was a well-known pattern, first produced by the manufacturer in 1910, and worth only a small part of the price asked. I suppose she is still the proud owner.

Many people will tell you a piece is over 100 years old. The age all too often, however, may have been arrived at in much the same dubious manner. If made during the 1860s, it is a bit over 100 years old. Most of the old pressed glass found in our shops today was produced between 1870 and 1900 and is not particularly old.

Several English and foreign creamers are shown here. This is to assist collectors and dealers in differentiating between American and foreign pressed glass. Since World War II there has been a rapid increase in the quantity of English glass imported into the United States. Shops everywhere now have pieces in stock. Most of it is easy to distinguish from domestic ware. Some, however, will baffle the most expert. Perhaps a general idea can be found here as to what most of it looks like. If the reader can do this, he will not buy English or foreign glass thinking it is American, and the space so devoted will have been worthwhile.

The system used by Minnie Watson Kamm for showing pattern titles will also be used here. Where a new title is assigned, it is shown in italicized capitals. Roman capitals have been used for titles previously assigned.

As Mrs. Kamm did, I have used creamers when available. She used them almost exclusively and Dr. Millard illustrated only goblets. Mrs. Lee illustrated and used whatever items were available in a pattern. In some ways her choice of articles was preferable. Because of its radically different shape, a creamer, goblet, or plate may show such a different arrangement of the pressed pattern that it is almost impossible to say any two are of the same pattern. By showing all three together, the difficulty is avoided. The disadvantages of the system lie in the increased space, and the added cost of the necessary art work. These can well price a book out of circulation. By and large, creamers show the design as well as any other item of a pattern. In my case, creamers were available and were, therefore, used.

Black-and-white pen-and-ink drawings are used exclusively in this volume. They are, in most instances, far superior to photographs for showing the details of a pattern. The art of photographing glass has made great advances in recent years, but it still leaves much to be desired. Because of its crystal clearness and its characteristic of reflecting light, glass presents many problems to the photographer. In a photograph of a clear hollow piece such as a goblet or creamer, the design is often confusing because it shows the design on both the anterior and posterior side. This sometimes makes it impossible to identify the pattern from the picture. This disadvantage is not present in a black-and-white drawing. In illustrating marbled glass, both photography and drawings have effect, but the design cannot be seen. In the drawing, the exact opposite will result. Many of the photographs in our glass literature are so indistinct it is impossible to identify the pattern. They thus defeat their sole purpose.

A few items shown in this volume are borrowed. This is noted in the discussion of each such individual pattern. All other patterns are from my collection of approximately twenty-six hundred pattern glass creamers, representing some twenty-one hundred patterns. The collection was presented to the Little Rock Museum of Science and Natural History, where it will be on permanent display.

1— HARP

The writer considers this piece, which is sometimes called LYRE, to be about the oldest and rarest pressed glass creamer he has encountered and thinks it dates from the 1830s to 1840s. The creamer is unknown to authorities on pressed glass, though they are familiar with the pattern and recognize it as being one of the most venerable. This piece was pressed in a spillholder mold without the base. The upper part was first tooled into the rim and lip, and then the handle was applied. Pieces in this pattern are seldom seen on the market, though the spillholder is most often found. Spillholders sat on the mantlepiece in the living room and were not as regularly handled and washed as the table articles. Thus, they escaped many chances of being broken. This creamer was bought from a shop on Cape Cod, Sandwich, Massachusetts.

Ruth Webb Lee, in her *Early American Pressed Glass*, Pattern 48, pages 141-43, Plate 14, shows pieces of the pattern and calls it HARP. She says it was made by McKee Brothers of Pittsburgh during the 1850s, but she believes it was also made at Sandwich at an earlier date. Samuel T. Millard in his *Goblets*, Plate 37-4, shows a HARP goblet which he says was of the 1850s, but it appears to be of a later period than this creamer. On page 153 of his *ABC's of Old Glass*, the late Carl W. Dreppard shows a spillholder with a round stemmed base which he calls HARP or LYRE. Alice Hulett Metz shows a later goblet as No. 95 in her *Early American Pattern Glass*. She says it was made by Bryce Brothers of Pittsburgh.

Very probably this pitcher is an offhand piece made by a workman in an early glass factory for his own use. The mold for the spillholder was altered to eliminate the round stemmed base. The creamer may well have been the only piece made. This is open to doubt, however, since table pieces were in great demand. The quality of the glass is excellent, but it has the saddened appearance that results from a long period of burial or submersion. At first glance the glass seems filled with myriad minute bubbles. This effect results in a beautiful silvery sheen on the glass when the light hits it. On closer inspection it is seen there are no bubbles at all, but what might be infinitesimal white flecks. Further scrutiny seems to rule out bubbles and flecks and reveals the effect of saddening as mentioned above. Every aspect of this creamer indicates bygone days.

The outside of the body is hexagonal and almost uniform in size from base to neck. The inside is cylindrical. Each of the six wide, flat panels extends from half an inch above the base to half an inch below the neck. Centered in each panel is a raised harp with four strings or reeds in high relief. At the top and bottom of the panels is a 9/16-inch-wide raised, flat molding with a narrower, half-round, convex figure superimposed on it. The moldings are straight and mitred at the corners. They extend around the body. Above the upper one the piece has been left smooth and plain. It is first constricted and then flares widely all around into a slightly saddled rim. The lip projects far forward and is ungainly. This portion of the piece was tooled while the glass was too cold and as a result, shows numerous wavy hairlines.

The handle is applied and is somewhat small for more than a two-finger grip by a man. It is sturdy enough and nicely tooled at the lower attachment so as to have crossbars and still have a triangular opening through the center of the coil. It is applied on top of a harp. The piece sits flat on a wide hexagonal base which has a well-rounded and shallow dome beneath. In the center of the dome is a high rough pontil mark. The glass is heavy flint.

Creamer: 3-part mold; 1 pound, 3 ounces; 5 3/8 inches tall, 3 1/4 inches wide, and 5 3/4 inches long.

The following articles are known to have been made in the pattern: butter dish, honey, goblet, lamps in two sizes, footed salt, creamer, sauce dish, spoon or spillholder, and a sweetmeat dish with cover, 6 inches on low foot. Judging by similar pieces in other old patterns such as EXCELSIOR, BAND, and INVERTED PRISM AND DIAMOND POINT, the sweetmeat dish is the missing covered sugar bowl.

2—STAR AND PUNTY

This is a great-great-granddaddy of our early American pressed glass. It is heavy, brilliantly clear, and scarce enough to be welcome in most museums. The possessor of an item in this pattern has indeed something to be proud of.

In *A Fifth Pitcher Book*, page 86, No. 115, Minnie Watson Kamm shows a different treatment of the shape. Her low flat-bottomed creamer tapers in to the shoulder and lacks a molding at the bottom of the body. It appears to have been pressed in a cologne bottle mold, then handtooled into a creamer. She attributes the pattern to Sandwich since the Massachusetts Institute of Technology, Boston, Massachusetts, has fragments of it in their collection found at the site of the old Boston and Sandwich Glass Company, Sandwich, Massachusetts.

Ruth Webb Lee, in *Sandwich Glass*, Plate 206, shows a full page of toilet bottles from the collection of Albert E. Shaw. Nos. 3, 4, and 6, middle row, from left to right show one clear and two colored bottles, which, from the photograph, appear to be of this pattern. Kamm's creamer has a body shape identical to these. We know a cologne bottle was made. Lee does not cover the pattern other than to list it on page 537 as identical with fragments from the Sandwich site.

George S. and Helen McKearin, in their *American Glass*, Plate 196, No. 1, show a canary yellow cologne bottle and mention it on page 386. This bottle was made in a mold for a lamp font and tapers in from base to shoulder as lamps do. Lee's bottle tapers in as did Kamm's creamer. On Plate 198, No. 18, the McKearins show a lamp with a pressed font, the top being handcrafted to accommodate the burner. While hot, a tall standard was fused to the font. This lamp is described on page 390, No. 18. The McKearins say the pattern came in clear and in six colors. On page 385 they caution against tenuous attributions of early whale oil lamps to any one company and quote Mrs. Laura Woodside Watkins to the effect that lamps made at the New England Glass Company, East Cambridge, Massachusetts, could not be differentiated from those produced at the Boston and Sandwich Glass Company. Men who worked at both factories were unable to do so at the time. They pointed out the possibility of this being true of products of other factories.

The creamer shown here is interesting because it was pressed in a spillholder mold. Spillholders varied little in shape irrespective of the company of origin or pattern. This is seen frequently in spillholders in SANDWICH STAR, SANDWICH STAR AND BUCKLE, HARP or LYRE, SAWTOOTH, and others. It is not certain that a spillholder was made in this pattern, but one probably was. The magnificent quality of the heavy flint glass and the workmanship of the piece are of a high order that suggests the quality produced at Cambridge instead of the slipshod and inferior methods often used at Sandwich. The only blemish on the piece is a large rough pontil mark on the base. This does not rule out Cambridge as the maker, but indicates it may be one of their earlier products. On this point, Laura Woodside Watkins, in *Cambridge Glass 1818 to 1888*, page 43, has this to say:

> From the beginning to the end the New England Glass Co. produced glass equal to the finest made in any country. Whether an article was intended for table use, for decoration, or for some serviceable purpose, it was invariably made of a glass of crystal clearness and purity, without bubbles or flaws, beautifully finished,

smooth to the touch and to the eye. Only the earlier pieces are pontil-marked. To have this rough scar seems to have been the accepted practice at the time, but as the cutting and engraving became more elaborate each piece was ground off on the bottom. Pressed ware was firepolished into smoothness and rough edges ground down.

STAR AND PUNTY clearly falls into one of the earlier patterns, and the McKearins think it dates from 1836-1860. The rough pontil mark does not confirm it as a Cambridge piece, but neither is it ruled out. The quality is better than is found in much Sandwich glass. After being removed from the spillholder mold, which carried all the patternwork, the body of the creamer was not altered. The gaffer had many manipulations to make before the finished creamer emerged. He had to raise and shape the plain top, shear the rim to give it shape, round the rim off by further heating in the glory hole, depress the lip and shape it, then smooth the piece by firepolishing. A base had to be prepared by hand and fused on at the waist while both were hot. A separate gather of metal was necessary to form the applied handle.

At base and shoulder an attractive molding surrounds the body. It is built up by a high flat band, with a raised ring in half-round relief on it. The body flares a little to the shoulder and has six flat panels from molding to molding. This gives the main portion of the bowl a hexagonal shape. Alternating panels contain a highly raised and beveled oval figure, the surface of which is hollowed out. In each such depression is a five-point star in high relief, with four short rays and a longer one that points straight down. The rays have sharp crests. Each alternate panel has two circles with beveled edges, one above the other. Their entire surfaces are covered with a round concave depression which our forefathers called a punty. Today, we call them thumbprints. The upper punty is left plain and smooth. The lower one has a raised five-ray star. Above the top molding the body ceases to be hexagonal and becomes round. This part is smooth, plain, and flares slightly to the rim.

Below the lower molding the piece tapers in rapidly in six flat panels to the narrowest part of the waist. At this point the base was fused to the body. The foot is thick and quite heavy. It is almost flat and is slightly rounded at the edge. A thick rounded wafer is in the center and on top this upper paneled stem is joined. The base is mirror smooth and beautiful. It shows no mold marks and has been hand tooled.

The base is hollowed out underneath enough to permit the creamer to sit on a wide ring at the edge of the footing. In the center a large, uneven,

1

Bottom
3-2

3-2

2

Bottom
4

4

3-1

5

6

though not rough, pontil mark is left. The rim has a deep dip near the back portion of each side, then rises to a large, high, V-shaped scallop at the upper handle junction. From its lowest point, it soars a full inch in front, then curves down into a rather wide lip. The too large handle was finely shaped and executed with beautiful curves, but it would have been more pleasing had it not been extended as far to the rear. It is almost round in cross section and is sturdier than most. The heavy upper attachment was sheared off square, turned under, and applied to the large smooth scallop provided for that purpose. The lower attachment is made on top of a star and in one of the small punties. It was so expertly crafted that no interstices remain to catch dirt, despite the fact it was applied over an irregular surface. The tab was coiled in on itself to make an attractive curlicue. The outer surface was tooled into three crossbars. No trace of a mold mark can be found on the entire piece. Since it is hexagonal, a three-part mold would have sufficed.

Kamm's creamer: weight unknown; 5 7/16 inches tall. This creamer: 3-part mold; 1 3/4 pounds; 6 3/8 inches tall; 3 3/8 inches wide; and 5 7/8 inches long. The only articles known to have been made in the pattern are a tall lamp, two types of creamers, two types of toilet bottles, and a spillholder.

3—DIAMOND THUMBPRINT

Here are two choice and scarce morsels that are seen on few tables. Their crudities, crimping of the lower attachment on the applied handles, their ground and ringed base at the pontil position, treatment at throat and rim, extreme weight and the brilliance of the heavy flint glass all indicate a very early pressing date. They probably were made during the 1830s and certainly not later than the 1850s.

The low-footed compote in this pattern is somewhat plentiful and is not too attractive. All other pieces in the pattern are extremely rare. As an index of their rarity, goblets are today quoted at $35 to $100 each depending on their condition; wine glasses $65; celery vases $35 to $50; and the creamer $35 to $100. A celery vase once in my possession was made in three segments and fused together while hot. It was the finest piece of early American pressed glass I have had the pleasure of seeing. It required twelve years of diligent search to find the two creamers shown here. We know practically nothing as to what factory made them. Fragments of the pattern were found at the old site of the Boston and Sandwich Glass Company,

which may or may not assure us that Sandwich produced it. All glass factories bought tons of broken glass (cullet), a necessary ingredient in making glass. Some of it would inevitably have been scattered about the premises to be discovered later. Steel mills buy thousands of tons of scrap iron necessary for making steel. If a knife blade were unearthed years later, it would not prove knives were made at that particular plant. The fine quality of this pattern indicates it may have been made by the New England Glass Company of East Cambridge, Massachusetts. Unfortunately, we do not know they made it. We do know they made much superior quality glass that is now erroneously attributed to other factories, Sandwich among them.

S. T. Millard, in his *Goblets*, shows a goblet in DIAMOND THUMBPRINT as a frontispiece together with a MORNING GLORY goblet. He did not describe it, but in his acknowledgments he said it belonged to Mrs. Edward C. Bowen who had a splendid and rare collection. Minnie Watson Kamm had not seen the pattern and did not mention it in her series of eight pitcher books on pattern glass. Ruth Webb Lee, in her *Early American Pressed Glass*, Pattern 5, pages 29-30, and Plates 3 and 25, describes the pattern and illustrates a creamer, low-footed bowl, tumbler, two types of covered sugar bowls, a quart decanter with matching stopper, and a goblet.

George and Helen McKearin, in their *American Glass*, list the items known to have been made on page 404. On Plate 205, No. 6 they show a canary yellow celery vase; on Plate 206, No. 1, they show a decanter with stopper; in No. 2, they show a deep bowl and in No. 3 a pitcher; in Plate 208, No. 11, a large handled whiskey tumbler is depicted; and in Plate 209, No. 3, a large wine glass.

Metz, in her *Early American Pattern Glass*, shows a goblet and covers the pattern on pages 10-11, No. 36.

The body of creamer No. 1 is almost cone-shaped as it flares from waist to rim. Instead of being constricted at the neck as is No. 2, it flares into a triangular top. This feature is unusual and encountered only in very early pieces which required much handcrafting after being removed from the mold. Above the figurework there is a wide, plain band to the rim. The mold marks show here but not on the design. Usually, the reverse is true because the tops are smoothed out more by fire polishing since they get hotter in the glory hole than do the bowls. The rim is deeply saddled and has a large scallop at the rear to accommodate the handle. At the front the rim rises abruptly, then levels off to an unbecoming spout which is off-center. The lower part of the body is covered by six wide, flat panels with arched tops that taper in sharply to a narrow waist.

The main motif was achieved by deep V-shaped grooves crisscrossing to form large, highly beveled diamonds, which stand on their corners. Three bands of these encircle the body, and their size is accommodated to the contours of the bowl. In the center of each diamond a beautiful deep thumbprint has been impressed. In the upper row the thumbprints are large, oval, and their long axes are vertical. In the middle row they are smaller, oval, and horizontal. In the lower row they are much smaller and round.

At the waist the wide columns curve out sharply on top of the base, which is low and almost flat. These flat panels are rounded on the end and extend to the edge of the base, causing it to be scalloped into six wide lobes. The edge of the foot is vertical and one-fourth inch thick. The piece rests on a wide, flat surface. No. 1 has a slight dome underneath, with a ground and polished pontil mark. No. 2 has no pontil mark, but there is a round thumbprint in the center of the bottom, and it is surrounded by six raised, concentric circles.

The applied handle is round and the inside is flattened. The large attachment is turned under at the top. The curves are pleasing, but the handle is a little frail for the weight of the creamer. The lower attachment is very long and beautifully tooled into crossbars to form a corduroyed effect. With No. 2 the treatment of the lower attachment is different. The thin tip end is turned back upon itself to form a small open coil. (See drawings for details.) The glass is heavy and brilliantly clear. It has an occasional black fleck and a few minute bubbles. There is no discoloration. The lower handle attachment was applied on top of the figurework and as a result has some inaccessible cavities which are now filled with grime. This flaw contraindicates the New England Glass Company as the maker. The workmanship of No. 2 is superior to that of No. 1; it was also made at a different factory. Both are prized possessions.

Creamer No. 1: 3-part mold; 1 5/8 pounds; 6 1/4 inches tall; 3 3/16 inches wide; and 5 13/16 inches long.

Creamer No. 2: 3-part mold; Weight 1 3/4 pounds; 6 1/4 inches tall; 3 1/2 inches wide; and 6 inches long.

The following articles are known to have been made in the pattern: covered butter dish, two types of covered sugar bowls, two types of creamers, spoonholder, cake plate, shallow footed bowl, deep footed bowl, compotes in several sizes, champagnes, large and small cordials and wines, goblets, pint and quart decanters with stoppers, honey dish, whiskey tumbler with handle, two sizes of water tumbler, sweetmeat jar, sauce dish, handled mug, water pitcher, and milk pitcher.

4—KAMM SUNK DIAMONDS*

Here is a treasure, indeed! This jewel of a creamer is compact, smaller than most creamers of its generation, heavy, thick, and just about the most attractive pattern in American pressed glass. As a tribute to Minnie Watson Kamm for her superlative work on pressed glass, the exquisite pattern is named KAMM SUNK DIAMONDS. A few of us still remember the dark, dismal railroad stations and their waiting rooms on a bleak day. While we waited for the Local, the tall, rusty, pot-bellied stove, bearing many chalk marks, warmed our icy fingers. That relic of the past had a girth and shape much like this creamer.

Pressed glass in DIAMOND POINT and SAWTOOTH patterns was very popular for decades. Their diamond points were raised, had sharp points and corners, and were quite uncomfortable to touch. It was easy to make the molds for these patterns. In this instance the diamonds are sunk into the surface to produce a perfect optical illusion wherein they appear to be raised and pointed. This piece is pleasant to touch, and in this way the marked difference in the patterns may be easily detected. There are no sharp points to become bruised or chipped by careless handling. Why was so little of so lovely a pattern made? The answer lies in the making of the molds. The inside of each, except for the pattern, must be cut away to leave the pattern raised above the surface. This would present difficulties to the most highly skilled artisan. In addition, far more labor would be required than for intaglio cutting. The latter, of course, would result in raised figures on the article pressed therein. See DIAMOND IN POINTS in Kamm's *A Fourth Pitcher Book*, page 80, No. 94, for a similar piece, but one that is probably not so old.

The bulbous body rests on a wide, round base. The base has a slight dome underneath, with a magnificent 10-point star made up of sunk diamond points. The outer border is formed by ten-

*Patterns in italics were named by the author.

11

pointed arches. There is a blank center space which is also formed by ten arches. (See cut.) The decoration shows through on the base and appears to be on the topside. In the clear center space is a large, rough pontil mark. The base and the body were made separately and fused together while hot. While still on the pontil rod the creamer was shaped around the neck, the rim was sheared to the desired shape, and the handle was applied. There is a shelf where the body rests on the base. It has nine sides and an equal number of flat panels, which starting there, curve in to complete the constriction at the waist and then curve out and up to approximately one-fourth the way up the body. The panels are plain, flat, and the top of each forms a pointed arch that meshes into the lower part of the sunk diamond motif.

Around the body is a band of small, swirled, sunk diamond points. Nevertheless they are graduated, smaller at top and bottom and large around the middle where the circumference is greatest. The band also has points at the top and bottom to conform to the arches that slash into it from above and below. The neck is narrow, and the glass shows a few fine hairlines and tool marks. Either the metal or mold was too cold. The rim flares out and is unevenly scalloped as shown. The forepart of the rim and lip is high, winged, and the lip appears too large for a small piece. The scallop at the back of the rim is high and forms a base for the upper attachment of the applied handle. The handle is round and has a turned up tab at the bottom attachment, but shows no tooling.

All the writers on American pressed glass have mentioned and described DIAMOND POINT. Only Kamm has mentioned *SUNK DIAMOND POINT*. This creamer and the water pitcher she used are not contemporary. This piece is the older and dates from 1840 to 1860. It was purchased at Avon, Massachusetts. Mrs. Kamm's pitcher came from Rutland, Vermont. They probably were made in the same locale. At the time this pattern was made, three glass factories were operating in that area, all making excellent quality pressed glass tableware. They were the Mt. Washington Glass Company of South Boston; the New England Glass Company of East Cambridge, Massachusetts; and the Boston and Sandwich Glass Company of Sandwich, Massachusetts. The glass is clear and of heavy, sparkling flint. There are few imperfections and even fewer small bubbles. It was a quality product when manufactured and still is today.

Small creamer: no mold marks show; 1 1/8 pounds, 5 5/8 inches tall, 2 7/8 inches wide, and 4 7/8 inches long.

Probably a covered sugar bowl, goblet, decanter, celery vase, egg cup, master salt, bar tumbler, and whiskey tumbler were made.

5—BULL'S EYE WITH DIAMOND POINT

This magnificent old creamer was shown in a catalog of 1869 and put out under the name of UNION by the New England Glass Company. Because they insisted on putting out only the very finest quality flint glass tableware and refused to lower their standards to compete with cheap, soda-lime glass made in a slipshod manner, this company gradually lost ground financially and was forced to suspend operations in 1888.

Pieces in the pattern are so perfect and scarce that they bring fantastic prices—almost as much as Carnival Glass—such as $80 for a pair of celery vases, or $100 for a creamer. For over-all quality, including glass, workmanship, design, finish, this pattern ranks well up in the top five of the best ten patterns of pressed glass ever manufactured in America. The pair of tall celery vases on high, knopped stems, with their clear, sparkling beauty is an arresting sight. The creamer is superior by every quality standard.

The pattern was shown as UNION in Laura Woodside Watkins' *Cambridge Glass, 1818 to 1888*, Plate 43. Five pieces were shown from the old catalog which listed many items as having been made. Nowhere in our literature is a creamer in this pattern previously illustrated. Mrs. Lee, in *Early American Pressed Glass*, Pattern 54, pages 158-60, Plates 27 and 49, gave the name used above. The McKearins in *American Glass*, Plate 208, Nos. 15 and 19, show a tumbler and a small hand lamp. Millard, in *Goblets*, Plate 161-2, shows a goblet and calls it BULL'S EYE AND DIAMOND POINTS. Do not confuse this aristocrat with the plebeian soda-lime pattern given the same name by Mrs. Kamm in *A Third Pitcher Book* page 100, No. 150, or with a pattern called BULL'S EYE AND DIAMOND PANELS by Mrs. Metz.

The shape of the creamer dates it. Not many heavy flint glass pitchers were produced during the era when this piece was made. The general shapes of all are strikingly similar. They are narrow at the waist, bulge out in the middle of the body and then are constricted at the neck, like the old potbellied stove. The bottom of the body stops where the waist panels end in rounded arches. Above each waist panel is a long, convexed triangle, shaped like an arrowhead. The glass is thick and heavy. Between the figures are beveled shields with a bull's-eye in their upper portions. The lower portions are filled with rather large diamond point. The triangles between the top of the shields have arched tops and are filled with still larger diamond point. Above the figurework is a high beveled ridge with six sweeping arches. The top 1 1/4 inch of the body is left smooth and plain. It is constricted and then flares out to a rim that is beautifully saddled. The lip has flowing curves, but projects a little too far forward. The glass at the rim is 3/16 of an inch thick.

The handle is applied and well proportioned. The top attachment is trimmed into a sharp point. The bottom attachment is long, coiled into a spiral, and then pressed into an intricately tooled arrangement as shown in the drawing. The stem is short and thick. Six flat panels flow out on the base and end in a high, round shelf. The top of the base shows how the mold lines swirl. There is a slight hollow beneath the base and the pontil mark has been completely ground and polished out. No mold marks show on the body. On the base they are barely perceptible.

Creamer: 3-part mold. 1 5/8 pounds, 6 1/8 inches tall, 3 3/16 inches wide, and 6 inches long.

The following articles are known to have been made in this pattern: flat bowls in four sizes, high-footed bowls in five sizes, low-footed bowls in five sizes, celery vase, champagne, cologne bottle with stopper, creamer, decanter with stopper in two sizes, celery vase, champagne, cologne bottle with sizes, eggcup, goblet, honey dish, low hand lamp, lemonade glass, sauce dish, spoonholder, sugar bowl with lid, two sizes of tumblers, two sizes of wines and water bottle with tumbler up. It would be surprising if a water pitcher and butter dish were not made. The market should have been flooded with this exquisite pattern.

6—BULL'S EYE

BULL'S EYE is one of the early, massive, flint glass patterns all dealers and collectors have heard of. The name is probably the most familiar and widely known of all pressed glass. Yet, a surprising number of people have never seen it. The pattern is one of the great-granddaddies of pressed glass. Its descendants are numerous. For instance, S. T. Millard lists twenty patterns with BULL'S EYE as part of the title. Minnie Watson Kamm lists thirteen patterns so named. Ruth Webb Lee lists eighteen. Dreppard also lists it, as do most writers on early American pressed glass.

This particular pattern is described in Mrs.

Lee's *Early American Pressed Glass* as Pattern 51, pages 153-54, Plates 48 and 49. She lists thirty items in the pattern and says the glass lacks the glow and sparkle of other early patterns. However, for brilliance and sparkle, the creamer shown here will hold its own in the most select company. Enos shows the pattern on Chart 4. Metz shows it as No. 60. Millard shows a goblet in *Goblets*, Plate 162-1, which he calls BULL'S EYE, KNOP STEM NEAR FOOT. This is believed to be the same pattern. Dreppard uses the pattern in his *ABC's of Old Glass*. The McKearins and Mrs. Kamm do not describe it. The author has seen only two pieces—a goblet in a private collection and this creamer.

The New England Glass Company manufactured this pattern under the name of LAWRENCE. (See Laura Woodside Watkins' *Cambridge Glass 1818 to 1888*, Plate 44 and 45.) They probably did not make this particular creamer; if they had, it probably would have a ground pontil mark, and the handle attachment would not have been applied on top of the figurework. The pattern is known to have been produced by the Boston and Sandwich Glass Company. It was probably made at other glass houses as well. There is no way of knowing who crafted this creamer. It is a very early pattern and dates from at least the 1860s. Compare it with COLONIAL in Kamm's *An Eighth Pitcher Book*, page 9, No. 15, and note the similarity of the two patterns.

The large body is inverted, bell-shaped and has a slight constriction at the neck. Six panels encircle the body, each outlined by a large, inverted V-shaped ridge which forms a large loop from near the base to the neck. Inside and at the top of each loop is the familiar bull's-eye—a large, convex disc in high relief with a deep, round, concave thumbprint impressed into the center of its top. Beneath each eye is a raised, rounded, baggy pouch which implies imbibing—not cream. Above each panel is a rounded arch, the lower edge of which is beveled. Above this, the body is plain and smooth. The rim and lip are adequate, but not remarkable.

The narrow waist is a short, hexagonal stem. Each flat panel swells up on the base of the bowl and ends in a high rounded arch. Below, each flows out on top of the base and ends in a high, round shelf. The base is round, thick, heavy, and adequate. Underneath is a small hollow, which is plain and has no pontil mark.

The handle is applied, massive, and comfortable to use. Its curves could have been improved. The lower attachment is different from any the writer has seen; it is applied on top of the figurework, then turned back on itself and pressed flat. Usually crossbars would have been tooled here. Just above the juncture of the lower attachment with the body is a well-defined and purposely made nipple which projects out for 1/4 inch and joins the face of the bull's-eye. (See details in drawing.) Why this was done remains an enigma.

Although the quality of the glass is superior, the craftsman was no true gaffer. He permitted either the mix or the mold to get too cold, and wavy lines resulted. The tooling of the rim and lip, and the shaping of the handle and lower handle attachment bespeak less than competent gaffer skill. The glass is clear, brilliant, thick, and quite heavy. Mold marks show only on the base.

Creamer: 3-part mold, 1 5/8 pounds, 6 1/4 inches tall, 3 3/8 inches wide, and 5 3/4 inches long.

Mrs. Lee says thirty items were made in this pattern, but all of them are hard to come by today.

7—THE CONFEDERACY

This is another magnificent, early heavy flint glass pattern that has escaped the authors who have written about early American pressed glass. It may be foreign, possibly English, and that could account for its not having been used. Foreign creamers were not as commodious as our American ones. It appears to be American, however, and has many characteristics of glass manufactured by the New England Glass Company, which ceased operations in 1888.

Here we find superb quality such as found in MIRROR, ARGUS, BULL'S EYE, BULL'S EYE AND DIAMOND POINT, ASHBURTON, DIAMOND POINT, SAWTOOTH, HORN OF PLENTY, EARLY THUMBPRINT, and early HONEYCOMB. The glass is beautifully clear, but has the slightly bluish cast often seen in our early glass. It has a clear resonance when tapped. The glass has the greasy or soapy feel often encountered in old flint glass. The workmanship was excellent. The obvious name for this pattern would be URN, but that title has already been used for another pattern and cannot be used again. The joining of the urn part with the creamer top forms an alliance that is akin to a confederacy. Because this piece was made during the early 1860s, it is contemporaneous with the Confederate States of America. Therefore, the pattern is assigned the title *THE CONFEDERACY*.

The lower two-thirds of the body is an attractive, urn-shaped portion which rolls out at the top like the scalloped rim of an urn or jardiniere. This section of the body is covered with twelve flat panels with a dewdrop near the top of each. Alternating between the flat panels are high inverted, V-shaped ridges. Over the top of each ridge is a raised, well-sculptured Gothic arch. Above the arches is a plain band which fills the interstices and extends up to twenty-four even scallops at the top of the urn. The top third of the creamer is plain, thick, and appears to be slipped down inside the top of the urn. At this junction the glass is 9/16 inch thick. The neck is constricted slightly, then flares to the rim. The rim is smooth, rounded over at the top, and nicely saddled. It is slightly pinched in at the lip and its curves are fluid.

The stem is hexagonal and thick. As depicted in the drawing, it is swirled, probably the result of constant rotation while hot and attached to the pontil rod. While this attachment was in place, the neck was formed, the rim was sheared and shaped, and the applied handle was put on. The stem ends on a high, round shelf on the base of the bowl and at the top of the foot. The foot is thick, round, and has a low instep. Underneath it is slightly hollowed out and has a large, ground and polished pontil mark. The beautiful handle is attached, large in diameter, but rather on the small side for handling. The large attachment is at the top. From there, with pleasant curves, it arches high and backward, then downward and forward to rejoin the body above the midpoint. The lower attachment joins the body higher than on most creamers. It has been expertly tooled into a series of crossbars and gracefully coiled back upon itself.

Creamer: 3-part mold, 1 5/8 pounds, 6 3/4 inches tall, 3 3/4 inches wide, and 5 3/4 inches long. Sugar bowl, covered: 3-part mold, 2 5/8 pounds, 8 3/4 inches tall, and 5 5/8 inches wide.

These are the only two items of the pattern known to the author. Doubtless such a grand old patrician comes from one of the best glass houses. Its every aspect attests to this. Other members of the family must be cherished somewhere. This is the type of piece to gladden the heart of any collector and grace the display cabinets of fine museums. It is exceedingly rare.

Fire or other calamity may have prevented much of this pattern being made. Otherwise, I would expect to find: goblets, celery vases, spoonholders or spillholders, wines, decanters, compotes, master salts, tumblers, whisky tumblers, water pitchers, eggcups, and other pieces. As this manuscript was being readied for the publisher, another creamer in the pattern made its appearance. The duplicate is on display at the

Restoration of the Territorial Capitol in Little Rock, Arkansas.

8—MAGNET AND GRAPE, FROSTED LEAF

This regal creamer is one of the rarest, most expensive, and desirable of any in early American pressed glass. It was made at an early date and must have been popular with our ancestors, for it was copied in many variants.

Ruth Webb Lee, in *Early American Pressed Glass*, Pattern 71, pages 197-98 and Plate 63, shows and describes this pattern. On the frontispiece of the book she shows an intricately constructed wine jug with a spigot, in this pattern. It is about as unusual as any piece of early pressed glass ever made. Mrs. Lee also describes a later variant of the pattern with "Stippled Leaf" in the same book. The McKearins, in *American Glass*, mention it on pages 395 and 397. On page 406 they list known items in the pattern.

In *Goblets*, S. T. Millard shows this pattern with "Frosted Leaf" in Plate 13-2. He also lists other variants: Plate 98-2, MAGNET AND GRAPE, STIPPLED LEAF; Plate 98-3 MAGNET AND GRAPE, CLEAR LEAF; and Plate 147-4, MAGNET AND GRAPE, FROSTED, TENDRILS ON GRAPE BUNCH. In his *Goblets, II* he shows: Plate 30-3, MAGNET AND GRAPE, IN MILK WHITE; On Plate 92-2, MAGNET AND GRAPE, SLAG. Mrs. Kamm had not seen a creamer in it but described MAGNET AND GRAPE, STIPPLED LEAF in *Two Hundred Pattern Glass Pitchers*, page 7, No. 5, and mentioned this pattern as being rarer than the one she was presenting.

This pattern is of the 1860s or a little earlier and was made at Boston and Sandwich Glass Company. It is not heavy or massive, but is of the superior quality that went into table glassware of that date. The glass is very brilliant, clear, smooth, and free of discolorations and defects. It was highly fire polished. It has a faint tinkle when tapped.

The body is long and ovoidal. It has a V-shaped groove near the rim and at the bottom of the body. The body is quartered by four wide, shallow concave flutes. Each quarter contains a wide loop shaped like a toy magnet. In the front and back quarters are well-defined magnet-shaped figures. The flat surface of each is filled with sunk diamond point. In the center of the magnet the space is smooth and slightly concave. Each side quadrant contains a large flat grape leaf, the surface of

which shows veins and is frosted. Coiled on each side of the leaf is a tendril. There is a short section of vine and stem below the leaf. Below this, a well-defined cluster of grapes is suspended. The top of each grape is flat and frosted. On either side of the grapes are more coiling tendrils which require a reading glass to be seen. The entire space around these figures inside the loop is plain. The upper portion of the creamer is plain, smooth, and beautifully polished. The plain rim soars high in front to form an upturned lip, which harmonizes well with the tall, slender body.

The large, tall stem is octagonal and ends in a shelf on the base of the body. It curves in, then out, to make a large knop at the lower end, where it terminates in a round-edged wafer. As shown in the drawing the stem has considerable swirl. The foot arches out to a wide, round edge which supplies stability for the tall piece. Underneath the base the piece sits on its outer perimeter. There is a slightly hollowed-out space in the center, and a large twenty-four-ray star is impressed there. The star lacks half an inch of reaching the edge.

The applied handle is beautiful. The large attachment is at the top and was sheared off on either side. It is wide and thin at the top and it tapers gracefully to the lower end. The handle soars high, arches over, and sweeps in to the lower attachment. This creamer has been nicely, though not elaborately, tooled. Its quality indicates Sandwich could produce superior quality when they so desired.

Creamer: 4-part mold, 1 pound, 7 1/8 inches tall, 3 3/8 inches wide, and 5 1/4 inches long.

The following items are known: covered butter dish, several types of open and covered compotes, celery vase, creamer, cordial, champagne, pint and quart decanters, eggcup, goblet, ladies' goblet, footed salt, sauce dish, spoonholder, covered sugar bowl, water tumbler, whiskey tumbler, small wine, large wine, and the rare wine jug, previously mentioned.

9—MAGNET AND GRAPE, STIPPLED LEAF

See MAGNET AND GRAPE, FROSTED LEAF above.

Minnie Watson Kamm in *Two Hundred Pattern Glass Pitchers*, page 7, No. 5, illustrates another variant of MAGNET AND GRAPE, STIPPLED LEAF. It differs in several details from the creamer shown here. Ruth Webb Lee in *Early American Pressed Glass*, pages 198-204 covers the pattern briefly but does not assign a pattern number. She illustrates a goblet on Plate 62. Millard illustrates a goblet on Plate 98-2 in *Goblets*. Metz, in *Early American Pattern Glass*, pages 78-79, No. 873, covers this pattern and says: "Only difference between the two is that in one the leaves are stippled, while in the other they are left clear." She is speaking of the "clear" and "stippled" variations.

This beautiful pattern appears in several variants indicating its popularity with our ancestors. The preceding pattern, by far the scarcest and most choice, was the first, and then other glass houses demonstrated their admiration by making differentiations. Someone with a penchant for solving difficult problems might well turn his acumen to tracking down and classifying these. When completed, he should switch to GRAPE AND FESTOON.

Probably the best way to describe this version of MAGNET AND GRAPE is to show the significant differences between the original (above) and this one. They are as follows:

(a) The preceding creamer dates from the 1860s. This appears to have been made between 1869 and 1875.

(b) This is not as tall and regal as the earlier example.

(c) The body shapes are completely at variance. (Compare drawings.)

(d) The glass of the original is flint and is clearer and heavier than that of the variant.

(e) This variant differs from Kamm's creamer in two respects: 1. It is heavier. 2. It has no tendrils.

(f) The handle of this piece is thicker, not as tall, and extends farther back than does the original. The tooling on the lower attachment of this handle is expertly done, whereas, it is only run-of-the-mill workmanship on the original.

(g) Mold marks show on the body of the original, but not on this one.

(h) The glass is thicker in the variant.

(i) The placing of the lip and handle alters the appearance of this piece. The lower handle attachment is in a concave flute and this permits a magnet and grape cluster to show on either side. The original has the handle placed in a magnet and shows only a grape cluster on each side with a magnet directly under the lip and another under the handle.

(j) The leaf of this piece is stippled, there are no tendrils, and the grapes are half round and smooth. The original has tendrils above and below

the stem. The tops of the grapes are ground flat and, together with the leaves, have been frosted by sand blasting. (Acid etching was first introduced in this country from France in 1876, after the original was made.)

(k) The stem of the variant is shorter, slimmer, entirely plain, and octagonal. It has no swirl and ends in loops on the base of the body and in an octagonal shelf on the top of the foot. The original stem is also octagonal, has a decided swirl with a large knop near its base, and is taller. It ends in lower loops at the top and in a rounded wafer on top of the foot.

(l) The base of the original is wider, more arched on top, and has a large 24-ray star impressed beneath. The variant has a plain foot.

Creamer: 4-part mold, 1 1/8 pounds, 6 5/16 inches tall, 3 1/8 inches wide, and 5 1/2 inches long.

These items are known to have been made in the stippled leaf variety: butter dish, open compote, cordial, creamer, goblet, salt, water pitcher, sauce dish, spoonholder, sugar bowl, and tumbler.

10—FOUR PETAL

Only a few articles are known to have been made in this beautiful pattern, before the War Between the States. We know only of covered sugars, creamers, round deep bowls, and a six-inch compote. Metz mentions a lamp and a covered jam jar. Strangely enough, with so few articles made, there were two types of creamers and two types of sugar bowls, the latter having slightly different shapes and radically different lids. The thicker, shorter sugar has a pagoda-shaped lid. The slimmer sugar has a rounded dome lid.

This pattern was made during the 1850s. In 1850 E. and J. McKee of the old McKee glass factory in Pittsburgh built a factory in that city for the manufacture of fine flint glass tableware. Apparently they produced this pattern. This particular branch soon became Bryce, McKee and Company. A reorganization occurred in 1853 or 1854 resulting in two firms being established—Bryce, Richards and Company, and McKee and Brothers. It is possible McKee and Brothers continued to make this pattern with one type of sugar and creamer and Bryce, Richards and Company also made it with a new and slightly different set of molds, thus producing two types of sugars and creamers. Other patterns known to have been made by the McKees in this period are ASHBURTON, PRESSED LEAF, FOUR PETAL, EX-

7-1

7-2

8

9

10

11

12

13

CELSIOR, and HORN OF PLENTY. Bryce, Richards and Company put out BELLFLOWER and PINEAPPLE as well as other early McKee patterns.

Mrs. Kamm described the more slender and lighter version of the creamer in *A Fifth Pitcher Book*, pages 26-28, No. 24. She also compiled some excellent data on the McKees as glassmakers. They first started making glass in Pittsburgh in 1834. In 1889 the plant was moved from Pittsburgh to Jeannette (named for the wife of the president), Pennsylvania, and it has remained in continuous production to the present time. It is now the McKee Branch of the Thatcher Glass Manufacturing Company of Jeannette. On pages 43-44 of *Early American Pressed Glass*, Ruth Webb Lee briefly covers the design as Pattern 10. On Plate 12 she shows the two types of sugar bowls and the heavier creamer. On Plate 213, No. 5 of *American Glass*, the McKearins show a sugar bowl with a round dome in a beautiful shade of blue. These, of course, are quite scarce; indeed no article in the pattern is plentiful. Alice Hulett Metz, in her recent *Early American Pattern Glass*, shows a tumbler as No. 2500 which seems to be in this pattern. (She thought it was of the early 1890s, and considered it to have no practical value.) She named it THUMBPRINT PILLOWS. She mentions FOUR PETAL on page 33. Millard does not show a goblet, and it is probable that none was made.

Mrs. Kamm's creamer, which is more slender, weighs five ounces less than the creamer used here. It is possible she had not seen a piece of the pattern and used an illustration of it. This conjecture arises from her statement, "Each petal is a raised ellipse with a sharp spine down its center and all petals meet others at their tip." Actually these sharp pointed ellipses are sunk and not raised. Rather than being cameolike, they are intaglio. The motif is composed of two simple designs—sunken petals and small, round thumbprints. There are four rows of thumbprints running horizontally around the body in staggered formation. In the three top rows, each is surrounded by four petals. The bottom band has two petals over each thumbprint. The petals are so arranged that the outer border of each forms a fourth of a circle, which in turn surrounds a thumbprint. Inside each circle is a four-cornered, raised pillow with a deep, round thumbprint impressed in its center. The pillow edges are curved. This four-petal band covers the bulbous two-thirds of the body.

The lower portion of the body is plain and curves into a short, thick waist. From the waist the foot slants to the edge in two planes, forming a high instep. The round base is large, almost flat, and quite stable. Underneath there is a wide, low, rounded dome with a nicely polished pontil mark. Above the four-petal figurework is a quarter-inch-wide band in high relief which surrounds the body. This band is not rounded and has a crest or ridge slightly below its center. Above this band, and with their bases resting on it, are eighteen somewhat rounded columns which extend to the rim and vary in width to conform to the contours of the neck. Under the lip is a flat panel with rounded borders equal in width to two of the columns. There is a considerable constriction at the neck, and from here the body flares to the rim.

The rim is irregularly scalloped with one particularly high and wide scallop at the rear to serve as an anchor for the large upper handle attachment. The back half of the rim has one wide scallop on each side. The front half curves up and far forward to form a wide lip. The rim is well rounded over the top, and the glass is quite thick, as indeed it is throughout the piece. The pleasing handle is ample in capacity and mass to complement the heavy creamer; it appears to belong. The top attachment is long, sturdy, and notched at the end. The handle curves high and then turns back to join the body at the middle of the petal band. The only fault with the piece is that no smooth surface was provided for the long, lower attachment. Some small, inaccessible pockets there are filled with dirt. The attachment itself was skillfully crafted into high crossbars and turned back upon itself in an open loop large enough to be kept clean.

Since this piece was not made before 1830, it is not, strictly speaking, an antique; nevertheless, I am proud to be the owner of this 1850 product. (I wish I had a shelf full of its siblings.)

The heavy flint glass is clear, sparkling, and without discoloration. It is brilliant and has a perfect firepolish. It has little resonance, as is customary in creamers where the handle interferes with the body's resonance. The quality and workmanship, except for the handle attachment, are superlative. The lower side of the quarter-inch band at the neck is the only place where mold marks can be found. They usually show also on the base and waist, but not here.

Slender creamer: 3-part mold, 1 pound and 13 ounces, 6 1/4 inches tall.

This creamer: 4-part mold, 2 1/8 pounds, 6 3/8 inches tall, 3 9/16 inches wide, and 6 1/4 inches long.

11—HAMILTON

This is a wonderful old pattern which Minnie Watson Kamm had not seen and did not use in her series of eight pitcher books. It is too bad such a desirable pattern should be so elusive and scarce.

The McKearins, in their *American Glass*, Plate 207, No. 4, show a creamer and in No. 6 a hat in the pattern. On Plate 209, No. 5, a goblet is shown. On page 405 they list the items in the pattern which they knew to have been made. S. T. Millard, in *Goblets*, Plate 117-4, shows a goblet, says it was made in the 1870s, came in clear only, and was already becoming scarce. Ruth Webb Lee describes it as Pattern 61, pages 173-174, Plate 56, in *Early American Pressed Glass*. The plate shows nine pieces. It is a photograph. Metz in her *Early American Pattern Glass*, pages 26-27, No. 242 shows a goblet and quotes prices on items in the pattern.

Everything about the piece, including its light, airy grace, indicates it to be a product of the late 1860s or early 1870s. The body is broad and bell shaped. From the shelf above the short, narrow stem, the body curves out rapidly then proceeds almost vertically to the rim. There are three main bands of figurework about the body of approximately equal width, plus ribbing under the lip. The bands are separated by horizontal V-shaped grooves. The lower band is composed of small, vertical fine ribs of uniform length which completely fill the band. The middle band is filled with raised lines which zigzag to form diamonds in the middle and triangles at the borders. The triangles are left plain. The sunk diamonds are filled with raised lines which cross to form smaller sunk diamonds. The upper band is in fine ribs of varying lengths so that the top is in peaks and valleys as in BLAZE and ICICLE. Under the lip is more of the icicle effect. It extends about a quarter of the way around the body.

The rim is plain, highly saddled, and makes a curvaceous and outthrust lip. There is an unusually high tab at the rear to accommodate the handle. The applied handle is wide, but thin at the top and narrow and thin at the bottom. The latter results in a fragile member which would not tolerate rough handling. The handle has a small capacity for a grip but has beautiful curves throughout. The lower attachment is turned back on itself and is well tooled as shown in the drawing.

The stem is short and hexagonal. It ends in a small round raised shelf on the bottom of the bowl and in a large, round shelf on the base. The foot is round and unusually wide. It is arched on top to form a high instep. The edge is thin and smooth. Beneath is a rounded dome with a large 27-ray star impressed therein. This is an authenticated Sandwich pattern, but there is no assurance that this piece was not made elsewhere. The glass is fine quality flint and has a faint tinkle when tapped. It is difficult to see the mold marks on the foot, where they are usually most easily seen. They show plainly on the body where, as a rule, they are polished off by fire or acid.

Creamer: 3-part mold, 13 ounces, 6 1/8 inches tall, 3 3/8 inches wide, and 5 5/8 inches long.

These items were manufactured: covered butter dish, caster set, variety of high and low open and covered compotes, creamer, decanters, 6-inch round dish, eggcup, goblet, honey dish, preserve dish, footed salt, variety of sauce dishes, spoonholder, covered sugar bowl, water tumbler, whiskey tumbler, two types of wines, syrup pitcher with metal top, cordial, and water pitcher. (Note: A later variant of this pattern has pressed handles.)

12—OVAL MITRE (LATE)

This creamer is not the heavy, massive type so characteristic of the 1850s and early 1860s. It has all the earmarks of belonging to the late 1860s or early 1870s. I have an oval pickle dish in this pattern which dates from the 1850s, and it differs markedly from this creamer. It is older, thicker, and heavier. The pattern was not described by Minnie Watson Kamm in her books, for she had never seen a creamer. Pieces in the pattern are scarce and seldom advertised or seen in shops. Years of diligent search were required to locate the creamer shown here. The heavier, more massive flint pieces are even more elusive. Goblets contemporary with this creamer are the most available items known.

Millard, in *Goblets*, Plate 48-2, shows a goblet. Mrs. Lee, in *Early American Pressed Glass*, Pattern 14, pages 48-49 and Plate 12, covers the design. A larger bowl than usually found and the short stem tend to give this creamer the appearance of being squat. Still it is tall as creamers go and has its own innate charm. The main motif covers the lower three-fourths of the body and is composed of rows of large thumbprints which encircle the body. Each such thumbprint is bound by beveled sides and these sides are mitred into the rows above and below. It is an effective design. In some of the items the thumbprints are round in order to fit into the space available. On this piece the top and bottom rows are very different in shape as shown in the drawing. There are nine ovals in each band.

Above the figurework, the body is plain and smooth. The rim is saddled, and near the front it rises sharply to form a lip. The stem has nine flat panels, each of which ends in points on the base of the bowl. All of the panels end on a high, straight-sided, wide shelf on the base. The base is large and rather thin. It is plain underneath, smooth, and slightly domed. The handle makes up in beauty for what it lacks in capacity. Only two adult fingers can be accommodated therein. The large blob is at the top. It arches high, then backward, then flows forward beautifully to the lower attachment which is nicely tooled.

The quality of the glass is excellent flint with considerable resonance when tapped. There is an occasional bubble. The batch of metal was a little cool, and an occasional hairline was left. The mold marks of this piece are set in a different position from where they are found on most pressed glass. Almost always one mold mark is directly under the handle. Here, it is to one side of the handle, and one is almost directly under the middle of the lip. This was probably caused by the way the gaffer cut and shaped the rim and lip. There is a charming simplicity to these early patterns. One never tires of having them around to feel, view, and admire. It is regrettable so few remain.

Creamer: 3-part mold, 15 1/2 ounces, 5 3/4 inches tall, 3 1/8 inches wide, and 5 1/2 inches long.

Very few pieces are known to have been made in this pattern, and they are: creamer, several open and covered compotes, butter dish, oval flat dish, goblets, sauce dish, spoonholder, covered sugar bowl. The pattern was made by the McKee Brothers of Pittsburgh.

13—GOTHIC

This is another of the magnificent early flint patterns Mrs. Kamm had not seen and did not use in her books. All pieces, except the goblet, are very scarce and are rarely advertised by dealers. It, apparently, was never made in large quantities. Ruth Webb Lee names the pattern in her *Early American Pressed Glass*, Pattern 60, pages 172-173 and Plate 35. She thought it was made by the Boston and Sandwich Glass Company about 1860.

S. T. Millard, in *Goblets*, Plate 125-4, shows a goblet. From his photograph it cannot be determined whether the goblet has a plain or rayed base. The goblet with the plain base seems not to have been made at the factory that produced the complete line. The McKearins, in their *American Glass*, page 405 and Plate 208, No. 5, show a goblet and list some of the items known in the pattern. Their goblet appears to have a shorter, thicker stem than that portrayed by Millard.

Anyone who loves glass would be thrilled to hold, admire, and work with this perfect specimen in its brilliant, sparkling early flint glass. Mrs. Lee thinks it was made about 1860; it is my opinion it was made slightly later. It is not of the heavy massive type like LOOP and HORN OF PLENTY of the early 1860s, and neither is it the light, graceful type of the late 1860s and early 1870s such as ARABESQUE and LOOP AND DART. It seems to fit somewhere between these dates as a transition piece. The quality of the flint glass is superior. It is crystal clear and brilliant. It has one small bubble. On the base, one of the mold marks is high and sharp. They are difficult to find on the body. The impression is slightly marred in one or two places, and this could have been caused by a cold mold, cool metal, or the way in which the piece was removed from the mold.

This urn-shaped, standard creamer has all its decorative motif confined to the lower two-thirds of the body. Two V-shaped grooves set off the two-inch-wide band around the middle of the body. The design here has erroneously provided the name. The arches are rounded, not pointed, and have a keystone at their apex, so they are not Gothic. Large, rounded loops based on the lower V-shaped groove make up most of the wide belt. There are six loops on the creamer with each outlined by an inverted V-shaped ridge. In the center at the base of each large loop is a large oblong, highly convex figure or jewel. The space between it and the outer loop resembles a rounded arch made of heavy, round-cut stones with V-shaped mortar joints. The large stone at top center is definitely a keystone. At the top of the band, the interstices between the loops are filled with raised fans. Below the wide belt and around the curved bottom of the body is a band of wide, rounded ribs alternating with narrow V-shaped ridges.

Above the wide belt, the body is left plain over the upper one-fourth of its surface. It is constricted slightly and then curves out to the beautiful, plain, saddled rim. The lip is narrow and is pursed upward. The rim rises sharply at the back to provide an anchorage for a top attachment of the applied handle. The handle is small but beautifully proportioned, and its curves are winsome. The top attachment is cut to a wedge instead of a round blob as was usually employed. The handle is not heavy or massive and blends perfectly with its counterparts. The lower attachment is beautifully tooled into crossbars. The lower tip is turned back but did not rejoin the handle. It leaves a quaint little hook at the base. (See drawing.)

The stem is short, thick, and has six sides. It ends in a round low shelf on the base of the body and in a round high shelf just above the base. The foot is round, rather low, and wide for stability. Underneath, the base is domed slightly and has impressed therein a 32-ray raised star. The star is the same diameter as the shelf on top. This type of raised star on bases of pressed glass is seldom encountered.

Creamer: 3-part mold, 1 1/4 pounds, 6 1/16 inches tall, 3 1/8 inches wide, and 5 1/8 inches long.

A number of items were made in this pattern, and the following are known: butter dish, berry bowls, caster set, celery vase, creamer, champagne, high or low, open and covered compotes, cordials, eggcup, goblet, oval dish, salt, spoonholder, sauce dish, sugar bowl, and tumbler. One might find a water pitcher, several sizes of decanters, honey dishes, whiskey tumblers, and a lamp.

14—RIBBED IVY

This is an illustrious member of the ribbed family of pressed glass. Many people consider the ribbed group the most beautiful and desirable ever made. Other members are RIBBED BELLFLOWER, RIBBED GRAPE, RIBBED ACORN and FINE RIBBED. They have almost as much shimmer and brilliance as Lacy Sandwich.

RIBBED IVY was made at the Boston and Sandwich Glass Company, and there is doubt if any other factory ever produced any items of the pattern. However, there is enough variation in pieces, such as compotes, to suggest the possibility that it was made by other glass houses. The bases on compotes, the ribbing, size, meandering of the vine, shape of veins on the leaves, and stems indicate a different point of origin for some items. The compotes are relatively plentiful and reasonably priced. So are the spoonholders, which make splendid vases for short-stemmed flowers. Creamers, sugars, butters, covered salts, and whiskey tumblers are difficult to find.

The lines of the creamer are attractive but tend toward plumpness. The body has the shape of an inverted bell and is ample in capacity. From stem to rim the body is covered with parallel and vertical ribs graduated in size to fit the contours of the piece. As a result, they are narrow at the waist but very wide where the body expands to form the spout. These fine ribs refract the light and give the piece its shimmering, silvery brilliance and sparkle. An ivy vine meanders about the middle of the body. It has three stemmed leaves above and three below the vine. Where the vine festoons, the leaves are above, and where it climbs, the leaves are below. The vines and leaves are left plain and are slightly dished. Only a faint trace of veining is present. Some pieces of the pattern are known to have raised veins in the leaves. From the well-rounded base of the bowl, the sides rise vertically to the rim except in front, where they flare high and protrude forward to form an overly large lip. The rim is deeply saddled with a high protrusion at the back and higher rise and forward thrust in front. When viewed from the side, the lip has graceful curves. When seen from the front, it is out of all proportion to the remainder of the piece.

The applied handle has the large blob at the top attachment and it is cut to taper to a thin sharp point. The lower attachment is turned back on itself and tooled into six crossbars. It was applied on top of the figurework and the interstices are filled with dirt. Repeated washings have failed to remove this accumulated grime.

The plain, round stem is small and short. It ends in a round, low, narrow shelf at the base of the body and flows out to a high circular shelf on the round base. The wide base is pleasingly arched on top. Underneath is a three-quarter-inch-high dome. At its apex is a dewdrop. Radiating from this, a many-rayed star is impressed whose rays extend almost to the rim. They show plainly through the glass and appear to be on top of the base. The piece sits on a narrow ring near the perimeter of the base.

The quality of this rather thin flint glass is superlative. No defects are found, and when tapped lightly it has a beautiful bell tone. This seldom occurs in creamers. The workmanship is on a par with the mix. Only after the most minute study under a strong light can a trace of a mold mark be found, except on the base, and even these are indistinct. This piece is magnificent.

Carl W. Dreppard, in *ABC's of Old Glass*, shows this creamer on page 149. Millard, in *Goblets*, Plate 16-4, shows a goblet. Ruth Webb Lee, in *Sandwich Glass*, Plate 214, shows four rare pieces in the pattern. In her *Early American Pressed Glass*, Pattern 37, pages 107-109, and Plates 33 and 39, she describes RIBBED IVY. She also mentions the pattern in her *Victorian Glass* on pages 14 and 390. Metz, in *Early American Pattern Glass*, pages 30-31, and No. 275, illustrates a goblet. She says the ware is of the 1850s and quotes prices on many items. Kamm did not use the pattern. Millard and Metz say the pattern was produced in the 1850s. I believe it was made somewhat later, possibly in the late 1860s to early 1870s.

Creamer: 3-part mold, 1 1/8 pounds, 6 5/16 inches tall, 3 3/8 inches wide, and 5 5/8 inches long.

Some of the many items manufactured in the pattern are: bowls, butter, caster bottles, celery vase, champagne, open and covered compotes of several sizes and heights, cordial, creamer, decanters, eggcup, goblet, honey dish, hat, lamp, mugs, salts of several types, spoonholder, sugar, two tumblers, and a whiskey tumbler. Probably a water pitcher was made, but it has not been listed.

15—*BUCKLE, FANCY*

This is a fancy version of the popular BUCKLE pattern which was made in several factories, each putting out its own particular version. It is known to have been made by the Boston and Sandwich Glass Company and also by Gillinder and Sons of Philadelphia, Pennsylvania. Others also made it, and we have BANDED BUCKLE, as well as pieces with and without rays on the lower part of the body.

Ruth Webb Lee, in *Early American Pressed Glass*, Pattern 123, pages 322-23, describes *Buckle* and lists the articles known to have been made. On Plate 62 she shows two different goblets, and on Plate 102 she made line drawings of a covered sugar bowl, creamer, eggcup, and a sauce dish. In her pattern the buckle design covers the lower three-fourths of the body. I have a spoonholder in her version, with scalloped rim. I also have a creamer with stem panels rounded over at the top and with rays at the base of the bowl. The pattern shown here is quite different.

Minnie Watson Kamm, in *A Fifth Pitcher Book*, page 8, No. 8, shows a creamer with the design covering most of the body and the tops of the stem panels having sharp points. Dr. S. T. Millard, in *Goblets*, Plate 110-3 shows a goblet with the design covering most of the body, and in the photograph no rays are seen on the bottom of the bowl. Edwin G. Warman, in *The Third Antiques and Their Current Prices*, page 18, shows what appear to be identical goblets and calls one *BUCKLE* and the other *BUCKLE WITH STAR*. The latter is the correct ti-

tle for both pieces he shows, and the pattern is different, later and worth less than the *BUCKLE* patterns under discussion. Metz, in *Early American Pattern Glass*, pages 122-23, No. 1370, shows a BUCKLE goblet.

The shape and conformation of this creamer would seem to indicate it dates from the late 1860s to the early 1870s, but the acid etching decoration proves it was made in the late 1870s by which time styles had changed, and this light, airy type was no longer in vogue. By a system of rather vague, circumstantial deductions we probably can say who made the piece. Gillinder and Sons, who were the makers of fine tableware, including some of our choicest patterns, had an exhibit at the Philadelphia Centennial Exposition in 1876. They erected a small glass factory at the fair and made novelties for sale.

At the same fair there was exhibited for the first time in America, glass with an acid-etched, satin finish from France. Gillinder immediately adopted this method of decoration and used it for a year or two, by which time most other companies followed suit. This piece appears to have been a sample of the early satin-finishing or frosting. Gillinder and Sons are known to have made BUCKLE pattern since they advertised a goblet in the early 1870s as their No. 15 ware. They could have made this creamer.

The lower third of the inverted bell-shaped body carries the six-buckle motif. The buckles are tapered and extend to the lower rounded portion of the body. Each has a large, low, beveled frame left clear and plain. The buckles are covered with diamond point, except in the center where there is a plain elongated thumbprint. The tops of these figures form a low, scalloped line about the body at its greatest girth. Above this, the sides are first constricted, then flare to the rim. The upper two-thirds of the body has a satinlike finish, commonly called frosted. Around the sides and front at the most constricted part of the body is a formalized floral spray band which was cut rather deeply and then polished. It was not etched. The clear design against the frosted background is refreshing.

The lower portion of the body is devoid of the ribs which appear on some variants. Where the stem panels blend into the bowl, they form flat-surfaced diamonds with curved sides. The saddled rim has a low scallop at the back for the handle attachment. In front the rim flares up and too far forward for the piece, and forms a wide spout. The stem is short and has six panels. The top of each is rounded over. They flare widely on the base and end in a large, hexagonal shelf. The foot is almost flat, is rounded on the edge, and hollowed out slightly underneath.

The applied handle is well shaped and proportioned—being a little on the delicate side. Such handles are subject to heat-checks just above the lower attachment, when they are subjected to sudden changes in temperature. The lower attachment is long, folded back on itself, and tooled nicely. (See drawing for details.)

Creamer: 3-part mold, 15 ounces, 6 1/16 inches tall, 3 inches wide, and 5 5/16 inches long.

This creamer may well have been a presentation piece, display specimen, or salesman's sample. For this reason no other items may have been made. However, a sugar bowl, spoonholder, and butter dish would be expected.

16—BLAZE

This magnificent small creamer is proof that the New England Glass Company turned out products of superlative quality. This piece was produced at their factory in the 1860s. It is of top quality in every detail—crystal clear, brilliant, and superbly finished. When lightly tapped with a pencil it rings like a compote or goblet. In fact, no creamer ever seen by the writer approaches the resonance found in this piece.

Mrs. Lee, in *Early American Pressed Glass*, Pattern 21, pages 63-64, Plate 13, covers the pattern. She compares it with STEDMAN and says they are very similar. (See STEDMAN write-up below.) Laura Woodside Watkins, in *Cambridge Glass, 1818 to 1888*, Plate 40, shows a spoonholder, creamer, covered sugar bowl, and a celery vase. These cuts were taken from an old New England Glass Company catalog dated 1869. In Plate 41 she shows a magnificent large compote. Millard, in *Goblets*, Plate 76-4, shows a goblet. George and Helen McKearin's *American Glass*, page 404, lists the items made in the pattern, and on Plate 208, No. 6 they show a goblet. Metz, in *Early American Pattern Glass*, page 53, No. 541, covers the pattern but does not illustrate it. Minnie Watson Kamm did not cover the pattern in her books.

This medium-sized piece originally had a lid, but it is not shown in the catalog illustration used by Mrs. Watkins. Slightly below the rim on the inside is a decided sloping ledge which follows the contour of the rim but dips low under the lip. (See broken line in drawing, and also, see FURROWS in this book which has an identical sloping ledge

to accommodate a lid.) The rim is well saddled. The lip is not remarkable.

The bell-shaped bowl has its decorative features on its lower portion. Parallel V-shaped flutes or grooves, side-by-side and vertical, ranging from short to long, provide a pleasing effect. The mold maker and gaffer worked so expertly that the figurework must be inspected closely to be sure it is not cut glass. These flutes in great peaks and deep valleys appear five times around the body. All figurework stops just short of where the handle is pressed on. This is one of the characteristics of glass made by the New England Glass Company. The upper portion of the body is mirror bright and smooth. The handle has an almost Spartan simplicity. It is six-sided and wider than it is thick. There is a well-designed protrusion at the top to assist in holding the piece.

The narrow, short waist is also hexagonal. The six flat panels are splayed on the bottom of the bowl and end at the blaze in rounded arches. These panels appear even more to have been cut than do the flutes of the blaze. Near the base the panels flatten out and disappear in a round shelf on top of it. The base itself slopes to a rounded edge. Underneath is a wide, arched dome which is so smooth it seems too perfect to have been fire polished. It seems that only grinding and polishing could have made it so smooth and mirror bright. Nevertheless, there is no evidence that a pontil mark was ground down. In actual fact, the entire piece was pressed with no portion tooled, and there was no need or excuse for a punty to be used. Most pieces manufactured by the New England Glass Company have ground pontil marks. They were seldom left rough.

Creamer: 3-part mold, 15 ounces, 4 7/8 inches tall, 3 1/4 inches wide and 5 3/8 inches long.

This piece is not thick and massive as were most of its contemporaries. The glass is thin, yet heavy.

The following items are known to have been made in the pattern: covered bowls in three sizes, on foot; open bowls in five sizes, on high foot; open bowls in five sizes, on low foot; celery vase; champagne; covered compotes in three sizes on foot; covered compotes in three sizes, on low foot; open compotes in three sizes on foot; open compotes in three sizes on low foot; cordials; custards with handles; dishes, oval in four sizes; dishes, covered in four sizes; eggcup; goblet; lemonade glass; salt, oblong; sauce dish in two sizes; spoonholder; sugar bowl; tumblers in two sizes; wines in two sizes.

17—STEDMAN

This tall, slender creamer has all the grace, charm, beauty, and simplicity of youth. Mrs. Lee said it was very similar to BLAZE, and was made by McKee Brothers in 1868. (See BLAZE above.)

In *Early American Pressed Glass*, Pattern 22, pages 63-65, Plate 12, Mrs. Lee shows this pattern. She had not seen a creamer. Millard in *Goblets*, Plates 13, 76 and 88, shows three slightly different goblets. The McKearins, in *American Glass*, Plate 208, No. 4, show a goblet. On pages 398 and 414 they list known items in the pattern, but they also had not seen a creamer. Mrs. Kamm never located a creamer and did not use the pattern in her books. Mrs. Metz illustrated a goblet as No. 542.

This is one of the tallest and most slender creamers found in early American pressed glass. (See McKEE'S COMET in this book and KALEIDOSCOPE, RUBY THUMBPRINT and HIGHTOWER for other tall but later patterns.) Despite its height, the creamer is quite stable. The body is long, cylindrical, and rounds under nicely to a hexagonal waist. Encircling the body and extending from the waist to within 3/4 of an inch of the rim are six series of raised figurework which look like stalagmites of random heights and widths. Some are rounded with round tops. Others are spined ridges which end in sharp points. In the center of each series are the three longest with sharp points. The two types then alternate and become shorter. They convey the impression of a pipe organ. At the top of the figurework is a ledge that surrounds the body. Here the glass becomes thinner; thickness is no longer necessary to take the impression of the figures. Above the ledge the piece is smooth and plain.

The rim has a high saddle. It rises high in the back for the handle attachment and unusually high in front and projects forward for the smiling lip. The handle is not ponderous, yet is sufficiently heavy to serve its purpose. At the lower attachment it is curled under in a spiral, then pressed and tooled into three crossbars. The one demerit of the piece is that this attachment is on top of the figurework and left pockets to catch and hold filth.

The waist is narrow and short for so tall a creamer. Six flat panels extend up on the base of the bowl and end in portions of circles. Below, they extend out on the foot and gradually disappear before reaching the edge. The base is round. Underneath, the base is slightly domed. At the apex of the dome is a small circular thumbprint. Radiating from this circle is a deeply impressed 36-ray star. The rays extend almost to the edge of the base and are visible from the top. The quality is excellent. Although this is fine quality flint glass, there is no resonance when tapped. All that is heard is a dull plunk. It is such a magnificent and delightful pattern, one can but regret its scarcity. It is impossible to find a mold mark on the piece.

Creamer: ?-part mold, 1 3/8 pounds, 6 7/8 inches tall, 2 7/8 inches wide, and 5 1/2 inches long.

The following items were made in the pattern: champagne, creamer, decanter, eggcup, goblet, lamp, 6 inch plate, footed salt, flat salt, sugar bowl, syrup pitcher, tumbler, wine in two sizes. In all probability a celery vase, spoonholder, butter dish, and a water pitcher were also made.

18—YOKED LOOP

A keen sense of joy comes from locating and acquiring a creamer as rare as this and in such a grand old pattern. It is contemporary with the earliest ASHBURTON and has the same characteristic greasy feeling. This feeling is peculiar to some of the early flint glass but entirely lacking in others. It is never found in soda-lime glass. Millard named the pattern YOKED LOOP in his *Goblets II*, Plate 54-4, and says it was made in the 1860s. In the same book on Plate 1-2 he shows SCALLOPED LOOP, which he says was made in the 1850s. It is impossible to distinguish one from the other in his photographs.

This piece was made during the 1850s. This is indicated by such features as: the greasy feeling, the fused-on base, the ground and polished pontil mark, the weight, the type of handle attachment, and the quality and brilliance of the metal as well as the general conformation. The simple, flowing lines and absence of fuss and feathers place this pattern in the class of COLONIAL, ASHBURTON, and ARGUS, all of which are imitations of earlier cut glass. The quality and workmanship were necessarily superb on these plain patterns, or they would have fallen from their exalted positions. Such a piece, in any setting, would be delightful to have around.

This creamer is rather squat and has an ample girth. To borrow a medical term, we could call it a 'pyknic' type. From a small waist the body swells outward and upward to the neck where it is again slightly constricted. The major portion of the body is covered with eight flat panels which are slightly rounded over on top. They extend down the body, through the waist, and out on top of the

14

17

18

15

19

21

16

Bottom
21

20

base where they end in a high, octagonal shelf. About halfway down each panel and where the bowl starts curving in to the waist is a raised ridge or yoke which loops across the panel. Above the panels is a plain band half an inch wide which curves in sharply. This is topped by a plain 3/16 of an inch rounded ring circling the body. Above the ring the body is plain and smooth.

The rim is beautifully saddled. It rises upward and forward to a pert and attractive lip. The lip was handtooled and is a little off-center which adds to the desirability of the piece. The applied handle is round and adequate, though not massive as are some of its relatives. The lower attachment is stuck on one of the flat panels of the body and the attachment turned in. It is also a little off-center and out of plumb—bless it!

The mold marks show on the lower part of the body. They are to one side of the handle and lip, rather than directly beneath them as is usually the case. The base is round, wide, and almost flat. It was made as a separate piece and fused to the body while both were hot. The pontil mark is ground smooth, but this did not remove all the scars of breaking and fusing. The piece is both thick and heavy. There are a few small bubbles and an occasional hairline. It was and is a quality product.

Creamer: 2-part mold, 1 1/4 pounds, 5 7/16 inches tall, 3 3/8 inches wide, and 6 inches long.

The goblet is the only other item known to have been made in this pattern. Since it is so lovely, it is unfortunate that it is also so rare.

19—VICKSBURG

Pick this beautiful creamer up in your hands and your fingers automatically start caressing it. It is smooth and comfortable to touch. Most pieces of glass feel cold, unfriendly, and forbidding. This medium-sized creamer is quite thick (from 1/4 to 1/2 inch) and very heavy. It is an early, brilliantly clear flint glass piece. I have a feeling it may be of foreign origin, possibly English, since some of its characteristics are unfamiliar. On the other hand, it resembles domestic glass in some respects.

Its decorative features have been used so often in the names of pressed glass patterns that no effort from that source was productive. Instead, consideration is given to its worth and sturdiness and the name *VICKSBURG* is assigned. The creamer was manufactured at about the time Vicksburg's sturdiness was being thoroughly measured.

The base of the piece is similar to no other in this volume. Underneath, an 18-ray star is impressed into a slight dome. Otherwise, the base is 1/2-inch-thick solid glass, and as massive as a paperweight. The curved waist is broad and short with nine flat panels extending throughout its length. Each panel has a rounded end on the thick, heavy, ringed base. On the bottom of the bowl the waist panels end in wide swags to conform to the figurework above.

The body swells slightly in its lower portion and is somewhat constricted above, thus forming a trim shapely bowl. Its lower half is covered by three horizontal rows of large, highly beveled, flat-topped diamonds standing on their points. They increase in size from bottom to top, the upper row being kite-shaped and an inch long. These bands stop abruptly in the rear where the handle is applied, providing a smooth, flat escutcheon for the handle attachments. No unseemly pockets resulted.

The upper half of the body contains nine large punties or thumbprints in a band which fills most of the space. The one directly under the handle is smaller and so placed as not to interfere with the handle attachments. The upper attachment was, in turn, sheared and tooled to conform to the shape of the punty. The punties increase in length from back to front. In fact, the two under the lip start out as punties, change to flat panels and then extend up to form an ungainly spout. The rim has eight deep V-shaped notches in its thick, flat top, thus forming seven large, flat-topped scallops. The long spout is tooled into a narrow, upthrust lip.

The handle seems large enough for the creamer's size, but small for the weight, since it weighs more than many twice its size. (See below.) The large blob is at the top attachment. All proportions and curves of the handle are pleasing. The lower attachment was well tooled but unfortunately the lower tip of the tab has been broken off.

The workmanship is excellent. Except for an occasional small bubble the flint glass is of fine quality. It has a ringing resonance when tapped. The escutcheon provided for the handle reminds one of the care lavished on pieces produced by the New England Glass Company. No such attribution is suggested, however. It is regretted that so little is known of this fine pattern. It should have been made in large quantities, but no other piece of the pattern has been seen by the writer.

Creamer, medium: 3-part mold, 1 3/8 pounds, 5 7/16 inches tall, 3 3/16 inches wide, and 5 1/4 inches long.

The pattern has not previously been described in our American pressed glass literature.

20—DIAMOND POINT WITH PANELS

This neat, compact little creamer is a fine old piece, contemporary with FOUR PETAL, HORN OF PLENTY, WAFFLE, etc. They are similar in body shape, contour of rim, the presence of ribs on the upper third of the body, and in having a scalloped base. The quality is that of excellent clear flint glass which gives a high sharp resonance when tapped. This creamer is smaller than the standard creamers of the patterns mentioned above. Perhaps two sizes were made as was true with HORN OF PLENTY. This piece is the size of the smaller HORN OF PLENTY creamer.

The grenade-shaped body rests on a heavy dome-shaped base which has six large scallops. There is a large ground and polished pontil mark underneath. The body is divided into three horizontal and nearly equal parts. The lower part has diamond point, the middle section is fluted up to a ringed collar, and the upper zone is vertically ribbed. The diamond point extends from the waist to a line one-third of the way up the body. The diamonds are not sharp at the apex as in cut glass, or other DIAMOND POINT patterns. Here, they are somewhat rounded.

The middle section is separated from the lower by beveled scallops from which nine plain and slightly concave flutes (note title) extend upward to a narrow, continuous high ring about the body. Above the ring and extending to the irregular rim are nineteen columns or ribs. The ribs under the lip are much broader than the others. The rim is cut as shown. It rises in front to a high lip, and has three wide scallops on the rear half.

The irregular scallop at the back of the rim affords an attachment to which the applied handle is affixed. It is not a massive handle as are many on this type of small creamer. It is 5/8 inches wide at the top, and 1/2 inch wide at the bottom. It is thin and has a delicate appearance. Fortunately the handle does not have a heat check. Heat checks are caused by a sudden change of temperature. Having less mass than the body, the handle contracts or expands more rapidly than the body. This causes the handle to crack at its weakest point—just above the lower attachment of applied handles. Why they are called heat checks instead of heat cracks is a mystery to me. These checks are so prevalent in early flint applied handles that we are almost conditioned to expect them. The upturned tab of the bottom attachment has two crossbars.

This grand old pattern has so many similarities to FOUR PETAL, HORN OF PLENTY, and WAFFLE it is easy to assume that they were, in all likelihood, made in the same factory and well may have been designed by the same person. This type of glass was made between 1850 and 1865. Millard, in *Goblets*, Plate 7-3, shows a goblet which he calls HINOTO and says it was made in the seventies and came in the clear only. Mrs. Lee, in *Victorian Glass*, Plate 20-4 and page 54, shows three pieces and mentions seven other pieces she knows to have been made. She says it was made by the New England Glass Company. Certainly it has all the fine attributes one would expect in a product of that company. Dr. Millard's name of HINOTO has the advantage of brevity and simplicity, but carries no significance in the English language. Mrs. Lee called it DIAMOND POINT WITH PANEL, and since this adequately describes the pattern the name is continued despite its length.

Small creamer: 3-part mold, 1 pound, 5 3/8 inches tall, 3 inches wide, and 4 3/4 inches long.

So little of this pattern is seen today that we must conclude it was neither made in large quantities, nor over a long period. It is difficult to find. Made when it was, it would not be surprising to find a four-piece table setting of two creamers, butter dish, spooner or spillholder, and covered sugar bowl. The following pieces also were probably made: celery vase, champagne, wine, several sizes of compotes, relish dish, honey dish, bowls, master salt, goblet, tumbler, pint and quart decanters.

21—HORN OF PLENTY

This is a fake—a reproduction that fooled the author $8 worth. (Caveat emptor!) It is one of the cleverest imitations possible and was made for no other purpose than to deceive. It is of the finest quality, beautifully clear, flint glass. It has a ringing bell-like resonance when tapped. The glass has the same greasy feeling as early flint glass. Only by the closest inspection can it be determined that the pontil mark which appears to have been ground was in reality pressed into the base. To make it more deceptive, a pontil rod was attached to the pressed pontil mark, and, after the lip was formed and the applied handle attached, the new pontil mark was left rough. (I have a faked EXCELSIOR whiskey tumbler with a pressed pontil mark that is even more difficult to detect than is this piece. It is, nevertheless, a fake and the ground-out place was pressed into the base.) Had this piece been produced at an early date, when its precursors were manufactured, the handle would have been applied in reverse, with the large blob at the top, and would have had an entirely different shape.

Ruth Webb Lee, on Plate 44 of *Antique Fakes & Reproductions,* shows this particular creamer in soda-lime glass. (Note that this piece is of the finest quality flint glass.) In Mrs. Lee's *Supplementary Pamphlet No. 1* to the above book she shows a reproduction of HORN OF PLENTY glass. If one confines his collecting of pressed glass to a single pattern and knows it is not being reproduced, he does not need the above books. If he collects several patterns, he should by all means own and study these books by Mrs. Lee. Elsewhere in this book is found a list of reproductions of pressed glass offered to the author at prices out of reason for acknowledged fakes.

Creamer: 3-part mold, 14 ounces, 3 3/4 inches tall, 3 5/16 inches wide, and 4 7/8 inches long.

A tumbler was made in HORN OF PLENTY but did not have an imitation ground pontil mark in the base, nor was the original mold used to make offhand creamers such as this.

22—LOOP AND MOOSE EYE

It is not surprising that Minnie Watson Kamm failed in her eight pitcher books to write up, name, and describe a large number of fine patterns. It is remarkable that she could locate and write up the fantastic total of almost sixteen hundred patterns. It was a herculean task for anyone and she did a superlative job. The pattern described here is one she did not find. S. T. Millard, M.D., in his *Goblets,* Plate 108-1, gave the pattern its distinctive name. There is no danger of confusing the pattern with any other name. He thought it was of the 1870s and came in clear only.

Ruth Webb Lee, in her *Victorian Glass,* page 176, Plate 57-2, shows a goblet, creamer, and eggcup. Although she did not particularly like it, she continued the name BULL'S EYE AND LOOP, which she had heard used for this pattern. Millard's title seems preferable. Metz, in *Early American Pattern Glass,* pages 18-19, No. 149, shows a similar pattern with the eyes directly over the loops. It is not the same pattern as shown by Millard, Lee, or the one used here. She did, however, call her pattern LOOP AND MOOSE EYE. Note the similarity of this pattern to the one that follows.

This is an old flint glass pattern and one that is seldom seen. Probably only a limited amount of it was manufactured, but where, when, or by whom remains an enigma. The type of glass, the shape, the handle, and mold marks seem to bear out Millard's belief that it dates from the 1870s. These and other aspects of the piece appear familiar and so closely resemble certain features in the patterns HUBER, BLAZE, and BALLOON that they appear to be contemporaries.

The wide, low foot on this creamer has a high instep and is plain and smooth. Underneath, the piece sits on a low, narrow ring at the perimeter of the base. The latter forms a low, flat dome.

Slightly above the base, the short, thick, heavy stem has a large round knop. Beginning half-way up the knop, the stem is paneled and also constricted to form a narrow, short baluster. The panels flare out and end in a high, hexagonal shelf on the base of the bowl.

The sides of the bowl are vertical after curving out broadly at the lower portion. The hexagonal shelf on the base of the body forms a foundation for six high, wide loops. Each loop starts at a corner and ends at another corner of the hexagon. The loops extend up to about the middle of the bowl. They are beveled on top and are separated from each other by sharp V-shaped ridges. The inside of each loop is slightly convexed and is left plain. (On some pieces they are frosted.) Centered over the junction of each two loops and slightly above them are six large, round, beveled "moose eyes" also slightly convex. Above the loops and around the moose eyes, the surface is plain and smooth. The rim is beautifully saddled, providing a high anchorage for the handle and a wide, generous lip. The edge of the rim is rounded and smooth. The handle has six sides and is the same size throughout its course, except where the excellent concave thumbgrip is placed on top. It provides a firm grip.

The mold marks on this creamer differ radically from any I have seen. The back one is straight and vertical, showing under the handle and on the foot. The two forward mold marks can be seen on the foot, over the knop, and on the edge of the stem panel. They then follow a meandering path, beginning on top of the V-shaped ridge between the loops and curving over the tops of the loops for 3/4 inch. From there they go vertically to the bevel of the moose eye above, skirt the eye on the crest of the bevel for one-third of its circumference, and then go vertically to the rim. What a headache it was for the mold maker. It was effort expended to produce a quality product by hiding the marks.

This piece is made of fine glass and has a slight ring when tapped. The convex discs and loops should serve as magnifying lenses and add to the overall beauty. Actually they do not, for their outer surfaces have a very minute pebbly, or grained, leather effect which prevents light from passing through, and so they do not magnify. This graining is not apparent and it feels perfectly smooth. The roughness results in little of the pattern being seen when looking through from the opposite side. This should have been an alluring feature. The mold lines show but are neither high nor sharp. The glass is clear, brilliant, and free of impurities and discoloration.

Creamer: 3-part mold, 14 ounces, 5 1/4 inches tall, 3 1/16 inches wide, and 5 3/16 inches long.

This design is infrequently seen. All items in the pattern are scarce. The creamer, sugar bowl, spoonholder, butter dish, eggcup, champagne, and goblet are known. Very likely other items may have been produced.

23—STAR-EYED

This pattern reminds me of the lovely song "Stars In My Eyes." Were it not so long, it would be a suitable title. I will shorten it to STAR-EYED. This pattern should be compared with the preceding one. Other than the stars, stippling, and shape of the base on this piece, it is identical with the pattern Dr. Millard called LOOP AND MOOSE EYE. Mrs. Lee, in *Victorian Glass*, Plate 57-2, named the Millard pattern BULL'S EYE AND LOOP. In LOOP AND MOOSE EYE the eyes are placed just above the junction of each two loops.

Mrs. Metz, in *Early American Pattern Glass*, pages 18-19, No. 149, shows a different pattern as Millard's LOOP AND MOOSE EYE, but used his title and reference. On her goblet an eye is directly over each loop. Note the large diamond-shaped interstices on her goblet. They are absent on the two patterns shown here. In this pattern the interior of the loops and the space above them, almost to the top of the eyes, is finely stippled. Each moose eye has a stippled six-point star for a pupil.

It is entirely possible that the same designer created STAR-EYED, LOOP AND MOOSE EYE, and the pattern shown by Metz. They may well have emanated from the Hipkins Novelty Mold Works at Martins Ferry, Ohio. This shop made molds for many factories and varied each set just enough to avoid patent infringements. They could

have produced the molds for all three patterns. The stem has six panels. They start from a hexagonal shelf on the base of the bowl and end halfway down the stem in a large round knop.

Lee said her pieces were flint. One of my creamers is light-weight and has no resonance. The other is flint. The resonance of a creamer, when tapped, is a poor indicator of whether it is, or is not, flint or lime-soda glass. The hollow body of a piece of flint glass vibrates and produces a bell-toned ring when lightly tapped. When handles are present, as on creamers and sugar bowls, they interfere with the vibrations of the resonator and as a rule prevent the bell-toned sound. Such articles as goblets, tumblers, spooners, bowls, sauces, celery vases, and compotes have the best resonance. This pattern seems to date from the 1870s.

Standard creamer: 3-part mold, 14 ounces, 5 1/2 inches tall, 3 1/16 inches wide, and 5 inches long.

I borrowed the creamer illustrated here from the Lutterloh glass collection in the Little Rock Art Center. Later I secured one for my own collection. No writer on American pressed glass has heretofore listed this pattern—an indication of how scarce it is. It is strange that the only two pieces seen or known of by writers on the subject are creamers, and both are in Little Rock.

24—PEARS' THUMBPRINT

The name *PEARS' THUMBPRINT* is assigned to this pattern to distinguish it from the larger, heavier, more massive, and earlier *THUMBPRINT* shown and named by Kamm in *A Seventh Pitcher Book*, page 2, No. 4 (which piece is in the author's collection). Ruth Webb Lee in *Early American Pressed Glass*, Pattern 67, Plate 15, shows this particular creamer in the four-piece table set as ARGUS from an early catalog of Bakewell, Pears and Company of Pittsburgh, Pennsylvania. The name *Pears* is used in the title here to date the piece. The Bakewell name remained in numerous company titles over a period of many years. They had been manufacturing magnificent flint glass for years before *PEARS* appeared in the name of the company. All books on American glass cover the Bakewell factories and their wares, so no attempt will be made to rehash them here. We are primarily interested in patterns of pressed glass in this volume.

It is well that the original name of ARGUS for this pattern was dropped and that of *PEARS' THUMBPRINT* substituted, since another regal old pattern still is known as ARGUS when it can be found. After working with pressed glass for twenty years, I have seen only one piece of pressed ARGUS pattern, and that is the creamer in my collection. I have a pair of cut-glass decanters in the ARGUS pattern, which antedated the pressed type and indeed are the originals which the pressed type imitated.

The sides of the bowl are almost vertical with a resultant cylindrical effect. The body curves in to the rather wide waist and then ever so slightly outward at the rim. Four rows of deeply impressed, somewhat misshapen thumbprints cover the lower three-fourths of the body. The impressions of the thumbprints are neither uniform nor perfect. This would seem to indicate a wooden mold (somewhat the worse from wear) rather than too small a gather of metal. Either could have produced this result, however. The upper part of the creamer is left plain.

The large waist has nine short, almost imperceptible panels which seem to disappear on the shelf atop the base. The rest of the base is thick and heavy. Underneath is a high, well-rounded dome that is perfectly smooth, but this is not from the polishing off of a pontil mark. The rim has a large, rounded scallop on each side. It also projects straight up at the rear, to accommodate the handle attachment. In front it soars to a high and rather haughty lip.

The handle is applied, large, round, and comfortable to use. It is more comfortable than attractive. In fact the general lines of the piece fall short of the overall beauty and symmetry of most of its contemporaries. It is a fine old piece, but no one would call it pretty. The lower attachment is rolled inward, then tooled down into several crossbars. It is applied over the figurework, which signifies a lack of refinement. I have a huge covered sugar bowl to match the creamer, and it is somewhat more pleasing in appearance.

The quality is of fine, early flint glass. There are a few bubbles, a few flecks of unfused sand discolorations, and in addition, the pressing was poor. The mold marks are high but not sharp. It has a wonderful resonance when tapped. This is unusual for a piece with a handle.

Creamer: 3-part mold, 1 1/8 pounds, 6 inches tall, 3 1/8 inches wide, and 5 1/4 inches long.

It is known that the four-piece table set was made in this pattern. Other items probably were made. Much excellent ware was made in the THUMBPRINT pattern. The author has an early THUMBPRINT celery vase made in three pieces and fused together, which is as fine as any pressed glass ever produced. It is truly magnificent. It is difficult to understand why there is not more demand for this pattern which is one of the most satisfactory ever produced. There is still some of it on the market, and it can be bought at prices lower than those of other pattern glass made between 1910 and 1920.

25—BELTED ICICLE

A stingy stepmother would never have purchased this commodious creamer, nor would she have used it had it been a gift. It bespeaks the large, generous, friendly rural family with its own cows to furnish all the cream desired. A large creamer was in order.

This beautiful old pattern has not been described by any of the writers on early American pressed glass. Yet it is, nevertheless, fairly plentiful and the prices are reasonable. Patently it is a transition pattern between the massive, heavy flint glass patterns of the late 1850s and early 1860s and the smaller, lighter, graceful soda-lime patterns of the late 1860s and early 1870s. The quality and workmanship are excellent, but it has a single bad feature in that the lower handle attachment is placed on top of the figurework. The interstices are filled with filth and grime which cannot be removed. This is a common fault, absent only on pieces emanating from glass factories that insisted on maximum quality. Even with this defect the piece is lovely.

All the figurework is confined to the lower two-thirds of the bowl. From the waist, a wide band of varying widths, with sharp-pointed flutes extends upward. The varying lengths cause the top of the design to undulate between high peaks and low rounded valleys. It is a type of design widely used in pressed glass patterns and was variously named ICICLE, BLAZE, etc. The base of the flutes is level and even. Above the peaks a 7/16-inch-wide belt of vertical, parallel prisms surrounds the body. Above it, the body is constricted to form a neck, and it then flares slightly to the rim.

The rim is smooth and flows up a little to the turned-up lip. It is also saddled and rises at the rear to receive the upper handle attachment. The waist is rather wide and beautifully curved. It ends on a large round shelf on top of a wide, round base. Underneath, there is a low dome.

The applied handle is one of the most interesting features of the piece. The blob at the top is much larger than the lower one. It diminishes rapidly in size, and the handle is decidedly delicate at the bottom. The lower attachment is turned up

22

23

24

25

Base of
Handle

26

26

27

28

29

and under, then pressed down and tooled into crossbars. The soda-lime glass is clear and sparkling. It has a few small bubbles, but no resonance.

Creamer: 3-part mold, 1 1/8 pounds, 6 1/2 inches tall, 3 5/8 inches wide, and 5 7/16 inches long.

The manufacturer of this excellent pattern is unknown. It is known to have been made in creamer, covered sugar, covered butter dish, and spoonholder. Do not confuse it with Millard's pattern, *ICICLE AND PRISM BAND*.

26—*ANANAS*

This attractive water pitcher is making its first appearance in our literature on American glass. The title *PINEAPPLE* would suit it admirably, but that name has already been used many times in the title of other patterns. It would only add to the confusion to apply it to this pattern. I will compromise by calling it *ANANAS*, the scientific name for pineapple. Note the striking similarity of this piece to the *BELTED ICICLE* pattern immediately preceding.

Instead of icicles below the band of prisms about the creamer, this water pitcher has three large, round medallions. In each is a life-like pineapple in high relief. Between the medallions and covering each mold mark are three erect, rigid, spiny-margined pineapple leaves. The pitcher is bulbous. The rim was handsheared and handtooled. Its curves complement those of the entire whole.

The massive applied handle (1 3/4 inches wide at the top and 1 1/8 inches at the bottom) has flowing curves. It is comfortable to heft, even when filled. The lower attachment is remarkable for both its merits and its demerits. The upper attachment is long and triangular. The lower has been turned up and under. While still hot, the gaffer, using a die, impressed a profile of a man's head and neck in high relief. (See drawing.) A raised oval line frames the figure. The man's head is completely bald. This is the first time I have seen this conceit used on an applied handle, though I have seen fern fronds so used. On pressed handles there are a half-dozen or more patterns with a head or a face pressed on the lower attachment.

I have an identical pitcher, minus the head. This piece is damaged. It was presented to me by Betty Toney of Little Rock. I bought the piece illustrated and described here from my good friend Joe Linderman of Middletown, Ohio. He wrote me

he had available an identical water pitcher minus any pressed pattern, but with the same head on the lower tab. These four variants are siblings and may assist in tracing the patterns to a particular manufacturer. The lime-soda glass is clear and brilliant. It is quite thick and has an excellent fire polish.

Water pitcher: 3-part mold, 3 pounds, 15 ounces, 9 inches tall, 5 1/4 inches wide, and 7 7/8 inches long.

The pattern dates from the late 1860s to the middle 1870s. I suspect it was made in a wide range of items.

27—LEAF AND DART

Mrs. Kamm used an 8-inch milk pitcher of this pattern in her *Two Hundred Pattern Glass Pitchers*, page 11, No. 11. It was of the same attractive shape as this creamer. Millard does not show a goblet. Mrs. Lee, in her *Early American Pressed Glass*, describes it as Pattern 184, pages 456-57, and Plates 95 and 149. Mrs. Metz shows a somewhat different goblet as No. 2022 in her *Early American Pattern Glass*.

The pattern is used again here, because I have the standard creamer and also to show the remarkable similarity existing between this pattern; LOOP AND DART, ROUND ORNAMENT; and LOOP AND DART, DIAMOND ORNAMENT, both of which follow immediately. This is another of the lovely patterns produced during the late 1860s and early 1870s. Mrs. Lee says it was manufactured by the Richards and Hartley Glass Company of Tarentum, Pennsylvania. Mrs. Kamm gave a glowing account of the grace and charm of the pattern and it was well merited. It is beautiful.

The lower half of the bullet-shaped, graceful body is covered by a band of stippling which is bounded by scallops above and below. The stippling resembles a multitude of minute, closely packed volcanic craters. The stippling is sectioned off by plain raised bands which form the main motif. At the top of the stippling the raised figures form almost a series of connected squares, each with a round, sunken, stippled space in its center. From each alternate square is suspended a dart which is similar to the minute hand on old clocks. From every other square is suspended a curled, formalized leaf. Above this figurework is a flat, raised, 5/8-inch band which encircles the creamer. Evenly spaced on this band are small daisies composed of eight raised petals surrounding a small dewdrop. Above this band the body is left plain to the rim.

The saddled rim rises in the rear for the upper handle attachment and in front to the lip which is attractive, though a little droopy. The stem is small, hexagonal, and ends at the top in a high shelf. Between this shelf and the points of the darts, the body is plain and not stippled. The stem ends in a wide, high, hexagonal shelf on the base. The base is round, rather flat, and shows the mold marks. This is the only place they can be detected. The base is plain and slightly domed underneath. The magnificent handle is applied with the large blob at the top. The lower attachment has been turned back and under, then tooled into crossbars. The quality of the glass is excellent, but there is no resonance. The workmanship is on a par with the glass.

Creamer: 3-part mold, 1 pound, 6 1/4 inches tall, 3 1/4 inches wide, and 5 11/16 inches long. These pieces are known to have been made in the pattern: water pitcher, 8-inch milk pitcher, creamer, covered butter dish, celery vase, eggcup, cordial, salt, covered salt, footed tumbler, covered sugar bowl, spoonholder, and sauce dish.

28—LOOP AND DART, DIAMOND ORNAMENT

Mrs. Kamm neither saw nor used a creamer in this pattern, though it is one of the aristocrats of pressed glass made during the late 1860s and early 1870s. It is known that the pattern was made at the Boston and Sandwich Glass Company. The stippling is not of the superb quality that created the term *Lacy* as applied to Sandwich glass. Doubtless, this particular piece was made by some other manufacturer about the same time.

Mrs. Lee, in *Early American Pressed Glass*, Pattern 181, pages 452-53, and Plates 124, 148, and 149, describes the pattern. The round 6-inch plate she shows on Plate 124 probably belongs with LOOP AND DART, for though it has diamonds around the rim, the design is entirely different. I have a footed tumbler or possibly a spoonholder in the same pattern as Mrs. Lee's plate, but not an item of the pattern shown here. The designs are entirely different, and the footed tumbler has a beautiful lacy-type stippling. The treatment of the hexagonal stem is also different.

S. T. Millard, in his *Goblets*, Plate 41-3, shows a very tall goblet and says it was made in clear only, during the late 1860s by Richards and Hotley. (Probably Richards and Hartley Glass Company of Tarentum, Pennsylvania.) Mrs. Metz shows a goblet as No. 2016 in her *Early American Pattern Glass*. The band of diamonds shows indistinctly in her photographic illustration.

The quality of this glass is extra fine, but the workmanship leaves much to be desired. Evidently too small a gather of metal was used to properly fill the mold, resulting in a poor impression. The figurework is distinct on the lower portion of the bowl but becomes progressively more indistinct toward the top. The diamonds are almost rounded. The stippling is poorly impressed and adds no beauty to the piece. The handle is too thin for its width, is too long, and has curves which indicate the gaffer was not on duty that day.

To work with and know the Loop and Dart group is a challenging task for the diligent searcher. Less studious collectors would do well to turn elsewhere or take the word of researchers. The group must have been highly popular since so many different types were produced. Nevertheless, large quantities of any one type were probably not made, or more would have been available today. It definitely is not plentiful, and it took years to locate this particular creamer which, incidentally, was purchased quite reasonably. Most of these pieces sell for less than "showy" pieces made forty years later. If "The Joneses" start collecting it, look out! You know who will have to keep up with them and what it will do to prices.

The shape of this creamer dates it. Many, many patterns were made in the same shape during that era. It is charming and has as beautiful a shape as was ever evolved by the pressed glass industry. The lower portion of the body contains the figurework. Raised plain ridges form the loops and darts and leave the sunken diamonds at their tops. Surrounding these figures the surface is lower and is covered with poor stippling which does no more than roughen the surface. The design, however, is pleasing. This creamer just happens to be one on which little care was expended.

Above the loops is a narrow plain band around the creamer; also, a 5/8-inch raised belt surrounds the bowl. A series of indistinctly formed, evenly spaced, raised, and pointed diamonds is centered on the belt. Above this, the body is plain and slightly constricted before it flares a little to the saddled rim. The lip is narrow and somewhat short, but has the best curves of the entire piece. The applied handle is too thin for its width. It is flat on the inside and convex on the outside. The large, tooled bottom crimp is too low on the body to give a neat appearance. The glass is thin, light, and without resonance.

Creamer: 3-part mold, 12 ounces, 5 1/2 inches tall, 3 1/4 inches wide, and 5 3/8 inches long.

These items are known: celery vase, covered butter dish, open and covered compotes, cordials, creamer, eggcup, covered sugar bowl, goblet, water pitcher, 6-inch plate? (see above), salt, spoonholder, footed tumbler, and a plain tumbler.

29—LOOP AND DART, ROUND ORNAMENT

This is another of the grand old patterns Mrs. Kamm had not seen or used. It is a beautiful member of the Loop and Dart group. Mrs. Ruth Webb Lee, in *Early American Pressed Glass*, Pattern 182, pages 453-54, and Plates 148 and 149, covers the pattern. She discovered it was designed and patented by William O. Davis and manufactured by the Portland Glass Company, Portland, Maine, between 1863 and 1873.

Millard shows a goblet in his *Goblets*, Plate 42-2. Mrs. Metz shows a goblet as No. 2019 in her *Early American Pattern Glass*. The quality and workmanship of this creamer are excellent. The molds gave a splendid impression with beautiful stippling of very small "donut" rings placed hexagonally so they form straight rows in all directions. The two creamers immediately preceding this show much poorer workmanship in their execution.

The loops and darts stand out in bold, high relief and form a pleasing contrast to the stippling which surrounds them. The loops, darts and bands from which they are suspended all have flat sunken spaces filled with stippling. The darts extend downward to the stem. Above this figure-work is a plain band. Like the two preceding creamers, this piece has a raised, flat belt 5/8-inch wide surrounding the body. Evenly spaced on this belt is a series of large, raised dewdrops. Above the belt the body is constricted and flares out to the rim.

The rim is smooth and has curves which sweep upward from a low back. The lip is ample and attractive. The handle is on the fragile side and is almost too long; its curves could have been more flowing. The small, hexagonal stem ends on the base of the body in a small hexagonal shelf. It ends on top of the round base in a large, high, hexagonal shelf. Underneath, the base is slightly hollowed out and left plain.

Creamer: 3-part mold, 14 ounces, 5 5/8 inches tall, 3 1/2 inches wide, and 5 5/8 inches long. At least twenty-six different articles were made in this pattern. Some out-of-the-ordinary pieces are: cup plates, cordials, lamps, footed salts, footed

tumblers, etc. Other patterns in the Loop and Dart group are: ARABESQUE; LEAF AND DART; DOUBLE LEAF AND DART; LOOP AND DART; DOUBLE LOOP AND DART; and LOOP AND DART, DIAMOND ORNAMENTS, etc. It is regrettable such a beautiful pattern should have been given such an unwieldy name.

30—DICKINSON

This is still another early pattern which Minnie Watson Kamm had not seen and did not use in any of her eight pitcher books. In *Goblets*, Plate 12-1, S. T. Millard shows a goblet with a plain base, says it was of the 1870s and came in clear only. In his *Goblets II*, Plate 6-1, he shows a somewhat lighter weight goblet with a rayed base which he considered contemporary with the plain-based goblet. In her *Victorian Glass*, page 65, Plate 23-4, Ruth Webb Lee shows a goblet, covered sugar bowl, and an open compote in the pattern and says it is a product of the Boston and Sandwich Glass Company, probably dating from the 1860s. In her *Sandwich Glass*, Mrs. Lee shows a DICKINSON goblet on Plate 218, and on page 520 she explains why the name was applied.

The quality of this early flint glass is only average since it has a slight bluish or smoky cast. The foot contains both bubbles and colored specks, though the bowl is free from such defects. The workmanship was considerably below par. The lower part of the mold was too cool, and this resulted in the foot of the creamer having more hairlines than ever before seen by this author on a piece of pressed glass. A few hairlines are also on the body. When the piece was removed from the mold, it was marred considerably around the beveled margins of the figure-work. Nothing in the way of fire polishing was done to soften or smooth out these rough places. Also the lower attachment of the handle was placed over the diamond point pattern indicating either a lack of know-how or an attitude of indifference. No one familiar with the quality of products which came from the New England Glass Company of East Cambridge would attribute this piece to them. To Sandwich? Yes!

The wide, round foot of this creamer is flat and underneath it has only a small, low, hollowed-out space. The nine-panel stem is short and small. The panels extend out on the base of the bowl and on top of the foot to end in wide, high, round shelves. The curved bottom part of the bell-shaped bowl is covered by twenty-four short, concave flutes of various lengths. They have rounded tops and are arranged so as to follow the outline of the figure-work above them.

The main motif fills a 2 1/2-inch-wide band around the body which is deeply scalloped on top and bottom. In reality, it is a series of tall, wide loops interlocking with another series of the same size, but upside-down. Inside each loop are two peculiarly shaped halves. One half is completely filled with fine diamond point. The other half is raised, rounded over the edges and flat on top, except for a long, concave thumbprint skewed into its middle. Six pairs of similar halves surround the body. Above this figurework the body is plain and smooth for an inch or more then flares out to a plain low rim. The creamer is wider than it appears in the drawing and also more squatty. The rim is adequate with average curves. The petite applied handle is the best feature of the piece. The handle is small and has the large blob at the rim. The lower attachment is long and has been tooled into an attractive appendage as shown in the drawing. It is too bad it was stuck on top of the design.

Creamer: 3-part mold, 15 ounces, 6 1/8 inches tall, 3 1/2 inches wide, and 5 3/8 inches long.

The following pieces were made in the pattern: two types of goblets, creamer, spooner, covered sugar, compote, butter dish, sauce dish, and water pitcher. Probably tumblers and decanters were also made. It was probably made between 1867 and 1875.

31—HONEYCOMB WITH OVALS

Dr. S. T. Millard, in *Goblets*, Plate 39-2, illustrated a goblet and named this pattern. The design extends much higher on the bowl of the goblet than on the creamer. Metz illustrated a goblet as No. 251 and said it was flint and of the 1860s. The height, design, and quality all indicate the pattern to be a product of the 1870s. Most creamers of this era are constricted slightly below the rim, but in this case the sides are straight and perpendicular after rounding out above the stem.

The design is confined to the lower third of the body. It consists of twelve, somewhat oval-shaped figures in high, rounded relief, which encircle the body. They sit in beveled frames, and these follow their upper and side circumferences. Their rounded tops form scallops on the body. Between these figures and the top of the stem the body is covered with honeycomb.

The top two-thirds of the body was left plain and smooth by the mold. An attractive, deeply

etched band of stems, leaves, and flowers was added after it had cooled. This extends over the sides and front. The rim was sheared so as to leave a high tab at the rear for the top handle attachment. It is saddled, flat on top, and extends upward and well forward for the lip. The applied handle is beautifully shaped and proportioned. The small, lower attachment is long and turned back on itself to form an open loop. Above the loop it is crossbarred. A gaffer was on duty to fashion this handle.

The stem is rather short and hexagonal. It curves nicely from the base of the body till it ends in a wide, six-sided shelf on the base. The top of each panel of the stem forms half a hexagon. This does not blend well into the honeycombing on the body. The base is wide, round, and almost flat. It slopes down slightly to the edge. It is hollowed out and plain underneath. The glass in this piece is of an excellent soda-lime base. This was adopted when the heavy, massive flint patterns were discontinued for being too expensive and impractical. The entire piece is without defect except for the poor design where the stem joins the honeycomb. There is no waviness to the surface and the mold marks are barely perceptible on the foot. They cannot be located on the body. We do not know where, or by whom this pattern was made. It is so lovely one wishes it had been produced in large quantity. It is quite scarce.

Creamer: 2-part mold, 1 1/8 pounds, 6 1/4 inches tall, 3 1/8 inches wide, and 5 3/4 inches long.

The goblet and creamer are the only items I have seen or am aware of. A sugar bowl, butter dish, spooner, and pitcher must have been made, however.

32—MELTON

Mrs. Ruth Webb Lee, in *Victorian Glass*, names and describes this pattern on page 106, Plate 38-1. She says it was made during the 1870s by Gillinder and Sons, Philadelphia. S. T. Millard, in his *Goblets II*, shows RECESSED OVALS in Plate 65-3, and RECESSED OVALS WITH BLOCK BAND in Plate 91-1. In his *Goblets* he shows FRETTED VAULT in Plate 108-4. A careful scrutiny of his three photographs, even with a magnifying glass, fails to show where each varied from the other enough to justify the three names. Except for height and shape of the bowls, no perceptible difference is noted. They all seem to be the same MELTON pattern Mrs. Lee has described. Perhaps line drawings would have accentuated differences that are not perceptible in photographs. Metz shows a goblet as No. 2473 and calls it RECESSED OVALS.

This tall, winsome creamer with its fluid curves is indeed a joy to behold. It is too bad more of this lovely pattern was not produced. Pieces of it are extremely rare and almost impossible to obtain. The elongated, bell-shaped body of this creamer is so typical of the 1870s, it all but dates it. Many glass factories put out similar patterns in almost the identical size and shape, all of uniform high quality and all very desirable. They were the thinnest and most delicate type of any pressed glass made—before or since.

The figurework covers the lower two-fifths of the body. At its greatest circumference are eight large flat-based, highly beveled arches. In the face of each arch is a large impressed thumbprint. Had they extended to the base, these figures would almost have been the shape of Folsom arrowheads. Below the arches is a band of rectangles. Each is slashed diagonally into four high triangular pyramids; one has a flat top while the other three have sharp apexes. The upper three-fifths of the bowl is plain and smooth with a slight constriction.

The stem is tall with eight flat, swirled panels as shown in the drawing. This is a feature often encountered in early pressed glass. The panels end in a high shelf at the top where each is slightly arched and also extend onto the base and end in a second octagonal shelf. The base is low, wide, and round, with a very slight dome underneath. The rim has a single scallop on each side. It rises to a high point in the rear to accommodate the large handle attachment. The rim is high in front and extends well forward to form an ample lip. The applied handle is beautiful and well proportioned. The basal attachment is looped back and under, and tooled into crossbars. The only defect of workmanship or quality on the piece is at the lower attachment which is applied on top of the figurework and thus leaves open spaces to catch dirt.

Creamer: 4-part mold, 1 pound, 6 7/8 inches tall, 3 1/16 inches wide, and 5 5/8 inches long.

Few pieces of this pattern are known today. They include the goblet in two or three variants and the four-piece table set.

33—BARBERRY

This fine old standard creamer with an applied handle has not previously been illustrated in our literature on American pressed glass. It is only infrequently encountered. Minnie Watson Kamm describes and illustrates a variant of the pattern which has a pressed handle. It is, however, some years later in origin than the piece shown here. She knew of the present creamer but had not seen it. In her *Two Hundred Pattern Glass Pitchers*, page 9, No. 8, she describes the earlier ware and indicates her piece was made by McKee in 1894.

Ruth Webb Lee, in *Early American Pressed Glass*, Pattern 169, pages 427-29, and Plates 135, 139, and 142, illustrates and describes the pattern but does not show a creamer. She does show a milk-white plate. She mentions three different goblets. S. T. Millard shows the three goblets and assigns each a name. In his *Goblets*, Plate 59-2, he shows BARBERRY, OVAL BERRIES, and in No. 4 of the same plate he shows BARBERRY, ROUND BERRIES. I cannot distinguish between the two from the photographs. In his *Goblets II*, Plate 61-1, he shows BARBERRY, OVAL WITH 3 ROWS, and this is the goblet which matches the creamer shown here. I am continuing the title used by Lee and Kamm, of BARBERRY. Metz shows a goblet as No. 999 and calls it BARBERRY without regard to whether the berries are round or oval.

This is the light type of tableware that was prevalent in the 1869-1875 period when manufacturers were getting away from the heavy, massive patterns of the preceding two decades. The body is bell-shaped with only a slight constriction at the neck. The lower portion is almost hemispherical. An inch below the rim is a slightly raised line which encircles the body. The neck is smooth and plain. Below the line are three sprigs of eight and nine oval berries and three stippled, crenulated leaves. Each sprig has two clusters of berries on top of the leaves, one with eight, the other with nine. The leaves are long, beautiful, and veined. They have deep serrated edges, and give the appearance of being blown in the breeze. The stippling is well done. The berries are in high, convex relief. Whether the leaves and berries are actually barberry is questionable. BARBERRY does make a short, unused title for a fine pattern. The surface around the sprigs is plain.

The stem is hexagonal with small and rather short panels. It ends in a low shelf on the base of the bowl and in a high hexagonal shelf on the foot. The latter is low and round. There is a slight hollow space underneath, but no pontil mark. By the time this piece was made, they had learned to hold the bottom with a clamp while applying and tooling a handle and cutting and shaping the rim,

30

31

32

33

34

35

36

37

and it was not necessary to use the pontil rod. The handle has its large blob at the rim. It arches high, then curves down and forward to the bowl. The lower attachment is stuck on top of the leaf figure-work which is in very low relief, and no open-end pockets are left to collect dirt. The attachment is turned back on itself and tooled into three crossbars. The rim is slightly saddled and the lip floats high and well forward.

I do not know where or by whom this fascinating pattern was made. The glass is of excellent quality, and the piece has been well finished off.

Early standard creamer with applied handle: 3-part mold, 12 1/2 ounces, 5 5/8 inches tall, 3 3/8 inches wide, and 5 1/4 inches long. Pressed creamer with pressed handle: 3-part mold, weight unknown, 6 inches tall.

The following items were made in the pattern: standard creamer; creamer variant; four-piece table setting also was probably made in the pattern; eggcup; butter pat or cup plate; footed salt; cordial; celery vase; goblet; footed sauce; flat sauce; 6-inch milk-white plate; high covered compote; low covered compote; honey dish; syrup pitcher; pointed pickle dish; and water pitcher.

34—PANELLED ACORN BAND

This is another beautiful old pattern which eluded Mrs. Kamm and thus does not appear in her eight pitcher books. Mrs. Lee refers to Acorn Pattern, Variants, in her *Early American Pressed Glass*, pages 438-39. She briefly discusses several variants and then calls this particular one, ACORN PATTERN, VARIANTS, PANELLED WITH LEAVES, as Pattern 174A, Plate 125. The name she assigned is too cumbersome.

Millard in his *Goblets II*, Plate 46-4, shows a goblet and names it as shown in the title above. He thought it was of the 1880s. In Plate 10-2 of the same book he shows another and somewhat similar goblet which he calls BEADED ACORN WITH LEAF BAND. Metz shows a goblet as No. 785 and calls it PANELLED ACORN BAND.

The impression of the figurework on this creamer is indistinct. It seems to have been pressed in a mahogany mold which had been used too long. Through repeated contact with molten glass, it may have charred enough to dull or obliterate some details of the pattern. It is also possible that the blob of molten glass used was too small to fill the mold properly and give a good impression. However, the latter usually results in imperfections about the upper portion of the

pressed object, rather than the lower. The motif as shown in the drawing is a composite.

A slinder limb or vine undulates about the upper part of the body. It seems to have been excessively pruned. Three pendant clusters of acorns are scattered around the body and attached to the vine. The clusters contain two and three acorns. The other figurework is 1/8 to 1/4 inch below the limb. Here, large, stippled oak leaves surround and underlie the acorns. The band of leaves undulates slightly, and this eliminates the stiffness which goes with straight bands. At the three mold marks on the lower part of the bowl a design of formalized, stippled leaves has been placed, and these figures seem to cut the piece into segments. The body is cone-shaped, and above the leaf band it is smooth, plain, and well fire polished.

The rim has a high saddle with a spur at the rear for the handle attachment. From far back, the rim starts its upward and forward journey to the high, wide lip. The applied handle is rather delicate and fragile for the size of the creamer. The lower attachment is beautifully tooled into a coil and crossbars. Its curves are exquisite. The stem is small, hexagonal, and ends in a high, narrow shelf on the bowl and a low, wide shelf on the base. The foot is round, very wide, and almost flat. There is only a small dome underneath.

This piece has every appearance of dating from 1869 to 1875. Where or by whom it was made is unknown to me. With the exception of the poor impresssion, the quality is good. It is soda-lime glass and has no resonance. It is a beautiful pattern.

Creamer: 3-part mold, 14 ounces, 5 5/8 inches tall, 3 1/4 inches wide, and 5 3/8 inches long.

The goblet, creamer, sugar bowl, spoonholder, and butter dish are known. A water pitcher, celery vase, wine glass, and compotes probably were made.

35—STIPPLED STAR

The magnificent creamer shown here is misnamed. The background is stippled but the stars are not. Mrs. Minnie Watson Kamm had not seen the pattern and did not list it. In her *Two Hundred Pattern Glass Pitchers*, page 103, No. 153, however, she does show a later copy which she calls STIPPLED STAR, VARIANT. There is little similarity to this piece. Mrs. Lee, in *Early American Pressed Glass*, Pattern 205, pages 494-96 and Plate 147, shows the pattern and names it. Mrs. Lee says the pattern was shown in a catalog of Gillinder and Sons, of Greensburg and Philadelphia, but unfortunately the catalog was undated. She thought it was possibly made before 1876.

Millard, in *Goblets*, Plate 38-1, shows a goblet. This pattern should not be confused with Dr. Millard's LINED STAR which has flat stars, each of which stands on a single point and is shown on Plate 107-2 of the same book. Metz speaks of the pattern as "unusually interesting" and shows a goblet as No. 1301.

This piece, in my judgment, dates from the late 1860s and early 1870s—a period of fine quality, light weight, and graceful patterns. It stands on a round base, has a tall stem, and all decorations are on the lower two-thirds of the body. The upper third is plain and the handle is applied. The rather small stem in this piece has nine flat panels which end on a round, high shelf both on the bottom of the bowl and the top of the round foot. The base is plain underneath and slightly domed. The mold marks show plainly on the base but are not found elsewhere.

Four rows of highly raised, five-point stars encircle the lower two-thirds of the body. Each ray has a sharp, raised spine in its center. The stars are beautifully graduated to match the size of the bowl at their elevation. They prove a master craftsman chiseled the mold. The space surrounding the stars is filled with fine stippling, and this imparts a frosty appearance to the glass. This, together with the clear stars shining through, gives a striking effect. The top of the stippling ends in a scalloped line which dips between each two stars of the upper row. The top third of the body is well shaped and plain. The rim is pleasantly curved to form an attractive lip.

The handle is applied and somewhat light, in keeping with the creamer. The large blob forms the upper attachment. The lower attachment shows a tooling I have not seen before. (See drawing.) The only defect found on this piece is that the lower attachment of the handle was applied on top of the stippling and stars. The dirt now encased there is captured for eternity. Many gaffers learned to leave a clear flat escutcheon for the handle attachments to obviate this demerit.

The glass is light, but clear and brilliant. The pattern demands that. It has a nice ringing resonance when tapped, despite the fact that it is made of soda-lime glass. The workmanship, except where the lower handle attachment was made, is exceptionally fine.

Creamer: 3-part mold, 13 ounces, 5 15/16

inches tall, 3 1/8 inches wide, and 5 1/16 inches long.

The following items are known in the pattern: creamer, wine, celery vase, spoonholder, covered sugar bowl, covered butter dish, open and covered compotes, eggcup, goblet, oval dish, and several sizes of sauce dishes. Evidently a water pitcher was made and tumblers may have been.

36—WASHINGTON CENTENNIAL

Mrs. Kamm, in *A Second Two Hundred Pattern Glass Pitchers*, page 124, shows an 8-inch water pitcher in this pattern and calls it WASHINGTON. Mrs. Lee, in *Victorian Glass*, pages 156-57, and Plate 51-4, shows the creamer but does not list it among articles made. She calls the pattern CENTENNIAL. On Plate 117 of her *Early American Pressed Glass* she shows a WASHINGTON platter. S.T. Millard, in *Goblets II*, Plate 20-3, calls it WASHINGTON CENTENNIAL. Metz shows a goblet on pages 112-13, No. 1295, of her *Early American Pattern Glass* and uses the Millard title of WASHINGTON CENTENNIAL. Bessie M. Lindsey, in *Lore Of Our Land Pictured In Glass*, Volume I, shows three platters in the pattern. Each has a different center and they are named: GEORGE WASHINGTON, No. 27; CARPENTER'S HALL, No. 28; and INDEPENDENCE HALL, No. 29.

Tracy H. Marsh, in her excellent new book *The American Story Recorded in Glass* (1962), on page 112, No. 92, shows a WASHINGTON OVAL BREAD TRAY. She says it was made by Gillinder and Sons of Philadelphia. WASHINGTON is not a suitable title since there is an earlier flint pattern so named, and one of the "State Series" carries that name. CENTENNIAL is not appropriate because almost every glass house in operation at some time put out a pattern or article celebrating some centennial. In addition, another well-known pattern commonly goes by the name of CENTENNIAL or LIBERTY BELL. The name WASHINGTON CENTENNIAL is a misnomer, for this centennial celebrated the Declaration of Independence—not Washington. Washington's likeness, however, is pressed in the center of one of the platters of this pattern. Around the border is the legend: "First in War, First in Peace, First in the hearts of his countrymen." Collectors know it far and wide as the WASHINGTON BREAD PLATE. The pattern is so well known for the many other articles manufactured in it, that Dr. Millard's inappropriate title is continued as the least assailable.

This tall, beautifully shaped, well-proportioned creamer has remained obscure, while its less appealing contemporary LIBERTY BELL is known wherever pressed glass is appreciated. This particular piece is neither marked nor dated and as a result is not well known. This perhaps is well since it is scarce. If active collecting should start, the price will skyrocket. This is soda-lime glass of superior quality. It gives a clear, sparkling brilliance that wins friends and influences people. The workmanship is of superlative caliber. The glass is thin, light in weight, and is without resonance. It was manufactured during the early 1870s and was probably not produced after 1876 since it commemorates 1776.

The body is beautifully bell-shaped, and the decorative motif is confined to the lower two-thirds. A band of six large, overlapping circles surrounds the bowl. Where they overlap they form long, flat, beveled, cigar-shaped figures whose surfaces are completely covered with minute diamond point. (The impression on this particular piece is indistinct.) In each beveled, shield-shaped area is a tier of three flat-surfaced, beveled cubes which stand on their corners. They are formed by V-shaped grooves. The circles provide a scalloped effect at the top and bottom of the figure work.

The tall stem of this creamer is hexagonal, has a large knop near its base, and plainly shows the high, sharp and swirled mold marks. The panels are rounded over at the top and do not quite reach the bottom of the circles on the body. The panels stop abruptly when they reach the wide, flat base. Beneath the base is a low, plain, hollow dome. Above the figure-work, the body is constricted and then flares slightly to a plain, saddled rim. Both rim and lip are blessed with winsome curves. The applied handle is well crafted from top to bottom. It soars upward, then backward, downward, and toward the body to reach the bowl at its greatest girth. A third of the way down the lower attachment a crossbar has been tooled. The treatment used on this long, lower attachment is one I have not seen before. The narrow tab is turned back on itself, and a crossbar has been tooled across it. Between the two crossbars the attachment has a deep vertical, V-shaped groove tooled up its center.

Creamer: 3-part mold, 1 pound, 1 ounce, 6 3/4 inches tall, 3 5/16 inches wide, and 5 3/8 inches long.

These articles are known to have been made in the pattern: syrup jug, fish-shaped pickle dish, pedestaled creamer, covered sugar bowl, spoonholder, covered butter dish, wine, goblet, water pitcher in two sizes, bowls, champagne, celery vase, sauce dishes in three sizes, three different platters, eggcup, three sizes of oval dishes, ten or more compotes in different sizes and heights with and without lids, and three sizes of cake plates on standards.

Between 1891 and 1907 the U.S. Glass Company put out a pattern named WASHINGTON in their States Series.

37—FORGET-ME-NOT IN SCROLL

A creamer in this charming pattern was never seen by Mrs. Kamm, so she did not describe it in her pitcher books. Mrs. Lee, in *Early American Pressed Glass*, Pattern 151, pages 387-88, Plates 77 and 86, describes and names the pattern. Dr. Millard, in *Goblets*, Plate 86-3, shows a goblet and calls it FORGET-ME-NOT IN SCROLL [*sic*]. Mrs. Metz shows a goblet as No. 602.

This slender, graceful piece sits on a tall baluster which gives it added charm. The bowl is conoidal in shape. It flares at the rim but is not constricted below, as is LOOP AND DART, ARABESQUE, and POWDER AND SHOT. This piece followed those old lovelies by about a decade. The bowl has an ample capacity. There is an appealing inch-wide sunken belt with a stippled background which encircles the body. The forget-me-nots and scrolls are formed by raised lines. The belt contains nine flowers, and each is surrounded by a swirling scroll. At the edges, the latter change to some type of leaf. Encircling the base of the bowl is a corona of formalized figures and flowers surrounded by stippling.

The rim is round, smooth, and slightly saddled. It rises to form a projecting lip. The handle is applied with the large blob at the upper attachment. The lower attachment has been turned back on itself and tooled into crossbars. This was not too skillfully done. The handle is round, sturdy without being massive, and comfortable to handle. The stem is small and six-sided. It ends in a narrow hexagonal shelf on the base of the bowl and in a wider one on the foot. The foot is wide, round, and almost flat. Underneath, it is hollowed out and plain. The quality of the glass is fine. There was, however, careless workmanship. Either the metal or mold was too cold, and this resulted in wavy hairlines on the lower half of the bowl. As if to compensate for this, the top was well fire polished. The manufacturer is unknown. It is probably a product of the mid-1870s to mid-1880s.

Creamer: 3-part mold, 14 ounces, 6 5/16 inches tall, 3 1/16 inches wide, and 5 5/8 inches long.

Pieces in this pattern are seldom seen today. Probably little was made, and the range of items must have been narrow. The four-piece table set was certainly made as was a goblet. One could also hope to find a water pitcher, celery vase, and wine glass.

38—AMAZON

Minnie Watson Kamm had not seen a creamer in this pattern. She illustrated one from an old advertisement of 1890 put out by Bryce Brothers of Pittsburg. The ad shows eleven items in the pattern and says, "This line consists of 65 pieces." AMAZON was the name assigned it by the company. They used this pattern as one of two for the Pittsburgh Glass Show of 1890. All indications are that the pattern was made as early as 1875.

Mrs. Kamm, not having seen a piece, could not show the correct shape, proportions, or details of the pattern. It is shown again here for that purpose. See her *A Third Two Hundred Pattern Glass Pitchers*, pages 9-10, No. 9, and Plate on page 141. She used the original name of AMAZON. She was able to secure much valuable information about the Bryces and their glassmaking (from 1841 to date) and included it in her write-up of the pattern.

Ruth Webb Lee, in *Victorian Glass*, pages 119-20 and Plate 42-1, illustrates a tumbler, sugar bowl, and creamer. She lists only the articles she had personally seen in the pattern. Millard, in *Goblets*, Plate 46-3, shows a goblet and calls the pattern SAWTOOTH BAND. This title is appropriate, but since it was already widely known as AMAZON, it is perhaps better to retain the earlier name. Metz shows a creamer as No. 341 and uses the Millard title of SAWTOOTH BAND.

This tall, slender, impractical creamer is strikingly beautiful with its simple, graceful lines. It is one of only a score of patterns (of thousands made) having very tall creamers on high balusters. It could so easily be toppled and broken. The bowl is long and cylindrical with straight, vertical sides which flare almost imperceptibly. On the lower part of the body is found the only figurework of the piece. It covers the lower portion and the bottom of the bowl and extends down to the high shelf at the top of the stem. There are five rows of sawteeth in high relief and graduated in size from top to bottom. (Mrs. Kamm thought there were three rows.) The sawtooth design is in such high relief that it forms a bulging band on the lower part of the body.

The baluster or stem is tall and slender. It ends in a wide, high shelf on the base of the bowl and a low, narrow shelf on the foot. (The underside of the upper shelf is the only place where even a trace of a mold mark can be found.) The foot is wide and round and slopes out and down to a rounded edge. It is hollow and plain on the underside. The rim is round on top with beautiful sweeping curves. It has an attractive saddle which ascends to a narrow, but pleasing lip.

The handle is an applied one and well executed. It is placed high on the piece with the small, plain upper tab turned under and applied at the rim. The large, round blob is applied midway of the body and avoids the high figurework. The only defects are the two small bubbles in the handle. This is top quality tableware, and great care was expended on it. It is very clear and has been fire polished to a sparkling brilliance.

Creamer: 2-part mold, 1 pound, 2 1/2 ounces, 6 7/8 inches tall, 3 3/8 inches wide, and 5 1/16 inches long.

The old ad tells us there were sixty-five items manufactured in the pattern. We know of the following: tumbler, molasses can, finger bowl, covered sugar, covered butter, spoonholder, creamer, tankard water pitcher, three sizes of cake plates on standard, celery vase, celery tray, champagne, claret, cordial, three sizes of open compotes, four sizes of flared scalloped-edged compotes, four sizes of covered compotes, four sizes of scalloped-edged bowls, covered dish, flower vase, goblet, four different types of jelly compotes, two types of salt and pepper shakers, three types of sauce dishes, and wine.

39—DIAMOND POINT

There are many DIAMOND POINT patterns. The "grand old creamer" shown here exemplifies one of the best of the group. The creamer is thick (1/4 inch), heavy, brilliant, and flawless. The resonance is sharp and high. The points of the diamonds are quite sharp. The body is cylindrical and rests on a flat base with a plain, shallow dollar-sized pontil mark underneath. The base is octagonal. It was not a separate piece applied to the body while hot (as was done on many of the earlier patterns), but the indentation on the base contains a pontil mark which was ground down and polished. The base is 7/16 of an inch thick with eight flat panels extending up the sides to the pattern itself. Above the panels, the body is round and covered by diamond point up to a

41

shoulder, where the design ends at a broad, flat, horizontal beveled band. The latter slopes outward slightly in the upper portion. The top part of the body is shaped as shown. The lip is long, and the rim is gently curved.

The beautiful applied handle of the early type is thick—1/2 inch wide in the lower part and 7/8 inch near the top. At its base is a long crimp with four cross-grooves. There is a plain, smooth inch-wide escutcheon on the back of the creamer which runs from the base to the shoulder. The diamond points were left off, so a smooth, plain surface would be available to receive the applied handle. This speaks well for the care lavished on this piece to produce a quality product. All who are familiar with handled pieces of early flint glass know how unsightly the pockets of dirt become after years of usage when the handle is applied over an irregular pattern. Such pockets are impossible to clean. This piece is one of the few patterns where the designer had sufficient foresight to take preventive measures against this unsightly and unsanitary situation.

Creamer: 3-part mold, 1 3/4 pounds, 5 1/2 inches tall, 3 1/4 inches wide, and 5 3/4 inches long.

This creamer is similar to a milk pitcher shown in Kamm's *A Fourth Pitcher Book*, page 134, varying only in details. The lips differ in outline when seen from the side, and the beveled line at the top of the diamond point, on the creamer, is wide and flat, whereas it is curved and bulged in the milk pitcher. The diamond point on the milk pitcher is also not quite as sharp as on the creamer. It is slightly graduated toward the base on each.

The bases of the two pieces differ, the creamer being octagonal with straight sides while the milk pitcher has six wide, thick scallops. The handles are comparable. The quality of the two is similar. The variations were probably the result of two different glass houses producing the same popular pattern. Both variants probably date from the sixties or earlier. Both were quality ware and expensive when manufactured.

Ruth Webb Lee, in *Early American Pressed Glass*, Plate 43, shows a celery vase, eggcup, open compote, tumbler, water pitcher, lamp, covered salt, pint and quart decanters, and a handled mug in this particular variation of the pattern. Surprisingly, Mrs. Lee does not show the creamer, covered sugar, butter dish, spooner, or spillholder. Elsewhere in the same book she shows a goblet and plates, etc.

Only an enduring affection for this pattern by the American public could have prevailed on so many manufacturers to continue the line for such a long period of time. This accounts for the many variations in shape, quality, quantity, and items produced. Each item required its own individual mold, and this was a time-consuming and expensive operation. Some idea of the tremendous effort spent on this pattern alone (and there were probably 3,500 additional patterns manufactured in America over the years, each with many items) can be gleaned from the number and variety of pieces in it. The following items were made: ale glass, three covered bowls, four open bowls, butter dish, five cake salvers, candlestick, caster bottles, two champagnes, six covered compotes, ten open compotes, two cordials, creamer, cruet, four decanters, four oval dishes, eggcup, two goblets, two honey dishes, jelly glass, four different jugs, lemonade glass, handled mug, mustard, pepper, eight pitchers with and without feet, eight plates, covered salt, sauce dishes, spoon holder, two covered sugar bowls, two tumblers, vinegar, and two wines.

The McKearins, in their *Early American Glass*, gave little space to this pattern but did show, as did Mrs. Lee, that it was made in colors which are exceedingly rare today. S.T. Millard, in his two books on goblets, shows many variations of the pattern. Laura Woodside Watkins, in *Cambridge Glass*, shows this creamer in Plate 37. The illustration is reproduced from an 1869 catalog of the New England Glass Company of Cambridge. They started producing this pattern in 1830, and the catalog shows four pitchers and a variety of other items. The company called the pattern SHARP DIAMOND, and that name is quite apt, since the pyramidal points are much too sharp to handle comfortably.

The late Carl W. Dreppard, in his *ABC's of Old Glass*, borrowed the cut from Mrs. Watkins' book and reproduced it on page 177. Rhea Mansfield Knittle, in *Early American Glass*, says DIAMOND POINT glass was made before 1864.

Frank W. Chipman, in *The Romance of Old Sandwich Glass*, states that DIAMOND POINT goes back to 1830 and was made at the Boston and Sandwich Glass Company. The pattern was later made by most glass manufacturers, each varying it somewhat. In the description of the No. 41 TOY SAWTOOTH creamer, the relationship of DIAMOND POINT and SAWTOOTH is discussed.

40—STEPPED DIAMOND POINT

This gem of a creamer calls for superla-

38

39

40

41

42

43

44

45

tives, like its sibling (No. 39 DIAMOND POINT). They were made at the same time, at the same factory, are of the same pattern, and are equal in value. In *A Seventh Pitcher Book*, page 5, No. 7, Minnie Watson Kamm calls this creamer STEPPED DIAMOND POINT. She did not know by whom or where it was made. Mrs. Lee, in *Early American Pressed Glass*, generally lumps all DIAMOND POINT together as Pattern 45, pages 135-37, and Plates 42, 43, 44, 45, and 153. In *Goblets II*, Millard shows a goblet of this pattern on Plate 64-1 and calls it DIAMOND POINT WITH RIBS.

In *Cambridge Glass 1818 to 1888*, Laura Woodside Watkins shows a cut from an old catalog of The New England Glass Company of East Cambridge, Massachusetts. They called the pattern SHARP DIAMOND and show this pitcher and the preceding one. Metz mentions this pattern under the Millard title of DIAMOND POINT WITH RIBS, as No. 321 but without illustration. The significant difference is the stepped arrangement of the pattern on the bottom of the bowl. Millard's goblet and a large compote I have; both show an arrangement identical with this one.

Every feature of this creamer bespeaks excellent quality. The early heavy flint is brilliantly clear and resonant. The fine escutcheon for the handle attachments, the almost obscured mold marks, the overall workmanship all are excellent. A good fire polishing has somewhat softened to the touch the tips of the diamond point.

Creamer: 3-part mold, 1 5/8 pounds, 6 1/2 inches tall, 3 9/16 inches wide, and 6 9/16 inches long.

I know of only three pitchers, a compote and a goblet in this pattern. It dates from 1830-1869.

41—TOY SAWTOOTH

The pyramidal diamonds on this toy creamer are exactly the same size as the diamond point on the two creamers immediately above. Yet, they are called DIAMOND POINT, and this is called SAWTOOTH. Many collectors and dealers become confused in trying to determine when a piece ceases to be diamond point and becomes sawtooth. They want an infallible rule of thumb—and there is none. In fact, there could not be. The motif is identical in both patterns and consists of a series of rectangular pyramids placed side by side. Such a pyramid on a large water pitcher would appear small, but a figure of the same size on a toy creamer appears huge. This brings us to the point of relative proportion. If the diamonds seem small

on a piece, you probably have DIAMOND POINT. If they look large, it is likely to be SAWTOOTH.

This pretty little toy creamer must have brought joy to some young girl. It is graceful and attractive and probably is like the large one mother had. Such pieces are exceedingly rare, for they did not last well in the hands of young owners. Many small creamers were made without a stem, but this one, LIBERTY BELL, and FROSTED LION are the only toy creamers with a stem to come to my attention. It could have been used as an individual creamer, for it is about that size; but this piece was made for a child's "play-pretty."

The sides of the body are vertical until at the lower third they curve gradually to the tall, plain, round stem. The lower half of the body is covered with sawtooth which is graduated to conform to the contours of the piece. The top band of sawtooth shows a design which is in fact "sawteeth."

There is a round raised shelf on the lower part of the body and another on top of the base. The latter is round, rather flat, ample in size, and domed beneath. The top edge of the rim is flat. The rim is saddled and sweeps up and forward to form a pinched lip. The pressed handle is six-sided and has a good thumbgrip on top. The glass is of only fair quality soda-lime metal. The piece is nicely conceived but the workmanship is poor. The mold marks show everywhere, and in some places, such as the handle and rim, they are high, thin, and razor-sharp.

Toy creamer: 3-part mold, 4 ounces, 3 1/2 inches tall, 2 3/16 inches wide, and 3 1/4 inches long.

The author knows nothing of the maker, though the creamer dates from about 1885. No other piece has been seen. The four-piece table set was undoubtedly made to sell only as a set.

42—SAWTOOTH

Here is one of the fine early massive flint glass creamers we seek so diligently today. Mrs. Kamm used a large milk pitcher 8 1/2 inches tall in her *Two Hundred Pattern Glass Pitchers*, page 4, No. 1. Note that she awarded it first place in her books on pressed glass pitchers. She said it was made during 1865-1875. The creamer used here may have been made thirty years earlier. This particular creamer was one of the first forms made in the SAWTOOTH pattern. It is shown in the upper right corner of Plate 40 of Mrs. Lee's *Early*

American Pressed Glass. Although the pattern was manufactured at the New England Glass Company, this piece was not made there or it would have had a pontil mark and probably a ground one. Instead, there is a large, 28-ray star impressed into the slightly hollowed-out base.

SAWTOOTH is such an old, revered, and long-loved pattern that it was kept in continuous production for a period of seventy or more years. During that time, innumerable glass houses produced the pattern—each differing in some detail from the pieces manufactured by their competitors. It would be impossible to relate each variant to the factory that made it. No attempt to do so will be made here.

This copious creamer is made of brilliant, clear, heavy flint glass. It is free of bubbles, hairlines, defects, and discolorations. It is so highly polished that only the faintest trace of mold marks can be found on the base and none on the body. It is very thick (3/8 inch in places) and much too heavy for practical, everyday use. It has a clear bell-toned resonance when tapped—unusual in creamers because of the handle.

The waist has eight broad, flat panels which extend up on the bottom of the bowl where each is rounded over its top. Below they flatten out and disappear on top of the base. The base is round and quite wide to give stability.

The body is mostly cylindrical. From just above the waist and for two-thirds of the way up the side of the creamer there is a 3-inch wide band of Sawtooth. Looking straight at the pattern, one wonders: why the name? After a look at the profile, the question is answered. Note the edges in the drawing. SAWTOOTH and DIAMOND POINT are exactly the same design, and the difference is only a matter of its size as compared to the size of the piece upon which it is used. The pattern is made of high, sharp-pointed, diamond-shaped pyramids set side by side. This places the pyramids in diagonal swirls and forms rows in all directions. The upper third of the body is plain and smooth.

The saddled rim rises slightly at the back for the handle attachment and sharply in front to form a broad, beautifully curved lip. The applied handle is massive and substantial. At the top it is 1 3/16 inches wide and tapers down to 7/8 inch at the lower attachment where it is tooled back and curled under to form fancy crossbars. The lower attachment is applied on top of the sawtooth design. This resulted in many "hard-to-get-at" spaces to catch and hold dirt. Had this piece been made by the New England Glass Company, they

would have provided a plain, flat surface for the attachment and this serious defect would not have occurred.

Creamer: 3-part mold, 1 5/8 pounds, 6 3/8 inches tall, 3 3/8 inches wide, and 6 1/8 inches long.

A great many items were made in this pattern. Some of the unusual ones were: water bottle with tumbler up, covered compotes with sawtooth edges and perfectly fitting lids, champagnes, egg-cups, lamp, pomade jar with ground stopper, covered salt, footed salt, spillholder, toy sets, trays, etc. Very infrequently it is found in colors.

43—CAMBRIDGE SAWTOOTH

This is a version of the SAWTOOTH pattern produced at the New England Glass Company, East Cambridge, Massachusetts. Laura Woodside Watkins, in *Cambridge Glass 1818-1888*, page 99 and Plate 40, shows and describes it. On Plate 41, she shows the water bottle with a plain tumbler up. The excellent line drawings she used for her illustrations were taken from an old catalog of the company which was of the 1860s. The pattern may have been made by them at an earlier date under their name of MITRE DIAMOND. This piece is more refined than the preceding SAWTOOTH.

It differs from the latter in several respects: (1) The design is level at top and bottom, not sawtoothed; (2) It has a wide bevel above the design; (3) The stem is smaller and is hexagonal rather than octagonal; (4) It has a shelf on the base; (5) It is not rayed under the base; (6) A smooth, plain escutcheon is provided for the lower handle attachment; and (7) It is lighter.

Ruth Webb Lee, in *Early American Pressed Glass*, pages 125-28 and Plates 40, 41, and 42, gives a good coverage of SAWTOOTH, but none of it can be identified as Cambridge though she knew it was made there. Minnie Watson Kamm shows the preceding variant as No. 1 in her *Two Hundred Pattern Glass Pitchers*. In *A Third Two Hundred Pattern Glass Pitchers*, page 22, she shows a much later variant and on page 34 shows a creamer with a pressed handle. In *A Fourth Pitcher Book*, page 15, she shows a later variety not akin to this piece. Elsewhere she shows a quite common early milk-white creamer. Her examples, together with the five types used here, show how widely products of different factories departed from the old originals in applying the same motif.

In both his *Goblets* and *Goblets II*, Dr. Millard shows five or six variants but none similar to this one. Since Lee, Kamm, and Millard did not find a single piece of *CAMBRIDGE SAWTOOTH* to illustrate, some conception of its scarcity can be gleaned.

The diamond-shaped, rectangular pyramids, in high relief, composing the sawtooth design, cover the lower two-thirds of the body. They are cut off abruptly at the top and bottom of the figurework so as to make triangular pyramids there and form straight, horizontal lines around the creamer. This treatment is not seen on any other variant. In the latter, the edges are sawtoothed. Just above the design is a wide bevel, flaring to the top. The upper third of the body is smooth, plain, and constricted before again flaring to the rim. The rim is superbly shaped and round on top. The glass there is over 3/16 inch thick.

The applied handle is a work of art. With the large blob at the top, it courses through graceful curves to the smaller, lower junction. Here it turns back on itself in an open loop. Its upper portion is tooled into four high crossbars. A wide smooth escutcheon was left free of figurework at the rear for the lower attachment, and because of this no unsightly crevices are present. This refinement is present on all pieces made at Cambridge that I have seen.

The rather small stem is hexagonal and ends in a rounded shelf at the base of the figurework on the body and in a similar shelf on the foot. The foot has a low shelf near the edge, a low instep, and a round edge. It is wide and of the same thickness as the rim. Underneath the base is slightly hollowed out and carries a pontil mark which has been fire polished into an irregular but smooth surface. This particular procedure has not elsewhere been encountered by the writer. Mrs. Watkins says only the very earliest ware from the New England Glass Company was released without the pontil mark having been handcut and polished. The brilliantly clear, heavy flint glass and the craftsmanship are superior. Mold marks show only faintly on top of the foot where there are three and on the bevel above the sawtooth where there are four.

Creamer: 3- and 4-part molds, 1 7/16 pounds, 6 1/2 inches tall, 3 7/16 inches wide, and 5 5/8 inches long.

In addition to the covered compote and covered sugar bowl, both with sawtooth edges, Mrs. Watkins illustrated the creamer and tumbler-up set. She also mentioned salt cellars, a water pitcher, and compotes with high and low bases.

44—LUMBERTON

The inhabitants of Lumberton, Mississippi, will understand why one of the SAWTOOTH variants of pressed glass was named for their friendly town. (There was a saw factory there.)

SAWTOOTH and DIAMOND POINT were two of the most popular patterns ever developed in pressed glass. They are basically the same pattern, the rectangular pyramids of SAWTOOTH being larger than those of DIAMOND POINT. Both are imitation cut glass motifs. The patterns were manufactured over a period of several generations and probably by more glass factories than any other design.

This creamer has the most portly shape of any in the series, though it might have been more attractive if the gaffer had made it a little more curvaceous at the rim. With a little more saddle, the piece would have been more attractive. The lip itself is attractive, but a little large. In the rear a large scallop was formed to anchor the upper attachment of the applied handle. The handle has the large blob at the top and curves over and back to form a comfortable if not commodious grip. It has been flattened till it is wider than it is thick. A veritable miracle was achieved with the lower attachment adhered so tightly to the underlying figurework that no dirt-catching pockets resulted. The attachment was beautifully tooled and then looped back on itself.

The body is shaped like a top and has a wide, plain constricted band at the neck. The lower two-thirds of the body is covered with square sawtooth with rounded tips. This was caused by the numerous reheatings necessary to constrict the neck, shape the rim and lip, and apply the handle, plus the further heating to fire polish the piece. It is magnificent, and no mold marks can be found anywhere except on the top of the foot.

The stem is small for the creamer and is longer than usual for its time. The hexagonal stem splays on the base of the bowl and mitres into the small sawtooth there. The lower end curves out into a wide, low hexagonal shelf on the round foot. The mold marks are plainly visible on top of the foot, and one is almost 1/8 inch high, though not sharp or rough. The foot was held in a clamp while the top was reheated, and these mold marks were not fire polished off. There is a slight hollow underneath the base. The latter has a very wide ring on which to rest and does so without rocking, though it has not been ground flat.

This is quality pressed glass throughout. It probably dates from the late 1860s to about 1875. It partially gets away from the massive, heavy flint pieces produced a few years earlier. It is of brilliantly clear and sparkling flint glass without defect of any kind. It is heavy considering its thinness. Fine flint though it is, there is only a sickening thud when it is lightly tapped.

Creamer: 3-part mold, 1 3/8 pounds, 6 3/16 inches tall, 3 9/16 inches wide, and 5 5/8 inches long.

Nearly all SAWTOOTH combines well. There is no way of determining all articles produced in this grand old pattern, but certainly a wide range is involved.

45—CROSSETT SAWTOOTH

This version of SAWTOOTH is so blessed with grace, beauty, charm, and elegance that it is completely regal. Everything about it is in complete harmony, which speaks well for the designer. It is named for the south Arkansas city of Crossett and the tremendous lumber industry there so dependent on saws for its success.

This piece has the slender curves of youth, while *LUMBERTON SAWTOOTH* shown above has a "middle-age spread." The figurework is almost identical on both pieces, but the contours vary greatly. The stem is slender, tall, and octagonal. At its top the panels mitre into the sawteeth. On the foot they end in a round, raised ledge. Note the swirled stem. The rim and lip are charmingly conceived. All curves flow smoothly.

The applied handle is a masterpiece of the gaffer's art of finishing off a piece. The large blob is at the top, and from it the handle tapers to its juncture with the body at the lower attachment. Unfortunately a portion of the lower tab is broken off, and we cannot know what it was like. Probably it was an open loop. The portion remaining was tooled into the most artistic and elaborate acanthus leaf I have ever seen. This partially shows in the drawing. The attachment was made on top of the sawteeth and meshes so perfectly that no openings remain to accumulate dirt.

The glass is fine flint, but without resonance. It is thick throughout and quite heavy, despite its airy appearance. Mold marks barely show on top of the foot. This was truly a quality product. It is probably a product of the 1870s. The manufacturer is unknown.

Creamer: 3-part mold, 1 pound, 6 3/16 inches tall, 3 1/4 inches wide, and 5 inches long.

This creamer will combine perfectly with much of the SAWTOOTH found in shops today. There are many items to choose from, yet none are overly plentiful.

46—BREWTON

This small creamer illustrates the English treatment given the SAWTOOTH motif. They combined flutes and panels with it, while most domestic glass manufacturers were content to use sawtooth alone. The piece is named for a fine southern Alabama lumber city, since SAWTOOTH and other descriptive titles are preempted. It resembles many other English patterns in conformation and size. This seems to hold for a large number of their patterns, as to shape and size. The surface design, of course, varies with each pattern.

The bullet-shaped body has its lower two-thirds covered with larger than usual rectangular pyramids. The upper third rises vertically to the rim and is made up of a series of alternating wide, flat panels and narrower concave flutes. The panels and flutes are rounded over their tops, and this makes the irregular scallops on the rim. The rim rises high and pushes well forward for the lip. The handle is adequate for its function. It is six-sided and diminishes gradually in size from top to bottom. The basal attachment has a curlicue standing well out from the body.

The nine-paneled waist is shelved on the lower part of the body and on top of the foot. Between them it is nicely incurved. The base slopes out to the round edge and is plain on top. Underneath is an 18-ray, raised star. The base has a peculiar adjunct; a raised ring is inset slightly from the outer edge. It has been ground to give a stable footing. It can be seen in the drawing. (See illustration of bottom.)

This piece of glass is clear early flint, but like so many of its compatriots is full of small bubbles and white flecks. The workmanship was poor. The mold marks are high and rough. It is quite heavy for its less-than-teacup capacity. It appears to date from about the 1860s to 1870s.

Creamer: 3-part mold, 13 ounces, 4 5/8 inches tall, 3 1/4 inches wide, and 5 7/16 inches long.

I know of no piece other than this creamer but would expect to find a sugar bowl.

47—BABY FACE

This is soda-lime glass at its magnificent best. Any item in this pattern is exceedingly rare. Furthermore, do not look for or expect bargains. Mrs. Lee admits that little of the pattern was made and that nothing is known as to the manufacturer. However, one can and does conjecture. See Lee's *Early American Pressed Glass*, Pattern 115, page

300, and Plate 89, where she shows a covered sugar bowl, spoonholder, and goblet. Mrs. Kamm has not described the pattern. Dr. S. T. Millard in *Goblets*, Plate 149-1, shows a goblet and says it was made in the 1870s in clear only.

The very similar pattern THREE FACE is much better known, and more of it was made. Even THREE FACE is rare, expensive, and was made first by George Duncan and Sons, of Pittsburgh, Pennsylvania, during the 1870s as their "No. 400." It also is of superb quality. The two patterns are so similar that there is some basis for assuming that the same factory may have produced both. Perhaps some day we will know.

The standard creamer and covered sugar are shown here to illustrate their relative proportions. They are among the tallest creamers and sugars ever manufactured. Because of their height they were easily knocked over, and casualties were high. This is the first time the creamer has been illustrated in glass literature. As on one version of THREE FACE, the sole figurework on the creamer appears on the tall, slender stem. The sugar bowl has the same design on the stem, and it is repeated as the finial on the lid. The sculpturing of this pattern is little more refined than that of THREE FACE. The stem on the BABY FACE creamer is taller and thinner than that on THREE FACE.

The bowl is severely plain with straight, slightly flaring sides. It is of medium capacity, despite its extreme height. There is no flaw of any kind in the piece and, fortunately, no etching was done. The base of the bowl tapers in at a sharp angle, forms a shelf, and continues at the same angle to the delicate stem.

From the top of the stem down, the creamer is frosted. Above the three baby faces there is a ring in high relief which encircles the stem. Below this are three chubby faces, all remarkably similar and with their hair streaming. A string of beads is festooned around each neck. Another ring surrounds the stem below the necks, from which wide and narrow ribs flow out on top of the base. The base is round, nicely shaped above, and slightly hollowed out beneath.

The mold marks are almost hidden, but close inspection shows them on the stem, and here they swirl one-sixth of a revolution. The piece does not have a pontil mark, and therefore had to have been held by the base with a clamp while the handle was applied and the lip tooled. Perhaps the turning motion during this operation was sufficient to twist the red-hot stem. The mechanics of chipping a mold with a hammer and chisel so as to form the faces with the twist in them would confound a mechanical engineer. I believe it was the turning motion and not the mold which caused the twist.

The handle is round and rather on the small or delicate side. The large blob is at the top, and the lower attachment has been tooled into three crossbars. The rim is plain and sweeps high to the front where there is a narrow lip with a jowl on either side. We have no knowledge of any item in BABY FACE ever being reproduced.

Creamer: 3-part mold, 14 ounces, 7 3/8 inches tall, 3 5/16 inches wide, and 5 1/8 inches long.

The following items are known to have been made in this pattern: four piece table set, celery dips, three different compotes, cordial, goblet, and water pitcher.

48—THREE FACE

This well-known version of THREE FACE is wrapped in assumption, legend, folklore, and myth to the extent that one becomes pixilated trying to unravel known facts from fiction. These few facts are known. Acid etching of glass was introduced in this country from France at the Philadelphia Centennial Exposition in 1876. It was taken up at once by the Duncans of Pittsburgh and Gillinder and Sons of Philadelphia. THREE FACE was put out in 1878 and continued in production into the early 1880s by George A. Duncan and Sons under one of its frequently changing company names. The pattern is one of the finest among the thousands of early American pressed glass designs. Mrs. E. C. Miller, wife of the designer for Duncan, served as a model for the faces. In 1900 Mr. Miller became a member of the firm which then changed its name to Duncan and Miller. The Duncans now own the company and are actively making glass today. An old Duncan catalog lists the items they produced in THREE FACE as "Pattern No. 400."

The McKearins and Kamm illustrate this version of the pattern as the Duncan product. Mrs. Lee and Mrs. Kamm knew two types of creamers were made—this one and the following creamer. This creamer has three faces on the frosted stem, a fourth in a beaded medallion under the spout, and a fifth on the base of the pressed handle. The other version has only three faces which are on the acid etched stem and has never before been illustrated in any book on pressed glass. (See following creamer for comparison. Also see the preceding BABY FACE for a much rarer pattern sometimes confused with THREE FACE.)

46

Bottom
46

47 - 1

47 - 2

48

Under
Spout

48

Base of
Handle

48

49

50 - 1

The stem of the creamer with five faces is almost 1/2 inch shorter than that of the three-face version. With its pressed handle and with mold marks on the body, which were not fire polished off, the creamer shown here gives the impression that it was made later than the following one, and perhaps to meet stiff competition. They probably were made by different factories.

See: (1) Ruth Webb Lee's *Early American Pressed Glass*, Pattern 114, pages 296-300, Plates 89 and 91, and her *Antique Fakes & Reproductions*; (2) Minnie Watson Kamm's *A Third Two Hundred Pattern Glass Pitchers*, pages 11-12, No. 12, and her *A Fifth Pitcher Book*, pages 93-95, for notes on George A. Duncan and Sons who made the pattern; (3) S. T. Millard's *Goblets*, Plate 149-2; (4) George S. and Helen McKearin's *American Glass*, pages 395 and 397, and Plate 207, No. 5; (5) J. Stanley Brothers, Jr., *Thumbnail Sketches*, page 47.

The sculpturing of the faces under the lip and at the base of the handle is decidedly poor when compared with that on the stem. They also differ from each other. (See cuts of these faces for differences, such as: earrings, hairdo, hair ornament, beading, and jabot.)

Both creamers have the shape of an inverted bell and are of about the same capacity. This one has no wheel-cut spray on the bowl. On the base of the body where it narrows in at a sharp angle to the stem, it is covered with twenty-four rounded ribs.

The rim is well saddled and the curves are pleasant. The lip is narrow and pinched.

The handle has six sides and is pressed. The side panels are narrow. On its top is a raised portion for a thumbgrip. At the lower attachment is another face.

The stem appears stubby and thicker than the stems of the preceding and following creamers. It ends in a rosette shelf on the foot, composed of nine rounded ribs. The foot is almost flat. The stem, foot, and underside are acid etched, leaving a satin smooth, frosted finish.

The mold maker did a wonderful job of chiseling the faces in reverse into cast iron by hand. The three faces on the stem are identical.

The glass is of a superior quality lime-soda base. A little better fire polishing on the body would have removed the mold marks which show plainly but are neither high nor rough. The mold marks indicate a five-part mold was used. The body was pressed in two parts. The foot and stem required three parts. The two upper parts joined the three lower ones just above the ribs on the base of the bowl. Their junction can be faintly seen directly under the spout. I have the impression that this piece was made after the following one struck the public fancy. This one is not so refined.

Creamer: 5-part mold, 15 ounces, 6 7/8 inches tall, 3 5/16 inches wide, and 5 9/16 inches long.

The original Duncan catalog listed the following: biscuit jar, covered butter dish, four sizes of cake stands, two types of celery vases, three types of sauce dishes, clarets, eight different sizes and shapes of open compotes, eight different sizes and shapes of covered compotes, creamer, goblet, six sizes and types of stemmed lamps, water pitcher, salt dips, salt and pepper shakers, two sizes of sauce dishes, spoonholder, covered sugar bowl, and wine.

Collectors should be wary of reproductions since the following are known to be reproduced today: champagnes in three types, butter dish, covered small compote, cordial, goblet, lamp, two sizes of sauce dishes, sugar bowl, and wine.

Do not confuse THREE FACE with a much later "Gone With The Wind" lamp which has three raised faces on the front and three on the globe. It is also called THREE FACE and is being made today. It is complete, electrified, and priced at $20 wholesale, at the present time.

49—THREE FACE, EARLY

This version of the aristocrat of pattern glass has only the three faces—on its stem. It has all the refinements and perfections of BABY FACE and is as difficult to locate. This is the first time this patrician of early American pressed glass has been illustrated in our glass literature. Although Mrs. Lee and Mrs. Kamm knew of its existence, there is a question whether either had seen an example. They made no effort to describe it and gave no illustration. Also, the creamer with five faces is the only article in that pattern with five faces to reach my attention. Necessarily, any covered item in the THREE FACE pattern would have six faces, three on the stem and three on the finial (as in the case of the covered sugar bowl).

A detailed description of this particular creamer will not be made, since it closely approximates the five-face piece. Instead, only those areas where there are differences will be listed:

(1) This piece has a beautiful applied handle, though the lower attachment was not artistically executed. The gather to make the handle seems to have been snipped too short, and the gaffer apparently tried to make it do. The other version has

a pressed handle with a face on its lower end.

(2) The rim here was handsheared instead of pressed as on the five-face piece. It has a flat place on either side near the handle attachment, and each ends in a small, almost unnoticeable, scallop. The jowls on the rim are flared more widely.

(3) There is an attractive engraved leaf-and-fruit spray around the front three-fourths of the body.

(4) This stem is almost a half-inch taller than that of the five-face version. The details of the sculpturing are more pleasingly executed.

(5) This piece is taller.

(6) The mold marks on this piece show faintly between the faces and nowhere else.

(7) At the stem's base are two scalloped shelves, the smaller atop the larger, each having nine rounded ribs.

(8) Where the base of the bowl tapers into the stem, there are eighteen rounded ribs. The five-face version has twenty-four such ribs in the same position.

With the exception of the lower handle attachment, this piece reaches the acme of perfection in quality of metal, excellence of designing, superiority of the work of the mold maker and the gaffer.

Both creamers have the soft, appealing satin finish accomplished by acid etching on the stem and base. This cool, frosted appearance harmonizes perfectly with the brilliantly clear and pure appearance of the remainder of the piece.

Creamer: ?-part mold, 14 ounces, 7 1/16 inches tall, 3 3/8 inches wide, and 5 7/16 inches long.

See above creamer for items made in THREE FACE. Either creamer goes well with other pieces of the pattern. This one is preferable if it can be found.

50—FROSTED EAGLE

In *A Fifth Pitcher Book*, pages 22-23, No. 23, Mrs. Kamm made her drawing from a photograph of the creamer. Many details were obscured, especially as to the base. She deduced that the pattern was made by the Crystal Glass Company of Pittsburgh, Pennsylvania, and Bridgeport, Ohio. There is doubt on this as will be brought out later. In her *A Sixth Pitcher Book*, page 62, No. 136, she used a water pitcher, and her drawing was more detailed. Millard does not show a goblet, and none is known to have been made in this pattern. If they were made, they probably go by another name. Mrs. Lee, in Plate 99 of *Early American Pressed*

Glass, showed a pair of covered compotes on tall stems with the FROSTED EAGLE finials on the lids. She gave no description.

The standard creamer and sugar bowl are used here to show the relationship. In several of the "animal" patterns there is an animal finial on the covered pieces, but on other pieces, such as the creamer, there is no way to show such a design and no way to identify them. Some of the patterns which give difficulty are: SNAIL, HAND, CHICKEN or FROSTED CHICK, JUMBO, ST. BERNARD, PHEASANT, one of the FROSTED STORK patterns, and of course FROSTED EAGLE (see CHICKEN in this book).

The bowl of the creamer is cylindrical with a slight flare from base to top. The sides are straight. It has a large capacity. The body is plain, though it sometimes is found etched. The rim has an uneven, but attractive scallop on the rear half. The front half is plain and flows upward and forward to form a pleasing lip. The handle is pressed, six-sided, and substantial. The front and back edges of each side have a raised edging which borders a flat sunken panel extending down either side. The edging is scrolled. At the base of the handle is an acanthus design splayed on the body. As large as the handle appears, it is still uncomfortable for a large hand. The waist is wide, short, curved, and has no panels.

The base sits on three short, scrolled feet. They are stippled and surround a large, convexed jewel. Above the scrolls on each mold mark is a sharp spear point which extends to the middle of the waist. They are also stippled. Around the bottom of the pieces is a heavy, plain round ring which has been wrapped, "barber pole style" with stippled ribbon. On plate 94-1, in *Early American Pressed Glass*, Mrs. Lee shows a covered JUMBO bowl with the identical base shown on this FROSTED EAGLE sugar and creamer. The plate also shows an odd spoon rack patented by David Baker, but with a foot entirely different. (See ORION THUMBPRINT in this book for more about David Baker.) The foot on the JUMBO creamer is not at all like those here. If we knew who made the JUMBO bowl that Mrs. Lee shows, we would be fairly certain who made FROSTED EAGLE. At least two companies made JUMBO bowls for the Christmas trade of 1883. They were the Canton Glass Company of Canton, Ohio, and the Aetna Glass and Manufacturing Company of Bellaire, Ohio. The latter company made and sold molds to other glass companies.

The quality is good, but it does not approximate that found in BABY FACE. The lower part of the bowl and the waist show hairlines and waviness resulting from cold molds or a cold gather of glass. It is hard, however, to locate the mold marks.

When seen together there is no doubt the sugar and creamer belong to the same set. The sugar bowl is shown to indicate the source of the name. The finial on the sugar lid is a large FROSTED EAGLE with wings half raised as if poised for flight. The eagle is sitting in the center of a round medallion on top of the lid. The medallion is covered with well-executed leaves and berries. Both medallion and eagle are frosted. Surrounding the medallion is a ring of egg-and-dart design. The "egg" shown here, however, is actually the hollowed out inside of small loops outlined by inverted V-shaped ridges.

Creamer: 3-part mold, 1 pound, 6 1/4 inches tall, 3 5/16 inches wide, and 5 3/8 inches long.

Probably many pieces were made in this pattern—but little is known of them. The only known pieces are: sugar bowl, creamer, water pitcher, and tall covered compote. The covered butter dish and spoonholder have been advertised in magazines on antiques.

51—JARVES GOTHIC ARCH

This is an authentic Lacy Sandwich creamer which has remained nameless all these years. No pattern has been named for one of the greatest men connected with American glass— Deming Jarves. Since this beautiful pattern was produced in the glass factory he organized and operated during his regime, it is only fitting that it should be named for him. Pieces such as this are seldom found outside private collections or museums. Even severely damaged specimens are cherished and preserved. It is one of the choicest finds for a collector of American pressed glass.

Mrs. Lee, on Plate 157 center of *Sandwich Glass*, illustrates this creamer in a photograph. She neither names nor describes the piece. Mary Harrod Northend, in *American Glass*, shows the same creamer in the lower left-hand corner of an unnumbered plate. It is shown in a photograph with seven other pieces of pressed glass. Details are not easily seen in either picture. It is hoped the drawings here, especially with the underlip view, will more clearly show the details of the pattern. George A. and Helen McKearin illustrate the creamer on Plate 163-5 of *American Glass*.

Like all Lacy Sandwich, this piece has the sparkling, shimmering brilliance which makes such glass popular. The fine stippling on the outer surface, together with its smooth, plain inner surface refracts the light to produce the characteristic silvery sheen. Stippling here reaches the zenith of perfection. It consists of very small, rounded dewdrops, placed close together in rows. Most stippling is more coarse and less beautiful.

This piece is rather small and sits on a wide, finely scalloped shelf-like base which protrudes beyond the sides of the lower body. In the hollowed-out center, underneath is a series of three raised and concentric rings. From these, and radiating to the ring base, are the large ribs of a raised star. (See cut.)

The lower zone of the body is covered by a series of six large Lancet arches, each in turn containing two smaller Gothic arches. The large arches are separated by columns of diamond point. Above the capitals, they fan out widely in high, spined ridges. Around the midriff is a row of large, closely spaced dewdrops. Above the latter is a half-inch belt filled with two crisscrossing ridges which form a heavy chain, with a diamond point where the links join. Above this belt is found a feature never before encountered by the author. It is a canal with sloping sides and a flat bottom which is sunk into the body. The bottom of the canal is corduroyed with vertical fine-toothing. Above it is a half-inch band of ribbed triangles and diamonds filled with four diamond points. This band extends two-thirds of the way around the body, but not under the lip. (See cut for the scrollwork there.) The top area of the body is filled with fine stippling except for the scrolls under the lip.

The back three-fourths of the rim is covered with low, even scalloping. The front portion is plain, rises slightly and extends far enough forward to become almost too lippy. On the inside of the creamer, at the height of the triangle band, is a wide, flat ledge to hold a lid—yet if such a lid was ever made for a Lacy Sandwich creamer, I never heard of it.

The handle is large, heavy, and somewhat ponderous for such a small vessel. Its lateral aspects are flat and stippled. The front and back are ridged and plain. On top of the handle there is a prominent knob which provides a secure thumbgrip. Near the base of the handle are two spurs. They are probably to simulate the crossbars put on applied handles in this era.

The quality of this heavy flint glass is superior. It is clear and brilliant with only an occasional fleck of discoloration due to a grain of sand failing to fuse in the pot. The designer and moldmaker produced a noteworthy achievement. The art of pressing glass had not progressed to the point of ensuring a perfect pressing. The mold marks and edges have the sharp, rough areas common to this period. Either the mold or the blob of glass was too cold, for it has numerous hairlines and wavy areas.

Creamer: 3-part mold, 1 pound, 4 1/4 inches tall, 3 1/4 inches wide, and 5 5/8 inches long.

Creamers in this particular pattern are more often encountered than other Lacy designs. This does not imply that these creamers are frequently found; all such pieces are quite scarce and priced out of the reach of most collectors. The sugar bowl and creamer were probably the only items in this pattern. This piece is probably of the 1830s.

52—LACY SCROLL AND DIAMOND

Here is a seldom encountered rarity in pressed glass. They are occasionally found in the New England states but few have survived the rigorous use to which they were subjected by their youthful owners. It is a child's toy or miniature Lacy Sandwich glass creamer. It was made during the 1830s at the Boston and Sandwich Glass Company, Sandwich, Massachusetts during the time that Deming Jarves was perfecting the use of the machine to press glass.

Ruth Webb Lee, in *Sandwich Glass*, Plate 80, middle row, extreme left, shows this pitcher, but does not name or describe it. It is not elsewhere covered in our literature on glass. It is only a child's toy and was made for that purpose. The body is constricted slightly above the narrow ring base and below the rim. The body bulges out a little in the middle. On each side there is a large diamond composed of nine, raised diamond points. Flanking the diamonds is a raised, flowery scroll. The rest of the body is covered with fine stripling and this accounts for the "Lacy" part of the name. The front mold mark, under the lip, is high and seems to form the shaft of a feather since each side is feathered with uniform, closely set fine-toothing.

The handle is round, uniform, and small—except for tiny fingers. The ring base is slightly hollowed out underneath. There is a narrow band of plain unstippled glass at the rim. The back half of the rim is flat. The front half rises, then dips forward for a lip. Inside the creamer and slightly below the rim is a wide, well-defined ledge which follows the contour of the rim. This ledge was made for a lid to rest on, but unfortunately it is missing— if it ever had one. A level teaspoonful of liquid fills this pitcher to capacity.

The glass is bright and sparkling, but has a few bubbles and discolorations. The mold marks are high, sharp and almost dangerous. The rim is rough and unfinished. The glass is heavy early flint, and when held in the hand the piece feels as heavy as if made of iron. It is very thick for a little fellow—being 3/8 inch at the base. This excessive thickness is often encountered in early Lacy Sandwich glass. It resulted from too much gather being snipped from the punty. It took much work and experimentation before a worker could gauge the exact amount of gather to snip off to make a perfect given article of pressed glass. Too much made the piece thick, heavy and expensive to ship. Too little resulted in the mold not being filled and in a poor impression of the figure-work or an incomplete article—a loss in either case.

Toy creamer: 2 part mold, 2 ounces, 1 9/16 inches tall, 1 1/2 inches wide, and 2 3/8 inches long.

No other articles in this pattern are known. Perhaps a sugar bowl was also made. An interesting speculation is that some of the much sought Lacy cup and toddy plates of today may have been toy plates which accompanied this creamer in 1830.

53—FURROWS

An early, unnamed piece such as this often evokes interesting speculation as to its origin, antecedents, and genealogy. It is not stippled so is not of the Lacy type, but it is of fine, brilliant, heavy flint glass of the same or a slightly later period. It is of the Sandwich type, but no such attribution can be hazarded. The concentric rings under the base (see cut), general conformation, etc., indicate that it is from one of the eastern glass houses, not a midwestern one. Its general appearance, size, and quality closely resemble the creamer shown on the upper right of Plate 158 in Ruth Webb Lee's *Sandwich Glass*. Nothing about it signifies a foreign origin. Undoubtedly it dates from the 1840s, and a covered sugar must have been made. This pattern has not been covered by any of our glass authorities in their literature. It is quite rare, in mint condition, and would be considered extremely desirable by most museums.

It is of the same capacity as many Lacy Sandwich creamers—yet the pedestaled base and the long sweep from lip to back of handle make it appear larger. The body is somewhat bell-shaped. Just above the waist are two adjoining V-shaped ridges which encircle the base of the body. From the ridges to slightly below the rim, the body is divided into eight panels which are separated by vertical ridges. They are entirely filled with small V-shaped *furrows*, which run at an acute angle to the vertical ridges to give a herringbone effect. There is a half-inch-wide plain band above the top of the figurework. It is also a ridge with a high spine cresting its middle, and follows the curves of the rim. The back portion of the rim rises slightly to accommodate the handle. It rises too high and projects too far forward. It is an unattractive lip.

The waist is small, short, and curvaceous. On the base it flows out to end in a low round shelf. From there it rounds off gradually to a wide, ample base. Underneath we find the furrows again, but here they are concentric circles, much like a target. (See cut.) The handle is round and climbs high. It sweeps backward and down and returns to the bowl in sweeping curves. Near the lower attachment the upper and lower portions are grafted together. At the lower attachment is a large protuberance or spur—ornamental perhaps. The handle is ample—but could be easily knocked off.

On the inside slightly below the rim is a well-defined sloping ledge to hold a lid. This ledge follows the sweep of the rim and is indicated by the row of small dots in the drawing. Note how it sweeps up to and then down under the lip. The odd shape of this ledge is rarely encountered and only on very early pieces. The identical feature is on the following patterns in this book: LACY SCROLL AND DIAMOND and BLAZE. It appears in a slightly modified shape in HEARTS shown in Kamm's *A Seventh Pitcher Book*. What a loss we suffer in not having this lid. It is amazing how competent artisans were in those early days in making lids to fit odd and difficult contours. A glance at an EXCELSIOR sugar bowl, THUMBPRINT small compote, SAWTOOTH or LOOP sugar bowls and compotes will convince any skeptic that artisans did a difficult job very well indeed.

The glass in this piece is quite thick and the creamer is unusually heavy for its medium capacity. The quality is what one would expect from the early pioneering days of pressing glass into molds. Many tricks of the trade were still to be learned. It is not Lacy glass, but the clear heavy flint has the same bright, silvery sheen as that of the Lacy type. There are many bubbles, some of them 1/8 inch in size. There are some discolored flecks here and there where the sand was not thoroughly fused. In pressing glass where a 3-part mold was employed, the mold was generally

divided exactly into thirds. On this piece the mold was divided into eighths. The part of the mold which formed the front of the creamer comprised two-eighths of the mold. The two parts of the mold which formed the back portion of the creamer each took three-eighths of the mold.

Creamer: 3-part mold, 1 pound, 4 ounces, 5 3/8 inches tall, 3 1/2 inches wide, and 6 1/4 inches long.

No other items have been seen by the writer.

54—OPEN ROSE (Late)

This is one of the better old patterns that Minnie Watson Kamm had not encountered and did not list in her eight pitcher books. There is a good reason for this—pieces in this pattern are difficult to come by. It took the writer years to locate this creamer, and it is the less desirable of the two varieties of the pattern.

S. T. Millard, in *Goblets*, Plate 54-2 and 3, shows a heavy and lightweight goblet in the pattern, saying the heavy was made during the 1870s and the light during the 1880s. Ruth Webb Lee, in *Early American Pressed Glass*, describes and names this as Pattern 145, pages 374-75, Plates 122 and 123. She shows a covered sugar, creamer, eggcup and a goblet. The stubby little creamer used here with the perky handle is not the same as the tall graceful creamer used by Mrs. Lee. It is almost an inch shorter.

OPEN ROSE is a beautiful and comfortable pattern (the roses have no thorns) and was bound to please the public. As a result, sales would be good; more than one factory would change the molds sufficiently to avoid patent infringements and go merrily ahead making the new variant. We do not refer to these later pieces as reproductions, though seventy or eighty years ago that is exactly what they were. How I cherish and welcome this "reproduction" into the "400" of my collection!

There is a V-shaped ridge and groove separating the upper 1/4 of the body from the lower 3/4. Above this band the body is smooth and plain. The rim is saddled, rising to a high point in the rear and just as high in front for the attractive lip. Below the band are three rose sprigs, each with a large, highly raised, open rose, stem, leaves, and two rosebuds but no thorns. Between the open roses are erect rose sprouts with three leaves and a bud. These straight stems cover and hide the mold marks on the body. The mold marks are placed so a mark does not fall under the handle as it does on most patterns.

The perky little applied handle is as cute as it

50 - 2

51

52

Lip
51

53

Bottom
51

Bottom
53

54

55 - 1

Lip
55

55 - 2

can be and is perched high on the side of the body. It does not provide a firm grip. The lower attachment was executed by a real gaffer and is a lovely thing. It is tooled into a crossbar and then turned up into an open loop, which is, in turn, tooled into a crossbar. The stem is quite slender and somewhat short. It is composed of nine flat panels which extend up on the lower part of the bowl, and each ends in a sharp point. This makes a large nine-point star. On the thin, flat foot the panels end in a straight-sided shelf. The base is slightly domed underneath.

The glass is of excellent quality soda-lime. It is brilliant, clear, sparkling, and free of discolorations and defects. The workmanship is of a high order. It is light in weight and appears to date from the period of 1875 to 1885.

Creamer: 3-part mold, 11 1/2 ounces, 5 1/2 inches tall, 3 1/8 inches wide, and 5 inches long.

This creamer and the light goblet pictured by Dr. Millard are the only items known to the writer in this late variant. Undoubtedly it was manufactured in about the same range of items as its precursor, the more stately, classical, and heavier OPEN ROSE pattern.

55—CROWE'S CHARM

This is a graceful pressed glass pattern which has escaped the attention of our glass writers, or perhaps they have purposely avoided it. This would be understandable, because there were several such patterns made with little to differentiate them, or to confidently relate different items in the same pattern with any degree of accuracy. Selecting a descriptive title is practically impossible.

The tall, slender pieces in patterns of this type carry little if any figurework. They rely for their charm on simple, pleasing lines, superior quality, and great brilliance. The bowls of the stemmed pieces are somewhat bell-shaped, rather large, and have almost straight sides—flaring out from waist to rim. On the creamer a well-raised palm (?) leaf is embossed under the lip. (See cut.) When seen from the side it is barely perceptible. This decoration is missing on the sugar bowl. On the other hand, there is no figure on the creamer even approximating the finial on the sugar bowl lid. On the latter, a reeded finial with a heavy ring in the center arches over an oblong, odd-shaped plateau. Neither of these features would be serviceable as a name. The palm on the creamer being absent on the sugar would not help. One wonders if it is on the cake stand, the spooner, or the goblet.

The slender stem is curved into the bottom of the bowl and into a slight shelf on the large, round base. The rim is severely plain but attractive. The lip is small. The mold marks are twisted around the stem. The pressed, reeded handles on both pieces present a superb imitation of an applied handle. Even on the ridges of the reeds, no mold marks can be found. Only at the top attachment can the imitation be detected, where the mold maker, of all things, allowed the reeds from the top of the handle attachment to continue on across the top of the rim in the identical size and shape of those on the handle. This caused three tiny scallops on the rear of the rim.

This is pleasing, quality lime-glass with no resonance. It was made between 1885 and 1895 and was a poor competitor at a time when the public demanded every available space on any article be completely covered with "fuss and bother." Little of it was made, less sold, and few pieces of it can be found today.

Creamer: 2-part mold, 13 ounces, 6 1/4 inches tall, 3 1/4 inches wide, and 5 3/8 inches long.

Mr. and Mrs. R. G. Crowe of St. Louis, Missouri, and Monroe, Louisiana, were kind enough to let the author include these two pieces in this volume.

56—FLAT DIAMOND

This tall, slender beauty is charming in its simplicity. Such an attractive pattern should have had a tremendous vogue. Nevertheless, pieces of it are never seen in southern shops nor is it often listed in advertisements.

Mrs. Ruth Webb Lee, in *Victorian Glass*, pages 88-89, Plate 32-4, names the pattern and shows the creamer, goblet and a tall celery vase. Her drawings vary somewhat from the creamer shown here, particularly around the lower part of the body and the stem. The latter she shows flowing out on a shelf on the base. She does not show a plain portion of the body below the panels of flat diamonds.

Millard, in *Goblets*, Plate 57-3, shows it as PANELLED DIAMOND, RED TOP and on Plate 89-2 of the same book shows a PANELLED DIAMONDS goblet. In *Goblets II*, Plate 59-2, he shows LIPPMAN. His illustrations are indistinct and positive identification is impossible. I am using the name Mrs. Lee assigned.

The tall, narrow, projectile-shaped body of this creamer is neat and would never grow tiresome. There is a half-inch-wide plain band around the base of the bowl. From the top of the latter six panels of flattopped diamonds extend three-fourths of the way up the body. The diamonds are formed by V-shaped grooves which cross each other at sharp angles from the vertical. Alternating with the diamond panels are smooth ones of the same width. A wide band above the panels is also plain and smooth.

The rim is rounded and smooth, low on the sides and sweeps up to high points at the lip and in the rear. The rim and lip are fetching. The hexagonal stem is small and of uniform size throughout. At its lower end it rests on a peculiar cavetto-shaped collar. The base is wide, flat, and round with a slight hollow underneath. The long, graceful, applied handle is compatible with the entire piece. Its long, flowing curves, its ample size and its sedateness all tend to improve the general beauty of the piece. The glass is scintillatingly clear, brilliant, and sparkling. No defect of any kind can be detected. The workmanship is also of a high order. This was never production ware. The maker of this creamer took pride in a quality product. It is soda-lime glass, light in weight, and has no resonance when tapped. It probably dates from 1875 to 1885.

Creamer: 3-part mold, 14 ounces, 6 5/8 inches tall, 3 3/16 inches wide, and 5 5/8 inches long.

We know the four-piece table setting was made as well as a goblet and celery vase. We have no inkling of where or by whom it was manufactured.

57—COLUMBIAN COIN

This is a pattern of strong contrasts with blunt contradictions and about which little is known. Most of what is known is not so—believe it or not. Perhaps the best way to cover the pattern is to show some of the differences between it and the pattern COIN, U.S. COIN, or FROSTED COIN as it is variously called.

This pattern is best known as COLUMBIAN COIN, but it is also called COLUMBUS COIN and SPANISH COIN. It is none of these. There is no coin of any realm represented. Instead, wretchedly sculptured medals were used which gave a poor impression to the glass. Six impressions surround the base of the body and in no way correspond to the nine columns above. The six medallions are as follows: two "1492 Christopher Columbus 1892"; two "Eagle and Shield"; one "Americus Vespucius"; and one "Crown and Shield," all gilded. On COIN, U.S. COIN, FROSTED COIN, THE AMERICAN COIN as it is variously called, the heads and tails of 5¢, 10¢, 20¢, 25¢, 50¢, and $1.00 United States coins dated 1892 were used. Thin impressions were either left plain, or were

frosted, silvered, gilded, or flashed with amber. Mint condition coins were secured and magnificent impressions resulted. The title COIN is short and appropriate, though its original name was THE SILVER AGE.

We know nothing of where or by whom COLUMBIAN COIN was manufactured. We know that COIN glass was manufactured by the Central Glass Works of Wheeling, West Virginia; and by Hobbs, Brockunier and Company also of Wheeling. (The latter became Factory "O" of the U.S. Glass Company, and they advertised the pattern widely.) See Plates 3, 4, 5, and 6 of Kamm's *A Seventh Pitcher Book* and also page 83 for four pages of illustrations and a page of notes on COIN. Also see Plates 58 and 59 in her *An Eighth Pitcher Book* for two additional full page advertisements of the U.S. Glass Company, on COIN. The Bellaire Goblet Company of Findlay, Ohio, also made COIN and there is some evidence a glass house in Wellsburg, West Virginia, made it. Molds for COIN were made by The Hipkins Novelty Mold Shop of Martins Ferry, Ohio.

COLUMBIAN COIN is supposed to be plentiful and, therefore, cheap. For years I have diligently searched the ads in our leading antique magazines, and I have been able to locate only one creamer—this one (it cost me $22.50). Of all the shops I have visited, I have been able to find only one additional piece. It was a creamer. COIN glass is supposed to be exceedingly scarce and very expensive. The myth of scarcity is carefully husbanded. The prices are fabulous as well as ridiculous with a creamer bringing from $95 up. None graces my collection. A trade journal of May 25, 1892, carried the following item: "A Government Inspector went to *Central* and *Hobbs* glass *factories* belonging to the U.S. Glass Co. They had been making a line of glass called THE SILVER AGE, with silvered glass facsimiles of coins of the U.S. in all denominations. The Inspector pronounced the molds illegal and *ordered* them destroyed. The ware was having a *tremendous run* and the molds cost several thousands of dollars (italics were supplied). The glass in the factories' *warehouses* was not destroyed but instead permission was granted to *complete* all sets and orders on hand. Even before the molds were destroyed (?) much COIN glass had reached the market. COIN was one of the best money makers the huge U.S. Glass Co. had." This informs us they had a tremendous sale of the pattern and reaped a big reward in profits. Without attempting to do so I have discovered three large collections of COIN in Fayetteville, Lonsdale, and Silver Hill, Arkansas.

Pieces of COIN are often found in shops. There seems to be no scarcity, but an insatiable demand. I once advertised a piece of it for sale and received twenty-two orders. A great many collections of it exist. Some pieces of COIN glass are being reproduced today.

No writer on pressed glass has ever tried adequately to cover COLUMBIAN COIN. Ruth Webb Lee devotes a chapter to the COIN pattern together with four full pages of illustrations in *Victorian Glass*. Minnie Watson Kamm describes and illustrates the pattern in one book and in another devotes a full page to notes on it. In addition she shows six pages of illustrations. Dr. S. T. Millard, George S. and Helen McKearin, Carl W. Dreppard, E. McCalmy Belknap, Josephine Jefferson, Edwin G. Warman, and Alice Hulett Metz all cover the pattern. Not unexpectedly we find facts liberally laced with pure legend and hearsay. It makes good listening and whets the demand, but unfortunately much of it is not true.

These items are known to have been made in COLUMBIAN COIN: creamer, sugar bowl, spoonholder, covered butter dish, goblet, lamps, water pitcher, tumbler, toothpick holder, and cruet. The COIN pattern was made in the following: footed ale; oblong bread tray; 6, 7, 8, and 9 inch flat covered bowls; covered butter dish; beer mug; tankard creamer; standard creamer; claret; flat cake plate; celery vase; champagne; compote using 20¢ piece; low open compotes; high open compotes in 6, 7, 8, 8 1/2 and 10-inch sizes; high covered compotes in 6, 7, and 8-inch sizes; candlesticks; candy or jelly dish; rectangular 8-inch dish; epergne; finger bowl; three goblets with dimes, quarters and halves; four types of square font lamps; four types of round font lamps; nappies in many sizes; night light with 20¢ piece; pickle dish; quart water pitcher; half-gallon water pitcher; salt and pepper shakers; flat sauce dishes; footed sauce dishes; spice set combination, four piece; syrup pitcher; covered sugar bowl; open sugar bowl; spoonholder; cake salver; tumbler; toothpick holder; waste bowl; water tray; small wine; and large wine.

This COLUMBIAN COIN creamer was made in the same mold as the COIN, though the COIN molds were *ordered* destroyed and are reputed to have been. Here the medals to make the medallions were substituted for United States coins. The round, raised medal decorations, all of the same size, are on six highly beveled, flat platforms. Between the platforms are flat-topped ridges. The top two-thirds of the body is vertical

and cylindrical. There are nine rounded columns with wide, inverted V-shaped ridges between. The rim, lip, handle, waist, and ringed base are plain and are of routine design. The bottom is plain and domed. The quality is excellent, except for the designing of the medals.

Creamer: 3-part mold, 1 pound, 5 1/8 inches tall, 3 3/16 inches wide, and 5 inches long.

58—ALHAMBRA

This pattern is shown again since it has now been authenticated as a product of the Iowa City Glass Company, Iowa City, Iowa. This was one of the few glass factories ever to be located west of the Mississippi River. Another known factory was located in California and it is reputed to have manufactured glass coins to be gilded.

An article by Donald A. Koehn of Rapid City, Iowa and Mr. and Mrs. Charles B. Righter of Iowa City, all collectors of ware from this factory, appeared with photographs and line drawings in the April, 1956, issue of *Hobbies*. A brief history of the factory was given from their vast store of knowledge about it, including photographs, old catalogs and cullet excavated from the site. This should be amplified and republished to obtain a wider audience. A line drawing of a spoonholder in the pattern was illustrated. At the lower part of page 80 a cut from an old catalog was used, which showed five different articles in ALHAMBRA.

Financed by local capital, this factory began operations in June, 1880. Although some experienced glass men were associated with the company and it produced considerable glass, it was never profitable. It finally failed after less than two years of production. Mr. Koehn assembled a list of known patterns produced, and this list should be amended and made public. The Righters have many excellent photographs of the factory and its products.

Dr. S. T. Millard calls the pattern TEEPEE in his *Goblets*, Plate 23-1, where he shows a goblet. In *An Eighth Pitcher Book*, page 11, No. 17, Minnie Watson Kamm illustrated and used the creamer I possess for her writeup. Since she had already named another pattern TEPEE in her *A Second Two Hundred Pattern Glass Pitchers*, she assigned the title WIGWAM to this pattern. Metz shows a photograph of a creamer as No. 1728 and calls it WIGWAM. Because of the confusion between TEEPEE and WIGWAM, I am returning to its original name of ALHAMBRA.

Section of Band
57

56

57

58

59

60

61

62

63

The body is bell-shaped with straight, flaring sides from the base of the bowl to the rim. Around the center of the body is a 1 7/8-inch geometric band of raised figurework. A series of triangular-shaped figures resembles an Indian village, though it is much too regular. They are formed by raised lines which zigzag up and down, and cross at their apexes to form smaller triangles above. In the center of each such small space is a triangular pyramid. Each interstice above the zigzag contains a Formée cross. The interior of each wigwam contains a raised, inverted T with a four-ray, raised fan on either side. Below the zigzag, four parallel lines surround the piece. The two center ones are spaced farther apart than the others, leaving a plain surface. In the space is a series of rectangular pyramids. The remainder of the body surface is plain.

The rim is deeply saddled, and rises well above the handle attachment at the rear. In front it climbs rapidly and pushes forward to form a wide, ungainly lip. The entire piece appears lanky and stiff. The large, complex handle is pressed and uses both angular and curved motifs. It is quite large. Almost half of the upper and all of the lower members are made up of cornucopia braces which point slightly upward. On both are wide concaved flutes, separated by V-shaped grooves. The lower portion ends in a well-rounded knob at the lower end. The remainder of the handle is six-sided with the two side panels much wider than the other four.

The tall, terete stem is the only really attractive feature of the piece. The body curves in sharply from the abrupt bottom of the bowl. A ring in high, rounded relief surrounds the stem at the middle, while below this the latter curves out gracefully and ends in a round shelf on the foot. The base is wide, round, and almost flat. The glass is dull lime-soda. It was not quite good enough, nor was the workmanship as refined as it should have been with so much plain surface left. The mold marks are high, show throughout their course, and were not fire-polished. There is no trace of the yellowish cast, so common in glass from this factory.

Creamer: 3-part mold, 1 pound, 6 1/2 inches tall, 3 11/16 inches wide, and 6 3/8 inches long.

A complete set of tableware was produced in this pattern.

59—ARTICHOKE

Minnie Watson Kamm used a covered compote, 10 inches high and 7 inches wide to illustrate this pattern in *A Seventh Pitcher Book*. She said it was unknown to Millard and Lee and did not appear in their books. She overlooked it as a pattern called FROSTED ARTICHOKE in Ruth Webb Lee's *Victorian Glass*, pages 65-66 and Plate 24-1.

Since the pattern is found in clear, clear and frosted, and clear with alternate flower bracts frosted, the title ARTICHOKE is shorter and seems more accurate than the longer title of FROSTED ARTICHOKE, and it is continued here. Metz mentions the pattern as FROSTED ARTICHOKE, No. 1155, but does not illustrate it. Do not confuse this pattern with two of similar motifs which Dr. Millard calls LAMINATED PETAL and ALLIGATOR SCALES.

Edwin G. Warman in his *The Third Antiques*, page 42, illustrates an open sugar bowl with an irregularly scalloped rim similar to that on Kamm's compote. The rim of this creamer is not scalloped. It is saddled with a cantle at the back and arches up and forward to form a droopy lip.

The body is barrel-shaped and has a list to the side where the handle is attached. The petals of the design start from the waist and extend well up on the body. The motif consists of the flower of an artichoke, with the bracts overlapping and the smaller ones at the bottom. Each bract is in high relief and has a raised, vertical spine up its center. The bracts and a portion of the handle have been acid etched and have a satin finish. They appear frosted. The finish was carefully applied and when seen closely, adds much charm to the piece. That portion of each bract which forms part of the upper edge of the figurework was given special treatment. When the upper portion of the piece was covered with "goo" in preparation for the acid bath, the goo was also applied on a narrow margin of the upper edge of each bract. It was applied very evenly. After the etching, each upper bract had its body etched but had a narrow clear border. It is a beautiful effect. (See drawing for arrangement of flowers.) The body is constricted at the top.

The ringed base is rounded under with a thick, heavy footing. Underneath it is hollowed out just enough to let it rest on the ring of the perimeter. The handle is ugly and impractical. It is similar to the handle of RED BLOCK. It is a poor imitation of an applied one with the large blob at the lower attachment. It is round in cross section.

We do not know where or by whom this quality product was made. It dates from about 1885-1892. If made after 1893 some decorator probably would have stained the plain upper portion ruby. Old goblets are unknown, though a new goblet is being made today. The pattern is not plentiful and brings high prices.

Creamer: 4-part mold, 15 ounces, 4 5/8 inches tall, 3 9/16 inches wide and 4 5/8 inches long.

The following articles are known to have been made: sugar bowl; butter dish; creamer; spoon-holder; bowls, shallow; cake stand; celery vase; compotes, open; compotes, covered; fruit bowls; lamps; rose bowl; sauces, footed; sauces, flat; molasses pitcher; water pitcher, tankard; water pitcher, bulbous; tumbler; water tray, large; and finger bowl with plate.

60—MCKEE'S COMET

This impractical, bean pole of a creamer was the most difficult of all to draw. Since it was hard to draw on paper, we can imagine the sweat and tears the artisan must have shed as he chipped the mold in reverse, in cast iron, with a hammer and chisel.

Mrs. Kamm drew the cut in her *Fourth Pitcher Book*, page 13, No. 14, from an old catalog of McKee Brothers dated 1887. It is shown on Plate 1, of the same book. Of course she had no measurements and could not show the exact details. The creamer shown here is from the author's collection. The catalog shows the following items manufactured as "Comet Set": 9-inch fruit bowl in assorted colors; 4 1/2 inch fruit (Sauce); 5 1/2 inch fruit; spooner; covered sugar; covered butter and creamer, all on high standards; 8-inch fruit, footed; and 9-inch fruit, footed. A water pitcher, gas globe, etc., were also made. The design is really something. It is late Victorian—with an effort!

Most of the body is cylindrical. The straight sides taper in slightly from base to rim. They are filled with an indescribably complicated cut glass effect. This was achieved by dividing the body into four equal parts with one-half inch wide, high, and inverted V-shaped ridges slewed or swirled from bottom to top. The crests of each ridge are strigiled with large and variously sized thumbprints. The space between the ridges is cut vertically, horizontally, and diagonally by V-shaped grooves. The distance between the parallel grooves varies and this further complicates the design. All this results in a large number of faceted figures of different shapes. Even the tops of the figures have been pressed differently.

At the base of the bowl is an unusual conceit. It consists of a flat, raised octagonal band over half an inch wide which encircles the round body. Superimposed on this is another raised shelf, with

the top and bottom edges widely scalloped. Evenly spaced in each of its surfaces are three large, inverted dewdrops. From this band, the body narrows rapidly to the round part of the stem. This area is free of ornamentation.

Midway of the stem is a large octagonal knop which matches the above described band, except that it has a single drop to the side. Below it the creamer is octagonal. The eight flat panels spread out at a 45-degree angle till they reach a width of one-half that of the base. They then flatten out in a slight decline to the edge . At the edge they drop almost vertically. The lower, outer edge of the base has been beveled. The tall stem is unusual, especially on such a tall body. The covered pieces have the added height of steepled lids with tall finials. The striving for novelty hit pay dirt there. Under the base is a low dome in the top of which is impressed a large, round 28-ray star.

The rim is level and unevenly scalloped with a wide scallop, then two narrow ones. They do not match the body design, but they do make it fancy. The lip is small and barely noticeable. The handle is large and ungainly. It is roughly six-sided and is a trifle larger at the lower attachment. The two faces on the back edge are covered with closely set, tiny thumbprints.

The lime-glass and workmanship of this pattern are of excellent quality, but the taste of the artisan who designed it is not that of today. When seen in a bright light it is scintillating in its brilliance. The mold marks show on the base of the bowl but not elsewhere. They are neither high nor sharp.

It is remarkable that this tall creamer, which could be so easily toppled over and broken, has survived some seventy-five years. Casualties in this pattern would be exceedingly high in the kitchen and especially with the steepled lids, which have a high finial perched at the zenith. Have you ever seen a covered sugar bowl or a covered butter dish in this pattern? I have not. Pieces in this pattern are seldom seen today.

Creamer: 4-part mold, 1 7/16 pounds, 7 5/8 inches tall, 3 3/8 inches wide and 4 1/2 inches long.

61—EXCELSIOR

The creamer in this exalted old pattern was shown and described in Kamm's *Third Pitcher Book*, page 32, No. 41. We are departing from the practice of showing only creamers, to show an item not previously shown in glass literature. The piece used here is a sugar bowl without a cover—also called a sweetmeat jar.

It had a high pagoda-domed lid, and with the added finial it must have stood almost 10 1/2 inches tall. A glance at the scalloped rim of the sugar bowl shows the insecure perch the lid had. Being high, and the lids insecure, they were easily broken by sliding off when the bowl was tilted in being passed. This explains why the lids are almost unobtainable though the bowls are not too difficult to find.

This pattern was made at several factories before the Civil War. It was very popular and was made in a great many items over a long period of time. There are a number of variants of the pattern. Some have differed sufficiently to warrant a name of their own as *HOURGLASS* shown in Kamm's *A Second Two Hundred Pattern Glass Pitchers*, page 8, and *TONG* in *A Fifth Pitcher Book*, page 24. *BARREL OF THUMBPRINTS* shown next is an adaptation of the same motif.

To give some idea how the glass houses catered to a pattern's popularity we need only list the items known to have been made in EXCELSIOR. They are: ale glass, bitters bottle, round flat covered bowl, 10-inch open bowl, 9 1/2-inch candlestick, smaller candlestick, celery vase, champagne, claret, cordial, covered butter dish, several sizes of covered compotes, caster set, creamer standard, creamer formed from tumbler, pint decanter, quart decanter, small footed decanter-like sauce bottle, large oval dish, small oval dish, eggcup, double eggcup, covered eggcup, many variations of goblets, jelly glass with glass screw lid, pint pitcher, syrup pitcher, syrup pitcher with tin top, 1-quart water pitcher, large and small handled mugs, footed salt, footed tumblers in several sizes, pickle or preserve dish, spoonholder, spillholder, medicine bottle, water tumblers in four sizes, wine glass in two sizes, water bottle or tumbler-up, vases, and pomade jar.

A few pieces have been found in fiery opalescent glass, but they are rare and expensive. No other colors are known.

See Ruth Webb Lee's *Early American Pressed Glass* Pattern 3, pages 20-25, and Plates 1, 4, 7, and 34. Also see George and Helen McKearin's *American Glass* which shows the EXCELSIOR pattern on page 404 and lists the many items in it. They also show illustrations of the pattern on Plates 206, Nos. 8 and 12; Plate 208, No. 16; Plate 209, No. 16; Plate 211, No. 6. Refer to S. T. Millard's *Goblet Book*, Plate 19, for BARREL EXCELSIOR, GIANT EXCELSIOR and FLARE TOP EXCELSIOR. In his *Goblets II*, he shows a goblet in Plate 2 as EXCELSIOR DOUBLE RING STEM.

62—BARREL OF THUMBPRINTS

The spoonholder shown here is of an obscure design made to imitate the famous EXCELSIOR pattern. Only a few pieces were made, and it is seldom found today. It is barrel-shaped and is in a neat, attractive pattern of excellent soda-lime glass. It is clear and brilliant, has no resonance, and is typical of the 1880s. It is both thin and light.

With the spoonholder as a guide, we may assume the creamer was of similar shape and had an applied handle. The spooner is widest at its middle and smaller at the rim and waist. It is covered with four horizontal bands of large shallow thumbprints, one above the other. They become progressively larger from the waist to the top, and are wider than they are high. Between each four thumbprints is a rectangular space filled with four raised and faceted pyramids.

The ring base is 1/2 inch wide and tapers out. On the upper portion of the base is a row of small, round thumbprints. Underneath, it is domed and plain. The top 3/4 inch of the body is left plain. The rim has deep notched, semicircular scallops.

The writer has a bar tumbler in this pattern, which was made to represent a much earlier age than the spoonholder. It is of fine flint glass and has a high fire polish, but there are many small bubbles and white flecks in the metal. When tapped it rings like a bell and has the appearance of early flint ware. A close observer will note that a "ground pontil mark?" has been *pressed* into the base. The reproduction fooled me to the sum of $5.

Spoonholder: 3-part mold, 14 ounces, 4 3/4 inches tall, and 3 3/4 inches wide.

The manufacturer is unknown. No other items of the pattern other than a creamer and a bar tumbler are known. A creamer, sugar bowl, butter dish, and goblet are the items most likely to appear. A water pitcher, celery vase, and decanter are the next most likely.

63—ORION THUMBPRINT

Ruth Webb Lee, in *Victorian Glass*, named this pattern ORION THUMBPRINT. Dr. Millard, in *Goblets*, calls it ORION INVERTED THUMBPRINT. Mrs. Lee's shorter name is used here as preferable. Here is a pattern of large and unusual pieces. The shape is rare. It is as tall as some water pitchers. The deep-domed base, the rim pattern, and the polka dots on the inside all tend to remove it from the ordinary run of pressed glass patterns. The quality is excellent. The glass is crystal clear, brilliant, thick (1/4 inch at places), and heavy, but not massive.

The ovate, globe-shaped creamer rests on a short, narrow waist. The latter is atop a high pagoda-like base which is hollow and plain underneath. On top it is covered with flutes and columns from the waist to the scalloped foot of the skirt. There are four wide flutes, each ending in a round daisy which is turned out slightly at the bottom. Six high, convex columns separate each two daisies. The outside ones are shorter and the two middle ones longer to form with the daisies the eight points on which the piece sits.

The ovoid body is widest around the middle, tapering in sharply downward to the waist and gently upward to the collar. The five bands of polka dots which decorate the piece are on the inside and progressively diminish in size toward the waist. They are well rounded. The outside of the body is smooth and quite plain.

At the top of the bowl is a concave 1/4 inch channel around the body, separating the bowl from the ornate rim. Around the inside of the piece and at the same level of the channel, a ledge is found to accommodate the missing lid. The latter, in order to have been seen above the rim, would have had to be as highly domed and with a superimposed finial. It probably was similar to the base. A half dozen or more types of this ornamental, but not utilitarian, ware were produced during the same period and all had lids.

The high collar is scalloped as shown. Each of the nine large, thick, arched scallops is centered by a sunken, three-lobed or club-shaped foil. Between them is a small erect fan or shell. The two front scallops have a high projecting extension which forms the lip. The round, attractive handle is attached at the bottom by means of a large, circular blob which narrows rapidly. The upper attachment has a turned-under tab with four furrowed crossbars. No mold marks can be found on the piece. The quality is so superior that all such marks have been obliterated.

Creamer: No mold marks show. Weight 1 7/16 pounds, 7 3/8 inches tall without lid, 4 1/4 inches wide, and 6 1/8 incles long.

Dr. Millard, in *Goblets*, Plate 151-4 shows a small goblet in this pattern. He considers it a product of the 1880s and says it comes in clear only.

Ruth Webb Lee, in *Victorian Glass*, page 66, Plate 24-3, shows a goblet, an oval platter with DAISY AND BUTTON center, and this creamer. She says the pattern was made by the Canton Glass Company of Indiana in 1893. According to her it was made in blue, amber, yellow, opaque blue, milk-white, and *black*, in addition to clear glass. Clear pieces are scarce and expensive. Colored pieces are almost unheard of. A 4-piece table set of spooner, covered butter dish, covered sugar bowl, and covered creamer was made. Other known pieces are platter, celery vase, compote, goblet, and berry set.

Bryce, Walker and Company put out a pattern in the late 1870s which they called ORION. It was made in clear, blue, amber, amethyst, and canary. Later the pattern became the popular CATHEDRAL. A CATHEDRAL creamer in canary was broken in shipment to me. It was one of the most beautiful shades of yellow glass I have seen.

This pattern closely resembles GLOBE AND STAR as shown in Kamm's *A Second Two Hundred Pattern Glass Creamers*, page 23. The unusual base, thick rim, daisies, handle, and general conformation are remarkably similar. Enough so, in fact, to arouse speculation that the same artisan designed both patterns.

The stem of the HEART STEM creamer shown in Kamm's *A Fourth Pitcher Book*, page 7, has hearts and four-lobed club or foil figures pressed into the stem. At first glance these depressions appear to be openwork, however, as is the case with the creamer being described, they are not. They are filled with thin panes of glass.

In Kamm's *A Sixth Pitcher Book*, in Plate 17 and on page 56, No. 128 is reproduced an advertisement of 1886 by the Belmont Glass Works of Bellaire, Ohio. It shows an elaborately designed covered butter dish and covered sugar bowl. Mrs. Kamm described the pattern from this ad without having actually seen a piece of the pattern. She called it BELMONT for the manufacturer. See description and cut of the actual creamer in the following write-up, and note the similarity between the two patterns.

In *Opaque Glass*, Dr. Millard shows a COLUMBUS 9 1/2-inch milk-white plate in Plate 11, left. In Plate 25, right,he shows a CLUB AND SHELL BORDER plate and says it came in four different sizes. The borders of the two plates are almost identical with that of the ORION THUMBPRINT creamer.

E. McCalmy Belknap, in his book, *Milk Glass*, on page 8, Plate 4-a, shows a milk-white plate which he calls SHELL AND CLUB BORDER. He says it came in four sizes and is presumed to be a product of the Canton Glass Company of Canton, Ohio. On page 9, Plate 5-a, he shows a handsome 9 1/2-inch, milk-white COLUMBUS PLATE with the club and shell border. On page 15, Plate 11-f, he shows a blue-white heavy plate in CLUB AND SHELL, WAFFLE CENTER. All these borders are identical with that of the creamer shown here.

J. Stanley Brothers, Jr., in *Thumbnail Sketches*, page 21, shows a cut of six beautiful milk-white plates. He says they were designed by David Baker and manufactured by the Canton Glass Company of Merion, Indiana, about 1893-1895. Two of them designed by Mr. Baker have borders exactly like that on the rim of this creamer and are called CLUB AND SHELL from the design. On the creamer the three-lobed foil, or club, figures appear to be openwork but are actually filled with thin panes of glass. The two plates have open lacy-edged borders.

The Canton Glass Company of Canton, Ohio, was established in 1883 and manufactured such patterns as PRIMROSE and BARRED FORGET-ME-NOT before they moved to Marion, Indiana, in 1890. While there they advertised: "Private molds a specialty." They had David Baker as their chief designer and artisan, and he designed the now rare and expensive JUMBO pattern. The Canton Glass Company joined the National Glass Company in 1898. It was heard of through 1903 and then was dismantled and shipped away to build still another glass house.

Given: (1) David Baker was the chief designer of the Canton Glass Company. (2) The Canton Glass Company manufactured ORION THUMBPRINT. (3) David Baker designed several plates with borders identical with that of ORION THUMBPRINT.

∴ David Baker designed ORION THUMB-PRINT. Q.E.D. (Or was it that simple?)

64—BELMONT

This most unusual pattern was listed and named by Minnie Watson Kamm in *A Sixth Pitcher Book*, page 56, No. 128 and Plate 17. She had not seen a piece of the pattern but had a cut made from an advertisement put out in 1886 by the Belmont Glass Works, Bellaire, Ohio. This cut shows a picture of the covered sugar bowl and the covered butter dish as their No. 100 pattern but does not mention other items or assign a title. The ad shows that C. H. Talmas was president and W. F. Snively was secretary of the company. They manufactured tableware, lamps, bar goods, blown tumblers, stemware, fine polka-dot and hobnail ware in assorted colors.

In *A Fifth Pitcher Book*, page 145, No. 191, Mrs. Kamm used a photograph of a water pitcher for her write-up. She called it DAISY AND BUT-TON, PLAIN. Since she had not seen a piece of the pattern for either write-up, it is not surprising that she failed to associate the piece in the photograph with the sugar bowl and butter dish in the ad. The creamer, butter, and sugar all have different shapes. Had Mrs. Kamm seen this creamer, she would have recognized the same pattern in the water pitcher. Without the pedestaled base, the creamer and water pitcher differ only in size. It is one pattern in a thousand where all handles have air twists through them.

GLOBE AND STAR, shown in Kamm's *A Second Two Hundred Pattern Glass Pitchers*, page 23, has so many striking similarities to this pattern including the air-twist handle, that it raises the question whether both designs may not have been designed by the same sculptor. They may even have been chipped by the same moldmaker. SWIRL, in Kamm's *A Third Two Hundred Pattern Glass Pitchers*, is also similar, but we know it was made by the Windsor Glass Company of Pittsburgh, Pennsylvania. They still could have been sculptured by the same hand and executed by the same moldmaker such as the Hipkins Novelty Mold Shop of Martins Ferry, Ohio, who could well have supplied all the molds. George Hipkins started making molds for the Belmont Glass Company in 1886, the year this pattern was advertised. He may also have supplied molds to the Windsor Glass Company.

Patterns such as this are often called *busy* and are spoken of disparagingly, especially by the avant garde and pseudoaristocrats. Had they lived in 1886, or if they owned this beautiful creamer today, their harsh judgment would be assuaged. The main motif is the *DAISY AND BUTTON* design which was a pressed imitation of the difficult-to-execute, scarce, and very expensive *RUSSIAN* cut pattern of genuine cut glass. It was once used in the White House and was discontinued only because it was too expensive. It is most effective in refracting light when the metal is clear and smooth.

The body of this creamer is shaped like a top and is covered with DAISY AND BUTTON design. The creamer is tall and sits on a high, ornate base. The waist is narrow, and it arches out widely to the base. The first arch has a band of highly convex ribs with rounded ends. Between each is a sharp-spined dart. At the base of this band is a heavy ring which encircles the base. Below it the base widens still more, then arches over and down. The bottom is formed by random widths and lengths of scallops. Each seventh scallop is wider than the others. The fourth and seventh scallops are long enough to form legs. Underneath is a dome over an inch high.

The neck is constricted. At its juncture with the body a raised and then a sunken ring surrounds the piece. The collar flares, and though it is more than half an inch in height, carries no figurework. The rim and lip are different from that on other patterns, as indicated by the drawing.

This handle is a rarity of pressed glass. It is an air-twist applied handle having four air passages which are twisted into a beautiful spiral. I know of only two other patterns with such a handle. The main defect of the piece is that the lower attachment of the handle was applied on top of the complex daisy and button figurework. Many open-end air pockets were left which have become filled with dirt through the years. It is impossible now to clean them. Later glass makers learned to provide a plain surface for such attachments.

This piece was quality ware when produced and was not made in large quantities. It is brilliantly clear and highly fire-polished soda-lime glass. In a bright light it appears to be fine quality cut glass. It has no resonance.

Creamer: 3-part mold, 1 1/8 pounds, 6 3/8 inches tall, 3 1/2 inches wide, and 5 1/4 inches long. Water pitcher: 3-part mold, weight unknown, 8 inches tall.

The pattern sometimes comes in amber and probably other colors, though they would be rare indeed. The covered sugar, covered butter dish, and water pitcher are the only other items known. The creamer and water pitcher were not mentioned or illustrated in the advertisement. It is likely that other articles not illustrated or named may show up. It would be reasonable to expect a tumbler, a goblet and a spooner.

65—DAISY AND BUTTON, CROSS-BAR

This golden amber individual creamer has not been illustrated in our glass literature. Because its base differs so much from the standard creamer and other pitchers in the pattern, it was deemed worthwhile to show it.

Kamm, in *A Third Two Hundred Pattern Glass Pitchers*, page 53, No. 74, shows a creamer with a high-domed pedestal which she calls DAISY AND

BUTTON, CROSS-BAR. She says it is too well known to require description. Ruth Webb Lee, in *Early American Pressed Glass*, Pattern 266, pages 592-94, and Plates 167, 168, and 170, describes the pattern and shows two tumblers, a goblet, celery vase, covered butter, creamer, and water pitcher in the pattern. S. T. Millard, in his *Goblets*, Plate 129-3, shows a goblet in the pattern and calls it DAISY AND BUTTON, WITH CROSS-BAR AND THUMBPRINT BAND.

This popular design was manufactured by the Richard and Hartley Flint Glass Company of Tarentum, Pennsylvania, between 1880 and 1900. Despite the firm's name this piece is not flint glass. It came in forty-five different articles—in clear, yellow, light and dark amber, and blue.

There are five noticeable differences between the individual and the standard creamers as follows: (1) The standard creamer has a narrow waist and a high-domed pedestal while the individual one has a flat base. (2) The sides of the standard creamer are straight and almost vertical, whereas they are curved and flare from the waist to the rim on the smaller one. (3) The handle of the individual creamer is small, round in cross section, left plain, and curves from top to bottom. The standard creamer handle is six-sided, very angular, and adorned with several motifs. (4) The crossbars join at their extremities on the large creamer and are widely separated on the smaller piece. The daisy and button motif forms squares on the large creamer and hexagons on the individual pitcher. (5) The large creamer holds almost five times as much as the smaller one.

A 3/8-inch-wide horizontal band comprises the base. It is filled with shallow, round thumbprints. It sits on a ring and is slightly hollowed out underneath. The hollow has a flat roof in which a beautiful daisy and button design is impressed. (See cut of bottom.) This feature is missing on the larger, pedestaled pieces.

There is a band below the rim identical with that around the base. Between the two bands are three large, convex crossbars, or Xs, which reach from band to band. They resemble sawhorses—upside down. When the bars cross, they form a flat surfaced diamond and two pyramids. The upper interstice of the crossbars contains a plain beveled triangle. The lower has half a daisy impressed. Between the X's are large hexagonal spaces filled with a symmetrical daisy and button pattern. The sides of the creamer bulge slightly at the middle, then curve into a somewhat narrower base.

Above the upper band, the rim has four pointed scallops, each with five much smaller scallops. The rims of the two creamers are identical. In front the rim is rounded and curves up to form a narrow, slightly dipped lip.

I know of no reproductions in this pattern, but this creamer is either a recent edition or a seldom used one. Mrs. Kamm says it has been reproduced, but she does not list such articles. It is of a particularly beautiful shade of amber. The glass is lime-soda and flawless. The workmanship is superb, and the fire polishing good.

Individual amber creamer: 3-part mold, 9 ounces, 3 3/16 inches tall, 3 3/16 inches wide, and 4 3/8 inches long.

Standard clear creamer: 3-part mold, 1 1/16 pounds, 6 1/16 inches tall, 3 5/8 inches wide, and 5 1/4 inches long.

Of the forty-five articles manufactured in this pattern, some of the more unusual ones are: large and small mugs, four sizes of lamps, water trays, waste bowl, several sizes of cruets, cordial, finger bowl, ketchup bottle, toothpick holder, molasses can, and small sugar dishes. The finials and stoppers of all are in the shape of Maltese crosses.

66—DELTA DAISY AND BUTTON

Let us start with the premise that this beautiful sapphire-blue creamer is a reproduction. No particular effort will be expended to prove that conclusion. From 1880 to 1900 every glass house in America that made tableware (and most of them did) produced some version of the DAISY AND BUTTON motif. It was probably the most popular motif ever used on pressed glass. By 1879 there were sixty-four glass factories in and around Pittsburgh, Pennsylvania, and the possible variants can be imagined. However, the motif did not lend itself too well to variants and was usually changed by altering the button. Thus we find low flat-topped buttons, high beveled buttons, sunken buttons, and buttons with a star or daisy. With so few opportunities to vary the figurework, the manufacturers made use of the avenues open to them, and there were three broad ones. (1) Color: We find about as wide a range of color in this pattern as in any ever made, including amberette. (2) Shape: More different shapes appear in DAISY AND BUTTON than in any other pattern. Several are shown in this book. (3) By cutting the design into segments by means of V's, X's, panels, ovals, triangles, squares, diamonds, circles, etc.

The surface has only been scratched insofar as illustrating, describing, listing, authenticating, and differentiating this beautiful imitation of cut glass. It is, of course, an imitation of RUSSIAN cut in genuine handcut glass. The pattern is so difficult and expensive to cut by hand that little of it was produced. Some future collector or lover of the pattern will have an interesting, difficult, and rewarding field before him when he starts covering it properly.

Frankly, I am not sure this is a reproduction. It may have been recently pressed in a mold of the 1880s. Creamers are seldom reproduced since only one is sold to a customer. Also the pattern has to be both popular and scarce to create sufficient demand to justify the expense. This pattern meets only one of these requirements—scarcity. It has not been previously mentioned in our glass literature. There is no demand for it at the present time. No manufacturer today would make a mold for a creamer only in the size, shape, and fashion of the 1880s. I believe this creamer was probably a feeble effort by some company to "get in on a good thing." For some reason they did not persist.

This is one of the few patterns made in a triangular shape. (See drawings of bottom.) The shape of the piece is its outstanding characteristic. From rim to waist the sides are curved slightly and covered with the daisy and button. At each corner is a narrow, rounded column from rim to base. Beneath the handle is a wide, flat panel of the same height as the columns.

The rim is flat on top but rounds up a little to the narrow, upthrust spout. There is no dip for the lip. Below the rim is a plain, narrow band which widens into a 1/4-inch-wide band beneath the semblance of a lip. The pressed handle is commodious and has a thumbgrip on the upper member. In both front and back, the handle has two flat panels. The sides are rounded over the highly convex relief. The waist is much narrower than the rim and is concave. It ends in a low shelf on the base which itself is a convex ring. The narrow, round columns at each corner follow the contours of the waist and base. It makes an attractive footing. (Note drawing for details.) Underneath the foot is a dome with a slightly arched roof. It is filled with daisy and button and is pretty.

This sapphire-blue glass is of good quality, but it has a few scattered bubbles. The firepolish makes it difficult to locate the mold marks, but faint ones can be found on each corner and above the handle. Nothing is known of the ancestry of the piece.

Creamer: 4-part mold, 1 1/16 pounds, 5 inches tall, 4 inches wide, and 5 1/2 inches long.

I have seen no other items.

64

65

Bottom
65

66

Bottom
66

67

Bottom
68

68

Bottom
69

69

67—BYARD DAISY AND BUTTON

I cannot escape the feeling that this is quite recent ware, produced as a novelty, and that only the sugar bowl and creamer will be found. With many glass houses making DAISY AND BUTTON and each one striving to be different and to strike the public fancy, I could not say this is not an old piece. This creamer appears to have been blown in a rose bowl mold. A depression was made in the rim for a lip, a handle applied, and presto—a creamer! This particular version of DAISY AND BUTTON has not previously been covered in American glass literature.

These creamers, clear, and canary colored, are especially beautiful, and it is regrettable that such poor craftsmanship was used in applying the handles. Otherwise the workmanship was splendid, and diligent search is required to locate the mold marks. The glass is brilliant, sparkling, and free of defects. The drawing accurately illustrates the shape of the piece, but on actual inspection it appears even more squatty than it does here. The cauldron-shaped creamer is very constricted at the throat. The bulbous part of the bowl is covered with the design in low relief, the buttons being low, wide, and flat-topped. From the throat the rim arches out until it is almost flat and quite wide. It is smooth and unadorned. The front dips slightly as a concession to a lip.

The handle has the large blob flattened widely and applied to the edge of the rim—a rather unusual treatment. The lower attachment is flattened on top of the figurework. No effort has been made to decorate it. The angle of the handle belongs elsewhere. The wide base is domed underneath to provide a ring at the perimeter for it to rest on. The dome itself carries the daisy and button motif.

Creamer: 3-part mold, 14 ounces, 3 5/8 inches tall, 3 13/16 inches wide, and 4 7/8 inches long.

I know of no other items in the pattern.

68—DAISY AND BUTTON, V-ORNAMENT

We are fortunate in knowing when, where, and by whom this version of the DAISY AND BUTTON family was made.

This creamer has not been illustrated in our glass literature before. Mrs. Kamm knew of it but had not seen it. See *A Fifth Pitcher Book*, page 112. S. T. Millard, in *Goblets II*, Plate 73-2, shows a goblet and erroneously lists it under the name of this pattern. The goblet he shows is neither a daisy nor a button, but does have the V-ornament. It is another pattern entirely.

Ruth Webb Lee, in *Early American Pressed Glass*, Plate 167, upper left, illustrates the goblet Millard used and cautions against confusing it with DAISY AND BUTTON. She did not know of a goblet in this variety of DAISY AND BUTTON. See her Pattern 265, pages 591-92, Plate 168, upper right, for a tumbler, and see Plate 171, lower, where a celery vase, finger bowl, sherbet cup, and oblong deep dish are shown.

This pattern came in several colors, but not in milk-white glass. It was introduced in 1886-1887 by the Steubenville Flint Glass Works (A. J. Beatty and Sons) of Steubenville, Ohio, before they built and began operating the A. J. Beatty and Sons factory of Tiffin, Ohio, in 1890.

The standard creamer in this pattern is large, cylindrical, and resembles a celery vase. The sides are vertical and, except for a narrow band below the rim, are covered with figurework. Four large V's made up of highly convex ribs, half an inch wide, extend down to midway on the body. Around the base are four similar but inverted V's which extend from the base to the same level. The two bands are staggered and produce a wide band which zigzags around the piece from its base to near the rim. The band and the interstices are filled with daisy and button design. The buttons in this pattern are high, and beveled with small flat tops.

Above the plain band at the top, the rim is almost level. It rises slightly over the handle and at the lip. Most of the rim is covered by half-inch-wide low scallops. The pressed handle is round, thick, and large. Only a slight effort was made to imitate an applied handle. It was left completely unornamented. There is an almost imperceptible ring at the base, wider than it is high, on which the piece rests. Inside the ring, the bottom is slightly hollowed out and filled with a beautiful, symmetrical daisy and button motif. (See drawing of bottom.)

The glass itself is a superior quality of lime-soda, and is brilliantly clear and sparkling. There are no bubbles, discolorations, or other defects. It is so well fire polished it is difficult to locate the mold marks except on the handle. The moldmaker and gaffer did excellent jobs.

Creamer: 4-part mold, 1 1/8 pounds, 4 15/16 inches tall, 3 5/8 inches wide, and 5 3/4 inches long.

This variety was made in a large number of articles, none of which are plentiful today. If goblets actually were made, they are, for practical purposes, nonexistent.

69—EVENING SHADE

This beautiful little electric blue creamer looks as cool and refreshing as the peaceful valley that shelters Evening Shade, Arkansas, and it is therefore named for it. It is almost a toy and should be classed as a "whimsey" since it evidently was pressed in a "hat" mold. While still hot the brim was turned up, a depression was made for a lip, and a handle applied. In this manner a creamer appeared.

The crown of the hat is covered with a well-executed Daisy and Button design. (See cut of bottom.) As a "hat," intended to sit on its top and serve as a match or toothpick holder, the underside of the brim would be visible so it also carries the motif. When the brim was turned up to make a rim, that portion on the inside left a 3/4-inch-wide plain band around the top. The pattern shows through. The small round handle was applied over the figurework. The large blob is at the bottom, and the top attachment is turned under.

The glass is of excellent quality and is a beautiful blue. It is unusually thick and heavy for such a small piece and is free of any defect. No mold marks show. There is no way to tell how old this piece is. It may be quite old, or it may have been "made last night"—though it was bought as "old."

Small creamer: no mold marks show, 7 ounces, 2 15/16 inches tall, 2 5/8 inches wide, and 3 7/8 inches long.

70—PASS CHRISTIAN

I can hardly believe it myself, but here it is—a good example of how far glassmakers would go in their heyday to create a new and striking design. The hope was to create a pattern that would capture the public fancy and return a handsome profit in a business where competition was terrific.

This is the first time this pattern has appeared in our glass literature. It is named for the lovely summer home of President Wilson. The concept may have occurred to the designer after seeing a plain pitcher stacked in a fancy sauce dish before being washed. The same idea was employed on THE CONFEDERACY creamer. No mold marks show, and I am unable to understand how it could have been removed from the mold after being pressed. The part of the mold above the sauce

dish could only have been raised vertically—not opened by hinges on the sides. I am indeed perplexed.

In her *A Second Two Hundred Pattern Glass Pitchers*, Mrs. Kamm, on page 23, shows GLOBE AND STAR which has the same motiff. In *A Sixth Pitcher Book*, page 54, No. 124, she shows DAISY AND BUTTON, PETTICOAT. Mrs. Lee calls the latter pattern DAISY BAND in her *Victorian Glass*, page 162 and Plate 53-3. The pattern seems better named by Lee since no buttons were present. Many similarities exist between her pattern and the one shown here. Perhaps the molds for both patterns were designed and made in the same shop.

The upper portion of the body is plain and tankard shaped. It tapers in slightly to the rim which has three large round scallops on either side. At the rear a wide scallop provides anchorage for the top handle attachment. The forward part of the rim is slightly scalloped and shaped into a narrow lip.

About the waist is a tilted band of highly beveled, flat-topped cubes. Above this the design flares widely and is covered with daisy and button design with half-buttons showing. The top of this flaring rim is scalloped over each daisy and extends a full 9/16 inch from the side. Between this projection and the body is a deep trough encircling the creamer as though to catch the drip. Below the band of cubes is a row of daisies which flare down and out to form the base. It has a scallop below each daisy.

The handle is round in cross section with the large blob at the bottom. It fits well on the smooth side of the bowl. Under the base is a high, flat-topped dome impressed with a large, many-rayed hobstar which has a plain rayed star in its center. (See drawing of bottom.)

This pattern dates from about 1880-1890. It is quality ware, and great care was lavished on it when it was produced. No sign of a mold mark can be found. The designer let his imagination run riot and produced a curiosity. The glass is brilliantly clear and without defect.

Creamer: ?-part mold, 1 pound, 2 1/2 ounces, 5 5/8 inches tall, 4 5/16 inches wide, and 4 7/8 inches long.

The creamer is the only item known to me, and the only others I would expect to find are the sugar bowl, butter dish, and spoonholder. It was undoubtedly expensive to make and probably few pieces were manufactured. It is very scarce. The wide-swept wings have a high casualty potential and the design itself is impractical.

71—BATESVILLE

This unlisted pattern is named *BATESVILLE*, a good town to live in on the banks of the White River in the Arkansas Ozarks. The tall, strangely constructed creamer with a narrow base is unstable and definitely accident prone. With all its oddities, it is still attractive and is to a collector "out of this world."

The bowl is a deep cylinder with flat bottom and vertical sides. Except for the figurework at the rim, the body was left plain and smooth—a perfect target for the decorator. On this piece a large spray of stems, leaves, and clusters of flowers was enameled and baked on. As a welcome relief, the painting was expertly done. At the top is a peculiar raised band with alternating large and small sawteeth on both edges. (See drawing for details.)

The small waist is curved and recurved into a lovely standard. Below the waist the foot flares widely to near the edge, where it turns down to form the base's perimeter. The latter is formed by a series of slightly flaring, large and small scallops, with the smaller left plain. At the base of each large one is a round cabochon in high relief. Each of these is framed over the top by a low, raised line which arches up and meets its counterpart over the center of the jewel. A similar raised line outlines the tortuous lower border of the foot. The six scallops extend down to form the fragile feet on which it stands.

Underneath the base is a high, hollow space which extends well up into the stem. The rim is topped with an exaggerated scalloping as shown. Because of the deep saddle, a high lip is formed. There is a decided rise at the back where the handle is attached. The round applied handle is a symphony of curves which only an expert could have achieved. The large round blob is at the bottom, and this dates the pattern fairly well.

The glass, the workmanship, and the decoration are all of high order. The mold marks can be seen only on top of the foot. It is a quality product. It is not common, and it seems to be found mostly in the central states. The maker is unknown, but it has characteristics of the period of 1875-1885.

Creamer: 3-part mold, 1 1/8 pounds, 6 3/4 inches tall, 3 1/4 inches wide, and 5 1/2 inches long.

I know of the following articles in the pattern: creamer, large covered sugar bowl, covered butter dish, spoonholder, large footed sauce dish, 10-inch low open compote with vertical sides, 10-inch low open compote with flaring sides, etched.

72—SPRADDLE LEGS

One wonders how this novel curiosity has survived without a major amputation. A short period of regular use would have resulted in one. The long, projecting legs would be broken off with the first bump. The fact that it has remained unbroken probably is due to its having been kept as a showpiece in a cabinet. That is where it had been for years when I found it with an old family that was breaking up.

The caldron-shaped body seems to sit on a spider with widely spreading legs as if to cook hominy over an open fire in the yard. The lines of the body and handle are beautiful, but those on the legs—well that is a different matter. The bottom of the bowl is hemispherical and widest at the spider. From there the piece rounds in and is much more constricted at the neck. The top portion is left smooth and plain. This area may originally have been etched or decorated with enameled flowers on some pieces. A groove encircles the body immediately above its junction with the base. The member joining the legs is rounded on the sides, but on its bottom is a row of deep, sharp sawteeth.

The four long spraddled legs remind one of a new-born foal. They are oval in cross section and are left plain. Near the top of each leg, on the outside, is a noticeable depression which does not belong. These marks were made by the tongs which held the piece while the hand tooling was done on the top and handle. A mold mark shows on either side of the legs, but nowhere else. The end of each leg has been flattened for the piece to rest on, but the angle is so acute that it stands on the heel rather than its plantar surface. This shows in the drawing. With the widespread legs this creamer has excellent stability. If the feet are prevented from sliding the piece can be tilted over to a 45-degree angle and will still right itself. When laid on its side the legs prevent rolling.

The rim is rounded on top and soars high and wide to the attractive lip. At the rear a high scallop is provided for the upper handle attachment. The handle is applied and is a work of art. An accomplished gaffer shaped it well. The large blob is at the top and the smaller at the bottom where it was turned back on itself and tooled into crossbars.

The bottom of the pitcher is something to behold. (See drawing for details.) On the center of the bottom a medallion the thickness and size of a nickel was placed. Into this a twelve-point rosette was impressed. A portion of the bottom seems to have had contact with fine sand, when hot, with

70

Bottom
70

71

72

Bottom
73

73

Bottom
72

74

75

76

some of the sand adhering. It gives a stippled effect. How this occurred is beyond my knowledge.

Great skill was used in shaping the top portion of the bowl and in forming the rim and handle. The bowl could not have been pressed because the plunger could not have been removed. It was not made by the Hipkins' patent since the top shows handwork. The glass is sparkling, clear, and brilliant. It was expensive to produce and could not have competed in a highly competitive market, so probably little was made. I do not know where or by whom it was made, but I believe it to date from 1880-1890.

Creamer: ?-mold marks, 14 ounces, 4 15/16 inches tall, 5 1/4 inches wide, and 5 1/4 inches long.

I have seen only the creamer.

73—MAPLE LEAF

In *A Fourth Pitcher Book*, pages 143-144, No. 194, Mrs. Kamm describes a water pitcher in this beautiful pattern. She also describes what she calls a variant of MAPLE LEAF. This latter piece has all the earmarks of an entirely different and inferior pattern. I have the small tankard creamer, and its quality is about what you would expect in a container for marketing condiments. I also have the standard MAPLE LEAF creamer shown here for the first time. As Mrs. Kamm so aptly put it: "No botanist would recognize the foliage as . . . any known leaf." It is neither maple nor grape— merely the artist's conception of a pretty leaf.

Mrs. Kamm knew that CLASSIC and MAPLE LEAF were both produced by Gillander and Sons of Philadelphia, Pennsylvania, at about the same time and that Mr. P. J. Jacobus sculptured CLASSIC along with WESTWARD HO!, FROSTED LION, etc. CLASSIC is one of the finest pieces of sculpturing in American pressed glass. She indicated MAPLE LEAF, too, was probably designed by Mr. Jacobus. The hypothesis is certainly tenable.

Ruth Webb Lee, in *Early American Pressed Glass*, Pattern 170, pages 429-35, Plates 143 and 144, describes and names the pattern. She says the lack of demand is a mystery. It is so beautiful that one wonders why he never sees a collector of it. Mrs. Lee devotes a great deal of space to the colors available—more than there are in any other pressed glass pattern. Plates 143 and 144 show an oblong bowl on four feet, a tumbler, a large platter, and a large plate. The center of each base has a grilled or diapered pattern. (See drawing.) In *Vic-*

torian Glass, Plate 73-2 Mrs. Lee shows a MAPLE LEAF goblet. It has a stem resembling the trunk of a tree with three branches to support the bowl. The body of the bowl is covered with the same leaf effect, reaching almost to the rim, as on the creamer used here.

S. T. Millard in *Goblets*, Plate 56-1, shows a goblet with a leaf design covering the lower third of the bowl and calls it MAPLE LEAF. I have a goblet like Dr. Millard's and it definitely is not this pattern. It seems to be a product of at least a decade later. The stem of his goblet is unusual and probably was intended to represent the bole of a tree. Metz shows the same type goblet as Millard and calls it MAPLE LEAF.

This attractive creamer is oval-shaped, and much longer than it is wide. The leaves are stippled and veined resulting in a cool and refreshingly frosted appearance. The odd feet and handle are similar to those of CLASSIC. The legs are impractical. Four huge leaves practically cover the bowl of the creamer, except for a narrow, smooth space between the lower margin of the leaves and the waist. Other leaves form the background around the top.

Below the waist, the base and feet are made to represent branches of trees with the bark intact. The legs are bent and widespread. The pads on the feet are rounded instead of flat. The flat underpart is marked off in a diamond-diapered or grill effect. The diamonds are formed by raised, well-rounded lines. This leaves a small sunken diamond in the center of each large one.

The large handle is oval in cross section and the stippling and graining show plainly on the lower half. It fades out on the upper half until the surface is almost smooth. There is a smooth, round knop on top of the handle for a thumbgrip. The handle follows a crooked course. It is rather large to heft. The back two-thirds of the rim, except at the handle, is as finely scalloped as the edge of the leaf. The front portion is round and arches over to form a wide, generous spout.

The glass is soda-lime of good quality. The workmanship was also good. The molds were excellently chipped. The pattern was made in canary, light amber, dark amber, vaseline, pale blue, sapphire blue, dark blue, clear, and apple green.

Standard creamer: 2-part mold, 14 ounces, 5 3/16 inches tall, 2 3/4 inches wide, and 6 inches long.

Water pitcher: 2-part mold, weight unknown, 9 1/2 inches tall.

We know the following items were made in the pattern: creamer, sugar bowl, butter dish, spoonholder, water pitcher, tumbler, goblet, two sizes of sauce dishes, large footed oval bowl, celery vase, 10-inch plate, 13-inch platter, many compotes, oblong tray, etc.

74—RECTANGLES

Here is a large creamer in an angular pattern which has escaped writers on early American pressed glass. In this and similar patterns, the appeal depends almost entirely on the brilliance, clarity of the glass, and superior workmanship. The pattern is too rigid to have a wide appeal and perhaps little was ever made. It is seldom seen in southern shops.

This tall creamer sits on a circular base, is plain underneath, and highly domed. The stem is somewhat small and slightly curved, departing in this respect from the main motif. From the stem the lower part of the body flares out and up in a vertical line, then turns at a sharp angle and ascends the body to the rim with only a slight flaring.

The same design extends from top to bottom and follows the contours of the piece. Single V-shaped grooves alternate with groups of three similar grooves which run vertically and horizontally over the entire body. The vertical grooves are closer together than the horizontal ones. This creates many beveled, flat-topped rectangles. Where the grooves intersect a variety of crosses is found.

The curves of the saddled rim are quite pleasing. The lip is high and narrow. The rim rises in the back to accommodate the top attachment of the many-sided and unusual handle. There is a rounded, upthrust knop at the top of the handle. A deeply sunk triangle is impressed on each side just below this knop. This thumbgrip, with the ample size of the handle and knop in the center, gives a secure grip on the piece when in use. The lower part of the handle curves in and has a knop at the base.

The glass is brilliant and clear. The metal was a little too cold when dropped into the mold and this resulted in some hairlines and waviness. It was not properly firepolished (or acid polished) as one mold mark stands nearly 1/8 inch high on the base and is dangerously sharp.

Nothing is known by the author as to where or by whom it was manufactured. It could have been made by any of scores of glass factories making production ware at the time. It has all the characteristics of the period between 1875 and 1890.

Creamer: 3-part mold, 1 1/8 pounds, 6 11/16 inches tall, 3 5/16 inches wide, and 5 1/2 inches long.

No other items in the pattern are known to the writer. Certainly the 4-piece table set was produced. Like other patterns which have been described and given a name, we may expect other items in this pattern to eventually make their appearance.

75—CHRONISTER

This fine old unlisted pattern is named in honor of Lieutenant Lawson Renfrom Chronister whose brilliant career was terminated in a raid over Tokyo. These tall clean-cut creamers on high standards are particularly attractive and desirable even though they are unstable and easily toppled over and shattered.

The stem is simple and beautiful. It is hexagonal and its flat panels are beautifully curved. They are vertical through the middle and curve out at top and bottom, to terminate in large, high shelves. The foot is plain, wide and almost flat. It is hollowed out underneath and rests on a ring at the perimeter.

The handle departs from the norm in having seven sides. Two wide panels comprise the inside, a narrow panel is on each side and three medium width panels make up the back portion of it. It is large and provides a good grip. The top member extends straight back and rises into a bulbous knop for a thumbgrip. On each side there is a large dewdrop. From the top the handle makes a sweeping, irregular curve to the lower part of the bowl.

The large body has a round, bowl-shaped bottom resting on top of the stem. The sides are straight and flare slightly to the rim. Banding the creamer at the middle is a two-inch belt of complicated, geometrical figure-work. The borders at both top and bottom are marked by two raised and closely placed lines. The interior is cut in triangular segments by zigzag figures of four tiny inverted V-shaped ridges which are parallel and adjacent to each other. Where they meet and cross, at the ends, they form triangles which are filled with diamond point. The large triangles, formed by the zigzags, are filled with an intricate pattern of faceted imitation cut glass design. The areas above and below the pattern are left plain.

The rim is slightly saddled and rounded on top. It is so superbly pressed it appears to be hand tooled.

It would be difficult to imagine a more brilliantly clear lime-soda glass. The workmanship is good. Mold marks show only under the handle and around the stem and foot. It probably dates from 1875-1885.

Creamer: 3-part mold. 15 1/2 ounces, 6 1/2 inches tall, 3 7/16 inches wide, and 5 1/4 inches long.

This creamer is the only piece of the pattern to come to my attention. Other items, however, are to be expected.

76—STAR IN HONEYCOMB

Minnie Watson Kamm, Ph.D., had not seen a piece in this pattern and drew a water pitcher with an applied handle from an early catalog of Bryce Brothers while they were still in Pittsburgh, Pennsylvania. It was their "No. 80" pattern, and must have been of an early date. See Kamm's *A Second Two Hundred Pattern Glass Pitchers*, page 122, wherein she describes the pattern and assigns the above name.

In *Goblets*, Plate 168-3, Dr. S. T. Millard names the pattern LEVERNE, and says it is of the 1880s, and is a pattern common in Pennsylvania. It is not common through the south and is seldom encountered in ads. Neither Mrs. Lee nor Mrs. Kamm had seen it. I own the creamer but have seen no other article in the pattern.

Metz shows a goblet as No. 1334 and calls it LEVERNE as does Millard. She says the creamers have applied handles, but my creamer has a pressed one. The main motif is an adaptation of one found on many patterns both earlier and later than this one. Millard shows three patterns with the same motif in *Goblets*, Plate 49-1, 2 & 3. They are GEDDES, PEERLESS, and DIAMOND BAND.

The figurework on this creamer is quite "busy." Also, there is plenty of it. There is so much to be drawn, one has the feeling, when it is reduced for printing, that it will appear as a black daub. Please study the handle of the creamer and note what the designer did there. (The handle of the water pitcher is an applied one.) The handle in various portions is straight, bent, curved, round, hexagonal, swollen, ringed, jointed, ribbed and splayed. It also has a knop on top for a thumb-grip.

This tall creamer has a large body with straight, vertical sides which round under sharply to a narrow stem. The lower 3/5 of the body is blanketed with figurework. The main motif is a series of large erect diamonds standing on end and joining at their side corners. The diamonds are

outlined by high inverted V-shaped ridges. They are cut, top and bottom, by two parallel ridges of the same type. This results in the diamonds becoming hexagons and triangles. Each hexagon has a six-point, raised star in its center. Surrounding the star is fine, sunken diamond point completely filling each hexagon. The inside of each triangle is plain and flat. Festooned across the tops of the diamonds are two V-shaped ridges with a single row of sunken diamond point between them. The latter is graduated to conform to the size of the festoon. The lower third of the body has six tall narrow arches filled with fine ribbing running horizontally. Alternating with them are six wider arches filled with sunken English or printed hobnail, a very unusual feature. The wide arches fit tightly and the narrow ones loosely into the lower part of the diamonds.

Above the figurework the body is severely plain for 1 1/4 inches or more. The back three-fourths of the rim is evenly scalloped similar to that on the base. The rim is saddled and rises to a narrow lip.

The stem is small, tall, and well ornamented. It begins at a shelf on the base of the bowl and has six short panels well rounded over at the top. They narrow in to a small stem then swell out on the upper half of a large knop. The lower portion of the knop and stem is round and bulbous. It flows out into a round shelf on the base which is large, thick, and has a scalloped edge. The edge of the base is slightly beveled to prevent scratching furniture and has twenty-one small scallops. The base is slightly hollowed out underneath.

The glass is of excellent quality soda-lime with no resonance. The workmanship is fair. It is an attractive pattern with a lacy effect.

Creamer: 3-part mold, 14 ounces, 6 1/4 inches tall, 3 3/16 inches wide, and 5 1/2 inches long.

The water pitcher, creamer, goblet, sugar bowl, butter dish, and spooner are the only pieces known. Undoubtedly other items were made.

77—TREE OF LIFE

Like the HONEYCOMB and DAISY AND BUTTON motifs, TREE OF LIFE was made by so many manufacturers, in so many different variations, a book would be required to adequately identify the pattern. I am including OVERSHOT and CRAQUELLE as variants of TREE OF LIFE.

This particular creamer is known to have been made at the Portland Glass Company, of Portland, Maine. The company organized in 1864 and was destroyed by fire in 1873. During this period William O. Davis was employed as superintendent and did some of the designing. He came to this factory from the fine old O'Hara Glass Company, of Pittsburgh, Pennsylvania. We have considerable circumstantial evidence to indicate he may have designed this pattern. The old records of the U.S. Patent Office show he created and patented a pattern with a similar surface treatment. (LOOP AND DART, WITH ROUND ORNAMENT.) Some pieces of this pattern, produced at Portland, carry the name *Davis*. The name is difficult to locate since it is small and follows the veining of the pattern.

The pattern came in clear, green, light amber, light blue, blue, dark blue, purple, and yellow. The tall, slender creamer shown here is a light-golden amber and sits in a britannia metal holder. (An alloy of tin, antimony, and copper, with the first predominating.) Pieces with this type of "silver holders" are occasionally found in little rural shops where they are least expected. For instance, I found this creamer in a rural shop near Neosho, Missouri. The sugar bowl, creamer, celery vase, fruit bowl, and a bowl six inches deep (possibly for holding ice) are known to have such holders. The metal part carries no name, mark, or number.

The bowl of the creamer is the only portion made of pressed glass. It is conical in shape with the sides curved gently. The shape resembles the nose of an artillery projectile. Where the glass stem would have been attached, it is smooth and has been polished.

The rim is deeply saddled and rises to a high point at the back near the handle. It curves up even higher toward the front to a well-shaped lip. There is a 1/4-inch plain band just below the rim which follws the contour of the latter. It is the distinguishing mark of the Portland TREE OF LIFE. The bowl does not have the melon-shaped vertical lobes which appear on most pieces in this pattern.

The bowl fits well into the tall ornate metal holder. It is not sufficiently snug, however, to prevent falling out if held upside down. There is no locking device to hold it in place and this lack has probably contributed generously to the casualty list of such pieces.

Mrs. Kamm in *A Third Two Hundred Pattern Glass Pitchers*, pages 120-21, No. 181, describes a water pitcher of the Portland variety of TREE OF LIFE. She mentions these pieces with the metal holders but apparently had not seen one. In *A Fifth Pitcher Book*, page 24, No. 36, she illustrates a tall slender creamer with a ring at the waist and a

narrower ring around the rim. The piece is lobed.

S. T. Millard in *Goblets*, Plate 80-3, shows a goblet with a double-knopped stem and says it was marked "P. G. Co." beneath the base. In *Goblets II*, Plate 48-1, he shows a goblet with the TREE OF LIFE motif extending entirely to the rim. He says they were made in the 1870s.

Ruth Webb Lee in *Victorian Glass* devotes Chapter IV to the TREE OF LIFE pattern. On Plate 11 she shows four sizes of drinking glasses and a covered sugar bowl in the pattern and says they were made by Portland Glass Company.

The Pittsburgh variety of TREE OF LIFE is not difficult to differentiate from this variety. It is lobed and most of the pieces have a hand holding a ball, for either the stem, the handle, or as a finial.

The glass is thin soda-lime and has no resonance. It is free of bubbles and discolorations. Further fire polishing around the rim would have helped, though no mold marks show on the piece.

?-Mold Marks, weight with holder, 1 1/8 pounds, 7 3/16 inches tall, 2 7/8 inches wide, and 5 11/16 inches long.

Many items were made in this pattern and in a wide range of colors. They are not too plentiful today. Note the standard creamer in this pattern, which follows.

78—TREE OF LIFE

Mrs. Kamm used a water pitcher to illustrate and describe the Portland variety of TREE OF LIFE. See *A Third Two Hundred Pattern Glass Pitchers*, pages 120-22 and No. 181. See also Chapter IV of Lee's *Victorian Glass* on THE TREE OF LIFE and S. T. Millard's *Goblets*, Plate 80-3, where a goblet is shown.

The standard creamer, without its lid, is used here to show measurements and proportions. This version of the TREE OF LIFE pattern was produced by the Portland Glass Company, of Portland, Maine. The company was established in 1864 and destroyed by fire in 1873. (See preceding writeup for another version of this pattern.) TREE OF LIFE is known to have been made by the Boston and Sandwich Glass Company, of Sandwich, Massachusetts. I am unable to identify individual items they produced.

The sides are straight. They flare slightly toward the top and curve in sharply to the waist. Twelve slightly convexed columns cover the body and are roughly arched over at their tops. A 1/4-inch band is placed below the rim and around the perimeter of the base which is plain and smooth. The remainder of the body is covered with the motif known as TREE OF LIFE. Round raised lines meander over the surface, crossing and joining in an irregular pattern to form small "rice-paddy" compartments. These segments are filled with raised triangular pyramids which are frosted. It is not stippling.

The base is wide and tapers to the round edge and disappears as it approaches the latter. Underneath is a plain, hollow dome.

A round ring was pressed on the edge of the rim which softens and enhances its appearance. The rim sweeps up in a lovely curve to terminate in a wide lip. Seen from the front it is "jowlly."

The handle is six-sided and comfortable to use. On top is a broad thumbgrip with sunken diamond point impressed into it to prevent slipping.

Below the rim, on the inside, is a wide well-defined ledge to hold a lid, but alas, there is no lid.

This pattern was produced in many colors but is seldom seen today in anything but clear. It originally came in green, purple, blue, light blue, dark blue, yellow, light amber, dark amber, clear, and possibly milk white. The glass is not flint and the quality is not particularly good.

Standard creamer: 3-part mold, 12 ounces, 4 3/4 inches tall, 3 3/8 inches wide, and 5 inches long.

Water pitcher: 4-part mold, weight unknown, 9 inches tall.

These articles are known to have been made in the pattern: goblet, wine, champagne, mug, oval bowl, sauce, honey dish, high open compote, low covered compote, flat dish, epergne, water pitcher, milk pitcher, finger bowl with a plate, covered sugar bowl, creamer with a lid, covered butter dish, spoonholder, celery vase, ice bowl, fruit dish, footed salt, and several items to fit in metal holders similar to the creamer shown above.

79—BLOCKADE

This lovely old pattern illustrates the difficulty in assigning appropriate names to patterns of pressed glass. Three writers have described this pattern. Each has assigned a different title and none has referred to a name used by others. All three titles are inept and stimulate one to give still a fourth name—which is exactly what I will not do.

(a) S. T. Millard in *Goblets* (1938), Plate 136-2, shows a goblet and calls it DIAMOND BLOCK WITH FAN though there is no diamond-shaped figure in the pattern. He had previously named another pattern BLOCK HOUSE in the same

book, on Plate 133-1, which is better known as HANOVER.

(b) Ruth Webb Lee in *Victorian Glass* (1944), pages 209-10, Plate 65-4, calls the pattern BLOCKADE to avoid confusion since there are so many blocks and cubes in pattern glass. STOCKADE, BLOCKHOUSE or LIGHTHOUSE would have been suitable—but BLOCKADE—no! One gets the feeling that Mrs. Lee had not personally seen this pattern and may have used a cut from an old catalog of Challinor, Taylor and Company of Tarentum, Pennsylvania. Her description of the pattern so indicates, though she does not say so.

(c) Minnie Watson Kamm in *A Fourth Pitcher Book* (1946), page 12, No. 29, says she had not seen a piece and that she used the old catalog for a guide. The catalog carried the pattern as "No. 309," and Mrs. Kamm called it CHALLINOR NO. 309 which the general public, glass buyers and dealers will remember only briefly. Numbers are difficult for most people to keep in mind, and our government has given us so many that we are mere numbers. The piece she redrew, from the old cut, was a water pitcher. The Lee title is shorter and is used here.

This willowy creamer has a very tall stem or baluster. In fact, it is in a group of a score or more of pressed glass patterns which are remarkable for the height of their stemmed pieces. All are fragile and they seldom become old if kept in the rigors of regular usage. They are all quite appealing and attractive. Other pressed patterns with equally tall stems are: WESTWARD HO!, PAVONIA, DART, SEASHELL, IONA, PSYCHE AND CUPID, WHEEL AND COMMA, HARMONY.

None of the above named writers has mentioned that this pattern has one of the most unusual features found in American pressed glass—a hollow stem. PAVONIA is the only other pattern known to this writer to have this feature. Underneath, the base is domed and plain for a wide band about the perimeter. The stem has a thimble-shaped hollow space over an inch deep, and this recess readily admits the thimble finger. Another unusual aspect is a round raised ring underneath, where the stem and base are joined. This could lead the unwary to believe that base and stem were pressed separately and later fused. This, however, is not the case. The entire piece was pressed in a single operation.

The base is severely plain on top and slopes at a slight angle to a round edge. The lower portion of the stem is shaped like a pineapple or ancient straw beehive. Its exterior is covered by three

77

78

79

80

81

82

83

84

85

rows of graduated beveled, flat-topped hexagonal buttons. In the interstices between the buttons are triangular pyramids. On top of this beehive dome is a heavy ring, above which the stem is constricted to its least diameter. From this constriction, the stem arches out onto the bottom of the bowl as shown in the drawing.

The sides of the bowl are straight and vertical. They are completely covered from top to bottom with geometric figurework. The upper half has nine large, beveled, flat-topped hexagonal figures surrounded by triangular pyramids and fans. The lower half of the body also has nine hexagonal figures, but they are surrounded by beveled rectangles and triangular pyramids.

The rim has a low, sweeping scallop over each fan, except at the lip. Here, the rim is plain, rises gently, and is pinched into a narrow spout. The handle has six sides. The two wider side panels are covered with a row of hexagonal buttons and triangular pyramids, except at the acute angle on top. Here, the space is filled on either side by an impressed fan.

This pattern was produced between 1875 and 1885 and may have been continued after the absorption of Challinor, Taylor and Company by the United States Glass Company as Factory C in July, 1891.

The soda-lime glass and workmanship are both excellent. The glass is clear, brilliant, and free of impurities or discolorations. It has a good fire polish. A table setting in this pattern would scintillate under a well-lighted crystal chandelier.

Creamer: 3-part mold, 14 1/2 ounces, 6 3/4 inches tall, 3 1/16 inches wide, and 4 3/4 inches long.

According to the old catalog, at least the following items were manufactured: several high open compotes, several high covered compotes, creamer, covered sugar, spoonholder, covered butter dish, water pitcher, goblet, water tray, tumbler, waste bowl, 7-inch flat dish, pickle dish, several round stemmed covered bowls or low compotes, finger bowl, quart pitcher, and half-gallon pitcher.

Compare the PAVONIA creamer made in 1885 by Ripley and Company of Pittsburgh, Pennsylvania, with this one. They are quite similar in shape, size, and stem. The hollow beehive-shaped stems are almost identical. They were manufactured by different companies, but their marked similarity makes me wonder if the same designer and moldmaker did not create both patterns—quite possibly at the Hipkins Novelty Mold Shop of Martins Ferry, Ohio.

80—CABBAGE LEAF

Millard did not show a goblet in this pattern and Kamm did not use such a creamer. Ruth Webb Lee in *Early American Pressed Glass*, Pattern 171, pages 435-436, and Plate 65-4, covers the pattern and lists the known items. In the August, 1955, issue of *The Spinning Wheel*, Mrs. Lee says that goblets, wines, and compotes are being reproduced today. I suspect other items may be included. Metz covers the pattern as No. 1156 without illustration. She, too, warns of reproduced ware in all items and colors in this pattern.

The beautiful golden or honey-amber creamer shown here is stippled rather than frosted. It has a "new" appearance and either really is new or has had little usage. The tall creamer has a small, round stem. The bowl is shaped like a growing cabbage. The rim is uneven, simulating leaf edges. Three leaves cover the body. Where they overlap and curl up the glass is 1/2-inch thick. Each leaf has a number of heavy raised veins, and the surface about them is stippled. There are no rabbits on the creamer as on the covered sugar, covered butter, and lidded compote.

The base flares out and arches down from the small stem to a wide round foot. The upper surface of the base is covered with raised and grained figures all pointing toward the stem. Unless they are chufas I have no idea what they were meant to be. They certainly bear no resemblance to the roots of a cabbage plant. Underneath, is a high arched dome.

Inside the bowl and near the top is a flat ledge which appears to have been made to accommodate a lid. It has two unusual rises near the front which would make it difficult to provide a well-fitting lid. If a lid actually was made, it probably carried the rabbit motif.

The handle is large, round in cross section, and adequate. A curved or rustic handle would have been more appropriate. The one it does have changes directions at decided angles and in the overall picture does not seem to belong. The glass and workmanship are excellent. There are no bubbles or defects, and the mold marks are difficult to see.

The pattern once was quite scarce. Suddenly it began to appear in shops, a piece here and a piece there for no apparent reason. Reproductions are plentiful. I can end this paragraph with no better advice than *caveat emptor*.

Creamer: 3-part mold, 14 ounces, 5 13/16 inches tall, 3 15/16 inches wide, and 6 inches long.

The creamer, covered sugar, covered butter dish, spoonholder, celery vase, pickle dish, tall covered compote, and sauce dishes are known to have been made at about the time of the Columbian Exposition in Chicago in 1893. It came in clear and amber, both frosted and stippled. Surprisingly it was not made in a light shade of cabbage green which would have been more realistic and attractive than an amber cabbage.

81—GULFPORT

This sedate pattern has not previously pushed its way up to the threshold of recognition as a member of the American pressed glass family—a family which, by the way, grows and grows and grows.

In the absence of a good descriptive title, I have given it the name *GULFPORT* for the lovely city from which, as a small boy, I saw the entrancing broad, blue expanse of the Gulf of Mexico. Its beauty and grandeur still enthrall me. The cylindrical body has straight and almost vertical sides. They flare slightly near the rim and round under abruptly at the waist. The sole decoration on the piece is a half-inch wide band which follows the contours of the rim. It consists of a series of raised U's placed side by side with a raised tongue in the throat of each. The rim is sway-backed, the curves rather placid, and the lip is wide.

The handle is hexagonal, but seems to have only four sides—much in the manner of mortised Mission furniture. Each side panel is outlined by a raised line which produces an attractive channel and at the same time relieves the angular structure. The waist and foot make up in beauty and flow of line for that lacking in rim and handle. Through curves and over ledges, the outline cascades to the base which is thick and wide. On the underside is a high, hollow dome. The plain sides are not etched, and the piece depends on the sparkling beauty of the clear glass for its appeal. Mold marks are visible, but are low and smooth. This piece dates from about 1875-1885.

Creamer: 2-part mold, 14 ounces, 5 3/8 inches tall, 3 1/8 inches wide, and 4 13/16 inches long.

The creamer is the only piece I have seen. A sugar bowl, butter dish, and spoonholder were almost certainly made. Many items may appear now that it has a name and can be identified. It is not common.

82—FROSTED FLEUR-DE-LIS

This grand old milk-white creamer is rare today. Even with the large number of opaque white pieces covered by Millard in his *Opaque*

Glass and by Belknap in his *Milk Glass*, no piece of this pattern was covered. Perhaps little was manufactured.

Mrs. Kamm in *Two Hundred Pattern Glass Pitchers*, page 85, No. 118, described a clear stippled creamer and named it FROSTED FLEUR-DE-LIS. This name was evidently given because the fine stippling imparted a frosted appearance to the piece. It was not because an acid bath had been given over the stippling, which was pressed in the mold. The title is a misnomer when used on milk-white glass, which will not show a frosted aspect. Kamm knew the pattern was made in a deep bottle green and a deep muddy amber, but did not know it was also made in milk-white glass. Amethyst and blue could be expected. She considered the pattern contemporary with, and similar to, FLOWER FLANGE or DEWEY. The latter was made to commemorate Dewey's entry into Manila Bay on May 1, 1898. From the quality of glass, the manner of stippling, the size and general conformation, I would think this pattern dated from ten to fifteen years earlier.

This large, round creamer has a somewhat narrow beaded waist. The lower part of the body is rounded under to the waist and changes to straight sides on the upper part. The body is decorated with long, slender fleur-de-lis. These are staggered so they swirl in two directions. The fleur-de-lis are in tiers of one, two and three respectively. The flowers have been touched with a pale blue enamel and the center with tan. They were then baked on. It was not expertly applied, but it does have the saving grace of being applied sparingly.

Around the body, below the rim an inch-wide band was left without stippling. This covers the back three-fourths of the body and is a modification of the egg-and-dart motif. Here, the sharp-pointed dart has been replaced by three club-shaped figures. The border is in well-rounded relief. On the front fourth, under the lip, the stippling reaches the rim.

The rim, formed by the top of the band, is attractive. The lip rises and extends forward slightly to make a well-designed spout. The pressed handle is round in cross section and looks much like an applied one with the large blob at the bottom. The mold marks show. The curves on the upper part of the handle are not too pleasing and would have benefited from some softening by the designer.

The piece appears clumsy and off-balance in the drawing. This is true in all three-legged items. There are three horseshoe-shaped loops in round relief which form the legs. Each loop contains a round and well-convexed cabochon. Between the feet at the base is a rounded scrollband and above it is some stippling and then a short beaded waist. It has a flared skirt. Underneath, the base is plain with a high hollow space.

The quality of the milk-white glass is superior, and it has a clear belltone ring when tapped. This is seldom found in creamers, even flint ones. It is snow-white with no opalescence whatsoever. It appears chalky where stippled. On the plain surface it looks like fine porcelain. The designer and decorator should have exercised a little more care. The moldmaker and gaffer were alert and competent. The mold mark on the handle is the only one present. A three-part mold probably was used. The stippling is as well executed as any I have seen and is actually a series of minute craters and not tiny dewdrops.

Creamer: ?-part mold, 12 ounces, 5 5/16 inches tall, 3 5/8 inches wide, and 5 3/8 inches long.

I do not know where or by whom this piece was made. It was produced in clear, green, amber, and milk white. These items are known: large creamer, sugarbowl, spoonholder, butter dish, and goblet.

83—DOVER

Both Mrs. Kamm and I have felt that this creamer was of European origin and probably English. It is a magnificent piece of milk-white glass with a satin finish. It is snow-white, chalklike, and has no opalescence. It gives the effect of billowy, cumulus clouds drifting in over the White Cliffs of Dover. For this reason, the above name is given. The creamer is unlike any other milk-white pressed glass creamer which has come to my attention. The shape, texture of glass, etc., indicate a point of origin outside the United States.

The jug has a melon-shaped body with six wide, low, convex lobes which extend from near the base to the lower part of the neck. There are two billows on each lobe. The lower edges of these billows are scalloped like a shell and resemble spring showers in the making. One line of scallops is near the base and the other is at the base of the neck. The edges of the scallops were daubed with gilt, and now are badly tarnished. Perhaps this represented sunshine on the clouds. Between the bands of scallops the piece is decorated (?) with a large number of small blue leaves and tiny brown,

circular flowers. The latter are formed by circles of minute dots with a larger dot for the center. The enamel was baked on and cannot be removed (an abominable job if I ever saw one).

The neck is quite constricted and is attractive. A plain rim sweeps high and forward to form the small lip. The front half of the rim and lip is thicker than the remainder. The creamer sits on a low, wide ringbase and is plain underneath. The applied handle is well executed with the large blob at the lower attachment. At the top it is flattened on the inside. It is attractive and matches the jug.

The glass is of superior quality, and the workmanship is as fine as I have seen. With imagination, a single mold mark (or where one should be) can be detected below the handle. The "mud-dauber" with a brush should have expended his efforts catching spiders instead of trying to decorate this little symphony. His work was decidedly inferior and done with a slapdash and abandon that should have resulted in his being fired.

Creamer: no mold marks can be found, 8 1/4 ounces, 4 7/8 inches tall, 3 3/8 inches wide, and 4 inches long.

This beautiful piece was bought with the covered sugar bowl. No other items are known to the writer.

84—ALBA

This magnificent milk-white pressed glass creamer was cherished for years and thought to be Bristol glass. It is radically different from most American pressed glassware in shape, in texture, and in finish. It is very rare and seldom seen in shops. Imagine my delight, when I learned from an old advertisement that it is not Bristol glass but early American pressed glass. It was made between 1885 and 1900 by Dithridge and Company (Fort Pitt Glass Works) of Pittsburgh, Pennsylvania. This company made much of our finest early flint tableware. Unfortunately we know very few of their patterns from lack of research. This is, for the most part, unavoidable since the former site of this glass house is now a part of the choicest real estate in Pittsburgh's Golden Triangle and much too expensive to justify excavation for research. Also, the company did not put out an early catalog of their products. They used only small ads which covered only a portion of their late ware and none of their earlier products. Some of their "lacy" type glass was as fine as ever produced and carried the name of R. B. Curling and Sons on the bottom. It is too bad this practice of marking glass was not more widespread.

Minnie Watson Kamm never saw a piece of this glass. In *A Sixth Pitcher Book*, Plate 78, she shows a cut from an old ad dated 1894 of Dithridge and Company (Fort Pitt Glass Works), Pittsburgh, which illustrates many salts, peppers, casters, toothpick holders, molasses cans, etc. A molasses can in this pattern, with a metal lid and spring, is shown. It is almost identical in shape to the creamer shown here. It is advertised as solid-color glass. Two types of salt and pepper shakers are also shown in the pattern.

In *An Eighth Pitcher Book*, Mrs. Kamm, on page 76, No. 150, drew the pattern from another old ad of the 1880s that illustrated a creamer and sugar shaker. The company called it ALBA or PATTERN A. The drawings in the ad were poor, but since Mrs. Kamm had not seen a piece of it, they were her only guide.

I have the standard creamer, and the illustration here shows its pressed design, but not the enameled floral spray which was baked on. The decoration would vary from piece to piece.

A noticeable feature of this creamer is the thinness of the glass. Also note how white, free of opalescence, polished and porcelainlike it is. Also the bulbous convoluted lower half of the bowl and the tall wide vertical neck are uncommon. This quality and type of glass is also seen in COSMOS and COREOPSIS as shown on the following pages. All three patterns could well have emanated from the same factory.

The bottom half of the creamer is bulbous or cantaloupe-shaped with nine high well-rounded lobes. This portion is covered with a design of raised netting similar to that of the muskmelon family. The upper half of the body is somewhat constricted and rises vertically to a plain flat rim. The netting and lobes end abruptly, without completing their design at the juncture of the two halves of the body. A delicate enameled floral spray has been painted on the neck. It cannot be removed. The colors are green, orange, blue, and tan and are applied in round dots and irregular daubs.

The rim is level and flat. It appears to have been sheared off and not reheated to round it over. Only a trace of a lip shows.

I have seen no other handle attached to a piece of pressed glass with the technique used on this creamer. It is hard to believe, but in this case a pressed handle was applied to the creamer. The handle was too cold to fuse with the body, and pressure was applied to make it stick. This pressure almost punctured the body at the two attachments and resulted in two large rough lumps

on the inside. The handle, nevertheless, is poorly fused to the body and a dirt filled space is present between them. The handle is six-sided, angular, and too small for the pitcher.

Without the bent rim for a lip and with the handle left off, this piece would have been a spoonholder. With a plain rim and two handles, it would have been a sugar bowl. Indeed, all three pieces could have been pressed in the same mold. As expensive as molds were, it is surprising this practice was not resorted to more often.

There is no pontil mark on the piece, but the contours show a plunger from the top could not possibly have formed this shape and been withdrawn through the narrow neck. After Mr. George Hipkins of the Hipkins Novelty Mold Works, Martins Ferry, Ohio, invented a method for making such bulbous containers by fusing two pressed glass pieces together, such pieces as molasses cans became popular. (This was at the time when hot cakes for breakfast were a national dish.) The Hipkins Works did sell molds to the manufacturer of this creamer, and they at that time were specializing in the production of just such molasses cans. Almost certainly the Hipkins people made the molds for ALBA.

This piece sits flat on a low but wide ring and is slightly hollowed out beneath. It has a nice resonance when tapped, indicating it is of fine flint glass.

Creamer: 3-part mold, 9 ounces, 4 inches tall, 4 1/16 inches wide, and 4 3/4 inches long.

Only the following items are known to have been made in this pattern: creamer, sugar bowl, butter dish, spoonholder, salt and pepper shakers in two styles, sugar sifter, and molasses can.

85—COSMOS

This pattern is shown for comparison with ALBA and COREOPSIS, two similar milk-white pieces. The name of the manufacturer is unknown, but a comparison with these two patterns may well indicate where and when COSMOS made its debut, since we know where and about when one of them was produced.

Mrs. Kamm, in *A Fifth Pitcher Book*, page 53, No. 60, wrote up the pattern using a line drawing and photograph. Millard, in *Opaque Glass*, shows a water pitcher in Plate 146; a milk pitcher in Plate 150; a tumbler in Plate 191; an open sugar bowl in Plate 214; and a small low lamp in Plate 252.

E. McCalmy Belknap, in *Milk Glass*, Plate 83, shows a two-quart water pitcher, and in Plate 206, a silver-plated pickle caster and tongs with a COS-MOS filler. He says the combination of silver and milk glass was rare.

We know Dithridge and Company (Fort Pitt Glass Works), of Pittsburgh, made ALBA between 1885 and 1900. The shape and treatment of the pattern, the porcelainlike glass with no chalkiness, the thinness of the metal, the absence of a pontil mark, and the fact the design shows in reverse on the inside, all indicate such a striking similarity that they invite the conclusion that Dithridge and Company probably made this pattern. The Hipkins' patent made all three of these patterns possible, without a pontil mark. This concern did furnish molds to Dithridge. Research may clear up this quesiton eventually. This is quality ware. It is not plentiful and it brings a high price.

Creamer: 4-part mold, 14 ounces, 4 15/16 inches tall, 3 7/8 inches wide, and 5 inches long.

The following items are known to have been made in this pattern: water pitcher in 2 sizes, milk pitcher, creamer, covered butter dish, covered sugar bowl, spoonholder, tumbler, caster set, inset for pickle caster, salt and pepper shakers, syrup pitcher with metal lid and spring, low and tall footed lamps, berry bowl, lamp shade, and sauce dish.

86—COREOPSIS

This is a larger creamer than Mrs. Kamm used in *A Fifth Pitcher Book*, page 52, No. 59, wherein she named and described this pattern. It is used again for comparison with ALBA, COS-MOS, and *LAZY LAGOON*, three very similar milk-white patterns.

This is the finest quality milk-white glass with which the author has worked. It is exceedingly thin and porcelainlike rather than chalky. The surface shines like and appears to be china. There is no showing of fiery blue or opalescence when held to a bright light. The workmanship of the moldmaker and the gaffer was highly skilled and commendable. A dauber made swipes at the piece with a paint brush to add color. He painted the raised flowers as if they were round rather than shaped like flowers as shown in the drawing. Certainly a more appropriate term than *artist* could be used to describe him and his ilk. It is too bad the colors are baked on and cannot be removed. The flowers are pink with reddish pigments and mustard-colored centers. The leaves (?) are grayish purple and green. The neck is colored chartreuse.

The handle is applied and has the large blob at the lower attachment. It is round in cross section and beautifully proportioned and curved. (See drawing for the painstaking manner in which the upper attachment is tooled.)

This creamer was made in a three-part mold, but was not pressed. No plunger was used and there is no pontil mark. The flowers and beading are raised on the outside but depressed on the inside. The shape, quality, and type of glass and decoration are so similar to the other three patterns a definite possibility exists that they were designed in the same shop and made in the same factory. We know that ALBA was made by Dithridge and Company (Fort Pitt Glass Works), Pittsburgh. We also know this company bought molds from the Hipkins Novelty Mold Works, of Martins Ferry, Ohio. The Hipkins' patent for making this shape of containers was almost certainly used. This piece, together with ALBA, COSMOS and LAZY LAGOON, was in all probability designed and made by the same moldmakers and manufacturers.

There is a band of large raised dewdrops around the waist and at the bottom of the neck. The body is quite bulbous. The base is somewhat narrow and plain underneath. The dewdrops show up as sunken areas on the inside—proof that it was blown in a mold and not pressed. The neck is small, straight, and tall.

In *Opaque Glass*, Plate 215-1, S. T. Millard shows a covered sugar bowl in this pattern and calls it APPLE BLOSSOM. He shows two other patterns in milk-white glass in the same volume and calls each of them APPLE BLOSSOM, though neither are of that pattern. This glass is believed to have been made between 1885 and 1898. The creamer Mrs. Kamm used was 4 3/4 inches tall.

This creamer: 3-part mold, 14 ounces, 5 1/2 inches tall, 4 3/4 inches wide, and 5 5/16 inches long.

The only items known to the author in this pattern are: 4 3/4-inch creamer, 5 1/2-inch creamer, and covered sugar bowl. It is not found as frequently as is COSMOS.

87—*LAZY LAGOON*

This creamer is probably a sibling of ALBA, COSMOS and COREOPSIS. The Hipkins' patent made its advent possible, and the mold in which it was blown was almost certainly a product of the Hipkins Novelty Mold Shop of Martins Ferry, Ohio. They made molds for Dithridge and

Company (Fort Pitt Glass Works) in the golden triangle of Pittsburgh. The latter firm specialized in making this type of superior milk-white and dead-white tableware. (See Kamm's *A Fifth Pitcher Book*, page 108, for notes on the Fort Pitt Glass Works.)

In an effort to clear up a confusing situation I have named this pattern *LAZY LAGOON* and hope it does not result in compounding the confusion. It is usually preferable to retain a rather inappropriate title unless it is also confusing. We have that situation in this pattern. Fortunately, Mrs. Lee and Mrs. Kamm did not assign titles inasmuch as they had not seen the pattern.

Dr. S. T. Millard published his *Goblets* in 1938 and on Plate 152-3 named a late pattern WATER LILY. In 1941 he published his *Opaque Glass* and on Plate 217 showed a four-quart water pitcher in this pattern and called it WATER LILY, WATER PITCHER. This resulted in two patterns with the name WATER LILY.

In his *Milk Glass Addenda* published in 1952, Edwin G. Warman showed a molasses pitcher with a metal lid, a covered cracker jar, and a covered butter dish in this pattern and called them WILD IRIS. See Plate 14-B-C-D. There are numerous other patterns with Iris in their title.

In 1946 Minnie Watson Kamm published her *A Fourth Pitcher Book* and on page 136, No. 180, named a beautiful pattern WATER LILY. Some "furriner" who had never seen a magnolia blossom later called this same pattern FROSTED MAGNOLIA. This is not only a desecration; it is intolerable. No rebel could ever imagine frost on a magnolia blossom, or recognize a similarity between the pattern named and the stately flower they love.

LAZY LAGOON is a quality product of a high order. Little milk-white glass of this quality was made. It is often mistaken for china. The interior and handle show the lovely texture of the glass. Some would-be decorator gave this gem the "works." The lower portion of the body is painted an abominable brownish pink. The upper half is yellow with light blue flowers. None of the flowers, leaves, or buds have a botanical entity. Why the leaves, buds, and their background were painted such a jaundiced shade of pink is hard to explain. The care lavished in making this quality product clashes violently with the slapdash abandon with which the colors were applied. Unfortunately the latter was baked on and cannot be removed. The flowers seem to be growing in quiet water and this suggested the above name.

The body is bulbous with all patternwork beginning at the base. Each second flower extends well up on the surface of the rounded shoulder. The taller flowers have four petals, the two shorter have five. A third of the body, around the handle, has the leaves and buds, but no flowers. The pattern is well raised on the outside, with corresponding depressions on the inside.

The neck is generous, but still much narrower than the body. No plunger could possibly have pressed the body and been removed through the smaller neck. The Hipkins' patent made it possible to manufacture such pieces. The rim is round on top, smooth, and slopes up from the handle to the front where it is depressed into a pleasant lip.

The round applied handle has its large blob at the lower attachment, which is stuck on a smooth, plain surface. The upper tab is turned under, flattened, and tooled into a fern frond. Fortunately the handle is not daubed with paint. The glass and workmanship of this piece are excellent, but my hypertension prevents further comment about the "finisher" who painted it. The mold marks are visible, but difficult to feel.

Creamer: 3-part mold, 12 ounces, 4 3/4 inches tall, 4 inches wide, and 5 3/16 inches long. We know the following articles were made in this pattern: creamer, covered sugar bowl, covered butter dish, spoonholder, covered cracker jar, water pitcher, molasses can, and a three piece condiment set, including a tray with a metal handle sticking straight up through the center. On the tray were salt and pepper shakers and a mustard jar. Articles one would expect to find are: small lamp, sugar shaker, dresser bottle, large dresser tray, covered box, pickle caster in metal stand with tongs, bowl, sauce dish, tumbler, waste bowl, water tray, compote, etc.

88—PASCAGOULA

Belknap, in *Milk Glass*, page 84, Plate 74-c, shows a tall milk-glass molasses can in this pattern with a metal lid and says it is a "beaded heart jug." No other writer apparently has seen or used the pattern. Mr. Belknap's name for it was inappropriate, for there are no true heart-shaped figures on the piece. There are some large concave teardrop-shaped areas outlined with beads. Underneath, four of them are so placed as to suggest, but not actually represent, a four-leaf clover. A descriptive title for this pattern would be too cumbersome.

Anyone who has ever driven along the Gulf shore drive in Pascagoula, Mississippi, on a clear spring day will understand why this beautiful pattern was given the name of *PASCAGOULA* by the author.

The milk-white molasses jug, and the beautiful clear creamer shown here, both have bulbous bodies and small necks and could not have been pressed by a plunger nor machine produced until after the Hipkins' patent. The dead-white molasses jug in this pattern and shape is the type of product specialized in during the 1890s by Dithridge Glass Company (Fort Pitt Glass Works), of Pittsburgh, and it is probable that this pattern was made by them in a Hipkins' mold. They also made quality tableware, and this creamer is certainly that.

The lower half of the creamer is bulbous both inside and out. Six large teardrops with their points up encircle the creamer's bulge. Each is deeply concave from side to side, but not from top to bottom. A row of tiny beading outlines each. Between each two drops there is a narrow protruding fin, where the glass from outside to inside is more than half an inch thick. Around the smaller upper half of the creamer are six highly convex columns with thickened, rounded bases which mesh into the tops of the teardrops below. In the center of each column a small floral spray was hand cut with a wheel and carefully gilded. The gilt was not baked on and is easily removable. The residue which remains is dark, tarnished and worn by washing.

The rounded tops of the three rear columns make wide scallops on the rim. The three in front flare up and slightly out to form the lip. The glass at the rim is 1/8-inch thick. The attractive applied handle is round in cross section and is of a late type with the basal attachment the larger. Both were attached to the smooth surface of the rear column, which is not engraved. The upper tab is sheared into a V-shape, turned under, flattened, and left unadorned.

The girth is ample and the base is wide for stability. The low base forms a ring on which the piece rests. Underneath, it is slightly hollowed and an attractive design is impressed. Four small, beaded teardrops, similar to those on the outside of the creamer, meet at their points. It is quite effective. (See drawing of bottom for details.) The glass and workmanship are of superior quality and make an article anyone would cherish. It belongs to the 1890-1900 era. There are indistinct mold marks on the base.

Creamer: 3-part mold, 1 1/16 pounds, 5 inches tall, 3 15/16 inches wide, and 4 13/16 inches long. The milk-white molasses jug and this creamer

are the only items known by the writer. Certainly a sugar bowl, butter dish, and a spoonholder were made. This pattern probably was produced at the same factory and at approximately the same time as *LAZY LAGOON*. We could expect a similar range of items, but they are not likely to be plentiful.

89—*YAZOO CITY*

In *Opaque Glass*, Plate 134-2, S. T. Millard shows a covered sugar bowl in this milk-white pattern and says it is of the 1880s. On Plate 206-2 and 3, he shows a creamer and open sugar bowl and says it is an Atterbury Company product, but does not give his source of attribution. Atterbury Glass Company of Pittsburgh, Pennsylvania, was famous for making fine milk-white glass. T. B. Atterbury obtained Patent No. 17192 on March 15, 1887, for the well-known Atterbury Duck.

Belknap, in *Milk Glass*, Plate 128d, shows a milk-white ribbed sugar bowl with lid. It is similar to this piece and could be used with it. He believed his piece might be a Westmoreland product. The two could easily be confused.

This pattern of milk-white glass has the appearance of glassware of the 1880s. It may have been made at that early date but unfortunately, it is still being made. Gift shops are full of it. The glass is different and the workmanship is better now. When old and new pieces are seen together, there is little difficulty in determining which is which. My advice, however, unless you are an expert, is to buy the pattern only from a gift shop and with the manufacturer's label still on it. It is beautiful and is now made in a wide range of articles including: footed tumblers, 10-inch plates, covered soup tureens, candleholders, cups and saucers, etc. Today it is also made in a new and beautiful pink milk glass. All pieces come with the maker's name attached, but the stickers wash off easily. It is too bad they do not use a pressed trademark. Such quality ware should have its own permanent mark. This pattern is now produced by the Fostoria Glass Company of Moundsville, West Virginia.

The big body of the creamer resembles a gravy bowl. Its flared rim is decorated with a border of Gothic arches over open portals. In the valleys between the arches are dewdrops. The front third of the rim is not perforated. The arches and dewdrops make the rim unevenly scalloped. The lip is fairly high and unattractive in its profile view.

The upper half of the body is plain and quite smooth. In earlier days, some pieces probably had

86

87

88

89

90

Bottom
88

Base of
Handle
91

Top View
90

92

91

Bottom
92

flowers painted there. The lower half of the body has such a simple and striking design one wonders why it has not been imitated more widely. This is particularly true when we remember some of the atrocious patterns which have been copied. A band of rounded ribs and alternating narrow spined ridges are placed vertically around the piece.

The waist starts at a shelf on the lower part of the body and curves in, then out, to the wide sloping foot. When the piece was removed from the mold by tongs, to be taken to the lehr, it was too hot and was pinched by the tongs. As a result it is misshapen at the waist and foot. There is a high, round dome underneath. The handle is terete. Its lower fourth is ribbed and flares into the large lower attachment.

The milk-white glass of this pitcher is flint and has a belltoned ring when tapped. The glass is pure white with no discoloration or opalescence. It resembles porcelain. It does not have the fine texture or expert workmanship of the newer pieces. The mold marks are prominent.

Creamer: 3-part mold, 15 1/2 ounces, 4 1/2 inches tall, 4 7/8 inches wide, and 6 inches long.

In addition to the articles listed above, many others were made.

90—*BLUEHAVEN*

The rim of the *YAZOO CITY (above)* milk-glass creamer is lacy and flares out and upward at an acute angle. Its openings can be seen from the side. The wide rim of this piece flares horizontally, and the holes can only be seen from above.

This small creamer with its fantastic rim and lip is in a soft shade of light blue glass which changes to opaque blue as it approaches the top of the lip and edge of the rim. This particular shade is very rarely seen in glass. This is the first appearance of this pattern in a book on pressed glass, and the name assigned is suitable for the color.

A more simple design could hardly be devised. It is formed by a series of horizontal V-shaped grooves, evenly spaced about the body. They are crossed by similar diagonal grooves running both to the right and left. This results in a design composed of highly beveled, flat-topped triangles side by side. This geometrical figurework covers the tapering body from below the rim to above the waist.

A raised ring at the base of the triangles separates the body from the waist. Below, it flares

sharply to the skirted base. The top of the foot is covered by vertical fine rib. The base has a well-rounded ring on which to rest. Underneath is a high flat-topped dome. The small six-paneled handle is not decorated and is so small that only a single adult finger can be accommodated.

Under the rim a prominent ring surrounds the body. Although Millard and Belknap show many plates with perforated borders, in none of them is the egg-and-fan motif (shown here) found. It is piquantly beautiful. (See drawing of rim for details.) In front, the flaring rim terminates, and a high square-jowled section rises almost vertically, then dips into a narrow lip. This appendage sticks out like a sore thumb and is about as attractive. This is good quality ware for gift shops. The glass is free of bubbles and other defects. I do not know where or when it was manufactured, but believe it to be between 1920 and 1930.

Creamer: 4-part mold, 8 1/2 ounces, 3 3/4 inches tall, 3 3/4 inches wide, and 4 1/8 inches long.

I know of only the creamer. Possibly a sugar bowl, vases, and nappies were made. It may have come in various colors.

91—SEQUOIA

S. T. Millard in *Goblets II*, Plate 140-2, calls this pattern SEQUOIA. Ruth Webb Lee in *Victorian Glass*, page 173, Plate 56-1, showed the type creamer used here, but grouped it with a goblet and wine glass in a pattern she named HOURGLASS. (Do not confuse with an earlier flint pattern which Mrs. Kamm called HOURGLASS.) A casual reader may misunderstand Mrs. Lee. She did not name the creamer HOURGLASS; in fact, she did not give a name—she merely indicated it would combine well with the pattern she was describing. Mrs. Metz showed a SEQUOIA nonflint glass goblet of the late 1880s as her No. 1807.

The glass of this creamer is a thick brilliant early flint which is quite heavy and without defect. I suspect it preceded the Millard and Metz goblets by a decade or so. It scintillates as brilliantly as any specimen in my collection. The goblets were evidently not made of flint glass or it would have been mentioned.

The lower two-thirds of the body is cylindrical, with vertical sides. It rounds over to a narrower neck and then flares widely. The design appears complex but is actually an imitation cut glass pattern, easy to lay out and easier to cut. To cut the mold the iron was marked off in half-inch squares by evenly spaced horizontal and perpendicular lines. The diagonal lines running to the left and right were drawn at one-fourth inch intervals. Each straight line would then be cut and polished as a V-shaped groove and the pattern was finished. The final result is a composite of innumerable triangular pyramids in different relative positions which in turn form squares, stars, and swirls.

A single band of this imitation cut glass design extends above the neck. From there to the flared rim the piece is left plain and smooth. The body has the shape of the "little brown jug." The rim is level throughout. There are seven rounded scallops on either side. For the handle there is a wide scallop at the back. The rim is plain and dips slightly in front to form a lip. The handle is an applied one with the smaller attachment turned under at the top. The only defect of the piece, and the one which keeps it from the pinnacle, is found at the lower attachment. A plain surface was not provided for the latter, and the huge blob was applied on top of the figurework. As a result, there are innumerable small orifices which have filled with dirt over the years.

The wide base is slightly hollowed out underneath. The outer ring has been ground smooth for a perfect footing as would be done on a quality product. A huge 32-ray star has been impressed in, and covers all but, the narrow outer ring on the base.

Creamer: 4-part mold, 15 ounces, 4 3/8 inches tall, 3 1/8 inches wide, and 4 3/4 inches long.

Since a goblet and creamer were made, we may assume there were a sugar bowl, butter dish, and spoonholder. The creamer is flint, though the goblets are of lime-soda glass, so it is probable they were made at different factories.

92—CLEATS

This early flint glass water pitcher is a type that museums cherish—as do proud owners. It has been called *Wistar glass*, but this could hardly be true. Casper Wistar established a glass house in South Jersey in 1739, and it was in operation for forty years. He produced window glass and bottles primarily but did make some tableware, though we do not know the designs. Any attribution of glass to Wistar is at best speculative. All Wistar glass was blown and handcrafted, and furthermore was produced at least forty-eight years before a machine to press glass in a mold was invented (1827). His glass was quite thin and most of it was

colored. This piece is very thick and heavy, and close inspection reveals two mold marks on the base. This proves that the present pitcher was formed in a mold and must have been blown. It could not have been pressed at that early date because of its bulbous body and narrow neck. The invention for pressing such bulbous shapes came many years later.

N. Hudson Moore, in *The Collector's Manual*, Plate 128, illustrates twenty-four pieces of American glassware. This pitcher is shown in the center of the top row, but is not mentioned in the text. It must be rare or else the McKearins, Lee, Watkins, Kamm, Millard, Belknap Brothers, Knittle, Northend, Metz, or Revi would have located it. Somehow, I have a suspicion it may be foreign though Moore calls it American. It has some characteristics of English glass.

The lower portion of the body is bulbous, and the upper portion is constricted through the long neck. The rim flares and protrudes far forward to form the lip. Four horizontal bands of large cleats, standing erect and in high relief, surround the piece. One band is around the neck, two encircle the bulbous part, and one is about the base. The cleats of the different bands are in tiers. The surrounding surface is plain and mirror smooth. The cleats are from 5/8 to 1 inch apart in the bands. Each cleat is a long, rectangular protrusion with a rounded top. They resemble the cleats (the English call them hobnails) used long ago on shoes to prevent slipping on ice. They are also similar to the football cleats of a generation ago.

This pitcher presents several perplexing questions as to how it was made. The pattern was not blown in a mold, or there would be an indentation on the inside beneath each cleat. It seems the pitcher probably was blown in a mold with recesses provided to receive the preformed cleats. The cleats have the appearance of having been applied to the outside. The necessary pressure to make them adhere to the outer surface caused the interior of the piece to have a noticeable protuberance opposite each cleat—particularly in the bulbous area.

There is a highly raised ring, 1/4-inch wide, around the throat; above it, the neck flares and is smooth. The front portion of the rim bears a decorative device I have not seen before. A deep crease has been tooled in front of the lip and half an inch from the rim, which it parallels. It appears to be the edge of a folded-under rim—but is not.

The beautiful applied handle is adequate, but massive. It is three times as wide as it is thick. The lower attachment is simple, but expertly done. No attempt was made to ornament it by tooling. The only defect on the piece is at this attachment. It was applied on the top and side of a cleat. Open and inaccessible pockets remain, which over the years have filled with dirt and grime that cannot be reached. The bottom is shown in the drawing and consists of a lower radial band of cleats joining a ring that slopes inward. The piece rests on the perimeter of this ring. In the center is a large, deep ground and polished pontil mark which, however, was not ground deep enough to remove all the roughness.

This piece is of brilliantly clear heavy flint glass which received much handcrafting to shape and finish it. It evidently dates from the 1840s through the 1850s. It is a magnificent specimen.

Water pitcher: 2(?)-part mold, 3 1/2 pounds, 8 9/16 inches tall, 6 1/16 inches wide, and 8 1/4 inches long.

This water pitcher is the only article of the pattern known to the glass writing fraternity. Other items may have been made, but they would be rare indeed. It is one of the rarest items discussed in this book. Mr. and Mrs. R. E. Jones, of Chino, California, are the justly proud owners of this pitcher, and their courtesy made it available for inclusion in this book.

93—EVANGELINE

This is a magnificent little canary yellow individual creamer which has escaped writers on pressed glass. Perhaps it was somewhat late in making its debut.

Kamm, in *Two Hundred Pattern Glass Pitchers*, No. 85, shows STARS AND BARS with two bands similar to the lower band on this creamer. Lee, in *Victorian Glass*, Plate 69-4, shows DAISY AND CUBE. It has two bands similar to this one, but with a middle band of bars not present here. Millard, in *Goblets II*, Plate 66-1, shows DAISY WITH AMBER STRIPE, which has a lower band of figurework similar to this, but with the stippled leaf spray missing from the top.

The sides of the creamer shown here are straight and vertical. They curve in to a round shelf on the wide waist, then flare to a plain, round thick footing. There is a low hollow space underneath bearing a raised, 16-ray star.

The lower portion of the body is decorated by a 3/4-inch-wide band composed of bars similar to a lieutenant's insignia. They alternate with squares containing a single, large faceted hobstar. Above this band, a leaf spray encircles the upper part of the body. I have not seen this decorative device

before. It is very effective. The leaf and stem effect is formalized and contains both veining and stippling. The band glistens in a bright light.

The rim is plain and saddled. It rises considerably in front for a lip. The handle is terete, small, and simulates an applied one with the larger attachment at the bottom. The mold marks show through. The handle is small, but suits the piece.

The quality is excellent. The color is yellow—not vaseline. Other colors may have been used. It is well polished and the mold marks are hard to find. It probably dates from between 1905 and 1915. Nothing is known of its antecedents.

Toy creamer: 3-part mold, 4 ounces, 2 15/16 inches tall, 2 1/8 inches wide, and 3 1/4 inches long.

This individual creamer is the only piece I have seen in the pattern. Undoubtedly the other three pieces of the four-piece table set were made. Art glass such as vases, rose bowls, ruffled edge bowls, trays, bonbons, etc., are likely to show up and perhaps with opaque borders. These little fellows are so attractive individually, and so space conserving that they almost tempt one to dispose of his collection of standard creamers and start over again specializing in them.

See also the following pattern, STARS AND BARS.

94—STARS AND BARS

I feel confident that this small amber individual creamer is one that went with a doll-house set of sugar, creamer, butter dish and spooner with the latter now called a toothpick holder. They were probably made in the late 1870s. Mrs. Minnie Watson Kamm, in *Two Hundred Pattern Glass Pitchers*, page 64, No. 85, named the pattern STARS AND BARS and illustrated a standard creamer. The specimen she used was clear. It had an applied handle and two bands of hobstars and bars about the body. The smaller creamer has space for only one band. The smaller creamer does not have the beautiful beaded tab on the turned-up lower handle attachment.

S. T. Millard shows a goblet in this pattern in his *Goblets II*, Plate 66-1. He calls it DAISY WITH AMBER STRIPE. His specimen is also of clear glass with its bars flashed with amber, whereas the individual creamer is of amber glass. This title, therefore, is not completely descriptive. He uses the term *daisy* for faceted figurework, better known today as *hobstar*. Mrs. Kamm's title seems preferable and is used here.

In *Victorian Glass*, Ruth Webb Lee shows a similar, but more ornate, pattern on page 244, Plate 69-4. She calls her pattern DAISY AND CUBE—and like Dr. Millard, she calls hobstars *daisies*. The individual creamer is shown here for contrast with the standard creamer and to enable the reader to compare it with the preceding creamer. It is reasonable to assume that the molds for the four different variants of the pattern came from the same place, and this probably was the Hipkins Novelty Mold Shop. Nevertheless, the four variants could have been pressed in as many different factories.

The conformation and size of this piece closely approximates that of the already described *EVANGELINE* creamer. There are, however, certain differences, the most important of which is the absence of the raised, stippled leaf band on this piece.

The base of this creamer is domed underneath and left plain. Both the standard and *EVANGELINE* creamers have round raised stars of many rays impressed into the base. The upper portion of the individual creamer is left plain, as was Millard's goblet. It has a single belt of squares filled with hobstars, the latter being separated by prisms similar to the bars of a lieutenant. The standard creamer is also illustrated.

The quality of the glass and workmanship in my three specimens are excellent. The standard creamer is definitely old and dates from the 1870s. The amber individual one has a new appearance. It may have remained unused for years on a top shelf, or it may be a "Johnnie come lately."

Individual creamer: 3-part mold, 4 ounces, 2 15/16 inches tall, 2 inches wide, and 3 1/16 inches long.

We know the pattern was made in goblets; standard creamer, sugar, butter, and spooner; individual creamer, sugar, butter and spooner; and in a small night lamp. The standard version was made in a wide range of items as was customary at that time.

95—BLEEDING HEART

This old pattern was so popular it was kept in production for years, and variants of it were produced by several factories; each factory changed the shape. Probably it is best to do as Dr. Millard did and give each variant a specific name. Otherwise a collector has difficulty in telling just which version he is dealing with.

We know the pattern was made from the mid-dle 1860s through 1898. Also that it was made by the Boston and Sandwich Glass Company, the King Glass Company, the Specialty Glass Company, and the U.S. Glass Company. Perhaps other glass houses also manufactured some variation of it.

The tall, slender, attractive tankard creamer shown here has not been described or illustrated in American pressed glass literature. It seems to date from 1875-1885. It has an attractive applied handle.

Mrs. Kamm described the earliest version of the creamer in *Two Hundred Pattern Glass Pitchers*, page 8, No. 7. It had an applied handle and a tall paneled stem and was probably first made prior to 1864 at Sandwich. The date was set by Chapman and Knittle. On Plate 82 of *An Eighth Pitcher Book*, Mrs. Kamm reproduced an advertisement of the Specialty Glass Company (1888-1889) showing a goblet, with or without a tin lid, and a mug with such a lid. These were made as containers for marketing jelly or condiments. The creamer shown here fits chronologically between the Sandwich creamer and the container items.

Mrs. Lee, in *Early American Pressed Glass*, Pattern 154, pages 399-401, Plates 123 and 128-1 and -2, covers the pattern. Plate 123 shows a goblet with a double knop stem made by the Specialty Glass Company. Plate 128-1 shows a creamer with a pressed handle which apparently dates from considerably later than the one used by Mrs. Kamm, or the one shown here. Dr. Millard covers three different goblets in his books. In *Goblets*, Plate 43-3, he shows BLEEDING HEART KNOB STEM. On 43-4, he shows BLEEDING HEART PLAIN STEM. In *Goblets II* Plate 91-4, he illustrates BLEEDING HEART WITH FLUTED STEM, the Specialty Glass Company's version.

Pieces of any of the variants combine well with the others though the earlier one is more refined and to be preferred. None of them is plentiful. This creamer has a deep bowl, a short waist, and a wide base. The attractive bleeding heart motif is confined to the lower half of the bowl. It is separated from the upper half by an unusual mold mark which surrounds the body and above which the glass is 1/16 of an inch thicker. The top has been handtooled into a slight constriction and from there flares to the rim.

The rim is deeply saddled, rising high at the rear to receive the large upper blob of the handle. In front, it curves upward and slightly forward and does not dip for the lip. Around the top of the bowl some waviness is found on the surface, indicating the glass was too cool when tooled. The long graceful applied handle matches the height of the bowl. It is wider than it is thick. The lower attachment was stuck on top of the raised figurework. The tooling is adequate but not outstanding.

The narrow waist is incurved and short. It ends in a low shelf on top of the foot. The base slopes out and rounds over into a wide, thick foundation. It is plain and hollow underneath. The glass is clear and without defect. The waviness of the upper surface is the piece's only demerit. We do not know just which glass factory made this particular variant, but it seems to date between 1875 and 1885.

Tankard creamer: 4-part mold (one around body), 1 1/8 pounds, 6 inches tall, 3 5/16 inches wide, and 4 7/8 inches long.

No attempt is made to list the articles in each version. Only a student or collector of the pattern could do that. I will list only the items known to have been made: covered berry bowl, waste bowl, butter dish, cake stand, high covered compote, low covered compote, oval covered compote, cordial, three types of creamers, oval dish, eggcup, three types of goblets, honey dish, mug, oval pickle, 4-section pickle relish, milk pitcher, water pitcher, plate, oval platter, master salt, round flat sauce, oval sauce, spooner, sugar bowl, footed tumbler, water tumbler, and wine.

96—BRUCE

This piece is pressed, but not pattern, glass. It has no design pressed on its surface. It is a beautiful honey amber glass, very thick in places, and combined with simple curves, giving a pleasing overall effect. As light plays through its sides it produces many shades of amber with pleasing overtones.

This is a small vase-shaped novelty. The sides, at the shoulder, are almost half an inch thick. The inside is small and straight and its capacity is minimal. It has a constricted waist with a thick base. The neck is also constricted and the rim flares widely. The latter is level but for the slight rise over the protruding lip. The round handle, with a curlicue at the top attachment, dates the piece. No really old pattern used this conceit.

The quality is good. No defects are found in the glass. The mold marks are almost invisible. The surface has a waviness which indicates that the metal, or mold, was too cold to be worked properly. It probably dates from 1940-1950.

Toy creamer: 2-part mold, 4 ounces, 2 inches tall, 1 13/16 inches wide, and 2 5/8 inches long.

This little pitcher may have been the only item made, but it well may have come in assorted colors.

97—TAPPAN

Mrs. Kamm never actually saw a piece in this attractive pattern. She mentions it briefly in *A Third Pitcher Book*, page 127, No. 187, and uses a cut from an 1894 catalog of the McKee Glass Company, of Jeannette, Pennsylvania. The cut shows a child's set of creamer, sugar, spooner, and covered butter dish. She continues its original name of TAPPAN. On page 131 of *A Fifth Pitcher Book*, she raises an interesting speculation as to the name's origin. The Aetna Glass and Manufacturing Company, of Bellaire, Ohio, was in business from 1880 to 1891 and produced some fine pressed glass. The company's president was named Tappan. Did he later become associated with McKee, and was the pattern named for him?

These toy creamers are occasionally found in shops today in amber as well as clear. They are quoted at high prices. The amber are priced between $6 and $12. (Why? It is neither that old nor that scarce.) The sets are nice for use on sick-room trays.

The body is cylindrical with vertical sides which curve under to a narrow waist. On the lower curved part of the body is a band of convexed columns, rounded over at top and bottom. Above these and below the rim, is a band of highly beveled, octagonal buttons with small pointed pyramids at their corners. Between the two are two bands of highly beveled squares—one with plain flattop and the other covered with minute round beading. Mrs. Kamm, not having seen the pattern, called this feature "fine diamond point." The figurework is arranged in vertical tiers.

The waist is narrow, short, and plain. The base flares and is domed underneath. The rim is plain and level but rises slightly to form a thumbgrip. The handle is six-sided and has a row of well-spaced dewdrops down the front and back facets. The glass is brilliant and sparkling. The amber color is an attractive shade and very desirable. The mold marks are high, and those on the handle are sharp.

Toy creamer: 3-part mold, 4 ounces, 2 3/4 inches high, 1 7/8 inches wide, and 2 7/8 inches long.

Probably the four known pieces of the table

93

95

98

94 - 1

96

Bottom
98

94 - 2

97

setting were the only items made in this toy size. If standard sizes were made, they are not now known to me.

98—THE SUMMIT

This tall tankard pitcher is an excellent example of pressed glass at its best. Kamm, in *A Sixth Pitcher Book*, page 22 No. 29 and Plate 40, covered the pattern and continued the company name, THE SUMMIT. In Plate 40 an 1895 advertisement by the Thompson Glass Company of Uniontown, Pennsylvania, is shown. It illustrates a four-piece table set and a tankard water pitcher similar to that shown here. Mrs. Kamm had not seen a piece of the pattern and made her drawing from this advertisement. The pattern is shown here again to discuss measurements, quality of glass, and workmanship, and for comparison with the following pattern—*STAR CITY*.

The piece is widest at the lower portion where all the figurework appears. The sides taper in to the rim. The large expanse of plain glass above the figures is not marred by etching or color flashing. The glass is clear and flawless.

The figured band at the bottom of the bowl is 3 1/4 inches wide. It is composed of eight elongated lobes in high convex relief. The top and bottom of each is arched and the sides are straight and vertical. The figures are framed above and below by deep bevels. These form scalloped lines. Each of the thick lobes has a quatrefoil deeply intaglio pressed into its surface. Each has a four-leaf clover in the center. Extending from the interstices in the clover leaf are four fern fronds. (This identical quatrefoil figure is used in combination with other figures on *STAR CITY*, which follows.)

The piece sits on a circular ringbase. The bottom is recessed and has a five-part figure similar to the quatrefoil impressed there. (See drawing of bottom.)

The applied handle is perfectly crafted. It is flattened until it is twice as wide as it is thick. The lower blob is very large and flows in all directions. The upper tab is flattened, turned under, and left plain. The handle portion of the rim has three low, wide scallops, each of which is flanked by small pointed ones. The spout soars high. The lime-soda glass is of top quality. The gaffer earned his title. The mold marks show only at the base and indistinctly there.

Tankard water pitcher: 4-part mold, 3 5/8 pounds, 10 3/16 inches tall, 5 inches wide, and 6 9/16 inches long.

It is too bad pieces of this pattern show up so seldom.

99—*STAR CITY*

This is a beautiful pattern not previously covered in our American glass literature. Because of two unusual types of stars in the pattern, I have named it *STAR CITY* for the pleasant Arkansas city of that name.

This individual creamer is somewhat drum-shaped and with a smalller diameter at its middle than at the top or bottom. The sides are filled from above the waist to the rim with alternating wide and narrow vertical panels. On either side and beneath the lip are wide panels. In the center of each is a round concave thumbprint. Above and below this is a quatrefoil composed of four fern fronds and a four-leaf clover. There is a narrow panel at each quadrant which contains two square stars in the lower two-thirds and is left plain in the upper portion. Each star is made up of faceted fine-cut.

The back three-fourths of the rim is level and finely scalloped. The front is plain. It curves up and out to form a dainty lip. The handle is applied, and it attests to the high degree of skill and workmanship achieved here. A large, plain escutcheon was left for the handle attachment. This eliminated openings under the attachment that could catch and hold dirt. In addition, the handle is beautifully proportioned and executed. There is a large lower blob from which the handle tapers rapidly to a delicate upper attachment. It is round in cross section and small, though adequate for such a small pitcher.

The body cuts in sharply to the wide waist at the base of the bowl. Below this is a ringed base. There is a 24-ray star on the flat bottom, with alternating long and short rays.

Nothing is known of where or by whom this piece was made. The quatrefoils on *STAR CITY* and THE SUMMIT (preceding) are the same. The two patterns were in all probability designed by the same person and produced at the same factory. The glass and workmanship of both patterns are of superior quality. This piece appears to be of the 1905-1915 period, or perhaps a little earlier, and probably came from the upper Ohio Valley. This was never merely production ware. It is quality glass.

Toy creamer: 4-part mold, 5 ounces, 2 3/4 inches tall, 2 1/2 inches wide, and 3 5/8 inches long.

This individual creamer is the only item in the pattern known to the writer. Doubtless, the rest of the miniature four-piece table set was made, as well as the standard one. If the manufacturer followed the usual practice of the period, as many as 125 items may have been made.

100—CHILD'S SWIRL

This individual creamer is another of the numerous swirl patterns. No attempt will be made to differentiate between them as it would merely create further chaos. It is the creamer from a child's table set of sugar bowl, butter dish, and spoonholder. These small sets were also popular for use on sick-room trays, and for individuals at home, or at hotels. Many patterns carried such four-piece sets in the period of 1890-1910. Today they are often seen in the shops, bring fair prices, and are actively collected.

This creamer sits on a high ringbase, which has a dome underneath. The waist is constricted. From the waist to just below the rim, the entire body is covered with convex ribs, which swirl from right to left. At the top they are rounded over and arched. The rim and lip are severely plain. Below the lip is a poorly pressed four-lobed fan of tapered and rounded ribs.

The handle is molded but intended to simulate an applied one. It is round in cross section. The quality of the piece is only fair. The mold marks show distinctly but are not sharp. The rim is rough and unfinished. The glass is clear but not sparkling.

Toy creamer: 3-part mold, 5 ounces, 2 3/4 inches tall, 2 1/8 inches wide, 3 3/8 inches long.

No pieces other than the four-piece table setting are known in this pattern. Complete sets, including plates, compotes, etc., were sometimes made in these miniature sets and could have occurred in this case. (See also the swirled creamer described next.)

101—SWIRL WITH DEWDROPS

Compare this individual creamer with the preceding one. A glance shows the resemblance. The rim, lip, handle, base, size, and quality are identical. They very likely were designed by the same artisan and pressed by the same glass house. This pattern is the more pleasing of the two. The swirls are wider and go from left to right. They are highly rounded with wide arched tops and narrow down to sharp points which wrap around the waist. Each convex rib is outlined by a graduated row of dewdrops, decreasing in size from top to bottom.

Millard, in *Goblets II*, Plate 79-1, shows a goblet similar to this pattern and calls it BEADED SWIRL. Lee, in *Victorian Glass*, Plate 41-1, shows three pieces of the same pattern as the goblet Millard shows. She, too, calls it BEADED SWIRL. Kamm, in *A Third Two Hundred Pattern Glass Pitchers*, page 95, No. 142, shows a pattern with beads, swirls, and a band of cabochons at the rim. She also calls her pattern BEADED SWIRL.

Since this particular pattern has not been named, I have called it *SWIRL WITH DEWDROPS*. There is a plain 1/4-inch band below the saddled rim which makes deep inverted U-shaped dips into the tops of the swirls. It is not particularly attractive.

Toy creamer: 3-part mold, 4 ounces, 2 3/4 inches tall, 2 1/8 inches wide, and 3 3/8 inches long.

The manufacturer is unknown, and only the four-piece table settings have been seen. The sugar bowl has no handles and would be mistaken for a toothpick holder unless seen with the creamer.

102—MINIATURE GRAPE

This dainty toy must have made small children happy, for it has a great deal of charm. It is one of the smallest pressed glass creamers the author has seen and is shown in its actual size in the illustration. I have, however, seen a pressed imitation cut glass sugar bowl, with two handles, no larger than a medium-sized thimble. The latter is owned by Ellis Doyle Herron, former director of the Museum of Science and Natural History, Little Rock, Arkansas.

The creamer sits on a thick, heavy round base, which is slightly hollowed out and plain underneath. Each side of the body has a symmetrical grape design. The vines spiral round each other like the serpents of a caduceus. The bunches of grapes are natural looking, rounded, and stand out distinctly. The tendrils look natural except that some of them coil in the wrong direction. The leaves could be those of the sweet gum tree (Liquidambar Styraciflua) or of the English ivy, but they bear no resemblance to a grape leaf. The design, nevertheless, is pleasing and attractive.

The rim carries no ornamentation and rises slightly in front to form a broad lip. The handle is six-sided, plain, compact, and has a thumbgrip on the top. Inside the bowl and near the top is a slight ledge which arches up on either side and dips down slightly below the lip. It evidently held a lid in bygone days. The only creamers the author has seen with this type of ledge have been authenticated Sandwich pieces. No such claim is made for this piece though the coincidence is interesting—and possibly suggestive. The quality of the glass and the workmanship of the piece are excellent. It is clear and free of bubbles.

Toy creamer: 2-part mold, 2 ounces, 2 3/16 inches tall, 1 7/16 inches wide, and 2 1/4 inches long.

Nothing is known of the manufacturer. It probably dates from 1875-1885 but could be of a later period. This enticing pattern stimulates one to speculate on a possible counterpart in a standard-sized creamer. Would it be as dainty?

This pattern has not been listed before in American glass literature. No other pieces are known, though a four piece table setting was probably made.

103—FANCY LOOP

This pattern was described by Mrs. Kamm in *A Second Two Hundred Pattern Glass Pitchers*, page 97. She had not actually seen it but used a cut from the 1897 catalog of the Heisey Glass Company of Newark, Ohio. It is illustrated here to show a line drawing, dimensions, and pattern variations since the figurework is sometimes reversed to fit the shape.

This piece does not bear the Heisey trademark. It varies greatly from the creamer shown by Mrs. Kamm, and it also differs from some forms of the pattern shown on Plate 31 of Kamm's *A Seventh Pitcher Book*. The pattern of this piece is the same as that of the toothpick holder and molasses can. The patterns of the cruet and butterdish are also different. The remaining pieces in the plate are the same as on the creamer in *A Second Two Hundred Pattern Glass Pitchers*, wherein the name was first applied. It comes in clear with gold trim and possibly in custard, emerald green, and clear flashed with ruby.

To avoid confusion with the variants made by Heisey Glass Company, the pattern should be compared with the pattern of Northwood's CRYSTAL QUEEN, as shown in Kamm's *A Sixth Pitcher Book*, page 36, Plate 25. The patterns are sufficiently alike to be used together. Both manufacturers ordinarily used a trademark, but this piece was produced about 1897, and Heisey did not adopt a trademark until 1902.

The quality of the glass is brilliantly clear and sparkling. It is of superior quality and heavy for its size. The base has a thin rim to sit on, and a plain 16-ray star is impressed underneath. The body is covered by loops that continue around the creamer, forming teardrop-shaped spaces. They contain cross hatching which results in five highly raised and flattopped squares in each loop. The crosshatching and rim are gilded, with the tops of the squares left clear. This makes the latter appear as brilliant jewels. Most of the creamer was also left clear. The loops are formed by a beveled ridge which is fine-toothed on its crest. The spaces between the loops are filled with a motif of cane design.

The rim is scalloped in wide arches to conform to the tops of the loops. The scallops in turn are crenulated. There is a 1/4-inch plain band below the rim which is slightly raised. The creamer appears rather squat. The handle appears to be applied but actually is pressed—clearly showing the mold mark. It is tiny, round in cross section, and provides a poor grip even for such a small creamer as this is.

Individual creamer: 3-part mold, 5 ounces, 2 1/4 inches tall, 2 5/8 inches wide, and 3 1/2 inches long.

It came in many items, some of them out of the ordinary. Among them were: individual, hotel, and standard sugar and creamer; bar tumbler; champagne; claret; sherry glass; punch bowl and glass (cup); toothpick holder; butter dish; spooner; individual and master salt; many square berry bowls; many sizes of nappies; handled jelly dish; large and medium-sized cracker jars; tankard water pitcher; cruet; molasses can; celery vase; tall slender vase (for drugstore straws?); and a handled triangular nappy. Although the list contains many different drinking glasses, no mention is made of ordinary tumblers or goblets. A goblet as a rule is the item most likely to be found in a pattern.

104—MEDALLION SUNBURST

This small creamer shows the same unique handle as found on INTAGLIO FLEUR-DE-LIS in this book and on V-IN-HEART in Kamm's *A Sixth Pitcher Book*, page 26, No. 39 (also in this book). These similar handles and patterns could well have been designed by the same artist. They appear to be contemporary.

The above name is given by Millard in his *Goblets II*, Plate 114-3. He says it is a product of

99

100

101

102

103

104

the 1880s. One should be careful of the tricky nomenclature used by Dr. Millard to name this pattern MEDALLION SUNBURST, because he calls a much different pattern by the inverted name of SUNBURST MEDALLION in Plate 52-3, of the same book. Metz, in *Early American Pattern Glass*, pages 228-29, No. 2590, shows a goblet in MEDALLION SUNBURST. (Mrs. Metz also shows DAISY AND BUTTON WITH FINECUT PANELS as No. 2590 on pages 224-25.)

The manufacturer's name for this pattern has not been established, though some of the ware is of recent origin. From the large number of such creamers found on the market today, plus their "new look," it is likely they are being produced today.

The glass is brilliantly clear, and the many facets of the pattern make it sparkle in the light. It is of fine quality soda-lime glass and is well finished. The body has five multiple circles, each of which surrounds a faceted, radial sunburst. The inner circle is filled with fine rib and the outer with small diamond point. Where the circles overlap they form an oval filled with large diamond point. The base is hexagonal. The top is octagonal and is formed by eight plain, vertical panels which make up the upper third of the body. Each panel arches over at the top to form a scallop in the rim. The lip is low and wide.

The unusual handle imitates an applied one, but it is not. There is a large blob at the bottom attachment which tapers to a small round handle. The latter curls up, inward, and down, till it returns to the basal attachment. It has a row of small thumbprints on either side. The handle is terete with a flattened top for a thumbgrip. The lower attachment is a large blob which fits exactly into the center of one of the medallions. The base is flat, has no ring to sit on, and contains an 18-ray impressed star.

Individual creamer: 4-part mold, 8 ounces, 3 1/8 inches tall, 2 1/2 inches wide, and 3 5/8 inches long.

The pattern shown here is similar to that of the small creamer STAR-IN-BULL'S-EYE shown in Kamm's *Two Hundred Pattern Glass Pitchers*, page 100, No. 145. It is even more like the goblet shown in Millard's *Goblets*, Plate 99-1, where it is also called STAR-IN-BULL'S-EYE. It is different from them, however, as they, in turn, differ from each other.

105—TEPEE

Mrs. Kamm, in *A Second Two Hundred Pat-*

tern Glass Pitchers, page 78, named and described this pattern. S. T. Millard, in *Goblets II*, Plate 128-4, shows a goblet in the pattern and calls it NEMESIS, with no explanation of his reasons therefor.

Do not confuse this imitation cut glass pattern with the tall angular pattern which Millard shows in *Goblets*, Plate 23-1, and also calls TEEPEE. Mrs. Kamm, in *An Eighth Pitcher Book*, page 11, No. 17, named the Millard pattern WIGWAM since she had already designated the pattern shown here as TEPEE. (The original name for Millard's TEEPEE and Kamm's WIGWAM has been found. It is shown in the present book under its restored original name of ALHAMBRA.)

Mrs. Kamm used a tall round creamer to illustrate this pattern. The petite oval individual creamer shown here seems too charming for the utilitarian purpose of serving cream. The piece is longer from lip to handle than it is wide. It would hold cream for coffee, but not for cereal too—unless the user was slenderizing at the time. It sits on a flat oval base which is slightly hollowed out underneath and has an oval-shaped 22-ray star impressed therein.

The body is covered with an imitation cut glass effect. Bands of cutwork half an inch wide sag from near the rim to the base. As they cross each other they form large diamonds, each filled with strawberry diamonds. Outside the bands a suspended fan is found underneath each apex, and larger erect fans fill each valley. On the steep inclines the bands are filled with diamond point. At the bottom of each valley the bands split into either two or three narrow bands—depending on the shape of the article. Some of the latter are topped with fine rib, and alternate ones with diamond point.

The small round handle is pressed but simulates an applied one, with the large blob at the bottom attachment. The back three-fourths of the rim is covered with low, wide, and even scallops. The front rises gently, then dips low for a lip. There is a narrow plain band below the rim which probably was gilded on some pieces.

It is quality ware and beautifully fire polished. A close scrutiny is necessary to find the mold marks. The manufacturer is not known. It probably dates from 1890-1900.

Individual creamer: 4-part mold, 5 ounces, 2 5/16 inches tall, 1 15/16 inches wide, and 4 1/4 inches long.

I know of only two small creamers and a goblet in this pattern. Many other items almost certainly were produced.

This particular creamer was presented to the author's collection by the Paul G. Snow family of North Little Rock, Arkansas.

106—THUMBPRINT BLOCK

A tall cylindrical creamer in this pattern was illustrated and described on page 57, No. 67, of *A Fifth Pitcher Book* by Minnie Watson Kamm. In *A Seventh Pitcher Book*, page 19, No. 35, she describes an especially tall tankard creamer with two rows of thumbprint block around the lower part of the body. The short, squatty creamer shown here is as a "toad" to the "giraffe" just mentioned or the exceedingly tall pitcher (also pictured). The first, third, and fourth of these pitchers are definitely of the same pattern. The extremely tall tankard may not have come from the same factory, but it probably did. In any event, they match and can be used together.

Mrs. Kamm assigned the name THUMB-PRINT BLOCK to the pattern, and it is descriptive. It is a tricky title, however, and must be used with care to avoid confusion with a much older aristocrat—BLOCK WITH THUMBPRINT. The latter is of early flint glass and of an entirely different pattern, though the motif is the same.

We have here for description the small creamer, the standard creamer, and two much taller pitchers of the pattern. All four are in my collection. The individual creamer is hassock-shaped, with a cup handle and tiny lip. It sits on a wide flat ringbase. Underneath the base, a large, six-petaled flower is impressed. (See drawing of bottom.) Three of the pitchers have this design, but it is missing on the tankard.

The midriff bulges in the small creamer and is completely covered by three horizontal bands of beveled blocks. The standard creamer (with straight sides) has six rows; the tankard two rows; and the very tall pitcher twelve. There are twelve to fifteen blocks to each band. All blocks are identical and in tiers. The flat surface of each block carries a somewhat square thumbprint.

There is a plain band at the rim of the individual creamer. The latter is level and rises just enough in front to form a "skimpy" lip. On the tankard, however, the lip soars high and is indeed something to see.

The pressed handle on the small creamer is round, small, and simulates an applied one. Its curves are not attractive. The others have beautiful applied handles. The small handle is a type found on punch and custard cups, but seldom encountered on pitchers.

The lime-soda glass is of excellent quality. It is clear, brilliant and beautifully fire-polished. There are no defects or discoloration. The manufacturer is unknown. It probably was made between 1885 and 1895. It is difficult to locate mold marks.

Individual creamer: 3-part mold, 6 1/2 ounces, 2 3/16 inches tall, 3 1/4 inches wide, and 4 3/8 inches tall.

Standard creamer, straight sides: 3-part mold, 1 pound, 5 3/4 inches tall, 3 1/16 inches wide, and 4 9/16 inches long.

Tall tankard, applied handle, creamer: no mold marks show, 1 1/8 pounds, 8 1/8 inches tall, 3 1/2 inches wide, and 4 1/8 inches long.

Tall pitcher: ?-part mold, 1 13/16 pounds, 9 1/8 inches tall, 2 13/16 inches wide, and 4 3/4 inches long.

With four pitchers known to have been made in the pattern, it is possible a wide range of items was produced.

107—HEART WITH THUMBPRINT

This probably ranks next to FEATHER as the pressed glass pattern most in demand. It is hard to understand the great popularity of either pattern, for we have patterns of finer quality and of far superior designs. HEART WITH THUMB-PRINT probably has a sentimental appeal in its symbolization of an imprint left on someone's heart. The pattern comes in clear and emerald green glass—plain and gilded. Miniature pieces of the set are much more plentiful than those of standard size.

Kamm, in *A Second Two Hundred Pattern Glass Pitchers*, page 102, described and named the pattern. She had no knowledge at that time of the manufacturer and did not know it came in colors. By the time her *A Fifth Pitcher Book* appeared, she knew it was made by the Tarentum Glass Company, of Tarentum, Pennsylvania, as their pattern for 1898-1899. She later obtained a small advertisement showing the rose bowl, cup, and individual creamer. The makers called it COLUMBIA, but almost every glass house put out a pattern with that title. Production of the pattern must have continued for some time after 1899, for pieces are still plentiful and comparatively inexpensive.

In *Victorian Glass*, page 59, Plate 23-2, Ruth Webb Lee gives a short write-up. She illustrates a goblet, berry bowl, and jelly dish and lists other articles. Millard, in *Goblets*, Plate 63-3, shows a goblet and assigns it the name BULL'S EYE IN HEART. He says it was produced in the 1870s and comes in clear, dark green, and blue. (We know it was first made in 1898, and what he called *bull's eyes* are, in reality, thumbprints.)

The main motif consists of large beveled hearts standing on their apexes. Three of them encircle the body. They reach from the base to a short distance from the rim. The surface of each heart is plain except for the concave thumbprint. The spaces separating the hearts resemble somewhat inverted V's, and extend from base to rim. Each V is filled with small hexagonal buttons which have been fire polished until they are almost dewdrops. In the valleys of the upside down V's, are beveled triangles, each of which has a round thumbprint impressed therein.

It rests on a wide almost imperceptible ringbase and is quite stable. Underneath is a hollowed out space just sufficient to form the ring at the perimeter. On the base a large 20-ray hobstar, in low relief, has been rather poorly impressed. (See cut of bottom.) Around the body, which is slightly constricted at the neck, is an irregular band just below the rim. This was often gilded. The rim is uneven, with wide sweeping scallops over the hearts, and these are crenated. Between them are very narrow inverted V-shaped scallops. The rim is rounded on top, arches up and then dips into a narrow lip.

The handle is small, round, and imitates an applied one. It deceives no one. The mold marks show plainly but are neither high nor sharp. The glass is of fine quality, and the green is a pleasing shade. A portion of the piece is fire polished too highly, and the handle not at all.

Individual creamer: 3-part mold, 6 ounces, 2 1/2 inches tall, 2 9/16 inches wide, and 3 5/8 inches long.

The following articles are known to have been made in the pattern: individual creamer, sugar bowl, butter dish, and spoonholder; standard creamer, sugar bowl, butter dish, and spoonholder; tumbler; water pitcher; 6-inch plate; 10-inch plate; berry bowl; sauce dish; cup; large rose bowl; individual, squatty rose bowl; wine; 6-inch bowl; tall vase; cordial; syrup jug; cruet; salt and pepper shakers; goblets; and handled jelly dish.

108—QUIXOTE

Millard, in *Goblets II*, Plate 89-2, shows a goblet in this pattern and calls it QUIHOTE (*sic*). He thought it was of the 1880s and says the flat surfaces are sometimes gilded or flashed with ruby.

Minnie Watson Kamm, in *A Sixth Pitcher Book*, page 38, No. 84, Plate 51, lower left, calls it TARENTUM'S HARVARD. She had not actually seen the pattern, but used a small 1898-1899 advertisement of the Tarentum Glass Company of Tarentum, Pennsylvania. The company called the pattern HARVARD. She made no drawing but continued the original name of the pattern by adding Tarentum's.

There are now three pressed glass patterns with the name HARVARD. There is also an expensive pattern of cut glass with the same title. This causes confusion, especially when the pattern is bought by mail. Dr. Millard's title has no duplicate in pressed glass, so I am using the name he supplied—with a minor change in orthography.

I have a small creamer and an open sugar bowl without handles in the pattern. The sugar is considerably larger than the creamer though they belong to the same set. Both pieces are squatty and are about midway between the standard and individual items in size. A half-inch band about the top and rim was originally gilded but is now worn off. This left plain still another band of the same width just above the figure-work.

The piece sits on a narrow low ringbase. It is hollowed out slightly underneath and has a round 24-ray star impressed there.

The waist is short on the creamer and is filled with a single narrow row of sharp diamond point. On the sugar, the band of diamond point is half an inch above the waist, and the latter is left plain.

Covering the lower half of the body is a wide convex bulge in high relief. This is cut into six segments by deep V-shaped slashes extending the full height of the bulge. On the crest of each segment is a 3/8-inch band of small sharp diamond point. At the top of the bulge is a high ridge cut by closely placed U-shaped slashes. Above it is a narrow band of sharp diamond point, similar to that at the waist. The upper half of the body above the figure-work has straight vertical sides to the rim.

The rim is not attractive. There is a large, wide scallop above the handle attachment which serves no useful purpose. The sides are level and covered by small even scallops. The front of the rim rises and pushes forward slightly to form the lip. The handle is small, has six sides, and is not remarkable. The quality of the glass is fairly good. There are no bubbles or discolorations, but there also is no brilliance. The mold marks are not fire polished off. The open sugar weighs eleven ounces.

Small creamer: 3-part mold, 8 ounces, 3 inches tall, 3 1/16 inches wide, and 3 15/16 inches long.

105

106-2

106-1

Bottom
106

106-3

106-4

107

Bottom
107

108

The only pieces known to have been made are: small open sugar bowl, small creamer, standard spoonholder, standard creamer, and a goblet. One would expect other items.

109—QUARTERED BLOCK

Mrs. Kamm described a medium-sized creamer (3 inches high) and gave it this name in *A Third Two Hundred Pattern Glass Pitchers*, page 96, No. 145. We now know who made the pattern. At the time she described it, she knew of a huge creamer 6 inches long. This is the individual creamer in the same pattern.

This little fellow is oval-shaped and squatty. It is longer than it is wide. Three bands composed of blocks standing on their corners encircle the body. The upper and lower rows are filled with uniform, small diamond point. The top row tapers off thin toward the top and the bottom tapers off similarly to the base. The blocks in the middle row are scored through the center by three grooves which result in quartering of each block—hence the name. Above the squares is a band of impressed fans, each of which is nestled between two blocks. The same relative positions are flat and plain at the base.

There is a plain band below the saddled rim. It sweeps up gently to a narrow but attractive lip. The handle is plain and round and is an excellent imitation of an applied handle—though the mold marks show. The base is oval, long, and contains a large deeply impressed 20-ray star. The quality and workmanship are superior. It is brilliant, clear, and free from defects.

Small creamer: 2-part mold, 5 ounces, 2 3/8 inches tall, 2 inches wide, and 4 inches long.

The pattern was put out as "NO. 24 WARE," by the George A. Duncan's Sons Company, of Washington, Pennsylvania, but, unfortunately, we do not know the date of the catalog. (They were seldom dated.) The glass appears to be of the period 1880-1890. The following pieces were made: hotel creamer, hotel sugar, 8-inch plate, icecream tray, 7-ounce syrup, horseradish with lid, ice tub, 1/2 pint tankard, and pint tankard. Undoubtedly other pieces were also made. The plate in this pattern could easily be mistaken for a number of other patterns.

110—PRISM AND DIAMOND BAND

This creamer is shown because Mrs. Kamm had not seen a piece of this pattern and had to draw and describe it from an old catalog. (See her *A Third Two Hundred Pattern Glass Pitchers*, page 50, No. 69, wherein she calls the pattern by one of the original company names—CENTRAL 438.) The latter is not descriptive and the second company name, STAR AND DIAMONDS, would have been more meaningful. Samples of the pattern were sent to the San Francisco Exposition in 1881. The creamer has a great deal more grace, charm, and refinement than is shown in the old cut. Compare the drawing here with that of Mrs. Kamm and you will note it is a lovely pattern. Thank goodness it has not been reproduced.

S. T. Millard, in *Goblets*, Plate 100-2, shows a goblet in the pattern and calls it by the above name. The author is not inclined to change nomenclature unless it adds materially to ease of classification. There are already four names for this pattern.

Josephine Jefferson, in her *Wheeling Glass* first edition, page 84, has a full-page reproduction of an early advertisement by the Central Glass Company, of Wheeling, West Virginia. It shows that eighteen items were manufactured in this pattern, starting from about 1875. (We now know many other items were made.) It was called STAR AND DIAMONDS, or 438 PATTERN. (See *American Antique Journal* for an article on the pattern.)

Kamm, in *A Seventh Pitcher Book*, page 65, No. 131, and Plate 86, shows a pitcher in a similar pattern made by the Imperial Glass Company of Bellaire, Ohio. The motif is so similar it could be confused with this pattern or combined with it.

The quality of the metal is superb for soda-lime glass, but it has no resonance. It is brilliantly clear, sparkling, has a mirrorlike polish, and no bubbles, discolorations, hair, or wavy lines. The fire polish almost removed the mold marks, but some can be seen faintly on the base.

The body of this tall, slender creamer is somewhat bell-shaped. The primary motif is a band of twelve large diamonds around the body. Each is outlined by sharp-ridged flutes which in turn form four-point stars between the diamonds. The rays of the stars taper to sharp points. Eleven of the diamonds are filled with large diamond point. The one at the lower handle attachment is left plain. Mitred into these diamonds are twelve flat panels above and a like number below. The upper ones extend to the rim—the lower ones to the bottom of the body. In each instance the flat panels are bent at an angle at both top and bottom of the diamonds. This controls the shape of the body and is evident in the illustration.

The rim is saddled and has a thick ring encircling it. It rises slightly at the back for the handle attachment. In front it dips slightly to break the upward sweep. The lip is high and graceful. The applied handle is well proportioned and beautifully shaped. It is thicker at the top than at the bottom. The bottom tab is turned up and instead of the usual tooling into horizontal bars, is tooled into an inverted tree with a distinct bole and nine outspread branches. No similar tab has come to the writer's attention.

The tall stem is double-knopped and has nine flat panels which begin just below the top knop and extend over the lower one. They end in a raised shelf of nine sides which sits atop the base. Above the top knop the piece arches out sharply to form the bottom of the bowl. The base is round, plain, and rather flat. Underneath, it is plain and domed just enough to give a good bearing around its outer edge.

Standard creamer: 3-part mold, 15 ounces, 6 3/8 inches tall, 3 1/8 inches wide, and 5 1/2 inches long.

Other items known to have been made in the pattern are: eight different types of high covered compotes; three low covered compotes; water pitchers in two sizes; salt and pepper shakers; covered sugar bowl; spoonholder; covered butter dish; 4- and 5-inch, open nappies; 5-, 6-, and 7-inch covered nappies; odd shaped pickle dish; 7-, 8-, and 9-inch, octagonal relish dishes; 7- and 8-inch round cheese plates, and goblet.

With two water pitchers known in the pattern, one would expect to find tumblers and perhaps a water tray. It would not be surprising if one also found bowls, celery vases, wines, cordials, decanters, toothpick holders, and other items.

This pattern was in production for at least fifteen years, and pieces should not be too scarce. It is a beautiful pattern.

111—JEWELLED PENDANTS

This large schooner-shaped creamer is in a pattern seldom seen today. Though too many conflicting motifs were mixed on the piece it still has some allure.

S. T. Millard, in *Goblets II*, Plate 133-3, shows a goblet and gives it the name used here. He says it comes in clear only and is a product of the eighties. In *Victorian Glass*, Ruth Webb Lee shows a drawing of this creamer (Plate 79, No. 10) where she shows odds and ends of pressed glass which might be found in other items. On page 247, she mentions a sugar bowl and says its ornate stem is hollow. She does not name the pattern. The writer

recently was able to add this creamer to his collection from a shop in Conway, Massachussets. Soon thereafter a small open compote, 6 inches wide and 5 inches tall, was seen in a shop in Arkadelphia, Arkansas. The knowledge that the creamer, sugar bowl, compote, and goblet were made lends credence to the belief other items may have been produced.

The tall thick odd-shaped stem of this creamer is unique. Nothing similar is known on other pressed glass stemware. It has fifteen concaved flutes which run its full length. They taper out from a round shelf on the base to the bottom of the body. It is 1 inch thick at the base and 1 1/2 inches thick where it joins the bowl. Mrs. Lee mentions that the stem is hollow. On this particular creamer and the compote, the upper end of the stem is hollow for only 1/4 inch. Between the round shelf on the base and the edge of the base proper is an unusual arrangement of long sharply tapered teardrops. They are arranged in pairs, the edges of each pair being contiguous. This, too, is unique in pressed glass. The base is slightly domed underneath.

The lower zone of the body has no decoration. The upper two-thirds is covered by a band of ornate figurework 2 inches wide. The design is an imbrication (*i.e.* an overlapping of the edges) similar to that used with tile or shingles. Below the rim is a band of twenty-one well raised and rounded raindrops. Below these are three rows of fans which alternate with two rows of shields, both fans and shields appearing to be draped. Each fan is composed of four highly faceted figures. The shields are well rounded over.

The back half of the rim is level and evenly scalloped. It follows the contour of the raindrop band. The scalloping shows as a faint mold mark under the lip. The front half of the rim rises slightly, and its scallops broaden into the narrow lip. The handle is roughly hexagonal and on either side there are ten large highly raised evenly spaced dewdrops. The quality of the glass is good, but the workmanship is only average.

Standard creamer: 3-part mold, 15 ounces, 5 5/8 inches tall, 3 5/8 inches wide, and 5 1/8 inches long.

The manufacturer's name is unknown. It probably dates from the 1875-1895 period.

112—*SHINGLES*

The imbrication motif used here is almost identical with that of JEWELLED PENDANTS.

So many pressed glass patterns were manufactured, designers and artisans were hard put to find a new and original motif. This design seems to have been copied verbatim from the dictionary.

The standard creamer is entirely covered by a design of overlapping shingles. The sides of the body are straight and almost vertical. Bands of fans, each fan containing five faceted prisms, alternate with bands of shields of the same shape. The shields have flat surfaces but are rounded on the edges. Both fans and shields stand erect. At the bottom of the bowl, the sides round in to a rather narrow waist.

Below the waist the base flares to form a stable foundation shaped like a truncated cone. The base carries the same pattern as the body, but upside down. There is a plain high, rounded dome underneath.

The rim is level and plain over the rear three-fourths. Here, where scallops would have been simple, they were omitted. The front fourth of the rim is higher and forms an almost vertical lip.

The handle is round, adequate, and comfortable to use. There is a rough mold mark, outlining a rectangle, on top of the handle. It may have been intended for a thumbgrip.

This piece probably dates from the period of 1870 to 1890. It was production ware with a lost opportunity for making a quality product. It also contains bubbles. The glass is not too clear and is not brilliant. A mold mark shows plainly on the handle, but elsewhere they are obscured by the nature of the design. This is soda-lime glass "at work."

Standard creamer: 3-part mold, 13 ounces, 5 3/8 inches tall, 3 1/4 inches wide, and 4 5/8 inches long.

The manufacturer is unknown to the writer. Since a creamer was made, one might expect a sugar bowl, butter dish, spoonholder, and perhaps a goblet. Other items are probable.

Since this pattern has not previously been named or described in our literature on pressed glass, I am assigning it the above name.

113—GRAINED SPRING

This creamer dates from the era when manufacturers thought it enhanced the appearance of the glass to have plenty of engraving in addition to the figure work. The customer could take his choice of the ware, with or without the engraving, and the price would still be the same. This idea was prevalent during the 1880s and lingered on into the 1890s. The glass of this pattern is good average-quality soda-lime for everyday use. It is lighter than usual because by etching a leaf-and-berry spray around the body, not much was needed elsewhere, which allowed the glass to be thinner.

It is an attractive, moderately large creamer with ample base, ample capacity, and a large handle. The body is widest at the rim, from which the straight sides taper in slightly to just above the waist. The waist itself is narrow and has a plain round stem which is shelved above and below. Under the lip and beneath the handle is a stiff, vertical, and poorly designed grained sprig covering the mold marks. In the center of each sprig is a seven-petaled formalized flower. Above and below it is a grained figure which may or may not represent leaves and stem. (See cut.) When seen from the side, little of the pattern is visible.

The large base gives stability to the piece. It is plain and slightly domed. The only unusual features are the mold marks. On the body they are hidden by the grained sprigs, but on the base they show plainly and are twisted down the stem and onto the base (more than 1/2 inch out of plumb with those on the body).

Around the rim is a fine-toothed band, almost obliterated except in front. It gives the appearance of a cord. With better pressing it would have been attractive. The handle is commodious, roughly four-sided, and severely plain—except for small nubs at the top and bottom attachments.

Standard creamer: 2-part mold, 13 ounces, 5 3/4 inches tall, 3 1/4 inches wide, and 5 1/8 inches long.

This pattern has evidently remained unseen by other writers on pressed glass. It is rarely found in shops today and is the type of glass which antedated the tremendous output of colored glass near the turn of the century. The manufacturer is unknown. No other piece has been seen by the writer, though it may have been produced in a wide range of articles. The four-piece table setting is the most probable.

DART, a beautiful pattern described in Kamm's *A Third Two Hundred Pattern Glass Pitchers*, page 4, No. 1, shows figurework employed in the same manner as on this creamer. On DART, the only decoration is to cover the four mold marks. BEAD COLUMN, in Kamm's *A Seventh Pitcher Book*, page 12, No. 21, shows a similar device on a 3-part mold creamer. In this case the design is used on a 2-part mold piece. It was exceedingly difficult to chip a pattern into the iron mold at the edge of the seams where the pieces of

109

112

Bottom
114

110

113

114

111

Detail
Under
Lip

113

115

the mold join. If an attractive symmetrical pattern resulted, it denoted great skill on the part of the moldmaker.

114—FROSTED BLOCK

Mrs. Kamm has warned that this pattern was first put out around 1913 and has been in continuous production since. It is made by the Indiana Glass Company of Dunkirk, Indiana. Despite its extreme youth, it brings high prices in our shops—especially the colored pieces. (Only in antiques is youth anathema.)

In *Two Hundred Pattern Glass Pitchers*, Mrs. Kamm, on page 98, No. 141, describes and illustrates a stiff, ungainly milk pitcher in this pattern and assigns the above name. In *A Third Two Hundred Pattern Glass Pitchers*, page 26, No. 34, she describes and illustrates the far more attractive clear creamer. She says it is made in a disagreeable yellow-green, faint pink (sassafras), apple green, amber, yellow, and blue.

Alice Hulett Metz, in *Early American Pattern Glass*, pages 230-31, No. 2626, illustrates a square plate. She is not complimentary to the pattern and says it was made for the "dime store trade" thirty years ago. She describes it as coming in sticky pink, bilious green, and clear glass.

Marion T. Hartung, in her *Second Book of Carnival Glass*, page 42, illustrates a low rose bowl in this pattern. She says iridescent pieces were made during the Carnival Glass era of 1910 to 1922 or 1924, and that they are older than some of the shiny garish pieces we encounter. She likes the pattern and so do I.

Pieces in sassafras color show up on the market more often than the others. Why? Probably because the more attractive colors were purchased and the pink allowed to sit unwanted. While sassafras color is acceptable in tea, it is not appealing and has a pallid appearance in glass.

In the majority of pieces the blocks are grained and appear frosted. I have a clear and also a sassafras creamer with frosted blocks (grained). The creamer shown here is apple-green with the rim, lip, and top of handle opalescent. The blocks are left smooth and have a high fire polish. It is beautiful, even if new.

There are ten vertical tiers of blocks which graduate from small to large as they ascend the bowl. They are also in three horizontal rows. Each block is framed by a low raised line which leaves the face of the blocks sunken. Running horizontally and vertically between the blocks are high,

inverted, V-shaped ridges with their tops strigiled. The bowl is roughly cone-shaped.

The stem is narrow and of a height that becomes the piece. It is octagonal and spreads out to a wide shelf on the base of the bowl and a narrow one on the foot. The top of each panel is rounded. The foot slopes gently to the edge of the base, then drops vertically to the bottom. The vertical edge is finely crenulated. FERRIS WHEEL is another pattern with a similar base. Beneath, the base is slightly hollowed with a large 22-ray star impressed. The ridges between the rays have been strigiled, and they show through the foot as if on top. This is an especially attractive treatment. (See cut of bottom.)

The back half of the rim is level, rounded on top and crenulated. The rim rises high in front to an attractive lip. The top is opalescent, and this adds to the desirability of the piece. The handle is small, six-sided, and uniform in size from top to bottom. Its upper portion also is opalescent. The handle juts upward slightly, then backward, and turns at an acute angle to arch back to the body.

These pieces are well made and are of good quality lime-soda glass. An occasional small bubble is the only defect found. This piece has been fire polished until the mold marks are barely discernible.

Creamer: 2-part mold, 10 ounces, 5 inches tall, 3 3/8 inches wide, and 4 9/16 inches long.

Milk pitcher: 4-part mold, weight unknown, 5 3/4 inches tall, other measurements unknown.

The only pieces known to the writer are: milk pitcher, creamer, 6-inch square plate, 6-inch bowl, 8-inch bowl, iridescent rose bowl. Probably many other articles were made.

The motif here is almost identical with that used by the Iowa City Glass Company, and a wine glass made by the latter is illustrated in the October, 1954, *Antique Journal*, page 19. The pattern is also similar to BERLIN.

115—FAN AND STAR

This is a standard creamer in a fine old pattern, and we know something about its antecedents. In *A Fourth Pitcher Book*, pages 28-29, No. 33, Mrs. Kamm illustrates and describes this pattern from an old catalog of Challinor, Taylor and Company, of Tarentum, Pennsylvania. She calls the pattern CHALLINOR NO. 304. Her drawing is not too accurate. The pattern was produced in a large number of items—perhaps from the late 1870s through the 1880s. (Challinor, Taylor and

Company joined the huge U.S. Glass Company, of Pittsburgh in 1891.)

In *An Eighth Pitcher Book*, pages 14-15, No. 24, Mrs. Kamm again presents the pattern, this time from a catalog of the U.S. Glass Company. She calls the pattern U.S. No. 304, overlooking the fact that she had previously called it CHALLINOR NO. 304. (She was quite ill at the time.) The U.S. Glass Company produced it in opaque white glass with a baked on enamel decoration. They kept it in production only a short time before discontinuing it. Mrs. Kamm never saw a piece of the pattern.

Mrs. Lee, in *Victorian Glass*, page 211, Plate 66-3, illustrates a goblet, celery vase, and water pitcher. She calls it FAN AND STAR and I prefer this title to either of Mrs. Kamm's. Mrs. Metz, in *Early American Pattern Glass*, pages 148-149, No. 1671, calls it FAN AND STAR and illustrates a celery vase.

The creamer is large and rests on a high domed base (1 3/8-inch high). The narrow incurved waist ends in a round shelf at the bottom of the bowl and on top of the base.

The lower half of the bowl and the domed base carry identical designs. They consist of large X-shaped crosses whose points adjoin those of the next such figure. In the diamond-shaped interspaces are small intricate, four-pointed stars. The triangles between the diamonds are filled with deeply impressed fans.

The body of the creamer is inverted and bell-shaped. About the middle of the body immediately above the figurework, is an unattractive bulge which detracts from the overall design. Above it the body is plain, smooth, and tapers out. The rim is scalloped in high triangular points, each of which is slightly crenulated. This type of rim is seldom encountered. It rises sharply in front and the lip has pleasing curves.

The handle is six-sided and starkly plain. At the top is a slight bulge which gives a better thumb grip. The handle is comfortable and easy to hold. The glass is clear, brilliant, sparkling, and without defect. The mold marks are barely perceptible. It is fine quality soda-lime glass.

Standard creamer: 3-part mold, 1 pound, 6 1/4 inches tall, 3 3/4 inches wide, and 5 3/4 inches long.

The following pieces are known to have been made in the pattern: creamer, sugar bowl, butter dish, spooner, goblet, water pitcher, small bowl, high covered compote, low covered compote, and celery vase.

116—SHERATON (variant)

S. T. Millard, in *Goblets*, Plate 127-4, shows a goblet in this pattern and names it SHERATON. He says it was common in Pennsylvania, apparently was made during the 1880s, and that it came in clear, amber, and blue.

In her *Victorian Glass*, Plate 55-3, Ruth Webb Lee shows a goblet, octagonal platter, and footed sauce dish. Mrs. Kamm, in *A Third Two Hundred Pattern Glass Pitchers*, page 38, No. 49, describes a quite different creamer. Which variety came first, or where or by whom either was made is still unknown.

The handle of the creamer used by Mrs. Kamm simulated an applied one. It was round, with no thumbgrip at the top, and was less comfortable to hold. The handle is hexagonal. It has somewhat rounded corners and a thumbgrip. The base of this piece is thicker and matches the body shape better, than in Mrs. Kamm's piece. The stippled area between the beaded bands is not as wide on this variant.

These pieces probably were made in the Ohio River Valley, and there is a good possibility the Hipkins Novelty Mold Shop, of Martins Ferry, Ohio, made the molds for both (one set for each factory). MELROSE, in this book, is a good example of this practice. In its case, three sets of molds were made for as many factories. Mrs. Kamm's description suffices for the remaining details. This piece is of good quality soda-lime glass. It is clear and there is no discoloration. The mold marks are not prominent.

Standard creamer: 3-part mold, 15 ounces, 5 3/8 inches tall, 3 5/16 inches wide, and 5 inches long.

117—KNOBBY BULL'S EYE

S. T. Millard, in *Goblets*, Plate 166-3, calls this pattern KNOBBY BULL'S EYE, and the name is appropriate. It is found in bowls, goblets, sauces, water pitchers, tumblers, spooners, covered butter dishes, sugar bowls, plates, berry sets, etc.

Mrs. Metz covers the pattern as No. 2443. She says a typographical error in Millard's *Goblets* has caused endless confusion. She, therefore, calls it BULL'S EYE AND DAISY and another pattern KNOBBY BULL'S EYE. Whether she helps the confusion is questionable.

The pattern sometimes comes with the bull's eye gilded, or flashed with amber, green, purple, or red. All have gilt rims. It is a striking pattern.

The creamer is rather thick (3/16 to 1/2 inch in some places) and because of the extra thickness is heavy for its size. It is also larger than the average creamer, with a diameter of almost 4 inches. It rests on a high base above which is a narrow waist. The base itself has eight wide scallops, is plain and is domed underneath. The outside of the base has eight columns in high convex relief which extend through the waist and well up on the bowl. Each column ends in a thick rounded bulge as shown.

Above the bulges a heavy 1 1/2 inch band carries the main motif of large, round, and deeply concave eyes. Each of the latter is centered in a large hexagonal button in high relief. The button itself has ribbed, sloping sides with a steep outward thrust. These 'eyes' carry the color. The band extends around the body. Eight knobby eyes thus appear, one above each convex column. A vertical panel of faceted figures in high relief separates them and extends above and below the band of knobs to form pyramids in each case.

Except for the deep slashes, the upper third of the body is plain and has been gilded. The rim is unevenly scalloped as shown. The lip is at the highest part of the rim. It thrusts forward at a 90 degree angle and extends half an inch out from the body. The handle curves out widely and is plain, with an inside nub where the top is attached. It is somewhat larger near its base and has six panels, with the two inside panels slightly rounded.

Standard creamer: 4-part mold, 1 3/16 pounds, 5 inches tall, 4 inches wide, and 6 inches long.

The knobby bull's eyes of this pattern are similar to those of RUFFLED EYE in Kamm's *A Sixth Pitcher Book*, page 58, No. 129.

The shape as well as the size of a piece to be decorated determines the way a particular pattern will appear. The more one works with glass, in its myriad shapes and sizes, the more evident this is. An example is FROSTED EAGLE, in this book. The creamer could not be identified by its name, so a cut of the sugar bowl was shown. Only lids, of the covered pieces, could show the design. Other patterns present diverse problems in the distribution of the motif. Small pieces carried less, and large pieces more, of the design as a rule. The water pitcher of this pattern has two bands of large knobby bull's eyes. There is a single band on the creamer and other small pieces. The pitcher has six knobs to the band whereas the creamer has eight. The creamer is from a four-part mold, while the water pitcher is from a three-part mold. The water pitcher does not have the narrow waist, and its sides are straight with only a slight flare. The

contour of the creamer is anything but straight. The pitcher weighs 3 pounds, 8 ounces.

It is assumed that this pattern was manufactured about 1890-1905, but mystery still cloaks the particular glass house that produced it.

118—AURORA

This pattern is used to show a tankard creamer which has not previously been listed. It is more appealing than the other creamers and pitchers in the pattern. Mrs. Kamm wrote about the pattern a number of times and established the fact that the molds were made by the Hipkins Novelty Mold Shop, of Martins Ferry, Ohio. The pattern was manufactured as AURORA by the Brilliant Glass Company of Brilliant, Ohio, and later by its successor, the Greensburg Glass Company, of Greensburg, Ohio. In Plates 61, 62, 63 and 64 of her *An Eighth Pitcher Book*, she carried four pages from a Brilliant Glass Company catalog, which illustrated many articles in the pattern. See also her *A Second Two Hundred Pattern Glass Pitchers*, page 110; *A Fifth Pitcher Book*, page 48; *A Seventh Pitcher Book*, page 96; and *An Eighth Pitcher Book*, page 59. Mrs. Metz covered the pattern as No. 2215 and changed the title from AURORA to DIAMOND HORSESHOE.

I have been unable to identify the pattern in Dr. Millard's goblet books, though a goblet was made. In Plate 55-4, No. 2, of her *Victorian Glass*, Mrs. Lee illustrated a goblet among a number of odds and ends which she did not attempt to describe or name. The second article from the left is an "odd goblet." On page 176 she refers to it as "an unusual goblet." It is of the AURORA pattern.

Notice the BUNGALOW tankard creamer, immediately following in this book, for its striking similarity. The creamer is tall, has straight sides, and tapers to a rather narrow neck and rim. The body is big enough to hold a large supply of cream. On the base of the body are two, high, inverted, V-shaped, parallel ridges, an inch apart, which surround the body. The space between is ornamented by eight large beveled flat-topped diamonds that join at their longer points. Above the diamonds and extending to the rim are four high looping arches, each of which has a narrow band similar to the wide one below. The large inside panels are plain, smooth, and sometimes etched. On this piece they are left plain. At the top of the loops and filling the notches are narrow fan-shaped wedges.

The rim is unevenly scalloped and has a

116

117

118

119

Bottom
119

Bottom
118

120

121

Northwood

122-1

Northwood

pursed and narrow lip. The waist is wide, curved, and has no panels. The base has four large curved feet composed of six ribs which are rounded on the underside and flat on the outside. Between each two feet is a short leg made up of two rounded ribs.

A beautiful, unusual, and complex raised star is underneath the base. The center is round, flat, and smooth. From it twelve rays of raised, triangular pyramids form the figurework of the star. (See cut of bottom.) With its long and short rounded ribs surrounding the star, the bottom easily becomes the most attractive portion of the piece. (It is surprising that this happens so often.)

The handle is round, applied, and of the later type, with the large round blob at the lower attachment. The upper attachment is turned under and applied to, and over, the low figurework.

The quality of the glass is excellent. The workmanship on the creamer is inferior to what one would expect on a tankard creamer. Such pieces were difficult and expensive to make, and manufacturers lavished skill on them, as a rule, to produce a superior product. For this individual item, however, the gather of metal was too small and an imperfect impression resulted. The metal was also too cool, and hairlines and waviness resulted. The piece was not well polished, and the mold marks are therefore too prominent.

Tankard creamer: 4-part mold, 14 ounces, 6 1/8 inches tall, 3 1/8 inches wide, and 4 3/16 inches long. The following pieces are known to have been made in the pattern, coming either plain or engraved: standard creamer; tankard creamer; covered sugar; spoonholder; covered butter dish; 10-inch round bread plate; goblet; wine; tumbler; handled tumbler; 4-inch compote; pickle dish; olive dish; salt and pepper shakers; water pitcher; water tray; waste bowl; decanter with stopper; wine tray; celery vase; 6-, 7-, and 8-inch open compotes; 6-, 7-, and 8-inch covered compotes on high stems; quart pitcher; 5- and 6-inch flat square sauce dishes; and a stemmed cake stand. Perhaps other items were made.

119—BUNGALOW

Dr. Millard named this pattern in *Goblets*, Plate 24-3. He must have had a reason for calling it BUNGALOW, but it is not known to me. Mrs. Kamm, in *A Fourth Pitcher Book*, page 101, No. 124, described a cylindrical tankard creamer and complained of, but continued, the inept name. Mrs. Metz illustrates a goblet in the pattern as No.

1758. The present creamer has a different shape and also a beautiful design on the underside of the base. Mrs. Kamm's creamer had straight vertical sides which imparted an aloofness to the piece. This creamer tapers in sharply from base to neck. Above the neck it flares slightly to the rim, the back portion of which is made up of large regular scallops. The lip (and what a lip) extends so far forward that any drip would miss the table and hit the floor.

The lower part of the figurework is well impressed but becomes less distinct as it approaches the top. Four large beveled, rectangular panels with chamfered corners cover most of the body. They are separated by large, inverted V-shaped ridges. Below the panels is a band of complicated figurework simulating cut glass. Following their chamfered contour at the bottom is a band about the body with a large V-shaped ridge that has smaller similar ridges above and below. Directly below the flat panels is a beveled, horizontal bar, whose top is covered with fine rib. Below the V-shaped ridges is a large cube filled with small triangles and four beveled hexagons. Each of the latter is stamped with a daisy on top. Below the imitation cut glass design is a 1/4-inch-wide inverted, U-shaped ring around the body and then a V-shaped ring. The base flares to make the piece stable.

Under the base is a slightly hollowed out space filled with a beautiful imitation cut glass effect. This is the most attractive feature of the piece. (See cut.) There is a large cross made up of beveled cubes, each of which has a daisy impressed on its crest. Between the arms of the cross large fans are deeply impressed.

The handle is the late type, wherein the large blob is attached over a V-shaped ridge at the lower attachment. The resulting pockets are filled with dirt that cannot be reached or removed. The upper part of the handle was tooled while too cold and is not attractive. (See drawing.) The glass is of excellent quality soda-lime. The workmanship is the worst I have seen on a tankard pitcher. This type of pitcher was difficult and expensive to manufacture and almost uniformly of superior quality. This piece falls far below what usually was expected.

Tankard creamer: 4-part mold, 1 pound, 6 9/16 inches tall, 3 5/16 inches wide, and 4 9/16 inches long.

The only known articles are: two types of tankard creamers, individual creamer, standard creamer, milk pitcher, water pitcher, and goblet.

120—*ARCADIA*

This charming little creamer is almost devoid of pressed figurework. It has not previously been described in American glass literature. Edwin G. Warman, in *A Third Antiques and Their Prices*, illustrates a sugar and creamer but neither names nor describes them. This is the first time I have seen a piece of pressed glass with this color of metal. It may be of foreign manufacture; but from where? Some call it clam broth, others camphor glass, and still others paraffin glass. It is smooth and soft to the touch but has a greasy feeling. Much early flint and some frosted glass have a greasy feeling, but this piece is neither. It is translucent, but not opalescent. It is so pleasing and attractive, one wonders why more was not made.

This tall, slender piece has a small capacity—approximating that of an individual size. The bowl is shaped like an eggcup and is of about the same size. Its sides are round and smooth. The tall stem and the handle contain the only figurework, which is made up of six flat flowing panels. From the narrow stem the panels arch out to the base of the bowl. Thier upper edges are rounded. They flow out on the base to the edge of the hexagonal foot. The edge of the foot is beveled at the top and bottom. Underneath the base is a large circular dome.

The rim is slightly saddled and flows upward to a prominent lip. The glass, at the rim, is almost a quarter-inch thick. The top of the rim is gilded, but this is not seen when viewed from the side. The handle has six sides and is wider than it is thick. Its curves are pleasing.

A small formalized spray of forget-me-nots has been painted in harsh green, blue, and yellow beneath the lip and then baked on. This enamel cannot be removed.

The quality of the glass is excellent, but there are a few small bubbles in the base, and the mold marks show plainly. On the handle they are high, sharp, and punishing. There is a slight tinkle when tapped. Nothing is known about this piece—except what it chooses to tell.

Individual creamer: 3-part mold, 8 ounces, 4 13/16 inches tall, 2 9/16 inches wide, and 4 1/8 inches long.

No other items are known in the pattern. It may have been made to sell as a novelty with no counterparts.

121—ARGONAUT

This unique custard glass creamer is again used to illustrate a different and rare trademark of the Northwood Glass Company. This particular one was probably used at their Wheeling, West Virginia, plant. This plant was moved a number of times and finally wound up at Indiana, Pennsylvania. I have been unable to find a reference in our books on American glass to the script trademark of Northwood illustrated in the cut. It is also found on the PUMP creamer which follows. No other Northwood pattern is known to have used this seldom seen mark to my knowledge.

Most pressed glass fanciers are familiar with the other Northwood trademarks: (1) the underlined N; (2) the underlined N inside a raised circle; (3) the underlined N inside two raised concentric circles; and (4) the raised circle found on some items of a pattern which has other items bearing a Northwood trademark. We do not know the exact period that this script trademark was used (or any of the others for that matter), but it was certainly between 1888 and 1922 and probably was during the earliest part of the years he was in operation. Many of his later authenticated patterns carry one of the better-known trademarks (1) to (4).

Minnie Watson Kamm, in *A Fourth Pitcher Book*, page 32, No. 37, called this pattern ARGONAUT. Dr. S. T. Millard, in *Opaque Glass*, Plate 247, illustrated two oblong sauce dishes and a large, low oblong compote in custard glass. He called the pattern NORTHWOOD SHELL and declared: "It is getting scarce and much sought after." E. McCalmy Belknap, in *Milk Glass*, page 308, Plate 281, called it ARGONAUT SHELL and illustrated two tumblers and a large water pitcher in custard glass. In addition he had seen another pitcher in blue with an opalescent top.

Mrs. Kamm had a Ph.D. degree in Protozoology from the University of Illinois. Another of her great loves was American pressed glass. When she encountered both in the same specimen, as she did in this case, her genius for description and illustration took charge. Please refer to her write-up of the pattern and see how beautifully she has drawn the word picture and the actual picture of this creamer. Since I cannot compete with her, I have made no effort to describe it.

Most of the custard glass in this pattern was a deep cream or custard color. The yellow color used in this piece has a smoky gray tinge but has a clear resonance when tapped. Despite this off-color defect, the piece has a magnificent fiery opalescence when held to a bright light. It was also made in clear with opalescent top, aquamarine with blue opalescent rim and handle top, clear blue with opalescence, and deep opaque turquoise. This creamer is decorated with dark green paint and gilt.

The workmanship of the designer, moldmaker, and gaffer was excellent. The glass was equally good, but after it cooled the color was not what they expected it to be.

Standard creamer: 4-part mold, 1 pound, 4 7/8 inches tall, 3 5/16 inches wide, and 5 15/16 inches long.

Other items may have been made but only the following are known: creamer, sugar bowl, covered butter dish, water pitcher, tumbler, footed sauces, footed compote or berry bowl, small compote, and large oval compote. I also have a creamer with a translucent cream color and an opalescent top in my collection.

(On December 4, 1966, I saw a small oval custard glass pickle dish in CHRYSANTHEMUM SPRIG. It bore the Northwood script trademark.)

122—THE TOWN PUMP TROUGH

A piece of this pattern has now been found bearing the script trademark "Northwood." Many of these PUMP creamers are unmarked, and this is the first definite proof that this particular pattern is a Northwood product. (See cut.) Harry Northwood had his own factories from 1888 to 1922. He moved his factory four or five times and so produced glass in several cities. Local supplies of fuel and sand often determined the location or relocation of glass factories. Further research is needed to determine when the script trademark was used. (It probably preceded the *N* versions.) This piece was produced about the same time as ARGONAUT and both bear the script trademark.

In *A Second Two Hundred Pattern Glass Pitchers*, page 108, Minnie Watson Kamm named this pattern THE TOWN PUMP and described it. She did not know the maker. Ruth Webb Lee, in *Antique Fakes and Reproductions*, pages 116-17 and Plate 64, illustrated two versions of the pump and trough. She said the one shown here was the original and the one with the flattopped rim was a fake. She did not know the manufacturer.

Marion T. Hartung, in *Third Book of Carnival Glass*, pages 122-23, mentioned it. She said it came in purple and marigold (iridescence). This would date it between 1910 and 1922. However, the pattern could have been made earlier and continued in production until 1910 or beyond. I had always assumed the script Northwood trademark was used in the 1890s, but apparently both this and the following pattern were made after 1910.

There is a possibility Northwood made both versions. I know he made two varieties of PANELLED CHERRY creamers for I have them, and they proudly bear the same trademark. I have seen five types of PANELLED CHERRY tumblers together and all with trademarks. There is an even stronger likelihood that the molds were made at the Hipkins Novelty Mold Shop, of Martins Ferry, Ohio. The Northwoods and Hipkins were old friends from England. When Harry Northwood brought his bride to America in 1885, they stayed at the home of Stephen Hipkins till they could locate a home of their own. We also know most of the molds used by Northwood came from the Hipkins shop. A third possibility is that Hipkins may have made the same pattern for several glass houses and varied each just enough to prevent a lawsuit for patent infringement. The type pump now being made may have come from another glass factory using Hipkins molds.

Some of us remember when every town had its pump and drinking trough in front of the big store on main street. Hitching posts were scattered up and down the street. In those yesteryears water troughs were the service stations. Many a horse was traded, much of the news was passed along, and considerable business was transacted, at this meeting place—the watering trough.

The present pitcher was made to represent a pump. It was fashioned from the sturdy stump of a tree with four heavy lateral roots chopped off to form the legs. The body is covered with bold, irregular corrugations in high rounded relief which meander up the sides. Their surfaces are smooth with small high nodules placed irregularly along the crests of the undulations. It does not resemble the bole of any known American tree.

The pump handle and spout are formed as crooked limbs. The sugar bowl of this set resembles a water trough hewed by hand from a large split log.

The present creamer is a beautiful electric blue with the upper part of the rim and the top of the handle an opaque blue. Other sets were made in clear glass with white tops, green with white, yellow with white, cream with opalescent tops, and others in amber. Amethyst also may have been used. The glass is thick and heavy. Many small bubbles are scattered throughout the piece, but they are difficult to see because of the irregular surface.

Novelty creamer: 4-part mold, 1 1/8 pounds, 6 3/4 inches tall, 3 3/4 inches wide, and 4 3/8 inches long.

Trough sugar bowl: no mold marks show, 10 ounces, 2 3/16 inches tall, 2 1/2 inches wide, and 5 1/16 inches long.

This was novelty ware with no thought of practical use. On the whatnot shelf, it was a source of conversation—a vanishing art. These two items are the only ones I expect to find in the pattern.

See the following piece for another example of a novelty pump. It too was made by Northwood and probably at a later date. He started making iridized glass in 1910 and continued doing so till 1922. I also have a pump creamer in a translucent cream color with an opalescent top in my collection.

123—*IVIED PUMP*

This rare relic was found in a secondhand store at Hot Springs, Arkansas. It has been badly broken and expertly mended. This is unusual for pressed glass, which when broken is usually discarded. I still glow with pleasure at finding this piece. THE TOWN PUMP, previously illustrated, is frequently seen, but this pattern had not been covered in the glass literature and was new and intriguing to me. *IVIED PUMP* is the obvious name for it. It is similar in size and shape to THE TOWN PUMP, but the body is round, and without the corrugations and small nodules; the latter are, however, found on the handle.

I recently received a copy of Marion T. Hartung's *Third Book of Carnival Glass*, published in 1962. She shows this piece on her cover and on pages 122-23, where she calls it NORTHWOOD's PUMP. Northwood made two quite similar pumps and her title could apply to either. My coverage of this particular pump was completed several years ago, and it was titled *IVIED PUMP*. Calling one THE TOWN PUMP and the other *IVIED PUMP* should avoid confusion.

The rim is flat across the top and serrated into deep narrow scallops. It has no pouring spout and was probably made for use as a vase. The body is stippled, except where an ivy vine trails over it with fullface leaves, none of which overlap. The leaves are raised, have beveled edges, and are veined. The vines are formalized and do not look natural. They extend over the entire body. The latter tapers in a bit toward the base, then swells into a thick round bulge.

The base is round and does not have the four lateral roots for legs, as does THE TOWN PUMP. It is wide, flat, and ringed. There is a slight hollow underneath, left plain, which forms an outer ring for the piece to rest on.

The round handle is similar to that of the preceding creamer. It resembles the bent limb of a tree and serves as a convenient pump handle. The spout also simulates a limb. It has an elbow bend. The hole is missing here, of course.

On the inside bottom the well-known raised *N* within a raised circle is found—one of the trademarks of Northwood.

It is made of amethyst glass and has been iridized by flashing it with bronze spray and baking. The metallic colors are pleasing. The gold and bronze of the leaves make them look like ivy in the early fall when the foliage begins to turn yellow and brown. Other colors may also have been used in this pattern. Evidently little of it was produced or it would be found more often. Its being listed here and by Mrs. Hartung may bring other pieces to light. The glass is quite heavy.

Novelty creamer: 4-part mold, 15 ounces, 6 5/16 inches tall, 2 9/16 inches wide, and 4 3/8 inches long.

I would expect to find the trough and no other article—but who can tell?

124—*PILASTERS*

Some American pressed glass authorities will consider this pattern, produced about 1910, too modern to be listed. They would, however, praise PANELLED THISTLE, which was made at the same time, or later, and which has far less grace and charm. I have given this the name of *PILASTERS*. In magazines on antiques I sometimes see a pattern advertised as NORTHWOOD'S DRAPE, though no such title is listed in our American glass literature. The word *drape* has so often been used in the titles of pressed glass that it is confusing. The pattern advertised may be the pattern covered here. *PILASTERS* seems to be a better title on all counts.

Again we have an authentic piece of glass made by Harry Northwood and proudly bearing the trademark of his company—a raised and underlined *N* within a raised circle impressed in the bottom. (See drawing.) The pattern is shown here for the first time.

The glass is of fine quality soda-lime metal and is a delightful azure or electric blue. The upper portion of the handle, the pilasters, and the rim change to a fiery opalescent blue in a strong light. It creates the illusion of blue skies with high billowing cumulus clouds drifting by. There are no bubbles or other imperfections in the glass. It is well sculptured, finely molded, and highly fire polished. The mold marks are barely perceptible.

The creamer is round at the rim and hexagonal at the base. From the rim the body curves in gradually to a long curved waist, then out rather sharply to the base. There are six prismatic pilasters in high relief, which reach from just below the rim to the bottom, where they splay and make the base six-sided. Their tops are rounded and their faces have a high spine. The panels between the pilasters are filled with uniform drapes which sag into crescents. The latter are even, rounded, and were not intended to simulate draped fabric. They extend almost from top to bottom.

The rim is practically identical with that of the PEACH pattern which follows. There are five high, rounded scallops on either side, and the front curves up to form a pouring lip. The handle is round in cross section and simulates an applied one, though the mold marks show. The creamer has a small liquid capacity. The bottom is slightly hollowed out so that it sits on an outer ring. The Northwood trademark is placed there.

Standard creamer: 3-part mold, 1 pound, 4 3/4 inches tall, 3 7/8 inches wide, and 5 3/4 inches long.

With the appearance of this standard-size creamer, we can be certain that a sugar bowl, covered butter dish, and spoonholder were also made. I would also expect to find water pitchers, tumblers, and bowls. They probably came in clear and a variety of colors, with opalescent tops. Some may have been iridized.

125—FERRIS

Eureka! Here is a simple, effective, and pleasing pattern shown for the first time in any book on American pressed glass. I have given it the title FERRIS, in honor of a close friend—Dr. Eugene Beverly Ferris, medical director of the American Heart Association—who died at his desk of a heart attack.

Do not confuse this with another and less worthy pattern called FERRIS WHEEL. Fortunately, this one bears the proud trademark of a raised and underlined N within a raised circle, assuring us that it is a product of the Northwood Glass Company.

As to its antecedents, it is only necessary to refer to the frontispiece of Goeffrey W. Beard's *Nineteenth Century Cameo Glass* to discover the eminence as a glassmaker of John Northwood the elder—father of the famous Harry Northwood. Actually, John Northwood reached the very pinnacle in the art of fine glass production, though his

son is better known. The latter also spent a lifetime in the business of glassmaking and developed many improvements (especially in colored glass)—innovations, techniques, new machines, and methods. He made valuable contributions to the American free enterprise system while operating his own factory from 1888 to 1922.

The glass of this creamer has a slightly yellowish tinge. The color was achieved deliberately, and the same type of glass is found in other Northwood patterns, such as INTAGLIO, THE TOWN PUMP, and ARGONAUT. (See Kamm's *A Second Two Hundred Pattern Glass Pitchers*, page 110, and *A Seventh Pitcher Book*, page 58.) I have two creamers in this pattern. One is a translucent cream with a white opalescent top. The other is emerald green with a similar top. The latter colors are ineffective in combination. A single glance at the green creamer informs one why it was manufactured in limited quantity. It literally appears jaundiced. The upper portion of each is an opalescent white which emits fiery flashes when held to the light. In most places the glass is unusually thick to have taken vigorous pressing. It is heavy but without resonance.

The body is tall, tankard-shaped, and constricted about the middle. Here it is surrounded by a half-inch-wide horizontal band of highly beveled flattopped cubes. There are two cubes to each panel. Above and below this band are nine wide and flat panels. Each panel is well rounded over on top and slightly less at the bottom. Above the low, wide waist the panels are sliced off at a sharp angle. Below this the body cuts in almost horizontally to the waist.

The base is formed by a low rounded ring. Into its bottom is impressed a beautiful 24-point hobstar which has a still smaller hobstar in its center. (See cut.) On the inside bottom is impressed the Northwood trademark described above. Compare it with another Northwood trademark used on the ARGONAUT and THE TOWN PUMP patterns above. The handle is terete and appears to be applied, except for the telltale mold marks which can be seen and felt.

The rim is almost horizontal, and over each of the six rear panels is a wide, low scallop. Over the three front panels the rim arches up and forward, then dips to form a deep lip. The plain band below the rim is attractive and shades from an opalescent white to clear with a yellowish cast. The pattern is an imitation of early cut glass and is remarkably beautiful. It is unfortunate that it is so seldom encountered, and this reminds me of an old bit of doggerel (probably by Abe Martin) which goes as follows:

"Ain't it funny there's some folks you cain't love,
An' some folks you just love a pile,
An' the folks you cain't love, you see lots,
An' the others—jest once in a while?"

Standard creamer: 3-part mold, 14 ounces, 4 11/16 inches tall, 3 1/4 inches wide, and 5 inches long.

These are the only pieces of the pattern I have seen. Certainly a covered sugar bowl, covered butter dish, and spoonholder must have been made. Other articles probably also were made. It would have to date between 1888 and 1922, and I believe it is a product of the mid-1890s.

126—NORTHWOOD PEACH

This is still another attractive pattern of pressed glass made by Harry Northwood. A large, clear water pitcher with a nacre iridescence (now called White Carnival) was used and named NORTHWOOD PEACH by Minnie Watson Kamm in *A Fifth Pitcher Book*, page 132, No. 172. The soft tints of mother-of-pearl made her piece attractive, despite the large amount of gilt on the rope bands and fruit sprigs. She knew of only one other item in the pattern. In Montgomery Ward and Company's catalog of 1920 a large elongated bowl in this pattern was listed at 98¢. White Carnival glass brings fantastic prices today.

Marion T. Hartung, in her *Second Book of Carnival Glass*, pages 115-116, shows a tumbler in iridescent cobalt blue. It bears no trademark. The creamer shown here is of emerald-green glass. The water pitcher, drawn by Mrs. Kamm, had three leaves at the top and three peaches. This creamer has two leaves and two fruits, with half of a leaf below the cluster. They have the same number of pruned stems. Emerald green and gold, when used together, make a striking display. The wide band around the rim and lip was originally gilded, but is now worn and tarnished.

The body is stubby, cylindrical, and the same size from top to bottom. Above the waist and below the rim are two heavy cable designs in high rounded relief. Each cable is bordered, above and below, by raised parallel lines. Between them are twelve short flat panels. In drawings they appear dished, and this optical illusion caused Mrs. Kamm to describe them as concave. Actually, the panels are quite flat. The apparent concavity is a result of their arching at top and bottom.

The fruits are in high relief, and PEACH is as good a name as any, though the figures are as round as cherries. The leaves have beveled edges, stippled surfaces, and raised veins. The stems are round raised lines. The leaves and fruits are gilded. The waist is wide and short. The base tapers out slightly but is not as wide as the body. The hollow space underneath is left plain.

On the inside bottom is found the Northwood trademark of a raised underlined *N* within two raised concentric circles. This version of the Northwood trademark is infrequently seen. Below the rim is a smooth gilded band. The back of the rim is covered by even rounded scallops—two to a panel. A larger scallop is placed above the handle attachment. The front part of the rim sweeps up gracefully, then turns forward and down for the lip.

The handle is round in cross section but admits only two large fingers—inadequate for so heavy a piece. It is shaped like an applied handle. The glass used was fine in quality, of a beautiful color, and contains no bubbles or discolorations. It is well sculptured, molded, and fire polished.

Creamer: 4-part mold, 15 1/2 ounces, 4 13/16 inches tall, 3 3/4 inches wide, and 5 7/8 inches long.

Water pitcher: 3-part mold, 3 1/2 pounds, 8 inches tall, 5 1/2 inches wide, length unknown.

The following pieces are known to have been made in the pattern: water pitcher; tumbler; covered butter dish; covered sugar bowl; spoonholder; and a large bowl, 12 1/2 inches long, 9 1/2 inches wide, and 3 1/2 inches deep.

127—WIDE PANEL

Marion T. Hartung, in *Carnival Glass*, page 52, called this pattern WIDE PANEL. I would have called it *WIDE FLUTE* since the figures are not as flat as panels would be, but are noticeably concave, or dished as are flutes. The concavity was not as pronounced on the low bowl she used as it is on the large pitcher shown here. On page 128 of her *Third Book of Carnival Glass* she shows a small piece and calls it TOOTHPICK. I do not know whether this was the name of the item shown or of the pattern.

The large raised ring on the inside bottom (see drawing) must be a trademark since it is in no way connected with a mold mark. The Fostoria Glass Company used such a trademark but is not known to have made iridescent or Carnival Glass. The Westmoreland Glass Company produced Carnival Glass without a trademark but usually only as small containers for condiments, etc. Only in recent years have they adopted a trademark. (Bless them!) Of the three large firms making Carnival

Glass in quantity between 1910 and 1922, we can eliminate two, because they did not use the raised circle. The Fenton Art Glass Company never used a trademark, and they have no present intention of doing so. It is not known whether they are making Carnival Glass today. The Imperial Glass Company, though it had several trademarks and used them on most of their glass, never used the large, raised circle. They never marked their Carnival Glass. They stopped making it in 1922, but, to supply the tremendous demand, put it back in production about 1960.

This leaves only the Northwood Glass Company. They used many trademarks, and most of them contained the raised circle in some manner. They are reputed to have used a large raised circle as a trademark, but this claim is not based on facts. Some pieces of a pattern carry their trademark; other pieces of the same pattern have the raised circle; and still other pieces are unmarked. Many Northwood pieces are not marked at all. This is true of their earlier patterns such as ROYAL IVY, ROYAL OAK, INTAGLIO, etc. I am inclined to believe this is a Northwood pattern.

The glass is a deep amethyst. The surface is plain and has the deepest iridescence of any Carnival Glass known. All pieces show vivid and striking greens and purples. The large water pitcher is always the first piece seen in any group. It is beautifully colored.

This massive pitcher is larger at the rim and base than it is in the middle. There is a plain 1-inch band just below the rim. Both margins are scalloped. The figurework is comprised of ten wide and deep flutes which extend almost from top to bottom. The lip is narrow and attractive. There is a wide overhang to the body just above the low, round ringed base.

The heavy, commodious handle is six-sided, and wider than it is thick. The glass and workmanship are excellent, and the color is particularly beautiful. The inside and the bottom were not iridized. Mold marks are hard to find, except under the handle.

Water pitcher: 2-part mold, 3 7/8 pounds, 8 9/16 inches tall, 5 7/16 inches wide, and 8 3/8 inches long.

I know of a punch bowl, berry bowl and dishes, low bowl, tumbler, and water pitcher. All are in the same deep green and purple iridescent colors.

128—PANELLED STRAWBERRY

A dealer in pattern glass, who is a serious student of the subject, assures me she has seen several pieces of this pattern with the Northwood trademark. This piece is unmarked, as are many of their items. The creamer has some characteristics which are common to Northwood products. The arrangement of suspended fruit sprays, as well as the band surrounding the middle of the bowl, are motifs used by Northwood on many patterns. (Several years after this was written, I personally saw a small compote bearing the Northwood trademark.)

Minnie Watson Kamm, in *A Fourth Pitcher Book*, page 89, No. 105, described, illustrated, and named this pattern, but did not show the design under the base, nor did she know the maker. The pattern is used here to make attribution to Northwood, and to illustrate the attractive intaglio design on the bottom. The pressing of the latter helps to date the pattern. (See drawing.)

Millard, in *Goblets II*, Plate 19-4, illustrated a goblet which he named STRAWBERRY WITH ROMAN KEY BAND. The photograph he used was indistinct, and identification from it was impossible. It does, however, show the shape, and this indicates its origin may have been much later than estimated by him (the 1880s). He also mentions a band about the center of the body which he calls a Roman Key.

Metz covered the pattern as No. 964 and used the long Millard title, in preference to the shorter Kamm title. Unfortunately she provided no illustration. She also spoke of a Roman Key in the central band. Kamm called the band on her creamer, which is identical to the one shown here, a Greek Key.

The unabridged dictionary illustrates four Greek frets and one Japanese fret. Number 2 of the Greek frets is called a Greek Key, but it is not the type used here. I do not know what a Roman Key looks like. The ornamented band of this creamer seems more like an Egyptian or a Navajo design. I doubt the goblets of Millard and Metz were of this pattern, despite the fact Mrs. Metz did have the clear drawing of Kamm's available and thought they were.

Eight wide, flat panels, rounded over their tops extend from below the rim to the base. The body bulges above the waist, then rises almost vertically to the rim. It is constricted just enough to soften the stiff, erect appearance. Surrounding the middle of the body is a 9/16-inch ornamental band. Its upper portion is pressed intaglio, and the lower is cameo. Mrs. Kamm calls it *Greek Key*, but it only resembles that beautiful motif. This band was gilded. On each side of the body are two fruit sprays, which overlap adjoining panels. Each has

122-2

End
122

123

124

Bottom
125

125

126

127

128

Bottom
128

Bottom
129

129-1

three sunken leaves at the top. They are stippled and veined but are definitely not strawberry leaves. Drooping from the leaves are two raised stems, each of which supports a luscious strawberry in high, rounded relief. Their surfaces are stippled to closely approximate the natural fruit. They cover and obliterate a considerable portion of the formal band. The leaves and stems are gilded, and the fruits are flashed with maroon. The remainder of the panel is left plain.

Above the panels, the glass is thick, and there is a plain 3/8-inch band surrounding the body. It is gilded. The rim is thick and it is flat on top. It has eight wide low scallops, one over each panel. Over the two front panels, the rim rises slightly, projects far forward, and is depressed into a narrow lip.

The waist is short, merely a V-shaped groove. The base is adequate and has a double bevel. It follows the octagonal outer shape of the body. At the corners, the sharp points are flattened, thus forming small diamonds. Beneath the base is a low, wide, and round dome. Into it six leaves have been intaglio pressed, along with stems and three strawberries, all stippled. (See cut.)

The pressed handle is hexagonal, shaped like a rabbit's ear, and provides a good grip. The glass is brilliantly clear soda-lime and has no defects. The surface is smooth and the mold marks are indistinct. From the intaglio pressing, I believe it to date from between 1905 and 1915.

Standard creamer: 4-part mold, 1 pound, 4 5/8 inches tall, 3 5/8 inches wide, and 5 5/8 inches long.

A covered sugar bowl, spoonholder, covered butter dish, this creamer, and a small compote are known to have been made. Other articles are to be expected. This creamer was presented to me by Mrs. Vera Gibson of Little Rock, Arkansas.

129—MEMPHIS

Still another Northwood pattern that has not previously been described in our literature on glass makes its appearance here. Usually we cannot determine the individual factory that produced a specific pattern, but in this instance we do have the trademark of the Harry Northwood Glass Company of Ohio, West Virginia, and Pennsylvania. It probably was made between 1905 and 1915, though the company ceased operations about 1924. The creamer is not marked, but the covered sugar bowl, also illustrated here, is marked on the inside bottom with a raised underlined N within a raised circle. The pattern is named for Memphis, Tennessee, the lovely city on the eastern bank of the Mississippi River.

This standard creamer and sugar are in a beautiful shade of emerald-green glass. This is unusual since imitation cut glass was rarely pressed in colors. Such pieces depend for their beauty on their ability to refract light. Clear glass excels over all colors in this respect and was more extensively used. This pattern also comes in Carnival Glass (iridescent) and this dates it as having been produced between 1910 and 1922. The glass had to be thick and heavy to receive the deep impression, which results in such high relief.

Added to the above is a lavish and slapdash use of gilt. Some of it extends to, and has been smeared on, the body a full half-inch from the figure it was intended for. It may not have been decorated in the Northwood factory but, since it carries their trademark, they must bear the onus. From this it is easy to see why manufacturers of fine porcelain were loath to put their mark on pieces to be decorated elsewhere. It would drastically improve the appearance of gilded *MEMPHIS* pieces if the gilt were removed. I prefer to let it remain, although it is tarnished, to illustrate the likes and dislikes of bygone days. Also, I have never seen it successfully removed.

This creamer is squat and has a middle-aged spread. The rim and base are smaller than the girth. The main motif is a series of four large ovate and highly raised shields reaching almost from rim to base. Those on the sides and under the lip are bounded by high beveled bands filled with printed hobnails and triangles. Each shield is dished from top to bottom, but not horizontally. A beautiful many-pointed hobstar has been fitted into each shield. Between the shields we find a new type of imitation cut figurework. It has high beveled octagonal buttons, each with a daisy impressed on its crest. The diagonal bands between the buttons are wide, flat, and sunken. The vertical and horizontal lines are deep V-shaped grooves. At the top and bottom of the figurework are figures shaped like matched steers' horns.

The body is circular with a narrow, thick octagonal base that flares, in flat panels, to the bottom. Underneath is a slightly rounded dome, into which a 28-ray hobstar is impressed. (See drawing.) The rim has broad scallops, each of which is crenulated. The front part of the rim is flat and slopes up to a high pinched lip.

The handle has a small opening for such a heavy piece, and especially is this true of the sugar bowl. It is six-sided and wider than it is thick. It also becomes wider from top to bottom and flattens out on top for a thumbgrip. A groove with fine-toothed rims runs down each side panel. The handle is mounted on a shield, which was left smooth and flattopped, as was done on quality ware where the handle was to be applied. The grooves of the handle, the shields, the rim, a band around the top, the base, and the top of the finial have all been gilded.

Standard creamer: 4-part mold, 1 pound (sugar, 2 pounds), 4 1/4 inches tall, 4 3/16 inches wide, and 5 3/4 inches long.

The items shown here, plus an iridescent amethyst cup, are the only articles known to the author. Certainly the cup had a saucer, and there must have been a butter dish and spoonholder. It may have come in a wide range of articles, but it is not plentiful today. I have recently ascertained that a water pitcher, tumblers, and a punch bowl and punch cups were also made.

The naming of this pattern illustrates how badly titles are needed. I originally named this pattern *MEMPHIS* in 1955. Later a dealer from Georgetown, Massachusetts, sent me a shipment of creamers from which to select what I wanted, with the request that I supply her with the name for any I returned. I told her I had named this pattern *MEMPHIS*, and today it is known all over the country by that name. Hartung, in her *Second Book of Carnival Glass*, page 48, wonders about the title, but she uses it.

130—INTAGLIO

This pattern was shown as FLOWER SPRAY WITH SCROLLS and was thought to be a product of the Indiana Tumbler and Goblet Company of Greentown, Indiana, by Mrs. Kamm when she wrote *A Second Two Hundred Pattern Glass Pitchers*. (See page 110.) Thirteen years later she published *A Seventh Pitcher Book* and again used the pattern because she had found some authentic material on it. On page 58, No. 118, she applied the original manufacturer's name of INTAGLIO and described the pattern but did not illustrate it with a drawing. Instead, she used a reproduction of the original advertisement. On Plate 100, she showed four covered butter dishes exhibited at the Pittsburgh Glass Show of 1898. One of them was INTAGLIO, which had been placed on display there by Northwood. On Plate 107, of the same book, she showed a full-page ad of the Northwood Company, which included a covered sugar and creamer in the INTAGLIO pattern. The ad said: "It comes

in ivory and gold and green and gold" and "The line is best of them all." It has been found in opaque blue, cream with opaque top, in custard glass, and in clear with opaque top.

E. McCalmy Belknap, in *Milk Glass*, page 310, Plate 283, carried a full-page illustration of a covered sugar and creamer. He called the pattern GOLDEN DAISY AND ROSE CUSTARD. His pieces were of custard glass and decorated with green and gold.

Alice Hulett Metz covered the pattern as No. 846, with a photograph of a creamer. She recommended removing the gilt and used the original title assigned by Kamm.

Since three titles have been assigned with one to five words, I have chosen the original Northwood title, INTAGLIO. Those who advertise pattern glass for sale at so much per word will appreciate the shorter title.

The pattern is included here to show a line drawing, correlate the name, and provide measurements. This transparent standard creamer has a slightly yellowish tinge. A wide band at the rim, lip, and top of the handle is opalescent. This is neither canary yellow, vaseline, nor custard glass. It is almost clear, with only a faint trace of color.

Note the creamer's base in the drawing. This is the view at eye level and it appears angular. When seen below eye level, as it usually is, four large, thick, rounded lobes are noted. Actually, they form four short feet. There is a raised, irregular scroll in indistinct relief near the edge of each.

The body is conical. It is round at the top and has lobes on its lower portion. The eight well-rounded lobes diminish and then disappear as they ascend. On each side, and beneath the lip, is a poorly impressed intaglio flower spray that resembles no specific flower. Below the rim and suspended between the floral sprays are highly raised scrolls with complex and irregular shapes.

The waist is constricted and is encircled by a highly raised band containing a single row of large dewdrops on its face. Below the band the waist narrows, and still further down it slopes out rapidly to the edge of the four-lobed foot. Underneath is a plain high and hollow dome. The rim is uneven and follows the raised figurework on the body. It is round over the top and has a half-inch band of fiery opalescent color around it.

The handle is an odd mixture of motifs. At the top are lobes that end in rounded loops. Over the top arch, it is round. The back side represents a heavy strand of rope. Below it the handle swells and has six short ribs ending above a large raised

117

ring about the member. Below the ring the handle splays in a wide medallion edged with first a large, long scallop and then a smaller short one.

To bring out the opalescence at the top, the piece was reheated very hot, and in so doing the scroll designs were leveled out. It is a Northwood product but made before the company adopted a trademark. (Although the trademark is shown in the drawing near the base of this creamer, it does not appear on the piece.)

Standard creamer: 4-part mold, 1 pound, 5 3/16 inches tall, 3 7/8 inches wide, and 5 3/4 inches long.

The only items known to this writer are creamer, sugar bowl, covered butter dish, spoonholder, jelly compote, bowl, and sauce dish.

131—NORTHWOOD'S GRAPE

This striking bronze and purple iridescent standard creamer is another Carnival Glass pattern made by the Harry Northwood Glass Company of Wheeling, West Virginia. The company's trademark is pressed on the bottom on the inside. Today it is popular, widely collected, and brings a good price in shops. I recently saw a 10-inch bowl priced at $42.50 and a punch bowl with a $250.00 price tag.

Larry Freeman, in his *Iridescent Glass*, page 111, reproduces a page from an old Butler Brothers (of St. Louis) catalog which lists the pattern in a Rose and Nut Bowl Assortment. The latter consists of a dozen 5-inch crimp-topped rose bowls with six feet, at $1.05, and one dozen deep 5 1/2 inch nut bowls or jardinieres, at the same wholesale price. On page 118 of the same book, Freeman shows a water pitcher in a similar grape pattern, but it is known to have been made by the Imperial Glass Company.

Marion T. Hartung, in her *Carnival Glass*, page 98, illustrates a tumbler and names the pattern *NORTHWOOD'S GRAPE*. We shall use the title Mrs. Hartung assigned. (Note: In buying by mail, remember any of Northwood's various grape patterns may be advertised as *NORTHWOOD'S GRAPE*.) Hartung mentions that the pattern is also called GRAPE WITH THUMBPRINT. That title is preempted by another grape pattern—one described by Kamm.

The glass is a beautiful shade of amethyst and was originally iridized by spraying a coating of metallic oxide on the outside while the glass was red hot. As a result, the bottom and inside are amethyst, and the exterior is iridescent with flashes of gold, bronze, and deep purple. Other pieces are of clear glass sprayed with luster gold. Still others are of cobalt blue sprayed with metallic colors. All have a bright mirrorlike sheen.

The piece shown is a standard creamer. The body is cylindrical with vertical sides and sits on a low ringbase. The latter has a scalloped, many-rayed star pressed into the bottom of its rounded dome. (See cut.) Above the base is an inch-wide thick convex band that surrounds the creamer. It has been deeply slashed with alternating V- and U-shaped notches. The upper three-fourths of the body is covered with a bold grape-and-leaf motif which seems to be suspended from a cable about the body an inch below the rim. This cable or band effect occurs on many Northwood patterns and is, in fact, almost a trademark. Each side of the creamer has a cluster of twenty-four raised grapes. Flanking each cluster are large raised veined and stippled grape leaves. Both grapes and leaves are from a well-pruned vine. A plain flat band above and below the design accentuates the highly embossed grape motif.

The rim is level, except where it rises to form an ample lip. It has large scallops which themselves are scalloped. Just above the upper attachment of the handle the rim is low and not scalloped for 3/4 inch. The handle is round.

Standard creamer: 4-part mold, 15 ounces, 4 1/2 inches tall, 3 1/2 inches wide, and 5 1/8 inches long.

This creamer was produced between 1918 and 1924. The pattern comes in many pieces including: spooner, covered butter dish, covered sugar bowl, creamer, rose bowl, nut bowl or jardiniere, large covered cracker or cookie jar, water pitcher, tumbler, shallow 8-inch bowl, deep 8-inch bowl, sauce or ice-cream dish, powder box, dresser set with bottle, wine decanter, wine glass, large punch bowl, punch cup, teacup and saucer, footed compote, candy dish, etc. It would be surprising if vases, cake stands, salt and pepper shakers, and platters were not made. No goblet is known in this pattern. Indeed, few Northwood patterns with goblets are known to me. A notable exception is the beautiful cream and brown custard glass goblet in the CREAM GRAPE pattern.

This creamer was used through the courtesy of Mrs. Helen Wycoff of Little Rock, Arkansas, who has an extensive collection of this pattern and of other pressed iridescent glass. She has been exceedingly helpful to me in the classification of iridescent glass—most especially that of Northwood. I have a covered sugar bowl of this pattern in my collection but to date have failed to locate a creamer.

129-2

130

131

132-1

132-2

Bottom
131

133-1

Bottom
133

133-2

132—PANELLED CHERRY

We are often too quick to decide whether a piece is a reproduction or a fake. If a company uses their own original molds to produce a pattern over a period of years, should the later pressings from these same molds be called reproductions? It is a question not easily answered. A plant may have closed down for years and later resumed production. Another may have produced the pattern for a year and gone bankrupt. A third may have bought the molds at a bankrupt sale and waited half a century to use them. Under such circumstances, would the later pressings (from the same molds) be reproductions or originals? Frankly, I do not know.

Sometimes we find two articles which vary only in minor details. Does this mean one is a variant, reproduction, or fake? If so, which one? A case in point is the present creamer. The two drawings appear identical, but many minor differences exist. In answer to the above question, neither was a fake. To supply an expected great demand, the Northwood Company had at least two molds producing these creamers and quite possibly even at two separate plants. Both are in my collection and both bear the Northwood trademark. Neither was a reproduction.

The following differences will be noted:

1. The lip of the first creamer is narrower and droops more.
2. The upthrust angle of the handle is greater in the first one.
3. The first has a low, flat cord about the body, whereas the second has a high, round cord.
4. The leaves also differ:
   a. On the first, the edges are highly serrated. The leaves are outlined and veined by tiny raised lines. Their tops are flat and stippled.
   b. On the second, the leaves are highly convex, are not stippled, and do not have the raised outline.

For a complete description of the pattern, see Mrs. Kamm's *A Fifth Pitcher Book*, page 63, No. 78, where she illustrated the first creamer and named it PANELLED CHERRY. The creamer used had no trademark and she did not know its maker. Fortunately, both pieces shown here carry the Northwood trademark. The pattern was not described by Lee, Millard, or Metz.

There is much confusion of titles involving this pattern, and I do not know how to correct it. The following references may help the collector. If the pattern shown here is desired, it would be well to ask for Northwood's PANELLED CHERRY.

Marion T. Hartung, on page 104 of her *Second Book of Carnival Glass*, illustrated a NORTHWOOD'S CHERRY bowl. She thought it matched the pattern discussed here under the name of PANELLED CHERRY described by: (1) Lee in *Early American Pressed Glass*, pages 474-75, Pattern 192, and Plate 79-4. (2) Millard in *Goblets*, Plate 132-1. (3) Metz in *Early American Pattern Glass*, pages 90-91, No. 990.

The PANELLED CHERRY described in (1), (2), and (3) above is called CHERRY WITH THUMBPRINTS by Kamm in *A Fourth Pitcher Book*, page 104, No. 128. The pattern under discussion is frequently called PANELLED CHERRY WITH THUMBPRINTS, which proves my point.

Standard creamer: 4-part mold, 1 1/16 pounds, 4 5/8 inches tall, 3 7/8 inches wide, and 5 1/4 inches long.

I have seen only the four-piece table setting and tumblers in this pattern. Hartung's bowl may belong to it. Other items probably were made. The cherries are flashed with a reddish color, and the rims, leaves, stems, and cable are gilded.

Mrs. Nell Gibson operates an antique shop in Malvern, Arkansas. Her specialty is American pressed glass. She has a set of five tumblers in this pattern. Each of the five was pressed in a different mold. They all differ, one from the other, as much as the two creamers shown here. Each of the five bears the Northwood trademark. (See DAISY MEDALLION which follows.)

133—DAISY MEDALLION

The two creamers illustrated under this name are shown with PANELLED CHERRY, inasmuch as they further expand the point made there. The differences, however, are more apparent in this instance.

In *A Fifth Pitcher Book*, page 35, No. 37, Mrs. Kamm described the upper creamer and named it DAISY MEDALLION. She thought that little of it was made.

Millard, in *Goblets II*, Plate 52-3, illustrated a goblet, but just which variant it was cannot be determined. He called it SUNBURST MEDALLION. Also see, in this book, another entirely different pattern, which Millard called MEDALLION SUNBURST. This can lead to confusion between such tricky titles, especially in indexing. When ordering by mail, the buyer should be alert to the two patterns.

Metz illustrated a creamer as No. 1429 and chose the Millard title of SUNBURST MEDALLION in preference to the Kamm title of DAISY MEDALLION.

The principal differences between the two variants are:
1. The first creamer has a scalloped rim; the second has a plain one.
2. In the first creamer the ribs of the stem are shorter.
3. The nubs on the handle of the first creamer are more prominent.
4. The dewdrops under the base of the first are dangerously sharp-pointed. On the second they are rounded.
5. The egg-and-dart bands surrounding the tops differ as shown.

Neither bears a trademark. We have no catalogs, advertisements, cuts, descriptions, or documentation and, therefore, no means of ascertaining what we would like to know. Certain questions inevitably arise such as just which is the variant, fake, or reproduction; or were both made at the same time? (The PANELLED CHERRY variants were probably made simultaneously.) Little of this relatively unattractive pattern was, or should have been, made. There was little incentive to fake it. Today it is scarce, but not high priced. Creamers are seldom faked in any event. Could the same mold maker have sold slightly different molds to different firms? I do not know.

See Kamm's write-up for this early, poorly made production ware. Her description covers it adequately.

Standard creamer: 3-part mold, 10 ounces, 4 3/4 inches tall, 3 3/4 inches wide, and 5 5/8 inches long.

I have these creamers in my collection. A goblet also was made. No other items are known to me.

134—DRAPERY

As in PANELLED CHERRY and DAISY MEDALLION we have here two similar creamers, though one is obviously a late copy of an older original. The latter was, in all probability, made by the Boston and Sandwich Glass Company, of Sandwich, Massachusetts.

Mrs. Lee, in *Early American Pressed Glass*, shows a covered sugar bowl and goblet of the older pattern. She also shows a crude and much later creamer and spoonholder similar to our second creamer. She discusses them together as if they were contemporary. Mrs. Kamm, in *A Fifth Pitcher Book*, page 9, No. 9, shows and describes the older creamer. Millard, in *Goblets*, Plate 133-3, shows a goblet belonging with the earlier and more refined creamer. Mrs. Metz, in *Early American Pattern Glass*, shows a goblet of the earlier type as No. 2058.

The creamers differ as follows:

1. The first is a product of the 1869-1875 period, while the second had its origin ten to twenty years later. (Also, the latter was probably put out as a copy.)
2. The general shape differs.
3. The handle of the older creamer is applied, delicate, beautifully shaped, and handtooled. The more recent has a run-of-the-mill six-sided pressed handle.
4. The figurework is higher on the later creamer. Also, the wide plain band above the figurework of the first creamer is the more attractive.
5. The second creamer has a corona of raised icicles about the lower part of the bowl. This is absent on the first one.
6. The drapery and stippling of the upper creamer are artistically designed and executed. The stippling of the second consists merely of straight rows of small dewdrops, with little similarity to draperies.
7. The rim of the first is attractively saddled. That of the second is not so curvaceous.
8. The first was designed and sold as a quality product. The second was nothing more than production ware.
9. All pendants on the second creamer are tassels and dangle from long cords. The earlier type has shorter pendants, and only a portion of them are tassels.

It is easy to tell which piece has seniority. Was the second creamer put out as a reproduction, or was it an out and out fake? The latter is doubtful; surely a better job of forgery would have been done. Did one company try to cash in on a popular product of another? If the second creamer was a fake, when did it gain respectability and sales value? (My own cost $4.50 in 1952.) Will other fakes become valuable antiques? If so, how old would they have to be? These are difficult questions to answer. (There is, similarly, an early and a late version of TULIP AND SAWTOOTH.)

Earlier creamer: 3-part mold, 10 1/2 ounces, 5 7/8 inches tall, 2 7/8 inches wide, and 4 5/8 inches long.

Later creamer: 3-part mold, 9 ounces, 5 1/4 inches tall, 3 inches wide, and 4 7/8 inches long.

I know of a matching sugar bowl and goblet for the older creamer, but of only the spoonholder to match the younger one. This latter creamer is now about eighty years old.

135—ROANOKE STAR

Millard, in *Goblets II*, Pate 38-4, called this pattern ROANOKE STAR. He thought it dated from the 1880s and came in clear only. His goblet does not have fans above the meandering bands. Since a plain band was essential at the top of a

121

goblet, this may explain why the pieces shown differ slightly from Millard's piece.

Marion T. Hartung covered this pattern in her *Second Book of Carnival Glass*, pages 46-47. She became lost in the jungle of imitation cut glass patterns, failed to locate it in our glass literature, and settled on the name CARNIVAL HOBSTAR. (which incidentally is an excellent title). The word *Carnival* dates it after 1910, though Millard considered it of the 1880s. His title ROANOKE STAR is retained here since it was the first assigned. Lee and Kamm did not cover the pattern.

Two creamers from my collection are shown here to illustrate minor differences in the rims, handles, and lips. The first creamer is clear, and the second is Carnival Glass flashed with marigold luster. Few imitation cut glass pieces are iridized. There is good reason for this. Cut glass and imitation cut glass depend for their beauty on clarity of metal and the ability of their many facets to refract light. When such glass is iridized it loses both attributes and becomes one of the least attractive types of Carnival Glass.

I believe this glass was made at least thirty years later than Dr. Millard estimated. It probably was made by the Imperial Glass Company of Bellaire, Ohio. They never marked their Carnival Glass with a trademark. They were organized in 1902, and they still produce fine tableware. The gold iridescent creamer shown here has certain aspects which indicate it is of comparatively recent origin.

I would like to refer the reader to the differences between the two NORTHWOOD'S CHERRY creamers already described. The two ROANOKE STAR creamers also have their differences and open the same speculation—i.e. they were probably made by the same company.

The principal motif consists of two half-inch-wide bands which meander up and down as they encircle the body. They crisscross and, in the process, form three large ovate spaces on the body. The bands are composed of strawberry diamonds which have triangular pyramids in their interstices. The ovate spaces have a small fan impressed into their sharp ends. The central space is covered by a huge hobstar. There is a 7-ray fan above and below the interstices where the bands cross. The vertical sides round under to a narrow waist. A large hobstar is impressed on the underside. (See drawing.)

The rim of the first creamer is unevenly scalloped and plain. The second has similar scallops but they, in turn, are finely scalloped. The first handle is more rounded and lacks the upthrust of the second. The handle of the iridescent creamer also has a manufacturing defect I have never before seen. While still hot and malleable, it was picked up by the handle with a pair of pincers, leaving two noticeable depressions on the round, lower blob. The lip of the clear creamer is narrower and deeper than on the iridescent one. Both handles have imitation "St. Louis cut" on the back surfaces. The glass and workmanship of both pieces leave much to be desired.

Standard creamer: 3-part mold, 14 1/2 ounces, 4 5/16 inches tall, 3 3/8 inches wide, and 5 inches long.

Only two creamers, a punch bowl, and a goblet are known to the writer. Mrs. Hartung mentions bowls and a table set.

136—ENGLISH HOLLY

This beautiful purple marble glass creamer is as British as cricket. It probably belonged to a child's milk and mush set. Like the *ILEX* pattern shown next, it has neither trademark nor Registry mark. Nevertheless, everything about it bespeaks an English origin.

On Plate 288-b of *Milk Glass*, E. McCalmy Belknap shows a reproduced photograph of a sugar bowl in this pattern. The illustration shows the marbled effect of the colored glass, but does not delineate the fine pressed pattern. The drawing we use shows the pressed pattern, but not the marbled effect. The sugar bowl may or may not have had a lid.

The bowl of this small pitcher is deep, shaped like a kettle, and stands on three legs similar to a washpot. The legs represent well-pruned boles of trees in half-relief. They extend as pilasters almost to the top. The tree trunk, at the rear, grows away from the bowl, then bends back to it to form the handle. At the top and bottom of the body are well-defined areas of raised overlapping figures which resemble scalloped shingles or clouds. Their significance is unknown to me.

All limbs of trees except one on either side are lopped off. One limb grows out and diagonally up on each side and crosses the one growing from the next tree almost at right angles. Each twig bears a few stippled, raised holly leaves and clusters of berries in half-relief.

The rim is well saddled, the glass thin, and the top rounded over. It curves upward in front, then dips slightly to form a small, narrow lip. Under the bottom are six raised concentric rings. (See drawing.)

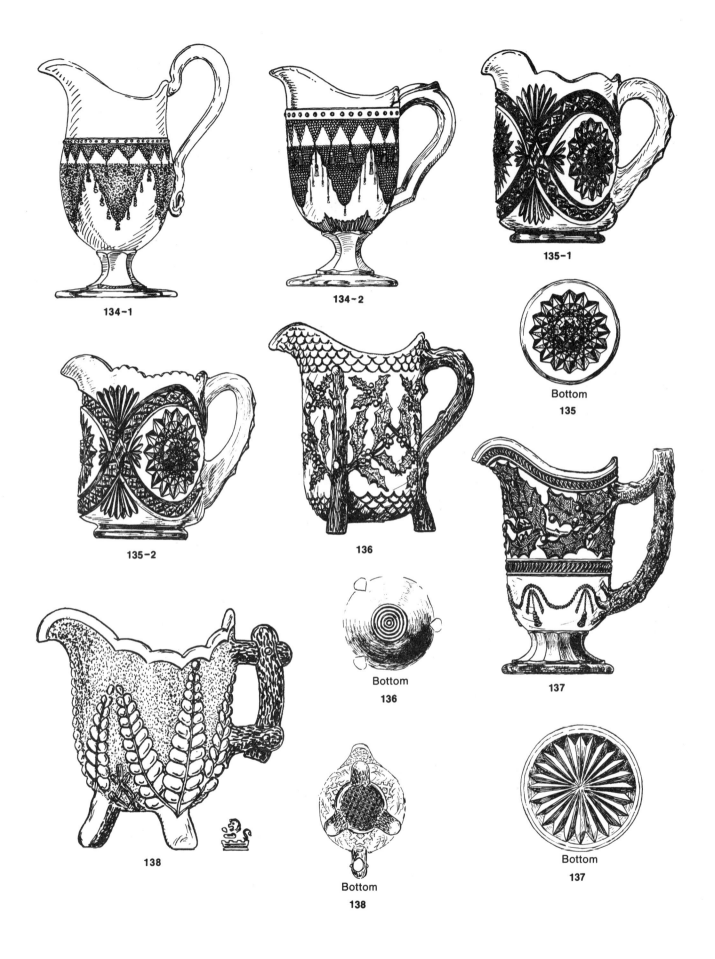

134-1

134-2

135-1

Bottom
135

135-2

136

Bottom
136

137

138

Bottom
138

Bottom
137

The purple marble glass of this piece is beautiful indeed with the purple predominating over the white. The moldmaker was an excellent artisan and the piece is well finished off. It is flint glass and has good resonance when tapped. I believe it to date from the 1870s.

Small creamer: 3-part mold, 8 ounces, 3 15/16 inches tall, 2 9/16 inches wide, and 4 1/4 inches long.

The sugar bowl and creamer are the only items known to me.

137—ILEX

Can you visualize a more fascinating design for pressed glass than this? The leaves are stippled and the outer surface of the bowl is crinkled just enough to impart a silvery sheen.

The piece is undoubtedly of English origin though it carries no registry or trademark. Many of its characteristics differ from those found in American glass.

A milk white sugar bowl without a lid in this pattern was illustrated by E. McCalmy Belknap, on Plate 222-d of his *Milk Glass*. He also thought it was English and beautiful.

This pattern should actually be named Holly; however, we already have too many patterns with the word *Holly* in their title. In an effort not to enlarge this list I have named it *ILEX*. The preceding pattern also is of English origin and covered with holly, so I named it *ENGLISH HOLLY*.

The body is long and cylindrical. The lower portion rounds under to the waist. Below the middle, a heavy rope band surrounds it. There is also a small raised line just above and below the rope. Beneath the rim, and following its contours, is a similar, but narrower, band which encircles the body. In the wide area between the two bands a beautiful design of holly leaves and berries in high relief is found. They look quite natural until you notice the strange placement of the berries. The berries themselves are large dewdrops. The leaves are highly beveled serrated edges, with veined and stippled surfaces. The stippling consists of minute beads. The background is plain, but under a powerful magnifying glass it appears frosted, or covered with microscopic beading over the entire surface.

Below the lower band, a wide portion of the body is left plain. This contains a cord-and-tassel design, similar to that of the American CORD AND TASSEL pattern. In the rear it stops at the lower handle attachment. The rim is well saddled and flat on top. The glass here is quite thin. It rises high in the rear for decorative purposes—not to accomodate the handle attachment. The rim curves upward and forward, in front, to form a good pouring lip.

The waist is thick and short. It begins at a high, round shelf on the lower part of the body. Twelve flat panels curve in slightly through the waist, then sharply out and eventually slope gently to a high shelf at the edge of the foot. (See drawing.) The base is rounded into a thick ring on the edge, giving the piece a wide stable base. The bottom is hollowed out underneath and a large star pressed therein. As with most pieces of English glass, the twenty-four rays are in high relief, rather than sunken as is so often true in domestic pieces.

The handle is round in cross section and simulates a branched limb of a tree—one branch for the upper attachment and one for the lower. The junction of the two branches provides a good thumbgrip. The lower branch splays on the body in the form of eight heavy twisted roots. They appear to be covered with bark, as does the handle. The roots are chopped off at various lengths from the bole of the tree. The upper attachment also splays on the body as six large pruned limbs. A large limb meanders about the body, bearing leaves and berries.

The glass is clear early flint and has a good resonance when lightly tapped. The mold marks are rather prominent but not incisive. A little more care in finishing it off would have improved it. Nevertheless, it is a strikingly beautiful piece. It was probably made during the 1870s.

Standard creamer: 3-part mold, 13 ounces, 5 7/16 inches tall, 2 15/16 inches wide, and 5 7/8 inches long.

Since this clear creamer and a milk-white sugar bowl are known, I assume other pieces of the four-piece table set were made and perhaps in purple marble or other colors. Other items may be available in England.

So many English (and other foreign) patterns of pressed glass are finding their way into our shops today that I have thought it advisable to include a few. Many collectors of pressed glass never have a real opportunity to adequately study the admittedly vast subject. Perhaps the listings in question may help clarify some of the problems in determining the patterns that are American and those that are foreign. I hope so.

138—BRACKEN

This small, pot-shaped English creamer has

all the appeal of spring in the wildwood, where white violets nod. It is not ashamed of its parentage and carries a Lion and Crown trademark on the inside bottom. Many such beautiful foreign pieces are finding their way to our shops. Perhaps a dozen are shown here to illustrate how European patterns differ from our own. Not knowing which English manufacturer used this trademark (see drawing), and not having access to the original name, I have given it the title *BRACKEN*.

It sits on three short log-shaped feet which are peeled on the outside and show bark on the underside. (See cut.) The handle represents three mortised tree limbs with the bark left on. A group of three large fern fronds, in high relief, centers over each leg. The central frond extends from base to rim. Between adjacent groups and descending to the mold mark at the base, twigs have been crisscrossed in an unusual arrangement. The surface around the figurework appears almost cold. The stippling causes a frosted effect.

The rim is coarsely scalloped and rises to a high narrow lip. The base is filled with sunken diamond point. Both quality and workmanship are excellent. The piece has a slight forward list. It is believed to be a product of the 1870s.

Small creamer: 3-part mold, 5 ounces, 3 5/16 inches tall, 2 5/16 inches wide, and 4 inches long.

No other items in the pattern are known to me.

139—SANDWICH IVY

This beautiful small creamer has escaped all American writers on pressed glass with the single exception of Alice Hulett Metz. In her *Early American Pattern Glass*, pages 14 and 15, No. 86, she illustrated this creamer and a small compote, assigning the name SANDWICH IVY. She priced the creamer at $65. By inference, she attributed the pattern to Boston and Sandwich Glass Company, Sandwich, Massachusetts, but gave no basis for it.

I purchased my own specimen from a dealer in Buzzards Bay, Massachusetts, in 1956 for $4.50. It was an unlisted creamer—one of a group of English creamers, some of which were marked. I had given a title before Mrs. Metz's book reached the market. Her title of SANDWICH IVY, however, is continued here to avoid the confusion of duplicate titles.

I believe this to be English glass. It has two racial characteristics quite common in English pressed glass of the same age group. I have never seen them on American glass. One is the band, below the rim, composed of vertical ribs with a scallop over each long rib. The other is the stippling, which bears no resemblance to that of Lacy Sandwich.

This tiny individual creamer is shaped like a coal scuttle. It is stippled and has well-formed ivy leaves but is not one of our American ivy patterns (STIPPLED IVY, BUDDED IVY, SPIRALED IVY, SOUTHERN IVY, or RIBBED IVY). It is a much different pattern. It reminds one of the restfulness of a cool green valley.

The waist is narrow but swells to a wide, ringed shelf on the base of the bowl. Below, it slopes out to a rounded edge on the foot. The hollowed out space underneath is filled with a highly raised star of sixteen rays. Such stars as these on American glass are usually impressed.

The sides of the body are straight, and they flare sharply from the shelf on the lower end of the bowl. There is a sunken belt, 1 1/2 inches wide, which surrounds the body. Near the center is a raised, meandering vine that winds about the piece. The leaves are raised and veined but otherwise plain. There are no berries. Except for the ivy, the entire band is stippled, giving a dew-covered appearance to the vine.

At the top, the glass is thicker to permit the figurework there. On each side are seven rounded ribs in high relief, which stand erect on the top edge of the stippled belt. They vary in length— first a long, then a short one. In the rear is a high, wide, arched scallop that serves no purpose and is not particularly attractive. In front, the rim rises gently and pushes forward to form a lip. The front third of the band, around the top and under the lip, is left plain.

The handle is severely plain, round in cross section, runs straight, and turns at sharp angles. It is thickest at the lower attachment. Its capacity is too small to admit the finger of an adult, but pressure of the thumb and finger is sufficient to hold it. The small liquid capacity—about a jigger—indicates that it was intended to be a toy.

The glass is fine, clear, heavy flint and has a musical resonance when tapped. Its only blemish is the presence of bubbles, some of which are rather large. The moldmaker did an excellent job, but the gaffer needed a rap on his knuckles. He left the high mold marks and some of them are quite sharp. There was no fire polishing. This creamer was probably manufactured between 1865 and 1875. A table setting in this pattern, if made, would be a delight.

Toy creamer: 3-part mold, 4 ounces, 2 13/16 inches tall 2 1/16 inches wide, and 3 3/8 inches long.

No other articles have been seen by the writer. Mrs. Metz shows the compote. The pattern is too appealing to abandon hope of finding other items.

140—MOON AND ARCH

The source of small creamers of this type has never been established conclusively. This one appears to be of English origin. It does not matter greatly whether they are foreign or domestic. Further investigation and research may well clarify the matter, but indications are that they are foreign. It is known that some have been possessed and cherished in this country for over a hundred years. They are so attractive that their popularity will continue.

At first glance this appears to be identical with SUNK BULL'S EYE, as shown in Kamm's *A Fourth Pitcher Book*, page 145, No. 196. On closer inspection, however, they can be seen to vary greatly. The present one is small, compact, and ovoidal. It has a narrow waist and spreads out into six wide panels above. The base also spreads out and terminates in six large heavy scallops. Underneath is a deep, smooth concave dome. The base is narrow, even for a small pitcher.

The rim is unevenly scalloped in keeping with the six side panels. The lip is high and narrow. Below the rim is a horizontal row of six large convex irregularly moon-shaped figures, one to each panel. Below each moon is a depressed arch that points upward and whose base terminates at the midline. Below these is still another series of arches—six in number. Each is concave with a deep finger impressed in its face.

The handle is pressed, small, round in cross section, and severely plain. It has mold marks that are high and sharp.

This creamer is too thick for its small size, being 5/16 inch at the rim. It is brilliant, clear, flawless, and has a high pitched ring when tapped.

Small creamer: 3-part mold, 13 ounces. 4 1/2 inches tall, 2 3/4 inches wide, and 4 3/4 inches long.

See *STAR IN THUMBPRINT*, immediately following. It is a creamer of the same general type. A sugar bowl, or a bowl for a milk and mush set, was probably also produced.

141—STAR IN THUMBPRINT

This quaint little flint glass creamer has a high, sharp resonance. It is heavy and has many tiny bubbles, indicating that it probably predates the Civil War. It may or may not be an American piece. The unusual shape, the radically different handle, and small size indicate it to be of foreign origin and probably English. On the other hand, the pattern, glass, and workmanship could well be American. The handle is so beautiful, unusual, and impractical that it makes the entire piece attractive. It is also clumsy and difficult to hold, since the opening will not admit even a child's finger. It is hexagonal, and a deep groove runs from top to bottom down each side panel. I know of no other pressed glass creamer with a similar handle. The evidence indicates it is a foreign piece.

The creamer is thick (3/8 inch at the rim and 7/16 inch at the middle) and heavy. Its small size was adequate for the era when heavy thick cream was used in tea. In all probability the sugar bowl was larger since it was made for the days in which only unrefined sugar was available. Those were the days of brown sugar, maple sugar, and "Y.C." (yellow clarified) sugar, all of which contain large, hard, uneven lumps.

The body rests on an octagonal base. It is wider in proportion than is found on most American pieces. The base has a rough pontil mark on its domed underside. It was made separately and fused to the body while both were hot. The body has eight flat sides that extend from rim to base, except through the waist. The latter is round and is the narrowest part of the creamer. The upper half of the body has eight flat panels which end at the deeply saddled rim. The lip is high and pinched. The rim is high at the back to provide for the upper handle attachment. The handle extends higher than the tall lip.

The glass of the lower half of the body is almost twice as thick as that of the upper half. It begins with a wide sloping shelf near the middle and descends to the waist. Each panel of the lower half contains a deep ovate punty, or thumbprint. In each thumbprint a raised six-pointed star is found.

Small creamer: 3-part mold, 11 ounces, 4 inches high, 3 inches wide, and 5 inches long.

I know of no other pieces of this pattern. The name *STAR IN THUMBPRINT* is used for this little gem since STAR AND PUNTY was an original name used by Kamm in *A Fifth Pitcher Book*, page 86, No. 115, to describe an equally venerable American pattern also covered in this book. The pattern resembles SANDWICH STAR AND BUCKLE, in Kamm's *A Second Two Hundred Pattern Glass Pitchers*, page 8. (See write-up of *MOON AND ARCH*, immediately preceding, for discussion of similar creamers.)

142—*WHEELS*

Another lovely English creamer is shown here. In size it is midway between the American standard and individual creamers. The main motif covers the lower three-fourths of the body and comprises two bands of large wheels. The upper wheels are larger than the lower, with which they are paired—one directly above the other. The tire of each wheel is a raised inverted V-shaped ridge. Eight convex spokes, or teardrops, meet at the hub. The space between each four adjoining wheels is filled with beveled, flattopped cubes, sixteen in number. The body is plain and smooth above the wheels, except for two unusual swags of fine vertical ribbing, which extend downward for a short distance from the rim, one on each side. There are two similar figures near the lip. (They are not well centered, and one extends to the middle of the lip.) I have seen this conceit on a number of English creamers but never on an American pattern.

The rim is deeply saddled and rises as high in the rear as at the lip, but this additional height is not used for a handle attachment. The lip is narrow. It arches high and projects forward. The handle is convoluted and appears to consist of six round parallel rods. They splay on the body at both attachments. The handle has a small capacity, and its curves are not particularly attractive.

The stem is short, thick, hexagonal, and twisted. It ends in a round raised shelf on the bottom of the bowl and on the upper surface of the foot. The foot itself is round and plain. Underneath is a low dome, the roof of which is ceiled with a large 24-ray star which is raised rather than impressed.

This pattern does not have the refinements of most early English pieces. It is made of thin early flint glass and has some resonance when tapped. The mold marks are high and rough but not sharp. The glass is not smooth, and the outer surface has a grained-leather effect. The inside bottom is as pocked and harsh as coarse sandpaper, with many black specks embedded in the metal. It would be impossible to keep this creamer in a sanitary condition. It probably dates from between 1865 and 1875. It may have matched a large sugar bowl, or it may have been the pitcher of a milk and mush set.

Small creamer: 3-part mold, 8 1/2 ounces, 4 13/16 inches tall, 2 5/8 inches wide, and 4 3/8 inches long.

The writer has seen no other item in this pattern.

143—*TARTAN*

This superb little creamer is from the British Isles. The plaid (albeit diagonal) in the motif accounts for the name. Finding suitable descriptive names for innumerable patterns of pressed glass becomes a headache as the titles, one by one, are found to have been preempted. This goblet-shaped creamer is almost completely covered with decorative material. Taken together, the parts are homogeneous and blend into a pleasing unity. It is a beautiful piece.

The bowl is bulbous. It starts from a round flat shelf at the top of the stem, curves out rapidly to its widest part, then curves in to a somewhat narrower neck. From the shelf, three high V-shaped ridges make long sweeping loops, almost to the rim, before returning to the shelf. They divide the body into large, oval-shaped spaces. A single ridge loops over each oval, while the central one extends up as a stem and expands into a wide fan. The latter has four ribs and stops at the rim. The loops are filled with V-shaped grooves placed at a 45-degree angle to the horizontal. These grooves divide the loops into innumerable large and small cubes imprinted on their tops. This gives the Tartan effect.

The stem is unusual and not, to my knowledge, found in American pressed glass. It is octagonal throughout, with eight flat panels. It starts at the round shelf on the base of the bowl, constricts to a narrow stem, swells to a large knop, and is again constricted. Below the latter it flares sharply to form a wide octagonal shelf on top of the base. The panels drop off the shelf and continue to the edge, ending in eight scallops around the foot.

Beneath the base there is a narrow raised ring at the perimeter on which the piece rests. From it a curved dome arches high in its center. Covering the space inside the ring is something different in star formation. (See cut of bottom.) A high ridged prism forms each ray of the 20-ray star, and each prism is outlined by a V-shaped groove. The beautiful star shows through the foot of the creamer and can be clearly seen from above.

The rim is unevenly scalloped, conforming to the figures on the body. The lip is high, narrow, and curvaceous. The handle is six-sided and is made up of three curved members joined together near their ends. The two back and two side panels of the handle are smooth and plain. The two inner panels are filled with short parallel slashes across their faces. At any angle from which the handle is seen, the reflection of these slashes shows up as if covering the entire handle.

This is a fine sparkling piece of clear early flint

glass. It has a beautiful belltone when tapped. It is neither heavy nor massive. The glass itself is thin. There is an occasional small bubble or spot of white discoloration. It dates from about the 1860s.

Creamer: 4-part mold, 10 1/2 ounces, 5 11/16 inches tall, 3 1/16 inches wide, and 5 inches long.

I know of no other item in this pattern.

144—KENT

The English have produced much of the world's finest glass, in many categories. Here is worthy testimony to this claim. It was bought from an eastern shop but is a recent importation from the old country. It is as English as *Kent*.

This is a creamer of limited capacity and almost as small as individual American creamers. It may have played an important role in the British tea ritual and for this purpose was ample in size. Here, it would hold coffee cream for two but not enough for cereal or dessert.

It is charming in its entirety. The overall pattern blends into a classic gem. The bowl holds less than a small teacup and is somewhat conoidal in shape. Covering most of the body is a wide band of nine large overlapping ovals. Where they overlap they form large almond-shaped spaces that are surrounded by a wide flat frame filled with large uniform dewdrops. In each such figure is a smaller space of the same shape filled with fine stippling. Within the ovals, and where they do not overlap, long convex double-headed clubs are found. At the upper end of each club is a fan of five rounded ribs. At the lower end is a fan of three rounded ribs. Above this figurework a 1/4-inch plain band encircles the body. It is smooth and level at its top, but is scalloped over the ovals. Above this is a half-inch band that contains figures resembling the rising sun with heavy vertical ribs for rays.

The upper portion of the rays helps form the top of two small scallops on each side of the rim. There is a plain high scallop in the rear, and the upper attachment of the handle is below this projection. The rim rounds up in front and is pinched into an attractive narrow lip. The stem is thick and short. It begins on a high shelf on the bottom of the bowl, and curves in and out to end in a high shelf on the base.

The foot is artistically domed and reminds us of those seen on our capitols. The dome is made up of three elements. At the bottom is an inclined ring which serves as a footing for the second element of short vertical and convex columns. Above the columns is a level 1/4-inch gallery surrounding the piece. From the gallery, highly convex ribs

arch up into the shelf of the stem. Underneath the base is a high plain dome.

The handle adds grace and charm to the whole. At the top it has a slight upthrust and also a round bar with a large knop on the end. This provides a secure thumbgrip. From the knop, the handle curves in to rejoin the side where there also is a knop. A raised thread band outlines the handle on each side and also ends in a knop at top and bottom.

This is fine early pressed glass of clear sparkling flint. It has a soft ring when tapped. The mold marks are high and somewhat rough but not sharp. I think it dates from about the 1860s.

Small creamer: 3-part mold, 8 1/2 ounces, 4 13/16 inches tall, 2 3/4 inches wide, and 4 9/16 inches long.

I know of no other item in this pattern. It may have been one of a long list of articles, including a four-piece table set, or perhaps it had a bowl to form a milk and mush set.

145—WEEPING WILLOW

This dainty creamer has the silvery sheen and airy laciness of a particular type of American glass that is world famous—Lacy Sandwich. I am convinced, however, that this piece was made in England about forty years later than Lacy Sandwich originated in this country. One glance will show clearly the basis for the name I have assigned.

It has the most beautiful foot of any creamer in my collection of over 1,800 patterns. It is round and flat. Beneath it is a broad low dome, the roof of which is adorned with the whorled lacy design shown in the drawing. (See cut of bottom.) Two rows of minute beading encircle the base near the perimeter. Inside this ring is a beautiful whorl of tiny beading. The beadwork shows through the base so that light is reflected from the design in a brilliant silver sheen. This is also true of the bowl.

The stem is small, of uniform size, and one inch long. It is covered from top to bottom by vertical fine ribs. Each rib is rounded over the top.

The body is similar to a cup in size and shape and has a lacy dewdrop motif that swirls from near the rim to the narrow stem. Each ray of the swirl is outlined by two low raised lines 1/8 to 1/4 inch apart. The space between them is filled with minute beading or dewdrops. Inside each such design is a long, slender nondescript sprig which seems to wave gently in the breeze. This gives a weeping willow effect. The rays of the swirl are

139

140

141

142

143

Bottom
143

144

145

Bottom
145

Bottom
146

146

graduated to conform to the shape of the body and there are nine of them. The top of the rays forms a scallop near the rim. Between the beaded figures are narrow plain stripes that are the same width for most of their length. Above the beaded figure-work is a narrow plain band considerably wider beneath the lip than elsewhere.

The rim has four large uniform scallops on either side. There is a wide scallop at the back, which is higher than those of the sides. All are filled with short vertical ribbing that extends from the top of the rim to a level line a short distance below it. Here it ends abruptly. This is a charac-teristic English motif. (See *KENT* and SAND-WICH IVY for other illustrations of the same feature.) The rim is plain in front and rises to a high narrow lip.

The handle is generally round throughout and of approximately the same diameter. It has no decoration but is comfortable to use. The creamer is made of thin, brilliantly clear flint glass which has a good resonance when tapped. No defects are discernible. The workmanship, especially of the moldmaker, is good.

Creamer: 3-part mold, 10 ounces, 5 inches tall, 3 1/16 inches wide, and 4 1/2 inches long.

Nothing is known as to when, where, or by whom this piece was made. Neither do we know of the items that may have been produced. It seems to date from between 1865 and 1875.

After World War II, a great deal of old English and European glass was imported into this coun-try and sold through antique shops. This is one of a small number of such pieces used in this book to help buyers compare domestic and foreign pieces. Lacking the time and opportunity to make an ex-tensive study of such ware, the collector may occa-sionally acquire a foreign piece, believing it to be American. I do not know how the ordinary collec-tor can expect to differentiate between early American and early foreign pressed glass, but in any event, the latter will be of fine quality and worth cherishing. This is truly a fascinating little creamer.

146—*ESSES*

This tall attractive barrel-shaped creamer is European and probably English. It is shown here for comparison with early American pressed glass. Collectors must take cognizance of such ware, which is often encountered in our shops to-day.

The upper two-thirds of the body is covered by a band of large reversed S's. Each S is formed by two meandering V-shaped grooves which leave a high inverted V-shaped ridge between them. These curlicues form fancy letters. Below the S's is a band of high-relief apostrophes formed in the same manner. Above the S's is a band of variously sized fans, each of which contains four convex ribs shaped like teardrops. There is also a 1/4-inch plain band below the rim.

The rim itself is low, level, and plain, for a short distance on each side. It rises high at the back for the handle attachment. The lip is low, narrow, and matches the plainness of the entire rim. The handle is pressed, round and unadorned. An S-shaped handle would have been more suita-ble.

The creamer sits on a thick, heavy ringbase, which spreads out from a rather massive foot. Un-derneath is a flattopped dome with a design of whorls and hearts. This is the most beautiful part of the creamer. (See cut of bottom.) The glass is thick heavy flint and has a good resonance when tapped. There are few imperfections. The mold marks are high and rough, but not sharp. The workmanship is substandard. It was probably pro-duced between 1865 and 1875.

Creamer: 3-part mold, 12 ounces, 4 1/8 inches tall, 2 11/16 inches wide, and 4 3/16 inches long.

The creamer is the only item I have seen in this pattern.

147—*SHEFFIELD*

This is an old English piece in an appealing pattern. It is of brilliant, clear, sparkling glass, and the stripes disappear into shimmering light rays. The name is assigned to indicate its origin. The pattern could easily be mistaken for a well-known American pattern called CURTAIN.

The glass is thick, heavy early flint. It is clear, but has an occasional speck of discoloration or bubble. The surface appears smooth until seen under a strong magnifying glass. It is then found to be grained, almost as if frosted. It is difficult to see through one thickness and impossible to see through two. This imparts a silvery sheen to the piece. There is considerable resonance when tapped.

The body is somewhat conoidal in shape—nar-row, and elongated. It has a small capacity, holding less than a teacup. Outwardly it appears to be paneled, though the body is round. This illusion is produced by the drapes that meet in straight lines down the side of the body. Near the rim are six large pecan-shaped figures. Below each is a series of six heavily draped ridges extending downward to the top of the stem. Around the rim and under the lip is a band of plain surface.

The stem is tall and rather heavy for the piece's size. It is hexagonal and commences in a high shelf on the base of the bowl. The edge of this shelf is curved like the draped bars. The stem curves in and then out to a large short knop. It then curves in again, and the panels start a counterclockwise swirl. This is exaggerated as shown in the drawing. No tooling was done on the rim lip, or handle, and the piece was not fire polished, so no force was applied to produce this twist. Only the mold could have imparted such an attractive distortion. What a trying job the moldmaker must have had in chipping three mold sections to get this odd twist. The stem ends in a high shelf on the foot. The edges of the latter are arched inward making the corners project. From each side of the shelf, a wide panel extends to the edge of the foot. They are concave, with rounded ends.

The foot is large, round, and has a heavy ring about the bottom edge. It sits on a still smaller ring. There is a low dome with a large 18-ray star impressed in the base. (See cut.) The rim is scalloped unevenly and has an extra scallop at the back. The lip is narrow and well curved. The pattern probably dates from between 1865 and 1875.

Small creamer: 3-part mold, 13 ounces, 5 3/8 inches tall, 3 inches wide, and 5 inches long.

I know of no other article in this pattern. Perhaps a sugar or mush bowl may have been made.

148—DEWDROP BANDS

This small creamer has characteristics that indicate it is of foreign extraction. A few of its siblings and other relatives are shown in this volume. It does not have a trade or registry mark for positive identification. Nevertheless, there is little to indicate that it was made in this country. It probably is an English "cousin."

It is of clear, thick, flint glass and unusually heavy for its small capacity. There are several bubbles and a few flecks of discoloration. A soft resonance is discernible when lightly tapped. The surface shows that the metal or the mold was too cold when pressed. The numerous wavy hairlines could have been caused by either. The workmanship is mediocre—as illustrated by the stem which is awry. The weight of the body on the stem before the piece was placed in the lehr caused both this

and the "bumpy" effect on the inside bottom of the bowl. Also, the weight of the handle, acting as a fulcrum, forced in the plastic side resulting in a rounded mound on the inner surface.

The body has a quaint attractiveness, though the decoration, admittedly, is overdone. The pouting lip and mule-eared handle give the creamer a rather gawky and top-heavy appearance. The base is round, plain, and slightly domed beneath, where a 20-ray star is deeply impressed. There is a 3/8-inch plain circle in the center of the star. English pieces sometimes use this space to mold their trademark. In American pieces the rays usually meet in the center.

The stem has six flat panels that flow out on the base of the bowl and the top of the foot to form a scalloped raised shelf on each.

The body is bell-shaped. Starting just above the panels of the stem are twenty-four short convex ribs, rounded at the top. They cover the base of the bowl. At the top of these ribs, and slightly below the rim, are two 5/8-inch bands of dewdrops. Each band is bordered by a row of regular-sized dewdrops with four rows of smaller ones in the top band and three rows in the lower. Between these bands a 1 1/8-inch-wide belt encircles the body. It is filled with beveled flattopped cubes standing on their corners. There are three rows of them.

At the top of the body is a narrow plain band which extends from the upper band of dewdrops to the broadly scalloped rim. The rim itself rises sharply at the back to accommodate the top handle attachment. In front, it soars sharply, arches over, and forms a narrow, ugly lip which seems to pout.

The pressed handle simulates an applied one, but the mold marks are so sharp and obvious that the illusion is dispelled. The handle itself is not unattractive, though the shape is poor. It is reeded and splayed at the bottom attachment into a large and attractive blob. The rear projection of the handle shows no reeding, but the upper attachment is both reeded and splayed. Few pressed glass creamers have reeded handles, and still fewer are splayed at both attachments.

Small creamer: 3-part mold, 10 ounces, 4 1/2 inches tall, 2 1/2 inches wide, and 5 1/2 inches long.

No other pieces of this pattern are known, but a sugar bowl is to be expected. This piece is early flint ware and probably dates back as far as the 1860s. It was presented to me by Mr. Charles A. Jacobus of Little Rock, Arkansas.

149—LOVERS

Time was when young couples strolled or went by buggy to cast pebbles from the bridge that spanned the local river. At the foot of the bridge a huge birch tree bared its bole to the blade of young swains. The universal symbol of undying love was that of twin hearts carefully carved into the yielding bark. A name or two, some initials, or a piercing arrow completed the troth. This design appears to have been lifted from the trunk of such a tree. The pattern has not been shown before in American glass literature.

The wide rim has been gilded and each heart has two daisies, with a leaf and crossed stems enameled and baked on. Hearts of this type indicate a product of the 1890-1900 period.

With the flaring top, large lip, and heavy handle, the piece appears top-heavy. It is low and wider at the top than at the bottom. Most of the body is covered by four large well-shaped hearts. Their surfaces are smooth and plain, except for the enameling, and they lack half an inch of joining at the sides. The surface surrounding these figures is finely crinkled, giving the effect of strippling. The upper portions of each heart are outlined with a 1/4-inch band of this crinkling.

The tops of the hearts form eight large rounded scallops. Between these and the rim, the body is smooth and gilded. The rim has three high, wide, and rounded scallops on each side. They do not conform to the scallops over the hearts. The front of the rim rounds over to form a wide-jowled and too generous lip.

The handle is round in cross section and resembles an applied one. It is thick and short. Despite its mass it is an impractical handle since the opening admits only one finger.

The body swells somewhat near the bottom, is beveled slightly, and then cuts in almost horizontally to the short waist. The base is a low ring. Underneath the base is a flat hollow space about which is a wide plain star. This star was quite a problem for the moldmaker who could not fill the available space properly. He reached a point where he could either complete the star and have a wide space remaining, or add another ray and crowd the design. He chose the latter. I have not seen this done before. It is probably the work of an apprentice.

The glass is of excellent quality. The design could have been improved by a few refinements. However, refinements would not have satisfied the highly competitive market existing when this piece was made. Competition was lethal then (about 1890-1900).

Standard creamer: 2-part mold, 15 ounces, 4 1/4 inches tall, 3 3/4 inches wide, and 5 3/4 inches long.

A sugar bowl certainly was made in this novelty pattern and a covered butter dish and spoonholder probably finished out the four-piece table set.

150—PANELLED MEDALLION

This is an early and very fine pattern that is seldom seen today. Apparently little of it was made. The general appearance is one of uprightness and stability in an attractive combination of motifs.

S. T. Millard, in *Goblets II*, Plate 76-4, shows a goblet in this pattern and assigns it the above name. He considered it to be a product of the 1880s. No other glass authority has encountered it.

The body is inverted, bell-shaped, and has straight sides that flare considerably between bottom and top. The bottom of the bowl is plain and flares rapidly from the waist. The sides then turn upward at a less acute angle. Running horizontally around the body, just beneath the rim, is a small raised line. Below it a 5/8-inch stippled band encircles the body. Evenly spaced in the band is a series of beautiful small flowers. Each flower consists of seven dewdrops with one serving as the center. The two front mold marks are covered by formalized sprays of leaves with a beaded flower in the center. These sprays divide the body into three sections, one of which is directly under the lip. The sections are left plain and smooth other than for the attractive, oval medallion in the center. The long axis of each medallion is vertical. An oval band surrounds each and is formed by small beads around the outer border and smaller ones on the inner border. The interior band is cut into rectangles by small raised lines. Each rectangle contains a pyramid which varies in shape according to its relative radial position from the center of the oval. The center is filled with a many-rayed, oval star.

The rim undulates and rises high in front before dipping to form an ample lip which has the appearance of a determined one. The waist is round, vertical, and undecorated. It has a wooden look as if turned on a lathe.

The base slopes out at an angle to form a wide foot before rounding over to terminate in a thick ring. The base is plain and smooth on top. Underneath is a high hollow dome with a stippled band like that about the top of the creamer. (See draw-

147

**Bottom
147**

148

149

**Bottom
150**

150

151

152

**Bottom
153**

153

**Bottom
154**

154

ing of bottom.) This band shows through and appears to be on top. This makes the foot very appealing.

The handle is large, hexagonal and commodious. It has a knop on top for a thumbgrip and a similar one at the bottom for balance. The glass is good quality and of soda-lime composition. It is free of specks and has few bubbles. The mold marks show plainly but they are smooth. The gaffer did not do too good a job of finishing the piece off, but the moldmaker did an excellent job in chipping the molds. We do not know where, or by whom, it was made. I agree with Dr. Millard that it probably dates from 1880-1890.

Standard creamer: 3-part mold, 15 1/2 ounces, 5 3/4 inches tall, 3 11/16 inches wide, and 5 15/16 inches long.

I know only of a goblet and this creamer. With the latter there should have been a sugar bowl, butter dish, and spoonholder. Other items may have been produced also, since in the 1880s glassmakers were prone to produce many articles in each pattern.

151—DELAWARE

This is one of the "States" series and was put out in 1899 by the U.S. Glass Company of Pittsburgh, Pennsylvania, using the above name and also "No. 15,065." See other information in this book about the "States" series.

Minnie Watson Kamm is the only author on pattern glass who has covered this pattern. In her *Two Hundred Pattern Glass Pitchers*, page 103, No. 152, and Plate VI, she used an individual custard cup-shaped creamer to illustrate the DELAWARE pattern. In Plate VI she reproduced an old ad showing a tall vase, individual creamer, oil bottle, toothpick holder, puff box with cover, and an 11-inch oblong fruit bowl. The ad gave the above name and number and also stated: "Made in Crystal with Rose and Gold decoration, and in Emerald, decorated with Gold." It is seen in pink, apple green, and in many items not shown in the ad or mentioned there. Round bowls in silver-plated stands are frequently found. The standard table setting of creamer, sugar bowl, spoonholder, covered butter dish, and sauce dish was made. The clear standard creamer with a gilded top is shown here. (The gilt is badly worn.) This creamer has more attractive lines than the individual creamer, and the pattern shows more distinctly.

Above the waist, and below the level rim, are plain surfaces which encircle the body. Toward

the middle, each has an irregular wavy, beveled edge. On this particular piece, only the top band is gilded, and no color has been applied to the flowers. Between these serrated edges is a wide band with a stippled background—not expertly executed. Suspended from the upper band at each mold mark is a poorly formalized leaf, fruit (?), and flower spray which represent no known variety of plant. Beneath the handle are three leaves and a fruit. In front are four leaves, a fruit, and a flower. On the reverse side are four leaves, a fruit, and two flowers. The fruit (or perhaps buds) are suspended on long raised stems, are somewhat cherry-shaped, and resemble the seed pods of a strawberry bush. The four-petaled flowers also are on long stems and in relief, with frosted surfaces and a design of "exclamation marks" scattered over the petals and radiating from the crown. The leaves are long, veined, and serrated on the edges. All leaf edges are beveled, but some are in high relief, presenting a sawtoothed effect to the touch. With a little more care in design and execution a better pattern would have been obtained. Overall, the round body is shaped like a tall cup or mug.

Most of the rim is flat and level with a rounded edge. In front there is a slight rise and dip where it forms a narrow lip. The handle is somewhat triangular in cross section. It is unusual in that the wide back face carries one of the long serrated leaves similar to those on the body. The serrated edges stand out in high relief, and the tip furnishes a secure thumbgrip. The mold mark inside the handle is high and sharp. The piece sits on a low, narrow ringbase. Underneath, a 20-ray round star is stamped into the flat base.

Although we know the United States Glass Company made this pattern, we have no inkling which of the many factories of the huge combine actually produced it. The overall quality is below that expected of the late 1890s. By then there was no excuse for manufacturing such a mediocre product. If a goblet was made in the pattern, it has a passion for anonymity.

Individual creamer: 3-part mold, weight unknown, 2 1/2 inches tall, other measurements unknown.

Standard creamer: 3-part mold, 13 ounces, 4 inches tall, 3 5/16 inches wide, and 4 15/16 inches long.

152—WASHINGTON

Edwin G. Warman, in *The Third Antiques and Their Current Prices*, pages 132-33, illustrated a large tankard pitcher as WASHINGTON and listed known items. Like several other "States" patterns he covered, he did not show the attribution.

Do not confuse this with a much earlier flint pattern called WASHINGTON and probably named for our first president. The flint version belongs to the pristine era before Washington was admitted to the Union in 1889. Pieces of the earlier pattern are so scarce, there is little likelihood of confusing the two. Even the later version is not plentiful and is described here for the first time in American glass literature. This pattern is similar to OHIO, a known member of the "States" series. (See appendix.). The size and shape are similar, but the curves are softened on this piece, resulting in more charm and minus the austerity of OHIO. Overall, this pattern fits into the "States" series.

The body is cylindrical on the inside and almost so on the outside. The lower portion is encircled by a bulge. They are in three-fourths relief and could easily be damaged in regular use. Above the bulge, the body flares to the rim. The entire upper portion was left unadorned by etching. The curves of the rim are so smooth and flowing that they seem to almost possess rhythm. There is some saddle present, and the lip is attractive. There is a shelf just below the bulge. From this the stem curves in rapidly to a smooth, round waist, then out to the plain base. Beneath, there is a large, hollow dome.

The applied handle is beautifully executed with a large blob at the bottom and a small one at the turned under, upper attachment. Its capacity is one adult finger or two small ones.

This is quality ware, with every precaution taken with metal and workmanship to insure good results. The glass is brilliantly clear and sparkling. Two mold marks show faintly on top of the foot, but the dewdrops would have prevented it from being removed from a two-part mold. It has all the earmarks of the period between 1890 and 1907. If Mr. Warman was correct in naming the pattern, it was manufactured by one of the numerous factories of the U.S. Glass Company of Pittsburgh, Pennsylvania.

Creamer: 4(?)-part mold, 1 pound, 5 3/16 inches tall, 3 7/16 inches wide, and 5 1/6 inches long.

Warman shows the following articles in this pattern: covered bowls in several sizes, open bowls in several sizes, butter dish, cake stand in several sizes, celery tray, champagne, claret, covered compotes in several sizes, open fruit compotes in several sizes, cordial, creamer, cruet,

oblong dishes in several sizes, goblets in two sizes, olive dish, pickle, half-gallon tankard pitcher, three pint tankard pitcher, quart tankard pitcher, half gallon water pitcher, three pint water pitcher, quart water pitcher, pint water pitcher, half pint water pitcher (evidently another creamer), sauce dishes in several sizes, spooner, covered sugar bowl, toothpick holder, tumbler, and wine. In all, fifty-five items were made.

153—CALIFORNIA BEADED GRAPE

This pattern is shown here as CALIFORNIA, one of the "States" series put out by the U.S. Glass Company of Pittsburgh, Pennsylvania, as their "No. 15,059 or CALIFORNIA pattern." It dates from the latter part of the period between 1891 and 1907. It comes in clear, but more often is found in a beautiful emerald green and in a bewildering number of items in round, square, and rectangular shapes.

The following references show this pattern to be better known as BEADED GRAPE. The U.S. Glass Company made and named a pattern for each state between 1891 and 1907. This one's historical interest justifies the listing under the state title. As CALIFORNIA it will be of interest to residents of the state and to collectors interested in assembling specimens of "State" patterns.

1. Lee, in *Early American Pressed Glass*, Pattern 75, pages 207-209, Plate 63, called the pattern BEADED GRAPE. She mentioned it as having been made by the U.S. Glass Company, as their CALIFORNIA pattern.

2. Kamm, in *A Fourth Pitcher Book*, pages 94-95, No. 114, listed it as BEADED GRAPE and apparently was not aware that it was one of the "State" patterns. She said it was given as premiums at the time it was made.

3. Millard, in *Goblets*, Plate 79-4, shows an emerald green goblet as BEADED GRAPE.

4. Enos shows the pattern as BEADED GRAPE on his Chart 1.

5. Metz, in *Early American Pattern Glass*, page 83, No. 928, mentions, but does not illustrate, this pattern as BEADED GRAPE. She says there is a flood of reproductions—both in clear and green.

The low, square creamer bears one of the more pleasing grape designs found in American pressed glass. It was appropriately named CALIFORNIA, but the design is botanically incorrect. The grapevines on the sides are shown as limbs rather than vines, and few tendrils are shown. The large, nearly flat, and roughly square panels have five beautifully executed, veined and stippled leaves.

135

There is a small and a large cluster of grapes, all well rounded and in high relief.

Below the lip a large 15-ray, shell-shaped fan of rounded ribs is splayed over much of the upper part of the panel. A grapevine, showing vine, leaves, tendrils, and fruit is festooned about and beneath the fan. On each side of the rear panel a grapevine starts from the upper attachment of the handle and spreads out on the body, drooping below the lower attachment. The vines are well pruned.

The corners and rim are outlined by a row of large, well-spaced dewdrops—some in three-quarter relief. The rim is level, and the dewdrops extend from the top, down over the sides. The front portion arches up and over to form a spout. The handle is rustic, to simulate a pruned vine, with laterals growing out and bearing fruit on the body. It is round in cross section and has raised nodules scattered over the surface and is minutely lined to appear as bark on a vine.

Underneath, the base is square, flat, and has a grape sprig, intaglio impressed. This type of pressing helps date the pattern. The pressing on the base is inferior to that on the sides. (See cut of bottom.)

The glass is fine nonflint, in a beauftiul shade of emerald green and is fairly well finished off. The mold marks are difficult to find, except on the handle. Just which factory of the U.S. Glass Company made the pattern is not known. The original goblets are very scarce.

Creamer: 3-part mold, 15 ounces, 3 1/2 inches tall, 3 9/16 inches wide, and 5 1/16 inches long.

These articles were made in the pattern: butter dish; cake plate on standard in two sizes; celery tray; celery vase; open compotes on high standards in 7-, 8-, and 9-inch sizes; covered compotes on high standards in 7-, 8-, and 9-inch sizes; shallow compote; small jelly compote, open and covered; cordial; creamer; cruet; dishes, oblong in many types; dishes, square 5 1/4, 6 1/4, 7 1/4, and 8 1/4 inches; goblet; olive dish with handles; pickle dish; oblong platter in different sizes; square 8 1/4-inch plate; square pitchers in several sizes; round pitchers in several sizes; tankard pitchers; salt and pepper shakers; square flat sauce dishes in 3 1/2-, 4-, and 4 1/2" sizes; sauce dishes with handles; spoonholder; square footed sugar bowl; square sugar bowl with flat base; toothpick holder; tumbler; oblong trays in many types; and vases. There may be other items.

See Appendix for other information on the "States" series of pattern glass.

136

154—ALABAMA

The small individual creamer in this pattern was illustrated in Kamm's *Two Hundred Pattern Glass Pitchers*, page 81, No. 112. The standard creamer is shown here for comparison as to size, proportion, etc.

During the depression that gripped the nation around 1890-1891, most glass houses in this country ran into financial difficulties. Eighteen of the largest and some of the best known combined in 1891 to form the United States Glass Company, of Pittsburgh, Pennsylvania. Between 1891 and 1907 this corporation put out a "States" series of tableware. One pattern was to have been named for each state in the union. The project was not completed, though a large number of "States" patterns were manufactured by one or another factory of the combine. (See a list of the factories elsewhere in this book, which joined this group. Also see table showing a list of the names of states known to have had patterns named for them.)

Lee and Millard do not show this pattern. J. Stanley Brothers, Jr., in his *Thumbnail Sketches*, page 42, shows a covered sugar bowl in the ALABAMA pattern and lists the items made. In the same article he discusses the patterns TEXAS, COLORADO, CAROLINA, MARYLAND, MISSOURI, and NEW JERSEY.

The figurework is bold. Six large, highly-raised bull's eyes encircle the upper third of the body. These figures have a large cabochon for a center. A crown of dewdrops surrounds each one. Each eye is on a large, round wafer that completes the eye. They are connected by short, horizontal V-shaped slashes. Each eye is supported at the top of a large, tapered pilaster in high relief. The sharp spine of each figure has been fine-toothed. The sharp point is at the top. The wide portion extends downward and bends on the under side of the base, providing the footing for the piece. On the base the spines are crossbarred. (See drawing of bottom.) A heavy, jeweled necklace is festooned from one bull's eye to another. Above the figurework a wide band is left plain to the rim. More often than not, this was gilded or flashed with ruby.

The creamers are cylindrical and appear stiff. The bottom is flat, with highly raised figures as shown in the drawing, and it is attractive. A raindrop is in the center.

The rim is rounded on top and unevenly scalloped. The lip protrudes well forward. The handle is six-sided and not unusual. The standard creamer does have a good thumbgrip, which is absent on the smaller piece. My individual creamer has a much better fire polish than my standard one. The latter has high, sharp, uncomfortable mold marks. The lime-soda glass is brilliant, clear and sparkling.

Individual creamer: 3-part mold, 6 ounces, 3 1/8 inches tall, 2 1/2 inches wide, and 3 5/8 inches long.

Standard creamer: 3-part mold, 14 ounces, 5 inches tall, 3 1/2 inches wide, and 5 1/2 inches long.

As was the custom in the "States" series, many items were made in this pattern. We know of the following: individual creamer, covered sugar, covered butter, spoonholder, standard creamer, covered honey dish, three sizes of oblong relish dishes, handled jelly, water pitcher, and several compotes. Many other items were made and probably included goblets and tumblers.

155—FLORIDA

FLORIDA was one of the original "States" series put out by the U.S. Glass Company of Pittsburgh. It is widely known as EMERALD GREEN HERRINGBONE—whether in green or clear glass. I am using the state name to fill another gap in the list of known patterns in this series.

Ruth Webb Lee, in *Early American Pressed Glass*, Pattern 230, page 536, and Plate 164-1, presented this pattern and assigned its widely known name. She especially liked its color and thought it had the appearance of being of the 1800s. It may well have been an old pattern given a new name. She did not know the name of the maker. On Plate 164-1 she illustrated an emerald green goblet.

Minnie Watson Kamm, in *Two Hundred Pattern Glass Pitchers*, page 46, No. 61, described and illustrated a small water or milk pitcher. She knew little about the pattern. In her *A Sixth Pitcher Book*, Plate 93, she showed cuts of two full-page advertisements of 1898, by the U.S. Glass Company. The four-piece table setting in the patterns LOUISIANA and FLORIDA was shown. No pattern numbers were used, and no mention was made of other items in the patterns. In the cuts for the ads, the covered butter dishes similar in shape were interchanged, and the FLORIDA piece was shown in the LOUISIANA cut.

S. T. Millard, in *Goblets*, Plate 87-4, named the pattern PANELLED HERRINGBONE. He said it was a product of the 1870s, and came in clear and emerald green. He used a photograph of a goblet, and some aspects of it are indistinct. In his *Goblets II*, Plate 137-3, he illustrated a similar pattern and named it PRISM AND HERRINGBONE.

In *A Fourth Pitcher Book*, page 114, No. 144, Mrs. Kamm called Millard's PRISM AND HERRINGBONE by the title PANELLED HERRINGBONE. She knew her pattern was made by the Imperial Glass Company of Bellaire, Ohio, about 1902. It should not be confused with the FLORIDA pattern.

Alice Hulett Metz, in *Early American Pattern Glass*, pages 176-77, No. 1992, showed a goblet in this pattern and used the Millard title of PANELLED HERRINGBONE. Also as No. 1992, but without an illustration, she covered EMERALD GREEN HERRINGBONE as if it were a different pattern and listed prices for both. She said the latter was being reproduced.

The standard creamer shown here is a beautiful emerald green shade of glass. Although it is not shown in the original ad to have a lid, there is a well-defined ledge for one on the inside at the top. The spoonholder quite possibly had a lid; the LOUISIANA spoonholder clearly shows a ledge for a lid in the ad. With lids, all four pieces of a table setting could be marketed as containers, and this added feature would give a decided boost to whatever commodity they contained. Lids on spoonholders were uncommon, but a few were made. STIPPLED CHERRY is an example.

The creamer is low, cylindrical, with straight, almost vertical, sides. At the bottom, they curve in to the waist, and at the top they flare slightly. There are twelve columns on the body, and they reach from waist to rim. At the foot of each column is a large, highly convex figure with its point up and its base at the waist. These figures look like bamboo sprouts. Each alternate column is filled with highly raised, coarse herringbone, arched like the top of the convex figures, on which they rest. The remaining columns are convex and are left smooth.

Each column on the body ends in a wide, low scallop on the rim. The lip rises slightly and thrusts too far forward. The herringbone column under the lip extends higher than the others do and almost reaches the edge of the lip. At the lower part of the body is a rounded constriction, to what might be called the waist, but which immediately spreads out into a low ringbase. Underneath, the piece is flat and has a round, 30-ray star impressed. It covers the entire base except for the outer ring.

The handle is large and almost round in cross section. It is flat on top and an Anthemion leaf has been impressed there for a thumbgrip. This figure is formed by raised outlines, with the interior space sunken. The mold marks on the handle are high and sharp on the inside. This is production ware, with several scattered bubbles, high mold marks, and only a fair polish.

Creamer, without lid: 3-part mold, 14 ounces, 4 1/4 inches tall, 3 3/4 inches wide, and 5 7/16 inches long.

These articles are known to have been made in the pattern: syrup pitcher, plate with turned up corners, milk pitcher, berry bowl, covered butter dish, celery vase, covered sugar bowl, spoon-holder, high compote, cordial, creamer with lid, cruet, toothpick holder, pickle dish, 7 1/4-inch plate, 9 1/4 inch plate, sauce dish, salt and pepper shakers, tumbler, cake stand, wine, water pitcher, etc. It is being made today and sold in our gift shops. It can be found in emerald green, clear, amber and blue.

156—NEW HAMPSHIRE

Three authors have each assigned a different name to this particular pattern. In selecting one as preferable, I intend no criticism. S. T. Millard, in *Goblets II* (1940), Plate 63-3, showed a goblet and named it MODISTE. He thought it was of the 1880s and came in clear only. Minnie Watson Kamm, in *A Third Two Hundred Pattern Glass Pitchers* (1943), page 97, No. 148, described the pattern and named it appropriately BENT BUCKLE. She knew neither the maker nor that it was made as late as the 1890s to 1907. She knew some pieces were flashed with different colors. Edwin G. Warman, in *The Third Antiques and Their Prices*, illustrated a tumbler and listed the items known under the title NEW HAMPSHIRE. He did not give the source of his title or attribution.

The U.S. Glass Company of Pittsburgh put out a series of pressed glass patterns from 1891 to about 1907 and named a pattern for each state of the Union as of that time. Arizona, New Mexico and Oklahoma were admitted to the Union after 1907, so no pattern was named for them. A pattern was named DAKOTA for both North and South Dakota. Another was called CAROLINA for both the Carolinas. Possibly the pattern VIRGINIA was also used for both Virginia and West Virginia, since we know of no pattern named for the latter. The list is almost complete, but we have no knowledge of patterns named for Arkansas, Mississippi, Montana, Nebraska, New York, or Rhode Island. What a thrill it would be to discover one of the missing six patterns. Imagine, if you please, the historical value of a collection made up of specimens from each pattern of the "States" series. (See appendix.)

Mrs. Kamm used an individual creamer to illustrate the pattern. Since I have both the individual and standard creamers, I will use the latter. The standard creamer sits on a flat base. The upper two-fifths of the cylindrical body is plain and smooth. Often, this surface was gilded or flashed with cranberry, ruby, purple, and possibly amber or green. The lower three-fifths of the body has the pressed pattern. Four large, arched buckles dominate the design, extending from the top of the pattern to the bottom where they bend under and end in fans. In the center of each buckle is a long, narrow thumbprint with a slightly raised rim on each crater. About the thumbprint the surface of each buckle is covered with small diamond point. The spaces between the buckles are filled with imitation cut glass figures such as diamond point, fan, hobstar, fine-tooth, and cane.

The rim is thick, round, and lacks style. It has a slight saddle and slopes up to an unattractive lip. The base has a beautiful imitation cutwork design—as would appear in a kaleidoscope—with four, rather than six, segments. The pattern is too complex to describe, but its symmetry is delightful. (See drawing of bottom.)

The handle permits a secure grip. It is large and six-sided. Each side panel is covered with fine rib. A small area on top is flat and covered with small diamond point, to provide a better thumbgrip.

Some pieces found in the pattern are of brilliantly clear lime-soda glass. Others have a decidedly dingy appearance. The glass is soft and easily abraded in use. When flashed with color or gilded, the work was done with care, though it really has too much surface to be gilded. This pattern is probably of the "States" series and was made by one of the many factories that joined the U.S. Glass combine. We have no facts on which to make attribution. We will, however, use Warman's title, call it NEW HAMPSHIRE, and consider it one of the series until we receive information to the contrary. It is an attractive pattern.

Individual creamer: 4-part mold, 10 ounces, 3 1/8 inches tall, 2 7/8 inches wide, and 3 7/8 inches long.

Standard creamer: 4-part mold, 1 pound 2 1/2 ounces, 4 15/16 inches tall, 3 1/4 inches wide, and 5 3/16 inches long.

The following items are known to have been made in this pattern: covered biscuit jar; standard creamer, sugar bowl, butter dish, and spoonholder; individual creamer, sugar bowl, butter dish, and spoonholder; bowls, flared 6 1/2-, 7 1/2-, 8 1/2- and 10-inch; bowls, round in same

155

156

156

Bottom

156

157

Bottom

157

Top
(inverted)

158

159

158

160

161

160

Bottom

160

four sizes; bowls, square in same four sizes; tall celery; champagne; lemonade cup; large mug; small mug; three pint water pitcher; half-gallon tankard water pitcher; three-fourths-gallon water pitcher; round deep sauces; four-inch flared round sauce; square sauce; flared square sauce; tumbler; wine and napkin holder.

It would not be surprising to find salt and pepper shakers, carafe, water tray, waste bowl, molasses pitcher, sugar sifter, pickle caster, decanter, vase, compote, relish dish, and cruet.

157—THE STATES

This pattern is unusual in that we have information about it that we would like to have about all pattern glass. We know when, and by whom, it was manufactured, but not exactly where. We do not know which of nineteen factories of the huge combine actually made it.

The U.S. Glass Company of Pittsburgh put the pattern out on February 9, 1905, with full-page advertisements saying it was "The Winner of the Year." They called it THE STATES and assigned it company number "15,093." Evidently this was at, or near, the end of their series of patterns for different states of the union. There are several gaps in our information about the "States" series. They all, apparently, fell between the company's "No. 15,001" and "No. 15,093." This subject is dealt with more fully, elsewhere in this book.

Minnie Watson Kamm, in *A Fifth Pitcher Book*, pages 142-43, No. 188, used the massive water pitcher to illustrate and describe the pattern. On Plate 25 of that book she reproduced the original advertisement which showed several items of the pattern.

The standard creamer shown here serves to give proportions, measurements, etc. It is squatty and looks ponderous but is not excessively heavy.

Eight wide columns in high relief make the predominant motif. They bend under the bottom where they taper to points and meet in the center. Each point has a three-lobe fan impressed into it. (See drawing of bottom.)

The heavy columns extend a third of the way up the body. Atop each is a large round medallion. (The medallions are ellipses on the water pitcher.) Under each medallion is a large crescent drape, in high relief, with a strigiled crest. The highly beveled medallions are alternately filled with a cane design of hexagonal buttons and deeply impressed 12-ray irregular stars set in a background of fine rib. The ribs radiate from the center. The

columns do not reach the rim. There is a half-inch irregular band about the top which probably was gilded in some cases.

The glass is thick at the rim, and the latter is double scalloped. There is a high, wide scallop over each disc, each of which has five smaller scallops. In front, the scalloping extends nearer the spout than is usually found. The thick lip is flattopped.

The handle is thick and massive with a limited finger capacity. It is six-sided and has a strange arrangement at the widely splayed, plain upper attachment. Mold marks are found there which are difficult to interpret, since no mold marks are found elsewhere on the piece. It is wider than it is thick and has been further widened on top, where there is a medallion the size of a dime, which is filled with cane design, and similar to the large ones on the body. This makes an attractive thumbgrip. The outside corners of the handle are heavily strigiled. The lower attachment is not flared to the extent of the upper one, but it does make a high shelf.

The glass is of superlative lime-soda quality, is brilliant and clear, and has no defects. It has been so highly firepolished that the number of mold marks cannot be determined.

Standard creamer: ?-mold marks, 1 1/16 pounds, 3 7/8 inches tall, 3 7/8 inches wide, and 5 15/16 inches long.

Water pitcher: 3-part mold, over 4 pounds, 8 inches tall. Other measurements unknown.

The following items are known to have been made in the pattern: standard creamer; sugar bowl; covered butter dish; spoonholder; water pitcher; celery vase; tumbler; tall, footed fruit bowl; an odd, square, sanitary, toothpick dispenser; 7-inch square plate; and a low, oval, individual creamer.

158—DIAPERED FLOWER

This creamer is again used to show it complete with its lid. What a charming little compote the lid makes when it sits on its finial. (See drawing of lid.)

Mrs. Kamm, in *A Sixth Pitcher Book*, page 44, No. 101, showed this creamer without a lid and assigned it the above name. She said her piece was "opaque blue, a rather dull 'Eleanor Blue,' with occasional streaks and swirls of opaque white through it." My creamer is of the same dismal color. Millard, in *Goblets II*, Plate 102-4, showed a goblet that appears to belong to this pattern and named it KNOTTED CORD. He said his pattern was made in clear only and was of the 1880s.

This creamer is made of an odd shade of opaque blue milk glass which appears dark green under fluorescent light. It is not a pretty shade of blue. Indistinct streaks of light and dark glass run through it. Note the similarity between this and the following creamer. Both are of the same dull color, and they are similar in size and shape.

In the 1907-1908 catalog of the Indiana Glass Company, of Dunkirk, Indiana, some glass steins were shown. They were made of the same colored glass as the two lidded creamers shown here. These particular steins were not shown with lids, but they sometimes are found with them. They were containers for marketing condiments, as are these creamers.

The lower two-thirds of the body is covered with a trellis effect which has forget-me-nots at the junction of each two slats. The trellis and flowers are in well-raised relief. Around the top third is a smaller type of trellis without flowers. The two sections are separated by a raised ring. The piece sits on a small ring at the base. Underneath is a wide, deep, and flat-roofed dome. The handle is six-sided and angular. A quick glance indicates it is square. Inside the body, and below the rim, is a well-defined ledge to accomodate the unusual and attractive lid.

We do not know who made this container. I think it was the Indiana Glass Company. The Westmoreland Specialty Company specialized in making similar ware during the 1890s, but never with finials like this. I have never heard of their products being made in glass other than clear, turquoise blue, and milk white. This, of course, does not mean other colors may not have been used.

Covered creamer: 4-part mold, 13 ounces, 4 7/8 inches tall, 3 inches wide, and 4 inches long.

This jewel of a covered creamer is the only piece I have seen in the pattern. I am unable to say whether Millard's goblet belongs to the same pattern. The only other articles in the pattern likely to turn up would be a covered sugar, covered spoonholder, or perhaps, a covered water pitcher.

159—*AZURE*

Dr. Millard, in *Goblets*, Plate 81-3, gave the title LATTICE AND OVAL PANEL to the early flint pattern that follows. The latter is called FLAT DIAMOND AND PANEL by Mrs. Lee. Regrettably, the pattern he used had neither lattice nor oval panels. The pattern used here fits his descriptive title perfectly since it does have such figures. However, he has preempted the title, and it should not be used again to further confuse glass nomenclature. This little blue fellow with the lid is therefore named *AZURE*.

Warman, in *Milk Glass Addenda*, Plate 54 B and C, shows a two-handled, open sugar bowl in this pattern which from the photograph appears to be about the same shade of blue as my creamer. He calls it ROSE SWAG, but the creamer, as well as the sugar bowl, are devoid of either. Apparently, the titles of his exhibits B and C were accidentally switched. Under B, which is milk white, he has the title OVAL PANEL, BLUE. Acting on that assumption we will accept the title OVAL PANEL as the one he intended this pattern to have. Other patterns have been named OVAL PANEL, however, so a new name seems necessary.

This creamer is so similar to the one immediately preceding that we feel certain they came from the same glass house, at about the same time. Their color, size, conformation, lids, quality of glass, workmanship, and the raised trellis figurework all bespeak a close familial relationship.

This piece is somewhat constricted through the middle and is wider at the base and rim. It is also thicker and shorter than the preceeding pitcher. Their liquid capacities are the same.

Four large, plain ovals on the body reach from rim to base. Their surfaces follow the contours of the creamer and are smooth. White streaks are mixed through the blue. Each oval is surrounded by a highly raised band. Between the ovals, all space is filled with latticework in high relief.

The handle is round and of uniform size. Under the wide base is a sagging, domed roof.

Inside the body, and below the rim, is a well-defined ledge to hold the lid. The lid is devoid of decoration, except on top of the finial. This lid does not form a compote since it will not sit on its finial. The two lids are not interchangeable. Probably other and similar containers were made.

The metal and workmanship are good. These are attractive pieces that anyone would cherish. They would under no circumstances be dropped into a garbage can when empty, as happens to empty bottles today. If such pieces were disposed of in such manner, they would certainly make the garbage look stylish.

Covered creamer: 3-part mold, 15 ounces, 4 7/8 inches tall, 3 3/8 inches wide, and 4 5/8 inches long.

I know of only this creamer and a two-handled, open sugar bowl. The latter probably had a lid. We would expect a spoonholder and possibly a covered water pitcher.

160—FLAT DIAMOND AND PANEL

This magnificent, stately creamer is a fairly well authenticated product of the Boston and Sandwich Glass Company of Sandwich, Massachusetts. It is contemporary with SANDWICH STAR. In her *Sandwich Glass*, Plate 216, lower left, Ruth Webb Lee shows a goblet with a round, instead of a faceted, knop on the stem. On page 536 she lists it as a pattern identified from Sandwich fragments. In her *Victorian Glass*, page 54, and Plate 21-1, she shows a decanter with metal stopper, an eggcup, covered eggcup, and goblet. It is difficult to identify the pattern from her drawings. She supplied the above title and thought the pattern dated from the late 1850s and early 1860s.

On Plate 81-3, of his *Goblets*, S. T. Millard shows a goblet of sparkling glass and thought it was of the 1870s. He assigned the somewhat inappropriate title of LATTICE AND OVAL PANELS. I agree with Mrs. Lee as to the approximate date of manufacture.

Alice Hulett Metz, in *Early American Pattern Glass*, page 29, No. 252, mentions, but does not illustrate, the pattern. She uses the Millard title in preference to that of Lee. Mrs. Metz quotes prices for the pattern in clear, milk white, and opaque colors.

This is one of the finer patterns of early flint glass. It was produced near the end of the era of the heavy, massive types we enthusiastically garner today. This transition piece maintains the weight and mass that is distributed evenly to impart more grace. It is unfortunate that the pattern is so scarce.

The tall, slender body has a small capacity. The lower two-thirds of the body carries the pattern. The unusual mold marks follow the high points of the pattern and can be traced on their tortuous course. One mold mark surrounds the creamer at the top of the figurework. Above this, the glass is thinner and has been hand tooled into shape. Around the lower portion are three large, roughly oval-shaped figures formed by deep V-shaped grooves. The ends of these ovals are pointed and their surfaces are flattened till they resemble tatting bobbins. Alternating with these are panels of what Dr. Millard called lattice and Mrs. Lee called diamonds. They are not lattice work, but highly beveled, flattopped diamonds which stand on their long axes. The top row has three diamonds and the bottom row one. In between they vary from one or two per row, increasing in size as they near the top. The plain band at the top is pinched-in slightly and then flares to the rim.

At the rim the glass is thick and rounded over the top. On the rear half there is a wide scallop on each side and a still larger one at the back, which provides anchorage for the upper handle attachment. The front half of the rim swells in a high, beautiful arch and then is depressed into a spout.

The thick handle is applied with the large blob at the top. The lower attachment was made over the diamonds, and it left many pockets to catch dirt. The gaffer apparently did not have the proper know-how, for in shaping the rim he could easily have formed it so the handle would fall on a flat, smooth oval. The lower attachment was sheared to a sharp point, then doubled back on itself and left plain. It serves its purpose but was not expertly done.

The stem, with a large faceted knop, is attractive. The goblet has a large round knop instead of a faceted one. I know of only a few creamers with this type of stem; they are TULIP AND SAWTOOTH, SANDWICH STAR, TALL ARGUS, and WAFFLE AND THUMBPRINT. Imagine how difficult it must have been to chip a mold with the mold lines following the high points of the pattern, and the task of making such knops may be better understood. This also probably explains their scarcity. The stem ends on top with a sharp-pointed star that mitres into the lower part of the body figures. It is six-paneled above and below with the panels swelling out to a wide knop in the middle. This is an imitation cut glass motif. The lower part of the stem flows out and ends on a low, round shelf. The piece was held at the foot by a clamp, while the handtooling was done on top. It had to be kept rotating, and this caused a twist of the stem.

The base is wide, round, and thick. Midway on top, it arches up to the stem shelf. Underneath, a star with twelve rays is impressed which shows through when seen from above. (See cut of bottom.)

The glass is brilliantly clear, early flint, very heavy, and yet has no resonance when tapped. The work of both the designer and moldmaker was superb. The gaffer left some hairlines and pulled a 'booboo' on the handle.

Creamer: 3-part mold, 1 9/16 pounds, 7 inches tall, 3 5/16 inches wide, and 5 1/2 inches long.

These articles are known to have been made: creamer, sugar bowl, celery vase, champagne, goblet, eggcup, covered eggcup, footed salt, and spillholder. Certainly a spoonholder, covered butter dish, decanter, wine, and water pitcher must have been made.

161—FLICKERING FLAME

Mrs. Kamm, in *A Second Two Hundred Pattern Glass Pitchers*, page 92, shows this creamer in milk-white glass and calls it FLICKERING FLAME. The creamer shown here is of clear glass. This is another interesting container creamer with a lid. Undoubtedly it made its debut full of pungent, tangy prepared mustard, horseradish, or other condiment. Probably a covered sugar bowl was the only additional item manufactured in this pattern. Butter dishes, plates, bowls, etc., do not lend themselves well to the marketing of prepared mustard or horseradish.

The low, oval, medium-sized body sits on a slight ring and is quite stable. The bowl is covered with graceful, swirling figurework, which Mrs. Kamm called FLICKERING FLAME. The body has nine convolutions and, except for the swirl, is similar to a cantaloupe. Each convolution is covered by three sets of three inverted V-shaped ridges, with each separated from the next by a row of small, closely placed dewdrops. The latter do not extend to the bottom of the ridges. The ridges, in turn, do not extend to the base, but leave a plain space at the bottom of each column.

Above the flames is a half-inch band that flares to a rim with nine broad scallops to conform to the columns of the body. Two of them, on either side, are finely scalloped. The large scallop at the handle has a smaller one on each side. The three broad scallops in front are plain, higher than the rest of the rim, and form a broad lip.

On the inside of the bowl, near the top, is a wide level ledge to hold a lid. The lid has the same flickering flame figurework as the body. The finial is oval and eight-lobed with a large dewdrop on top. It provides a firm grasp, and there is little likelihood of ever dropping the lid. The underside of the base is plain and smooth. It was here the manufacturer placed his sticker, listing the contents. The handle has six sides. The two lateral faces are ornamented with a row of dewdrops.

Covered creamer with lid: 4-part mold, 1 1/16 pounds, 5 inches tall, 3 5/8 inches wide, and 5 3/4 inches long.

This creamer may have been marketed with a surface coating of bright, flashy, and easily removed paint, though none now shows.

The quality is fair. There is a decided tinge to the glass. It probably was produced between 1890 and 1910. The Westmoreland Specialty Company is known to have made many similar containers.

162—*SWIRL AND CUBE*

This creamer is shown to present its appearance when accompanied by a lid and also to comment on the nomenclature involved. The title is changed from SWIRL AND DIAMOND to *SWIRL AND CUBE*.

In *A Fourth Pitcher Book*, page 94, No. 113, Minnie Watson Kamm covered two similar patterns in a single write-up and named both SWIRL AND DIAMOND. (Her upper creamer was the one shown here.) This caused confusion between the two patterns and shows the difficulty one is confronted with in assigning suitable names to patterns of pressed glass. Consider the following:

1. In her *A Second Two Hundred Pattern Glass Pitchers*, page 106, she previously assigned the same title, SWIRL WITH DIAMOND, to an entirely different pattern for which it was more appropriate.
2. In her *A Sixth Pitcher Book*, page 32, No. 58, Plate 11, Mrs. Kamm reproduced a full-page advertisement of 1890 by the Riverside Glass Works of Wellsburg, West Virginia, which presented eight items in the pattern mentioned above. The company called the pattern AMERICA. This pattern was also made under the same title (AMERICA) at the same time, by the American Glass Company of Anderson, Indiana, who also gave it the same stock number (348).
3. At the time Kamm was covering the first-named pattern, SWIRL AND DIAMOND, Dr. Millard was preparing his *Goblets II*, and on Plate 131-2 he showed a goblet of the AMERICA pattern and called it SWIRL AND SAWTOOTH.
4. Metz, in *Early American Pressed Glass*, pages 212-13, No. 2433, illustrated a goblet and used the Kamm title of SWIRL AND DIAMOND.

This creamer with lid has no diamonds in its figurework. The so-called *diamonds* are really beveled squares or cubes. For this reason I have called it *SWIRL AND CUBE*. This leaves Mrs. Kamm's large creamer shown in her second, fourth, and sixth books with the SWIRL AND DIAMOND title.

Mrs. Kamm did not know how this creamer was made when she wrote of it. The mold marks indicated it was pressed in a mold. The bulbous interior shows the pattern in reverse. Pressing could not have formed the bulbous portion. Mrs. Kamm later learned this shape of container was made possible by a patent of the Hipkins Novelty Mold Works of Martins Ferry, Ohio. The neck of these pieces was pressed and left smooth inside. The bulbous portion was machine blown in a mold, and the two pieces were fused together while still viscous. I have both creamers, and the larger shows plainly where the parts were fused together. The metal was too cold to flow freely, and this resulted in a poor fusion where the neck joins the body.

We have no idea where these containers were made, but they date from about 1890-1900. They probably were not marketed as table ware, but rather as containers for a product. Condiments, preserves, tea, baking powder, olives, pickles, gherkins, pearl onions, and other goodies were sold, for the most part in such containers. (A practice recently renewed by a manufacturer of peanut butter who uses goblets.) Both Jewel Tea and Larkin used a large quantity of such ware in those days.

The small, vertical neck is covered by nine bands of beveled, flattopped cubes, which stand on their corners. This causes diagonal lines to both right and left. The inside of the neck is smooth and round. The lower part of the creamer is bulbous and is covered with regular, counterclockwise swirls in high convex relief. On the inside the swirls are concave.

The small lid fits snugly on a flat ledge on the inside, immediately below the rim. Its figurework is on the underside and shows through. It simulates the cubes on the neck. The effect is achieved by slightly raised lines that cross each other at regular intervals. The rim is uneven. The lip is "uppity." The base is low and has a slight ring. The handle is small, round in cross section, and uniform in size. The glass is of excellent quality, and the workmanship indicates an expensive product was packed in this piece. It has every appearance of quality and none of production ware. The glass is quite thin and the piece is light.

Covered creamer with lid: 4-part mold, 10 ounces, 4 3/4 inches tall, 3 1/8 inches wide, and 3 11/16 inches long.

In addition to the creamer, I have seen a spoonholder and sugar bowl in this pattern. It is doubtful if other items were manufactured, unless possibly a water pitcher.

163—DIAMOND SWIRL

I am tempted to put this creamer back on my shelf and select another. This write-up will explain why.

Minnie Watson Kamm used an individual sized creamer to cover the pattern in *A Fourth Pitcher Book*, page 93, No. 112, and called it DIAMOND SWIRL. The details are not too clear in her drawing. I have the standard creamer with a ribbed applied handle. The present drawing is more distinct, exact measurements are given, and cross references listed.

In this pattern, the swirls run counterclockwise. Three heavy prisms (the middle one notched

or strigiled) alternate with three rows of huge diamond point, or small sawtooth, to form the figurework.

Kamm, in *A Sixth Pitcher Book*, page 33, No. 59, and Plate 33, gave a short written coverage inasmuch as she had not seen the pattern. On Plate 33, she reproduced an 1895 advertisement of the U.S. Glass Company showing their "15,042" pattern. A large punch bowl and eight punch cups are seen sitting on a huge matching tray. She named it ZIPPERED SWIRL AND DIAMOND. In this pattern the swirls run clockwise. The general motif varies slightly from that of DIAMOND SWIRL. The punch bowl shows five prisms and five rows of diamond point, while the punch cups show three prisms and three rows of diamond point, as on this creamer. I believe they belong to the same pattern. (The negative for the ad may have been reversed as often happened in pictures of those days.)

In *A Second Pitcher Book*, page 106, Mrs. Kamm illustrated a beautiful tall tankard with a plain top, in a similar motif and called it SWIRL AND DIAMOND. (Note the tricky nomenclature.) Her drawings show five prisms and many rows of diamonds all swirled counterclockwise. In *A Sixth Pitcher Book*, page 32, No. 58, and Plate 11, she made no drawing, but used a reproduction of an old advertisement instead. The full-page ad was by the Riverside Glass Company, of Wellsburg, West Virginia. It showed several articles and listed many others in SWIRL AND DIAMOND. That is not the pattern shown here. The ad was dated 1890. (See preceding pattern.)

Dr. Millard, in *Goblets II*, Plate 131-2, shows a goblet with etching around the top and an elaborate stem. It is identical with Kamm's SWIRL AND DIAMOND; nevertheless, he named it SWIRL AND SAWTOOTH. The difference between diamond point and sawtooth is relative and variable. Both are rectangular prisms or pyramids. Large diamond point on a small piece would be called sawtooth. Small sawtooth on a large piece would be called diamond point. ("You pays yer penny an' you takes yer choist.") These patterns combine well. If you are collecting any of the variants, you should become familiar with all—especially those with the tricky, reversed titles.

This squat bulbous creamer is very attractive. It has a plain band below the scalloped rim. It sits on a wide ringbase narrower than the body, but still providing ample stability. The bottom is slightly hollowed and has a large, 22-ray daisy impressed therein.

Mrs. Kamm did not mention the handle in her

write-up of the small creamer. It is plain and, from her drawing, appears to be applied. On this standard creamer a large, beveled square was provided for the large blob at the lower attachment. The handle is ribbed, swirled, applied and attractive. The upper attachment was turned under and fastened to the plain band below the rim. When this attachment was made the glass had cooled too much, and the ribs did not flow out. With only the crests of the ribs joining the body, there are numerous deep pockets, now filled with dirt that cannot be removed. The piece is a quality product. It is clear, brilliant, and smooth.

Individual Creamer: 4-part mold, weight unknown, 2 3/4 inches tall, other measurements unknown.

Standard creamer: 4-part mold, 1 pound, 4 1/16 inches tall, 4 7/16 inches wide, and 6 inches long.

The pattern was made in about thirty articles.

164—GRAPE JUG

This beautiful jug is used again in the hope someone may carry on, where I met an impasse. Mrs. Kamm used and named this covered jug in *A Fifth Pitcher Book*, page 95, No. 128. I have the creamer and also a water pitcher with a lid. It is similar to the creamer, though larger. I have also found a family who have a similar covered water pitcher which they had purchased from the Jewel Tea Company some forty or fifty years ago full of tea.

A letter, with a drawing of the creamer, was sent to the Jewel Tea Company, of Barrington, Illinois, with a request for help in determining when it was used, where it was purchased, etc. They wrote that they had no knowledge of it. They said in the past that they had purchased most of their glassware from three companies, whose names and addresses they furnished. None of the three had knowledge of the piece. One company suggested that I write the McKee Division, of the Thatcher Glass Manufacturing Company, Inc., of Jeannette, Pennsylvania. This was done, and their longtime employees could not identify the pattern as made by McKee. This, of course, does not mean McKee did not make it. Someone who reads this may be able to help trace the time and place of its origin and the name of its manufacturer.

We know of a dozen patterns of this general type. The glass is thin, all pieces originally had lids, and all have small necks with large bulbous bodies; also all were containers. We have no information as to who made them. Probably all or most of them emanated from a single factory. They are named and described by Mrs. Kamm in her pitcher books as:

1. QUILT AND FLUTE, KI-71-98 (Also in this book.)
2. LATE PANELLED GRAPE, VARIANT, KI-117-189.
3. CHERRY SPRIG, K2-56 (Also in this book.)
4. STRAWBERRY WITH CHECKERBOARD, K4-103-127.
5. CHERRY WITH THUMBPRINT, K4-104-128.
6. GRAPE JUG, K5-95-128, this write-up.
7. GRAPE WITH THUMBPRINT, K5-96-129.
8. SHASTA DAISY, K6-23-35.
9. STRAWBERRY JAR, K7-17-33.
10. LITTLE FLOWER, K7-53-108.
11. JAM JAR, K8-28-48.
12. SUNFLOWER, CONTAINER, K8-29-49.

A description of this creamer will not be given since Mrs. Kamm described it so well in *A Fifth Pitcher Book*. The drawing is sufficient. Measurements are given for comparative purposes.

Covered creamer: 2-part mold, 12 ounces, 5 3/4 inches tall, 3 5/8 inches wide, and 4 3/8 inches long.

Covered Water pitcher: 2-part mold, 2 3/8 pounds, 9 5/8 inches tall, 5 3/4 inches wide, and 6 5/8 inches long.

No other items in this pattern are known to the writer. A covered sugar bowl, marmalade jar, spoonholder, or pickle jar would be the other items most likely to have been used as containers.

165—PANELLED THISTLE

This is a late pattern which either has been in continuous production, or has been widely reproduced. It still remains a very popular pattern. This is surprising because the quality is only fair and the design is a mixture of divergent motifs which do not harmonize. Is the demand due to the moderate price? A moderate price is almost prerequisite for widespread collecting of a pattern today.

This pattern, fortunately, was produced by a company that identified most of its products by a trademark. It was made by The J. B. Higbee Glass Company of Bridgeville, Pennsylvania. This is a company about which we have little accurate information. Moreover the available data is conflicting. Apparently it was established after 1899 and soon adopted a trademark of a small bee formed by raised lines. On the left wing is an *H*, on the abdomen an *I*, and on the right wing a *G*, thus forming HIGbee. They did almost no advertising. It is known that they did not join the U.S. Glass Company trust, nor did they later enter the National

Glass Combine. (See Appendix for list of companies joining these corporations.)

Another well-known pattern carrying the Higbee trademark is CANE AND SPRIG, also shown in this book. Some writers frown on CANE AND SPRIG but praise PANELLED THISTLE highly. Why? They were both made by the same company and at approximately the same time. Neither is reproduced more than the other. This may be due to the mistaken impression, by the general public, as to their relative ages. In my opinion, CANE AND SPRIG is a slightly more desirable pattern.

A milk or lemonade pitcher was used by Minnie Watson Kamm in *Two Hundred Pattern Glass Pitchers*, page 83, to illustrate and describe PANELLED THISTLE. The standard creamer is used here to illustrate, show measurements and proportions and for comparison with other patterns with a thistle motif. PANELLED THISTLE was shown by Ruth Webb Lee as Pattern 168, pages 424-26, and Plates 114 and 141, in her *Early American Pressed Glass*. In her write-up she pointed out the pieces being reproduced.

S. T. Millard, in *Goblets*, Plate 163-1, shows a flared goblet in this pattern and says it is a product of the 1890s. In his *Goblets II*, Plate 77-1, he shows a straight-sided goblet. Alice Hulett Metz, in *Early American Pattern Glass*, pages 68-69, No. 746, covers the pattern. She says it was made in Pittsburgh, and calls it a pitfall pattern because so many of its items have been reproduced.

Mrs. Kamm thought the milk pitcher and standard creamer were identical except for height. They also differ in appearance, however, for the milk pitcher with six prism buttresses seems to be hexagonal. The creamer with four appears square.

On page forty-six of the June, 1940, issue of *Hobbies—The Magazine for Collectors*, Jennie Lloyd had an article entitled "Join Up With Panelled Thistle." Little data was given about the pattern, and the fact that it is trademarked was not mentioned. The article was slanted toward collecting the pattern, not toward describing it. On the cover was a fine picture of a cabinet filled with pieces of the pattern from the author's collection.

The large buttresses stand out in high relief and extend from rim to base. They are notched immediately above the base, and in a way, form clumsy-looking feet. They bear no relation to the remaining figurework, except to divide the sides into segments—which could have been done more pleasingly. Two of the segments carry the thistle motif with the flower being unmistakable. The intaglio stem, buds, and the absence of leaves resemble a form of cactus. The stems are deep V-shaped grooves which meander from base almost to the top. The sides of the channel are pressed with fine rib, thus making the stems appear to be herringbone. The buds are not of the thistle and are purely ornamental. The intaglio pressing helps date the pattern as after 1900.

The other two segments carry half a sunburst at the base and a complete one at the top. In the center of each is a beveled pentagon, with a daisy pressed into its face. About this are a number of triangular pyramids. From each corner of the pentagon, a 1/4-inch band radiates outwards. Each top is filled with fine cut design. Between the wide rays are numerous smaller ones extending outward from the corona.

The handle is formed on top of the rear buttress. It is six-sided, and the side panels have a row of flat-surfaced, beveled, hexagonal buttons, with triangular pyramids between.

This particular creamer does not carry the trademark, and the collector of this pattern quickly learns that not all pieces of the pattern did.

The back portion of the rim is thick and has a flat top. It is double scalloped to resemble cut glass. The front portion is rounded over. It first arches up, then down in curves that tend to soften the stiletto like buttresses.

The glass and workmanship of this piece are only fair. It is below the level of technical excellence that had been attained at that time.

Standard creamer: 4-part mold, 14 ounces, 4 5/8 inches tall, 3 1/2 inches wide, and 5 1/8 inches long,

Milk or lemonade pitcher: 2-part Mold(?), weight unknown, 7 inches tall, other measurements unknown.

The collector should be on guard, since several items in this pattern are being made today. The articles known to have been made are: wines, two types; bowls, many sizes, footed and flat, round and square; water tumbler; lemonade tumbler; covered butter dish; creamer; covered sugar bowl; two handled spoonholder; water pitcher; milk or lemonade pitcher; vases in two sizes; tall cake stand; celery vase; celery tray; cordial; cruet; cheese dish; sherbet cup; punch cup; (Was a punch bowl made?) sauce dishes in several sizes; compotes, open, many sizes; salt well; salt and pepper shakers; pickle dishes in two sizes; plates, square and round in four sizes; goblets, two types; dishes, many sizes, both oval and square. These pieces are pressed in the original mold, and the pattern has been in continuous production, rather than being lately reproduced.

162

163

164

165

Bottom
165

166

NEAR CUT

167

168

Bottom
166

166—LATE THISTLE

We know definitely who manufactured this pattern and approximately when. Mrs. Kamm, in *Two Hundred Pattern Glass Pitchers*, page 116, illustrated and described it, using a milk pitcher. Her piece bore the trademark *Near Cut* impressed on the inside of the bottom. I have the smaller and more graceful standard creamer and it carries the same trademark.

The colossus which resulted from the combining of 19 large glass factories into the National Glass Company in 1898, built only one new factory and it was at Cambridge, Ohio. It was later known as the Cambridge Glass Company. From 1901 to 1906 they used a trademark of a *C* inside a triangle. In 1906 they adopted the trademark Near Cut and called their factory 'The Home of "Near Cut" '. Since 1916 they have made only the finest tableware. This pattern, therefore, was made between 1906-1916. In 1960 the Imperial Glass Company of Bellaire, Ohio purchased both the Cambridge Glass Company and the A. H. Heisey Glass Company of Newark, Ohio. Both were kept in production.

The pitchers sit on wide, flat bases without a ring. The creamer's shape is more comely than that of the larger piece. It is constricted above the base and near the rim. Between them, it curves in a shape that suggests a vase.

On either side is a large formal thistle spray in deep intaglio pressing. From a central shaft, a fullblown thistle droops toward the front and rear while a third one stands stiff and erect in the center. From the stem of each drooping bloom a formalized leaf, (which is anything but thistle), curves about the upper flower. At the base, two stiff leaves are placed on each side of the erect sprigs. All are deeply impressed. Unusually thick glass was necessary to permit this impression. The same design, minus the drooping flowers, appears beneath the spout. A much different spray, made up of symmetrical leaves, is found beneath the handle.

The wide base makes the creamer stable. It has a low, arched dome with an intaglio design impressed therein. (See drawing of bottom.)

The handle is attractive and comfortable. It simulates a late, applied handle with the large blob at the bottom and the upper tab turned under and pressed flat. High, noticeable mold marks betray it for what it is—a pressed handle. On either side of the round handle, a long, slender leaf and stem design has been impressed. It resembles a weeping willow twig.

Above the flowers the surface is smooth to the rim. A high scallop at the rear is used for the handle attachment. On each side of the rim two low, wide scallops are separated by narrow ones. The front portion curves up and over, then pushes forward into a narrow, pinched lip.

Standard creamer: 4-part mold, 1 pound and 2 ounces, 5 inches tall, 3 3/4 inches wide, and 4 9/16 inches long.

Milk pitcher: 4-part mold, weight unknown. 6 1/2 inches tall. Other measurements unknown.

Compare this pattern with PANELLED THISTLE just above.

In addition to these pitchers many other articles were made which are not scarce today—particularly tumblers without the attractive basal design.

167—THISTLE

This graceful creamer is in a pattern that is scarce today, though a wide range of articles were originally made. It is of a type and shape known to have been manufactured by the Boston and Sandwich Glass Company of Sandwich, Massachusetts. The mere finding of a few pieces of shard on the site of a former glass factory is not sufficient basis for attribution of a pattern. Similar ware was made by most other glass factories, all of which bought broken glass by the ton. This creamer has never been illustrated in American glass literature.

Ruth Webb Lee, in *Early American Pressed Glass*, Pattern 164, pages 420-21, names and describes the pattern and on Plate 140 illustrates a goblet, tumbler, spoonholder and eggcup. S. T. Millard shows a goblet in Plate 132-2 of his *Goblets*. The reproduced photograph is almost too indistinct for identification, except by the title THISTLE. Mrs. Metz covers the pattern in *Early American Pattern Glass*. She shows a better photograph on page 68, No. 749, than that of Millard. Her description of the pattern is found on page 71. Mrs. Kamm did not cover the pattern in any of her eight pitcher books.

The tall, slender body is shaped like a projectile. The upper half of the body is smooth and plain. Probably this portion was never etched. A small rounded ring flanked by a groove, above and below, encircles the body at its midportion. Below this dividing line is a 1 1/2-inch band of easily recognized THISTLE with stems, flowers and leaves. The latter are both veined and stippled. Their arrangement is attractive. Below it, the body is rounded and plain.

The stem ends in a six-point star shelf at the bottom of the body. The six flat panels extend

148

through the slender stem and well out on the base, ending in a raised hexagonal shelf.

The base is round, almost flat and shows mold marks. Underneath is a low, hollow dome, which is left plain.

The rim is saddled with easy curves that rise in front to form a spout and in the rear to form an anchorage for the handle. The glass is thicker at the rim than is usually found in this type of ware.

The applied handle is sturdy and almost uniform in thickness. The upper attachment is turned under but is not massive. The lower attachment is turned back on itself and crossbarred.

This pattern dates from the late 1860s to the early 1870s. It is clear, brilliant, and nonflint. It has an enchanting grace. The workmanship and the quality of the glass are excellent. Mold marks show on the base and lower body. They were fire polished off the upper portion.

Creamer: 3-part mold, 12 1/2 ounces, 5 1/2 inches tall, 3 inches wide, and 4 13/16 inches long.

Compare with PANELLED THISTLE and LATE THISTLE. Do not confuse this pattern with an early flint pattern also called THISTLE, and made by Bakewell, Pears and Company. The latter is listed under that title in Plate 190, of Ruth Webb Lee's *Early American Pressed Glass*. A more appropriate name of PILLAR AND BULL'S EYE was given by Minnie Watson Kamm, in her *A Fifth Pitcher Book*, page 142, No. 187.

These items are known to have been made in the present pattern: berry bowl, cake plate on high standard, open compote, covered compote, cordial, creamer, eggcup, goblet, oval pickle dish, flat 4-inch-deep sauce dish, milk pitcher, covered butter dish, covered sugar bowl, spoonholder, footed salt, tumbler, footed tumbler, water pitcher, and wine.

168—INDIANOLA

This is a rare and beautiful pattern of early American pressed glass. It also presents a headache in nomenclature. When a name has become well established, it is presumptuous to change it. The following are some of the problems with which we are confronted.

On Plate 79 of Ruth Webb Lee's *Victorian Glass* a goblet in this pattern is shown as No. 4. On page 247 she calls it OAK LEAF BAND WITH MEDALLION, and says it is very attractive. Dr. S. T. Millard, in *Goblets II*, Plate 13-2, shows a totally different pattern and calls it OAK LEAF BAND. Throughout New England the pattern is called OAK LEAF. We find this name preempted in

Millard's *Goblets*, Plate 164-2. Dr. Millard also used such names as FROSTED OAK LEAF BAND and OAK LEAF BAND AND LOOPS. Kamm and Metz did not cover the pattern.

The logical solution seems to be in the selection of a new name. It should be short but not necessarily descriptive—since such a title too often expands into several words. (See Introduction with regard to difficulties encountered in the nomenclature of patterns of pressed glass.) There is a beautiful small city in Mississippi where most of the homes are white, with well-kept yards. They nestle beneath broad, sheltering oaks. The beauty of this pattern is matched there, so I have called it *INDIANOLA*.

This is not flint glass, but it is definitely of the period between 1869-1875. It could be Sandwich glass, but I do not believe so. It probably came from the New England Glass Company of Cambridge, Massachusetts, or one of the glass factories in and around Pittsburgh. In every respect it is the equal of PRESSED LEAF which we know to have been made in Pittsburgh.

The bowl is shaped like an inverted bell. There is a 1 1/4-inch band around the middle of the body which is outlined above and below, by a small raised line. The band contains stippled and veined oak leaves, whose stems are turned to the left. They are in pairs and overlap. In turn, each pair covers the stem of the pair on the right. Where two pairs meet, slender stems extend upward and downward, some with two acorns, some with one acorn, and some with only an acorn cup. The acorn stems are longer and slimmer than their real-life counterparts.

The lower third of the bowl is rounded in to an octagonal shelf on top of the stem. Covering the three mold marks are symmetrical, plain-surfaced, leafy scrolls that extend the full height of this portion of the creamer. Each of the three segments, thus formed by the scrolls, has a medallion with an in-scalloped, beaded border. Each medallion has a sprig of oak with a stem, two leaves, three acorns, and a bud. The background space between the scrolls and medallions is stippled.

The upper third of the body was left plain and is smooth and highly polished. The rim is saddled with curves that are not exaggerated. The lip is wide with a tiny dip. A pointed elevation on the back of the rim provides an anchorage for the top handle attachment.

The dainty handle is beautifully executed and curved. It is so delicate that one is forced to wonder how it has stood the hard knocks of the world it has lived in for the past ninety years.

(Perhaps by being loved—and kept in a cabinet—as I intend to do.) The larger attachment is at the top. It was sheared to a point, then applied and flattened. The handle soars high, drifts backward, then glides in to join the body at the middle. The lower attachment is wider than the upper, despite the fact that the handle itself becomes progressively more slender as it descends. The lower tip is thin and narrow and coils back on itself to form an open loop. Above the latter is a beautiful attachment. It is tooled into a perfect acanthus leaf such as only a consummate gaffer could have produced. His skill can be imperfectly seen in the drawing.

The stem is shorter and thicker than of most pieces of this era. It has eight flat panels which end in a low shelf on the base of the body, and in a high wide shelf on top of the base. The base is low and wide. Underneath is a low, plain dome.

The glass is light, brilliantly clear, and has no defects. Surprisingly, for a lime-soda glass creamer, it has a clear ringing resonance when tapped. This type of delicate ware followed immediately after the era of 1840-1865 which produced the magnificent heavy, massive flint pieces so desired today. The work of both the moldmaker and the gaffer was outstanding. This is the type of ware with which the market should have been flooded.

Creamer: 3-part mold, 13 ounces, 5 5/16 inches tall, 3 1/8 inches wide, and 4 7/8 inches long.

We know of a goblet and this creamer in the pattern. Since a creamer was made, we can assume a sugar bowl, butter dish, and spooner also were made. Time may turn up other items, but probably not many.

169—DALLAS

"Big D" is a neat clean city which this creamer seems to well represent. The massive handle is also such a one as DALLAS likes to seize upon to handle a situation. The pattern is shown here for the first time in American glass literature. The bowl is shaped somewhat like an inverted bell, with the upper two-thirds left severely plain. The glass was too cool when it was worked, and the piece was not sufficiently fire polished to flow out all waviness on the surface.

The lower third of the body carries all the decorative motif. Fifteen short panels surround this portion, with the top of each rounded over and the bottom pointed and mitred into a band of diamond point immediately below. As shown in the illustration, they appear similar to the sharp teeth of an ice saw. The combination of panels and diamond point gives a pleasing effect.

The stem is slightly thicker than usual on creamers of this era. It consists of nine slightly concave flutes that end in a low round shelf on the base of the bowl and in a slightly larger shelf on top of the foot. The stem seems to be a little short for the bowl.

The base is round and low. There is a hollowed out plain space underneath, and the piece sits on a ring at the base's perimeter. The rim is deeply saddled and somewhat flat on the sides. It soars high and forward to form a lip. A high, wide scallop at the back receives the handle. The glass at the rim is 3/8-inch thick.

The high applied handle appears heavy when viewed from the side. When seen from the rear it seems particularly ponderous for this type of creamer. It is in marked contrast to the delicate, slender handle of INDIANOLA. The thick, lower tab is rather well tooled, but one gets the idea the gaffer may have stepped out for a moment and been replaced by a newly indentured youth when the handle was made, for its lines lack grace. Aside from this, the creamer has a simple piquant beauty and neatness of design that is fascinating. The quality of the glass is excellent, and the workmanship otherwise is good. It is almost a top quality product. It is nonflint glass and dates from between 1870 and 1880.

Creamer: 3-part mold, 1 pound, 6 3/16 inches tall, 3 1/8 inches wide, and 5 inches long.

Since a creamer was made we can assume a sugar bowl, butter dish, and spoonholder were also produced in this pattern. Other items may also have been produced. It is quite scarce.

170—SQUARE FUCHSIA MARSH PINK

This pattern is presented to resolve the confusion between it and the following one. Some items not previously listed in our glass literature are also listed. I collected this pattern for years and had a table setting for twelve that consisted of 185 pieces.

The pattern is widely known over the country as SQUARE FUCHSIA. It is square, but not fuchsia. The flowers have no botanical entity, though there is a slight resemblance to the marsh pink, as Mrs. Kamm indicated. Little effort was made to achieve botanical accuracy. (See the following pattern for a similar problem in nomenclature.) I feel that a well-established and widely known name, though inappropriate, is preferable to a new and slightly more accurate title. It is therefore still called SQUARE FUCHSIA.

Minnie Watson Kamm, in *A Second Two Hundred Pattern Glass Pitchers*, page 30, describes this pattern and calls it MARSH PINK. She was not well acquainted with it. Ruth Webb Lee, in *Victorian Glass*, page 58 and Plate 23-1, calls the pattern SQUARE FUCHSIA, provides an excellent list of known items, and illustrates a celery vase and covered sugar bowl. She shows a goblet but says it does not match the pattern well. This led many to believe her "ladies-size" goblet was the round version of SQUARE FUCHSIA. This is not correct. Despite years of diligent and painstaking search I have never found a SQUARE FUCHSIA goblet. I did turn up six small goblets that were supposed to be SQUARE FUCHSIA and which brought a correspondingly high price. They were of the scarce but much less expensive *BAY ST. LOUIS* pattern which follows immediately.

Mrs. Metz calls it MARSH PINK and lists the pattern as No. 713.

All pieces of this pattern that I have seen are square, but the goblet would probably be round. The body has four wide panels, one to a side, which flare as they ascend to the rim. On each panel a stippled, veined, and slightly raised floral spray is impressed. On the creamer, a corner was pushed out and ribbed to form the spout. The opposite corner bears the handle. Each corner has been sliced off, and is fluted and columned. This softens the ware to the touch. The corners change to flat panels when they reach the lower part of the bowl, continue through the waist, then out on the foot and down to the bottom.

The waist is angular with the sharp corners chamfered. It is short, but the beveled shelves above and below give the illusion of greater height. The foot angles out in a sharply sloping ledge to the bottom.

Underneath is a square, high dome whose ceiling is covered with a grill of closely placed, raised lines crossing at right angles. In the center of each square is a raised dewdrop. (See drawing of bottom.)

The rim is flat and the edges are rounded over. In front a small concession is made to curves where the rim arches slightly to the lip. The handle is six-sided and of an odd shape, which is easy to grasp but uncomfortable to heft.

The glass is of good quality, as is the workmanship. It is a delightful pattern and one of the most admired designs known. It is supposed to have been produced in blue and amber, but I have

neither seen nor heard of such a piece. It dates from about 1870-1880. I doubt a goblet was made. The large dinner plates and covered sugar bowls are not particularly scarce. The other items are. I have found only one celery vase. It was badly bruised, but expensive. I would prefer a pair.

Creamer: 2-part mold, 1 pound, 5 5/8 inches tall, 4 1/4 inches wide, and 5 7/8 inches long.

The following articles were made: 5 x 8 1/8-inch bowl with handles in middle of long side; 5 x 8 1/4-inch bowl with no handles; 6 x 9-inch bowl with side handles; covered butter dish; cake plate on standard; celery vase, creamer; covered compote, 7 1/2-inches wide and 10 1/2 inches high; compote 5 inches wide and 6 3/4 inches high; open jelly compote; covered jelly compote; goblet; marmalade jar with glass lid; pickle caster with metal lid, holder and tongs; plate with square, chamfered corners, 10 1/2 inches wide; 4-inch footed sauce dish; 4-inch footed sauce dish, handles on corners; flat sauce dish, handles on sides; 4 inch sauce dish, no handles; 3 1/2-inch footed sauce dish, no handles; 3 1/2-inch flat sauce dish, no handles; footed honey dish with lid; 6-inch square honey dish, flat, with lid, holds 1 pound of honey from a patent hive; spoonholder; covered sugar bowl; salt and pepper shakers; and water pitcher. A few other items may be expected.

171—BAY ST. LOUIS

Ruth Webb Lee, in *Victorian Glass*, used a "lady's sized" goblet of this pattern with SQUARE FUCHSIA to show how the two patterns would combine. (See Plate 23-1 and page 58.) Goblets in SQUARE FUCHSIA are virtually nonexistent. Most items of *BAY ST. LOUIS* are even more scarce, but small goblets in it are occasionally found.

At first glance, one might call the flower in this pattern a nasturtium, but a more careful inspection will reveal it to be neither nasturtium nor any known blossom. The flower was evidently sculptured by the same hand that designed the molds for SQUARE FUCHSIA. The leaves are nondescript. The stems are almost as willowy as the thorns of the honeylocust and as lethal.

Pieces of this pattern are round instead of square. The body arches out from the waist, and then the straight sides rise with a slight flare to the rim. There is a small, raised line which touches the rim and runs horizontally around the body. Below it is a band of alternating large and small dewdrops, spaced about 1/4-inch apart. Suspended from each large dewdrop is a nine-ribbed, open fan with a tiny bead at the lower end of each rib.

Covering the two front mold marks on the body are rigidly erect tree boles in high relief, crinkled, with their branches pruned to stubs. They separate the body into three segments. Each contains a diagonally placed stiff floral arrangement consisting of an unbending branch, four leaves, five buds, and two full-blown flowers. They are either veined, crinkled, or stippled. The background of the spray is smooth and plain.

The plain handle is round in cross section, almost horizontal on the top, and permits a good grip. The top of the rim is flat and broadly saddled. The lip is narrow. The bottom of the body curves in through the waist, then out on top of the foot, which is round and wide. Beneath the base is a hollow dome wth an eight-point star impressed therein. Each point of the star is made up of six point, sharp-spined rays. The center is round and plain. (See drawing of bottom.)

This attractive piece probably dates from 1875-1885 and is of good quality. It is regrettable that such an attractive pattern is so scarce. No colored pieces are known to have been made. It is an excellent example of early American folk art, and I give it its present title in honor of the beautiful little Mississippi coastal city, Bay St. Louis.

Creamer: 3-part mold, 13 ounces, 5 3/4 inches tall, 3 5/16 inches wide, and 5 1/4 inches long.

Other than the six goblets, a spoonholder, and the creamer in my possession, no other items are known to me. It is described here for the first time. A sugar bowl and butter dish were almost certainly made. There could be many causes for so small a production.

172—BLOCK AND FAN

Here again is a brilliant old pattern. It is presented for comparative purposes and also to point out certain errors.

Minnie Watson Kamm had not seen a creamer in this pattern and made her drawing from an old woodcut of a water pitcher. She used it in her description in *A Third Two Hundred Pattern Glass Pitchers*, page 75, No. 107, and the Plate on page 143. The Plate is from an old advertisement of Richards and Hartley Glass Company of Tarentum, Pennsylvania, and shows six articles of the pattern. In this advertisement, the creamer, sugar bowl, and spoonholder are correctly drawn. The details on the water pitcher and celery vase are not correct. The butter dish is so poorly drawn that no

identification can be made. The woodcut is wrong in several important details. On the water pitcher and celery vase, the fans are shown centered over V-shaped gooves between the large blocks. This is erroneous since the fans are always centered directly above the large blocks. The woodcut also incorrectly shows the blocks on the handles. (See drawing for correction of these details.)

In *Early American Pressed Glass*, Ruth Webb Lee shows a 10-inch plate in this pattern on Plate 187 and page 645. In *Victorian Glass*, Plate 41-3, Mrs. Lee shows a goblet correctly drawn, but the details are not correct on the high and low compotes she illustrates. On page 118, she calls the pattern BLOCK WITH FAN and lists the items shown by the advertisement of the 1880s. She may have copied some of her drawings from the same advertisement. On Plate 85, she shows a table setting of BLOCK WITH FAN. It should be noted that two other patterns have been combined with it. One shows a fan in each corner of a long relish dish, and the other is a large berry bowl, with plain columns.

In an effort to clear up the confusion, Mrs. Lee wrote an article entitled, "Block With Fan and Oregon Pattern Glass," published in *Spinning Wheel*, a national magazine about antiques, in May, 1956. With it, she used the old original woodcuts from her illustrations. The goblet and tumbler are correctly depicted. The so-called celery vase (it is a spoonholder) is incorrectly drawn. The actual celery vase (I have a celery vase and spoonholder before me) has three horizontal rows of cubes between the base of the fans and the tops of the large blocks. The illustration shows two. The fans are also centered over the large blocks and not over the grooves, as shown. There is one large block per fan—not two. There are, furthermore, six rows of beveled cubes between the large blocks and the waist on the celery—instead of four, as shown.

In *Goblets*, S. T. Millard shows a BLOCK AND FAN goblet on Plate 135-4. He shows another goblet in the pattern on Plate 57-4 with the fans and some of the blocks flashed with ruby. Do not confuse this pattern with an entirely different one shown by Dr. Millard in Plate 66-2, called MILK WHITE BLOCK AND FAN. Metz, in *Early American Pattern Glass*, pages 154-55, No. 1731, illustrates a creamer and describes the pattern.

This barrel-shaped creamer of the 1880s has an imitation cut glass design. To be effective, it must be made of top quality metal, and that is exactly what we find here. The glass is brilliantly clear, free of defects, and sparkles superbly. It was given

169

170

Bottom
170

171

Bottom
171

172

173

174

Bottom
173

175-1

175-2

a superior fire polish, and this obliterated all mold marks, except one under the handle.

The lines of the pattern are simple and appealing. The body is covered wth beveled, flat-faced cubes, in line both horizontally and vertically. About the middle is a belt of much larger cubes. The rims and edges of all pieces, except drinking vessels, are covered with large fans that slice into the cubes. The tops of the fans form a double scallop of large and small undulations.

The pieces sit on a wide, flared base composed of a single band of blocks. Underneath is a hollow dome with flared sides and a flat ceiling. The handle is six-sided, and the two side panels are covered with beveled blocks shaped to fit the contour.

Creamer: ?-part mold, 1 1/8 pounds, 5 1/6 inches tall, 3 5/16 inches wide, and 5 3/16 inches long.

Mr. and Mrs. Young M. Orsburn of North Little Rock, Arkansas, have a 73-piece collection of this pattern, consisting of: 10-inch plates, covered sugar bowl, creamer, cruet, sugar shaker, syrup pitcher, covered butter dish, water pitcher, tumbler, 9 1/2-inch berry bowl, flat sauce dishes, footed sauces, celery vase, covered cracker jar, 8-inch vegetable bowls, open compote, 10-inch cake stand, and spooner.

The following articles are known to have been made: 6-inch bowl, 10-inch bowl, 7-inch compote with collared base, 7-inch open compote with high foot, goblet, wine, 4-inch flat sauce, 5-inch flat sauce, celery tray, caster set, salt and pepper shakers, handled decanter, and rose bowl.

Very little of it was flashed with ruby. Goblets and wines are difficult to secure.

173—SKILTON

Dr. S. T. Millard, in *Goblets II* (1940), Plate 59-1, shows this pattern and calls it SKILTON in honor of the E. B. Skiltons of Dowlington, Pennsylvania. He did not know the manufacturer and was not aware the blocks were sometimes flashed with ruby.

Ruth Webb Lee, in *Victorian Glass* (1944), shows and describes this pattern on Plate 44-3, page 131. She had seen an old advertisement of the Richards and Hartley Glass Company of Tarentum, Pennsylvania, put out during the 1880s advertising this pattern under the name of OREGON. She did not check Millard's listing and therefore, continued the company name. Minnie Watson Kamm does not cover the pattern in any of her eight pitcher books. Alice Hulett Metz in

Early American Pattern Glass, pages 154-59, No. 1734, illustrates such a goblet and uses the title OREGON, in preference to SKILTON.

During the 1890s and into the early 1900s, the huge glass combine, the U.S. Glass Company of Pittsburgh, produced a "States" series of patterns and named one pattern for each state in the Union at the time. In their trade catalog of 1907, they show a pattern in the series named OREGON as No. 15,073. This pattern is shown by Lee, Kamm, and Millard as BEADED LOOP. Oregon has two patterns originally named for it, though only one is of the "States" series. In addition, at least five companies put out a pattern called VIRGINIA, but only one of them belongs to the "States" series. Since this pattern is not of the series, I am using the name SKILTON which Dr. Millard assigned.

This attractive pattern is glass of excellent quality and on a par with BLOCK AND FAN or PLUME AND BLOCK, which came from the same factory about the same time.

The body of the creamer is generally cylindrical and divided into three equal sections. Each contains two large convex columns, separated by a high sharp-spined ridge. They extend from the rim to a band of rounded figures on the lower part of the body. Between each two such groups is a wide level-topped fan which forms part of the rim and is mitred into highly beveled, flat-surfaced cubes below. On either side of the fan is a large beveled triangle. Below, are four large cubes. The bulge around the base of the body has been cut into rounded lobes in high relief. They do not match the panels above.

There is almost no waist to the piece; the rounded lobes above are cut off horizontally. It sits on a thick, heavy ring considerably narrower than the body. The rounded ring base is slashed at regular intervals with V-shaped notches.

Under the bottom is a beautiful pressed design which has little relation to the design on the body. In the center is a large beveled hexagon and around it a Star of David with fans in the interstices. (See drawing of bottom.)The rim is unevenly scalloped, to conform to the figurework on the sides. It is almost level across the top but dips slightly in front to form the lip. The handle is large and six-sided. It neither adds to, nor detracts from, the pattern.

Creamer: 3-part mold, 1 pound, 5 inches tall, 3 1/4 inches wide, and 5 1/16 inches long.

The following articles are known to have been made in the pattern: bowl, collared base, 7 inches; bowl, collared base, 8 inches; bowl, 4 inches; bowl, 5 inches; bowl, 6 inches; bowl, 8 inches; covered butter dish; celery vase; celery tray; compote, open, high, 7 inches; compote, open, high, 8 inches; compote, covered, high, 7 inches; compote, covered, high, 8 inches; creamer, dish, deep oblong, 7 inches; dish, deep oblong, 8 inches; dish, deep oblong, 10 inches; goblet; salt and pepper shaker; sauce, footed, 4 inches; spoonholder; sugar bowl, covered; sugar shaker; tankard pitcher, quart; tankard pitcher, half-gallon; water pitcher; pitcher, quart; pitcher, half-gallon; and wine.

It is probable that a molasses pitcher, covered cookie jar, rose bowl, cruet, handled decanter, water tray, etc., were also produced.

174—PLUME AND BLOCK

This creamer belongs with the BLOCK AND FAN and SKILTON creamers above. All three were made by the Richards and Hartley Flint Glass Company of Tarentum, Pennsylvania. This particular pattern was made both before and after the company was absorbed by the U.S. Glass Company in 1891.

Mrs. Kamm, at the time she wrote *A Third Two Hundred Pattern Glass Pitchers* (see page 74, No. 104), had not seen a creamer in this pattern, and she used an illustration from an old catalog to make her drawing. Some of the details are in error. For example, she shows the rim to be plain and horizontal, whereas, only the back two-thirds is level, and this is covered with small scallops. In *An Eighth Pitcher Book*, Plate 73, she shows a cut of pattern No. 189 from an old advertisement of 1891-1892 by the Richards and Hartley Flint Glass Company. This is of a quart pitcher, has the scalloped rim, and shows the blocks flashed with ruby.

The pattern is used here to furnish an accurate drawing (with measurements) and for comparison with the two preceding patterns which are often confused with it. Note the shape of the body, the skirted base, and handle, and see how closely these features resemble those of BLOCK AND FAN.

Ruth Webb Lee, in *Victorian Glass*, pages 193-194 and Plate 61-4 illustrates a spoonholder, covered butter dish, and creamer. She knew little of the pattern other than its maker. She listed only items she had seen.

The size and shape closely approximates that of BLOCK AND FAN. The body narrows in somewhat to the waist but is for the most part straight with vertical sides. Up each of the four mold marks is a plume that is 11/16 inch wide, in high relief. Flanking the plume on each side is an inverted V-shaped prism with fine-toothing on the spine. There is a plume in the center on either side, another under the spout, and still another under the handle.

Above and below the plumes are fine-toothed prisms which surround the body. The lower appreciably constricts the waist. The space formed between contains two large, beveled, flat-surfaced rectangles. The latter have deep slashes in each corner which radiate toward the center. The two in each panel are separated by a fine-toothed ridge. These large rectangular areas are occasionally found flashed with ruby stain. At the top of the body is a plain wide band. This may also be found flashed with ruby in some pieces.

The waist is short and wide. Below it the apron arches out to the bottom, where an adaptation of the body motif is repeated. Underneath is the same type of hollow dome found on BLOCK AND FAN. The rim is simple and almost unattractive. The back is level with many small scallops. The low upward curves of the lip and its slight dip are pleasing.

The handle is of the same size and shape as BLOCK AND FAN. The top and bottom members have odd curves with an up-thrust. The handle has six sides with two front and two rear facets left plain. Down the center of each side panel is a row of large dewdrops. Raised fine-toothed lines outline each side panel. The top member has four raised bars across the top for a thumbgrip. A similar device, with three bars, is on the lower end of the upright member.

The glass is clear and without defect. It is not, however, a quality product like its two contemporary patterns. Here the mold lines are plainly visible, and all plain surfaces are wavy resulting from the metal, or mold, being too cold when pressed. They were not removed by firepolishing. This pattern is not frequently seen today.

Creamer: 4-part mold, 1 pound and 1/2 ounce, 5 3/8 inches tall, 3 1/4 inches wide, and 4 7/8 inches long.

The old catalogue of 1891 shows the following articles were manufactured: creamer; covered sugar bowl; covered butter dish; bowl, collared base 7 inches; bowl, collared base 8 inches; celery vase; goblet; sauce, collared base 4 inches; tumbler; water tray; water pitcher; quart pitcher; and half-gallon pitcher. This does not necessarily mean other items were not made.

175—SELBY

This attractive pattern is shown in Millard's *Goblets*, Plate 67-2. He named the pattern in honor of Mrs. Bertha M. Selby of Kirkwood, Missouri, who had been of great assistance to him in assembling patterns for his books. My own search for a creamer for illustration and use in this volume resulted in something of a chain reaction. Mrs. Selby informed me she had never seen a piece in this pattern though she had dealt in pressed glass for years. She referred me to Miss Pearl B. Henshaw, The Old House, Buzzards Bay, Massachusetts. Miss Henshaw wrote she had no pieces but that, in the past, she had sold pieces of SELBY pattern to Miss Mary L. Selby of Washington, D.C. She, in turn, wrote to Miss Selby about my request. I learned that Miss Selby had six goblets and a master salt cellar or small sauce dish but had not seen other pieces in the pattern. Miss Selby graciously loaned the goblet and salt cellar, illustrated here, to me.

The pattern was not described by Kamm, Metz, or Lee. Millard says it came in clear only and was made during the 1880s.

If it were not for the salt cellar, it would be easy to assume the goblet was the only piece manufactured, as was often the case. The scarcity of pieces in the pattern indicates few were made. We can be certain, however, that other pieces were made or planned. The black and white illustration here may assist in identifying other pieces that have gone unnoticed, since the only photograph of the pattern is not too clear.

There is a band of sparkling clear glass around the rim of the goblet. The lower three-fourths of the bowl is covered with three wide flat panels, slightly arched at top and bottom. Each panel is framed by two highly raised, inverted V-shaped ridges. They, too, frame three alternating wide panels, which are filled with a fine cut design. The latter is composed of highly raised, sharp-pointed, triangular pyramids.

The base is ample and slightly domed underneath. On top of the base is a slight shelf. From this shelf, a tall, hexagonal stem rises to the base of the bowl, where it ends in a second shelf. Near the top of the stem is a large knop which adds to the attractiveness of the piece. The quality of the glass and workmanship are all that could be desired. It is brilliantly clear, sparkling, and free of bubbles, hairlines, or discolorations. It has been fire polished, and no mold lines are visible except on the base.

Goblet: 3-part mold, 10 ounces, 6 1/4 inches high, 3 3/8 inches wide.

Master salt: 3-part mold, 4 ounces, 1 13/16 inches tall, and 3 1/2 inches wide.

The master salt cellar (or small sauce dish) carries a form of scalloping on its rim that the author has not seen on other patterns. It is not rounded over but is flat on top. Instead of three flat and three fine-cut panels as on the goblet, it has five of each. The short stem is hexagonal, without the knop, and the base is more domed than that of the goblet.

176—ABERDEEN

Mrs. Lyndall Harlow of Lewisburg, West Virginia, suggested the name KEYHOLD BAND for this pattern. It has also been called INTERLOCKING BANDS. Millard, in *Goblets*, Plate 174-3, called it ABERDEEN and said it was a pattern of the 1880s which came in clear only. Millard's title is used here. Metz showed a goblet in the pattern as ABERDEEN, No. 1431.

I have a spoonholder in the pattern, but it is the only piece I have seen. Of necessity it is used instead of a creamer. Perhaps in the north and east it may be as plentiful as this simple, restful pattern deserves.

During the period of 1869-1875 innumerable spoonholders of this type were made. Most were of excellent quality and well designed. They have never been widely collected other than as part of a set. Many of these fine old pieces are still to be found in shops and at prices much lower than other pressed glass items. When the flower lover learns how well they hold short-stemmed flowers, the demand will increase. For honeysuckle, nasturtiums, sweet peas, violets, home-grown roses, camellias, and cape jasmine, no other holder surpasses them.

The sugar bowl in this type of ware is today called a *buttermilk goblet*. Actually they are sugar bowls without a lid. Both sugar bowls and creamers have tall slender stems as do the spoonholders. The base of the piece is broad, stable, and severely plain. It is slightly domed underneath and sits flat on the ring of the base. The slender stem is composed of nine flat panels which spread out on top of the base to form a raised shelf. Their top ends spread out onto the bottom of the bowl and are rounded over. They form a scalloped cup on which the body rests.

The body is somewhat goblet-shaped. Around the middle is a narrow raised band which appears to be a cord but is not twisted and is topped with fine ribbing. The lower half of the body contains the decorative design. It consists of two formal, round, raised bands which meander about the bowl and interlock. The bands are similar. In the space between the bands is a narrow ribbon of stippling. Above and below the decorative band, the pattern is outlined by a row of minute dewdrops. Above the cord-like band the piece is severely plain. Occasionally this part was hand-engraved with a leaf spray. The rim has low, even scallops.

Spoonholder: 3-part mold, 10 ounces, 5 inches tall, and 3 inches wide.

With a goblet and a spoonholder made, there must have been a creamer, sugar bowl, and butter dish. Other items may have been produced also. The name of the manufacturer is unknown.

177—BEADED SWIRL

Mrs. Kamm had not seen a creamer in this pattern so she made a drawing from a cut in an old advertisement of George Duncan and Sons, of Pittsburgh, which showed this creamer and a finger bowl in a pattern they called No. 335. The advertisement said "N. B. We continue to make a full line of 335 Pattern." This came out in the summer of 1889, before they joined the U.S. Glass Company in 1891. The advertisement was reproduced as Plate 31 of Kamm's *A Fifth Pitcher Book*. In *A Third Two Hundred Pattern Glass Pitchers*, page 113, No. 171, she described the pattern and called it SWIRLED COLUMN. She suspected milk-white and opaque-cream pieces existed, but none in emerald green, like this, with gilded beads and feet. On page 95, No. 142, she called another pattern BEADED SWIRL, although that title is as applicable to this pattern.

S. T. Millard, in *Goblets II*, Plate 79-1, showed a goblet of this pattern which he called BEADED SWIRL. He said it was made in the 1880s and came in clear only. I have continued his title.

The manufacturer produced one type of the pattern, which rests on three scrolled feet, and a second type with flat bottoms. Mrs. Lee in Plate 41-1 of her *Victorian Glass*, page 116, illustrated a spoonholder, covered sugar and creamer of the squatty variety and called it BEADED SWIRL, LOW FORM. She listed items available in both forms and called the footed pattern BEADED SWIRL. The latter is the more attractive.

Metz covered the pattern without illustrations on page 201, No. 2296. She did not mention colored pieces. She called it BEADED SWIRL.

This creamer is of a particularly beautiful shade of deep green glass. The beaded swirls and scrolled feet have been gilded. It has an arresting

appearance. The body has the shape of a high velocity projectile with its nose pointed down. The inside is round and smooth. The outside is covered with nine wide convex columns in high relief that start at the rim and swirl around the body and end at the tip of the base. Separating the swirls are rows of graduated beading, minute at top and bottom, but increasing to BB size dewdrops at the middle. (See drawing of bottom for the attractive base.)

The three feet splay on the base of the bowl like well-convexed shells. At their lower ends they curl into tight coils. The back two-thirds of the rim has six low wide scallops, one over the top of each column. The three columns in front are somewhat taller and form the low narrow lip. The handle is round in cross section and simulates an applied one with the large blob at the bottom. The mold marks on the piece are high enough to dispel such an idea but are not sharp.

The quality of the glass is excellent, and the creamer is heavy for its size. If the workmanship had been just a little better, it would have been an outstanding piece. I have seen clear pieces in this version of the pattern. The 'low form' is seldom encountered. It tinkles when tapped, but is not flint glass.

Creamer: 3-part mold, 1 1/8 pounds, 5 1/8 inches tall, 3 1/4 inches wide, and 4 7/8 inches long.

The following pieces were produced: four-piece table set, water pitcher, goblet, finger bowl, cruet (the article most often seen in the pattern), and sauce dish. Probably other items were also made. Since we now know the ware was made in emerald green, we may expect to find it in blue, amber, canary, and milk white.

178—BANDED STAR

This odd, impractical standard creamer is presented to show its dimensions and proportions. Minnie Watson Kamm, in *Fourth Pitcher Book*, page 110, No. 136 illustrates and describes an individual creamer and calls it BANDED STAR. She lists the known pieces of the pattern, including this one and says it was made in 1882.

Ruth Webb Lee, in *Victorian Glass*, pages 213-14 and Plate 67-2, shows a sauce dish, water pitcher, and spoonholder. She calls it BANDED STAR. I have been unable to identify the pattern in S. T. Millard's books.

Alice Hulett Metz, in *Early American Pattern Glass*, pages 120-21, No. 1352, illustrates an identical creamer. She calls the pattern LEGGED BANDED STAR and says there was another pattern called BANDED STAR. She does not show the latter in her booklets 1, 2, 3 and 4.

M. Ray Doubles, in his *Pattern Glass Checklist*, lists a single pattern called BANDED STAR—the one shown here. Judge Doubles does, however, list two slightly different variants of the pattern as STAR BAND #1 and STAR BAND #2. Mrs. Kamm, in her first and fourth books, names both patterns STAR BAND.

Most pieces of this pattern rest on four curved ball-feet. Casualties were terrific for such feet in ordinary kitchen usage. It is surprising that any survive.

This piece sits on four legs that are ribbed longitudinally, with the exception of the pad on which they sit, and the round ball on the end of each leg. These spaces are left plain. The ribbing is expertly executed and gives the effect of a large shell splayed on the lower part of the body. Underneath is an intriguing design produced by the legs, the shape of the body, and the square, raised star. (See cut of bottom.)

The body has straight sides, is narrower at the bottom, and flares considerably to the rim. Four large, rounded lobes compose the sides. From above it looks like a four-leaf clover. Down the center of each lobe runs a narrow cigar-shaped figure, formed by low, sharp, ridged lines with sharp ends. The inner surface also has a raised cigar-shaped figure. The remainder of the lobe is smooth and plain. Below the rim is a decorative band or tape whose margins are irregularly scalloped, and stippled on each side. The tape is divided into even segments by short, vertical, raised lines. In each compartment is a small, raised star.

The rim is smooth and slightly saddled. The handle provides a secure grasp with its large upthrust thumbgrip and huge size. It is roughly six-sided, with a rounded crease impressed throughout its length, in the center of each side. At the lower end of the handle is a suspended knob, similar to a beginning stalactite. The soda-lime glass and workmanship are average and indicate that this was production ware. It dates from about 1875-1885.

Standard creamer: 4-part mold, 15 1/2 ounces, 5 7/8 inches tall, 3 7/8 inches wide, and 5 3/4 inches long.

The manufacturer is unknown. The following articles were made in the pattern and possibly others: standard creamer, water pitcher, sugar bowl, covered butter dish, spoonholder, two types of sauce dishes, celery vase, high and low open compotes, high and low covered compotes, individual 4-piece table set, two different covered dishes, and a jam jar. A goblet and tumbler are not known, but may have been produced.

179—CHURCH WINDOWS

The United States Glass Company of Pittsburgh put out this pattern as "a 1903 Winner" under their "No. 15,082." (See Plate 28 of Kamm's *A Sixth Pitcher Book* for a full-page reproduction of the company advertisement.) They again advertised it in 1907 under "No. 15,082" and then called it COLUMBIA. (See Kamm's *A Third Two Hundred Pattern Glass Pitchers*, page 107, No. 161, where the standard creamer is described, illustrated, and named COLUMBIA.)

In *A Fourth Pitcher Book*, page 115, No. 146, Mrs. Kamm showed a water pitcher in this pattern and calls it CHURCH WINDOWS. She said it was quite similar to COLUMBIA, in her third book, overlooking the fact that they were the same "No. 15,082," by the same company.

The title CHURCH WINDOWS is descriptive, different, and more suitable than COLUMBIA— so the latter name will be dropped. COLUMBIA is not suitable because too many companies have used the title, as the following list indicates:

(a) The present pattern was named COLUMBIA by the United States Glass Company, in 1907.
(b) The original name of HEART WITH THUMBPRINT, as given by the Tarentum Glass Company, in 1898-1899, was COLUMBIA.
(c) Dalzell, Gilmore and Leighton made a pattern with sixty items which they called COLUMBIA. It is described in this book as DALZELL'S COLUMBIA.
(d) The Co-Operative Flint Glass Company, of Beaver Falls, Pennsylvania, produced a pattern in 1900 called COLUMBIA.
(e) The Indiana Tumbler and Goblet Company, of Greentown, Indiana, put out a pattern in 1899 as "No. 140" which they called COLUMBIA.
(f) The Beaumont Glass Company, of Martins Ferry, Ohio, put out pattern "No. 100" in 1893 called COLUMBIA. Their large advertisements of the pattern show that many articles were made.

The standard creamer shown here was illustrated in the old advertisement. Its rim, however, differs from that of Mrs. Kamm's creamer. It is a simple pattern, whose long flowing curves make it particularly attractive. With such clear brilliant glass, free of defects, and with an excellent fire polish, plain patterns can be very appealing.

Around the bowl, and extending from the bottom to a level line near the top, are eight slightly concave flutes. They follow the contours of the

176

177

Bottom
177

178

Bottom
178

179

Bottom
179

180

181

Bottom
181

body, being sharply arched at the top, narrow at the waist, and rounded over at the base. The rounded ends produce the scalloped base. The flutes are shaped somewhat like Folsom points. (Very early Indian arrowheads and spearheads.) Each flute is outlined by V-shaped grooves which form beveled edges. Above the top arches, the body is plain and probably originally came flashed with ruby or in some instances, gilded.

The waist is constricted and much narrower than the bowl, which arches up and outward to a large rim. The base flares slightly and has eight broad scallops on which the piece rests. The glass is thick on the edge, but much thinner in the ends of the flutes, which are concave and directly above the hollowed out figures underneath. (See drawing of bottom.) The base is divided into eight segments, deeply concave, and rounded on their outer ends. V-shaped grooves separate the figures.

The handle is round in cross section and makes a slight effort to simulate an applied handle. The mold marks show. The rim is flat on top, and slightly saddled near the rear. It sweeps up, forward, and down, into a wide jowled, narrow lip.

Standard creamer: 4-part mold, 15 ounces, 4 11/16 inches tall, 3 3/4 inches wide, and 5 13/16 inches long.

Water pitcher: 4-part mold, weight unknown, 7 1/2 inches tall.

The following were included in the forty items produced in the pattern: toy creamer, toy sugar, toy butter dish, toy spoonholder, toy mustard pot, standard creamer, covered sugar, butter dish, spooner, water pitcher, tumbler, berry bowl, sauce, goblet, rose jar, custard cup, handled jelly, tall 8 1/2-inch bowl, half-gallon pitcher, tall vase, and 10 1/2-inch low orange bowl.

180—*BON SECOUR*

We have here an example of two reputable glass manufacturers simultaneously putting out identical patterns. The McKee Glass Company of Pittsburgh advertised this pattern in their trade catalog of 1894 and showed "1/2 gal. tankard pitcher, packed 2 doz. to the bbl." There were tumblers to match. Nothing was said of other items. It was continued in production by McKee and was still shown in their catalog of 1915. The McKee Glass Company adopted a trademark of "Press-Cut" before 1894 and enclosed it in a circle by 1905. This particular creamer carries the trademark "Krys-Tol" impressed on the inside bottom. The Ohio Flint Glass Company of Lancaster,

Ohio, and of Dunkirk, Indiana, used this trademark from about 1906, and it was on most pieces they made. They combined with the National Glass Company, but later withdrew, and eventually became a part of the Hocking Glass Company. Evidently the latter stopped using the trademark after the merger, for it was soon adopted by the Jefferson Glass Company of Follanbee, West Virginia.

Mrs. Kamm, in *A Sixth Pitcher Book*, page 65, No. 142, calls the pattern MCKEE'S NO. 140. She had not seen and did not illustrate the design. In Plate 98 of the same book she shows a catalog cut with the pitcher illustrated. She did not know of this small tankard or that colors were used. This is not the McKee piece, and Mrs. Kamm's title for the pattern is, therefore, not suitable.

This pitcher dates from about 1906 or a little later. It is an excellent example of gilding the lily. The quality, workmanship and the custard glass were all superlative, but some decorater (?) daubed on a bright red rose, ghastly green leaves, brown stems and scattered blue dots. It was baked on and cannot be removed. The center jewel in the hobstars and the rim were gilded. It was a beautiful piece as it left the lehr and needed nothing to embellish it.

I have another tankard of the same height, but it is slightly thicker. It is clear, with the plain upper portion flashed with ruby. Etched thereon is "Souvenir of Coney Island." In front is an enameled rose spray superimposed on the ruby. The piece has no trademark, but was made by the Ohio Flint Glass Company of Lancaster, Ohio, and Dunkirk, Indiana.

I also have a toy or individual creamer with the printed legend "Souvenir of Coney Island." Below the spout is an enameled rose spray. This piece is made of custard glass with the trademark Krys-Tol. It also was made by the Ohio Flint Glass Company.

The tall tankard illustrated here has straight sides which taper in from base to rim. All pressed decorations are on the lower fourth of the body and on the bottom. Around the lower portion of the body are six large, highly beveled, kite-shaped areas, each containing a well-formed hobstar. At the top edges of these hobstars are highly raised, pointed figures with fine-toothed crests that meet at a raised diamond. In the interstices below the kites are highly beveled fans. Above this figure-work, the body is severely plain and beautiful—except for the daubing.

This piece sits on a small ringbase, slightly domed underneath. The roof of the dome is covered by a magnificent 20-point hobstar. The rim is plain and rises somewhat toward the front to form a narrow lip. The applied handle has the large blob at the bottom. It is terete and perfectly formed. No tool marks of any kind show.

Individual creamer: 3-part mold, 4 ounces, 2 3/4 inches tall, 1 15/16 inches wide, and 3 inches long.

Standard tankard creamer: no mold marks visible, 1 1/8 pounds, 5 11/16 inches tall, 3 inches wide, and 4 1/16 inches long.

Pitchers are the only items definitely known to have been produced in this pattern. One would expect a standard table setting—toothpick holder, goblet, tumbler, cruet, and perhaps various novelties.

Under an ultraviolet light this creamer shows a brilliant and beautiful fluorescence.

181—NOONDAY SUN

This is a quality product that is not congenial to the patina of fine old furniture. Undoubtedly this had an effect on its production. With only slight demand for it, few pieces were made. The piece sits on the points of a ring of pointed hobnail around the perimeter of the base. When the creamer was filled it must have marred the finish of any article of wooden furniture on which it was placed.

Mrs. Kamm described and named the pattern in *A Second Two Hundred Pattern Glass Pitchers*, page 107. The bottom of the piece carries the only figuration by which the pattern can be identified, and she did not draw it. The design is beautiful enough to deserve an illustration. (See drawing.) In the center is a dime-sized disc or sun. Around this is a corona composed of: first, petal-shaped rays; second, three rows of beveled, flattopped cubes; and third, a circle of high hobnails. The hobs are higher than the other figures, and the piece sits on their sharp points. The base is much wider than the rest of the body. It appears as a thick, straight-edged wafer. Above it the sides curve in and taper gradually to the rim. Inside, the body is larger at the bottom than at the top, indicating that after the pressing plunger was removed, considerable handtooling, shearing, and shaping were done.

The glass, at the rim, is thick and has been sheared and shaped into classic curves. The rim is deeply saddled and soars high and forward to a pronounced lip. Throughout, the glass is very thick.

The handle is applied, and of the later type—with the large blob at the lower attachment. It is well proportioned and adds to the simple beauty of the piece. The handle, round in cross section, is flattened at the top. It was turned under and applied flat at the rim in a long fixture which was left plain. Around the sides and front, a horizontal band of leaves is etched. Pieces in this pattern could be bought both plain and etched—at the same price.

This is a tankard creamer of superior quality in every respect. The glass is especially clear and brilliant. It has been firepolished inside and out till no vestige of a mold mark shows. The workmanship is on a par with the quality of the glass.

Tankard creamer: ?-part mold, 1 1/8 pound, 5 15/16 inches tall, 3 3/4 inches wide, and 5 3/8 inches long.

The tankard creamer is the only item of the pattern known to me. One would expect a series of graduated pitchers from small to the size of a water pitcher. A four-piece table set may well have been made.

182—*CHAPEL*

Unnamed and unlisted patterns, such as this, continue to make their appearance. The figurework reminds one of church windows. Since we have a fine old pattern named CATHEDRAL, this pattern will be called *CHAPEL*. The two are similar.

Some features of this pattern indicate that it is an American product, though others hint that it may be foreign. Its provenance is an enigma. The cone-shaped lower part of the body, together with the vertical paneled stem, resembles a funnel. The rigidity of this portion contrasts markedly with the free-flowing curves of the rest of the body.

The stem is uniform in size, narrow, and has nine flat panels. At the lower end it rests on a wide and circular shelf. The foot is low, round, and plain, above and below.

Above the cone on the body, the sides are straight and flare to the rim. At the base of the body there is a raised horizontal band with a beveled upper margin and a below-center, small, raised cable. Above the beveled margin and joining it, is the church window figurework. Included therein is a band of erect, pecan-shaped prisms with sharp spines. The lower interstices are filled with triangular pyramids. Above the prism band are wide arches filled with large diamond point or

161

small sawtooth that mesh with the pecan-shaped figures. Above the diamond point, the body is first beveled, then plain and smooth to the rim.

The rim has a low saddle and is well finished. The lip is shallow and rather wide. The applied handle has the large blob stuck to the plain band at the rim. The small end is attached to the figure-work, and an excellent bond was obtained. In crafting this fancy tab, the gaffer closed the upper loop a little too tightly, and a small orifice that was left has filled with grime over the years and now cannot be removed.

The glass is above average in quality. The piece was well fire polished, but the mold marks still show on the upper band. It is an attractive piece and probably dates from 1875-1885.

Creamer: 3-part mold, 10 ounces, 5 inches tall, 3 1/4 inches wide, and 5 1/4 inches long.

I have seen no other items in the pattern.

183—PANELLED RIB

This odd pattern is neither practical nor pretty. It is so similar to Kamm's CHECKER-BOARD BAND, in *A Seventh Pitcher Book*, page 60, No. 122, that one is justified in suspecting the same man designed both and that both were made at the same factory. Challinor, Taylor and Company of Tarentum, Pennsylvania, made PANELLED RIB about 1885.

Ruth Webb Lee, in *Victorian Glass*, page 186, Plate 59-2, named this pattern and showed the spoonholder, sugar bowl, and creamer. She thought that little of it was made, which resulted in its scarcity. It is easy to see why there was little demand.

Alice Hulett Metz, in *Early American Pattern Glass*, pages 170-71, No. 1932, illustrated a creamer and called it FOOTED PANELLED RIB because the Lee title was similar to that of another pattern.

The body is almost cylindrical, with straight sides that flare slightly from base to rim. It is completely covered with an unusual design extending from the bottom of the bowl to the narrow raised ring at the rim. The design is composed of three elements. The first consists of seven wide, convex columns that extend below the bowl and end in round, tapered legs some half-inch long. They are flat on the bottom. Second, there are two sharp-spined, V-shaped ridges that continue under the base but are not as long as the legs. There are fourteen of them, one set between each column and panel. The third feature has seven highly beveled, flattopped panels that end in sharp, rectangular

pyramids under the base. (See cut of bottom.)

The rim is plain, flat, and has a narrow ring around it. The lip pushes forward and is "nosy." The handle is six-sided and has a U-shaped channel down each side face. The margins of these channels are so sharp that the handle is uncomfortable to hold.

The bottom is by far the most attractive part of the piece. The band around the outer perimeter is filled with low projections from the side motifs. There is a smaller clear band with a round, deeply impressed, 18-ray star in the center.

The quality of the lime-soda glass is excellent. The workmanship could have been improved. Only the mold mark under the handle can be located. A good job would have required that the sharp margins on the handle be fire polished off.

Creamer: parts of mold unknown, 12 ounces, 4 1/2 inches tall, 3 1/4 inches wide, and 5 1/8 inches long.

At least three pieces of the four-piece table set are known to have been made, leaving the covered butter dish yet to be found.

184—CROW FOOT

The design on this pattern appears complicated, but actually it is simple. Except for the handle, the entire creamer is covered with staggered, horizontal rows of large, highly convex, adjacent moons that vary in size to fit the topography. Each moon has a sunken five-point fan impressed on its lower right half. These figures provide the name.

Dr. Millard, in *Goblets*, Plate 68-2, named the pattern CROW FOOT, and said it was made in blue, probably in the 1880s.

In *A Third Two Hundred Pattern Glass Pitchers*, page 126, No. 188, Mrs. Kamm used a full-page cut from an 1894 trade catalog that announced the pattern as YALE, by the McKee Glass Company of Jeannette, Pennsylvania. She used the YALE title. Because negatives were used, the pattern was shown in reverse in the picture. Using the print for her source material, she erroneously said the crows' feet were on the lower left side. The pattern is used here to furnish an accurate line drawing and measurements.

Ruth Webb Lee, in *Victorian Glass*, pages 51-52, Plate 19-3, shows a goblet, spoonholder, and sauce dish. She lists the items she has seen and uses the name CROW FOOT.

The sides of the upper part of the body are vertical. On the lower part they curve in to a narrow waist. Five bands of moons cover the body. The waist has a single band of small moons. The high,

182

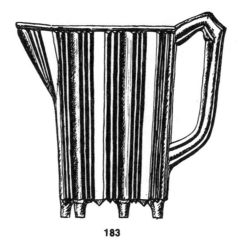

183

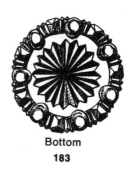

Bottom
183

184

185

Bottom
185

186

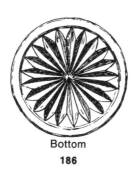

Bottom
186

187

skirted base also has one row. The moons of the upper four rows are staggered, though those in the lower three rows are in tiers. Beneath is a high, round dome.

The handle is charming. It is nearly round in cross section and ample in capacity. On top is a well-designed and executed, seven-lobe leaf. Each lobe is concave. They curve gracefully over the sides and up at the body. A similar, smaller, five-lobe leaf is found at the base of the handle. A row of large dewdrops extends down each side of the handle from leaf to leaf. The rim is scalloped over the top moons. The lip is slightly higher than the rim and is narrow.

The glass is clear and brilliant but not highly fire polished. The complicated molds necessary for this creamer had to be the work of a master. At the rear the mold mark is vertical. The two front mold marks pass vertically between the three lower moons, then skirt the border of the next moon and ascend vertically to the second row above, where they skirt a second disc and rise vertically to the rim. To chisel such a tortuous mold in cast iron, so that the parts fitted together so perfectly that the resulting mold lines are barely perceptible, required a high degree of skill.

Creamer: 3-part mold, 14 ounces, 5 5/8 inches tall, 3 1/4 inches wide, and 4 1/2 inches long.

The following articles are known to have been produced: covered butter dish, covered sugar bowl, creamer, spoonholder, open compote in several sizes and with imitation cut glass bases, covered compotes in several sizes with ribbed columnar stems and crowfoot bases, footed sauce, flat nappie in two sizes, half-gallon pitcher, water pitcher, goblet, tumbler, and a pickle dish.

185—WASHBOARD

A standard creamer is used for comparison with the water pitcher used by Mrs. Kamm. It is then possible to put additional data together. (See her *A Second Two Hundred Pattern Glass Pitchers,* pages 127-28 and Plate 12 of her *A Sixth Pitcher Book.*)

Mrs. Metz, in *Early American Pattern Glass,* pages 142-43, No. 1595, covered this pattern and illustrated a celery vase. She said the pattern had been known for years as PLEAT AND TUCK. However, she used the title WASHBOARD.

We know this pattern was introduced in 1897 as ADONIS by McKee and Brother after they had moved from Pittsburgh to Jeannette, Pennsylvania, in 1889. Other manufacturers also had patterns called ADONIS; The Aetna Glass and Manufacturing Company of Bellaire, Ohio, was one. The old original company name is therefore not suitable because of duplication. The name WASHBOARD, supplied by Mrs. Kamm, is better since it can be recognized at a glance, and that title is continued here.

The water pitcher originally had a lid. The creamer may likewise have had one since there is a well-defined ledge for a lid on the front fourth of the rim on the inside near the spout. This is still problematical because the back three-fourths of the lid would have had to mesh with the scallops. Many earlier flint patterns did do this, such as: LOOP, HONEYCOMB, THUMBPRINT and SAWTOOTH. Such lids are not known to exist on later, nonflint glass.

From the curved waist, the straight sides flare slightly almost to the rim. In this area around the body the design is a simple geometric one that is striking, but not too pretty. There are long triangles with their bases at the waist which mesh with six similar ones based near the top. Those based on the waist are filled with uniform, V-shaped, horizontal ridges in high relief. The meshing triangles are filled with similar ridges, except that they are perpendicular and taper enough to fill the space they occupy. Around the body, above this design is a wide ring, almost in half-relief. It is notched at regular intervals with deep, vertical thumbprints. Under the rim is a row of dewdrops that follow the scallops.

The rim is evenly scalloped in wide low arches. In front it arches up and forward to form the lip. The beading around the top stops before reaching the lip.

The six-paneled handle is ample for holding and has a flat top for a thumbgrip. The two side panels are pressed with fine ribs.

The curved waist flows out on the base and ends in a round shelf that is edged with a row of beading. It then rounds into a heavy ringbase. The bottom has a modified version of the body design pressed on it. (See drawing.)

The glass is fine quality, brilliantly clear, and sparkling. Had it been fire polished, it would be top quality ware.

Standard creamer: 3-part mold, 13 ounces, 5 inches tall, 3 3/8 inches wide, and 5 inches long.

Water pitcher (without lid): 3-part mold, weight unknown, 8 7/8 inches tall, other measurements unknown.

The old ad lists the following articles: 4 1/2-inch footed jelly, 4-inch round dish, 4 1/2-inch round dish, 8-inch round dish, molasses can, quart jug, half-gallon jug, tall celery, tumbler, oval dish, caster salt and pepper. The creamer was not listed but since it was made, we would also expect a sugar bowl, butter dish, spoonholder, goblet, and perhaps other items.

186—BELLE

Minnie Watson Kamm used a cut from an old advertisement to illustrate and describe this pattern in *A Fifth Pitcher Book*, page 64, No. 80, but she had not seen it. In the ad a negative was used which reversed the pattern so the swirl was shown slanted clockwise instead of counterclockwise.

This makes it difficult to identify by her drawing. On Plate 101 of *A Seventh Pitcher Book*, she shows a cut of four leading patterns at the Pittsburgh exhibit in 1898. The plate shows four covered butter dishes, with the one on the lower right, of this pattern and identified as a product of the Ohio Flint Glass Company of Dunkirk, Indiana.

This pattern was advertised by this company in 1899 as BELLE, their No. 999, before they joined the National Glass Company in 1900. Later they moved to Lancaster, Ohio, withdrew from the combine and began marking their ware with the trademark "Krys-Tol." This pattern was made in more than sixty articles. About 1906 or 1907 the company joined the Hocking Glass Company and started making a Pyrex-type cooking ware, tumblers, and specialties in great quantity.

The creamer is an ordinary one with neither the glass nor the workmanship good enough to lift it above other forgotten patterns. The curves on the swirl are stiff and ugly.

The handle served its purpose but is poorly designed, and its curves do not blend. The handle is different from the upthrust one shown by Kamm. This one is six-sided, wider than thick, and has a row of tiny thumbprints down each of the two side corners. It projects too far. A long, raised escutcheon was provided for the attachments. It extends from the rim to the lower swirl pattern.

From a wide ringbase the sides round out moderately then flare slightly to the rim. The lower third is covered with a swirl design made up of concave figures with high, ridged sides. Each ridge is notched with fine teeth. The top and bottom of each is rounded and plain. Three-eighths of an inch below the rim is a band around the creamer except at the escutcheon. Mrs. Kamm, not having seen a piece, called it a raised rope band. Actually it is a sunken band of small figures

without fine-toothing, similar to the lower swirl. The remainder of the body is smooth and plain. The quality of the glass did not warrant etching.

The rim is round on top and has a slight saddle. The curves are a little more comely here than elsewhere. The lip is wide with a slight dip. Below the lip, a protrusion on the body was provided which adds nothing to its beauty or utility. It would have been better omitted. Under the base is a deeply impressed 21-ray star. (See drawing.)

Creamer: 3-part mold, 13 1/2 ounces, 4 7/8 inches tall, 3 5/8 inches wide, and 5 5/8 inches long. The pattern was made in more than sixty articles. Why?

187—CONLEY

Minnie Watson Kamm, in *A Fifth Pitcher Book*, page 102, No. 138, used an old advertisement to make her drawing since she had not seen the two containers illustrated. She called them "SPECIALTY" CONTAINERS. On Plate 83 of *An Eighth Pitcher Book*, she used a cut of the old advertisement of 1890-1891 by the Specialty Glass Company of East Liverpool, Ohio, which showed this creamer with the following comment: "No. 1. Tankard Creamer, Finished. Hold 6 oz. Liq. Meas.; used largely by packers of mustard, honey, horse-radish, etc. Mouth to be corked."

We know that other commodities were packed in these attractive pickle bottles such as: gherkins, small dills, olives, relishes, queen onions, piccalilli, chowchow, baking powder, etc.

The creamer is used here to provide a description and measurements. There must have been thirty or forty different patterns of these pitchers made. With the exception of one named LUTZ, which was of poor quality, the twenty or so others in my own collection are of uniformly good quality. They are not of superior quality, but all are good enough not to have been thrown away when empty.

The tall, slender, cylindrical creamer is plain and smooth with vertical sides for more than four inches at the top. The sole decoration is a heavy 1 3/8-inch band at the base. The top and bottom of the band are formed by heavy rings in half-round relief. Between them a series of rounded ribs extends vertically from ring to ring. The creamer sits on the lower ring. Underneath is a high dome with walls that taper in toward a roof which is flat and plain. The glass of the dome is 3/4-inch thick.

The rim is slightly saddled and the curves are

becoming. The top was made to take a large cork and look well at the same time. The handle is round in cross section, sits low on the body, and is comfortable to grip. The glass is a clear and brilliant lime-soda. There are no bubbles, no discolorations, and no waviness on the surface. The mold lines show plainly, but are not sharp. On a more expensive product, they would have been fire polished off.

Creamer: 2-part mold, 1 1/16 pounds, 6 1/8 inches tall, 2 5/8 inches wide and 4 1/16 inches long.

The six-ounce creamer was probably the only article made in this pattern. There might have been similarly shaped creamers with a four- or eight-ounce capacity. This pattern is named in honor of Sheridan Caraway Conley.

188—WINONA

Tankard pitchers were very expensive to make and manufacturers could not afford to make them of poor quality glass or workmanship. This tall tankard is no exception. It was made by the Greenburg Glass Company of Greenburg, Pennsylvania sometime between 1885 and 1895.

Mrs. Kamm had not seen a piece of this pattern and reproduced a portion of a company advertisement of about 1890. See her *A Third Two Hundred Pattern Glass Pitchers*, page 135, No. 196, and *A Fifth Pitcher Book*, Plate 7. She used the company name of WINONA. A newspaper editorial of 1888 attributed the pattern to the Central Glass Company of Bridgeport, Ohio, and said the pattern was "taking better than Barnum's Circus." Evidently the editor had his facts mixed. (The Central Glass Company was in Wheeling.)

I have the standard tankard creamer, and it is used here for descriptive purposes and for measurements. The sides of this very tall and narrow creamer are straight and taper in slightly from base to rim. They were given a splendid firepolish. Originally, pieces of the pattern could be bought both plain and etched, at the same price. Thirty-five items without etching and forty-five engraved ones were illustrated in the advertisement. The engraving is of the typical fern frond and meandering line type so widely used then. No mold marks show on the body. All pressed figurework is confined to the extreme lower portion of the bowl and to the bottom. On the corner of the bottom there appears to be a band of well-rounded, thick discs standing on edge. They are, however, in three-fourths relief, and are similar on the sides and bottom. Above it are two half-inch-wide bands, in half-round relief which encircle the body.

Beneath the base are two concentric rings similar to the two bands above. They are graduated in size to fit the available space. (See drawing for details.) The glass at the rim is thick and rounded on top. It is beautifully shaped and tooled. The rim is deeply saddled with a high scallop for the upper handle attachment. From the sides, the rim soars to an extreme height and pushes forward to form a shovel-shaped lip. The sweep is in keeping with the tall body.

The applied handle is attractive and comfortable to use. The large, round blob is at the lower attachment. The upper end is turned down and in and applied flat. The handle is round, expertly crafted, and no tool marks show. The glass and workmanship are of superior quality. The mold marks are only faintly perceptible on the figurework.

Tankard creamer: 3-part mold, 1 3/8 pounds, 7 3/4 inches tall, 3 1/2 inches wide, and 5 1/8 inches long.

The advertisement shows the following articles to have been manufactured: tankard creamer, tankard milk pitcher, tankard water pitcher, sugar bowl, spoonholder, butter dish, eggcup, custard cup, two cake plates, goblet, celery vase, several nappies, pickle caster, pickle dish, cordial, claret, champagne, wine, finger bowl, low salt, seven sizes of high covered compotes, four sizes of low covered compotes, four sizes of high open compotes, three sizes of low open compotes. Many pieces of the pattern bulge below the middle.

189—HIGHTOWER

This slender, upright creamer is named in honor of Dr. Jesse Robert Hightower, of Itta Bena, Mississippi. The name is also descriptive. This is the first time the pattern has been shown in American glass literature. It is a tall, slender piece which probably was intended for use as a vase, since it is too top heavy to give useful service as tableware.

The conical body has a plain, smooth outer surface with a spray of flowers etched thereon as illustrated. Where the body joins the small stem is a low ring about the piece. The only pressed figurework on the piece consists of ten, slightly raised columns on the inside, which extend from rim to bottom and show through to good advantage on the outside.

Bottom
188

189

188

191

190

Bottom
191

192

193

194

Front
192

The stem is terete and flows out on top of a wide, round base. The rim is curved with an upward and forward sweep to the lip. The side of the rim has been etched with scallops. The elongated handle is hexagonal, with the large attachment at the bottom. It has a "wrong-way curve" just above the upper attachment.

The quality of the glass is excellent. The workmanship could have been better and the mold marks should have been firepolished off. It would be difficult to identify bowls, plates or sauces in this pattern, if they were made.

Tall creamer: 2-part mold, 15 ounces, 7 inches tall, 3 inches wide and 4 15/16 inches long.

I have a feeling this novelty creamer may have been the only item made in the pattern. The shape would not be suitable for a sugar bowl because of the depth.

190—BULGE

Another unlisted pattern of pressed glass is shown here. I wonder just how many still remain undiscovered and unlisted. Because of its prominent feature, I have called the pattern *BULGE*.

On the inside bottom we find a familiar trademark—a raised diamond surrounding a raised *H*. It is that of the A. H. Heisey Glass Company, of Newark, Ohio. (Purchased in 1960 by Imperial Glass Co., of Bellaire, Ohio, and continued in production.) This piece appears to date from the 1890s.

The design is simple and effective even if it is rather overdone. The upper two-thirds of the body is plain, smooth, and flares slightly to the rim. The lower third displays a pronounced bulge as shown and the glass there is unusually thick. Above and below the bulge is a narrow, beveled ledge which is covered with fine-toothing. They accentuate the bulge.

The rim is fairly attractive. It would be homely but for the rear half, which is covered with dewdrops. The foot is low and ringed. On the bottom is impressed a small, round, 20-ray daisy. The applied handle has the large blob at the lower attachment. It is simple and well crafted. The glass is clear, brilliant, smooth, and heavy. I have seen the four-piece table set, and its simple beauty and attractive sparkle make it pleasing to the eye. The mold marks show only on the foot.

Standard creamer: 3-part mold, 1 1/8 pounds, 4 7/16 inches tall, 3 3/8 inches wide, and 5 3/16 inches long. It was probably also made in custard glass.

191—ORSBURN HOBSTAR

One July, years ago, a young bride of Okolona, Arkansas, accompanied her husband to Little Rock to do the Christmas buying for their drugstore. The pitcher shown here was seen by her in a Little Rock jewelry store and greatly fancied for its sparkling beauty. Without her knowledge, her husband purchased it secretly and figuratively slipped it in her Christmas stocking. It was cherished through the years by the late Mrs. Madison M. Orsburn, who graciously presented it to me for inclusion in this book and in my collection of pressed glass pitchers.

A special effort has been made to describe and illustrate only creamers. Occasionally a creamer is unobtainable and then the next best available article in the pattern is used. In this instance a lemonade pitcher.

This medium-sized, imitation cut glass pitcher is of the finest quality I have ever seen in such ware. Infinite care and skill were expended on both the design and mold, and a superior quality of metal was employed. Expert workmanship used these three factors to produce a beautifully clear, sparkling piece without defect, which closely resembles cut glass. Indeed many people, including some who fancy themselves as experts, are unable to distinguish between the genuine and this imitation.

Except where they round under slightly at the bottom, the sides are straight and flare to the rim. The body is completely covered with various figures of imitation cut glass. Three large modified hobstars are centered round the bowl, each with thirty-one points. In the center of each is an additional hobstar an inch in diameter. The big hobstars would require infinite patience and skill to chip the mold out of cast iron with a mere hammer and cold chisel. Separating them are 3/4-inch-wide panels. They are cut into highly beveled, flat-topped pentagons whose large surfaces are filled with minute diamond point. The panels extend almost the entire height of the piece. Elsewhere are pyramids, fans sunbursts, etc., which cover all of the remaining surface.

The back three-fourths of the rim is unevenly scalloped and these are themselves crenulated. The front of the rim is flattopped and arches up into a narrow pinched lip. The handle is pressed, but only a close scrutiny convinces the examiner it is not applied and cut. A plain escutcheon was provided for the two attachments and these heighten the effect of being applied. The back surface of the handle is covered with imitation "St. Louis" cut, or honeycomb design. The waist is wide and flares to an even wider, low flaring skirt. Underneath the base is a high, rounded dome, with a large hobstar impressed in its ceiling. (See cut of bottom.)

Lemonade pitcher: 3-part mold, 1 7/8 pounds, 7 1/2 inches tall, 4 3/16 inches wide, and 6 1/4 inches long.

The author knows of no other article in this pattern, although lemonade glasses certainly must have been made to go with the pitcher. A water pitcher, tumblers, and various other items may have been manufactured. It is thought to be of the 1905-1915 era, but could be earlier. It bears no trademark.

192—MARIGOLD WINDMILL

In 1951, while on a trip to the Ozark mountains I stopped at a small second-hand store in Morrilton, Arkansas, and found, to my delight, this MARIGOLD WINDMILL in gold iridescence, among other pieces of pressed glass from nearby mountain homes. It was priced at $2.50. Fifty or sixty miles further north, I made a second stop at a shop which stocked and frankly sold reproductions as such. There, on their shelves, were three milk-white glass pitchers in the pattern. Mr. Carl Gustkey, President of Imperial Glass Company, told me in 1960 that his company made no Carnival Glass between 1920 and 1960.

Mrs. Kamm described and named this pattern in *A Fourth Pitcher Book*, page 88, No. 140. She knew it was made in tremendous quantities by the Imperial Glass Company, of Bellaire, Ohio, between 1910 and 1920. She thought the formula for iridizing glass was lost. Imperial revived the making of Carnival Glass in 1960 to supply the great demand.

The milk pitcher is used here to let it be known the pattern was still being made in milk white as late as 1951, and also to show the design under the lip.

Marion T. Hartung, in *Carnival Glass*, page 88, shows a pitcher. She says there is a water set which should include tumblers and bowls. In his *Milk Glass*, page 97, Plate 87, E. McCalmy Belknap shows a milk-white water pitcher in this pattern. Mrs. Kamm says it was also made in blue and purple iridescence.

Milk pitcher: 3-part mold, 1 5/8 pounds, 6 1/2 inches tall, 3 7/8 inches wide, and 6 3/8 inches long.

Water pitcher: 3-part mold, weight unknown, 8 1/2 inches tall, 5 inches wide.

193—BURGER

This pattern shows up occasionally throughout the Middle West and deserves a name. A creamer is not available so a sugar bowl, without its lid, is used. The pattern can readily be identified from the drawing.

The bulbous bowl contracts into a narrow throat and a still narrower waist. It is urn-shaped. The body is divided into four sections with a large, eleven-ray fan impressed around the bulge. These fans extend from just above the waist to slightly above the neck. Separating them at the top are long, elliptical slashes, each with two, ridged prisms. Below each slash is a large triangle with straight sides and an arched base. Their surfaces are covered with small diamond point. At the base of each fan is a large, highly beveled, flattopped diamond. The diamonds round the waist are covered with diamond point.

From the waist the piece angles sharply out and down to a wide, high foot which makes it stable. The foot has impressed in its top the reverse pattern of the bowl, as if reflected in a quiet pool of water. The base is wide and has a high, tapered dome with a flat top, underneath.

Above the neck the rim flares widely and is lobed into four segments. Over each long slash is a large, pointed scallop. Between each two of these is a low, wide scallop covered with eight smaller scallops. Near the top, on the inside, is a ledge provided for a lid. There are no handles. The quality of the glass and the workmanship are both good. The piece appears to date from 1885-1895.

Sugar bowl without lid: 4-part mold, 15 ounces, 4 5/8 inches tall, and 4 7/16 inches wide.

The pattern is known to have been made in the following items: covered sugar bowl, covered butter dish, spoonholder, creamer, wine, 8 3/4-inch tall vase, 4 3/8-inch footed sauce, 5-inch flat sauce, 9 7/8-inch-wide flaring bowl, other size bowls. I would expect to find a water pitcher, tumbler, water tray, waste bowl, carafe, goblet, lamp, open and covered compotes, salt and pepper, plates, celery vase, pickle or relish dishes, pickle caster, etc.

This piece was loaned to the author by Mrs. Myrtle G. Burger of Washington, Missouri. It is named in her honor. She has been very helpful in assisting me to locate unnamed and unlisted patterns of pressed glass creamers for use in this volume.

194—GARDEN OF EDEN

The standard and the individual creamer which follow are shown for comparative purposes and also to prevent further confusion. S. T. Millard originally assigned a different name to each. His goblet books show one. Mrs. Kamm showed the two creamers in separate books but assigned one of Millard's titles to both varieties. They are shown and described here to illustrate what I consider two distinct, though similar, patterns. One may well be a variant of the other, but if this be true, we do not know which has precedence.

S. T. Millard, in *Goblets II* (1940), Plate 8-1, named this pattern GARDEN OF EDEN. He indicated that it was not plentiful and that it dated from the 1870s. In his index he listed it both as LOTUS WITH SERPENT HEAD, and as GARDEN OF EDEN.

Minnie Watson Kamm, in *A Third Pitcher Book* (1943 and 1946), page 58, No. 80, described and illustrated the standard creamer. She continued the GARDEN OF EDEN title assigned by Millard.

Alice Hulett Metz, in *Early American Pattern Glass*, pages 76-77, No. 839, showed a goblet in this version and used the title LOTUS WITH SERPENT. She said this version was a twin of the pattern LOTUS which followed. (Certainly not an identical twin—possibly a sibling or cousin.)

Ruth Webb Lee did not describe either variant.

The standard creamer illustrates how far designers went, in the 1870s, to produce a novelty to appeal to the public fancy. Innumerable patterns were produced by a large number of glass manufacturers, each striving to capture his share of the market. Some of the results were fantastic— and this pattern verges on it.

The conical body tapers in from the rim to the waist. At the latter a nondescript animal, with large prominent eyes, sticks its head out from under a log. The head has a pebbled surface and could be that of a dolphin, fish, frog, turtle, salamander, snake, or what have you. At the back, beneath the handle, the end of a large log projects. It has been chopped off by a woodsman of real skill and a sharp axe. The end of the log is stippled and shows radial seasoning checks, but no annular rings.

From the end of the log to the rim, the body is covered with a "tree-of-life" effect. All bark segments are outlined with low, wide inverted V-shaped ridges. The segments are small and irregular. The surfaces are covered with small graining. The entire appearance is that of a frosted drink. Down each side of the body is a long stippled leaf-shaped figure composed of tapering, sharp-ridged lines.

The jagged rim is not found on any other pattern. Little care was expended in its execution. It partially follows the "tree-of-life" motif on the body. Some of the interstices, however, are free of glass, some are partially filled, and still others are completely filled with clear glass. The rim is rough, ragged and unfinished, especially over the ugly, nose-shaped spout. It could not be kept sanitary.

The base is round, thick, and wide. A shelf extends to within one-half inch of the perimeter and curves up through the waist to the base of the body. Its top is grained. Under the base, the piece is plain and hollowed out.

The handle is roughly round in cross-section, is almost the same size throughout, and is made to resemble the limb of a tree. At the top there is a chopped-off limb for a thumbgrip, similar to the log at the waist. The handle is ample and comfortable.

The quality of the glass is good. The mold maker also did fairly well. The gaffer should have been fired. Being soda-lime glass, with a crinkled surface, it has a cool, shimmering appearance. There is no resonance.

Standard creamer: 3-part mold, 14 ounces, 5 1/8 inches tall, 3 3/16 inches wide, and 5 1/4 inches long.

These items are known to have been made: creamer, sugar bowl, butter dish, spoonholder, water pitcher, bread plate, mug, eggcup, salt, honey dish, and a most unusual cup and saucer, goblet, 3 sizes of flat sauces, 2 sizes of oval relishes, some relishes with handles, 6-inch plate with bar handles, and an open compote.

195—LOTUS

In his *Goblets* (1938), Plate 14-2, S. T. Millard named this pattern LOTUS. He said it came only in clear glass and was of the 1870s. In *A Seventh Pitcher Book* (1953), Minnie Watson Kamm, on page 12, No. 22, said this was the individual creamer to the pattern shown just above and continued the name GARDEN OF EDEN. Let us compose the differences.

Mrs. Metz covered this variant as LOTUS on page 77, No. 840, of *Early American Pattern Glass*. She used no illustration. She said it was exactly the same as LOTUS WITH SERPENT, without the serpent.

The rim of this piece is flat and straight, not jagged as in the preceding. There is a barely perceptible rise to the lip instead of the sharp rise of

GARDEN OF EDEN. This piece has a round segment with two arched segments supporting it under the lip. The large one has a chopped-off log.

The bodies are similar in shape but were treated differently. The odd leaf-shaped areas have flat stippled centers instead of tapering, sharp-pointed ridges as in GARDEN OF EDEN. The segments of the "tree-of-life" in this case are large and generally triangular or rectangular, rather than small and irregular. On GARDEN OF EDEN, the bark segments are grained. On LOTUS they are filled with small, V-shaped, raised lines.

The waist is round, smooth and plain, with a circular shelf on the base. There is no serpent, log or fine graining on top of the shelf. The hollow space under the foot is entirely different. The handles are similar though the chopped-off limb for a thumbgrip shows a roughened surface without radial seasoning checks.

The glass is much thinner in this piece. We do not know who made either piece. I have a feeling this piece and the preceding one above may have emanated from separate factories, with this little one making the first appearance. Possible some designer saw it, liked it and adopted it by adding the embellishments.

Individual creamer: 3-part mold, 8 ounces, 3 1/2 inches tall, 2 3/4 inches wide, and 4 3/16 inches long.

We know only that the small creamer and goblet were made in this version. Probably some of the items listed above would belong to this pattern if they were closely examined and reclassified.

196—BOUQUET

This is another instance where Minnie Watson Kamm used a water pitcher to name and describe a pattern of pressed glass. See *A Fourth Pitcher Book*, pages 137-38 and No. 183. She called it NARCISSUS SPRAY.

Ruth Webb Lee illustrated a goblet in this pattern on Plate 153, No. 8, of her *Early American Pressed Glass*, and on page 628 listed the articles she knew of in the pattern, but did not name it.

A photograph of the goblet is shown in S. T. Millard's *Goblets*, Plate 62-2. He thought it came in clear glass only and was of the 1880s. He assigned it the appropriate name of BOUQUET. He supplied that name in 1938, whereas Mrs. Kamm gave her title in 1946. I have used the original and shorter title. Dr. Millard used photographs to illustrate his books. Unfortunately, photographs are not too suitable as a means of showing designs on glass. One authority on pressed glass will take exception to this statement. In this instance, though I had seen Dr. Millard's illustration of this pattern hundreds of times and had a creamer of the pattern in my collection, I could not discern enough detail from the photograph to identify the two pieces as being of the same pattern. Mrs. Kamm apparently had the same difficulty. It was only by studying the black and white line drawings of Mrs. Lee's goblet that the shape of Millard's goblet became familiar till it could be recognized for what it was.

Alice Hulett Metz, in *Early American Pattern Glass*, pages 66-67, No. 725, covers this pattern under the Millard title of BOUQUET. Her photograph of a goblet is far superior to that of Millard's, but she overlooked Kamm's NARCISSUS SPRAY.

I have a standard creamer in this pattern, and it is similar in shape to the water pitcher. (Note: Mrs. Kamm in her drawing did not complete the band of figurework around the water pitcher.) There is also a tall, slender, individual creamer in this pattern. It is pedestaled and of much the same shape as the goblet. From the shape of the various items in the pattern, plus the intaglio pressing (see drawing which shows even the band is depressed), it is my belief this pattern did not originate in the 1880s, but dates from about 1905-1915. The glass is clear and brilliant but very soft and thus, easily abraded. After regular use it develops a dull, cloudy appearance. This destroys the formal floral effect. With top quality glass, it would have been superb ware. The mold maker did a superlative job.

The waist curves in, then flares somewhat to a wide, thick base. The glass of the bottom is 1/2 inch thick. Under the base is a low, wide dome. Into this dome is impressed one of the most beautiful motifs found in pressed glass. (See drawing of bottom.) Three ellipses overlap to form a six-pointed star, with a hexagonal daisy in the center and curved plumes in the points. Diamond point fills the outer spaces to the ring on which the piece sits.

The body is round, with almost straight sides, flaring slightly from waist to rim. Centered on each side and covering much of the surface is a formal, stylized bouquet. It begins at the bottom as a fleur-de-lis and changes to an anthemion at the top. Above this are three six-petaled flowers, shown full face. On each side of the posy are three small, impressed fern fronds. This design is intaglio pressed with a raised outline on the larger figures. The center of each flower is a large, sunken dewdrop, and the petals are veined with tiny raised lines. Under the lip and the handle is an inch-wide, horizontal band which is simple and effective. It is bordered at top and bottom by inverted V-shaped ridges. Through the center and running horizontally, is a band of vertical, sharp pointed prisms standing side by side. Above and below is a band of small diamond point. There is considerable undecorated space on the body which would be lustrous if it were not badly clouded.

The back portion of the rim is scalloped, first by a low, narrow one, then a low, wider one. The front arches up and over to form a narrow, deep lip. The handle is six-sided. The two side panels are about half as wide as the other four. It turns up at an angle to provide a thumbgrip, then curves back to the body and flares slightly as it descends.

I know nothing of when, where, or by whom the pattern was manufactured.

Standard creamer: 4-part mold, 1 pound, 4 15/16 inches tall, 3 5/16 wide, and 5 5/16 inches long.

Water Pitcher: 4-part mold, weight unknown, 8 1/2 inches tall. Other measurements unknown.

These items are known in the pattern: individual creamer on a pedestal, goblet, standard creamer, covered butter dish, spoonholder, covered sugar bowl, small bowl, 10-inch plate, celery dish, small jelly compote. There must be a sugar bowl to match the individual creamer. I suspect many other items were produced.

197—THISTLEBLOW

Mrs. Kamm said this pattern was known by the euphonious name of THISTLEBLOW, and she used that title to describe the pattern in *A Sixth Pitcher Book*, page 45, No. 104. She thought, from the imitation cut glass band round the top of the creamer, that it dated from 1895-1910.

S. T. Millard, in *Goblets II*, Plate 48-2, named the pattern PANELLED IRIS (*sic*). He thought it came in clear glass only, and was made during the 1880s. He said the flowers were irises.

Mrs. Metz, in *Early American Pattern Glass*, pages 230-31, No. 2644, covered the pattern under the Millard title. She overlooked Kamm's coverage as THISTLEBLOW. She illustrated a tall stemmed vessel which could have been a wine or sherbet. She did comment, however, that when she saw a pattern in a 1915 catalog, with no characteristics of the 1880s, it was difficult to accept the latter as the date of origin.

The formalized floral spray was not intended to represent a botanical entity, but was solely ornamental. Since the flowers were intaglio pressed, I would date the ware as not earlier than 1905-1915. The name THISTLEBLOW is continued as more suitable.

The standard, flat-based creamer is used here to show the attractive design on the bottom, details of the pattern, proportions and measurements. I once had a tall, slender, pedestaled creamer in the individual size, shaped much like Millard's goblet. It is the only specimen of my collection that I have been unfortunate enough to break—so far. See PANELLED HEATHER for a similarly shaped and identically sized, individual creamer. Both patterns may well have come from the same factory.

The base is a low, wide ring. Underneath is an eight-point, many-rayed star in a hollowed out roof. (See cut of bottom.)

The lower two-thirds of the body has four narrow, flat panels alternating with four wide, slightly convexed ones. They extend from the waist almost to the band of figurework at the top. The narrow panels are low and arched at the top. The wide panels have swagged tops, and a floral spray centered in each. These symmetrical sprays have a fleur-de-lis as their stem; they are clamped together tightly at the middle with an impressed rosette; and they have a bud on each side with an erect, open flower at the top. The figures are deeply intaglio pressed and may have been painted a garish color when originally placed on the market. Around the top third of the body is a chain design of ovals and buckles. Where two such figures meet they overlap and form beveled, flat cubes. The oval figures are framed with wide bands of faceted figures in high relief. Their centers are filled with oval rosettes, the end of each petal being well rounded. The petals are concave, with a raised line as a margin. The buckles are odd-shaped and framed with diamond point bands. Their centers have round rosettes composed of sharp-pointed and spined faceted figures.

The rim has a peculiar form of scalloping. There are three wide, low scallops with very small, low scallops on top. Over the two buckles on the sides, but not following their contours, are high, narrow scallops, each three-lobed. The glass is thick at the rim and flat on top. It rises up and forward to form the narrow lip.

The handle is six-sided and well arched, being somewhat larger at the lower attachment than at the upper.

The glass has an amethyst tint and would color well from exposure to the sun. It is free of defects and is a good quality production ware. Nothing is known as to where or by whom it was made.

Creamer: 4-part mold, 1 pound, 4 5/8 inches tall, 3 1/2 inches wide, and 5 1/2 inches long.

The goblet, standard creamer, and individual creamer are the only pieces known to me. Certainly there should have been a four-piece table set in the standard, as well as the individual, size. One would expect to find many other articles.

198—FLEUR-DE-LIS, INTAGLIO

The fleur-de-lis motif has been used on many patterns of pressed glass, but never before have I found such a deeply impressed intaglio design as on this piece. The stylized flower appears four times round the body of the creamer. They are deeply slashed (1/4 inch), probably so that gilt or coloring could be applied, though in this case, none was.

Between the flowers is a complex loop-and-twist design. The figurework of this design is topped with fine-toothing and small diamond point. The tops of each goat horn curve over and meet the tips of the adjoining one to form a curved arch over each fleur-de-lis. Between the apexes of these arches, and 3/4 inch below the rim, is a small, deeply slashed fleur-de-lis figure as shown.

The creamer is somewhat barrel-shaped. The handle half of the rim is double scalloped. The lip half is plain. It rises, then thrusts forward to form the lip.

The handle is oval in cross section and notched down each side with small thumbprints. It is an unusual handle which, to my knowledge, is found on only two other patterns. It is identical with the one on V-IN-HEART shown in Kamm's *A Sixth Pitcher Book*, page 26, No. 39. (In fact, the two creamers are alike in many respects.) The handle of MEDALLION SUNBURST, shown in this book, is also the same. All three patterns were probably conceived by the same designer and made in the same factory. They are all late ware—1910 or later. For some reason this piece looks as fresh as if baked last night. Perhaps it sat on a shelf for a long, long time, and so accumulated no battle scars.

There is a ring round the base, and underneath there is a deeply pressed, intaglio quatrefoil, as shown in the drawing of the bottom. The quality is good. The glass is clear, brilliant, and quite thick in places to take the deep impressions. It is not flint.

Creamer: 4-part mold, 13 ounces, 4 1/4 inches tall, 3 inches wide, and 4 3/4 inches long.

Dr. Millard, in *Goblets*, Plate 97-4, shows a goblet he calls FLEUR-DE-LIS. The flowers on his pattern are similar in size, shape, placement, and general appearance to those on the creamer shown here. There is an 11-inch, somewhat square-shaped bowl of very brilliant glass in this pattern. Sauce dishes and tumblers are also found. There must have been a spooner, sugar bowl, and butter dish to go with the creamer. Probably a water pitcher, water tray, and numerous other items will eventually turn up.

199—EVERGREEN

This small, attractive, apple-green creamer has only one demerit—its extreme youth. It probably is not over thirty-five years old. In pressed glass, youth is the unpardonable sin.

It has not been described in any reference book on glass. Mrs. Kamm, in *A Seventh Pitcher Book*, page 80, No. 156, illustrates a plate in NORTHWOOD'S SUNFLOWER. That plate is emerald green and similar to the piece used here. The bottom and the graining on the leaves, however, are different. (See drawing of bottom.)

The name *EVERGREEN* is applied because it matches the color of the glass, the leaves on the piece, and the little Alabama city of that name, which has developed a thriving enterprise of supplying wholesale florists with bracken, similax, holly, autumn leaves, mistletoe, lichen, fungi, magnolia leaves, yaupon, acorns, pine cones, Spanish moss, etc.

The impression given is that of a large flower showing only the calyxes and petals. The former make a crown extending from the base up some one-third of the body. They are leaf-shaped, show raised veins, and have high, beveled edges. They stand erect, joining each other side-by-side with an irregular top margin. The petals are long, slender, and overlapping. Each petal has a raised spine down its center and ends in a sharp point at the top. These points form the unevenly serrated rim. The petals are attractively grained. At the bottom of the body is a zigzag band of dewdrops round the bowl.

The base is round and narrow. The sides flare widely to the rim. It sits on a ringbase, and the underside is slightly hollowed out. A large cabochon is in the center with a ring of zigzag dewdrops around the perimeter. The rest of the bottom is filled with meandering, radial veins. The sides of the lip are high. The lip then dips deeply and is quite narrow. The plain pressed handle is oval in cross section. It increases in size as it approaches the bottom attachment.

I do not know the name of the manufacturer. It could have been made by Northwood since it is contemporary with, and closely approximates, some of his products. The glass is a beautiful shade of light apple green, and together with the grained petals, gives a cool, refreshing appearance. There is an occasional bubble, but no discoloration. The mold marks show plainly on the handle but are not sharp. The spines of the petals obliterate such marks elsewhere.

Creamer: 2(?)-part mold, 9 ounces, 3 1/8 inches tall, 3 3/4 inches wide, and 5 1/4 inches long.

This creamer is the only piece of the pattern I have seen. A few other items probably were made. Certainly a sugar bowl must have been manufactured.

200—TIGER LILY

This is a pretty, but very late pattern of pressed glass. Larry Freeman shows a picture of this water pitcher along with twenty-six other pieces of iridized glass in Plate 122 of his *Iridescent Glass*. He lists many names but gives no key as to which name matches what piece. I have a feeling this pitcher may be the one he calls IMPERIAL 494-1/2. I do not know why.

Marion T. Hartung, in her *Carnival Glass*, pages 71-72, names the pattern TIGER LILY. She illustrates a tumbler. Rose M. Presznick, in her *Carnival and Iridescent Glass Price Guide* (1962), shows the water pitcher on Plate 203. On page 92 she gives prices on the following items of the pattern: 3 sizes of bowls, butter dish, decanter, goblet, lamp, mug, 2 sizes of plates, water pitcher, milk pitcher, and tumbler. She says other pieces of the pattern have been reported and attributes it to the Imperial Glass Company.

Most iridescent pressed glass tableware was made by the following companies: (1) Northwood Glass Company of Martins Ferry, Ohio and Indiana, Pennsylvania; (2) Imperial Glass Company of Bellaire, Ohio, and; (3) Fenton Art Glass Company of Williamstown, West Virginia. Westmoreland made some in lesser amounts. Much of the Northwood glass is trademarked, and in general it was made somewhat earlier than that of the other companies. The Imperial Glass Company produced such glass in tremendous quantities. This pitcher may have been one of their products.

This type of glass is known by a different name by everyone familiar with it. (And who isn't?) Some names are unprintable. Others are marigold, luster, nancy, carnival, iridescent, tiffin, tiffany, gold luster, etc. It is now becoming generally known as Carnival Glass. It was popular ware, and much of it was made until about 1922. It is being reproduced today to supply a renewed demand.

This is a large water pitcher iridized with a marigold luster. In the deep places are soft reds and purples that glimmer in different lights. A trace of iron was added to the spray solution to produce such shades.

The floral figurework is in deep, well-executed intaglio. The glass is thick to take these impressions. They are formalized and of two types. Though quite attractive, they represent known flora. On each side and under the lip are erect plumelike stems of leaves, adorned at the top with two large, six-petaled flowers—tiger lilies. The petals are curved and veined. An erect spike separates the flowers. At the base two more such flowers are separated by the plume. Above each of these are sprays of slender leaves and several deep-sunk, many-petaled little flowers.

There are two large scallops on each side of the rim, each with five to seven smaller scallops. There is a high, rounded scallop at the rear for a handle attachment. The rim rises abruptly in front to form the high sides of the lip, which itself is wide and depressed.

The handle is large and commodious. On each side is half a fern frond in high relief. Close study shows the handle was pressed, not applied. The large, round blob is at the bottom attachment. The shape of the pitcher is one quite common in later wares. It is constricted at the waist and the base is larger. The glass there is 3/4-inch thick. Underneath, it is slightly hollowed out with a beautiful formal design intaglio pressed. (See drawing of base.) This piece is of excellent quality for iridescent pressed glass. It is clear and flashed with marigold inside and out.

Water pitcher: 4-part mold, 3 pounds and 6 1/2 ounces, 8 3/8 inches tall, 5 3/4 inches wide, and 8 7/8 inches long.

Since a covered butter dish was made, we might expect to find a sugar bowl and creamer in the pattern. By the time Carnival Glass was made, our styles had changed. Sugars and creamers were produced in only a few of the many Carnival Glass patterns.

201—DARLING GRAPE

There is considerable confusion about this pattern. It is regrettable, for the pattern is attractive, though late. It might be better to omit it since

195

Bottom
196

196

197

Bottom
197

198

Bottom
198

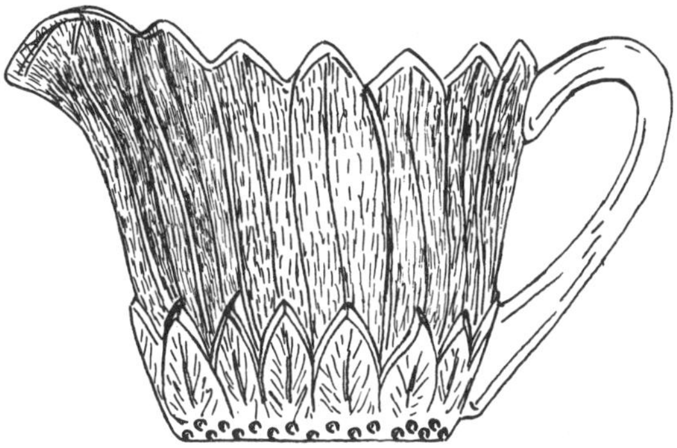
199

Bottom
199

201

200

Bottom
200

Bottom
201

I cannot clear up the confusion. On the other hand, it might help some future collector if I cite the references we have.

Ruth Webb Lee, in *Early American Pressed Glass*, first named this pattern LATE PANELLED GRAPE, as Pattern 74, pages 206-207 and Plate 65. She knew that some had been made around 1890 and some about 1900. (35 years before.) She listed six pieces. In her line drawings on Plate 65-1, she showed a butter dish in this pattern as determined by the scalloping on the base and the vine suspended from the large, rounded band. She also showed a covered bowl and goblet in a different paneled grape design. Her write-up indicates she thought there were two or more variants of the pattern.

S. T. Millard, in *Goblets*, Plate 120-2, showed a tall, slender goblet in the pattern and named it DARLING GRAPE (for Mrs. Mary A. Darling of Gary, Indiana), and said it was of the 1880s. In the same book on Plate 86-1, he shows a goblet which he names LATE PANELLED GRAPE and considered it to be of the 1890s. This latter goblet is similar to the goblet and covered bowl in Lee's Plate 65-1.

Minnie Watson Kamm, in *Two Hundred Pattern Glass Pitchers*, page 96, No. 136, shows LATE PANELLED GRAPE. She uses a creamer, the same as used here, and matching the butter dish of Lee and the DARLING GRAPE goblets by Millard and Metz. In the same book she shows, and describes on page 117, No. 187, a LATE PANELLED GRAPE, VARIANT, which matches the Lee goblet and covered bowl. It also matches Millard's LATE PANELLED GRAPE.

Larry Freeman, in *Iridescent Glass*, showed a cut reproduced from a mail order catalog of 1910-1920 listing this pattern at $6.50 per bbl. of 10 doz. pieces. The cut showed: sherbet, sauch dish, spooner, covered butter, covered sugar, creamer, deep bowl, celery tray, footed bowl, covered jelly compote, tumbler, and water pitcher. He inferred the ware was iridized, which could have been true, though I have never seen an iridized piece and know of only clear glass being used in this pattern or its variants.

Alice Hulett Metz, in *Early American Pattern Glass*, pages 80-81, No. 891, showed a goblet in DARLING GRAPE and said it is of the 1890s. On pages 78-79, No. 864, she showed a goblet of LATE PANELLED GRAPE.

The body of the creamer is almost cylindrical, but flares slightly near the top. Twelve wide, flat panels extend from above the waist to below the rim. Each panel is rounded over at top and bot-

tom. Near the top a round, smooth, raised ring, or straight vine surrounds the body. Coiled about and suspended from this support are alternating large bunches of grapes and large grape leaves. Tendrils are suspended from the support, the grapes, and also the leaves—a truly remarkable phenomenon. The embossed designs are somewhat smoothed and rounded out, so a clear-cut impression is not shown.

The back half of the rim has a scallop over each panel. One on each side is plain. Flanking the plain scallops are others bearing three small scallops each. The front of the rim rises slightly and extends well forward to form a copious lip.

The handle is six-sided, large, substantial, and wider than thick. There is a perceptible waist and a ring below it that serves as a base. Underneath is an intriguing deep intaglio leaf and grape design. The margins of this figurework, like that of the sides, are softened. (See drawing of bottom.)

Since Millard, Lee, Kamm and Freeman have all suggested dates of manufacture and I have no additional evidence, I will not add to the confusion.

Creamer: 4-part mold, 15 ounces, 4 5/8 inches tall, 3 3/8 inches wide, and 5 5/8 inches long.

202—GRAPE WITH VINE

Minnie Watson Kamm used this pattern in *A Second Two Hundred Pattern Glass Pitchers*, page 60. The specimen she used had a poor impression, and she was unable to depict the pattern accurately. Having a creamer with an excellent impression, I am using it for the drawing alone. It is a beautiful pattern, with all details well executed.

Mrs. Metz, in *Early American Pattern Glass*, pages 82-83, No. 927, illustrated a creamer and said it was of the 1890s. Her photographic illustration was not too clear. I am unable to determine whether Millard, or Lee, used this particular version of the large number of patterns employing a grape motif.

It is a beautiful, well-executed design that is rather plentiful and also reasonable in price. Fortunately, it has not been reproduced as has the HEAVY PANELLED GRAPE pattern which it somewhat resembles.

This squatty creamer sits on a wide base, scalloped by rounded ribs, which start at the edge of the base and extend through the wide waist and up onto the base of the bowl.

The body is divided into three divisions at the mold marks. A heavy, grained grapevine meanders around the top of the bowl, then drapes down

202

203-1

203-2

204

Bottom

203

207

205

206

208

209

210

211

to obliterate the mold marks. In each of the three panels are four well-formed grape leaves which are veined and stippled. Each panel contains a large bunch of nineteen rounded grapes. Tendrils are scattered along the vine.

The lip is upraised and plain. The back three-fourths of the rim is covered with large, graduated beads in three-quarter relief. The handle is scrolled, has dewdrops down the side panels, and is well buttressed at the attachments.

Creamer: 3-part mold, 12 ounces, 4 1/2 inches tall, 3 9/16 inches wide, and 4 15/16 inches long.

The glass is of fine quality for production ware. It is soda-lime, light, and has no resonance. Certainly the four-piece table setting was produced. There was a berry bowl with sauce dishes made and probably a water pitcher. It is believed to have been produced about 1890-1900.

203—BOGUE CHITTA

This pattern is named *BOGUE CHITTA* for the little Mississippi town close to the now vanished backwoods community of Cold Springs where I was born. Flowers similar to these could be found today in the thick forests along the banks of the beautiful Bogue Chitta River. This is another pattern not previously covered in our glass literature.

The sides of the body are almost straight, flaring gently to the rim. Two long, sharp-spined spikes cover each of the two front mold marks. Between each two spikes is a large dewdrop, flanked on either side by a smaller one. These figures extend from the base of the bowl to the geometric border at the top. They divide the bowl into three large panels. Each panel has a diagonal floral sprig with thorns or bracts, leaves, buds, and blooms. It is purely decorative and belongs to no known botanical species. Just under the rim is a 5/8-inch decorative band. Its upper edge is a round, raised line and its lower a sharp-spined, smaller one. This band surrounds the entire body, except the spout. The band is cut into squares by groups of two spined prisms. Inside each square is placed a diagonal cross with four sharp points. A dewdrop is centered in each corner around the cross.

The ring around the rim makes the glass there rather thick. The sides of the rim are plain, level, and flat. In the back is a high, wide upthrust apparently designed to permit the decorative band to rise above the handle attachment. In front, the rim rises abruptly, then levels off into a somewhat large and rather clumsy lip. The glass was not well pressed about the lip, and a depression was left

which is difficult to keep sanitary. The lip is over a nose-shaped bulge in the front of the creamer. It fits into the middle of the front panel, but the panel decoration does not include the nose. A band of dewdrops outlines the protrusion, whose surface is left plain.

The handle is six-sided with the two side panels the wider. It is undecorated, except by its many irregular curves. The waist is curved and shapely. It is formed by a reverse curve that sweeps from the bottom edge of the bowl to the outer edge of the wide, round base. It is smooth and plain.

Under the base is a comely design composed of a large whorl of rounded ribs, with a dime-sized center which contains six large dewdrops. (See drawing of bottom.) I believe this pattern to be a product of the 1875-1885 period. The designer was neither artist nor a botanist, but he did add to our folk art. The design is compatible with this era. The glass is fairly clear, but the piece was made in a hurry and poorly finished off. The four-piece table set, if made, probably would have retailed for about fifteen cents. Try to buy it for that price now!

Creamer: 3-part mold, 12 ounces, 5 1/8 inches tall, 3 1/4 inches wide. and 4 15/16 inches long.

The creamer and spoonholder are the only articles I have seen in the pattern. It was not a container since there was no provision made for a lid. Creamers of this type were never made by themselves: Q. E. D. There was a covered butter dish and a covered sugar bowl.

204—WILD BOUQUET

Alice Hulett Metz, in her *Early American Pattern Glass*, page 76, No. 849, named and illustrated this pattern for the first time but did not describe it. Her title is excellent. My creamer is probably the one shown in her photograph since I purchased it from her. The design is not too clearly shown in her book, especially about the handle, lower part of the body, and foot. It is hoped that our black and white line drawing will better depict these details.

The creamer is so similar to Northwood's IN-TAGLIO pattern with its yellowish tinge of the glass, the opalescent rim, conformation, and design which all combine to make one wonder if it may not be unmarked Northwood pattern.

The wide, sweeping panel on each side conveys the appearance of being oval but actually is round, as in INTAGLIO. Each large side panel is outlined by raised scrolls and beadwork. The surface is left plain, and a bouquet of flowers (try to name them) is pressed therein with low lines outlining the stems, flowers, and some of the leaves. The top leaf and one flower are rounded over in higher relief than the lines. All designs were originally painted with green paint some of which still adheres in places. The flowers probably were of a different color. The scrolls at the side and bottom of each panel are made up of beadwork, consisting of a series of tiny, beveled, flat-topped squares. Near the bottom the beads diminish and disappear—ending in well-rounded, horn-shaped scrolls which have a knob at the small upper end. In the space between the base of the scrolls is a round, raised wafer with a beveled, hollow, squared figure superimposed. Below the wafer is a raised heart with an ornate design covering its surface. Under the lip is a wide column which begins as a wide V-shaped trough at the waist and gradually changes into a well-rounded column as it ascends. This, too, is bordered by square beadwork. Flanking the panels on each side is a long cornucopia-shaped figure with a flat, stippled surface. At the top of each space is a wing-spaced design in rounded relief. This same winged treatment is repeated on each side of the body where the handle is attached.

The handle is five-sided, with two panels on the inner side, but appears square. Each side panel is outlined with square beadwork, and the lower attachment expands enough to accommodate a stippled wing design similar to those on the body. The handle seems to grow out of the lower end of the body.

The rim is unevenly scalloped with a large arch of graduated round beads. The largest bead is at the crest, over each panel. At the back and front, the rim rises and is outlined with square beading which stops at the handle and gradually disappears under the center of the lip. The lip is wide and erect. The rim and the top of the handle are opalescent white. The narrow waist is encircled by two closely placed rounded rings and is quite short.

Below the waist, the foot curves down and out to near the edge. This portion is covered with twenty ribs, the crests of which are finetoothed. Between the ribs are curved, concave channels. The base is wide, thick, and rounded at the edge. Underneath is a large hollow space with a ring at the edge to give a firm foundation. The design of this creamer is never idle.

The quality and workmanship are on a par with that of Northwood glass. The off-clear glass, which has a yellowish tinge and was used in some Northwood patterns, must have been deliberately used, because clear glass could be cheaply made when this piece came along. If it really were a product of Harry Northwood, the nation's leading authority on colored glass, everything would fit nicely into place. The mold marks can be seen but are neither high nor sharp.

Creamer: 4-part mold, 1 pound, 4 5/8 inches tall, 3 7/8 inches wide, and 6 inches long.

The other three pieces of the four-piece table set must have been made to go with the lonely creamer in this seldom seen pattern.

205—DIAMOND CUT WITH LEAF

Mrs. Kamm never located a creamer in this charming but rare pattern. Ruth Webb Lee, in *Early American Pressed Glass*, Pattern 130, page 337, and Plates 108, 109, 138 and 144, praised the pattern highly, assigned the above title and illustrated a creamer, three plates, a handled cup, and a goblet. She knew of blue, clear, and amber pieces. It is also known to have been made in yellow. Clear pieces are scarce, blue and amber pieces even more so, and yellow, exceedingly difficult to find.

Dr. S. T. Millard, in his *Goblets*, Plate 89-3, showed a goblet. Mrs. Metz showed a goblet as No. 1801 on pages 160-61 of her *Early American Pattern Glass*.

Do not confuse this pattern with the earlier DIAMOND POINT AND LEAF pattern shown by E. McCalmy Belknap, in his *Milk Glass*, page 230, Plate 214, where he illustrated a covered sugar bowl in milk-white glass. His piece was probably contemporary with PRINCESS FEATHER.

The naming of pressed glass patterns is not as simple a task as it may seem. To give a short descriptive, or otherwise suitable name may lead to unsuspected pitfalls. Mrs. Ruth Webb Lee, the dean of American pressed glass writers and a recognized authority on glass nomenclature, named this pattern DIAMOND CUT WITH LEAF. A glance at the drawing shows this title is unsuitable. Note that the pattern is pressed into triangles and pyramids, not into diamonds. Also, it is pressed, not cut. It would be impossible to handcut glass in such a design by means of a cutting wheel. To handcarve the pattern in a single piece would have required many months of work by an expert craftsman and would have been financially prohibitive. This title is continued, since it is not my mission to change well established pattern names no matter how inappropriate they may be. Would the ASHBURTON pattern have been better known if it had been given a descriptive title? I don't think so.

The surface of the glass of the body is almost imperceptibly roughened, giving it a cool, frosted appearance which is pleasing. The roughness does not extend to the handle or base.

The body rounds out just above the waist, then flares slightly to the rim. Six large leaves, their stem-ends at the waist, extend well up on the bowl. The leaves have no botanical identity. Their edges are beveled and serrated. Their surfaces are intaglio pressed, well veined, and stippled. The background above and between the leaves is filled with a seldom found decorative device, which consists of inverted V-shaped ridges running horizontally and diagonally to both left and right. This results in many small, ridged triangles, each enclosing a sharp-pointed, triangular pyramid.

The rim is level, except for the very slight rise at the lip. The back portion is covered with low, rounded scallops which bear no relation to the triangular design below. The front rises and arches over ever so little as a concession to a lip. The lip is one I have never before seen in pressed glass. Both inside and out, it is V-shaped, the inside forming a deep trough. On the outside, it extends well down on the body and has a sharp crested ridge.

The waist is short, thick, and surrounded by many vertical, rounded "bowed-in" ribs. The bowing causes a portion of the ends of each rib to show, and these form a high, round shelf on the base of the bowl and on top of the foot. The base is round and tapers down. The hollowed space underneath is plain and extends into the waist.

The handle is six-sided and angular. Its only curve is a slight rise, on top, which furnishes a thumbgrip. The lower attachment differs markedly from the simple upper one. It fits into the center of a leaf, and to receive it, a raised, elongated escutcheon was provided. (See drawing.) The mold marks on the handle are sharp and uncomfortable.

The glass is clear and of fine quality. The moldmaker did a good job. No effort was made to finish the piece off, however, after it was removed from the mold. The mold marks on the sides, rim, and handle are incisive. Nothing is known as to just which glass house made the pattern. It appears to be a product of the late 1870s and early 1880s.

Creamer: 3-part mold, 11 ounces, 4 3/8 inches tall, 3 1/2 inches wide, and 5 1/8 inches long.

The following items are known to have been made: creamer, covered sugar bowl, covered butter dish, spoonholder, cup, cordial, 7 1/2 and 9 1/2-inch round plate, goblet, and wine glass.

206—ROSE IN SNOW

The square version of ROSE IN SNOW has been authenticated as a product of Bryce Brothers, of Pittsburgh, Pennsylvania, and dates from the late 1870s through the 1880s. The round type is thought to be an Ohio product. Mrs. Kamm, in *A Fourth Pitcher Book*, pages 43-44, No. 49, describes and illustrates the round form. She was told the Indiana Glass Company of Dunkirk was still making both forms in a complete line of articles. Most articles found today in either form are likely to be new. The square piece shown here is radically different from the round type. It is possible that forms for both were products of the Hipkins Novelty Mold Works of Martins Ferry, Ohio.

Ruth Webb Lee describes both round and square versions together as if they were one and the same pattern, though they were originally made by two widely separated factories. See her *Early American Pressed Glass*, Pattern 143, pages 371-373 and Plates 73, 120 and 122. The collector of this pattern should see Mrs. Lee's *Antique Fakes and Reproductions*, wherein she makes several references to pieces of the pattern that have been reproduced. Also see her *Victorian Glass*, Plate 8.

Alice Hulett Metz, in *Early American Pattern Glass*, pages 54-55, No. 572, shows a goblet and cautions against reproductions. S. T. Millard, in *Goblets*, Plate 17-1, shows a goblet.

Except for plates and goblets (if such items were actually made by Bryce Brothers), all items in this particular version are square. The square creamer in my collection is much brighter and clearer than is my yellow-tinged round piece.

All parts of the square creamer fit into the shape. On the square bowl are four flat, slightly flaring sides with the handle on one corner and the spout on the diagonal one. Each side panel is dominated by a large U-shaped surface. These are stippled, except for the clear rose sprigs in relief, which are placed diagonally across each panel. The rose petals, buds, and leaves are veined. The design differs in many details from that of the round form, but not enough to prevent their being used together. Directly below each U-shaped panel is a large arc filled with vertical fine rib. The corners of the body are ornate. At the top the space is filled with a long, fancy prism in relief. The dart-shaped spaces on the lower corners are filled with imitation cut strawberry diamond.

The square waist ends in a shelf on the base of the bowl. It curves in, then flows out to the edge of the foot. Each side of the waist has three upended ovals in low relief and these are filled with sunk diamond point. The corners of the waist and foot are chamfered. The foot is left plain and smooth— even underneath where a high, hollow space remains. The round form has a large rosette with sharp points underneath, and its surface is stippled.

The rim is horizontal with a low scallop over three corners. A narrow, raised line outlines it. The rim over each side panel is in the shape of a large bracket. The spout extends out from the body, is high, and arches over the top. It was left plain.

The pressed handle is six-sided and ornate. A knop at the top, in the rear, provides a good thumbgrip. The upright member is similarly shaped to the brackets on the rim. A knop also adorns the lower end of the handle.

The piece is well made and of good metal. It comes in clear amber, blue, yellow, and milk-white glass, but colors are seldom seen. It is one of the most popular of pressed glass patterns.

Round creamer: 3-part mold, 14 ounces, 5 3/8 inches tall, 3 15/16 inches wide, and 5 5/16 inches long.

Square creamer: 4-part mold, 14 1/2 ounces, 4 3/4 inches tall, 4 9/16 inches wide, and 5 7/8 inches long.

The following articles in the square form are known to have been made: creamer, covered sugar bowl without handles, covered butter dish, spoonholder without handles, low-base compote, water pitcher, sauce dish, and flat square bowls in 8- and 9-inch sizes.

207—ANTHEMION

Probably the most beautiful 10-inch plate ever made in American pressed glass was in the ARCHED LEAF pattern. The goblets shown by Lee, Millard, and Metz, as ARCHED LEAF, have no stippling; have intaglio leaves instead of flat ones; and fans instead of cabochons. Their arches are framed with V-shaped grooves instead of beveled, flat-topped bands. Probably the two ANTHEMION 10-inch plates (square and round) with maple leaf centers are entitled to second place. (Lacy Sandwich excepted.)

Minnie Watson Kamm, in *A Fifth Pitcher Book*, pages 137-38, No. 178, used a tall water pitcher to describe and name this pattern. She learned it was made by the Model Flint Glass Company of Findlay, Ohio, between 1890 and 1900. Neither Kamm nor Ruth Webb Lee knew a 10-inch round plate was made in the pattern. Lee, in *Early American Pressed Glass*, Pattern 198, page 428 and Plate 58-3, described the pattern and listed the pieces she had seen. They did not include a creamer. On Plate 58-3 she illustrated a 10-inch square plate, a tumbler, and a sauce dish.

Mrs. Metz showed a covered butter dish as No. 842, pages 76-77 of her *Early American Pattern Glass*. A goblet in this pattern has not been shown or listed by Millard, Kamm, Lee, or Metz; nor has it been seen by this author. They may, however, have been made.

The standard creamer is shown here to give size, proportions, and record the fact that one was made. The shape is generally the same as that of the water pitcher, but on a reduced scale. The body pinches in to a narrow waist, above which the lower part of the bowl rounds out sharply. It then takes a straight line to to the rim, flaring slightly on the way.

Around the body are three long and three short foliations called ANTHEMION. The longer reach from two round scrolls at the waist almost to the rim. The shorter extend half way up the body from their scrolls. Each scroll has two cabochons. The background is filled with finely executed stippling. On this pattern is a stippling effect produced by arranging minute dewdrops in straight lines. The drops are staggered and appear in straight lines in three directions. Most stippling is made up of minute craters, or small doughnuts. These dewdrops make a pleasing, frosted surface and accentuate the Anthemions, which are left plain. The fronds are in three groups with a long, wide one, flanked by a short, narrow one on each side. Each leaf is concave and has a raised ring as an outline. There is an odd arrangement of small three-ray fans at the top of the stippling. They stand erect, and their bases look like a well-filed saw. Above the fans a plain band, about 1/4-inch wide, extends around the body, except under the lip. Here the fans are absent and the stippling almost reaches the rim. A smaller Anthemion covers most of the spout.

The back part of the rim is level, with even scallops, one over each fan on the body. In front the rim rises and juts forward to a curved spout which starts well down on the front of the body. The top of the creamer needed fire polishing but did not get it.

The base flares from the narrow waist to form a ring on which the piece rests. Underneath is a plain hollow dome. The handle differs from most.

At the top is a raised member for a thumbgrip. From this point almost to the bottom, the handle is four-sided. The two back faces are crossed by many small ribs with round ends set side by side. The inside faces are round and smooth, but the mold marks are sharp and punishing. The lower end of the handle has many ribs and splays onto the body.

The glass is soda-lime and of a beautiful, clear quality. The designer and mold chipper did an excellent job. The gaffer must have stepped out; an underling "goofed." Fire polishing to smooth out the harsh mold lines would have enhanced the piece.

Standard creamer: 3-part mold, 11 ounces, 4 15/16 inches tall, 3 1/8 inches wide, and 5 inches long.

Water pitcher: 3-part mold, weight unknown, 8 inches tall.

I do not believe a goblet was made in this pattern. The following items were: water pitcher, sugar bowl, spoonholder, butter dish, standard creamer, tumbler, flat sauce, 7-inch berry bowl, 7-inch flat square dish, milk pitcher, 10-inch square plate, 10-inch round plate, high cake stand, and triangular relish dish.

208—STIPPLED CHERRY

This is a good name for the pattern until you try to determine what variety of cherry is represented. Nothing about the limbs, foliage, or fruit resembles the cherry, and the fruits are not stippled.

Mrs. Kamm could not find a creamer, so she used a tall water pitcher. See her *A Fourth Pitcher Book*, page 132, No. 174. Millard did not show a goblet in his goblet books. Perhaps, like Lee and Kamm, he had not seen one. Goblets also may not have been made.

Ruth Webb Lee, in her *Early American Pressed Glass*, Pattern 193, pages 475-76, described and listed known items. On Plate 126 she showed a 6-inch plate. In Plate 145 she showed a large, round bread plate. In Plate 156-1 she illustrated a bowl, creamer, and celery vase or spoonholder. Metz showed a plate as No. 993, pages 90-91, of *Early American Pattern Glass*. She said no goblet was made.

The creamer sits on a high, domed base which adds stature to the tall cylindrical bowl. From rim to waist are three vertical stripes, an inch wide, which cover the mold marks and are made up of convex herringbone, or an inverted frond. These, plus the leaf stems and fruit, are well rounded and

left clear. The background is stippled. Three wide segments of the body carry the design. To the left, in each, is a long leaf spray. To the right is a shorter sprig with three trilobed fruits at the top and leaves near the base.

Most of the rim is level and covered with low scallops. It has a narrow, flat shelf on the inside at the level of the dips in the scallops. This may signify that the piece originally had a lid and was sold as a container. I have a pair of articles, identical with what Mrs. Lee calls a celery vase. They are of the same dimensions as the creamer and are too tall for spoonholders but too short for celery vases. Each has a rim ledge to hold a lid. I have never known a celery vase to be used as a container. Spoonholders? Yes.

The rim was not finished off properly and as a result, is rough and sharp. In front it arches high to form a thick, upthrust lip.

The creamer rounds in to a constricted waist, from which it again curves out and down to its base. On top of the base a heavy, round and raised line zigzags around it. Due to the shape of the latter, the line cuts the foot into small triangles above and larger ones below. The small triangles contain three large dewdrops, and the larger ones four.

The handle is large, round in cross section, and capacious. It simulates an applied handle with the large blob at the lower attachment. The upper attachment also has a large blob. This is unusual and would never occur in an applied handle and deceives no one with even a rudimentary knowledge of blown glass. The mold lines on the handle are high, rough, and uncomfortable.

The glass of this pattern is of good quality, but the craftsmanship was poorer than usually found, even in cheap production ware. None of my pieces of the pattern are well finished off. It seems to be of the 1875-1885 period. However, we have this to consider: It was made by The Lancaster Glass Company of Lancaster, Ohio. They were not widely known nor well established, and the only advertisement we know of was issued around 1910. See STARLIET, PLAIN in this book for another pattern made by this company.

Standard creamer: 3-part mold, 15 ounces, 5 11/16 inches tall, 3 1/2 inches wide, and 5 3/8 inches long.

Water pitcher: 3-part mold, weight unknown, 9 inches tall, other measurements unknown.

The following articles are known in the pattern: creamer with a lid, covered sugar bowl, covered butter dish, covered spoonholder or celery vase, 6-inch bowl, 8-inch bowl, mug, 6-inch plate, footed sauce, flat sauce, 9 1/2-inch round bread plate, water pitcher, and tumbler.

209—PANELLED DAISY

This is one of the choicer patterns of the 1870s. It is found in many items, including round and square plates.

Mrs. Lee, in *Early American Pressed Glass*, Pattern 161, pages 416-418, Plates 95, 134, 135, and 136 described and illustrated six pieces of the pattern. She had seen no variants. Mrs. Kamm, in *A Third Two Hundred Pattern Glass Pitchers*, page 65, No. 92, showed a creamer with the daisy design occuring only in alternate panels. She did not describe the piece but did give a brief history of the Bryce Glass Company. She is believed to have used an old catalog for the write-up. She knew the sprig sometimes appeared in all panels.

S. T. Millard, in *Goblets*, showed a goblet in Plate 25-4 and said it occasionally came in amber. In his index the pattern was listed as DAISY, PANELLED. Mrs. Metz in *Early American Pattern Glass*, pages 62-63, No. 671, illustrated a goblet. She noted the differences in her goblet and the piece Mrs. Kamm illustrated.

The standard creamer (all panels filled with sprigs) is used here for description, measurements, and illustration. This has not previously been done. Bryce, Walker and Company of Pittsburgh, Pennsylvania, made the pattern. This was the name of the company from 1855 to June 13, 1882. They had several names before that period as well as afterward. They are producing quality tableware at present. The standard creamer is tall and slender, with less capacity than most creamers of its day.

From the waist the straight sides flare slightly to the rim. Five rounded ribs, in high relief, extend from waist to rim. They are bordered on either side by scalloped bands with raised edges, which look like wattles. The surface of each wattle is stippled. Under the handle are three of the rounded ribs between the scalloped bands. Six wide rounded panels are placed around the body, alternating with the ribs. They fill the spaces between the scalloped bands. Each panel is filled with a formalized floral sprig which might as well be called a daisy as anything. The flowers are in high relief, and the center of each is a dewdrop. The veins of the leaves are prominent. There are two daisies to each panel.

The waist is of the same size as the lower portion of the bowl, and is filled with an odd-shaped ring in high relief. Below the waist the base flares to a wide, high foot which is left plain. Underneath is a 3/4-inch high, hollowed-out space with a flat roof. It too is plain.

The handle is angular, as is the creamer. Three stiff, round sections comprise the member. Two jut upward and outward from the body and are joined together by a vertical third. On the back and inside surfaces of the handle are the same rib and scallop-band figures seen on the body.

The rim is unevenly scalloped with the wide ones over the panels and the narrow ones over the ribs. The lip dips perceptibly. The quality is good. A little better fire polishing would have improved the rim.

Creamer: 3-part mold, 13 ounces, 5 3/4 inches tall, 3 1/4 inches wide, and 5 inches long.

Although thirty-five items were made in this pattern, none of them are plentiful today. The goblet is being reproduced and sold in gift shops today. I do not know whether other articles of the pattern are also being reproduced.

See Plates 1 and 2 of Kamm's *A Seventh Pitcher Book* which show two pages from an undated trade catalog of about 1891-1892. They show five items together with various pieces of other patterns. All pieces of this pattern, shown there, have a daisy sprig in each panel.

210—PRIMROSE

A milk pitcher was used by Minnie Watson Kamm to illustrate this pattern in *A Third Two Hundred Pattern Glass Pitchers*, page 119, No. 179. The milk pitcher differs in significant respects from the standard creamer shown here.

Mrs. Lee, in *Early American Pressed Glass*, Pattern 155, pages 401-402 and Plates 114 and 136, described the pattern and told of a variant. The difference is in the floral treatment.

S. T. Millard, in *Goblets*, Plate 138-4, showed a goblet. J. Stanley Brothers Jr., wrote an article for the December, 1940 issue of *Antiques* in which he attributed PRIMROSE to the Canton Glass Company of Canton, Ohio, during the 1880s, as their "No. 10" pattern.

Mrs. Metz illustrated a creamer as No. 584, pages 54-55 of *Early American Pattern Glass*. Her photographic illustration did not show the figure-work too clearly.

Colored pieces in this pattern are hard to find today. Clear pieces are not particularly scarce. Few patterns were made in such a wide range of colors as PRIMROSE. Those known to have been used were: clear, "crystal" (?), amber, yellow or canary, apple green, blue, opaque white, opaque turquoise, purple slag, and opaque black. This choice of colors, appearing in a pattern with an attractive design and several sizes of plates, made it a favorite pattern of collectors.

The sides of the body are straight. They flare to the rim and round under at the waist. The body is divided into three wide panels by raised figurework on the mold marks. Mrs. Kamm called these canthooks. Having worked many a long day with canthooks and peavies, I would call them something else. They look like arrows aimed in opposite directions, with feather ends abutting. In any event, they do cover the mold marks, and each is surrounded by a rectangle outlined with small beading. Each panel has a spray of flowers and leaves placed diagonally across its surface. The flowers appear in two slightly different treatments, but all are in low relief. The background, around the sprays, looks cool and frosted. It is not stippled, frosted, grained, or beaded. Under a powerful magnifying glass it appears to be a quality fabric woven of coarse thread. It is so uniform and of such a small and intricate design, one wonders if the mold to press it was actually chipped by hand in cast iron, using only a hammer and chisel. Even with the magnifying glass the pattern runs together. How it could be chipped—using the naked eye and maintaining the exact regularity from top to bottom—is an enigma to me.

Mrs. Lee says the bases of the bowls are fluted. On the creamer and milk pitcher this figurework is reeded, not fluted. The reeds alternate with first a rounded one with a rounded top, then a narrower, sharp-spined one with a pointed top. The reeding extends on to the underside of the bowl and up to the wide panels. The same design extends through the narrow waist, then flares onto the top of the foot, ending in a well-defined shelf midway of the base. The base is low, hollow, and plain underneath. The top of the creamer is level and flat, whereas, on the milk pitcher the lip, rim, and handle all are curved. The top of the creamer appears rigid and severe.

Around the body of the milk pitcher and below the rim is a plain band. On the creamer is a half-inch-wide band of figurework in high relief. The band is made up of the same type of reeding found on the corseted waist. There is the added factor that the top and bottom of the band are the same, with rounded and pointed reed ends alternating. The crest of each rounded reed carries a tier of four small dewdrops.

The rim of the standard creamer is level, flat, and not fire polished. The milk pitcher is irregularly scalloped with a curved, raised lip. The

lip is like a nose on the front of the creamer which has been sliced off flat, on top. Under the lip is a large bulge of the body which is covered with an eleven-ray palm. The latter splays on the body and is quite attractive.

The lower halves of the handles are alike. The handle on the milk pitcher arches over the top. That of the creamer juts straight back and appears to be mortised to the stiff, straight, upright member.

The glass is clear, brilliant, and free of discoloration. The workmanship brands the piece as cheap production ware. The mold marks under the handle are razor sharp and dangerous. The rim and all corners have uncomforatable feather-edges. The surface is not smooth, so transparency is impaired. (Either the mold or metal was too cold.) The mold chipper should have had a commendation. The gaffer should have lost a week's wages.

Standard creamer: 3-part mold, 9 1/2 ounces, 4 1/2 inches tall, 3 3/16 inches wide, and 4 15/16 inches long.

Milk pitcher: 3-part mold, weight unknown, 7 1/2 inches tall.

These articles are known to have been made: deep berry bowl; deep waste bowl; covered butter dish; cake plate on standard; flat cake plate with handles; celery vase; covered compotes in 6-, 7 1/2-, and 8-inch sizes; cordial; creamer; eggcup; goblet; pickle dish; milk pitcher; marmalade jar with lid; water pitcher; plates 4 1/2-, 6-, and 7-inch sizes; platter; footed sauces, 4 and 5 1/2 inches; flat sauce; spoonholder; covered sugar bowl; and water tray.

211—PANSY

Mrs. Kamm names this pattern PANSY in *A Sixth Pitcher Book*, page 24, No. 34. She says it is of the period between 1910 and 1920 and probably was made by the Imperial Glass Company of Bellaire, Ohio. She also says this is the first time violets, or pansies, were used as a motif on American pressed glass.

Marion T. Hartung, in *Carnival Glass*, page 65, shows an iridescent creamer and calls it PANSY SPRAY. She does not think it was made by Imperial. On pages 63-64 she shows a bowl she calls IMPERIAL'S PANSY. The bowl and creamer apparently belong to the same pattern.

Rose M. Presznick, in *Carnival and Iridescent Glass Price Guide*, Plates 143 and 144, shows two iridescent bowls. Plate 143 she calls PANSY, and Plate 144 PANSY SPRAY. I am unable to determine whether either or both belong to the pattern discussed here. The accompanying illustration will suffice for identification, and a detailed description is not necessary. The pattern is shown here because of two new items of information pertaining thereto.

First: The evidence today does seem to support Mrs. Kamm's belief that it was manufactured by Imperial Glass Company. About 1911 that company advertised "helios" a silver-green iridescent glassware. Also, about 1911 Butler Brothers, of St. Louis, Missouri, listed and illustrated a number of items of pressed glass in their catalogue, including this creamer with its matching open sugar bowl. It was labeled Silver Green Iridescent Ware. Silver-green iridescent ware is uncommon in Carnival Glass. Evidently, Imperial produced it.

Second: For years the pattern was rarely seen, but in the past year or two it has become more available and is now often seen in shops. It shows up in light green with a slight silvery iridescence, and also in luster-gold or marigold. I have a sugar and creamer in the latter, and a creamer in the green. I expect to eventually find a purple iridescent piece. I have a feeling that this ware is now being made and marketed. Imperial resumed the production of Carnival Glass in 1960, after an interval of forty years.

The piece is colorful and appealing. It carries no trademark. It is of light green color with a silvery iridescence inside and out. Millard, Lee, and Metz do not show the pattern.

Small creamer: 3-part mold, 10 1/2 ounces, 3 7/8 inches tall, 3 3/8 inches wide, and 5 inches long.

A sugar bowl, creamer, and a bowl probably were the only items manufactured in the pattern. The bowl Hartung shows may or may not belong to it.

212—DAISY AND BUTTON WITH NARCISSUS

This is one of the best known of all pressed glass patterns. It is easily found in shops, and I have yet to see an item in the pattern which was of average quality. I know of only one collector of it. It is attractive to lovers of pressed glass—but not to botanists. Such poor metal and craftsmanship were utilized that it has small appeal.

A creamer is shown here since Mrs. Kamm, in her *A Fourth Pitcher Book*, page 139, No. 187, used a water pitcher. According to her, a Sears, Roebuck and Company catalog of 1925 lists a decanter, tray, and wine glass, and a "grape juice set"—whatever that may consist of. Ruth Webb Lee, in *Victorian Glass*, pages 92-98, Plate 34-1, showed a covered sugar bowl, water pitcher, and creamer. She knew little about the pattern, but did name it DAISY AND BUTTON WITH NARCISSUS.

Millard named the pattern DAISY AND BUTTON WITH CLEAR LILY and said it was of the 1880s. I believe its origin to be ten to forty-five years later. Mrs. Metz covered the pattern as No. 722 and said that the quality of the glass, generally, was only fair. She warned that wine glasses were being reproduced in clear and green.

The lines of the piece are attractive. The standard creamer has a spray, with two flowers and two leaves, which reaches from base to rim on either side. Under the lip is a short spray with a single flower. The flowers have no counterpart in nature but are attractive as a pattern. The five-petal flowers and leaves are well shaped, beveled, and concave. This shows them to good advantage. The background is covered with a daisy and button design around the flower sprays.

The base is wide, flat, and the glass is 3/8-inch thick. The flat bottom has a modified hobstar impressed. (See cut of bottom.)

The back third of the rim is evenly scalloped. A portion of the rim on each side is shaped to fit the outline of the taller flowers. The front third rises rapidly and arches forward into a lip.

The rabbit-eared handle juts up and back, then arches back and down to its lower attachment where it splays widely. The handle is six-sided and undecorated. On top of the handle is a mold mark, or a thumbgrip—possibly both.

Creamer: 3-part mold, 1 pound, 4 7/8 inches tall, 3 3/8 inches wide, and 5 1/2 inches long.

The following articles are known to have been made: wine decanter with stopper, large tray, wine glass, goblet, grape juice set, water pitcher, creamer, covered sugar bowl, covered butter dish, spoonholder, milk pitcher, footed bowl, celery vase, jelly compote, oblong pickle dish, salt and pepper shakers, flat sauce dish, footed sauce dish, sherbet, two sizes of tumblers and two sizes of trays, as mentioned above.

213—CASSADAY

No descriptive title is adequate for this pattern. I have exercised an author's prerogative and given it the name of my favorite paper boy—Eddie Cassaday of Little Rock, Arkansas.

The blocky body is longer than it is wide and is roughly six-sided. The front and back are large, rectangular, flat, and plain. In some instances the rectangles would be engraved. Under the lip and near the handle, tall, convex columns alternate with concave flutes. These extend from the rim to a band at the bottom of the bowl. The flutes carry unusual figurework. Each flute is blocked off by groups of five closely placed fine ribs. In the two outer flutes, the fine ribs slope up and to the right. In the two inner flutes, they slope up and to the left. A column stands at each of the six corners.

At the bowl's base is a half-inch-wide band which encircles the body. It is bordered by raised lines and filled with raised circles containing a central dewdrop. The circles are separated by double spearpoints.

The piece rests on four flaring legs. The bottom edge is irregularly scalloped. On each leg is a winged shield outlined by a raised line. The interiors of the shields are stippled, and each has a many-branched cluster of berries arranged as a candelabrum. Between the shields is a long diamond, similarly stippled, but bearing a quatrefoil. Underneath is a low flat dome, covered with grillwork. Groups of three raised lines cross each other at acute angles to form it. (See drawing of bottom.)

The handle is hexagonal in outline and in cross section, adequate in size, and serviceable. The sides of the rim are level and plain. The spout and handle portions of the rim are high and rounded. The lip is pushed forward but has no dip.

The glass is brilliant, clear soda-lime. The mold marks are difficult to locate. Either the mold or the metal was too cool, because the flat rectangles show hairlines. It is a quality product and dates from the 1880's.

Creamer: 3-part mold, 1 5/16 pounds, 5 5/8 inches tall, 3 1/8 inches wide, and 6 inches long.

I have seen only this creamer, but certainly other items must have been made. *CASSADAY* should be compared with ETCHED RECTANGLE.

214—DIAGONAL FROSTED RIBBON

S. T. Millard, in *Goblets II*, Plate 23-2, illustrated a goblet and named this square pattern. (The goblets are round.) He considered it a very sparkling and pretty goblet probably of the 1880s. His goblet had raised figurework on top of its foot.

Alice Hulett Metz, in *Early American Pattern Glass*, page 171, No. 1928, covered the pattern but used no illustration. She did not say any articles in the pattern were square, but she did indicate the ribbon on the foot was not frosted.

I have this rather stiff creamer but without its lid. The figurework on the creamer is identical to that of Millard's goblet. This may be one of the few patterns in which both square and round hollowware was manufactured. Often a goblet was not made in square patterns. Also, in many patterns, a goblet was the only item made.

The waist is incurved, and the foot is thick and has vertical sides. Underneath is a square dome with alternating columns and panels. These panels are not frosted. (See drawing of bottom.)

The sides of the body are straight and vertical. There is a rounded column on each corner. Each flat side is covered with alternating convex columns and flat panels which run diagonally upward and to the right. The surface of each panel is frosted. This does not have the smooth, satiny finish of acid-etched pieces. It is as rough as sandblasted glass—the process of frosting in use before 1876. On this particular piece, the scarifications run lengthwise on the panels. This could have resulted from the use of a coarse abrasive wheel.

A narrow plain band below the rim flares to the top. The rim is covered with low even scallops. There is only a semblance of a lip and it is pursed.

A half inch below the rim, on the inside, is a flat ledge intended to hold a lid. Some of our oldest pressed glass creamers did have lids, or at least ledges in the throat to accomodate them. The latter was true even in Lacy Sandwich creamers, though I have never heard of an actual lid in their case. The practice of making lids was dropped for two or three decades and revived in 1889. This particular pattern was probably made between 1889 and 1895. The piquant thought persists: just how fetching would this piece have been with its lid?

The handle is shaped like a figure 7. It is six-sided, ample, and plain. The quality of the glass is only middling. The workmanship is fair. The piece is heavy and contains a few bubbles. Mold marks are obscure.

Creamer without lid: 2-part mold, 1 1/8 pounds, 5 1/4 inches tall, 3 7/8 inches wide, and 5 inches long.

Mrs. Metz quoted prices on: goblet, creamer, covered butter, and spooner. Certainly a covered sugar bowl was made.

215—CARROLL

This imitation cut glass creamer has not been described previously in American pressed glass literature though other patterns as recent

212

Bottom
212

Bottom
213

213

214

Bottom
214

Bottom
215

215

216

217

218

Bottom
218

219

NEAR
CUT

have been. It arrived on the scene after intaglio flowers became popular in cut glass. Pieces of this type were usually pressed and touched up on the cutting wheel to become what was euphoniously called "pressed cut." This piece has several undesirable features, but also one that is beautiful. It is named *CARROLL* in honor of Carroll L. Tucker of Little Rock, Arkansas.

The base of this creamer has the most beautiful design I have ever seen in pressed glass. It is a complex, kaleidoscopic and completely fascinating design. (See drawing of base.) The figure is too complicated to describe in words.

The sides of the piece are straight and taper in slightly from base to rim. Just below the rim is a half-inch-wide band with an irregular border left plain. Below this is an intaglio band of alternating hobstars and six-pointed stars, which is filled with faceted figures. The outlines of the band are sharp-toothed above and below. The lower two-thirds of the body is covered with pressed intaglio flowers and leaf sprays. These are sunk deep and have not been wheel polished. The flower petals are fluted and the concave centers of the flowers are crosshatched. The body curves under the bottom to form a flat base.

The rim is unevenly scalloped, and the arched front dips into a pinched spout. The handle is pressed but was intended to simulate both an applied and a cut one. It is round in cross section and the back half is covered with St. Louis cut (concave honeycomb).

The glass is thick, heavy, and very soft. It is susceptible to scratches, bruises, and abrasions. It has hairlines, so the mold or metal was too cold. There are also occasional bubbles, and black and white flecks which are inexcusable in glass of this late period. The surface has been partially frosted. For what reason? If the piece becomes wet, the frosting does not show, and it is clear and pretty. When dry it appears to be encrusted with soap powder. It would have been a handsome piece with proper metal and care. Actually, it was production ware of the most common kind. The designer must have winced when he saw this creamer peeled out of the mold he had so painstakingly crafted.

Creamer: 4-part mold, 1 1/16 pounds, 4 1/4 inches tall, 3 1/4 inches wide, and 5 1/4 inches long.

If the other items of this pattern deviated as much from what they could have been as this one, there is no use trying to locate or to enumerate them.

It is from the period of 1915-1925 and ema-

nated from any one of five factories which produced such ware—meaning, of course, type and not quality.

216—*SWEET BAY*

This unlisted creamer is cylindrical and has a beautiful shape. It is made of light green glass, and a few small, scattered bubbles are the only defects of the metal.

The large full-blown intaglio flowers and leaves, though formalized, look somewhat like a member of the beautiful magnolia family called *SWEET BAY*, and that name is assigned to the pattern.

On either side of the body, over the lower two-thirds, is impressed a formal floral spray. Centered on each side is a large full-faced flower. The flowers and leaves are similar to a type that was pressed and later touched up on the cutting wheel in the final phases of the brilliant cut glass era. With a little wheelwork, the figurework here would be similar to real cut glass. On the upper third is a stiff, wide, and ungainly swag of diamonds with diamond point surfaces. It ends abruptly at each end and does not encircle the body. It also is intaglio pressed. Under the lip are six wide, rounded petals which are not very pretty.

The base is a full half-inch thick and has a deeper green appearance. It contains an impressed star. The rim is slightly saddled, flat on top, and the wide lip is upthrust. The six-sided handle has a good thumbgrip, is of ample size, and is easy to handle. Suprisingly, this piece has some resonance when lightly tapped. This is not because it is made of flint glass. The quality and workmanship are deficient.

Creamer: 2-part mold, 1 1/8 pounds, 4 5/8 inches tall, 3 3/8 inches wide, and 5 1/4 inches long.

217—*BLUE MOUNTAIN*

This unlisted standard creamer is similar to the *SWEET BAY* pattern above, and there is little doubt they were made in the same factory at about the same time. They may well have been conceived by the same designer. I will name it *BLUE MOUNTAIN*.

This is very late ware which probably dates from 1905 to 1920. It is found in shops at reasonable prices and is much in demand because of its exquisite color. This particular piece is of a pleasing shade of electric blue. The glass has a few bubbles and the workmanship is below par. With a little more care it could have been a quality ware. It arouses derision in those who can afford Peachblow, Pomona, Burmese, Pink slag, Aurene, Quezel, Amberina, etc.

The piece is cylindrical with straight vertical sides that were left plain on the outside. At the top is a wide band also left plain on the inside. Below it on the inside, is a belt of low inverted columns around the middle. At their base they mitre into a band of inverted diamond quilting around the lower third of the inside. The design shows through the glass. The bottom is quite thick and because of this appears to be a darker blue.

The edge of the body is beveled slightly near the wide, flat base. It has no ring to sit on. A rather poorly formed 18-ray star has been pressed in the base. The handle is six-sided, large, and comfortable to use. At the top is an upthrust knob that serves as a secure thumbgrip. The lower attachment is larger than the upper, but no effort was made to simulate an applied handle.

The glass is thick and flat on the rim and the latter is saddled. It rises to a wide, upturned lip. Nothing is known as to where or by whom it was made. It was not well fire polished, and the mold marks are prominent though not high or sharp.

Creamer: 2-part mold, 1 1/8 pounds, 4 5/8 inches tall, 3 3/8 inches wide, and 5 1/4 inches long.

I have a creamer and a two-handled open sugar bowl in this color and pattern. I expect to eventually find it in yellow, apple green, sassafras, and light amber. Other items probably were made.

218—RED SUNFLOWER

Mrs. Kamm, in *A Second Two Hundred Pattern Glass Pitchers*, page 116, describes and names the standard creamer with four stubby, ungainly legs. All plain flat surfaces on the piece she used were flashed with ruby. This, together with the intaglio pressing of the flowers, dates the piece as having been made in the period between 1900-1910. The creamer shown here is clear with no red flashing, and also differs from Mrs. Kamm's in other respects. We know from the NEAR/CUT trademark that the pattern was made by Cambridge Glass Company of Cambridge, Ohio.

This creamer is oval rather than round and sits on a large, flat base instead of four heavy legs. It has the NEAR/CUT trademark in raised letters on the inside bottom. The shape of the body varies sufficiently to permit an extra half flower on the side panels, instead of the single flower found on the round piece.

This creamer is more comely than the footed one. About the body are four large, highly beveled figures shaped like tatting bobbins. In the center of each is a pressed hobstar, and at either end the bobbins are filled with grating. These figures extend almost from waist to rim. Between them are impressed intaglio leaves, stems, and flowers which Mrs. Kamm called sunflowers, but which more closely resemble Cosmos. They are an imitation of straight-line cut flowers and have their centers filled with grating. Under the lip is one such flower. On the panel nearest the handle are two flowers with upper petals intact and lower petals absent, as if a lover had played "She loves me. She loves me not."

The rim has a complex scallop effect which is becoming. The lip is narrow and pretty. The handle is of a late type and appears adequate, but affords only a precarious grip. It has six flat panels and spreads out in a large blob at the base. The handle has an upthrust at the top as is often seen on glass of this era. They do provide a good thumbgrip.

The oval base has a beautiful design that shows up well in the drawing. (See cut of bottom.) Two bobbin-shaped figures are crossed and at their four ends are hobstars. Where they cross is a squarish figure filled with irregular, rectangular pyramids. Poorly impressed fans fill the four corners around the bobbins. The glass is heavy, thick (5/8 inch in the bottom), brilliant, and sparkling, but without resonance. There are some hairlines and waviness but no discolorations. The mold consisted of two long sections and a shorter one—the latter for the narrow panel under the lip.

Oval creamer: 3-part mold, 14 ounces, 3 3/8 inches tall, 2 13/16 inches wide, and 5 5/8 inches long.

The two creamers described are the only articles known to have been made in this pattern. At the time they were produced, however, the Cambridge Glass Company was making a fantastic number of items in each pattern as shown by their advertisements. There is every reason to suppose this pattern was treated in a like manner. At that time they listed *nappies* which their ads described as: "8 3/4 inch nappie, C shaped; 10 inch nappie, D shaped; 9 1/4 inch nappie, E shaped; 7 inch nappie, F shaped, cupped." Do not be surprised if unusual pieces show up in this pattern.

219—HORSEMINT

S. T. Millard, in *Goblets II*, Plate 22-4, showed a pretty goblet in this pattern and gave it the name HORSEMINT. (Horsefeathers could have been used.) The name is short, handy, and not previously used so it has not been changed. Dr. Millard probably used a name by which the pattern was popularly known at the time.

Mrs. Metz covered the pattern as No. 726 but did not illustrate it.

The standard creamer is large and sits on a wide, flat base. It has straight vertical sides. The base is a sloping quarter-inch ring. Underneath is an impressed 20-ray hobstar.

The base of the body carries a rounded band which turns under to help form a wide waist. Above this, and below the rim, are two 3/4-inch belts of squares with alternating decorations. The first is scored diagonally with the tops of the flat figures covered with small diamond point. The adjacent squares are filled with highly beveled, geometric figures which extend upward from the band to form triangles in the clear band below the rim. Such extensions are absent on the lower band. The dominant pattern work is in a 2-inch wide space around the center of the body. Here are found three clumps of a nondescript shrub or bush with the stems, leaves, and flowers, all intaglio pressed. Dr. Millard calls this HORSE-MINT. Each clump is centered over and hides a mold mark.

There is a 3/4-inch plain band just beneath the saddled and slightly scalloped rim. One-third of the rim constitutes the lip. The handle is composed of six wide panels and increases in size as it descends to its lower attachment. It is left severely plain. The glass is brilliant and clear but contains a few bubbles. It was good, but cheap, pressed glass. Millard said it is of the 1880's and comes only in the clear. Because of the hobstar on the bottom and the intaglio pressing, I believe it was produced at least twenty to thirty years later.

Creamer: 3-part mold, 14 1/2 ounces, 4 5/8 inches tall, 3 3/8 inches wide, and 5 1/2 inches long.

The goblet and creamer are the only items known to me. Probably the number of items made was legion.

220—PANELLED HEATHER

These two creamers were made as production ware at a time when it was necessary to compete with much cheap glass. The pattern does not have the refinements of high quality ware. It is fairly clear, heavy, and thick. The surface has not been fire polished, and the base is poorly im-

pressed. It is of the 1900-1915 period. This is based primarily on the intaglio pressing.

S. T. Millard, in *Goblets,* Plate 152-2, shows a graceful goblet in this pattern, and he gave it the above name. I wonder if heather looks at all like the flower on this pattern. No other name seems more fitting, and it is already known by the present one. Millard says it was produced about the 1880's, and it came only in clear.

One other authority on American glass has fully covered the pattern. Alice Hulett Metz, in *Early American Pattern Glass,* page 67, No. 726, covered, but did not illustrate it.

My collection contains an individual and a standard creamer in this pattern. The individual creamer (see drawing) is the only piece I have ever allowed to slip through my fingers and break. Eventually another was found, and it is illustrated here with the standard creamer. The small one has six rather than seven panels; two instead of three flower sprays (modified to fit the smaller available space); stands on a pedestal; and is plain under the base. Its V-shaped channels do not extend to the base; its scalloped rim does not conform to the panels as on the standard size; there are no floral sprays on each side of the lower handle attachment; and it is far more graceful than the larger piece. Its shape helps to date it as later than Dr. Millard thought.

The standard creamer has something seldom encountered in pressed glass—seven wide, flat panels. Seven panels multiply the task of moldmaking many times. The panels extend from base to rim. Between each two panels is a V-shaped channel that runs from the base to within a fourth of an inch of the rim. A panel on each side and one beneath the lip carry a formalized intaglio flower spray called heather. There are three fullblown flowers at top and bottom of these panels. Stem, scrollwork, and nondescript leaves are also present. There is a small sprig on each side of the lower handle attachment. The body has a slight constriction just above the base. From there the piece swells gradually to near the top where it narrows slightly.

The base is ample and flat. Underneath is a slight depression containing a beautiful intaglio motif. The seven sides show plainly when seen from the bottom. (See drawing of bottom of the standard creamer for details.)

The handle is sturdy, six-sided, plain, and adequate. The rim has low, wide scallops over the panels with each scallop topped by smaller ones. The lip is high and protrudes well forward.

The manufacturer is unknown. I would expect

220-1

Bottom
220

220-2

221

Base
221

222

223

224

225

226

Bottom
226

Bottom
225

to find the glass advertised by either Montgomery Ward, Sears Roebuck, or Butler Brothers, between 1912 and 1920.

Individual creamer: 3-part mold, 10 ounces, 4 15/16 inches tall, 2 13/16 inches wide, and 4 5/8 inches long.

Standard creamer: 3-part mold, 1 1/8 pounds, 4 5/8 inches tall, 3 3/8 inches wide, and 5 3/4 inches long.

The only items I have seen are these two creamers. Albert Steel of Little Rock, Arkansas, has a collection containing a covered sugar bowl, goblets, water pitcher, wines, jam dish, cruet, and berry bowl. The pattern is not plentiful.

221—CREOLE

At first glance this standard creamer seems to belong to the STARRED COSMOS pattern shown by Minnie Watson Kamm in her *A Fourth Pitcher Book*, page 131, No. 172. She used a very tall water pitcher. Closer scrutiny reveals several significant differences, however. One gets the impression that no attempt was made to copy the ware of a competitor, but rather that two different glass manufacturers each purchased a set of molds from the same moldmaker. (Such as the Hipkins Novelty Mold Shop of Martins Ferry, Ohio.) The supplier varied the designs enough to avoid patent infringement. The two patterns are so similar that they appear to be the handiwork of the same designer. The mold chipping shows excellent workmanship.

CREOLE is the name given this pattern.

The treatment of the flowers in the diamonds is not the same in the two pieces. The water pitcher has a band of faceted figurework on the lower third of the body which is missing on the creamer. It also has a narrow belt of tiny faceted figures, below the rim and around the waist, which the creamer does not have.

Four large diamonds, standing on their corners and joining the others at their side corners, encircle the body. They are bordered by high, inverted, V-shaped ridges which give them beveled edges. The surface of each diamond is smooth and contains an intaglio-pressed formalized floral spray, resembling cosmos. The leaves and stems are stiff, rigid, and purely decorative. The petals of the full-faced flowers have ridged surfaces which resemble engraving. They radiate from the center, which itself is cross-hatched or grilled. These spaces on the water pitcher are filled by six-point stars in petaled flowers. All leaves and stems are below the flower on the creamer, and are both above and below it on the water pitcher. Occasionally, the flowers were painted.

The large triangles between the diamonds, above and below, are filled with figurework identical to that used on the large pitcher. It is slashed into squares, each alternate square having an octagonal, beveled button whose surface is covered with minute diamond point. The adjacent squares have been slashed diagonally each way by two V-shaped, parallel grooves which divide them into many faceted figures in high, sharp relief. These figures were sometimes painted, but, fortunately, it was not baked on (like enamel) and can be easily removed.

V-shaped ridges bound the figurework at rim and waist. The base of the creamer is not flared, as is the large pitcher, but rests on a high ring. Underneath is a low, wide dome with a magnificent kaleidoscopic figure impressed. The center is a hexagonal button with a rayed daisy stamped on its surface. It is surrounded by six similar buttons covered with tiny diamond point. It contains many triangular pyramids, and the perimeter is fringed with fans and crow's feet. (See drawing of bottom.) The same motif is on the water pitcher.

There is a half-inch plain band at the top of the body below the rim. This probably was originally gilded, or red-bronzed, on the inside. The rim of both pieces is identical. It is depressed on the sides and covered by low, wide scallops with smaller ones between them. The rim rises to form a rather attractive lip.

The handles are similar, six-paneled with the two side panels the narrower, and sometimes found in the shape of a figure "7." The quality of glass and workmanship are good. Nothing is known of its maker. It probably was produced between 1905 and 1920.

Creamer: 4-part mold, 14 ounces, 5 1/16 inches tall, 3 7/16 inches wide, and 5 inches long.

See RAYED FLOWER in *Kamm's Book VII* and FLOWER MEDALLION in Kamm's *A Fifth Pitcher Book* for similar patterns.

222—MOUND BAYOU

This small cone-shaped creamer is made of jet-black glass. Although it is unusually thin for pressed glass, it shows no translucence when held to a strong light. Its beautiful purple hue is different from that of black amethyst glass. I have named it for Mound Bayou, Mississippi.

Black glass was often used to make cheap bottles in the early days. Some vases and art objects were also made of black amethyst glass in that era.

Soon after 1900, Butler Brothers of St. Louis, Missouri, advertised dresser sets and a vase in enameled black glass. The vogue for black glass tableware came into being between 1905 and 1935, and some that I have seen bore the trademark of the Anchor Hocking Glass Company. I also have a black amethyst creamer, with a lid, and from certain characteristics of the latter I am reasonably sure it was made by the Westmoreland Glass Company. Evidently two or three other glass houses also produced black glass. It is regrettable they did not use a trademark, for the quality of the ware was very good.

This cone-shaped creamer has no pressed figurework except a highly raised round ring at the waist. Both inside and outside are plain, smooth and have an excellent polish. Above the waist, the sides curve outward and upward to the rim. The rim is round, flat, and dips forward slightly to form a small lip.

Below the ring of the waist, the base curves out into a wide flat foundation. It is hollowed out underneath and left plain. The decorative motif was achieved by painting a spray of flowers and leaves around the upper part of the bowl and a narrow band at the rim and base with silver oxide. It was then baked on and polished. The word *sterling* is printed in one of the small leaves. The bright silver, against the shimmering black background, is very effective. An overly zealous housekeeper has polished this thin layer of silver until it barely shows. The silver appears to be oxidized.

The handle is round and not remarkable except for its small size.

The creamer is made of fine flint glass and has a clear, bell-like tone when lightly tapped. The metal is heavy, but the glass is thin, thus accounting for its light weight. The workmanship and design are good.

Small creamer: 2-part mold, 7 ounces, 3 5/8 inches tall, 3 5/16 inches wide, and 4 1/8 inches long.

This is the only item I have seen in the pattern. I would expect a sugar bowl, ash tray, vase, tobacco jar, cigarette holder, and possibly plates, cups, and saucers.

223—SILVERY MIDNIGHT

The little square creamer is by far the most attractive and also the finest in quality of any black, or black amethyst, glass shown in this book. This particular piece, when held to a bright light, proves to be not jet-black at all but a beautiful deep amethyst color. Surprisingly, it has a clear,

ringing resonance when lightly tapped. It is thin and light. Because of its silver and black glass, I have named it *SILVERY MIDNIGHT*.

The piece is rectangular, and its four corners are cut with concave flutes from base to rim. The base is small. The body arches out to become much wider at the rim, which is flat.

The base ring and the top half of the bowl are covered with filigreed silver which has been appliqued on the surface. The silver is stamped *sterling* and by some method, unknown to the author, was fastened to the glass so securely that dirt and grime could never get between them. The filigree is complicated and attractive. The silver and black complement each other nicely and make an agreeable whole. The black glass has a slick mirrorlike smoothness which has unusual reflectibility. The soft, satiny surface of the silver gives a pleasing contrast.

The handle is four-sided and angular as is the body, but without the rounded channels at the corners, which the body has. It seems angular and stiff. This is flint glass. It probably was sold through jewelry stores from about 1905 to 1915. It is a quality product. The author knows nothing of where or when it was made—or by whom.

Small creamer: 2-part mold, 8 ounces, 3 7/16 inches tall, 2 15/16 inches wide, and 4 1/2 inches long.

It is possible that a sugar bowl, coasters, ash trays, and small cake plates were made.

224—BLACK MANTLE

This plain, simple mug-shaped creamer is made of jet-black glass which shows no trace of amethyst when held to a bright light. I have given it the name *BLACK MANTLE*.

It is devoid of any pressed, decorative motif, other than the light ribbing on either side of the handle. The semicircular handle has three raised lines on each side panel of the six-sided member. The appeal of the piece stems from its mirror smooth, black surface with its brilliant polish. The sides are straight and vertical. The body is cylindrical. It rounds under the base to sit on a low ring. Underneath is a low dome.

The rim is rounded and level. It originally had a 1/8-inch-wide silver band at the rim. The band was painted on, then baked. It is now almost worn off. The lip is narrow and small. It appears that a mug was made, and, while still hot, the front rim was pressed down slightly to form a lip.

Creamer: 2-part mold, 14 ounces, 4 3/8 inches tall, 3 1/16 inches wide, and 4 3/4 inches long.

The quality of the glass is fine. It has a good resonance when tapped. I believe it was made since 1920. I have no idea what other items may have been made. Some of them might be difficult to relate to this piece because of the lack of decorative figures.

225—RUBY TALONS

The pattern of this creamer presents such a mingling of motifs it defies selection of a short, suitable, descriptive name. However, *RUBY TALONS* was eventually chosen.

This low creamer is not an imitation cut; nor is it a floral design. It has some of the elements of both—well scrambled. It has the appearance of having been hastily assembled—a little here, a little there. It was then flashed with ruby and gilt to appeal to public fancy during the period when the public was much impressed by the ornate.

The base is in the shape of a six-ray star with rounded points for feet. (See cut.) It sits flat and a formalized intaglio flower with rays is impressed therein. The points of the star protrude beyond the body to form small feet, and add stability. They could easily be broken off. The writer knows of no other company except the Higbee Glass Company ever using this particular type of base. Other patterns on which they used the same, or a very similar type of footing are shown in this book as PERKINS and PANELLED THISTLE. They were in business at the time this piece was made.

This is the standard-sized creamer, and the body is cup-shaped. From each of the six feet, and extending two-thirds of the way up on the body, are highly raised, ridged, and sharp-pointed talons. These seem to grasp the bowl similar to the way the glass balls of table legs were held by brass lion paws during the Gay Nineties. Each talon has been flashed with ruby. Between each two talons is a large, highly beveled shield. The base of each shield is pointed, and from it a nondescript sprig of flowers emanates. The flowers are the same as those on the base, except that they have a stem and formal leaves. These flowers and stems are left clear. Surrounding the body, above the talons and shields is a 3/4-inch slightly convexed band. Within this and at the point of each talon, is a five-prong branch of agave, all six of which are gilded. In the same band, and directly above the sprig of flowers on each shield, is a flower similar to that on the shield, but without a stem. Each of these intaglio flowers has been daubed carelessly with deep ruby flashing.

The back two-thirds of the rim is level and covered with small scallops. The top of the rim was originally gilded. It rises toward the front to form a high, narrow, pinched lip.

The handle is small, six-sided, and attractive. It has a knop to make a secure thumbgrip. There is another such knop near the bottom. The handle carries no other figurework. Most of the handle is six-sided, but the lower attachment is round.

The quality and workmanship leave much to be desired. This is late ware—probably as late as 1915-1920—by which time all glass houses were able to turn out superior glass. This piece has bubbles, hairlines, prominent mold marks, flashings of gold and ruby carelessly applied, and the glass is neither clear nor brilliant. It is soda-lime glass and has no resonance. The glass is thick (1/4 inch in places), and the creamer is unduly heavy for its size. It was production ware, and nothing more.

Creamer: 3-part mold, 14 ounces, 4 1/4 inches tall, 3 3/4 inches wide, and 5 1/2 inches long.

The manufacturer is unknown. The only items in the pattern the author is aware of are: spoonholder, sugar bowl, covered butter dish, and creamer. Many other items may have been made.

226—JACKLYNN CARNATION

This ruby and gold creamer is the most arresting specimen in the author's collection of over 2,200 creamers and pitchers. No other fifty creamers in the lot cause such comment. Only a few decry its decore. The great majority consider it the most beautiful of all, and many suggest a codicil to my will with themselves as recipients. Some also mention stealing it from me. It is named *JACKLYNN CARNATION* in honor of 1st Lt. Jack Lynn Zelsman who was in South Vietnam and now lives in Little Rock, Arkansas.

This standard creamer sits on a low ring which seems small because of the width of the bowl. Beneath is a shallow dome and into this has been pressed a ten-ray, deep, intaglio whorl. (See cut.)

The bowl seems broader and lower than it actually is. The contours are graceful and pleasing. There are three large, and very realistic, deeply impressed, intaglio carnations on the body. Unfortunately, another pattern already bears the name CARNATION. For that reason it is given the name *JACKLYNN CARNATION*. The leaves are deeply intaglio pressed, also, and truly resemble those of a carnation. Few flowers on pressed glass bear any resemblance to the real flower, so this piece of pressing is to be highly commended. Had it been left clear, it would have been magnificent— but the decorator then took over. The beautiful flowers and graceful leaves were carefully gilded. Something is recollected about "gilding the lily." All smooth, flat surfaces were flashed with deep ruby. A ruby carnation with green leaves against a clear background would have been preferable.

The back three-fourths of the rim is level and evenly scalloped. The valleys between the scallops have been given a touch of gold. In front the rim rises and turns forward to form a wide lip.

The handle is comely, round, strong, and applied. Where a fourth carnation would have been placed on most patterns, it was left plain to provide a secure foundation for the handle attachment. The lower attachment is a large, round blob. The upper attachment is small and turned under.

The glass of this piece had to be at least 1/4-inch thick to take the deep intaglio impressions. It is too heavy to be practical and probably was made to be purely ornamental. The quality of the glass is excellent. The workmanship—especially that of the moldmaker—was superb. The coloring was carefully and painstakingly done. The handle was placed by an experienced gaffer, who turned out a well-finished product. A mold mark is visible in only one place—beneath the thickest part of the handle where the blob acts as a convexed magnifying lens.

This pattern has not been previously named or described in American pressed glass literature, and it is hoped the present listing and illustration will bring further information to light.

Creamer: 3-part mold, 1 3/16 pounds, 4 1/2 inches tall, 4 inches wide, and 5 3/8 inches long.

This piece is of the 1900-1910 period, when intaglio floral designs were replacing, by popular demand, the geometric designs of imitation cut glass which had been used so extensively that the public taste for it began to fag.

The author has seen a covered sugar, covered butter dish, spoonholder, large punch bowl, punch cups, ice cream dish, celery vase, and, of course, this creamer. The punch bowl was left clear.

227—IVORINA VERDE

Mrs. Kamm had not seen this lovely pattern. In *A Fifth Pitcher Book*, page 65, No. 83, she used a small cut from an advertisement of 1899 by A. H. Heisey and Company. Her details were incorrect in part as she suspected they might be. She called it IVORINA VERDE because the advertisement said it was "in opaque ivory colored glass . . . with green trim." It was trimmed with enameled roses.

In *A Seventh Pitcher Book*, page 25, No. 48, she still had not seen a piece of the pattern but had a full-page ad from which to make her drawing. The proportions, size, and shape again were not too accurate. (See Plate 37 and 100 of the same book.) Plate 37 showed nine separate articles in the pattern, all with enameled roses between the scrolls. Plate 100 showed four covered butter dishes exhibited in the Pittsburgh Glass Exhibition of 1898. The one in the lower left-hand corner was in this pattern with the flowers left off, though the scrolls may have been gilded as on my creamer and spoonholder. The Heiseys have preserved many items in the pattern at their plant in Newark, Ohio.

The standard creamer I have is in a beautiful shade of emerald green. The scrolls, the top of the rim, the fan at the base of the handle, and the small ring at the waist are all gilded. It carries no floral decoration. These pieces were made before the Heisey Company adopted their well-known trademark about 1902. (It is a raised *H* inside a diamond with a raised border.)

Mrs. Kamm shows an obese creamer. Its actual shape is much more graceful. The bowl has four lobes which do not show in the advertisements. From a narrow waist, the sides taper out, then round in sharply to the neck. The latter is constricted, but is still considerably wider than the waist. Centered in the four creases between the lobes are bound sheaves, or scrolls. Each is symmetrical and composed of numerous branches in high, rounded relief. They spread laterally on the body. The neck and waist are round and have no lobes.

The neck is plain and flares out in a wide band. The back portion of the rim is level and scalloped by shallow notches cut into the edge. The lip has irregular curves and is somewhat attractive. The narrow, short waist is surrounded by a narrow, inverted V-shaped ridge. The piece then flares out to form a ringed base. Underneath, is a low plain dome.

The handle is small, six-sided, and almost useless. The tip of a finger barely enters the aperture. The upper member thrusts backward and curves slightly upward. The other member crosses it, turns down, and then curves inward to the bowl. The glass is of excellent quality, and the workmanship shows skill and a desire for quality.

Creamer: 3-part mold, 15 ounces, 4 inches tall, 4 1/8 inches wide, and 5 11/16 inches long.

The following pieces are shown in the advertisement: molasses can, toothpick holder, salt and pepper, tumbler, spoonholder with two handles,

4 1/2-inch nappy, creamer, covered sugar, cruet with pressed or cut stopper, and a covered butter dish.

228—EMERALD VALLEYS

About 1897 the A. H. Heisey Company of Newark, Ohio, put out a catalog in which they called this their "No. 150" pattern. They said nothing of colors. Mrs. Kamm, in *A Fourth Pitcher Book*, page 90, No. 107, called it HEISEY, No. 150. She used the woodcut from the catalog—not having seen an actual piece of the pattern. She was unaware it came in colors. The original advertisement showed a large open pitcher and another with a lid. The advertisement did not mention that the creamer also had a lid, but the flat ledge for one is present on the inside at the level of the neckline. Without seeing the creamer, Mrs. Kamm could not know this. Regretfully, I admit the lid for my creamer is missing. Was this piece perhaps marketed as a container for prepared mustard, baking powder, or horseradish?

Several features of the pattern justify its use in this book, e.g. size, weight, color, lid, quality, etc.

The name HEISEY, No. 150 is not too good for identification of the pattern. No apologies are needed for the new name of *EMERALD VALLEYS*. It is in such sheltered, green vales as these that one expects to find wild azaleas in bloom.

This small piece is in a beautiful emerald green. The body is hassock-shaped, with a short skirt and low collar. Around the middle the glass is 1/2-inch thick. There are eleven deep V-shaped valleys slashed from waist to neck. Their faces are polished to mirror brightness and are the loveliest portion of the decorative motif. The spaces between follow the shape of the body and are filled with small, uniform, sunk diamond point. (Mrs. Kamm thought it was raised, from the catalog picture.) On the creamer itself these areas seem subdued, but by their very nature they become accentuated in the drawing.

The waist is large, short, and the base curves out slightly. Underneath is a 20-ray star in high relief. The rim is plain, level, and flares evenly. The lip is low and wide.

The handle is round and is an excellent imitation of an applied one. The figurework is absent from the wide panel under the handle. This is often true of quality pieces where the handle was applied—so the attachment would not leave fissures when applied over figurework. Even with this refinement, the handle was pressed and not applied as can be determined by a barely perceptible mold mark.

The quality is excellent, though a single bubble does show. It was made as quality ware and was manufactured before the company began to use their well-known trademark.

Small creamer without lid: 3-part mold, 12 ounces, 3 1/2 inches tall, 3 1/4 inches wide, and 4 1/2 inches long.

The original advertisement illustrated the following items: creamer, sugar bowl, covered butter dish, spoonholder, half-gallon open pitcher, half-gallon pitcher with lid, several nappies, etc.

229—CROESUS

This creamer is shown to give additional information about a popular pattern. In fact, it is so popular that its prices have skyrocketed. Today only Croesus himself could collect the lovely Imperial Emerald, or the beautiful Royal Purple. The few pieces of clear glass seem by me were expensive. It is so scarce, only "Uncle Sap" could buy a collection of it. All exaggeration aside, pieces in this pattern do bring fantastic prices.

Mrs. Lee and Dr. Millard did not use the pattern in their books. Mrs. Kamm, in *A Fourth Pitcher Book*, page 112, No. 141, described the pattern. In *A Fifth Pitcher Book*, Plate 92, she showed a page from a catalog of 1897 by the Riverside Glass Company of Wellsburg, West Virginia, which illustrated eight items in the pattern as No. 484 CROESUS WARE. The original name has remained. This factory put out good patterns of superior quality glass and workmanship. Their colored glass, which they used extensively, was among the most beautiful made between 1880-1900. A number of their patterns are shown in this book.

Mrs. Metz covered the pattern as No. 2528, but did not illustrate it. She quoted no price for a goblet, nor did she particularly care for the pattern.

On both emerald and amethyst pieces the scroll and shell work was gilded. The result was striking. Even today few patterns bring forth such praise as does CROESUS. Because of its three feet, it appears unbalanced in the drawing. Actually, when looking at such pieces they prove to be much more stable and balanced. The feet are short, stubby, fan-shaped and stippled on the underside. A shell is deeply impressed on each outer surface.

The lower portion of the body is cauldron-shaped and the upper is constricted below the rim.

227

228

229

230

Bottom
230

231

Bottom
231

232

234

233

235

The bulge is covered with figurework. There are three irregularly shaped smooth medallions around the body. Each is framed with deeply impressed V-shaped scrolls. The scroll work is augmented by a well-defined and impressed shell above and below. The space between the scrolls is irregular and filled with a waffle design in high relief. A wide band above the figurework and a narrow one below are left plain and smooth. The rim is saddled and the back four-fifths is covered by small, uniform scallops. The lip is high and plain.

The handle is of a late type with a large round blob at the basal attachment. It is terete, with the top attachment turned under and undecorated by tooling. The figurework is so arranged that both attachments are on a plain, smooth surface. It was made in a mold of three parts to form the sides of the body and an additional part to form the round disc of the bottom to which the three feet are attached. The quality is excellent and the Imperial Emerald, as the manufacturer calls it, is beautiful. The base has a few hairlines. The mold marks have almost been fire polished off.

Creamer: 4-part mold (see above), 1 3/16 pounds, 5 3/4 inches tall, 3 3/4 inches wide, and 4 3/4 inches long.

The following items are known to have been made in this pattern: small oil cruet, bulbous cruet, large cruet, individual creamer, berry creamer, standard creamer, half-gallon pitcher, covered sugar, covered butter dish, 7-inch berry bowl, 7-inch covered berry bowl, spoonholder, celery vase, jelly compote, sauce dish, tumbler, toothpick holder, salt and pepper shaker. Many other articles probably were made also.

Though goblets were produced in almost every pattern during this era, apparently none were made in CROESUS. A table set that would require one spooner would require six to twelve goblets. Casualties among goblets were higher than with any other item of pressed glass.

230— TRIPLE TRIANGLE

This ruby-stained, clear glass creamer dates from between 1891 and 1900 since the method of flashing glass with ruby was discovered in 1891. Such decoration became a favorite of the American public, and by the time of the Columbian Exposition in Chicago, Illinois, in 1893, it was produced in great variety and in large quantities. Pieces were sold as souvenirs at the exposition. The same thing occurred at the Louisiana Purchase Exposition at St. Louis in 1904. This particular pattern was made in ruby by Doyle and Company of Pittsburgh, Pennsylvania, before they combined with the United States Glass Company in 1891 as "Factory 'P'." It was continued in production by the huge combine for a number of years.

Dr. Millard first covered the pattern in his *Goblets*, Plate 165-1, and named it TRIPLE TRIANGLE, one of the most apt descriptive titles in all pressed glass nomenclature. He thought it was first produced in the 1880's, which may be correct, but it could not have been in ruby before 1891.

Ruth Webb Lee next described the pattern in her *Victorian Glass*, page 174, Plate 56-3, as a Doyle and Company product and shows a tumbler, covered butter dish, goblet, and a sherbet or punch cup (mug). She listed the articles known to her and used the title assigned by Millard.

Minnie Watson Kamm had not seen the pattern and made her drawing from an old Doyle and Co. catalog of 1891. Unfortunately, she assigned a less appropriate title, using the company's original number, and calling it DOYLE'S NO. 76 in her *An Eighth Pitcher Book*, page 36, No. 64. On Plate 6 she illustrated a full-page cut from the catalog as NO. 76 SET by Doyle. This showed the four-piece table set, all with handles. On Plate 7 was another full page showing a large, round bread plate, goblet, wine, odd shaped mug, low celery dish, and a half-gallon jug. On Plate 73 is shown a tall covered butter dish which she also attributes to Doyle and Company. This dish was markedly different from the one shown in Plate 6 and the one used by Mrs. Lee, both of which were squatty. Metz showed a goblet as No. 2519 and attributed it to the Pioneer Glass Company of Pittsburgh.

The pattern is shown here for descriptive purposes and to give accurate measurements and weight, as well as to illustrate the beautiful design on the bottom. The pattern is not particularly aesthetic. The gawky, ear-shaped handle was used profusely, and even the spoonholders and butter dishes had two of them. They are almost identical to the handles which detract so much from the RED BLOCK pattern. Also, the upthrust, "snooty" spouts on the pitchers could well have been toned down a little.

The creamer sits on a wide, flat, ringbase and has a very short waist. Under the base is an imitation cut-glass rosette composed of rectangular pyramids in high, sharp relief. Six long ones are at the center, six diamond-shaped ones surround them and six additional elongated pyramids form the periphery. (See drawing of bottom.) The entire figurework is an imitation cut glass effect.

The body rounds over from rim to waist, and this is most pronounced at top and bottom. The design covers the lower three-fourths of the bowl. There are five inverted V-shaped prisms in high relief which separate the body into segments. They have sharp, pointed ends, sharpest at the bottom. They extend from the waist to the top of the design. Between each two, and a half-inch below their crests, is a deep V-shaped groove running horizontally from one prism to another. The rectangles so formed in each segment have been diagonally grooved from corner to corner. This results in four large triangular areas, the basal one being grooved additionally to form a large sawtooth pattern. The flat surfaces of the three upper triangles have been flashed with ruby and thus the title TRIPLE TRIANGLE. At the back is a large, beveled, teardrop-shaped escutcheon to receive the handle. The latter simulates an applied one, but the mold marks show. Above the figurework, the body is smooth and stained ruby.

The rim is flat on the sides and has a poorly curved scallop above the handle. It rises sharply in front to form a narrow lip.

This pattern was produced as a quality product. The lime-soda glass is brilliantly clear and sparkling. Mold marks show under the handle. They are high, but not sharp. They also show faintly on the ringed base.

Creamer: 3-part mold, 14 ounces, 4 7/16 inches tall, 3 7/16 inches wide, and 5 1/8 inches long.

Other items known to have been manufactured and not listed above are: 9-inch flat circular bowls; 5-inch sauce dishes; 8-, 9-, and 10-inch flat rectangular dishes; mug; sherbet or punch cup; etc.

231—BEATTY HONEYCOMB

This little beauty was not covered by Mrs. Kamm, though she did use RIBBED OPAL and SWIRLED OPAL. All three were made at the same time by A. J. Beatty and Sons of Tiffin, Ohio, in the 1880's. All came in opalescent blue and only rarely in opalescent yellow, as in this piece, which is of slightly opalescent glass with all high parts white. Held to the light it has a fiery opalescence.

Ruth Webb Lee, in *Victorian Glass*, pages 218-23, Plate 69-1, named it as above, saying, "It was such an appropriate name." This is difficult to understand because it is not a honeycomb motif. Grill or waffle, yes, honeycomb, no. She described the pattern and listed the articles she had seen.

Alice Hulett Metz illustrated the creamer as

No. 1175 on page 100 of her *Early American Pattern Glass.* She evidently overlooked the fact that the pattern had been named by Mrs. Lee, for she called it CROSSBAR OPAL.

Either this creamer or a pattern almost identical was produced by Iowa City Glass Works, Iowa City, Iowa, during 1889-1892.

The design is simple and effective. Raised ribs start at the center of the bottom, extend to the edge, bend over the corner, and then ascend perpendicularly almost to the rim. Similar ribs circle the center of the base and concentrically follow the course of the upright ones. This results in many sunken, beveled cubes in tiers. The vertical ribs are enlarged slightly at the bottom curve to provide a ring upon which to rest. (See cut of bottom for details.)

The rim is horizontal and composed of low scallops. The lip projects forward and is not pretty in profile, but is more comely when viewed from above. The handle is pressed, plain, and round in cross section.

The pattern was made of excellent glass and highly firepolished to accomplish the white opalescence. This also obliterated all mold marks, except under the handle. At least four parts of a mold would have been necessary to press this design and permit its removal. It has a ringing resonance.

Small creamer: ?-part mold, 8 ounces, 3 1/8 inches tall, 2 5/8 inches wide, and 3 7/8 inches long.

These articles are known to have been made in the pattern: individual creamer, standard creamer, water pitcher, tumbler, 8- and 9-inch bowls, covered butter dish, sugar bowl, sugar shaker, spooner, toothpick holder, celery vase, sauce dish, salt and pepper shaker, box with cover, cologne bottle, large and small cruet, and 1 mug.

232—CANE AND SPRIG

Mrs. Kamm, in *A Fifth Pitcher Book*, page 97, No. 130, showed a molasses pitcher with a high finialed lid and assigned a temporary name of FLORAL OVAL to the pattern. This was in 1948. S. T. Millard, in 1940, showed a goblet in his *Goblets II*, Plate 69-4, and named it PITTSBURG DAISY because it had a variable type of daisy.

This pattern had been sold for years as CANE AND SPRIG from New England to California and from Minneapolis to New Orleans before Dr. Millard or Mrs. Kamm wrote their books assigning new names. The original name is restored here since it is much more suitable.

Mrs. Lee has nothing but contempt for the pattern which she speaks of as CANE AND SPRAY in her *Antique Fakes and Reproductions*. She shows a 7-inch plate on Plate 68. It must be remembered that this is a very late pattern, and it might be more accurate to say it was continued in production rather than reproduced. Strangely enough, Mrs. Lee devotes considerable and favorable space to PANELLED THISTLE (see in this book), which is no more venerable, no more attractive, and no less reproduced, and which was made by the same company, at the same time and carries the same trademark.

Mrs. Metz covered the pattern as No. 675 without illustration. She said it was "made in full setting, but not worth listing." She used the Millard title.

The pattern was manufactured by J. B. Higbee Glass Company of Bridgeville, Pennsylvania. Most of the larger and flat pieces carry the familiar trademark of a small, resting bee with an *H* on the left wing, an *I* on the body and a *G* on the right wing. (See drawing.) The company used this trademark until 1911. There is considerable evidence that it was adopted in 1905. Mrs. Lee says it was dropped when the Higbee Glass Company was absorbed by the United States Glass Company. This was in 1891 if they were in truth absorbed. We have no evidence to show the company joined either the U.S. Glass Company or the National Glass Company. (See appendix for lists of firms combining to form both corporations.) Research is needed to clear up such discrepancies as this, and the writer wishes he had the time and facilities to perform the task.

Mr. Charles A. Jacobus of Little Rock, Arkansas, assiduously collected this pattern from all over the United States, from 1920 to 1952, then he lost his entire collection of 183 pieces in a fire at his home near Hardy, Arkansas. During that time he bought every piece of the pattern he could, and had only the following: four 12-inch square plates; two dark blue, two amber, one peach, and one blue opaque 7-inch square plates; a very tall goblet shaped vase on an exceedingly tall, slender stem; 9 goblets, straight sides, no flared ones; two 2-handled celery vases; 7-inch high bonbon dish with applied basket handle; many sizes of bowls, all squarish; covered sugar bowl; four tumblers, straight and flared; five punch cups, straight and flared; compote on 1/2-inch by 7-inch long stem; butter dish with lid; syrup pitcher with lid; two creamers; dishes 5 x 8 inches in vaseline; pickle dish, long oval; banana dish on stem; cake plate on

stem; and wines. (The latter are made in atrocious colors today.)

Mrs. Kay has two clear 7-inch plates of this pattern in her famous *Plate Window* in Toll House, Silver Springs, Maryland.

The pattern is similar to PERKINS, which was also made by J. B. Higbee Glass Company. Millard assigned the name PERKINS to that pattern.

The soda-lime glass is light, exceedingly clear, and brilliant. The standard creamer is large, round, and urn-shaped. The waist is short and narrow for such a wide bowl. Surrounding the round waist are two V-shaped grooves. Below them the foot slants out to a wide base and is topped with eight flat panels with round ends. Underneath is a plain, high arched dome.

Around the bowl are four long, ovate figures 3 1/2 inches in length which reach almost from rim to waist. They are outlined by highly raised, V-shaped ridges, the tops of which are strigiled. Inside these, a large figure with highly beveled sides fills the entire space. Into the top of these is pressed a curvate figure of a formalized flowering spray or sprig. Between the ovate figures, the body is covered with a cane design similar to that of a cane seated chair. Above the cane and sprig are arches of V-shaped grooves and prisms. There are also fan-shaped spaces which are concave and left plain.

The back three-fourths of the rim has six large scallops, each of which is covered by three to five smaller scallops. At the front the rim rises and is plain. The lip is narrow.

The handle is small for so large a creamer. It is four-sided, and the two rear panels are filled from top to bottom with closely spaced, minute thumbprints. A square escutcheon is provided for each attachment to heighten the appearance of an applied handle. It is, however, a pressed one and the mold mark shows plainly. This piece does not have a trademark and has never had a lid.

Standard creamer: 4-part mold, 1 pound, 5 1/2 inches tall, 4 1/16 inches wide, and 5 1/2 inches long.

233—MITERED PRISMS

A low keg-shaped creamer is shown in this pattern. The design is simple and effective. Dr. Millard assigned the descriptive name to the pattern in his *Goblets*, Plate 68-3. He thought it was produced in the 1880's and came in clear only.

Ruth Herrick, in *Greentown Glass*, shows a mug in Fig. 330. In Fig. 332 she showed an open sugar and a tall piece, which appears to be a two-handled celery vase. She said it was Albany Glass. I cannot tell from her written material whether it was made by the Model Flint Glass Company or the Indiana Glass Company, both of which were located at Albany, Indiana.

Around the lower three-fourths of the barrel are three wide, zigzagging bands of highly rounded prisms. On the vertical lines, where the bars are mitred, a deep V-shaped slash has been made. Because some of the bars point up and some down, the slashes leave egg-shaped places in the design, alternating up and down.

The upper fourth of the body is plain, smooth, and about an inch wide, with the lower border following the zigzag of the pattern. It would be surprising if this band were not occasionally flashed with ruby or amber. It may have been gilded in some cases.

The rim dips slightly at the sides and is a wee bit high at the back and front. The lip is somber and depressed.

The wide ringbase is heavy and high. Underneath is a plain, wide, flat-topped dome.

The handle is by far the most attractive feature of the pattern, though it does not match the stubby, rigid prisms used. Some type of angular handle would have been more suitable, and this handle would have suited a rococo motif better. A series of large teardrops in high relief overlap on either side of the handle. The overall effect is pleasing. (See details in drawing.)

The quality of this piece is a good average for soda-lime production ware. It is brilliant, clear, and free of defects. It has a slight resonance when tapped and is of light weight. The mold marks show, and the piece is not sufficiently fire polished to bring out its merits. The moldmaker did a fine job. Millard says it was made in the 1880's. I think it dates from 1900 to 1910. It is not often seen in shops today.

Creamer: 4-part mold, 15 ounces, 4 7/16 inches tall, 3 7/16 inches wide, and 5 1/8 inches long.

The only items I am aware of are the goblet used by Millard and the pieces listed above. It would be logical to assume a butter dish and spoonholder were made. It is somewhat less likely, but still probable, that a complete range of articles was made.

quartz and well known as the City of Roses.) The figurework is composed of elements which have been overworked in pressed glass titles. It is midway between an individual and a standard creamer in size.

The glass is fine, of brilliant flint, and free of impurities. It was given a fine fire polish. It is unusually thick and heavy and has a clear ringing resonance when tapped. This is unusual in a creamer. But for the handle I would think the piece dated from the 1860's. Because of it, however, I must conclude it came along much later—probably about 1900. It is quality ware.

The piece sits on a low, wide ringbase. It is almost flat underneath, and has a round, 20-ray star impressed.

The body narrows at the waist and rim and has an attractive curved bulge two-thirds of the way down. The glass of the sides is very thick to receive the deep slashes of the figure work. The lower third is covered with three bands of highly beveled, flat-topped diamonds which stand on their corners. Above the diamonds, the body is slashed with deep V-shaped flutes which extend almost to the rim. Between the spikes are flat panels which round off near the tops of the spikes. Above the figurework is a plain, smooth surface.

The rim is deeply saddled with a graceful sweep up and forward to a narrow, pursed lip. The rim is flat on top, whereas on most pieces it is rounded. A wide plain escutcheon was left at the rear of the creamer. This was done on some high quality glass where the handle was intended to be applied. Here, however, the handle was pressed. It has six flat sides and is wider than it is thick. It increases in thickness toward the lower attachment. From the upper attachment, it curves up and back, then straight back, and finally turns at a 90 degree angle to descend in a long curve to the lower attachment. This type of handle is found on glass of the 1900-1915 era, but is it likely a creamer of such excellent flint glass was made at that late a date?

Small creamer: 3-part mold, 12 ounces, 4 3/16 inches tall, 2 7/8 inches wide, and 4 5/8 inches long.

No other pieces are known to the writer, but they should exist.

234—LITTLE ROCK

This ponderous little creamer so resembles rock crystal and is so beautiful that it would be hard to find a more suitable name than *LITTLE ROCK*. (World famous for its rock crystal or

235—FOLDING HATRACK

Here is a standard creamer in an unnamed pattern. It is somewhat appealing, and I am surprised it has remained nameless for so many years. It could be named dewdrop bands, but

Millard has already used that title for another pattern. The above name is assigned so it can be talked about in polite company. There is a chance an old catalog may turn up some day—giving its original name, manufacturer, siblings, and approximate date of birth.

It is not a large creamer, and its sides are straight—flaring slightly from waist to rim. Above the waist and a half-inch below the rim are 5/8-inch-wide bands composed of three rows of large high dewdrops arranged diagonally. The lower band encircles the body. The upper is interrupted at the handle attachment. Between the two is a 2 1/2-inch band filled with six large overlapping squares which stand on their corners. They are arranged like an old folding hatrack, with white porcelain-topped pegs, such as were always found hanging in the "dog trot." Where the large squares overlap is a smaller flat-topped, plain, and highly beveled square. In the center of each large square is a beveled square with finecut top. The large squares are bordered, inside and out, with raised ridges which are topped with minute beading. The remainder of the complex design (See drawing.) is filled with fine cut figurework. In the interspaces around the pattern are large, plain triangles.

Above the top row of dewdrops is a plain band half an inch wide which extends to the partially scalloped rim. The rim is raised a little and thrusts forward in front to provide the lip. There is a high, wide scallop over the handle.

The handle is six-sided and adequate. The side panels carry a single row of large dewdrops graduated in size from top to bottom. The lower attachment is well fitted into the design of a square. The girth is ample. A heavy ring provides the base and beneath it is a 1/4-inch deep curved, hollowed out space.

The glass is 3/16 of an inch thick at the rim, and the piece is heavy for its medium size. There is no resonance. It is production ware of unclear glass, which was neither fire nor acid polished. The mold marks are high but not sharp, and the rim and lip are rough. The latter has a deep, unexplained crease which is difficult to keep sanitary.

Standard creamer: 3-part mold, 12 ounces, 4 3/4 inches tall, 3 3/16 inches wide, and 4 3/4 inches long.

Nothing is known as to where or by whom it was made. It dates from about 1875-1890. I know of no other items. Perhaps assigning it a name will bring out of hiding other items in the pattern, as often happens. A little more nurturing in the form of a better mix, and more care in finishing it off would have resulted in a beautiful product.

This creamer was presented to the author for inclusion in this book by the late Mrs. O. E. (Kate Clark) Ward of Pascagoula, Mississippi, from her fine collection of pressed glass water pitchers. Her generosity is deeply appreciated.

236—SIAMESE NECKLACE

This standard creamer is shown here for the first time in our American glass literature. The individual creamer and water pitcher were shown with a standard creamer of a different pattern by Mrs. Kamm in *A Seventh Pitcher Book*, page 33, No. 65 and in Plates 16, 17, and 101. She named the pattern D&M No. 42. She used the same standard creamer in *A Fifth Pitcher Book*, page 70, No. 91 as DUNCAN, No. 42. The standard creamer she used was made by Duncan and Miller Glass Company of Pittsburgh, Pennsylvania from about 1894 to 1904. It was manufactured in a very large range of items.

This creamer is considerably more ornate, and also more comely. It differs from the pattern put out by Duncan and Miller and definitely belongs with the individual creamer and water pitcher used by Mrs. Kamm.

The decoration on the lower portion of the body is the same as on D & M No. 42, but there the similarity ends. High, wide, vertical prisms are topped with English hobnail. Alternating high, narrow prisms are finely notched. The pitchers in this pattern are jug-shaped, and their necks are ringed similar to Siamese ladies. Six rings of raised V-shaped ridges make up this feature. Above the ringed neck, an inch-wide collar flares to the rim. The collar on all pieces has an attractive border design of oval thumbprints alternating with long, deep slashes.

The rim is level and irregularly scalloped to conform to the decorative motif of the collar. The lip rises slightly. It is narrow and attractive. The handle is applied with the large blob at the bottom and the small attachment turned under at the top. This type of applied handle never appeared on early flint glass. Great care was lavished on it to insure a quality product. This is further shown by the plain, smooth escutcheon provided to avoid the necessity of applying the handle over the figurework. Even the rings around the neck stop where the handle is attached in the rear.

The piece sits on a low ringbase and is flat underneath where an irregular, but attractive, six-point, many-rayed star is impressed. The quality of glass and workmanship are superior. There is

236

237

238

Bottom
238

239

240

241

242

243

244

no resonance, but the glass is brilliant and sparkling.

Nothing is known to me about where, or by whom, the pattern was manufactured. The molds may well have been made by the Hipkins Novelty Mold Works. It is a product of the 1890's.

Standard creamer: 3-part mold, 15 1/2 ounces, 4 3/4 inches tall, 3 5/8 inches wide, and 4 7/8 inches long.

Four articles are known to have been manufactured in this pattern: individual creamer, standard creamer, water pitcher, and covered sugar bowl. Other items must have been made.

237—HEAVY DRAPE

Mrs. Kamm had not seen a creamer in this pattern so she drew it from a cut in the 1904 catalog of the Fostoria Glass Company, Moundsville, West Virginia. The company called it No. 1300, and Mrs. Kamm supplied the above excellent descriptive title in *A Seventh Pitcher Book*, pages 39-40, No. 78. She also showed a full-page cut on Plate 93 of *An Eighth Pitcher Book*. It was dated 1901. It is not covered elsewhere in our glass literature.

The pattern appears complex but is actually quite simple. The piece is hogshead-shaped, somewhat squatty, and both wide and heavy. The glass in most of the drapes is a full half-inch thick.

Around the rim are eight large elliptical figures which are thin at the rim, but which curve out to their lower edges to form the first fold of the drape. The ellipses were originally gilded, and the remainder of the body left clear. The gilt is now badly worn. Under each ellipse is a column of five heavy drapery folds. They show as well-rounded columns when seen in use. The design completely covers the body. The top of the five ellipses at the back make the high, wide scallops of the rim. The one under the lip plus the ones on either side of it are elongated and extend upward to form the raised, curved lip.

The piece sits on a wide, flat ringbase and is stable. Underneath is an unadorned, 1/4-inch-deep flat-topped dome.

The column of drapes, where the handle was to be applied, was made with a wide, thick platform to receive the large blob of the lower attachment. The upper turned under attachment of the applied handle fused well with the flat surface of the adjacent ellipse.

The glass is clear, brilliant, and heavy. It is of soda-lime and emits a dull thud when tapped. It contains several bubbles and an occasional fleck of discoloration. The work of the gaffer was somewhat better than that of the mixmaker. It was well fire polished and mold marks are visible only on the ringbase.

Note the striking similarity of the pattern FRISCO which follows immediately and which was made at the same time by the same company. It is shown in Kamm's *A Seventh Pitcher Book*, page 39, No. 77. The Fostoria Glass Company makes FRISCO in fine quality milk white glass today. The new pieces carry gummed labels, which are easily washed off, and lost. The company may also be producing this pattern in clear glass. It should be compared with QUEEN'S NECKLACE, since the two seem to have the same genealogy.

Creamer: 4-part mold, 1 1/4 pounds, 5 1/16 inches tall, 4 1/4 inches wide, and 5 9/16 inches long.

Many items were originally made in this pattern and some of the unusual ones which appear in the more modern patterns of today are: tall vases, rose bowl, handled nappies, toothpick holder, covered cracker jar, finger bowl, footed jelly, custard cup, sherbet cup, punch bowl, water carafe, and punch cups. The above are in addition to the many items routinely produced.

238—FRISCO

The Fostoria Glass Company of Moundsville, West Virginia made this pattern in 1904 (as their No. 1229) in thirty-three different articles, and called it FRISCO.

In *A Seventh Pitcher Book*, page 39, No. 77, Mrs. Kamm drew and described the pattern from a cut in an old catalog. She had not seen the pattern. In *An Eighth Pitcher Book*, Plate 94, she showed the actual cut, which illustrated seven articles. I have the clear creamer and will give a description and measurements.

In his *Goblets*, Plate 12-4, Millard showed an early flint goblet with the same motif, but inverted and without the dewdrops. He named it LAMINATED PETALS. The figures appear to overlap at the edges rather than to have been laminated. In *Goblets II*, Plate 12-3, he showed a similar, but older pattern than the one covered here. He called it ALLIGATOR SCALES.

This standard creamer is, in general, barrel-shaped, though it swells a little at the base. Encircling the top is a band of ten, large pecan-shaped figures in high, convex relief. The top fourth of each rounded figure is left plain. They form half of the rim scallops. Between each two, a large teardrop is wedged. The tops of the teardrops make up the other half of the scallops. The lower borders of the pecan-shaped figures are outlined by a band of graduated beading.

Below these rounded ellipses the body is completely covered with a design similar to alligator scales. Each scale is well rounded and has a vertical spine at the center. Three horizontal, interlocking bands of these scales cover the piece to the waist, and each scale is bordered by a row of fine beadwork. The waist also has a band of scales, but they are not as highly rounded and have no beading. They end at the bottom of the bowl.

The base is wide and the piece sits on a flat ring. On the underside is a formalized daisy made up of ten rounded, tapering ribs. (See cut of bottom.) The front third of the rim surges up and forward to a rolled, narrow lip. The handle is large, round in cross section, and applied. A large, plain escutcheon is provided for the attachments with the lower one receiving the large blob. The upper attachment is turned under. The quality of the lime-soda glass is excellent, and it has a perfect fire polish. The skill of both moldmaker and gaffer was superior. It is difficult to locate the mold marks.

In a gift shop in May, 1957, I found a covered sugar bowl, of excellent quality, in white milk glass in this pattern. It had a Fostoria sticker on it and was sold for what it was—a new, high quality product. We know, therefore, that this pattern has either been continued in production, or is enjoying a revival. It is no fake. It is regrettable that such fine quality is not permanently trademarked. Stickers are easily detached. I would not be surprised to find iridescent pieces. There is a possibility it may be made in colors.

Creamer: 4-part mold, 1 pound, 4 3/4 inches tall, 3 5/8 inches wide, and 5 inches long.

In addition to this creamer, thirty-two other items were made. Because of its late arrival, it is not surprising to find a cruet and three types of vases in the pattern.

239—QUATREFOIL

DERBY would be the obvious name for this pattern, but it has already been used. Mrs. Kamm restored the old factory name of DERBY to the well-known PLEAT AND PANEL pattern and it cannot be used again.

Alice Hulett Metz showed a covered butter dish in this pattern and named it *QUATREFOIL* in *Early American Pattern Glass*, pages 146-47, No. 1643. In her *Booklet No. 4 Studies in Early American Pattern Glass* she used three photographs. On the cover she showed a covered butter dish. On page 10 she illustrated a covered sugar bowl and creamer. She said the pattern was plentiful in Illinois.

This is production ware at its lowest ebb. The lines, design, metal, and workmanship, all are substandard. The body is cylindrical with a rounded, raised ring circling the rim. At the bottom it curves in sharply and changes from a round contour to one of eight flat panels. They extend through the narrow waist and disappear in the wide base.

Below the rim is a band of inch-high, four-lobed, nondescript, and stippled quatrefoils. Over each of the four mold marks is an enigmatic combination figure containing in sequence an arrowhead, mace, derby hat, and diamond—all stippled. The wide thick base adds stability to the piece. It is domed on the underside.

The Roman "proboscis" is one of the prominent identifying features of this creamer. It is not known to be particularly drip resistant. The handle, like the lip, is too large and too massive for a creamer of this capacity. It is six-sided and appears much wider when seen from the rear. It is comfortable to heft.

The glass is fairly clear soda-lime, but the piece has many bubbles—some of them more than half an inch in width.

Standard creamer: 4-part mold, 14 ounces, 5 inches tall, 3 inches wide, and 5 7/16 inches long.

It appears to date from 1885-1895. Few other items are known.

240—MIAMI

This is the rare occasion where it seems advisable to change the name of a pattern. Mrs. Kamm had not seen this design, but did find an advertisement in the magazine *China, Glass, and Lamps* of 1895, by Riverside Glass Works, Wellsburg, West Virginia. The four-piece table setting was illustrated as No. 436 TABLEWARE and called BRILLIANT. A full line of samples of No. 436 was said to be on exhibition in their showrooms.

Mrs. Kamm, in *A Sixth Pitcher Book*, pages 33-34, No. 63 and Plate 65, used the ad as an illustration and described it as well as she could without seeing an actual item. She did not make a drawing. She continued the name BRILLIANT. At the time this ware was produced, there was already a pattern of early flint glass, predating it by many years, made by McKee Brothers of Pittsburgh, Pennsylvania which was called BRIL-LIANT.

Ruth Webb Lee, in *Early American Pressed Glass*, Plate 153, No. 14, illustrated a goblet of the McKee Brother's pattern. She gave a brief write-up on page 628.

S. T. Millard, in *Goblets*, Plate 125-1, illustrated a goblet which he too called BRILLIANT. The title was already preempted when the Riverside Glass Works started making this particular pattern.

Since a new name is in order, it seems appropriate to name such a beautiful pattern for the lovely city of Miami, Florida, with its sparkling waters, beaches, and gold coast. The light amber panels of the piece give the appearance of actual gold. This type of ware is known as "amberette."

All patterns manufactured by Riverside, as far as I know, have been of superior quality. They must have employed a gaffer of consummate skill, who also had a wide experience, an infinite patience, and a consuming desire to excel. The pattern is of just such quality.

The body is constricted at the waist and neck. It is melon-shaped with six broad lobes which also extend from waist to neck. The alternate lobes are plain-surfaced, and these and the top of the rim are flashed with a light golden amber, which is baked on. Some items may have been flashed with ruby, light green, or amethyst. The three remaining lobes have a rectangular impressed design, the principle feature of which is a quatrefoil of four leaf-shaped figures outlined by deep grooves. The interior of each leaf has a formal daisy composed of faceted figures in high relief. The interstices on the sides have three-ray fans impressed. Those at top and bottom have large five-rayed fans.

The waist is short and low and the ringbase flares out therefrom. On the underside a flat-topped hollow dome is left plain. The rim flares from the neck and is round on top. It is irregularly scalloped in pleasing curves. The lip is low, narrow, and effective. The flashing on the rim was applied with care and restraint, and there is only a trace of it. At first glance it appears to be a reflection of the golden color from below.

The handle is round in cross section and imitates a reeded handle at both attachments. The lower is large and splays into a serrated medallion on the body. The flat panel which bears the handle is flashed with color, but not a particle reached the serrated handle attachment.

The glass is clear, brilliant, beautifully fire-polished, and no defect can be found. The only mold mark that can be seen is beneath the handle.

It was made as a quality product.

Creamer: 4-part mold, 14 ounces, 4 3/8 inches tall, 3 9/16 inches wide, and 5 inches long.

We know that a creamer, covered sugar bowl, covered butter dish, and spoonholder were made. The old ad informs us that "a full line" of tableware was manufactured. It is not plentiful, and this is the first time it has been described in American glass literature.

241—*DIME*

This modern piece is shown for the same reason that a known reproduction would be. Over twenty years ago, as a beginning fancier of pressed glass, I was sold this pitcher as "a very old pressed glass block and fan pattern." At the same time it was being sold in the 5¢ and 10¢ stores and is still sold there today. It is a great-grandchild of the cheap pressed glass of eighty years ago. Perhaps eighty years from now a few pieces of it may still be around and be worth something.

It is a variation of a very old theme but carried out rather subtly. The blocks are uneven, and some have curved beveling on the sides. The large, erect, petallike rays at the top are also unusual. The creamer is in the shape of a lemonade tumbler or vase, flaring upward slightly from above the base to rim. The thick base is flat, despite its appearance. On the underside is a large, plain, incised, and 12-ray star.

The rim is plain and horizontal over the back half, and then rises gently to a low lip. There is an unusual horizontal line on the outside of the front portion—a continuation of the remainder of the rim. The body is plain for almost an inch down from the rim, and from there on to near the base it is covered with a continuous pattern. At front and beneath the handle is an inch-wide, vertical panel of washboarding, similar to that on JACOB'S LADDER.

On either side, in high relief, are large diamonds arranged diagonally. These flat-topped diamonds vary considerably in size and margins, some incurved, others tapered. Above them and mitred into the blocks are long, broad fans composed of coarse rays.

Creamer: 2-part mold, 15 ounces, 5 1/8 inches tall, 3 1/4 inches wide, and 5 1/8 inches long.

The manufacturer is unknown. The quality of glass and workmanship are below that expected of today's manufacturers. It is believed that no other items were made. None have been seen.

242—ANGEL

This is still another of the many pressed glass creamers which have not been described in our books on glass. This particular one is not old enough to be "well-ripened." It probably is a contemporary of the Louisiana Purchase Exposition plate.

Bessie M. Lindsey, in Volume I of *Lore of Our Land Pictured in Glass*, No. 204, shows this creamer and calls it ANGEL. In No. 205 she shows a matching 5 1/2-inch plate with openwork border. This creamer presents several questions I cannot answer. Perhaps others may be more astute.

The sides of the bowl are straight and flare slightly to the top. Otherwise, it resembles a plain glass mug. The body is covered with a shallow acid-etched design. It is, in fact, so shallow as to be almost impossible to feel with one's fingers. In places it fades till it all but disappears. This type of etching makes us think it is of the 1900's. On the front side of the bowl are four angels—one directing and the others playing a violin, lute, and cello. Their wings are in motion though they perch on the small branches of a flowering tree. On the opposite side of the creamer the same picture is shown in reverse somewhat as if the negative had been turned over. In front the musicians are left-handed; in the back they are right-handed. Under the lip is a sturdy cupid without wings, but with a heavy bow and arrow. He appears to be shooting straight down. The etching is not deep enough to be effective, since it takes close observation to make out the figures.

The wide waist is curvaceous but short, and there is a shelf where the base of the bowl rounds in slightly to meet it. There is a second shelf on the thick, wide ringbase.

Underneath the base is a wide, rather deep, flat-topped dome. Its ceiling has a raised, 24-ray star, with rays of uneven length. Centered in the star is a raised trademark, as shown in the drawing. I am not familiar with the mark and know of only one American glass company whose name starts with a *T*. (Thatcher Glass Manufacturing Company, Inc., of Jeannette, Pennsylvania.) Is this their mark or a foreign one?

The rim is plain, round, and has a wide-jowled, narrow lip. The handle is round in cross section and except for a faintly seen mold mark, could pass for an applied one of the later type, with the large blob at the bottom.

The quality of the glass is only fair for a product made when technical skill and knowledge had made tremendous advances. There are scattered bubbles and a lack of clearness and brilliance—both of which should have been corrected. It was fairly well polished, but poorly etched. The design was placed on it with a stencil. The piece is ordinary, and better etching could have given it a sales boost. The mold marks are almost polished off. It could have been a container for marketing of jelly, or preserves. A tin lid could have been securely clamped over the rim.

Creamer: 2-part mold, 14 ounces, 5 1/16 inches tall, 3 5/16 inches wide, and 5 1/8 inches long.

243—ST. BERNARD

ST. BERNARD is one of the more desirable frosted animal patterns, such as JUMBO, FROSTED EAGLE, CHICK, DOVE, STORK, etc. On these patterns the frosted animal serves as the finial of covered pieces and they are also found in the bottoms of flat bowls and sauces. Creamers, spooners, celery vases, etc., have no finial, and their bases were not suitable for an animal design. They are, therefore, difficult to identify unless accompanied by covered pieces in the same pattern.

I show my large covered sugar bowl in the ST. BERNARD pattern because it shows clearly the frosted dog and other figure work. Most such pieces are engraved, but mine is not.

Mrs. Kamm had not seen a piece in this pattern and used a small illustration from an 1896 catalog of Montgomery Ward to make her drawing. She also showed a full-page advertisement from *China, Glass and Lamps*, which was issued in 1895. This shows the pattern to have been made by Fostoria Glass Company of Moundsville, West Virginia, as their 450 PATTERN. In the Montgomery Ward catalog the pattern was called ST. BERNARD. The four-piece table set of creamer, spooner, covered sugar, and covered butter was priced at seventy-five cents.

Please refer to Mrs. Kamm's *A Fifth Pitcher Book*, page 61, No. 75, and Plates 13 and 14. With such a small illustration for a guide for her drawing, it is not surprising that slight inaccuracies appear. Since pieces without the dog are difficult to identify at best, and can be done only by the other figurework, the figures should be accurately drawn. Her drawing is incorrect in three instances: (1) She shows a plain band separating the body figurework from the plain upper portion of the body. The line actually is made by a series of pointed slashes, two above each fan. (2) She shows similar fans in the interstices above and below where the large diamonds meet at their corners. The fans are not similar, except that each has its base at the bottom and spreads upward. (See drawing for dissimilar figures.) (3) She shows all squares in the large diamonds to be beveled, flat-topped cubes. However, only the four corner ones are like this. The other five are sharp-pointed rectangular pyramids.

Mrs. Metz, in *Early American Pattern Glass*, pages 148-149, No. 1665, illustrates a flat bowl from directly above. The angle from which the photograph was taken shows the dog plainly but the figurework is partially obscured.

Mrs. Lee, on Plate 99 in her *Early American Pressed Glass*, top row, center, shows a covered compote with a large frosted dog finial. On this piece the dog is half crouching. On ST. BERNARD the dog is lying down. She neither names nor describes the piece. It appears to be a somewhat earlier item than ST. BERNARD, but is not before 1876.

On covered pieces, the rim is plain, and the lids have a flange that fits into the throat. The glass is clear, highly polished, and brilliant. I am unable to find a mold mark on the sugarbowl. The frosting is carefully done.

Covered sugar: ?-Mold marks, 1 3/4 pounds, 7 1/16 inches tall, and 4 1/4 inches wide.

These items are known to have been made in the pattern: four-piece table set, low bowl, sauce dish, low covered compote, high covered compote, water pitcher, and tumbler.

244—CRY BABY

In so far as I have been able to determine, this baby cries incessantly. The name suggests itself. This is an attractive, medium-sized, figural creamer, well off the beaten path. The glass is of fine quality, clear, brilliant, and thin. It was blown in a mold, then the narrow neck was formed and the handle applied.

The bowl of the pitcher is in the shape of a baby's head and one who is crying lustily. It is cut off at the neck and sits flat on its chin. The small, vertical neck sits on top of the head.

Creamer: 3-part mold, 8 ounces, 4 1/8 inches tall, 2 7/8 inches wide, and 4 1/8 inches long.

This piece is not old. Nothing is known by the writer as to when, where, or by whom it was made or whether other items accompanied it. Probably none did.

245—LANTERN GLOBE

This is the largest of four similar creamers that have not been shown in our glass literature.

The other three follow in succession. Unfortunately, all are without lids. They were containers and probably were sold only when filled with spice, sage, baking powder, pickles, prepared horseradish, prepared mustard, jelly, or other condiments. Three or four glass houses specialized in supplying such containers. We have no clue as to which factory made these pieces, but probably they all came from the same one.

This standard creamer, without its lid, is in the shape of an old lantern globe. About its wide middle, a formalized leaf band has been etched with a wheel.

The waist is large, and a flared skirt descends from it to end in a beveled ring. On top of the skirt are short convexed ribs, which swirl in a clockwise direction. Underneath on the hollowed out base, is a second series of identical ribs, which swirl counterclockwise. One gets the effect of rounded diamonds when looking through the clear glass.

At the neck is a 1/4-inch-wide, highly raised, convex ring. Above it the collar flares to a saddled rim. The collar has the same rib treatment as the base but is wider and therefore more apparent and attractive. (See drawing.)

The back half of the rim is scalloped to conform to the top of the rounded ribs, with a tall scallop at the back for a handle attachment. The front half of the rim is not scalloped and flows upward to form the lip.

Inside the creamer and slightly above the level of the heavy ring at the neck is a well-defined flat shelf 1/8-inch wide to accommodate a lid. The lids of creamers are so attractive and so few of them were made, one must lament their high mortality rate. They slipped off and fell so easily. Somewhere, sometime, a single lid may have survived such a fall—but it has not been recorded.

The handle is terete and appears to be clumsy. However, it does give a secure grip when used, though the low thumbgrip on its top does not contribute to that security. The glass is soft and easily scratched. It is clear soda-lime of good quality. Some waviness and a few hairlines indicate that the metal was too cool for good pressing. The mold marks are plain but not sharp. It probably dates from between 1895 and 1905.

Creamer, large, no lid: 2-part mold, 13 ounces, 5 3/16 inches tall, 3 11/16 inches wide, and 4 11/16 inches long.

No other piece in the pattern is known. I would expect to find a sugar bowl, spooner, goblet, and tumbler. These could be easily fitted with a cover to be filled and sold in grocery stores. There may have been a moderate range of sizes and colors.

246—BILOXI

This creamer is similar to the preceding one except for the following: (1) It is smaller; (2) It is of honey amber glass instead of clear; (3) It has inverted thumbprints on the inside of the body; (4) It has not been etched.

Perhaps it was designed by the same person, and produced in the same factory, as the other three. The beautiful color reminds me of a sunset over the Gulf of Mexico as seen from Biloxi, Mississippi.

This is a little beauty when seen in the sunlight. The light honey-amber color is intensified to deeper ambers in the thickened places. The inverted thumbprints enhance its attractiveness. Here again we meet with a too common occurrence—a missing lid. One wonders what commodity this dainty piece housed, and carried to the dining table, as well as where and when. It probably was made between 1895 and 1905.

The large inverted thumbprints on the inside are staggered. There are seven in the top row and eight in each of the three lower rows. The thumbprints are graduated to conform to the space they occupy. The collar and skirt of this piece are similar to those of *LANTERN GLOBE*, immediately preceding.

The handle has a rudiment of a thumbgrip. It is round and simulates an applied handle but actually was pressed. There is a well-defined flat ledge inside the creamer at the top to hold a lid. It is believed a three-part mold was used, for the base would require a separate part so the piece might be lifted off when the lateral halves were thrown open. There is a mold mark around the middle of the ringbase. The other mold marks have been fire polished off.

This is a fine piece of quality glass, and both it and its contents originally retailed for a dime or probably no more than a bit.

Creamer, medium, no lid: 3-part mold, 10 1/2 ounces, 4 11/16 inches tall, 3 3/16 inches wide, and 4 1/8 inches long. Creamer, large, no lid: 2(?)-part mold, 12 1/2 ounces, 5 1/8 inches tall, 3 5/8 inches wide, and 4 7/8 inches long.

The pattern also came in a beautiful shade of blue. The following items are known: a water pitcher with a rim on the inside near the top to hold a lid, a round water tray, tumblers, and a waste bowl that would certainly be taken for a finger bowl if seen apart from the set. I have creamers in two sizes in this pattern.

247—BEER KEG

This amber sibling of the two previous container creamers above is most pleasing. Regrettably, the lid is missing. No description is necessary to show the close familial relationship between these three pieces and the one which follows. The body is keg-shaped and all decoration is on the outside of the body. The hoops, staves, and bunghole all show plainly. It definitely represents a beer keg, but what did it contain?

The skirt and collar are of the same shape but markedly different from the two preceding creamers in decorative motif. Here we have odd shaped sections side by side. Each has a plain center, surrounded by a band, or ruffle of fine rib. The rim is gently scalloped in accordance with the top of the previously described sections, except at the front where it is left plain.

The handle is terete, has no thumbgrip, and is a little more squarish than those of its kin. The glass is a beautiful golden amber, a very desirable shade. Amber glass is steadily increasing in popularity. Unfortunately, this soda-lime ware is soft, and easily scarred or marred.

Creamer, medium, no lid: 3-part mold, 10 ounces, 5 inches tall, 3 3/16 inches wide, and 4 1/4 inches long.

Only this creamer, without a cover, is known to the writer. Similar glass lids were easily adapted to sugar bowls. Tin or some other light metal was often clamped over the rim of goblets, tumblers, jelly glasses, and spoonholders, to make them suitable for marketing condiments or jellies.

248—LEPANTO

This beautiful creamer is made of yellow glass and has lost its lid. It is a sibling of the three preceding patterns and has a strong familial resemblance to each.

Never having been covered in glass literature before, it must be given a name. Therefore, I christen thee *LEPANTO* in honor of the little Arkansas town of that name.

As stated, all five of the creamers of this group of four types have lost their lids. None, however, have a chip or blemish of any kind. This leads me to believe the finials on the lids provided a poor grip, and that they easily slipped from the fingers and were broken. They were beautiful containers and finished off with care, so they must have been used to carry a superior product. Three of the specimens are large in size and two are medium. Other sizes may have been manufactured.

Compare this pattern with *LANTERN GLOBE* and *BILOXI*. It will be noted that the flared rim and skirted base of all three are identical. The shapes of the three are also the same. The body of *LEPANTO* has inverted columns on the inside, whereas *LANTERN GLOBE* is plain, and *BILOXI* has inverted thumbprints.

Of my five specimens two are of clear glass, one is of light amber, one of darker amber, and this one is of a beautiful yellow color. Other colors may have been used. The glass and workmanship are of a superior quality. They probably date from about 1895 to 1905.

Creamer, large, no lid: 4-part mold, 14 ounces, 5 1/4 inches tall, 3 1/2 inches wide, and 5 1/8 inches long.

I suspect that only hollow items, suitable for use as containers, were made.

249—GRENADA

Mrs. Kamm had not seen a piece in this pattern. She used a cut of an individual creamer from a 1905 catalog of the Fostoria Glass Company of Moundsville, West Virginia, listed as "No. 600." She called it FOSTORIA'S NO. 600 in her *A Seventh Pitcher Book*, page 43, No. 87. Since numbers are difficult to remember as titles, a new name is given it here. This particular creamer is a beautiful one, with its overall configuration and many deep slashes. It resembles the rolling countryside around Grenada, Mississippi, where erosion has cut enormous gullies in the deep loessial soil. Mrs. Kamm missed some minor details in copying the pattern from the small original cut.

This hassock-shaped standard creamer is an excellent imitation of cut glass. It probably was welcomed by a large segment of the population who could not afford cut glass and had to settle for something cheaper. The imitation is so fine it is difficult to determine whether it actually was cut or pressed.

On each side, and under the lip, is a large, beveled, hexagon. In each is centered a 16-point hobstar. Between the hexagons are stubby, cigar-shaped figures filled with English strawberry-diamond design, and flat-topped triangles. Around the lower part of the body, and extending downward from all interstices in the figurework, are fans which curve under to the base. The piece sits flat, and a large beveled square on the bottom is an extension of the pattern on the side. It is filled with a square hobstar. (See drawing of bottom.)

The handle is round and pressed. It is an excellent imitation of an applied one. A large escutcheon was provided for the handle. The lower attachment, with its large blob, looks so much like an applied one, it is deceiving. Mrs. Kamm thought the handle had small thumbprints down each side, but she had not seen a piece. Actually, the back part of the handle is covered with St. Louis cut. (A type of concave honeycomb cutting widely used in cut glass on handles, necks, and stems.)

The rim is irregularly scalloped like most cut glass. The wide scallops are covered by smaller ones. The rim rises abruptly in front to form a high lip. The glass and workmanship are of excellent quality. The piece is clear, brilliant, and sparkling. It is quality pressed glass.

Creamer: 4-part mold, 14 ounces, 3 3/8 inches tall, 3 7/8 inches wide, and 5 3/8 inches long.

Standard and individual creamer and sugar sets were made. Possibly salt shakers, carafes, bowls, sauces, goblets, tumblers, and nappies were made also.

250—NORTHWOOD'S HOBSTAR

Seldom does one find a Northwood pattern in imitation cut glass. This is one and *MEMPHIS* is another. Both are of superior quality. The imitation cutting is very deep. The glass is bright and shiny. When held to the light it has much of the sparkle shown by cut glass. The design is so well done that many people cannot tell it from genuine cut glass. This pattern has not been described in our glass literature, and the above name is assigned.

It is crystal clear, heavy, thick (1/4 inch), and without resonance. This is typical of glass manufactured when fine workmanship and the best basic materials are utilized to make a quality product of soda-lime glass.

The creamer is larger than usual, and is hassock-shaped. The base has eight sides and there is a large, 32-rayed star underneath. On the inside of the bottom is a raised N with a bar beneath and enclosed in a raised circle. This mark was used after 1906. Earlier, Northwood products were not usually marked. (See ARGONAUT and TOWN PUMP, in this book, for an earlier mark.)

The rim is double scalloped with sharp V-points. At the front the rim is plain and raised to form a narrow, incurved lip. The latter is the most graceful portion of the piece. The handle is

245

246

247

248

249

250

Bottom
249

251

252

253

Bottom
252

honeycombed with concave notches on both sides and in the rear.

The principal motif of the pattern is a series of large, diamond-shaped rectangles which extend from the base almost to the rim. Each is subdivided into four smaller ones. Their lower margins are curved. The upper and lower rectangles have sharp points and are filled with English strawberry-diamond. The side squares are topped with cross-hatching. Encircling the base and extending about a third of the way up the body are eight wide arches shaped like Folsom arrowheads. They are hollowed out. Below the rim and in the *V*'s formed by the rectangles is a band of large hobstars. Each has a deep concave thumbprint in the center. There are six of them.

Creamer: 4-part mold, 1 pound, 3 5/8 inches tall, 4 inches wide, and 6 inches long.

This creamer belongs to a four-piece table setting. Probably there are many items in existence, such as: rose bowl, vase, nappie, relish, punch bowl, cup, etc. There is a striking similarity between this pattern and HEISEY'S SUNBURST as shown in Kamm's *A Sixth Pitcher Book*, page 48, No. 110. There is also a resemblance between these patterns and SQUARED SUNBURST which is shown on the same page of the same book.

I believe this pattern will be found in various colors.

251—*MOURNING DOVE*

Another nameless standard creamer is shown here. It is pleasing, despite its great mixture of motif. The main motif is a well-rounded and executed mourning dove. (Or raincrow as it is often called in the South because of its low, plaintive coo.) I am naming it *MOURNING DOVE*.

The medium-sized, thimble-shaped bowl has straight sides which round in at the waist. At the rim is a 1/4-inch-wide plain, thickened band. The dove on either side is unmistakable, though it does not appear as real in the flat drawing as on the curved surface of the creamer. Aside from this, there is no really identifying feature in the pattern. The log on the obverse side could be the concept of a man who has never seen one. The botanical effect of the flowers, leaves, stems, branches, and boles is fantastic with no semblance to any known flower, tree, or shrub. In front of and behind the doves on either side are four exotic flowering plants. This is truly folk art.

Two ornamental bands 1/2 inch wide encircle the body at top and bottom. They are made up of rectangles that lean on a clockwise direction in the lower band and counterclockwise in the upper. Every other rectangle contains a flower sprig (of sorts) on a plain background—alternating in position, first upright, then inverted. The intervening spaces are filled with raised figurework and stippling. The motif of a dove standing on a log dominates the pattern. Both doves face toward the lip and are similar. The logs are entirely different, and their leaf sprays are from the "fourth kingdom"—belonging to neither animal, mineral, nor vegetable worlds.

The rim is severely plain, flat, level, and slightly pinched at the front to form the lip. The handle is heavy, stiff, and designed to represent mortised timbers, carved on the front and back. The other four sides have plain, flat surfaces. The carving effect is similar to that in the bands around the body.

The body curves in at the waist which is constricted. It is 1/4 inch high and has vertical sides. From the waist, the base slopes out to its full diameter, then drops vertically for 1/4 inch. Beneath the base is a dome half an inch high in which has been impressed, in slightly raised letters, the following words in reverse: PATENT APPLIED FOR. It can be read by looking down through the creamer and is a feature seldom seen in pressed glass.

This is production soda-lime glass and bears all the stigmata—high mold marks, hairlines, rough edges, a few bubbles, and an off-color. The piece is thick and heavy for its medium size (3/16 inch at the rim and 1/4 inch at the base). It appears to date from the period of 1875-1885.

Creamer: 2-part mold, 12 ounces, 4 3/8 inches tall, 3 1/4 inches wide, and 4 3/4 inches long.

Nothing is known of other items in the pattern. Probably many were intended and few resulted, possibly due to such prevalent disasters as fires, bankruptcy, or strikes. Pieces in this pattern are very scarce. At least, one should expect to find the four-piece table setting to which this creamer belonged.

The design so lightly traced and executed on glass is on the whole pleasing. Only when seen in the drawing, or when studied closely, do the anomalies become apparent. It definitely is an example of early American folk art. Nothing about it has a foreign accent.

The late Mrs. O. E. (Kate Clark) Ward of Pascagoula, Mississippi, generously presented this rare piece to the author's collection and so enabled its inclusion here. She had a large collection of early American pressed glass water pitchers—several hundred.

252—SPIDER

This is a fascinating old pattern which has heretofore escaped writers on pressed glass. Had I named it, it would be *Daddy Longlegs*, but SPIDER is the name by which it is commonly known. Perhaps its name plus the public's revulsion to spiders accounts for the scarcity of items in the pattern. Certainly it never made the "top ten," and most ladies would prefer something else.

The standard creamer shown here is bullet-shaped and rather large. The body tapers out sharply from the narrow waist and is smooth on the outside up to within 3/4 inch of the rim. At this level a 3/8-inch-wide sunken and stippled band encircles the creamer and dips under the lip. Evenly spaced in the band are flat-topped, vertical, elongated rectangles. To one side of these is a dewdrop and on the other an inverted, V-shaped prism. Above this are two narrower and rounded bands around the creamer just below the rim. Below the stippled band a plain, undecorated area 5/8 inch wide surrounds the body. Below it, nine large, high, inverted thumbprints are seen through the glass. Below these on the inside are two rows of large bodyless spiders with long, crooked, and widespread legs. Each has the proper number of legs—eight. There are nine spiders in the upper row and six in the lower. The figures of the spiders are raised on the inside of the creamer, and are as high as they are thick. The writer does not know how the inside mold (plunger) could have pressed these figures and then been removed without marring the figurework. Usually the figurework on pressed glass is on the outside of the piece and not touched by the contents. In this case, the spiders would drown in cream, and washing would be difficult.

At the base of the body is a high, rounded ring on which the body rests. The waist is narrow with a rounded ring or belt in its middle. The base flattens out and down over two shelves to form a large base for a stemmed creamer. It is as wide as the body of the creamer (3 1/2 inches). The base is hollowed slightly beneath, and has a ring of six large raised spiders. Each spider has a rounded dewdrop for a body. One spider is in the center of the ring. (See cut of bottom.)

Except for the lip, the entire level rim is covered with minute fine-toothing. This decorative motif has not been encountered on a rim before and adds nothing to its appearance. The rim rises slightly at the spout but juts forward one-half inch. The spout is V-shaped and detracts from the symmetry of the piece.

The handle is large, round, and of the same size throughout. It is comfortable to use. At the lower attachment are two rounded knobs. At the top of the handle a strange V-shaped wedge has been pressed between the body and the handle as though to reinforce the latter.

The glass is of fine quality, clear, brilliant, and contains few bubbles and no flaws. The workmanship was only so-so. The mold marks show plainly and the lip was left rough.

Creamer: 2-part mold, 14 ounces, 5 1/2 inches tall, 3 1/2 inches wide, and 5 3/4 inches long.

No other item in the pattern has been seen by the author. A sugar, spooner, and butter dish must have come with the creamer. Probably few items were made and still fewer sold. It has all the earmarks of belonging to the period of 1870-1880.

This cherished keepsake was graciously loaned by Mr. and Mrs. Clinton A. Sharp of Knoxville, Illinois, for inclusion here. However, after borrowing their creamer, I was later able to obtain one for my collection.

253—ARTESIA

This is another unnamed and unlisted pattern. The figurework is adequate, and with good quality glass and careful workmanship, it would have been very pretty. The glass, however, is the poorest quality I have ever seen in pressed glass. The workmanship is on a par with the glass. It is production ware at its worst and should never have reached the market, though some batches may have been of better quality. Only one who has waited in Artesia, Mississippi, from 4:00 to 10:00 A.M. between trains on a cold, dreary, winter morning could understand the reason for the above title.

The body is almost cylindrical. It is constricted slightly at the waist, and a little less so just below the rim. Around the top is a band of faceted geometric figures. It is two inches wide and almost too intricate to describe. (See drawing for details.) Above and below it are wide, short, and somewhat concave panels with rounded bottoms whose upper ends are mitred into the band. The lower panels are separated by pointed V-shaped slashes.

The base is flat and the glass there is thick. It is hollowed out underneath and contains an impressed 24-ray star. The rays vary greatly in length to form a hexagonal star. The rim has wide, uneven scallops. Its edge is rough and unfinished. The lip is wide with sharp edges. The handle has six sides, and there is a row of figurework, formed by crisscross lines, on each side panel.

Creamer: 3-part mold, 1 3/16 pounds, 4 5/8

213

inches tall, 3 3/4 inches wide, and 5 7/8 inches long. This is the only item I know of in the pattern.

254—EUDORA

Here is still another pattern that has remained unnamed and unrecognized to this time. I am naming it for the small city of Eudora in southeastern Arkansas. The standard creamer used here is without its original lid. It has a well-defined ledge to accommodate one. The piece has a narrow, curvaceous waist which flares below to form a wide, plain footing. Underneath is a high, unadorned dome.

The cylindrical body rounds out rapidly from the waist, then the straight sides ascend almost vertically to the rim where it flares slightly. At the upper and lower portions a band of beveled and slightly concave figures, shaped somewhat like football stadia with their straight sides and rounded ends, encircle the piece. Between each pair of these figures is a column in well-rounded relief. The ends of the columns are dished to conform with the other figurework. The design is simple and pleasing.

The back part of the rim is level, with a scallop over the top of each column. The front half rises on an inclined plane to the lip, which dips and curves slightly. The handle is terete with the larger blob at the bottom attachment. It is a poor simulation of an applied handle because the mold marks are high, though not sharp. The handle is comfortable to hold.

Unfortunately, the lid is gone. Lids have a high casualty rate. The design used here could have been lifted from drabness to a pinnacle of beauty with more care in the quality of the glass (poor) and in the workmanship (mediocre). With good glass and proper fire polish, it would have been beautiful. It was production ware, and the writer knows nothing of where, or by whom, it was made. It is thought to date from about 1895 to 1905. It is of "picklebottle" quality.

Creamer, without lid: 3-part mold, 12 ounces, 4 5/8 inches tall, 3 3/8 inches wide, and 4 5/8 inches long.

The creamer is the only piece of the pattern known to me. I would expect to find a covered sugar bowl; covered butter dish; spoonholder, probably with a lid; and a water pitcher with tumblers and goblets.

255—CURTAIN TIE-BACK

Mrs. Kamm, in *A Third Two Hundred Pattern Glass Pitchers*, page 118, No. 178, uses a water pitcher to describe this pattern. S. T. Millard, in *Goblets I*, Plate 35-4, shows a goblet and judged it to date from 1870 to 1880. Mrs. Metz, in *Early American Pattern Glass*, pages 130-31, No. 1451, also covers the pattern. She says it comes with two types of feet, and shows a spoonholder with four feet. My creamer has a flat round base. If the reader can imagine all glass to have been removed from the base below the cable, he will have an idea how the four footed pieces appear.

I have the clear standard creamer in this pattern, and it differs from the water pitcher in so many respects, other than size, that I have used it for comparative purposes. The more obvious differences are:

(a) The handle on the creamer is round in cross section, has no thumbgrip, and is curved throughout. The water pitcher has a six-sided angular handle with a thumbgrip.
(b) The creamer has five low scallops on each side of the rim, and the large pitcher has four.
(c) The water pitcher has a better lip which does not jut out as does the one on the creamer.
(d) The creamer has a ledge on the inside near the top to accommodate the missing lid. The water pitcher has no such ledge.
(e) The water pitcher has a wide band of down-pointing arrows just above the waist. This is absent on the creamer.
(f) The diamond point drapery on the creamer continues to the waist, becoming smaller and more rounded over the top as it descends. The lowest are mere beads.
(g) The larger piece has a plain curved waist. This is not true on the creamer.
(h) The creamer has considerable decoration on top of the foot. A cable design meanders about the base, and in its deep loops are crystal pendants of dewdrops and faceted figures. At the top of the meander are arcs of fine latticework formed by raised lines. The top of the foot is plain on the water pitcher.
(i) The underside of the creamer is plain, but the water pitcher has rounded bars, set side by side, which extend from the center to the edge. They show through from the top.
(j) The glass and workmanship of the creamer are superlative. The larger piece is somewhat off-color.

Nothing is known concerning the manufacturer of this ware. It appears to date from 1875-1885.

Standard creamer: 4-part mold, 14 ounces, 5 1/8 inches tall, 3 3/4 inches wide, and 5 1/2 inches long.

254

255

256

257

258

259

260-1

260-2

261

262

Bottom
262

263

Water pitcher: 2-part mold, weight unknown, 8 1/4 inches tall, other measurements unknown.

We know the following items were made in the pattern: standard creamer, water pitcher, goblet, tumbler, water tray, sugar bowl, spoonholder, butter dish, pickle dish, and two types of sauces.

256—PARIS

This pattern was advertised under the name PARIS in Montgomery Ward's catalog No. 68 of 1900-1901. The name probably was assigned by the manufacturer. The pattern was evidently being closed out by the manufacturer to make way for a new one. This, despite the catalog's statement of: "PARIS Pattern. One of the year's most popular patterns in medium priced goods; the color is pure crystal, very bright and sparkling, caused by each piece being thoroughly fire-polished inside and out."

Mrs. Kamm had not seen the pattern and used a very small cut from the catalog mentioned above to make her drawing in *A Fifth Pitcher Book*, page 40, No. 45. Because the drawing was from so small a cut, it is surprising that her work did not contain more inaccuracies. The standard creamer is used here to show the pattern in greater detail. On Plate 31 of her book, Mrs. Kamm shows a full-page reproduction from the catalog.

The creamer has a body shaped like a top and the neck is constricted. It has a narrow waist and sloping base. The drawing is accurate but gives an illusion of greater height.

The design is simpler than it appears. It has segments extending from rim to base. On the body and foot are nine wide, beveled, concave flutes, alternating with an equal number of prisms which have fine ribbed tops. The throat has two prominent steps. The neck flares and is slashed vertically and horizontally into nine sections. The short waist contains two bands of prismatic figures.

The foot slopes out at a sharp angle, and the top is covered with similar figures to those on the body. There is a high, hollow dome underneath.

The front fourth of the rim is rounded, smooth, and rises slightly to form a lip which has little depression. The remainder of the rim has both wide and narrow scallops over the tops of the corresponding body figures. In addition, the tops of the wide scallops are covered with smaller ones. The rim is not saddled.

The handle is round and applied. The lower attachment is a large blob. It was applied on top of the figurework, and the small cavities are impacted with grime which cannot be removed. The upper attachment is small, delta-shaped, and turned under.

As the catalog says, the glass is brilliant, sparkling, and of high quality. The excellent fire polish makes it difficult to locate the mold marks. They show faintly near the edge of the base.

Creamer: 3-part mold, 14 1/2 ounces, 5 inches tall, 3 9/16 inches wide, and 5 1/4 inches long.

These items are priced in the catalog: four-piece table set, 53¢; high, open bowl, 21¢; cake basket, 23¢; cake salver, 25¢; 5-inch square nappy, 54¢ per dozen; 9-inch square bowl, 21¢; half-gallon pitcher, 38¢; table tumbler, 60¢ per dozen; vinegar cruet, 15¢; round cake or bread plate, 8 inches, 8¢; 10-inch plate, 18¢.

257—CLIO

Mrs. Kamm and Dr. Millard had not seen and did not use this pattern in their books. Millard, in *Goblets*, Plate 142-3, does show a goblet in a similar pattern which he calls DAISY AND BUTTON WITH ALMOND BAND. His photographic illustration is indistinct, but the characteristic prisms of CLIO do not show in his pattern.

In her *Victorian Glass*, Ruth Webb Lee shows a spoonholder, covered sugar, and creamer on Plate 46-1. On page 135 she tells where the pattern was made and lists the items shown in an old catalog of Challinor, Taylor and Co. of Tarentum, Pennsylvania. She continues the original name of CLIO as given in the catalog.

As far as I can determine, no other pattern of American pressed glass has ever been given the name of a Muse. In Greek mythology, each of the nine goddesses was a Muse of one of the arts, sciences, music, or poetry. They were: Calliope, Muse of eloquence and heroic poetry; Clio, Muse of history; Erato, Muse of lyric and amatory poetry, Euterpe, Muse of music; Melpomene, Muse of tragedy; Polymnia, Muse of sacred music; Terpsichore, Muse of the dance; Thalia, Muse of comedy and bucolic poetry; and Urania, Muse of astronomy. (New Orleans has streets named for most of the Muses.)

The pattern in general appears stilted and stiff. The figurework and the clarity of the glass tend to soften the overall impression. It was drafted along geometric lines. The sides are straight and flare moderately from the waist upward. The wide bands at the waist and rim are straight and horizontal. The skirt is straight and flares sharply. The most pleasing feature of the pattern consists of two bands encircling the body. The upper band is 3/4 inch wide. Each is beveled, flat on top, and filled with evenly spaced, ovate slashes as if cut on a wheel. The body between the bands is divided into eight panels by long, sharp, and ridged prisms. At the top band the prisms are half an inch wide, and they taper to a very sharp point at the lower band. This tapering results in the intervening panels being of the same width from top to bottom. The panels are divided into three equal squares. Each contains an eight-point hobstar with a central design consisting of an octagonal button with a rayed daisy impressed in its top. (Not shown in drawing.) The entire hobstar is composed of highly faceted figures.

The rim begins at the top of the upper band. The back two-thirds is evenly scalloped with low narrow arcs. The lip curves up and out and is narrow. The flaring skirt is tall and its decoration is identical with that of the body. Underneath the base is a straight, flared dome 7/8 inch in height and with a wide, flat ceiling. The handle is plain, six-sided, and adequate. It is of the same size from top to bottom. The outer margin of each side panel is outlined by a raised line.

The water pitcher in this pattern is exactly the same as the creamer in shape and proportion, though larger. The glass and workmanship are good. It is of soda-lime glass and dates from the 1875-1885 period.

Creamer: 4-part mold, 1 pound, 5 9/16 inches tall, 3 5/8 inches wide, and 5 3/8 inches long.

The following pieces are known to have been made in the pattern: bowl, 6-inch nappy, 2 different covered bowls, 2 different butter dishes, celery tray, 2 sizes of covered compotes, creamer, plates in 3 sizes, sauce dish, spoonholder, sugar bowl, and water pitcher. It is probable that goblets and tumblers were also made.

258—CANE INSERT

In Mrs. Kamm's *A Sixth Pitcher Book*, page 38, No. 85, Plate 51, she assigned the above name to this pattern. She had not seen a piece and used a print from an 1898-1899 catalog of the Tarentum Glass Company, Tarentum, Pennsylvania, to show a covered sugar bowl. The pattern is not covered elsewhere in American glass literature.

This standard creamer is of medium size and about two-thirds as large as the sugar bowl. It sits on a wide ringbase, and has a 24-ray star impressed on the bottom.

The waist is slightly constricted and very short. It is entirely filled with a single row of small, sharp diamond point.

The main motif consists of six pointed arches extending from the waist almost to the rim. They are outlined by highly raised, and curved prisms whose upper halves have been strigiled. The lower halves (below where they converge) are flat-topped and scored with fine toothing. The arches are filled with a cane design, such as is found in a chair seat. At the bottom of each arch a 5-ray, upside down fan is mitred into the cane design. The top button of each arch is not octagonal, but extends upward into a sharp point. From the arches up to and including the rim, the piece is plain, and this area is usually found gilded.

The rim is level and evenly serrated. There is a wider scallop over the handle. The front third of the rim is plain, rises gently at the front, and pushes forward to form a lip. The handle is six-sided and plain. It is somewhat larger at the bottom than at the top. The lower attachment fits into a large octagonal escutcheon which is well beveled. The lid of the sugar bowl has the basal fans of each arch replaced by fine diamond point, but the fans remain at the base of the bowl.

The quality is good for soda-lime glass. It was made as quality ware and considerable effort was expended to make it attractive. The writer's collection contains a clear gilded creamer and an emerald-green gilded creamer with matching covered sugar bowl. The original ad lists only a sugar bowl as having been made. Perhaps the table setting as well as other items were made. It is a beautiful pattern.

Creamer: 3-part mold, 12 1/2 ounces, 4 1/4 inches tall, 3 5/16 inches wide, and 5 3/16 inches long.

259—POSSUM TAIL

This massive imitation cut glass creamer probably deserves first rank as bizarre among all the pressed glass shown in this volume. It approaches freakishness. Good design was certainly not the ultimate goal.

The ponderous handle is indeed something to behold. It starts at the back of the rim, descends to the base, wraps itself completely about the body, then ascends to the rim. It increases in size as it descends until it becomes quite wide and thick at the lower attachment. It is six-sided, and the two back and two front panels are left plain. The side panels are covered with hexagonal buttons whose surfaces are covered with impressed daisies. The spaces between the buttons are filled with triangular pyramids. Under the lower attachment, five long rays are impressed and they make up a fan.

With all its mass and weight, the handle only admits one adult finger. The handle resembles nothing so much as an opossum's tail coiled over its back.

The handle decoration necessarily covers much of the body surface. The remainder is covered with various motifs of imitation cut glass—particularly hobstars. They are all in high relief. The rim is slightly saddled and rises high to a narrow, curved spout.

The piece sits on a narrow ring which is half-round and in high relief. A hobstar is impressed on its underside. The quality of glass and workmanship are above average, but the designer undoubtedly was on a binge.

Creamer: 4-part mold, 1 5/16 pounds, 4 3/4 inches tall, 3 7/8 inches wide, and 6 5/16 inches long.

The creamer is the only article known to me, and I have abandoned the search.

260—*STAR OF THE EAST*

The above title was suggested for this pattern by Mrs. Rhoda and Mrs. Nelson of Oconomowoc, Wisconsin. The squat, square creamer has the appearance of fine cut glass. The outside surface is covered with faceted figures that refract the light and enhance the beauty of the crystal clear glass. The beveling on the figures is much deeper than usual.

The piece is thick in places (1/4 inch) and quite heavy. It is square in cross section and sits on a narrow, square base. There is a large, 20-ray star impressed into it, and the star conforms to the square pattern.

The two sides are identical and each is almost completely covered by a large, ornate, 8-ray, and highly beveled star. The points of the top and bottom rays are left plain. The three rays of each side have their points covered with small diamond point. In the center of the star is a large, octagonal, highly raised button with its top completely covered with raised hexagonal hobnails. The four corners of the creamer have thick fans arranged as shown in the drawing.

The front and back of the creamer bear the same motif as the sides but in modified form. In front, below the lip, a large palm leaf is spread. The back carries a large, plain escutcheon to receive the handle attachments. The front does not show the large octagonal button in the star that is found on the sides. A rectangle with a fan is pressed on its top. To show how the motif was

adapted to the shape of the creamer, we are also showing a front elevation.

The rim is unevenly scalloped to conform to the pattern. The handle is six-sided and has two rows of fine toothing on top to provide a secure thumbgrip. There is also a row of fine toothing down each outside corner of the handle.

The glass is clear, sparkling, and beautiful. The workmanship is excellent. It is late ware, probably from about 1915. By that time glass manufacturers had the know-how to produce superior products.

Creamer: 4-part mold, 1 pound, 3 3/8 inches tall, 3 3/4 inches wide, and 5 3/4 inches long.

The manufacturer is unknown. The only other items in the pattern known to the author are the sugar bowl and toothpick holder. Undoubtedly other items were made but probably not in colors.

261—PARACHUTE

A standard creamer in this pattern is used to illustrate size and shape and give measurements. It is also used to point out the striking dissimilarities between the way the design was employed on the creamer and the water pitcher. They differ so widely, one cannot escape the thought that perhaps one is a variant from another factory (possible but not very probable). It is a little-known pattern, and the variation may have resulted from an effort to fill space on the larger piece.

Lee and Millard did not use the pattern. Minnie Watson Kamm, in *A Fourth Pitcher Book*, page 130, No. 171, named and described it using the water pitcher as a guide. (The difference in size and shape is obvious.) These points of deviation exist between the two pitchers:

(a) The water pitcher has a scalloped rim. The creamer has a plain saddled one.

(b) The water pitcher has a wide band of fine ribbing around the body above and below the wide parachute figurework. On the creamer these bands are missing.

(c) The interstices around the figurework of parachutes on the water pitcher are filled with English hobnail. (diamonds with flat tops and four tiny cubes impressed on each). Similar spaces on the creamer are filled with sunk diamond point.

(d) The waist ends on a shelf on the foot of the water pitcher. This is lacking on the creamer.

(e) The handle of the water pitcher is oval in cross section and simulates an applied one with the large blob at the lower attachment. On the creamer, there is no simulation of handwork. Its handle is six-sided and wider than it is thick. The side panels are covered with cross-ribbing from top to bottom. At the top of the handle, and also half-way down, the side panels are pinched together and the cross-ribbing varies in length. It appears to be a noticeable defect, but it seems to have been accomplished purposely—perhaps for aesthetic reasons.

Nothing is known as to when, or by whom, it was made. It has the appearance of ware dating from 1880-1890. The glass has a brownish tinge and nothing about the piece achieves true quality. It is not fire polished.

Standard creamer: 3-part mold, 12 ounces, 4 7/8 inches tall, 3 inches wide, and 4 5/8 inches long.

Water pitcher: 3-part mold, weight unknown, 8 inches tall, other measurements unknown.

The two pitchers discussed here are the only pieces of the pattern known to the writer. Perhaps I should say the two pieces are the only ones known in either pattern.

262—JACOB'S COAT

Mrs. Kamm and Dr. Millard did not describe this pattern. Ruth Webb Lee, in *Early American Pressed Glass*, Pattern 227, page 533, and Plate 115, described and illustrated it. She considered the name absurd because the pattern was not multicolored, but nevertheless continued it. It has always been my understanding that Jacob had the "ladder" and Joseph the "coat of many colors." The name (by all that's holy), should have been Joseph's Coat. (Unless perhaps Jacob had a coat for winter wear.) Since the misnomer is well established and widely known, I am continuing it. I like the pattern a little better than Mrs. Lee did.

Belknap, in his *Milk Glass*, on Plate 202b, shows a covered butter dish in milk-white glass and calls it JACOB'S COAT.

The figure-work of the pattern is composed of tiny components in low relief which impart an overall open, lacy effect. The glass has a cool frosty appearance. The lines of the pattern were not conceived or crafted by an artist. It is pure folk art. The shape of the creamer is primarily composed of curves, while the covered butter dish is made up of straight lines and sharp angles. The pieces are not homogeneous except by configuration.

The standard creamer is almost cylindrical, curving in only slightly at the waist. The body is round, and the figurework is divided into six wide panels, separated by six narrow ones. The latter are a series of parallel, closely placed, small, raised, and tilted cigar-shaped figures. They are framed by a band of tiny dewdrops which loop at the top. The wide panels contain two large squares, each of which stands on a corner. They

are quartered into smaller blocks with the top and bottom ones filled with fine diamond point. The two side squares are filled with raised, formalized square daisies. Each panel also contains four large stippled triangles with a large dewdrop in the center. All triangles and squares are bordered by a row of minute beading.

There is a thick quarter-inch band around the top of the body at the rim. It is closely filled with vertical capsules in high relief. The rim has unusual curves which are not particularly appealing. It dips in front, then arches up again to a wide, stiff lip. The glass is thick on the flat rim and not well finished off—sharp edges were left.

The waist is wide, short, and vertical. It is filled with a quarter-inch belt of small prisms. From the ring waist, the base flares out and remains plain. On the underside the piece has a pretty lacy design. (See drawing of bottom.) This design is on the flat roof of a half-inch high dome.

The handle is six-sided with none of the angular corners rounded off. The two side panels are outlined with barely perceptible, but very sharp-pointed dewdrops. It has a knop well down from the top and another at the bottom. Neither is aesthetic or useful.

This is average production ware of the 1880's and probably into the 1890's. It is clear, not very brilliant, and the mold marks show but are not sharp. The pattern is similar to MOSIAC *(sic)* and JARDINIERE, two other patterns covered in Mrs. Kamm's books.

Creamer: 3-part mold, 14 ounces, 4 3/4 inches tall, 3 3/4 inches wide, and 5 5/8 inches long.

At least the four-piece table set, goblet, sauce dish, and celery vase were made.

263—CLARENDON

As more and more previously unnamed patterns of American pressed glass are located, one wonders if there ever will be an end. The creamer shown here invokes such thoughts. The task of naming them seems incredibly large and difficult until we remember what has been done by others in similar and more difficult lines. In the vegetable kingdom plants run into hundreds of thousands, but Linnaeus (Karl von Linné, the famous Swedish naturalist) took on the stupendous job of listing and naming them. He persevered and produced one of the great milestones of human knowledge and endeavour. Contrasted with such an undertaking, the task of naming several hundred out of fewer than five thousand patterns may seem trivial. Nevertheless, it needs to be done.

This pattern is named *CLARENDON* in honor of the little Arkansas city with tree-lined streets on the banks of the White River.

The standard creamer shown here is vaseline colored. No doubt it was also made in other colors. The pattern is somewhat attractive, but not sufficiently so to cause it to be purchased in preference to other more lovely patterns at no higher price.

The body has six convexed columns which start at the base in high relief and diminish until they almost disappear one-half inch below the rim. From the waist down, the columns are thick and flare widely to form the six heavy scallops that the piece rests on. Each column is rounded over at the end. Around the middle of the body is a raised, plain 7/8-inch-wide belt without decoration.

In this case, great restraint was used in the decoration. The wide band encircling the center, which provided such a good space for enameled or engraved flowers, was left plain. This was in an era when almost everything was decorated, fringed, or tasseled. When the gilt was added, it was applied sparingly and with care. Only the top of the rim was gilded. A hairline of gilt is seen on the narrow, beveled edges of the central band, and a similar line is found across the top of each scalloped foot. They are less than 1/16 inch wide, and no other gilt is found anywhere.

The glass of the rim is thin, but near the bottom it becomes massive. The bottom of the bowl can be seen through the sides and is 7/16 inch thick. The glass is heavy and of excellent quality. The workmanship is good. The design is not that of a prize winner.

The rim on either side has a large round scallop flanked by two smaller ones. There is a high rise in the back for the upper handle attachment. The front quarter of the rim rises slightly, then levels off to a lip which does not dip, and does not extend very far forward. Beneath the base is a large, wide dome left unadorned.

The handle is round in cross section and rather small for so heavy a piece. It increases in size as it descends and for the last inch spreads rapidly into a reeded end which splays on the body. The manufacturer is unknown to the writer, but it resembles ware of the Riverside Glass Company. It seems to date from 1885-1895.

Creamer: 3-part mold, 1 pound, 4 5/8 inches tall, 3 5/16 inches wide, and 4 3/4 inches long.

No other items are known in this pattern, but certainly the other three pieces of a four-piece table set must have been made.

264—CONCAVE BLOCK

This pattern was made after glass manufacturers had perfected the art of glassmaking. Clarity and brilliance by then had superseded the fancy work which all too often, in the past, had served to cover up imperfections of the mix. This glass was mirror polished by a final fluoric acid bath which added a sparkling beauty without extra handling. Its clarity and brilliance are unexcelled. The pattern has not previously been listed in glass literature, and the above name is assigned.

The creamer is hexagonal in shape on the outside and cylindrical within. The sides are vertical. It is heavy for its size and thick—1/2 inch at the base and corners and 3/8 inch at the rim.

The pattern has six panels, each composed of two large, rectangular blocks. Each block is deeply beveled on all four sides, and the front is concave from top to bottom. This results in two bands of blocks around, and covering, the body. The concave beveled blocks have the appearance of early cut glass. All margins are true, sharp, and well molded. The rim is flat and level. The front two-thirds rises to form an arched, outthrust spout. The spout is a little narrow and is neither graceful nor pretty.

The shape of the handle indicates the period in which it was made. (See CHIPPENDALE and ARCHED PANEL on page 107 of Kamm's *Two Hundred Pattern Glass Pitchers*, and ARISTOCRAT in this book, for similar handles.) These pieces were manufactured from 1907-1910. The handle has six flat, undecorated panels and is becoming in its simplicity. It is heavier and thicker at the bottom than at the top. The creamer's base is hexagonal and attractive. (See cut.) Underneath, it contains a large, plain, and sunken 32-ray star. Around the star is a flat band of radial fine rib on which the creamer sits.

On the bottom of the inside is a 3/4-inch slightly raised circle. Circles of this kind are often seen in the bottoms of pressed glass creamers and may or may not be a manufacturer's mark. Some known Northwood patterns have them. No mold marks can be found on the piece, but it must have been from a 3-part mold.

Creamer: 3-part mold, 1 3/8 pounds, 4 5/8 inches tall, 3 1/2 inches wide, and 5 3/4 inches long.

Undoubtedly a sugar bowl, butter dish, and spooner were made in the pattern. A water pitcher, water tray, tumbler, goblet, cracker jar, pickle jar, bowl, nappy, compotes, and other items probably will be found. A complete set of this pat-

Bottom
264

264

265

Bottom
266

266

267

Bottom
267

268

Bottom
268

269

270

Bottom
270

271

tern would make a magnificent table setting—but would be impractical for regular use because of its weight.

265—SAVANNAH

This simple, charming pattern is named in honor of the fine old city of Savannah, Georgia. It is one of many similar patterns that combine simplicity of design with superior quality and workmanship. Many have flat panels ranging from four to twenty-four. This particular one has six and is distinguished from the others by V-shaped flutes which separate the panels. Each panel is arched over the top.

The panels start below the rim and follow the contours of the piece down through the narrow stem and on to the edge of the hexagonal foot. The flutes stop short of the stem.

There is an incurved, 1/2-inch-wide, plain band around the rim. Here the creamer is round, but elsewhere it is hexagonal.

The handle also is six-sided, and it provides an inadequate opening for adult fingers. However, the piece is small and can be handled by gripping the handle between the thumb and finger.

The handle portion of the rim is evenly scalloped. The forepart arches up and then dips to form a lip.

Heisey made many patterns of this type, but most of them bore a trademark and were also of uniformly excellent quality. This piece is not marked and has a small bubble, so I suspect it is not Heisey ware. It probably dates from about 1905. The mold marks are hard to find.

Small creamer: 3-part mold, 12 ounces, 4 15/16 inches tall, 2 13/16 inches wide, and 4 9/16 inches long.

A large number of items were probably made.

266—KLONDYKE

In 1882 Mr. Stephen Hipkins founded a shop at Martins Ferry, Ohio, to manufacture molds in which to press glass. His molds were sold in great numbers over a period of many years to glass houses throughout the Middle West. His four sons worked in his shop most of their lives, and in 1951 two were still living. Mr. Howard Hipkins (then eighty-two years old), of Barnesville, Ohio, gave Mrs. Kamm much information about their molds and the glass manufacturers to whom they were sold. KLONDYKE was made in their shop. Strangely, molds of the identical pat-

tern were sold to, and used by, three other glass houses.

The piece shown here was manufactured under the name AMBERETTE by the Dalzell, Gilmore and Leighton Company of Findlay, Ohio. Their advertisement of 1897-1898 shows the four-piece table setting and has this to say: "Something entirely new and handsome, the panels are satin finished, figure bands are stained old gold, while the deep mitres on each side are bright crystal, giving the most striking and beautiful effect of anything ever placed on the market. The line consists of 40 pieces of the most beautiful articles for table use. Amberette Ware in crystal is known as 75D, it is an exceptionally bright pattern, the shapes are striking and original." See Kamm's *A Sixth Pitcher Book*, Plate 15, for a cut of the old ad. Also see her *A Seventh Pitcher Book*, Plate 96, for another view of the setting.

The A. J. Beatty Company of Findlay, Ohio, put the pattern out as KLONDYKE. They used a different method of decoration—baked on enamels. See Kamm's *A Second Two Hundred Pattern Glass Pitchers*, page 100.

The pattern was also manufactured by the Findlay Glass Company of Findlay, Ohio. We do not know how they decorated their ware or the name under which it was marketed.

There already are three or four patterns called AMBERETTE so I am using the KLONDYKE title instead.

A large square standard creamer is shown here. The four sides bulge a little between top and bottom. At the widest part of each side are two 3/4-inch wide bands which cross at right angles. They are made up of printed hobnail. The squares, formed where they cross, are filled with diamond point and are left clear. Radiating from each corner of the intersection is an intaglio fan. The bands are flashed with golden amber, and thus each side, as well as the base, displays a cross of gold. The base is square and has a pattern as shown in the cut.

The four corners of the creamer were slashed off and left clear. All other flat surfaces were acid-etched to a satin finish. The six-sided handle appears to be applied, but the mold mark shows and applied handles are never flat-sided. Both handle and lip stand higher than the rim. The rim has large, low, broad scallops.

The golden effect of the golden crosses against the frosted background is both striking and beautiful. The quality of the glass and the workmanship are excellent. The glass is neither thick nor heavy.

Creamer: only one mold mark shows, weight 1 pound, 4 1/8 inches tall, 3 5/8 inches wide, and 5 5/8 inches long.

267—BOGALUSA

This late pattern of the pressed glass fraternity made its debut about the same time as the above Louisiana city—between 1905 and 1910. It has not previously been named, and nothing is known of its background. The above name will serve until the original is known—if ever.

This small, squatty creamer is shaped like a custard cup and has some charm. A little more care in bringing the metal and mold to the proper temperature at the time of pressing would have improved it. The lower part of each panel shows hairline thumbprints containing whorls, valleys, etc., impressed in the glass. Either cold metal or a cold mold caused the defects. As any gaffer or Bertillon expert knows, fingerprints should be found on glass, not impressed in it.

The top of the creamer is large, round, and wider than the base. (See cut of bottom.) A smooth, concave 1/2-inch-wide band encircles the flat top. It has been gilded. The gilt is now worn off and the piece appears drab. The rim is round, level, and smooth, with a slight dip in front for a small, narrow lip. There is much about the piece to convince me it was originally designed as a punch or custard cup and later converted into a creamer by means of the slight dip for a lip.

The main motif consists of six wide, dished flutes with flat bases ending at the creamer's foot. They flare widely, and their tops are high, rounded loops. Where the flutes join they form high, sharp corners, and this makes the lower half of the creamer hexagonal in shape. Above the flutes, and below the plain band at the top is an irregular space which is filled with large sunk diamond point. The bottom of each depression is rounded rather than pointed.

The small handle has six sides as well as many curves and angles. It is enlarged at the lower attachment. The quality of the glass is all that could be expected of soda-lime glass. Poor workmanship resulted in the undesirable fingerprints.

Small creamer: 3-part mold, 6 ounces, 2 5/16 inches tall, 3 5/16 inches wide, and 4 7/16 inches long.

No other items are known to the writer. Because of its lateness we can expect to find a number of unusual items such as: rose bowl, tall vases, punch bowl and cup, handled nappy, covered cracker jar, toothpick and match holder,

custard cup, parfait, sherbet cup, and cup and saucer. The usual standard-sized items were almost certainly produced.

268—PANELLED PALM

S. T. Millard, in his *Goblets II*, Plate 37-2, named this pattern PANELLED PALM, and it is a good title. The panels on the goblet he used were flashed with amethyst. From this, it is likely that we will find pieces flashed with ruby, amber, green, and some with gilt. This feature dates the piece from 1893-1905. The writer has a creamer and water pitcher, but neither is colored.

The creamer is of good quality late glass, with a simple and effective pattern that has some of the features of cut glass. It is more pleasing than the overdecorated, imitation cut glass of the same period. The glass is clear and brilliant, but without resonance. It bears no trademark, and the maker is unknown.

The creamer is low, wide, and has six raised and rounded panels. Into each a palm frond is deeply impressed. The panels have Gothic arches at their tops and are framed by beveled prisms. The latter have 1/4-inch-wide bands of interlocking triangles on their crests. Where the borders meet between the panels, they mesh and make a 3/8-inch band of raised diamonds and triangles. They then bend and continue under the base as shown in the cut. The creamer sits flat, and in the center of the base is a hexagonal hobstar. (See cut of bottom.)

The handle has six sides and is wider than it is thick. It is severely plain but its type of attachments are not too often seen. The rim is unevenly scalloped as shown in the drawing. The lip appears "at home" on the piece.

Creamer: 3-part mold, 11 ounces, 3 3/8 inches tall, 3 1/2 inches wide, and 5 inches long.

Water pitcher: 3-part mold, weight unknown, 7 5/8 inches tall, 4 5/8 inches wide, and 7 1/4 inches long.

On the water pitcher the pattern does not bend under to form the base. It sits on a heavy ring 1/2 inch high, with a dome underneath. The waist is slightly constricted. With a goblet, creamer, and water pitcher known to have been made, other pieces may be expected to appear.

269—CANNON BALL PINWHEEL

This pattern is quite similar to the one that follows it, and the two are often confused. They are shown together to illustrate the differences.

Mrs. Kamm used a tall milk or lemonade pitcher to describe this pattern and named it CANNON BALL PINWHEEL. See her *A Fourth Pitcher Book*, page 140, No. 188, for details. She thought it was a product of the 1890's. Ruth Webb Lee did not describe or use the pattern. She did illustrate an earlier pattern but called it PINWHEEL; therefore the latter title is preempted.

In his *Goblets*, Plate 100-1, S. T. Millard shows a goblet, named it PINWHEEL, and thought it was made in the 1880's. His particular PINWHEEL pattern is the one described here and is not the same as illustrated and named by Mrs. Lee. Mrs. Metz shows a goblet and called it PINWHEEL but thought there was little value to any piece other than the goblet.

Because the title PINWHEEL was preempted when Millard called this pattern by that name, we now have two patterns with the same title. Mrs. Kamm realized this and tried to avoid confusion by calling this pattern CANNON BALL PINWHEEL. I have used her title.

The standard creamer differs in shape from the milk pitcher, and is smaller than the average standard creamer. It sits on a flat, wide ringbase and is quite stable, whereas the taller pitcher is easily overturned. In the low, flat, domed space underneath, a round 29-ray star is impressed. The odd number is intriguing.

The sides of the body curve in sl thtt the waist and flare from the latter to the rim. Above the waist and below the rim a plain band surrounds the piece. Most of the body is covered by a wide belt of figurework composed of four circles with alternating, vertical ellipses. Each ellipse overlaps two circles and cuts an arc from each. The top and bottom portions of each ellipse are filled with fine cut figures. The two lateral triangular segments are filled with short, wide ribbed fans. Each circle contains a beautiful whirling pinwheel with a large and highly raised cannon ball at its center. Above and below each pinwheel is a half-inch-wide arched prism topped by sharp pointed pyramids which resemble the meshed teeth of a shark.

The milk pitcher has a one-inch-wide band of impressed rays below the pinwheels. It was utilized to fill space on the taller pitcher, and is not found on the creamer. The rim corresponds in general to the top of the design. The wide scallops are crenulated and the narrow ones are left plain.

The handle has two features intended to be decorative, but which would have been better omitted. They have not been used on other patterns—for good reason. On the side panels of the six-sided handle is a row of sharp-pointed pyramids, similar to those around the circles on the body. They do prevent slipping, but they are also so sharp and uncomfortable that they must have been highly unpopular. On top and at the rear of this ugly handle is an arched dip with two sharp-edged V-shaped ridges on each side.

The quality of the milk pitcher is excellent. The creamer, however, is mere production ware of poor quality. Either molds or the metal were too cool, for the surface is rough and full of hairlines. The glass is not clear, is full of bubbles, and the piece was not fire polished. The mold marks are prominent, and the piece lacks luster. There was no necessity to make it—nor to write it up for that matter. Some pieces, however, may match the excellent quality of the larger pitcher.

Standard creamer: 4-part mold, 13 ounces, 4 inches tall, 3 3/4 inches wide, and 5 1/2 inches long.

Milk or lemonade pitcher: ART MOLD, WEIGHT UNKNOWN, 6 1/2 INCHES TALL, OTHER MEASUREMENTS UNKNOWN. The two pitchers and goblet are the only pieces known to the author.

270—BULL'S EYE AND FAN

Mrs. Kamm named and described this pattern using a tall, slender creamer in her *Two Hundred Pattern Glass Pitchers*, page 58, No. 75. She believed it was first produced in the 1890's, but she was aware it was still being made in 1908.

S. T. Millard, in his *Goblets II*, Plate 92-3, called it DAISY IN OVAL PANELS, PURPLE and thought it was made in the 1880's. In Plate 115-3 he again referred to it by that name because of the daisy in each panel. The round figures are really hobstars with round, flat, beveled centers rather than daisies or bull's eyes. Mrs. Kamm's title for the pattern is continued as slightly better than Millard's, though both are misnomers. Metz showed a goblet as No. 2467 and called it DAISIES IN OVAL PANELS.

The pattern is being used to furnish some additional information. The small creamer shown here is somewhat wider than the tall one used by Mrs. Kamm; also it differs at the waist and bottom.

Eight bobbin-shaped figures standing on end, and side by side, cover the body from the waist almost to the rim. In the center of each is a round hobstar with a round, beveled and flat-topped button. Above and below each hobstar is a whorled fan in high relief which fills the ends of the bobbins. Above them is an irregular, plain band extending to the rim. This was originally gilded but is now well worn. Below the bobbins are beveled triangular figures which extend through the waist and out to the base.

The waist is plain, round, and thick, but narrower than the body. The tall creamer of Mrs. Kamm's has a narrow, fluted waist and a skirted base which is hollow and plain underneath. The smaller creamer is lower, wider, and beneath the base has an attractive pressed design. (See drawing of bottom.)

The rim is rounded and irregularly scalloped. It inclines slightly forward to form the lip, which then droops straight down. This is an extreme I have not seen before on pressed glass. It could only have been so shaped after the piece was removed from the mold. It pouts.

The handle is small, six-sided, and provides a poor grip. The glass is fair quality lime-soda. The finishing is good. The mold marks are barely perceptible. The maker of this ware is not known to the author.

Small creamer: 4-part mold, 8 ounces, 3 7/16 inches tall, 3 1/4 inches wide, and 4 1/2 inches long.

Tall, slender creamer: 3-part mold, 10 ounces, 5 5/8 inches tall, 2 9/16 inches wide, and 4 inches long.

The pattern, as would be expected of glass tableware made as late as 1908, was produced in a wide range of articles.

271—OPTIC FLUTE

Minnie Watson Kamm, in *A Seventh Pitcher Book*, page 45, No. 91 and Plate 83, illustrated this creamer from an old catalog of the Imperial Glass Company of Bellaire, Ohio. She had not personally seen a piece of the pattern. Had she, she might have assigned a more appropriate name. Actually there are no flutes on the piece, though it does have raised columns on the inside that resemble panels rather than flutes when seen from the outside. The catalog illustrated the company's "No. 4" pattern, and it said their "No. 6" pattern was the same except fluted. It was probably produced between 1905 and 1915. It does not carry a trademark, though later the company used several trademarks. One such was 'Nu-Cut' with a flourish above and below on their imitation cut glass.

The standard creamer is a quality product. The glass is beautifully clear and sparkling, is quite heavy, and has some resonance. It is free of bubbles and impurities. The workmanship is excellent.

The outside of the bowl is cylindrical. The inside has ten wide, convex columns which do not reach the rim. They are arched on top. These inverted columns show to excellent advantage through the clear glass. The sides are vertical. On the front two-thirds of the body is an acid-etched, formalized leaf and vine design.

At the bottom of the bowl is a band of pressed design. On the sides it is represented by a series of small, raised cubes standing on their corners. The face of each cube has been crosscut to make four smaller cubes. When viewed from underneath, each cube is seen as the end, or cross section, of a highly raised prism that gradually disappears into the base. (See cut.)

The piece sits on a wide ringbase. It is flat underneath, except for a large 22-ray impressed star. The back two-thirds of the rim has wide even scallops which do not match the inside columns. The lip is raised to a considerable degree, then arches over and forward. The handle is round, and applied, with the large blob at the bottom attachment. Mrs. Kamm thought it was a pressed handle.

Creamer: 3-part mold, 1 1/16 pounds, 4 5/8 inches tall, 3 1/2 inches wide, and 5 1/2 inches long.

The catalog shows the following items to have been made: individual creamer, individual covered sugar bowl, standard creamer, covered butter, covered sugar, spoonholder, celery vase, two sizes of berry bowls, two sizes of footed compotes, two sizes of footed jellies, wine, goblet, three sizes of footed bowls, and a water pitcher.

272—BEADED ELLIPSE

In *A Third Two Hundred Pattern Glass Pitchers*, page 106, No. 160, Minnie Watson Kamm shows a round creamer in this pattern without a lid. The creamer shown here, also without its lid, is different from the one used by Mrs. Kamm, though it is still of the same pattern. Her creamer was round and this is oval. Her piece sat on a scalloped base conforming to the figurework at the bottom. This creamer sits on a wide skirted base encircled by a ring of dewdrops. There is a hollow, oval dome underneath.

The creamer shown here has twelve long, beaded loops about the body. (The Kamm creamer has nine.) The inside of each loop is in high convex relief with a tier of three thumbprints. Each thumbprint is ringed with a circle of tiny beading. They were given a treatment not seen elsewhere in American pressed glass. Instead of being left plain, to act as lenses, they were stippled. Where the dewdrop lines make a round loop at the base, they form large, stippled teardrops with long slashes up their centers. Small twin teardrops fill the interstices between the loops at top and bottom.

The rim is evenly scalloped to match the tops of the loops. In the rear it leans to become part of the handle. In front it spreads out to form a wide lip. The handle has six sides and, except for the thumbgrip, is left plain. At the top, on the inside, is a sharply defined ledge for a lid. This piece was manufactured as a container for prepared mustard or other condiment. It is of the same order as FLICKERING FLAME shown in this book. Regrettably, the mortality rate of the lids of these intriguing pieces is extremely high.

This is average production ware. When filled with prepared mustard it probably retailed for ten cents. The Westmoreland Specialty Company produced a great many varieties of this type of ware and may have made this piece. The mold marks are high and some are sharp.

Creamer without lid: 4-part mold, 11 1/2 ounces, 3 3/4 inches tall, 3 3/8 inches wide, and 5 13/16 inches long.

The round and oval creamers described above, each now lidless, are the only pieces of this pattern I have seen or am aware of.

273—BEVELED SLASHES

There are both large and small creamers in this pattern. They are similar and in the shape of bowls. The larger is shown here. The glass is necessarily thick and heavy to permit the deep slashes of the design. The bowl sits on a half-inch-high ringbase decorated on the underside by an attractive 12-ray, complex star. It has many faceted bits of varying shapes. (See cut of bottom.) The individual creamer has a plain star underneath.

The body has a unique and complex decorative motif, much of it resulting from a series of slashed U-shaped figures. These cross and interlace in a way difficult to describe. There are long, irregular, flat-topped, and beveled figures, in pairs, and with smooth edges. Between each pair are long, tapering, kitelike prisms (also in pairs) in high relief. Irregularly shaped and high raised figures fill the remaining spaces down to the waist.

There is a plain half-inch-wide band immediately below the flat rim. On the individual creamer the rim is coarsely scalloped. At the top of the body's figurework is a line of alternating round and pointed arches. The lip is low and

small. On the standard creamer the handle is applied. There is a raised, beveled escutcheon for the bottom attachment and the blob fills it exactly. On the individual creamer the handle is round, quite small, and pressed. The quality is excellent, and the creamers are attractive, though the design is sufficiently intricate to be confusing.

Standard creamer: 4-part mold, 1 pound, 4 inches tall, 5 inches wide, and 5 inches long.

Individual creamer: 4-part mold, 5 ounces, 2 1/2 inches tall, 2 1/2 inches wide, and 3 9/16 inches long.

No other item in the pattern is known to the author, though there must have been two sugar bowls. The manufacturer is also unknown. It bears no trademark. It appears to be a product of the 1885-1905 period.

274—CRESCENT CITY

This creamer was purchased by mail as BRITANNIC, a pattern which Mrs. Kamm shows in *A Fourth Pitcher Book*. On cursory inspection there is a resemblance, but the two patterns would not be confused by anyone familiar with either.

The low oval creamer shown here has not been previously described in our literature. The ridged crescents in high relief are the dominant feature of the pattern and suggest New Orleans, the exotic and lovely old city of the Deep South affectionately known as the Crescent City because it nestles in a great bend of the Mississippi River.

The bottom is elliptical and the piece sits flat on a wide raised base. Deeply impressed underneath is a large, 20-ray star which conforms to the basal shape.

The top of the bowl has a wide, plain band around it. It probably was often gilded or flashed with ruby stain. The lower two-thirds of the body is covered by a wide band of figurework. A series of eight pairs of "wet and dry moons" or crescents forms the pattern. Each crescent is in high relief and has a sharp spine. In the circular areas formed by the juncture of two opposing crescents are rosettes of cut glass figures. They consist of a single large rectangular pyramid, surrounded by eight smaller triangular ones. All interstices above, below, and between the crescents are filled with similar, raised pyramids. The high relief of the figures on the sides produces a definite bulge on the outside but not on the inside.

The rim is long and sweeping with no dip for the lip. It is flat on top with its corners slightly chamfered to knock off rough burrs.

A high-powered magnifying glass was neces-

272

Bottom
273

273

274

275

276

277

278

279

280

Bottom
280

281

sary before I was convinced the handle truly was pressed rather than applied. This particular handle would fool many authorities on pressed glass. The large round blob at the lower attachment is made so that it actually appears to flow into the figurework. (See drawing for details.) This blob has the rounded edge at the point of juncture we expect to find on applied handles. The handle is round in cross section and also in general outline. It is so clear it magnifies the mold mark on the inside surface until it can be seen. It cannot be felt.

The glass is magnificently clear, brilliant, and sparkling. It has no defects. The workmanship of the designer and mold chipper was of a very high order as shown to good advantage in the care taken with the handle. The gaffer made sure the finished product was put on the market with an excellent fire polish. The mold marks can only be found after a diligent search. This is definitely quality ware. Nothing is known as where, or by whom, it was manufactured. It has all the earmarks of having been made between 1890 and 1900 and probably was put out for the Columbian Exposition in Chicago during 1893.

Creamer: 4-part mold, 8 ounces, 2 3/4 inches tall, 2 3/4 inches wide, and 5 5/8 inches long.

No other item in the pattern is known to the writer. I would expect, however, to find a full range of tableware, and it would indeed be a charming ensemble.

275—BORDERED ELLIPSE

This pattern was described, illustrated, and named by Minnie Watson Kamm in *A Fourth Pitcher Book*, page 99, No. 121. A cursory inspection of the creamer she used and the one illustrated here would seem to indicate that they are identical, but close study will reveal a number of ways in which they differ. I have a feeling that a single mold maker, perhaps from the Hipkins Novelty Mold Shop of Martins Ferry, Ohio, designed and made similar molds for two, three, or more glass factories. Each varied in minor details from the others. This is known to have happened in many other instances. It is also known that the same company was sometimes furnished two or more molds for a single item and that there were differences in them. (NORTHWOOD'S PANELLED CHERRY is a case in point. I have seen five different tumblers in this pattern, all bearing the Northwood trademark.)

The following differences exist between our creamer and that of Mrs. Kamm. (Who may not have actually seen the one she described.):

(a) This creamer has never had a lid and was not designed to hold one. Mrs. Kamm's creamer has a well-defined ledge on the inside near the top to hold a lid. It was marketed as a condiment container.
(b) This creamer has eight pointed ellipses about the body. Mrs. Kamm's creamer had six.
(c) The ellipses in this instance are highly beveled and flat surfaced. The Kamm creamer had convexed ellipses.
(d) The handle of this creamer is thicker and shorter than that of the other one.
(e) The ringbase of this creamer is heavier than on the one Mrs. Kamm used and is also rounded.
(f) This piece has a 16-ray star impressed in the flat bottom, while the creamer of Mrs. Kamm has an 18-ray star.
(g) This creamer is slightly higher.

The two variants would match nicely in a complete table setting, and only an astute student of pattern glass could tell the difference.

This is excellent lime-soda glass, which is well fire polished. It is a quality product. It appears to date from 1889 to 1895 and to be from the Ohio Valley. Nothing definite is known as to its background.

Creamer: 4-part mold, 13 ounces, 4 4/5 inches tall, 3 1/2 inches wide, and 5 1/2 inches long.

The creamer shown here is the only item of this particular variety known to the author.

276—MOBILE

This is an attractive small creamer in a pattern not previously described in American glass literature. In *Goblets*, Plate 124-3, Millard shows a goblet quite similar to and yet different from this pattern. He called it FINECUT AND RIBBED BARS. As well as I can determine, Mrs. Kamm covered the same pattern, but called it LADDERS WITH DIAMOND in her *An Eighth Pitcher Book*, page 42, No. 79. In any event, this creamer is not the one described by either.

There is a band of six large, complex diamonds around the upper half of the body. They are outlined by long, faceted prisms whose tops are fine-toothed. Inside each such frame is a single diamond composed of nine smaller diamonds whose tips are flattened.

Below this band is another filled with six large concave boat-shaped slips. Separating the slips are two highly raised buttresses, or docks, whose faces are cross-ribbed. They are separated by long, deep V-shaped slashes. The entire effect resembles the docks of the beautiful city of azaleas—Mobile, Alabama. Above the diamonds is a plain zigzagged band, which was probably often gilded or flashed with ruby.

The body is slightly constricted in the middle portion and somewhat larger at base and rim. The rim has low, wide scallops over the diamonds and they in turn are scalloped. The front third of the rim is plain. It rises slightly, then tilts forward to form a small lip.

The bottom of the bowl curves under to form a wide and flat base. The glass at the edge of the base is a full 5/8 inch thick. Underneath, a large, deeply impressed, 12-ray star is found.

The handle is pressed, but it is an excellent imitation of an applied one. I, myself, thought it to be an applied handle until at long last I located an almost imperceptible mold mark. The handle is terete, with a large round blob for the bottom attachment and a smaller one turned under, for the upper.

This is quality ware of a standard consistent with the skill and technology of the era. It is brilliantly clear, sparkling, heavy, and has some resonance when tapped, though it is soda-lime glass. It is free of bubbles, specks, and discolorations and has a perfect fire polish. The workmanship of both the mold chipper and gaffer was outstanding.

Small creamer: 3-part mold, 11 ounces, 3 1/4 inches tall, 3 1/4 inches wide, and 4 9/16 inches long.

In size this piece is about midway between an individual and a standard creamer. Usually items of this size were not made in a pattern unless a large number of other articles was also produced. It is believed to date from 1905-1915. As many as 125 items (or more) may have been manufactured. It is an effective piece of imitation cut glass, and a complete table setting would have been a prized possession.

277—MALVERN
IMPERIAL No. 9

Mrs. Kamm, in *A Seventh Pitcher Book*, page 61, No. 123 and Plate 82, called this piece by its old catalog number and added the company's name. She had not seen a piece of the pattern, and her drawing was made entirely from the catalog. The pattern is shown again here for the purpose of description and measurement. Most collectors have difficulty in remembering patterns when numbers are used in the title. For this reason a name without numbers is assigned to this beautiful, but not very old, pattern. Its beauty reminds one of the tree-shaded streets of Malvern, Arkansas, and its seventy-five different items equal the products of that little industrial city. It

is, therefore, named *MALVERN*.

It was made by the Imperial Glass Company of Bellaire, Ohio (which still produces fine glass). They were organized in 1902, and this was pattern No. 9 of their first catalog issued about 1904. It was produced in clear and also with a wide gilded top band. The latter pieces were impressive.

The waist is wide, considering the small size of the individual creamer. It has eight wide, flat panels which arch out and down. They are rounded at the bottom and form a wide scalloped base for it to rest on. There is a high, flat-topped dome underneath with an 18-ray, round star impressed therein.

The waist panels extend well up on the sides and have curved arches which reach a sharp point 3/4 inch below the rim. The beveled faces of the arches cross and continue upward and laterally till they meet midway above the junction of the arches. They thus form eight elongated, kite-shaped figures, each of which is filled with hexagonal buttons, in both horizontal and diagonal rows. The small spaces between the buttons are filled with triangular pyramids. Above the kite-shaped areas, the body is smooth and plain with the bottom edge zigzagged.

The back portion of the rim has five large, low scallops, and each, in turn, contains three or four smaller scallops. The front part of the rim is plain. It rises slightly, then dips just enough to form a lip.

The top member of the handle juts back horizontally, then curves back to the body. The two top and back faces of the handle are filled with close-set thumbprints. The quality is excellent for soda-lime glass.

Small creamer: 4-part mold, 8 1/2 ounces, 3 3/8 inches tall, 3 inches wide, and 4 1/2 inches long.

The seventy-five articles produced in the pattern include: 7 1/2-inch water carafe; standard creamer; covered sugar bowl; covered butter dish; spoonholder; celery vase; covered pickle jar; tumbler; 1/2-gallon water pitcher; covered cracker jar; 7- and 8-inch covered compotes; 1/2-gallon bulbous water pitcher; quart pitcher; crimped compotes, 4 1/2, 7, and 8 inches; salt and pepper shakers; molasses can; rose bowl; cruet; custard cup; toothpick holder; eggcup; sherbet cup; goblet; low lamp with handle; globe to match lamp; tall lamp; electric light globe; wine; claret; champagne; water tray; two-handled oval lemonade tray; wine tray; wine decanter; sugar sifter; and many sizes of stoppered bottles, two to thirty-two ounces.

278—CORNELL

This is another pattern which Mrs. Kamm drew from an old catalog without having seen the creamer. She continued the original name given it by the Tarentum Glass Company of Tarentum, Pennsylvania. They were quite proud of this pattern and entered it in the Pittsburgh Glass Show of February, 1898. See Kamm's *A Seventh Pitcher Book*, page 37, No. 73, also Plate 95.

This small creamer is not the standard one used by Mrs. Kamm. It differs in size, shape, rim, and handle. The standard creamer is taller and more slender, while this one is rather squat and somewhat hassock-shaped. It sits on a broad, flat, ringbase and has a 22-ray star deeply impressed in the bottom. Above the base the body bulges, then again curves in near the rim. Most of the body is covered with an imitation cut glass effect. The top of the design is formed by large, highly convex figures which form *V*'s. Below the latter are large, flat-topped, and inverted V-shaped figures whose tops are covered with fine diamond point. Below these *V*'s are large, highly raised, beveled, and flat-topped cubes. The top of each cube is scored by two bands of three lines which cross the center of the cube at right angles to form a Greek cross. Below this is figurework in varying imitation cut glass designs.

The rim is unevenly scalloped as is also true of the creamer shown by Mrs. Kamm. There is a plain band above the pattern which has been gilded. The lip droops a wee bit. The standard creamer has a round applied handle. This one has a small, six-sided, pressed handle, which the mold marks prove.

The quality of the glass is excellent. The piece is thick and heavy for its small size. The workmanship in polishing and gilding is not particularly good.

Small creamer: 4-part mold, 12 ounces, 3 inches tall, 3 1/4 inches wide, and 4 7/8 inches long.

We know the four-piece table setting was made. Other items may show up. (Remember, the manufacturer thought so highly of this pattern he placed it in a glass show.)

279—SLIDELL

Have you ever sauntered through a longleaf yellow pine forest on a lazy summer afternoon? A delightful aroma comes from the pine. Slidell, Louisiana nestles in the midst of such sur-roundings and the pattern has been named by the author in that city's honor.

An attractive shape graces this imitation cut glass creamer. Many deride the imitation cut glass category in pressed glass patterns. Others love and cherish such pieces. Some antique dealers will not deal in pressed glass because it is so "late," but a glance about their shops will reveal a large array of more recent cut glass of the Brilliant Period. (Consistent?)

This piece rests on a wide base and is constricted just above it to form the waist. Above this it swells out somewhat, but is again constricted slightly at the neck. The rim has a moderate flare. Below it is a smooth, plain band, which has been gilded. Still below this are the different cut glass motifs. The outstanding figure consists of three large, highly beveled squares, one on either side and a third beneath the spout. In each square there is a well-executed 14-point, impressed hobstar. All parts of the hobstar are highly faceted. The surface of the square beneath the handle is left plain, as would have been done with high quality ware, for an applied handle. Since the squares meet at their corners, they make triangular spaces above and below them. Large fans fill the upper triangles. Four three-ribbed groups compose each fan. At the end of each rib is a thumbprint shaped like a teardrop.

The space below the squares and continuing down to the base is filled with conventional cut glass figures including squares, triangles and diamonds. Their surfaces in turn carry daisies, diamond point, fans, and finecut figures. The rim is unevenly double scalloped. In front it slopes up and forward into a wide jowl, then dips slightly to form a narrow lip. The base is hollowed out underneath and sits on a wide, thin ring. The dome sags a bit and has a large, round, 24-ray star impressed therein.

Usually this type of glassware has a handle which simulates an applied one. No such effort was made here. The handle has six sides and none of the attributes of a true handmade handle, despite the fact a smooth escutcheon was provided for the lower attachment. The top of the handle has a prominent protrusion that furnishes a good grip. It is an attractive handle.

I believe this pattern probably was produced between 1895 and 1910. There is no trademark to assist in dating it. The glass has a beautiful, sparkling clearness and is without defect. The mold maker did an excellent job. The glass must have been a little cool when pressed, for a few stray hairlines show here and there under the rim.

Standard creamer: 4-part mold, 14 ounces, 4 9/16 inches tall, 3 9/16 inches wide, and 5 3/8 inches long.

Only the creamer is known to the writer. There is a possibility the pattern may have been pressed in as many as forty-five or fifty items.

280—CIRCULAR SAW

Mrs. Kamm described a water pitcher of this pattern in *A Fifth Pitcher Book*, page 146, No. 193. A standard creamer is used here for comparative purposes. This is a thick, heavy creamer with a bulbous body. The glass is half an inch thick. The sides curve in from the bulge to form the neck and waist.

The decorative motif is bold and stands out in high relief. Six large, highly convex, teardrop-shaped jewels with their points down are spaced about the body. In the top of each is an impressed whirling figure like a circular saw, and each such figure has a beveled hobstar for its center. They extend from waist to neck. Separating each two jewels is an unusually high, beveled, and sharp-pointed escutcheon. The flat surface of each is covered with fine diamond point. Below each jewel is a short, wide fan which spreads out on the base.

The base itself is stable and wide, and the piece rests on a ring. Underneath is a wide flat-roofed dome with a many-rayed hexagonal impressed star. (See cut of bottom.) The rim is saddled, rising in front and rear. A narrow lip dips low in front, then droops as if sulking.

The handle is six-sided and has long, sweeping curves. It is wider than thick and increases in width toward the lower attachment. Because of the tremendous thickness of the figurework there is little finger room in the large handle. The two rear corners have been finetoothed.

Standard creamer: 3-part mold, 1 3/16 pounds, 4 1/4 inches tall, 4 1/16 inches wide, and 5 1/2 inches long.

Water pitcher: 3-part mold, 5 pounds, 7 1/4 inches tall, other measurements unknown.

This pattern is somewhat similar to SUNK JEWEL, and so similar to STARRED JEWEL they could be mistaken for each other. The water pitcher and creamer are the only items known to the author. Other articles probably were made.

281—ARISTOCRAT

This individual creamer is quite impracti-cal despite its classic beauty, symmetry, purity of line, superior quality, and excellent craftsmanship. It is unusual in that it is twice as long, and more than three times as high, as it is wide. With its narrow base it is, of course, easily toppled. The base is roughly rectangular in appearance but actually has ten sides. The side edges are considerably longer than the four front and back ones. (See drawing.)

The outside of the body is hexagonal with two wide convex side panels and two flat panels in both front and back. The vertical corners on each side of the wide side panels are cut off by concave flutes. There is a similar concave flute around the entire body just below the rim. The body flares smoothly to form the base.

Although the outside of the body is hexagonal, the inside is oval in cross section at the top and tapers until it is wedge-shaped at the bottom. The mold plunger on the pressing machine which formed the inside was exactly the shape of the cutting end of most prehistoric stone celts. The rim is curved and notched as shown, and the flat, six-paneled handle has a smart, upturned thrust, with an unusual thumbgrip.

The quality of the glass is excellent. It is brilliant, mirror polished, and flawless. The glass is 1/4 inch thick and the creamer is heavy for its small size.

Individual creamer: 2-part mold, 10 ounces, 5 1/4 inches tall, 2 inches wide, and 4 1/4 inches long.

This creamer resembles another one shown in this book. However, this is of top quality, and the other is similar only in general conformation. The handle is much like that of ARCHED PANEL in Mrs. Kamm's *Two Hundred Pattern Glass Pitchers*, page 107; and of CHIPPENDALE on the same page. Also see U.S. SHEARTON in Kamm's *A Fifth Pitcher Book*, page 100; and CONCAVE BLOCK in this book. The COLONIAL VARIANT in Kamm's *A Seventh Pitcher Book*, page 29, has a likeness. The similarity of these pieces indicates it is a ware manufactured between 1907-1915. It was probably made in many items including: the four piece table setting, water pitcher, goblet, compotes, bowls, sauces, etc.

282—WICKERWORK

This pattern resembles TILE, in Mrs. Kamm's *A Sixth Pitcher Book*, page 22, No. 30, and also BRICKWORK in her *A Fourth Pitcher Book*, page 58, No. 62. It differs, however, from both. TILE has rectangular, concave blocks such as found here, but lacks the upright, imitation, split-wood stakes present in this pattern. BRICK-WORK carries two courses of rectangular stippled bricks and ovate or circular stippled discs about the top of the creamer.

The present creamer is of average quality and rather tall, though lighter than usual. It is made of soda-lime glass. The creamer is thimble-shaped. It is widest at the top and tapers in gradually to a flat base. There is a ring of cable around the underside of the latter. In the center is an unusual star pattern composed of twelve raised rays. (See cut.)

The body of the creamer is covered by the pattern. The design consists of seven long rows of interlaced and concave rectangles. They are woven into a wickerwork with imitation wooden stakes lined to represent wood. The lip is low and narrow. The rim is flat and level. The handle is pressed but appears applied. It is round in cross section and completely plain.

Creamer without its lid: 3-part mold, 10 ounces, 4 inches tall, 3 3/8 inches wide, and 4 3/4 inches long.

The pattern was probably originated in the 1890s. The concave rectangles were painted bright green and red. Evidently this was done by a distributor of condiments and not by the manufacturer. The paint is easy to remove.

No other items are known in the pattern, but it would be surprising if goblets, berry sets, tumblers, water pitchers, butter dishes, sugar bowls, and spooners were not made. Nevertheless, it may have been produced solely as a condiment container, and thus could be the only item made. The manufacturer is unknown. This pattern has not previously been covered. It is illustrated here for the first time and I have chosen the name *WICKERWORK.*

283—STARLYTE, PLAIN

Mrs. Kamm described this pattern, using the handcut stars for a title (as did the manufacturer) in her *A Fifth Pitcher Book,* page 36, No. 40. She used a clumsy and ponderous water pitcher. Her specimen had a star cut in each panel near the top, and all panel edges were cut into notches. The piece shown here bears no such cutting, and a person seeing it is unlikely to associate it with STARLYTE, since it has no stars. The accompanying drawing shows how it appears and helps correct a minor error.

The glass is considerably thicker than is usual or necessary. It is half an inch thick at the rim and even thicker at the base.

Mrs. Kamm said the pattern had eight panels, but her drawing showed only seven (the same as this one). The base is flat underneath and has a treatment of thick heavy crystal such as I have never before seen. It has seven thick, rounded scallops which arch out on their edges from bottom to top. On top of the foot, each scallop becomes the rounded end of a panel. The panels extend upward through the narrow waist to the rim where they are rounded over and are unusually thick. The plain flat panels are very beautiful—the crystal-clear glass showing to excellent advantage. The two front panels join beneath the lip. The rear panel affords an excellent anchorage for the handle. The latter is applied and pleasingly curved. The lower attachment is a large blob while the upper attachment is turned under. The handle diminishes in size as it ascends.

The beveled rim is odd and, except at the lip, quite thick. The lip is attractively curved and the glass thinner there.

The glass and workmanship demonstrate the high standard glass technology had reached by 1910. The Lancaster Glass Company of Lancaster, Ohio, advertised three patterns in 1910, called CROWN, CARNATION, and STARLYTE (the present pattern). No previous or subsequent ads are known, and no other information is available about the company.

No mold marks are visible, even when minutely studied with a magnifying glass. It has a perfect fire polish. Great care was lavished on it to produce a quality product.

Creamer: ? mold marks, 1 1/8 pounds, 5 1/4 inches tall, 3 5/8 inches wide, and 5 1/4 inches long.

The following articles are known: creamer, sugar bowl, spoonholder, covered butter dish, plates, nappies, goblet, water pitcher, and tumbler. Doubtless other items were made.

284—HENDRICKS

This tall Mother Hubbard-shaped creamer has not been previously described or listed in American glass literature. It was presented to the author by John T. Hendricks of Little Rock, who illustrated this book.

I cannot escape the impression that this piece was marketed as a container for gherkins, olives, pickled pigs' feet, etc. The flat-topped rim with the ring in high relief would permit a flat metal lip to be clamped securely to it. If I correctly surmise that it was indeed manufactured and sold as a container, probably no other articles were made in the

282

Bottom
282

283

Bottom
285

284

285

286

287

288

289

pattern. It may or may not have been a mere pickle bottle. If not, a sugar bowl and spoonholder might exist.

I know of no other creamer with this peculiar shape. It resembles the loose, flowing dresses worn near the turn of the century. A creamer of this shape would have been possible only after the Hipkins' patent. Being bulbous at the base, a plunger could not have pressed it and then been removed through the narrower neck.

The rim is flat and is 1/4 inch thick on top. A 1/8 inch ring surrounds the rim.

Below the rim, it is constricted slightly to form a vertical neck. An inch-wide band of figurework covers this portion. The band is a modified version of the ancient egg-and-dart border. In this case we have five darts rather than the usual single one impressed between the eggs. The surface of each is flat and vertical.

On the inside the body has low, narrow columns below the neck. They disappear as the body flares toward the base. They do not show in the lower bulge.

The piece rounds under to form a wide and stable ring foundation on which it rests. In the center, underneath, is a large, rounded, 24-ray star outlined by a low, circular shelf.

The handle has six sides and is easy to hold. It is for the most part angular, with a few curves to alleviate its stiffness.

The writer knows nothing of where, or by whom, it was made. If it was a container, it would be a good guess that Westmoreland Specialty Company produced it. McKee and Brothers also made similar ware. The glass is of average quality soda-lime. It is neither very clear nor particularly brilliant. It is probably a product of the 1895-1915 period or even later.

Creamer: 2-part mold, 14 ounces, 5 inches tall, 3 11/16 inches wide, and 4 5/8 inches long.

285—DALZELL'S COLUMBIA

Minnie Watson Kamm had not seen a piece of this pattern. She used two old advertisements for her description. She did not illustrate a pitcher. In *A Sixth Pitcher Book*, page 39, No. 89, and Plates 43 and 44, she described the pattern as best she could. It was made by Dalzell, Gilmore and Leighton Company of Findlay, Ohio, and was advertised in *China, Glass & Lamp*, on January 17, 1894, as their COLUMBIA pattern. They were proud of the new method of crimping the rim by a machine which gave the pieces a handmade appearance. (Harry Northwood patented the

machine but had to resort to the courts to prevent unauthorized use of it.) Mrs. Kamm was confident that a tumbler and goblet were made in the pattern. I am not so certain. The sole distinguishing characteristic of the pattern (except on the bottom) is the crimped rim. A tumbler or goblet could not be used with such a rim and would have had to be left plain. The crimps are quite difficult to keep clean.

The pot-bellied, or rose-bowl-shaped standard creamer is shown here primarily to give accurate measurements. The sides of the bowl are constricted to a rather narrow waist. They flare to a bulbous body before curving in again to the neck. The sides are severely plain and so highly fire-polished that no mold marks show. They do show, however, on the base.

Above the neck the rim flares widely and is crimped on either side. It is left plain at the rear for the applied handle attachment and in front for the narrow pinched lip. The top is level. The lower part of the body curves in and ends in a horizontal plane just above the waist. From it the ringbase flares to the wide heavy ring on which it rests. Under the base is a wide, deep, arched dome in the center of which is a large cabochon surrounded by a ring of pear-shaped figures.

The handle is applied and is slightly awry. The large blob is at the lower attachment. The upper attachment is to the underside of the wide collar. The glass is clear and brilliant, but there are a few small bubbles and flecks of foreign matter scattered through it. More often than not, it came etched with floral sprays. This particular piece was left plain.

Creamer: 2-part mold, 1 pound, 4 9/16 inches tall, 3 13/16 inches wide, and 5 1/4 inches long.

We know these items were made in the pattern: water pitcher, standard creamer, covered sugar bowl, covered butter dish, spoonholder, and a large tall covered compote.

286—PLEAT BAND

Mrs. Kamm used a milk pitcher in *A Fifth Pitcher Book*, page 139, No. 182, to name and describe this pattern. A standard creamer is shown here. Ruth Herrick, in her *Greentown Glass*, Figures 17, 18, and 19, illustrated a plain spoonholder, cake stand, covered butter, covered sugar, small covered compote, wine, goblet, and an etched spoonholder. She did not describe the pattern.

It is hard to understand why this pattern was made. It would be less difficult if the quality of the glass were better, for the large plain surfaces would then have been more alluring. Enameled flowers might also have enhanced its beauty but, as it stands, the design is bleak and unattractive. The inferior glass mars easily; it is unclear, has a wavy surface, and is not properly fire polished.

The cup-shaped creamer has a plain bowl with straight sides which round under sharply at the waist. This portion of the pitcher also contains no decorative motif. The bowl has an ample capacity. The rear two-thirds of the rim is covered with small and unattractive scallops. In front, it rises sharply to form a curved lip.

The handle has a small finger capacity for so large a creamer. It is round in cross section, with a band of horizontal fine rib on either side of its descending portion. The waist is quite short. Below it the base rounds over to form a ponderous foot.

Underneath is a deep concave dome with a smooth roof. Around the inside base of the dome is a half-inch-wide band of vertical fine rib. (Sometimes called pleat or flute.) The design shows through the base and has a silvery sheen. When viewed from underneath, it acts as a reducing lens.

Standard creamer: 2-part mold. 1 1/16 pounds, 4 15/16 inches tall, 3 9/16 inches wide, and 5 5/16 inches long.

Milk pitcher: 2-part mold, weight unknown, 7 1/2 inches tall, other measurements unknown.

It is doubtful this pattern was ever popular enough to create a demand for it.

287—ENGLISH

Mrs. Kamm used this small creamer in *A Second Two Hundred Pattern Glass Pitchers*, page 109. It is shown here with a lid. Creamers manufactured with lids are fascinating to most people and especially so to the author.

An intriguing and prevalent glass story has to do with creamers with lids. According to it, they were made for use in the South, before the days of screens, to keep flies out of the cream. Strangely enough, milk pitchers were more often used and were not provided with lids. Actually, pieces of this type were manufactured as containers for the marketing of various condiments, such as prepared mustard, horseradish, etc. Imagine shipping by freight, and selling through countless stores, these little creamers without lids—all filled with prepared mustard. The Westmoreland Glass Company and their subsidiary, the Specialty Glass Company, manufactured many varieties of pressed glass containers. Some had metal lips clamped thereon. Except for goblets and tumblers,

they could not be reused and were subsequently discarded. Many, however, came with reusable glass lids. A filled sugar bowl and creamer, both with lids, could be bought for the price of two bottles of mustard (twenty cents). They were, of course, sold directly to condiment manufacturers and were never on the retail market as empty tableware.

The Westmoreland Glass Company illustrated this pattern in their 1896 catalog and called it ENGLISH. Mrs. Kamm had earlier called it DIAMOND WITH DIAMOND POINT, before she learned its original name. It was made in "opal ware" and clear. A sugar, spooner, and butter dish were made, as was a puff-box with lid—to keep the flies out, of course.

The base and rim have broad shallow scallops. The lip is slightly higher than the rim. The base is hollowed out to a depth of half an inch, and a plain 24-ray star is impressed therein.

The body is almost cylindrical with a slight flare at both top and bottom. It is smaller than the average standard creamer, but too large for an individual one. It was designed to hold a "dime's worth" of mustard. When viewed from above, it is seen to be octagonal with eight flat panels. When seen from the side, it appears round. Seven long narrow diamonds extend almost from rim to base. Each is centered on a line where two flat panels join. As a result, the four beveled diamonds contained in each differ—two have high spines through their axes, and two are flat topped. The space above and below is filled with diamond point. Beneath the lip is a fan composed of five long, sharply tapered, and pointed teardrops which extend from the rim to the middle of the bowl. The combined effect is pleasing.

The small domed lid rests securely on a wide ledge in the throat of the creamer. Except for the paneling, the designs on the lid and bowl are almost identical. The rim of the lid is plain—to permit a better bond by the sealant when full and packed for shipment. The figurework on the lid is on the inside of the high arched dome, with the outside left smooth. The finial is hollow and tapers the wrong way. It has fourteen rounded ribs and is difficult to grip. It is a type of finial so often seen on Westmoreland patterns, and indeed it almost constitutes a trademark of the company. The quality of the glass is excellent. The workmanship is good.

The handle is round and simulates an applied one, though the mold marks prove it is not. The panel for the handle attachment is plain.

Creamer with lid: 2-part mold, 13 ounces,

4 3/4 inches tall, 3 1/4 inches wide, and 4 1/2 inches long.

The lids of most of these little covered creamers fit interchangeably. Beware of those shopkeepers who fit a lid to a creamer even though it may not be of that pattern.

288—*WINSLOW*

I am calling this previously unlisted pattern *WINSLOW* for an enticing little town securely tucked away in a green valley of the Arkansas Ozarks. Winslow is a haven for a quiet, restful summer vacation, and the creamer appears as cool and refreshing as the morning dew I recall in that town.

The sides of the bowl flare slightly to the rim. The lower border of the body bevels under to a narrower, but still wide waist. To the right of each mold line is a raised, vertical panel with a plain surface. There is a raised, formal band between each two such panels which joins them at top and bottom. They are horizontal and follow a broken course but do not touch the verticals. The background is covered by a raised daisylike configuration which gives the piece a frosted appearance. The small facets do not refract light.

The rim is unattractively saddled. The spout has wide jowls and a lopped-off lip. The shape lacks grace, and any charm must come from other features. On a more graceful shape, the figurework would have been outstanding.

The pressed handle is heavy and round in cross section. It simulates an applied handle, but the mold marks show it is not. The ringbase is low, and a large, 20-ray daisy is impressed on the bottom.

Strangely enough, this creamer originally had a lid. It sat flat on the rear part of the rim. In front it arched up at each jowl and then down at the lip. Only these arched shelves held the lid in place—a precarious footing indeed. Many patterns made by the Boston and Sandwich Glass Company of Sandwich, Massachusetts, from 1830 to 1870, had similar lids. Lacy Sandwich creamers have this odd arrangement, but I have neither seen nor heard of one with a lid. Very definitely I am not trying to attribute this piece to Sandwich. It was made between 1893 and 1910, and the Sandwich factory closed in 1888.

The glass has a slight smoke-grey cast similar to some of our early flintware. This is the only defect of the glass. The designer (?) was untrained. The finishing off is only average.

Standard creamer without its lid: 3-part mold,

13 1/2 ounces, 4 1/2 inches tall, 3 5/8 inches wide, and 5 5/16 inches long.

I have seen two creamers and know of the three remaining pieces of the table set. One of the creamers was left plain and is clear. The other is clear, but the smooth, raised figurework and top of the rim were flashed with ruby. This feature established the above dates.

289—*FRANKFURTERS*

This is an individual tankard creamer that may be part of a large set of "colonial" glass. It is too fine in quality to have been used as a container and is somewhat small for that purpose. The glass is better than average, bright, fairly heavy, and has no sharp edges. There is no trademark.

The simple, effective design consists of a wide band of frankfurter-shaped vertical columns arranged side by side. Each is well convexed and arched at top and bottom. The band covers the lower two-thirds of the body. The upper third is plain and in some pieces may have been stained with ruby or gilded.

The rim is smooth, has a slight saddle, and is raised moderately at the lip. The base is a substantial ring and is domed underneath. It has a small impractical handle which imitates a later applied one. It flares at the lower attachment and turns under at the upper. It is round in cross section.

Small creamer: 3-part mold, 8 ounces, 4 inches tall, 2 1/4 inches wide, and 3 5/8 inches long.

The manufacturer's name is unknown. It was probably produced in the 1890's. No other pieces of the pattern are known to the writer, but there must have been a matching covered sugar bowl.

290—MADISON

A rare creamer such as this is encountered no more frequently than a childhood friend, and the experience is equally as pleasant. The pattern is extremely scarce, and neither the McKearins, Mrs. Lee, Dr. Millard, Dreppard, Brothers, nor Mrs. Metz covered it in their writings on early American pressed glass.

Minnie Watson Kamm, in *A Sixth Pitcher Book*, page 75, No. 159, named the pattern MADISON. Only a spillholder was known to her and this was used for her drawing. With dotted lines she projected the spillholder into a creamer (*i.e.*—by dotting in the top and handle.) Students of pattern glass incline to the belief a spillholder may, at times, be the only item manufactured in a certain pattern. However, the discovery of a creamer in

HARP or LYRE, STAR AND PUNTY, and this pattern tends to negate the theory. Perhaps other items were also made to match all spillholders. The matter would not be so open to question if other items in these patterns were more plentiful.

This creamer is as fine a specimen of early flint glass as can be found. It is of superior quality, heavy, brilliantly clear, well finished off, and beautiful. It was pressed in a creamer mold, whereas HARP or LYRE and STAR AND PUNTY were first pressed in a lamp or spillholder mold and later crafted into creamers.

The piece has four features which set it apart from its contemporaries:

1. While it appears to be round, it is actually hexagonal, both inside and out. The shape of the inside differs radically from that of other creamers in that the lower corners of the plunger, which formed the inside, were deeply chamfered. This produced a tapering of the inside bottom while still retaining its hexagonal shape.

2. Atop the huge applied handle, the gaffer pinched up a high thumbgrip without leaving a tool mark. Of all the applied handles I have ever seen, this is the only one with such a feature.

3. On the inside, and dipping low beneath the spout, a well-defined ledge spans the two forward panels to accommodate a lid. The rim over the other four panels is thick and flat. The back part of the lid would have needed a flange to fit into the throat. Note the topography of the rim and the deep dip of the ledge in front. How could a lid have been fashioned to fit properly and stay on? I simply do not know.

4. A three-part mold was used to form the creamer, but it was a very unusual one. One part formed two complete panels and two half panels; a second produced a full panel and two half panels; while a third pressed two half panels. Overall there are six panels. On the foot, through the waist, and between the pentagons on the base of the bowl, the mold marks are easy to locate. Above the pentagons there is no trace of them. They must have skirted the large ovals. Had they crossed the ovals they could not have been fire-polished off.

Each panel is covered by a large, deeply dished oval with a high border. All ovals contain a pair of parallel and inverted V-shaped prisms with sharp points. They are vertical and close-set. At the bottom of the ovals, large pentagons mesh with them. The pentagons rest on a high, hexagonal shelf on the base of the body.

The waist and foot are round. On the underside there is a large, impressed star with six points. (See drawing of bottom.) There is no pontil mark. The huge handle would be comfortable for a "ham-fisted son of the soil." It is also off-center.

This is a product of early pressed glassmakers. They were still experimenting with their mold structures. Eventually they discovered a much easier method than the complex one used for this piece, which was made between 1840 and 1860.

Spillholder: 3-part mold, 1 pound, 5 1/4 inches tall, other measurements not available.

Creamer: 3-part mold, 1 13/16 pounds, 6 1/2 inches tall, 3 3/8 inches wide, and 6 1/2 inches long.

The spillholder and creamer are the only known items. Since a creamer has been found, we can be sure other articles were made.

291—DOLPHIN PITCHER

Because of the handle and lip, this strange piece is called a creamer. It may have been marketed as a container for a condiment or candy. The lid has no notch for a ladle, so it is not a gravy boat. At a time when opaque and colored glass was very popular in this country, it was produced as a novelty to capitalize on the public fancy. The imagination of glass designers was given full rein in those days, as this piece attests.

S. T. Millard, in *Opaque Glass*, Plate 288, shows this covered milk-white pitcher. He thought it was probably made by the Westmoreland Glass Company but did not pursue the matter. The name used here was first used by E. McCalmey Belknap in *Milk Glass*, page 79, Plate 69. He said they were hard to obtain in pairs. This piece probably belongs to the period of 1890-1910 and there are indications it has been reproduced.

It is made of opaque white glass of good quality. It is not, however, the superior quality or finish of the smooth, shiny, chalk-white glass produced today. When held to the light some opalescence shows in the thinner places.

The body is elongated, oval-shaped, and its dominant figurework centers about an oval medallion on either side. Both are framed with a raised cord design. They may have been left plain so flowers or other decorations could be painted on, or to provide space for a label. On either side of each medallion are raised scrolls and lattice-work as shown in the drawing.

The rim consists of a series of scallops which simulate ocean waves. They are above and form a 3/8-inch undulating band which completely encircles the piece. The rim rises slightly in front to form a blunt lip. This part of the rim carries a row of tiny beading.

The handle is hexagonal and the sides are outlined with tiny beading. The top attachment of the handle seems to be a continuation of the rim of the pitcher and could be used as a second lip. The lower attachment of the handle simulates a leaf which splays on the body. Inside the creamer is an ample ledge to accommodate a lid. A raised swimming dolphin dominates the lid. The tail of the dolphin is curved back over its body to form the handle on the lid. The design is well done.

Creamer with lid: 2-part mold, 1 pound, 3 3/4 inches tall, 3 inches wide, and 7 1/4 inches long.

In addition to the covered piece, I have a second milk-white creamer which is almost identical, except it does not have a ledge to accommodate a lid. (See drawing.)

Being of a novelty type, it is unlikely that other pieces were made. The Indiana Tumbler and Goblet Company of Greentown, Indiana, was the only company to produce caramel- or chocolate-colored glass. They manufactured a strange DOLPHIN covered dish in caramel slag. There is also the well-known DOLPHIN pattern which came in many pieces and is well documented. The Boston and Sandwich Glass Company used the dolphin motif extensively in such articles as the RIBBON compote, candlesticks, etc. This piece is not of such ancient or exalted lineage however.

292—BERNARD

Still another unlisted and unnamed pattern of American pressed glass is presented here. Such a simple and plain design, exemplifying uprightness and rectitude, should no longer be neglected. I am naming it in honor of Bernard Lawton Collins of Montgomery, Alabama.

This piece was designed and pressed along purely geometric lines which lend themselves nicely to the media used. A plain design with large flat surfaces requires one of two things—either figurework to cover the surface, or a very high quality glass to make the area so attractive it needs no embellishment. The latter is true here.

The glass is of high quality soda-lime and has some resonance. It is brilliantly clear, sparkling, and free of defects or discoloration. It is highly fire polished. The weight is light, as would be expected. The name and location of the manufacturer is unknown to the writer, but the pattern probably dates from 1900 to 1910.

This small, round, squatty creamer has straight, vertical sides with a horizontal rim and base. The decorative motif is achieved by a series of two closely placed, parallel V-shaped grooves.

Seen in cross section they are W-shaped. One band of these grooves encircles the bowl near the top and another close to the base. The same design runs vertically and so divides the body into eight large beveled squares. Below the lower band the body slopes inward at a 45 degree angle to a wide waist, then slopes out to the base. The upper angle is segmented by sharp-pointed spikes.

The base is a tapered ring, wide and stable. Underneath, it is hollowed out to receive the impression of a large, round, 20-ray star. The rim is round, plain, and level, dipping only slightly to form a small lip. The handle has six sides and is unadorned. It is rectangular in shape and provides a secure grip.

Small creamer: 4-part mold, 10 ounces, 2 5/8 inches tall, 3 3/8 inches wide, and 4 3/4 inches long.

I have the creamer and an identically shaped, two-handled sugar bowl which never had a lid. I know of no other items in the pattern. I would expect many pieces to have been made, for the design could be so easily adapted to any item. In addition, the flat squares could well have been flashed with ruby or amber, which was a popular glass decoration from 1893 to 1915.

293—BROOKHAVEN

This beautiful clear creamer, with its mirror-smooth surface—most of which is covered by threading—scintillates in the light as few pieces do. The pressed threading provides a frosted appearance as cool as a mint julep. I have named it for the lovable Mississippi city of Brookhaven, near which I was born. It was our trading center, and occasionally we made the all-day trip in a buggy. Memories of those trips, lying on a pallet in the back of the buggy, are poignant ones. Watching the moon travel over the countryside, through the trees or behind a hill, never ceased to intrigue my youthful mind, for it traveled at the same speed we did and when we stopped—it stopped!

THREADING would be the obvious title, but it is already preempted.

I have two creamers in this pattern. One is more bulbous and squatty, while the other is tall and slim. Both are severely plain, depending on beauty of line, plain surfaces, and sheer brilliance for their appeal. The low creamer is illustrated.

They sit on wide and flat bases and could be overturned only intentionally. Few creamers are so stable. Underneath, a low arched dome reaches to the edge. The surface of the dome is so smooth and even that it resembles a concave mirror.

290

Bottom
290

291-1

291-2

292

294

293

The lower two-thirds of the body is bulbous and is covered from base to shoulder by fine, well-formed, imitation hand-threading. Even where the threads join at a mold mark they still match perfectly. From the shoulder, where the threading ends, to the rim, the neck is constricted and left smooth and plain.

Most of the rim is level and rounded on top. It arches slightly in front and is depressed in the center to form a lip.

The handles are applied and are perfectly crafted. The large round blob at the bottom is applied over the threading and many small inaccessible pockets are left and are filled with grime.

The glass is soda-lime at its best. The workmanship, except at the lower handle attachment, is on a par with the metal. The mold marks are barely perceptible. I would date it from 1900-1915, but it may be older.

Squatty creamer: 2-part mold, 14 ounces, 3 1/8 inches tall, 4 1/4 inches wide, and 5 1/4 inches long.

Slender creamer: 2-part mold, 1 1/8 pounds, 3 3/4 inches tall, 3 13/16 inches wide, and 4 15/16 inches long.

I have seen only the two creamers in this pattern. I have a feeling they may have been made in a graduated series of pitchers. This was frequently done at the time these pieces were manufactured.

294—GOLDEN PHEASANT

To name this pattern of American pressed glass was no problem. There is the pheasant etched in gold, and here is a title that has not been used before. Suitable names for unnamed patterns are often difficult to find since so many titles have already been used. A third, fourth, or even fifth choice sometimes must be accepted.

This low oval creamer was originally pressed plain and smooth, then given a fine fire polish and turned over to a decorator for embellishment. The latter did an excellent job, using a treatment not previously encountered.

The upper half of the body is covered with an inch-wide band of attractive figurework. On either side there is a long medallion within which is etched a pheasant, tree stump, and floral motif. In front and back a formalized full-blown flower and scroll motif is etched. The band is bordered at both edges by a round linked chain. The etching is well done. I cannot be sure whether it is wheelcut or acid-etched, though I suspect the latter. After the etching was completed, a band of black enamel was painted on the inside of the creamer, opposite

the etched band. On the outside the band was gilded except for the background of the two medallions. This was neither etched nor gilded, and the black enamel shows through with a glossy surface which is magnificent. The golden pheasant stands out against the jet-black background. The gilt is left with a pleasing Roman gold or satin finish, which is neither flashy nor shiny.

The sides of the rim are level and the top is flat. There is a scallop at the back for the handle. At the extreme front it rises and curves over into a small lip. The handle has six sides, is wider than it is thick, and is left plain.

The base is oval and without a ring. It was ground smooth to make it sit level, not to polish off chips. It has an 18-ray star impressed underneath. This was an item of quality ware and was sold through jewelry stores. Great care was expended on it. The manufacturer is unknown to the writer. I believe it was made between 1915 and 1925.

Small creamer: 2-part mold, 9 ounces, 2 1/2 inches tall, 3 1/8 inches wide, and 5 1/4 inches long.

I once owned the two-handled, open sugar bowl as well. I would not expect to find other items, except possibly salt and pepper shakers, which might have accompanied these two pieces on a tray.

295—POLYANGULAR

Yes, this too, is a creamer! A rather new and peculiar one, but still a creamer. It is strictly modern, but its life expectancy is short. A formal Italian Garden would run it a poor second for unbending rigidity, straight lines, and acute angles. Also, there are the deeply cut and beautifully executed intaglio rose sprays. To give a better idea, the creamer is illustrated in three elevations: (a) from the side; (b) looking down from the top; and (c) looking up from the base. It took imagination to conceive the pattern, and fortitude to produce it. It is occasionally found in shops today. The title POLYANGULAR is assigned.

It is small, as creamers go, but large enough for XX cream, at today's prices. It rests on a flat base with impressed grillwork. Later, it was smoothly polished off. The base is large enough to make the pitcher difficult to upset—even intentionally.

The body is oblong and contains eight straight sides. They are vertical from rim to center, then angle in sharply to the base. All but two planes on the surface are covered with straight ribs, V-shaped grooves, or fans. On each side of the

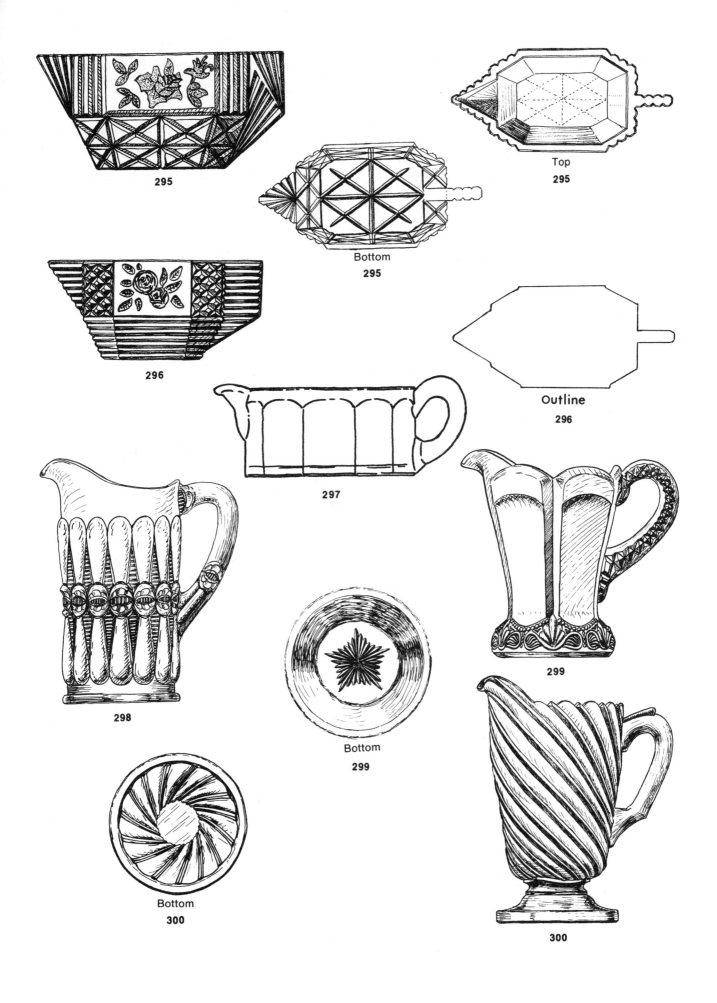

295

Top
295

Bottom
295

296

Outline
296

297

298

Bottom
299

299

Bottom
300

300

creamer a large rectangle 1 1/8 inches wide and 2 1/8 inches long is left flat and plain for later decoration. Into each a frosted and full-blown rose, rosebud, and several veined leaves were later intaglio cut to unusual depth. The surface of each is wheel polished.

The rim is level, flat, undecorated, and polished. The lip is delta-shaped and pointed.

The handle is an odd one as shown. It also is impractical since the empty creamer is too heavy for a thumb and finger grip to keep it from tilting forward when picked up.

It is made of excellent flint glass and has a good resonance. It is sparkling, clear, and free of defects. The workmanship on the mold is not top quality, but the intaglio cutting is. The glass is 1/4 inch thick. This was necessary for the deep pressing and cutting. It is heavy for its small size.

Small creamer: 2-part mold (mold marks polished off), 9 ounces, 2 1/8 inches tall, 2 3/8 inches wide, and 5 1/4 inches long.

A matching sugar bowl was made, but the writer is not aware of other items in the pattern. It was probably produced about 1920. It may be of American origin, but there is some possibility it was made in England. (See CORNERS which follows.)

296—CORNERS

This pressed and cut glass creamer is a small sibling of POLYANGULAR shown just above. The patterns are identical in shape. The modernistic pressed figurework is different as is the floral cutting. Because it has many corners, I will call it that.

The body has eight flat vertical panels around the top. On the lower half they slant in at an angle to the base. (See drawing of outline.) The handle, spout, end panels, and lower half of the body are covered with horizontal prisms arranged as steps. On the upper half, the four corner panels are filled with beveled cubes, and each side panel has deep intaglio cutting of two open roses and many well-executed leaves. The flowers and leaves were left frosted. After these areas were cut, the top surface was ground and polished, as were also the rim, back of the handle, and the bottom.

The two handles of the sugar bowl and that of the creamer project at a right angle from the body as thick wings. Each side of the handle has prisms that afford a safe grip on so small a piece.

The glass is clear, brilliant, and of excellent quality. The futuristic pattern is somewhat harsh. The workmanship is above average. The mold

marks are faint. This could be foreign ware—perhaps English. I believe it to be a product of the 1920's. It is novelty ware and does not "grow on one."

Small creamer: 4-part mold, 5 ounces, 1 7/8 inches tall, 1 13/16 inches wide, and 4 3/16 inches long.

Small open sugar: 4-part mold, 4 ounces, 1 7/8 inches tall, 1 13/16 inches wide, and 4 3/8 inches long.

These probably were the only two articles made, though in different sizes. I have found them only in Goodwill Industries stores.

Note the optical illusion in the drawing of the beveled cubes. At times they appear sunken, at other times raised. On the creamer they are raised.

297—MESA

This squatty novelty creamer is the most impractical I have ever seen. When full, it is impossible to pass without spilling a portion of the contents. It is like trying to carry a large shallow pan of water. Also, it has no charm. Nevertheless it was made.

The sides are vertical and the rim is level; therefore, the name MESA is assigned. It sits on a wide flat bottom with an odd decagonal-shape and many-rayed star impressed therein.

Ten wide flat panels cover the sides and round over near the top. Above the panels the piece is round, whereas the panels themselves make the lower portion ten-sided. The rim is rounded, level, and pinched forward to form a good spout. The small ring handle is round in cross section. It appears to be a cup handle.

The quality of the glass is excellent, and the workmanship is on a par with the metal. Where, when, by whom, or why it was made we do not know. I believe it dates from 1915 to 1920.

Small creamer: 2-part mold, 6 ounces, 1 5/8 inches tall, 3 1/4 inches wide, and 4 15/16 inches long.

If other items were made in the pattern they would be difficult to identify as related items. It is intriguing to contemplate what a tall celery vase or water pitcher would look like in this pattern. The shallow creamer could have been intended for use as a nappie.

298—BOW-TIE

This pattern is popular with collectors and is found in a wide range of articles. Dr. S. T.

Millard named and illustrated the pattern in his *Goblets II*, Plate 5-1.

Minnie Watson Kamm, in *A Sixth Pitcher Book*, page 50, No. 118, and Plate 17, discussed the pattern but used an old advertisement to illustrate it. On Plate 17 she showed a cut of a small ad by the Thompson Glass Company of Uniontown, Pennsylvania. This revealed a tall open compote, but the legend beneath it was too indistinct to read. She had on hand a 10-inch flat bowl similar to the compote. This glass company was organized in 1889 and went out of business about 1892. They made such patterns as TORPEDO, TILE, and a NELLY BLY plate. BOW-TIE came out in 1889 and was one of their first patterns.

Alice Hulett Metz covered the pattern as No. 2413 in her *Early American Pattern Glass* but did not illustrate it.

The creamer is shown here for the first time. The line drawing should help to identify the pattern.

It is tall, somewhat slender, and cylindrical. Almost all of the vertical surface is covered by a wide belt of figurework. The wings of the ties are rounded over at their ends. This results in scalloped borders, above and below. They are in high rounded relief, and each tie looks somewhat like an aeroplane propeller. The knot in the center is oval in outline and formed by two opposing crescents meeting at their points. The crescents are high, ridged, and their inner surfaces are impressed with three small thumbprints. A small elliptical figure is formed in the middle whose surface is covered by vertical fine ribs. The space between the ties is filled with long low dartlike figures which have flat tops and are covered with horizontal fine ribs. Above the design, the body is smooth and plain for about an inch. A similar plain quarter-inch band is found below the figurework.

The base extends a short distance beyond the body and consists of a round ring. Underneath, a ring surrounds a shallow depression into which has been impressed a cross made of a portion of a tie. The interstices are filled with four-ray fans. (See drawing of bottom.)

The rim dips slightly on either side, then rises rather sharply to the forward-thrust lip. The handle is round in cross section and oddly decorated. At the upper attachment there is half a bow-tie knot on each side, and two-thirds of the way down a full knot is pressed therein. Below this the handle splays on the body and is covered by six well-raised and rounded ribs.

The glass is of only fair quality. The workmanship indicates it was production ware. The mold marks are prominent on the plain surfaces but are neither sharp nor rough.

Creamer: 3-part mold, 1 pound, 5 5/8 inches tall, 3 inches wide, and 5 inches long.

The following articles are known to have been made: goblet, creamer, tall open compote, and a 10-inch bowl. There probably are many other items.

299—PENSACOLA

Still another pattern shows up for the first time to be described, illustrated, and given a name. We will, therefore, call this attractive pattern *PENSACOLA* after the beautiful Florida city of that name. It is not plentiful, and collecting a complete set will require diligent search. It is a pattern worthy of the effort. The shape diverges from the norm, and this alone places it in a special niche. The glass is very thick in places. This is necessary because of the deep pressing and the bulging base.

From the waist up, the sides are almost straight and flare to a wider top. The body is divided into six wide panels separated by deep V-shaped grooves which extend from waist to rim. Each panel is topped, first with a low arch, and then with a wide thick lintel. Both are plain and flat. The large smooth areas on the panels should have encouraged decorators to etch or enamel them, and we may find pieces so treated. It would not have increased the original price.

The rim has a wide low scallop over each panel, except at the front where there is a moderate rise to provide a wide and slightly depressed lip. The rim is thinner than the lintels just below it. The handle is adequate and gracefully curved. It is somewhat round in cross section and has a band of large diamond point pressed on either side. The back and front are plain.

The waist appears narrow because of the exaggerated flare above and below. The base arches out to a round, wide, and thick skirt, much as though bustles were being used. The panels extend a short distance out on top of the base and end in a drape of dewdrops. At the bottom of each V-shaped groove is an acanthus leaf in high round relief which is flanked by a scroll and beadwork. On this portion of the piece the glass is half an inch thick.

The creamer rests on a wide ring. On the underside is a wide dome with slanting sides and a flat roof on which a raised five-pointed star has been molded. The star is made up of many sharp-pointed spined ridges. (See cut of bottom.)

243

This was a quality article. The only place where a mold mark can be seen is around the handle. With its deep grooves, a four-part mold would have been required to permit its release after being pressed. The glass is brilliantly clear and free of defects. It is heavy, but not flint and appears to date from about 1885-1895. The work of both the moldmaker and gaffer was superlative.

Creamer: 4-part mold, 15 1/2 ounces, 4 3/4 inches tall, 4 inches wide, and 5 3/4 inches long.

The creamer is the only piece of the pattern known to me. Look for the companion pieces—sugar bowl, spoonholder, and butter dish. Often after a pattern is named and illustrated, other articles are then found.

300—VORTEX

Another pattern of pressed glass is shown here for the first time and given the title of *VORTEX*. The title SWIRL has been too often used and is confusing.

S. T. Millard, in *Goblets II*, Plate 20-2, illustrates a goblet and calls it DOUBLE LINE SWIRL. He thought it was of the 1880's. This creamer may be of the same pattern as the Millard goblet, but his photographic illustration of the latter is too indistinct to permit a positive identification. They, at least, are similar.

The large body rounds out widely from the waist, flares to about the middle, and from there to the rim the flare is less noticeable. The pattern is composed of rounded ribs in high relief alternating with raised inverted V-shaped prisms. The ribs and prisms have a violent upward and clockwise rotary motion and vary in size to fit the topography over which they travel. The entire body is covered with this design.

The top of each prism forms a small pointed scallop on the rim, and the ribs make rounded scallops at their tops. The front third of the rim is not scalloped but arches upward and forward to the spout.

The handle is round in cross section and, except for the flat thumbgrip on top, is severely plain. This contrasts with the simulated movement on the body much as the calm of the eye of a hurricane does with the surrounding vortex.

The waist is short and well curved. There is a shelf on the lower part of the body and another on top of the base. The piece was marred on the upper shelf while hot—as it was carried by tongs from the mold to the annealing oven. (See drawing for defect.)

The top of the foot has an ogee curve from the waist shelf which flattens out toward the edge. The foot is thick with a vertical edge. A large whorl is impressed on the under side of the base and shows through when viewed from the top. The design is the same as that of the body. (See drawing of bottom.)

This is average quality pressed glass containing a few scattered bubbles. It is clear, brilliant, and heavy. The manufacturer's name is unknown. The pattern appears to be of the 1875-1885 period.

Standard creamer: 3-part mold, 1 pound, 5 3/4 inches tall, 3 3/8 inches wide, and 5 3/16 inches long.

This creamer is the only piece of the pattern to come to my attention. Millard's goblet may belong. It is not plentiful or other writers would have found it. Certainly a sugar bowl, butter dish, and spoonholder were made. Quite possibly a large range of items may have been produced.

APPENDIX A
"STATES" SERIES

Between 1894 and 1907 the United States Glass Company of Pittsburgh, Pennsylvania, manufactured a "States" series of patterns. One pattern was named for each state of the Union. Arizona, New Mexico, and Oklahoma were territories at the time and were not included. There is a possibility that the series was not completed since we do not know of patterns for Arkansas, Iowa, Mississippi, Montana, Nebraska, New York, and possibly Rhode Island. Further research is necessary to determine whether they were produced and, if so, to locate them.

In the series one pattern, DAKOTA, represented both North and South Dakota; CAROLINA included North and South Carolina, and VIRGINIA may well have included West Virginia.

Several glass factories manufactured patterns which they named for individual states, but they made no series. Only the patterns made by the U.S. Glass Company are listed here with their references in our glass literature.

LEGEND

L VG 36-1: Ruth Webb Lee's *Victorian Glass*, Plate 36, No. 1 from left.

L EAPG Pat. 99, pp. 248-54, Pl. 75: Ruth Webb Lee's *Early American Pressed Glass*, Pattern 99, pages 248-54, Plate 75.

M 34-1: S. T. Millard's *Goblets*, Plate 34, No. 1 from the left.

M II: S. T. Millard's *Goblets II*.

K 7-10-17: Minnie Watson Kamm's *A Seventh Pitcher Book*, page 10, No. 17.

W 3rd Ant. p. 126: Edwin G. Warman's *The Third Antiques and Their Current Prices*, page 126.

B TS p. 43: J. Stanley Brothers Jr., *Thumbnail Sketches*, page 43.

Mz EAPG, No. 1747: Alice Hulett Metz, *Early American Pressed Glass*, No. 1747.

STATE PATTERNS

ALABAMA. K 1-81-112; B TS p. 42; and this book.

ARIZONA. Admitted as a state after series completed.

ARKANSAS. Have no data.

CALIFORNIA. L EAPG Pat. 75, pp. 208-209, Pl. 63, where she named it BEADED GRAPE, but mentions it was made by U.S. Glass Co. as No. 15059 and named CALIFORNIA; K 4-94-114 used Lee title; M 79-4 as BEADED GRAPE.

COLORADO. K 1-106-160 called it LACY MEDALLION; K 2-115 and 117 named it COLORADO; K 6, Pl. 94; B TS pp. 42-43; W 3rd Ant. p. 126.

CONNECTICUT. K 4-65-71; W 3rd Ant. p. 126.

DELAWARE. K 1-103-152; K 1 Pl. VI; and this book.

FLORIDA. K 1-46-61 called it EMERALD GREEN HERRINGBONE; K 6, Pl. 93 called it FLORIDA; L EAPG Pat. 230, pp. 536 and 638, Pl. 164, No. 1; M 87-4 called an almost identical pattern PANELLED HERRINGBONE; M II, Pl. 137-2 called it PRISM AND HERRINGBONE; and shown in this volume.

GEORGIA. K 1-77-105; L EAPG Pat. 250, pp. 565-66, Pl. 106 called it PEACOCK FEATHER; B TS p. 28.

IDAHO. B TS p. 44.

ILLINOIS. W 3rd Ant. p. 127.

INDIANA. K 4-105-130; L VG Pl. 39-3.

IOWA. No data available.

KANSAS. K 1-78-106; L EAPG Pat. 99, pp. 248-54, Pl. 75, called it JEWEL WITH DEWDROP; M 47-4, used Lee title.

KENTUCKY. L VG Pl. 39-4; K 4-68-76.

LOUISIANA. K 1-59-77; K 6 Pl. 93; B TS p. 44; M 92-4, where he called it GRANBY.

MAINE. K 4-86-103; L EAPG Pat. 166, pp. 422-23, Pl. 77-2, where she named it PANELLED FLOWER, STIPPLED; L VG Pl. 52-1, pp. 158-59, where she called it MAINE.

MARYLAND. Two very similar patterns have each been named MARYLAND by our authorities on pressed glass. On one, the large diamonds between the loops and fans were filled with diamond point. On the other they were left plain. The type with the diamond point has been covered as follows: K 1-60-73 MARYLAND; B TS p. 42 MARYLAND; L EAPG p. 628, Pl. 153-15 LOOP AND FAN; M 139-4 INVERTED LOOPS AND FANS; Mz EAPG No. 1746 LOOPS WITH FANS.

The type with plain diamonds was named as follows: L VG p. 105, Pl. 37-2 MARYLAND; and Mz EAPG p. 155 (not illustrated) MARYLAND.

The original catalog of the U.S. Glass Co., which I do not have, would be necessary to determine which type is MARYLAND.

MASSACHUSETTS. K 4-95-115; K 2-131 showed an oddity in pressed glass, a RUM JUG, and called the pattern CANE VARIANT; it is MASSACHUSETTS. M II, 59-3 called it ARCHED DIAMOND POINT, and in M II 131-4 called an apparently identical pattern GENEVA.

MICHIGAN. K 1-106-161; B TS p. 44; W 3rd Ant. p. 127; M II, 44-1, where he called it LOOP AND PILLAR.

MINNESOTA. K 8-51-99 and Pl. 107; W 3rd Ant. p. 129.

MISSISSIPPI. Have no data.

MISSOURI. K 2-113; B TS p. 42.

MONTANA. Have no data.

NEBRASKA. Have no data.

NEVADA. W 3rd Ant. p. 129.

NEW HAMPSHIRE. W 3rd Ant. p. 129; this book; M II, 86-3, where he called it MODISTE; K 3-97-148, where she called it BENT BUCKLE.

NEW JERSEY. W 3rd Ant. pp. 129-30; B TS pp. 42-43; M 165-3, where he called it RED LOOP AND FINE CUT.

NEW MEXICO. Admitted as a state after series completed.

NEW YORK. Have no data.

NORTH CAROLINA. K 2-28. It was named CAROLINA by the U.S. Glass Co. B TS p. 42.

NORTH DAKOTA. K 4-8-8 under the name DAKOTA given by the U.S. Glass Co.; L VG Pl. 67-1, p. 213; M II, 151-1 where he called it THUMBPRINT BAND, CLEAR; M II, 37-3 where he called it THUMBPRINT BAND, RED TOP; it is commonly known as BABY THUMBPRINT.

OHIO. K 5-33-34; L VG Pl. 31-1, pp. 104-105.

OKLAHOMA. Admitted as a state after series completed.

OREGON. K 8-18-30; K 3-87-130, where it is called BEADED LOOP; L EAPG Pat. 95, pp. 244-45, Pl. 76 where it is called BEADED LOOP; M 82-2 also calls it BEADED LOOP; See SKILTON in this book. It is not of this series.

PENNSYLVANIA. K 2-103; W 3rd Ant. p. 130.

RHODE ISLAND. Have no data. See M II 7-3, where he named a pattern RHODE ISLAND. Evidently not one of the "States" series.

SOUTH CAROLINA. K 2-28. It was named CAROLINA by the U.S. Glass Co.; B TS p. 42.

SOUTH DAKOTA. See under North Dakota.

TENNESSEE. K 3-62-86; M II, 5-2 where he called the pattern JEWELLED ROSETTES.

TEXAS. K 2-58; L VG Pl. 27-4, p. 74; W 3rd Ant. p. 131; B TS p. 42; M II, 44-4, where he called it LOOP WITH STIPPLED PANELS.

UTAH. W 3rd Ant. p. 131.

VERMONT. K 6-56-127 and Pl. 19; do not confuse with HONEYCOMB WITH FLOWER RIM.

VIRGINIA. This pattern was put out by the U.S. Glass Co. as their "No. 15,071." In 1907 they put out what was evidently a very similar pattern which they called MIRROR as their "No. 15,086." Mr. J. Stanley Brothers, Jr., wrote me that through an oversight the Mirror Plate was erroneously shown and labeled VIRGINIA on page 44 of his *Thumbnail Sketches.* K 3-89-133 shows the same MIRROR and calls it VIRGINIA. Millard calls it GALLOWAY. Warman shows an entirely different pattern as VIRGINIA. There is so much confusion about the pattern VIRGINIA, that only source material, not available to the writer, could untangle the "snafu."

WASHINGTON. W 3rd Ant. 132; and this book. Lee, Kamm, and Millard show a much earlier, flint pattern called WASHINGTON that is not of the series.

WEST VIRGINIA. See under VIRGINIA.

WISCONSIN. K 7-46-94; B TS p. 25; W 3rd Ant. p. 133; L EAPG Pat. 94, pp. 242-43, Pl. 57, upper right. She knew it was of the "States" series and named WISCONSIN but instead used its well-known name of BEADED DEWDROP; M 119-4 uses the title of BEADED DEWDROP.

WYOMING. K 2-49; B TS p. 28; M 140-4 where he named it ENIGMA.

THE STATES. K 5-143-188; and this book.

APPENDIX B
REPRODUCTIONS

Fakes and reproductions of early pressed glass are reprehensible, as they are for all antiques. Such practices are a menace and are employed so widely that everyone interested in antiquity should join in an effort to have the deceptions stopped. This can be done if our voices are raised loud and long enough to be heard by our legislatures. It might be said that the vogue of faking old pattern glass is no more prevalent than it is in paintings, furniture, ceramics, figurines, pewter, silver, early cut glass, or blown molded glass. Let any old article become scarce enough to command a high price, and the faker immediately steps in.

This subject is involved and complex and deserves much more attention than has yet been given it. Much research, study, and time will be necessary to cover the subject of American pressed glass reproductions alone. It is hoped some competent researcher will accept the challenge.

Reproductions are commented on throughout this volume. The subject presents many questions which I cannot answer. If an article was pressed in a mold in the 1880s and an identical one is pressed in the same old mold today, is the new one a fake or reproduction? Admittedly it is new and should be so marked in a manner that will not wash off. But is it a fake or a reproduction? Logical arguments can be made on both sides of the question.

The fact that the subject is not adequately covered here, does not mean the serious dealer and the purposeful collector have been completely neglected. On the contrary, there are excellent works available on the subject. Nevertheless, much more must be done before the reproduction racket is thoroughly canvassed. Three primary sources of information all glass students should have are listed in subsequent paragraphs.

Mrs. Ruth Webb Lee, over a period of many years, conducted a crusade against fakes and reproductions. She devoted a tremendous amount of time and a large sum of money to combat the evil. She even bought up old molds and destroyed them so new articles could not be struck from them. (See page 80 of the September, 1958, issue of *Hobbies, The Magazine for Collectors.*)

Mrs. Lee published *Antique Fakes and Reproductions.* Later she published *Supplementary Pamphlet No. 1* to the first volume. Throughout her *Early American Pressed Glass* and *Victorian Glass* she pointed out known articles then being reproduced in the pattern under discussion. Glass lovers should not deprive themselves of the pleasure of owning all her books. We mourn her untimely demise.

E. McCamly Belknap, in Chapter Ten of his *Milk Glass,* covered the subject of reproductions and thought it the most important chapter of his book. Every student of glass should read and reread the wealth of information it contains. Too late to be covered fully, he discovered that the John E. Kemple Glass Works, of East Palestine, Ohio, was actively making milk glass with old marks. The company possessed approximately 150 original pressed glass molds and could supply the demand. Most of the patterns used were originally made only in clear and not in milk glass. Their products were of superior quality. They refused to mark them as reproductions since they were pressed in the old molds. We all agree that their products are new, and most of us believe the ethical thing would be to permanently mark quality ware.

Mr. Belknap also devoted considerable space to the magnificent reproductions of the Westmoreland Glass Company of Grapeville, Pennsylvania. They used stickers on their products but stickers do not last long. Recently, however, I have seen a few of their pieces carrying a permanent trademark. They are proud of their fine handmade products and sell them only as reproductions. Every glass student should have a copy of their beautiful brochure entitled *Westmoreland Glass Company Handmade Reproductions of Choice Pieces of Early American Glass.*

The following is an alphabetical compilation of patterns in which some, or all, articles have been reproduced. Where prices are shown, they are taken from price lists of wholesalers who deal only in reproductions and sell only to dealers. The list is far from a comprehensive one, but it may help in keeping collectors from paying antique prices for new products.

ANCHOR AND YACHT, 7" milk-glass plate.

ANCIENT CASTLE, 7" milk-glass plate.

ANGEL, plates, milk-white, 8 1/2" in diameter, $2.25 each.

ANGEL AND HARP, 7" milk-glass plate.

ARCH BORDER LACY-EDGE, 9 1/2" bowl.

ARTICHOKE, frosted goblet, $2.50 each.

ASHBURTON, cordial, in early flint pattern.

ASHBURTON, square, footed cake stand, $4.00 each. Same as above in amber, $6.00 each. (Note that this is not the same as the early flint pattern.)

BABY FACE GOBLET? Probably not the same as the old.

BABY FACE, 10" ball lamp shades, milk glass or frosted, $4.40 each. (Not the old BABY FACE pattern.)

BABY FACE, matching fount shell for above, $3.85 each.

BABY FACE, milk white or frosted. Gone-with-the-wind lamps, electrified, $20.00 each. (Not the old pattern.)

BALL AND SWIRL, covered candy jar in milk glass. Also 18" round clear plate.

BALTIMORE PEAR, goblet $1.50 each; 9" plate $2.25 each; covered sugar bowl, $1.50 each; covered butter dish, $1.75 each; sugar and creamer, $3.00 set; 10" plate, $2.50 each; and 9" plate, $2.25. This is quite different from the original pattern.

BEADED GRAPE (CALIFORNIA), goblet in clear or emerald green, $2.00 each; 8" square plate, in clear or emerald green, $2.50 each; and 9" plate, $3.00 each.

BEADED EDGE, 10 1/2" round dinner plate in milk glass.

BEADED JEWEL or LACY DEWDROP, covered sugar bowl and covered butter dish, goblet, etc., in milk white. Most items being made in milk glass are pressed in the original 1880 molds.

BEEHIVE, square, covered honey dish, amber 6 1/2", $3.50 each.

BEEHIVE and old Lacy Sandwich, octagonal plate, now made in several sizes and in colors.

BENJAMIN FRANKLIN, from Sandwich original, cup plate.

BLACKBERRY milk white goblet. This is the early BLACKBERRY pattern. Clear creamer, goblet, water pitcher, and sugar bowl.

BLACKBERRY pitcher in milk glass. This is not the early BLACKBERRY, but made from old molds.

BROKEN COLUMN covered compote, 5" square, $2.50 each.

BUNKER HILL MONUMENT, Lacy cup plate.

BUTTERFLY, Lacy cup plate.

CABBAGE LEAF. I have no actual proof that fakes are being made in this pattern, but many pieces have shown up in recent years with a "new" look.

CABBAGE ROSE goblet, clear, $2.00 each.

CAMEL covered dish, blue milk glass, $3.00 each. White milk glass, $3.50 each.

CANE AND SPRIG, wines, in amberina, $1.50 each.

CAT 8" covered dish, milk white, lacy edged base, $7.50 each.

CHERRY clear goblet.

CHECKERBOARD, see under OLD QUILT.

CHICK eggcup, milk white, 50¢ each; 4" ash or pin tray in milk glass.

CHICKEN covered dishes in milk glass can be had in (1) Large hen, 6 1/2"; (2) Standing rooster, 9" high; (3) Medium hen; (4) Hen on Basket, 4 3/4" long; (5) Rooster, 5" long; (6) Small hen, 3" long; and (7) Toy chick, 2" long.

CHICK ON EGGS, 6 1/2" covered dish in milk glass.

CLUB, SHELL AND LOOP, 8" round plate in milk white.

COIN toothpick holder.

CONTRARY MULE, 7" milk-glass plate.

COW covered dish, milk glass, white, 7" base, $3.75 each.

CRYSTAL WEDDING goblet, $1.85 each; 5" square, covered compote, 10 1/2" tall, $2.75 each; covered compotes, 8" and 10" sizes, in milk glass; two sizes of covered compotes in clear with ruby trim.

CUPID AND PSYCHE, 7" milk-glass plate.

DAISY AND BUTTON vinegar cruet, blue, $4.50 each; tumbler in blue or amber, $1.75 each; pickle caster jar in blue or amber, silver plated top, 6 1/2" tall, $.75 each; 7" square clear plate, $1.00 each; the same plate made in blue, amber, vaseline, or green, $1.65 each; same in clear with ruby or amber daisies, $1.75 each; salt dips, $1.10 each; 4" baby shoe in blue, amethyst, or amber, $1.50 each; Gypsy Kettle mustard pot with ladle, blue, $2.25 each; Coal Scuttle in blue, green, or amberina, $1.00 each; 8" milk-white basket, $4.00 each; sauce dishes, 4" square in blue, amber, canary, or clear, $1.35 each; 10" round plates in canary, amber, blue, or clear, $2.50 each; butter pats in cobalt blue, clear, milk-glass, green, or camphor, 25¢ each; round, covered powder box in vaseline, 3", $1.00 each; High-Top Shoe, 4" tall, 4 1/2" long, in amber, blue, vaseline, amethyst, and milk glass, $1.50 each; Hat toothpick holder, 2 3/4" tall, in sapphire blue, cobalt blue, amber, vaseline, amethyst, amberina or blue milk glass, $1.00 each; 4 1/2" tall in blue or amber, $2.50 each; 6" tall, blue, $3.50 each; bow-tie slipper, 5", in blue or blue milk glass $1.00 each; slipper, 4", in blue, amber, vaseline, or amberina, $1.00 each; same in 2" size, 75¢ each.

DAISY AND BUTTON WITH NARCISSUS, wines in clear or emerald green, 75¢ each.

DAISY AND BUTTON WITH THUMBPRINT goblet in clear, blue, amber or vaseline, $1.75 each; same in amberina $2.25 each; stemmed wines in blue, amber, or vaseline, $1.50 each; sauce dishes in blue, amber, and vaseline, $1.50 each; cream pitchers, 5" tall, in blue or amber, $4.75 each; 7" round plates in blue, amber, or vaseline, $1.50 each; 10" round plates in blue, amber, or vaseline, $2.75 each; covered compote in blue or amber, 6" square, 9 1/2" tall, $7.75 each.

DAISY AND BAR goblet, emerald green, $2.25 each; same in clear, $2.00 each.

247

DAISY AND CUBE, miniature lamp, blue or milk-white glass, 9″ tall, not electrified, $4.50 each; goblet, moose etched, in clear, blue, or amber, $2.50 each; goblet, clear, plain, $1.50 each; same in emerald green, $2.00 each.

DEW AND RAINDROP, amber or ruby-top cordials, 75¢ each; goblets, clear, $1.50 each; wines, clear, 60¢ each; and sherbet cup.

DEWDROP AND STAR, salts, 50¢ each; and 7 1/2″ plate.

DIAMOND QUILTED goblets in blue, amber, and amethyst, $2.25 each.

DOLPHIN, covered dish, milk white, $3.00. (This is a Greentown pattern, usually found in caramel slag.)

DOLPHIN CANDLESTICKS, 9″ in black glass, and milk white.

DOLPHIN SHELL, 8″ compote in black glass. Also 8″ and 12″ compotes in white milk glass.

DORIC BORDER footed bowl, 7 1/2″ milk white, also 11″ plate; footed banana bowl; footed cake salver, 11″, with tripod stem and bell shaped bowl, 12″ wide.

DOUBLE HAND WITH GRAPES, 7 1/2″ card tray in milk glass.

DOVE milk glass, covered dish, 5 1/2″, $2.00 each; and 5″ individual salt in milk glass.

DUCK covered dish, milk white, 5″ split rib base, $2.00 each.

ENGLISH HOBNAIL, milk-white goblet; and many pieces in clear.

EASTER CHICK, 7″ square type, milk-glass plate.

FINE RIB goblet.

FLATTENED HOBNAIL tumblers in colors.

FLEUR-DE-LIS decorated, 7″ milk-glass plate with Watteau scene in colors; same plate without the decoration.

FORGET-ME-NOT triple bordered, 8 1/2″ plate in milk white.

FOX covered dish, milk white. $3.00 each.

FROSTED ARTICHOKE (see under ARTICHOKE).

FROSTED BLOCK, a pattern continued in production till at least 1958. It comes in clear, sassafras (pink), and apple green with white opalescence.

FROSTED CIRCLE, clear and frosted goblet.

FROSTED LION goblet, $1.50 each; 4″ sauce dish, 2 1/2″ tall, $1.50 each; eggcup, $1.50 each; and covered sugar bowl, spoonholder and celery vase.

FRUIT, made in white and blue milk glass, in goblets, sugar bowl, and cream pitcher.

GRAPE AND CHERRY, covered creamer and covered sugar bowl in milk glass.

GEORGE WASHINGTON Lacy cup plate.

GEORGE WASHINGTON 9″ milk-glass plate.

GREEN HERRINGBONE goblet, $2.50 each; and clear $2.00 each.

HAND pin tray, amethyst, blue, amber, vaseline or milk white, 4 1/2″, 75¢ each.

HAND VASE, 8″ tall, in milk glass.

HEART-shaped 8″ plate with heart border, lacy, in milk white.

HEAVY PANELLED GRAPE jelly compote, 3 3/4″ in diameter, clear, $2.75 each; same in amethyst or amber $3.50 each; small creamer, $1.50 each; milk-white goblet; sherbet or punch cup, $1.25 each; sauce dish, $1.25 each;

cordial, $1.25 each; lemonade tumbler, $1.25 each; tumbler, 75¢ each; wine, $1.25 each; parfait, $1.25 each; goblet, $1.25 each; water pitcher, $5.00 each; ale glass, celery vase, large creamer, salt, and covered sugar.

HEN covered dish, 7″ base, milk white, $2.75 each; same in blue milk glass, $3.75 each; same in 5″ size, milk white $2.00 each; blue milk glass, $2.75 each; and covered dish in amberina, amethyst, or amber, 7″ long, $6.75 each.

HENRY CLAY, a Sandwich variant, cup plate.

HERRINGBONE goblet, emerald green, $2.00 each.

HOBNAIL blue opalescent, and cranberry opalescent, 80 oz. water pitcher, $5.00 each; 9 oz. tumblers, $1.25; vinegar cruets green, or satin, $2.50; and sugar shaker, blue or amber, $3.00.

HOBNAIL covered sugar or candy jar, ruffled top, amberina, $3.50 each.

HOBNAIL goblet in amber or amethyst, $2.00 each; tumbler, blue or amber, 10-row hobnail, $1.75 each; and master salt, amethyst, 50¢ each.

HORN OF PLENTY tumbler, cordial, hat-bowls, and creamers. The last two were made from blanks pressed in the tumbler mold. They are flint.

HORSESHOE blown flask, "a perfect replica of Americana glass," with stopper, 10 1/2″ high, $4.50 each.

HUNDRED EYE goblet, in clear or nacre iridescent, with band of cranberry colored dots. Similar creamers can be had.

INDIAN HEAD (BEADED LOOP) 7″ milk-glass plate.

INVERTED THUMBPRINT tumbler, decorated with grape cutting and gold, in amethyst, ruby, blue, or green, $1.85 each; pickle caster with lid in cranberry, blue, amber, and green, $3.00 each; water pitcher, bulbous, cranberry, ruffled top, $8.50 each; tumbler in cranberry, blue, amber, amethyst, or green, straight sides, $1.75 each; candy jars, covered in cranberry, 6″ tall, $3.75 each; 7″ tall, $4.00 each; syrup pitcher, 5 1/4″ tall, cranberry, $3.75 each; wine, cranberry, barrel shape, $1.15 each; finger bowl in cranberry, $3.75 each; and tumblers, emerald green or amethyst, $2.00 each.

IVY IN SNOW, milk-white pitcher. Other articles in milk white are being produced in the old molds. Any milk-glass item is new. Some clear pieces have also been reproduced.

KINGFISHER toothpick holder, sapphire blue, $1.00 each.

KINGS CROWN goblet, $1.25 each; wines, 65¢ each (see under RUBY THUMBPRINT below for ruby version of these clear pieces); finger bowl, clear, $1.00 each; and 8 1/2″ plate, $1.00 each.

KITTEN covered dish, milk white, 5″, split-rib base, $2.00 each.

KNEELING HORSE covered dish, milk white, 5″, split-rib base, $2.00 each.

LACY DEWDROP (see under BEADED JEWEL).

LACY SANDWICH type decanter set, including 10 1/2″ decanter, 6 stemmed wines and glass tray, clear, $4.25 per set.

LATTICE EDGE milk-glass compote, 9 1/2″ in diameter, 7″ tall, $6.50 each; round bowl, 8 1/2″, milk white; 11 1/2″ flared open bowl; 11″ round plate; plate with handpainted wild turkey. (One of a set of 8 game plates such as bobwhite, grouse, snipe, woodcock, bluejay, redbird.)

LINCOLN milk-white plaque, 6 1/2" X 8" an "authentic copy of the original," $3.00 each.

LION milk-white or clear covered dish, 7" base, $3.75 each; clear butter dish; celery vase; creamer; eggcup, and goblet.

LION HEAD ball lamp shade, milk glass, 10", $4.40 each; matching fount shell, $3.85 each. (Not the FROSTED LION pattern.)

LOVE BIRDS 6 1/2" X 5 1/4" covered dish in milk glass.

MAPLE LEAF goblet in blue or amber, $2.00 each.

MAPLE LEAF tray in milk-white glass. Comes in 12", 9", and 6" sizes.

MARIGOLD WINDMILL milk pitchers in gold iridescence and in milk-white glass.

MILLEFIORI glass cruets with handcut polished stoppers, 7 1/2" tall, $8.50 each. (Not pressed glass.)

MOON AND STAR miniature lamps with matching umbrella shades, blue or amber, not electrified, 8 1/2" high, $4.50 each; salt and pepper shakers, $3.50 pair; covered compote, clear, 6" diameter, $5.00 each; same in amber glass, $6.25 each; covered butter dish, clear, $4.50 each; covered sugar bowl, clear, $4.25 each; cream pitcher, clear, $4.25 each; water pitcher, clear, $8.50 each; champagne goblet, flaring, clear, $1.75 each; goblet, clear, $1.75 each; tumbler, footed, $1.75 each; eggcup, $1.75 each; salt dips, clear or amber, $1.00 each; finger bowl, clear, $2.75 each; 10" plate, $2.75 each; sauce dish, clear, $1.50 each; and student lamp shade, 10", in blue or amber, $5.00. Amber lamps and shades are again on the market.

MOON AND STAR, VARIANT, made in milk glass, all of which is new, but made from old molds. Originally it was produced only in clear.

MOTHER EAGLE WITH YOUNG, 6" covered dish in milk glass.

NATIONAL 7" milk glass plate.

NEW ENGLAND PINEAPPLE clear goblet with both round knop stem, and faceted knop stem; and cordial.

NIAGARA FALLS 7" milk glass plate.

NOTCHED LACY EDGE oblong bowl, milk white, 8" X 5"; 8" bowl; and hen covered dish.

OPAL DOT cranberry covered butter dish, $5.25 each; sugar shaker, $3.00 each; vinegar cruet, $3.50 each; and cream pitcher in clear, 4" tall, $1.50 each. (Not pressed glass.)

OPAL HOBNAIL creamer, water pitcher, and tumbler.

OLD QUILT or CHECKERBOARD beverage jug and tumbler, 8 and 10 ounce, in milk glass; goblet; celery vase; covered butter; covered sugar bowl; 3 1/2" open sugar and matching small creamer; covered high footed square sweetmeat jar; and 5" square, covered, low compote.

OPEN SLEIGH 9" dish in milk glass; and matching candlesticks.

PANELLED DAISY clear goblet, $2.00 each.

PANELLED THISTLE goblet, clear, $1.35 each; 7" square plate, $1.75 each; 7" round plate, $1.50 each; 10" round plate, $2.25 each; salt dip, 50¢ each; goblet, $1.35 each; and goblet, flare top, $1.75 each.

PEACOCK covered creamer and covered sugar bowl in milk glass. Both come in iridescent colors also.

PILGRIM tumbler, in sapphire blue, lower half satin, $1.50 each.

PLEAT AND PANEL 7" square plate, $1.00 each; and goblet, $1.50 each.

PRISCILLA goblet, "an authentic copy of a lovely old pattern," $1.25 each.

PUMP AND TROUGH, sugar and creamer (not identical to one shown in this volume) in amber, blue, and green, $3.75 set.

PUSS IN BOOT slipper, in blue, amber, and blue milk glass, 5" long, $1.00 each.

RABBIT milk-white covered dish, 5", split rib base, $3.00 each.

RABBIT milk-white covered dish, 9", "from the original mold," $5.00 each.

RABBIT covered dish, 5" long, rectangular, in milk glass; same with eyes and ears pink.

RABBIT plate 7" milk white with clover and horseshoe border.

RAINDROP finger bowl in sapphire blue or ruby, $1.60 each.

RED BLOCK goblet, $2.25 each; same with blue or amber blocks, $2.25 each; and wine, red blocks, $2.00 each.

RIBBED compote with cover, 10" tall, in milk glass; and 6" high round, covered candy jar.

RIBBON goblet, clear and frosted.

RING AND PETAL milk white, square bowl, 11"; footed, 7" square bowl; 8" plate ; 10 1/2" salver, crimped edge; and 3 1/2" candlesticks.

ROBIN ON NEST blue milk glass, covered dish (reproduction of a French piece), $7.00 each.

ROMAN ROSETTE goblet, $1.50 each.

ROSE IN SNOW, round, goblets in clear, blue, amber, or vaseline, $1.50 each; plates in same colors, $1.75 each.

RUBY THUMBPRINT goblet, $1.50 each, or $15.00 per dozen; wines, 75- each; finger bowl, $1.50 each; 8 1/2" plate, $1.75 each. (See under KINGS CROWN above for clear version of these pieces.)

SANDWICH GLASS (pattern undetermined), covered butter dish, 6", emerald green, $3.00 each.

S BORDER game bird plates, assorted, 6 birds, $1.25 each; plates 8 1/2" square, milk white, $2.75 each.

SANDWICH 1831 EAGLE lacy cup plate.

SCROLL AND EYE bordered, 10" round plate in milk glass.

SHELL 6" nappie, three feet, milk glass.

SHELL AND TASSEL goblet, clear, round, $1.75 each.

SHELL AND JEWEL or VICTOR. Was first produced in 1893 by Westmoreland Glass Company and has never been discontinued. Iridized pieces of recent ware frequently appear.

SHELL LACY EDGE DISH, 7" long by 5" wide, in milk glass.

SPOKE AND RIM 10" round plate in milk glass.

SPOT RESIST art glass, 70 oz. ice water pitcher in cranberry color, $5.50 each each; 12 oz. lemonade or ice tea size tumbler, $1.50 each; vinegar cruet, clear, $2.75 each; same in blue or amber, $3.25 each. (Not pressed glass.)

SPANISH LACE (fern) tumbler in cranberry color, $2.00 each. (Not pressed glass.)

SPRIG AND CANE, square plate in clear and colors. See write-up of pattern in this book.

SQUARE PEG 8″ square plate in milk glass; and comes in black glass.

SQUARE 'S' border, 8 1/2″ plate in milk glass. (Also in black glass.)

S REPEAT amber toothpick holders, $1.65 each.

STAR WITH DEWDROP 7 1/4″ clear plate.

STIPPLED HEART Lacy cup plate.

SWAN covered creamer and covered sugar bowl with swan finial, in milk glass.

SWAN with raised wings, covered dish, 5 1/2″ X 10″, in milk glass.

THE WEDDING DAY lacy cup plate.

THREE BEARS 7″ milk glass plate.

THREE FACE covered compote, $6.00 each; goblets, $3.75 each; champagnes, $3.75 each; lamp, $9.50 each; and salt and pepper shakers, $4.00 pair.

THREE KITTENS looped border, 7″ milk-glass plate.

THREE OWLS, looped border, 7″ milk-glass plate.

THOUSAND EYE, tumbler in clear, amber, or amberina, $2.00 each; goblets in clear, amber, or apple green, $1.75 each; 8″ square plate in clear, blue, vaseline, or amber, $2.50 each; cruet in amberina, $3.50 each; same in amber, $3.00 each; lamps, No. 2, amber base and blue fount or vice versa, $12.50 each; also available in clear in complete table service, including 6″, 7″, 8 1/2″, 10″, 14″ and 18″ round plates.

TOP bordered, 8″ round plate in milk white.

TULIP cordial, flint.

TURKEY McKee-type covered dish, milk white, 5″, split-rib base, $2.00 each.

TURTLE covered dish, 8″ long, in amber $5.00 each.

TWO-PANEL goblet in clear, blue or amber, $1.85 each.

VALENTINE Lacy type cup plate.

VICTOR. (See under SHELL AND JEWEL.)

WESTWARD HO! low, oval, covered compote, $10.00 each; small lamp made from new goblet mold; and goblets, $1.50 each.

WICKET EDGE 9″ round plate in milk white.

WILDFLOWER tumbler, clear or apple green, $2.00 each; covered compote, 6″ wide by 9″ tall in blue, amber, or clear, $6.50 each; footed sauce dish in clear, or blue, $1.75 each; goblet, clear, $1.75 each; goblets in blue, vaseline, or apple green, $2.00 each 10″ square plates in blue, amber, or vaseline, $2.50 each; and wines, stemmed in blue or amber, $2.00 each.

With such an array of reproduced items, one may conclude that all pressed glass must be fakes. Remember, however, three important facts, as follows:

1. Fewer than 20 patterns have been reproduced in most items.

2. Fewer than 200 patterns have one or two items reproduced. These items are usually tumblers, goblets, plates, sauces, egg cups, etc., where a collector will want 4, 6, 8, or even 12 pieces. Creamers, water pitchers, etc., are seldom faked.

3. American glass factories produced between 3,000 and 3,500 patterns. In some of these as many as 165 items were manufactured, though most patterns were made with about 40 items. Subtract the above reproductions from the number of patterns made and we have from 2,800 to 3,300 patterns that have never been reproduced.

APPENDIX C
NAMING PATTERNS OF PRESSED GLASS

A descriptive name for a pattern in glass is generally most suitable. The exception comes when the descriptive title becomes too long or cumbersome, or has been preempted by another pattern.

In naming unlisted patterns in this book, short titles have been used almost exclusively.

Numerals in titles have been avoided because they have little significance and are difficult to remember. A few have been used in the past which are excellent as well as descriptive. Some of them are: EIGHT O EIGHT (808), ONE O ONE (101), and PANELLED 44. On the other hand, such titles as: NEAR CUT NO. 2692; JEFFERSON NO. 271; HEISEY'S NO. 343½; NU-CUT NO. 2508; FOSTORIA'S NO. 1231; DOYLE'S NO. 76; and U.S. NO. 304 are far too difficult for my feeble, recollective mechanism to master.

One of our authors on pressed glass used the old, original company title when it could be ascertained. This had both good and bad points. Unfortunately, the old company titles were advertised only in trade magazines or in catalogues which went to dealers. The original company titles did not

become known to the general public, so the people assigned their own names to patterns and these titles became widely accepted. Usually these titles were preferable to the originals.

A second author had an aversion to the type of nomenclature used by still a third writer. The latter used the word *variant* in many titles, for instance: DAISY AND BUTTON, VARIANT. There were ten or twelve variations of DAISY AND BUTTON. Therefore, if the word *variant* was appended, which one of the ten or twelve was meant? In an effort to correct the confusing situation he adopted a system of giving an individual name to each variant. As far as possible only descriptive titles were used, and some of these were inordinately long, as pointed out below. Where found inappropriate to use a descriptive title, he named patterns for persons who had assisted him in the work of assembling patterns, using their cognomen. This gave us one-word names that are most acceptable.

Short titles are economical. The late Myrtle G. Burger, a dealer of Washington, Missouri, recently wrote me and requested that only short titles be used in naming patterns in my book because of the cost of advertising an article. At 10-per word, a one-word title would cost 10- to advertise, whereas, a four-word name would cost 40-. Carrying this thought along, let us consider a ridiculous, but not impossible, example. As a mail-order dealer you have a collection of twenty-nine pattern glass sauce dishes to sell through advertising at 10- per word. The twenty-nine sauces are in these patterns: STAR IN BULL'S EYE, PURPLE TOP; BELLFLOWER, FINE RIB, FLARE TOP, PLAIN BASE; PRISM AND BLOCK BAND, RED TOP; DAISY AND BUTTON, RED TOP AND DOTS; FESTOON AND GRAPE, SMALL AMERICAN SHIELD; DAISY AND BUTTON WITH CROSS BAR; FERNS AND LILY OF THE VALLEY; DAISY AND BUTTON WITH "V" ORNAMENT; LOOP AND BLOCK WITH WAFFLE BAND; SERRATED BLOCK AND LOOP, RED TOP; DAISY AND BUTTON WITH SCROLL PANEL; DAISY AND BUTTON WITH AMBER STRIPES; BELLFLOWER, FINE RIB, KNOP STEM, BARREL SHAPE; DAISY AND BUTTON WITH OVAL PANELS; DEER AND DOE WITH LILY OF THE VALLEY; LOOP AND DART WITH DIAMOND ORNAMENTS; LOOP AND DART WITH ROUND ORNAMENTS; STIPPLED GRAPE AND FESTOON, STIPPLED LEAF; PRISM AND DIAMOND POINT, PLAIN STEM; PRISM AND DIAMOND POINT, ROUND STEM; BEADED GRAPE MEDALLION, DESIGN ON FOOT; DAISY AND BUTTON WITH CROSS BAR AND THUMBPRINT BAND; DAISY AND BUTTON WITH ALMOND BAND; PANELLED DAISY AND BUTTON WITH FLAT STEM; MAGNET AND GRAPE, FROSTED, TENDRILS ON GRAPE BRANCH; FESTOON AND GRAPE WITH VEINED LEAVES; DAISY AND BUTTON WITH CLEAR LILY; BULL'S EYE, KNOP STEM NEAR FOOT; and DAISY AND BUTTON WITH BLACK BAND.

On your first ad you sell fifteen sauce dishes. Two months later you advertise the remaining fourteen and sell eight of them. Eight purchasers failed, by a few cents, to include enough to cover postage. What was your net profit? We admit that a short descriptive title such as WAFFLE, THUMBPRINT, SAWTOOTH, FESTOON, HARP, PRISM, or ROSETTE is preferable. Regrettably, very few patterns are susceptible to such short and easy names. Since a descriptive title can become burdensome when too long, we have resorted in this book to using one- and two-word titles. That poses a question. Would any of the following patterns have been more widely known or recognized if their titles had been descriptive? ASHBURTON, BIGLER, HUBER, CROESUS, SAXON, HIDALGO, EXCELSIOR, EUGENIE, EUREKA, CRYSTAL, COLONIAL, ARGUS, VICTORIA, PILLAR, and HAMILTON. I doubt it.

Many patterns have multiple titles. In some cases it becomes confusing. Patterns are often purely decorative, and to call them one flower or another merely adds to the confusion. Take an example. Northwood produced a pattern with bark, burrs and lanceolate leaves. The only oak with a similar leaf is the live oak, but its acorns do not resemble the burrs on this pattern. Even the overcup oak does not have such an acorn. Yet this pattern has been assigned the following titles: NORTHWOOD'S ACORN BURRS, ACORN BURRS AND BARK, NORTHWOOD ACORN BURRS AND BARK, CHESTNUT BURRS, and HORSE CHESTNUT. Any short title would have been preferable.

APPENDIX D
PATTERNS OF THE U.S. GLASS COMPANY

The United States Glass Company of Pittsburgh, Pennsylvania, adopted a number series starting at 15,001 and continued it through 15,099. They are listed numerically below, along with the title, if known. Several of the glass factories that combined to form the U.S. Glass Company had their own number series and continued to use them during the same time that the 15,000 series was being produced.

No. 15,001 RUBY STAR K2-52; O'HARA DIAMOND K5-46-51 and in this volume; and SAWTOOTH AND STAR L. VG Plate 47-1.

No. 15,002 FLUTED RIBBON K3-95-143; NAIL K6, Plate 7.

No. 15,003 PLEATING K8-60-117, Plate 72; FLAT PANEL Lee's VG Plate 51-1.

No. 15,004 BARRED OVAL Lee's VG Plate 41-4.

No. 15,005 COIN K7, Plates 3, 4, 5 and 6; K8, Plates 58 and 59.

No. 15,006 POINTED JEWEL K1-97-137 and K6, Plate 1.

No. 15,007 FROSTED CIRCLE K4-19-22.

No. 15,008 RUFFLES K6-42-98 and Plate 36.

No. 15,009 FLEUR-DE-LIS AND TASSEL K3-50-68.

No. 15,010 BRICE Lee's VG page 87; K1-32-39.

No. 15,011 ALL-OVER DIAMOND K3-134-195; WESTMORELAND K1-117-188; and DIAMOND BLOCK Lee's VG Plate 66-2.

No. 15,012 FOUR THUMBPRINTS K5-57-66.

No. 15,013 U.S. THUMBPRINT K5-5-4.

No. 15,014

No. 15,015

No. 15,016 FAN AND FLUTE K8-63-122 and Plate 84; BUCKINGHAM K6-33-60 and Plate 33; and MILLARD Lee's VG Plate 42-2.

No. 15,017

No. 15,018 DIVIDED BLOCK WITH SUNBURST, VARIANT K2-73; DIAMOND AND SUNBURST VARIANT K3-84-125; also K6, Plate 30.

No. 15,019 This may possibly be PALM BEACH Lee's VG Page 178.

No. 15,020 BLOCKED ARCHES K6-25-37 and Plate 32; and BERKELEY Lee's VG Plate 45-4.

No. 15,021 NOTCHED RIB K3-94; BROKEN COLUMN K4-116-148; BROKEN COLUMN Lee's VG Plate 71-3.

No. 15,022 PANEL AND FLUTE Lee's VG page 98; and FLUTED RIBBON EAPG page 226.

No. 15,023 PRISM COLUMN K6-15-19, Plate 31.

No. 15,024 DOUBLE ARCH K5-73-96; and K6, Plate 31.

No. 15,025 DIAMOND WAFFLE K3-60-83; U.S. DIAMOND BLOCK K4-49-55; and PATRICIA Lee's VG Plate 58-1.

No. 15,026 SCALLOPED SWIRL K6-26-38, Plate 32; and YORK HERRINGBONE M II-141-3.

No. 15,027

No. 15,028 LOOP WITH DEWDROP K1-72-99 and K6, Plate 29; LOOP WITH DEWDROPS M 89-4; LOOPS WITH DEWDROPS Lee's EAPG Pattern 100, page 255, Plate 79.

No. 15,029 INDIANA K4-105-130; and Lee's VG 39-3.

No. 15,030 ROMAN ROSETTE Lee's EAPG page 499; and ROMAN ROSETTE B TS page 24.

No. 15,031 SUPERIOR K3-78-114.

No. 15,032 TEARDROP AND THUMBPRINT K3-23-30.

No. 15,033

No. 15,034 LEAFY SCROLL K4-90-109 and K6-36-75, Plate 59.

No. 15,035

No. 15,036

No. 15,037

No. 15,038 ELECTRIC K3-78-113.

No. 15,039

No. 15,040 U.S. NO. 15,040 K4-90-106.

No. 15,041 PINEAPPLE AND FAN K3-79-116; and CUBE WITH FAN Lee's VG Plate 44-1.

No. 15,042 ZIPPERED SWIRL AND DIAMOND K6-33-59 and Plate 33.

No. 15,043

No. 15,044 STIPPLED BAR Lee's VG Plate 63-2.

No. 15,045 U.S. NO. 15,045 K4-65-70; and BLOSSOM Lee's VG page 115, Plate 46-3.

No. 15,046 FLORAL DIAMOND K4-71-80; and this book.

No. 15,047 U.S. COLONIAL K3-51-71; and COLONIAL K4-33-38.

No. 15,048

No. 15,049 MARYLAND K1-60-78; and MARYLAND Lee's VG page 105, Plate 37-2.

No. 15,050

No. 15,051 KENTUCKY K4-68-76.

No. 15,052

No. 15,053 LOUISIANA K1-59-77; GRANBY M 92-4.

No. 15,054 CANE VARIANT K2-131 Rum Jug; MASSACHU-SETTS K4-95-115.

No. 15,055 MINNESOTA K8-51-99, Plate 107.

No. 15,056

No. 15,057

No. 15,058

No. 15,059 CALIFORNIA: BEADED GRAPE, EAPG 208, Pattern 75, Plate 63, originally named CALIFORNIA.

No. 15,060 VERMONT K6-56-127, Plate 19.

No. 15,061

No. 15,062

No. 15,063 BOHEMIAN K6-34-68, Plate 59.

No. 15,064 TENNESSEE K3-62-86.

No. 15,065 DELAWARE K1-103-152, Plate VI.

No. 15,066 MAINE K4-86-103; MAINE Lee's VG Plate 52-1; and MAINE Lee's EAPG Pattern 166.

No. 15,067

No. 15,068 CONNECTICUT K4-65-71; and JEWELED ROSETTES M II 5-2.

No. 15,069

No. 15,070

No. 15,071 VIRGINIA K3-89-133; MAIDEN'S BLUSH Lee's VG page 100; GALLOWAY M 7-1.

No. 15,072

No. 15,073 OREGON K8-18-30; BEADED LOOP K3-87-130; and BEADED LOOP Lee's EAPG Pattern 95.

No. 15,074 WASHINGTON K6-44-100 where it was briefly mentioned; and WASHINGTON W 3rd Ant. 132.

No. 15,075

No. 15,076

No. 15,077

No. 15,078 MANHATTAN K6-44-100.

No. 15,079 WISCONSIN K7-46-94; WISCONSIN B TS page 25; and BEADED LOOP Lee's EAPG Pattern 94; M 119-4.

No. 15,080

No. 15,081 WYOMING K2-50; B TS page 28; and ENIGMA M140-4.

No. 15,082 COLUMBIA K3-107-161; CHURCH WINDOWS K6, Plate 28.

No. 15,083 CAROLINA K2-28 and K5-5-4-13; and B TS page 42.

No. 15,084

No. 15,085

No. 15,086

No. 15,087

No. 15,088 PANAMA K2-49.

No. 15,089

No. 15,090

No. 15,091

No. 15,092

No. 15,093 THE STATES K5-142-188, Plate 25; and also this volume.

No. 15,094

No. 15,095

No. 15,096

No. 15,097

No. 15,098 U.S. REGAL K6-51-120 (of 1906), Plate 55.

No. 15,099

Other patterns known to have been made by the United States Glass Company are listed below. Some of them may have had numbers between 15,001 and 15,099 and indeed, may fit into the "States" series:

Patterns shown in Ruth Webb Lee's *Victorian Glass*: LOOP AND FAN, page 67; ATLAS, page 72; COMPACT, page 136; BULL'S EYE, VARIANT, page 139; SCROLL AND FLOWER, page 141; CUBE AND DIAMOND, page 142; TRILBY, page 169; PAVONIA, page 169; CRYSTALINA, page 169; TRIPLE TRIANGLE, page 174; FLEUR-DE-LIS AND DRAPE, page 187; BLOCK AND PANEL, page 190; DEWDROP AND FAN, page 196; PITTSBURGH, page 197; ROSETTE MEDALLION, page 205; TEARDROP, page 223; CLIMAX, page 226.

Patterns shown in Ruth Webb Lee's *Early American Pressed Glass*: FLATTENED SAWTOOTH, page 138; WISCONSIN, page 242; BEADED LOOP, page 244; LOOP

WITH DEWDROP, page 255; BLEEDING HEART, page 399; RED BLOCK, page 542; RUBY THUMBPRINT, page 542; LOOP AND FAN, page 628; TRILBY, page 639; KNIGHTS OF LABOR, page 633.

Patterns shown in the pitcher books of Minnie Watson Kamm: MASCOTTE, K1-18-19; LATE CRYSTAL, K1-19-20; BALTIMORE PEAR, K1-30-36; RIBBON CANDY, K1-32-39; ROMAN ROSETTE, K1-34-41; WILDFLOWER, K1-36-45; FLUTED DIAMOND POINT, K 1-37-46; COTTAGE, K1-38-47; WHEAT AND BARLEY, K1-41-53; FISHSCALE, K1-58-74; STAR IN DIAMOND, K1-62-83; HOBNAIL, THUMBPRINT BASE, K1-70-96; LATE JACOB'S LADDER, K1-98-139; CORDOVA, K1-105-157; WAFFLE, VARIANT, K1-118-189; LATE BLOCK, K1-118-190; ATLAS, K2-15; MITRED BARS, K2-33; FEATHER DUSTER, K2-42; EAR OF CORN, K2-62; SNAIL, K2-69; NAIL, K2-87; ROANOKE, K2-99; GIANT BULL'S EYE, K2-101; WHIRLIGIG, K2-103;

SNOWFLAKE, K2-104; ETCHED GRAPE, K2-122; ADAM'S SAXON, K3-8-7; LITTLE BALLS, K3-44-58; BROKEN BANDS, K3-48-65; NURSERY TALES, K3-63-87; U.S. COMET, K3-82-121; U.S. NO. 84, K3-91-137; OPTIC, K4-97-118; CLOVER, K4-98-119; CHURCH WINDOWS, K4-115-146; PAVONIA, K4-142-192; DUNCAN FLUTE, K5-30-29; KING'S NO. 500, K5-71-93; PARROT PITCHER, K5-71-93A; CRYSTAL ROCK, K5-96-130; U.S. SHERATON, K5-100-135; GRIDLEY PITCHER, K5-135-176; 45 COLONIS, K5-146-192; U.S. REGAL, K6-51-120; COMET, K7-9-14; U.S. RIB, K7-42-85; FILLEY, K7-72-143; U.S. NO. 304, K8-14-24; DOYLE'S SHELL, K8-20-35; DOYLE'S NO. 76, K8-36-64; RAINDROP, K8-47-90; DOYLE'S NO. 90, K8-48-91.

Patterns shown by J. Stanley Brothers in *Thumbnail Sketches*: RUBY THUMBPRINT, page 23; COLONIAL, page 44; ROANOKE, page 44.

APPENDIX E

GLASS COMPANIES IN AMERICA, 1888-1904

During 1888, 1889, and 1890 all American glass factories were experiencing financial difficulty. In 1891, eighteen of the better known ones joined together to form a huge combine and called it the United States Glass Company, with headquarters in Pittsburgh, Pennsylvania. The companies that joined were:

1 Adams and Company, Pittsburgh
2 Bryce Brothers, Pittsburgh
3 Challinor, Taylor and Company, Tarentum, Pa.
4 George Duncan and Sons, Pittsburgh
5 Richards and Hartley Flint Glass Company, Tarentum, Pa.
6 Ripley and Company, Pittsburgh
7 Gillinder and Sons, Greensburg, Pa.
8 Hobbs Glass Company, Wheeling, W.Va.
9 Columbia Glass Company, Findlay, Ohio.
10 King Glass Company, Pittsburgh
11 O'Hara Glass Company, Pittsburgh
12 Bellaire Goblet Company, Findlay, Ohio
13 Nickel Plate Glass Company, Fostoria, Ohio
14 Central Glass Company, Wheeling, W.Va.
15 Doyle and Company, Pittsburgh
16 A. J. Beatty and Sons, Tiffin, Ohio
17 A. J. Beatty and Sons, Steubenville, Ohio
18 Novelty Glass Company, Fostoria, Ohio

The U.S. Glass Co. remained in production until about 1907, when it ceased advertising. Some of the member companies disbanded; others combined, and some continued making glass.

Times became so difficult financially by 1898 that some move had to be made to avert disaster. Twenty large glass factories combined to form the National Glass Company, Pittsburgh. They immediately shut down some factories, and by 1902 only twelve of the original twenty remained. Some with-

drew and resumed the making of glass as a private concern. By 1903 the National Glass Company through mismanagement, supplanting experienced glassmen with outside managers, poor investments in ideas, was in trouble again. They reorganized with a new bond issue. Then natural gas played out in Indiana. In 1904 three plants were destroyed by fire and three were dismantled. None were rebuilt. By the end of 1904 the remaining plants were idle.

Firms that originally joined the National Glass Company were:

1 Beatty-Brady Glass Works, Dunkirk, Ind.
2 Canton Glass Company, Canton, Ohio, and Marion, Ind.
3 Carter Glass Works, Marion, Ind.
4 Central Glass Company, Summitsville, Indiana (formerly of Wheeling, W.Va.)
5 Crystal Glass Company, Bridgeport, Ohio
6 Cumberland Glass Works, Cumberland, Ind.
7 Dalzell, Gilmore and Leighton Company, Findlay, Ohio
8 Fairmont Glass Company, Fairmont, W.Va.
9 Greensburg Glass Company, Greensburg, Pa.
10 Indiana Tumbler and Goblet Company, Greentown, Ind.
11 Keystone Tumbler Works, Rochester, Pa.
12 Model Flint Glass Company, Findlay, Ohio
13 McKee and Brothers, Pittsburgh
14 Northwood Glass Company, Indiana, Pa.
15 Ohio Flint Glass Company, Lancaster, Ohio
16 Riverside Glass Works, Wellsburg, W.Va.
17 Robinson Glass Works, Zanesville, Ohio
18 Rochester Tumbler Company, Rochester, Pa.
19 Royal Glass Works, Marietta, Ohio
20 West Virginia Glass Company, Martins Ferry, Ohio

BIBLIOGRAPHY

BARBOUR, HARRIOT BUXTON. *Sandwich: The Town That Glass Built.* Boston: Houghton Mifflin Company, 1st Edition, 1948.

BELKNAP, McCALMY. *Milk Glass.* New York: Crown Publishers, 1949.

BROTHERS, J. STANLEY, JR. *Thumbnail Sketches.* Kalamazoo, Mich.: J. Stanley Brothers, Inc., Publications, 1940.

HARTUNG, MARION T. *Carnival Glass: One Hundred Patterns.* Salisbury, N.C.: Published by the Author, 1st Edition, 1960.

HARTUNG, MARION T. *Second Book of Carnival Glass.* Salisbury, N.C.: Published by the Author, 1st Edition, 1961.

HARTUNG, MARION T. *Third Book of Carnival Glass.* Emporia, Kan.: Published by the Author, 1st Edition, 1962.

HERRICK, RUTH, M.D. *Greentown Glass: The Indiana Tumbler and Goblet Company and Allied Manufacturers.* Grand Rapids, Mich.: Published by the Author, 1959.

HOUSE, COURTMAN G. *Relative Values of Early American Patterned Glass.* Medina, N.Y.: Published by the Author, Fourth Edition, 1944.

HUNTER, FREDERICK WILLIAM. *Stiegel Glass.* New York: Dover Publications, 1950.

JEFFERSON, JOSEPHINE. *Wheeling Glass.* Mount Vernon, Ohio: The Guide Publishing Company, 1st Edition, 1947.

KAMM, MINNIE WATSON. *Two Hundred Pattern Glass Pitchers.* Detroit, Mich.: Motschall Company, Fourth Edition, 1946.

KAMM, MINNIE WATSON. *A Second Two Hundred Pattern Glass Pitchers.* Detroit, Mich.: Motschall Company, Second Edition, 1946.

KAMM, MINNIE WATSON. *A Third Two Hundred Pattern Glass Pitchers.* Detroit, Mich.: Motschall Company, Second Edition, 1946.

KAMM, MINNIE WATSON. *A Fourth Pitcher Book.* Detroit, Mich.: Motschall Company, First Edition, 1946.

KAMM, MINNIE WATSON. *A Fifth Pitcher Book.* Detroit, Mich.: Motschall Company, First Edition, 1948.

KAMM, MINNIE WATSON. *A Sixth Pitcher Book.* Detroit, Mich.: Motschall Company, First Edition, 1949.

KAMM, MINNIE WATSON. *A Seventh Pitcher Book.* Detroit, Mich.: Motschall Company, First Edition, 1953.

KAMM, MINNIE WATSON. *An Eighth Pitcher Book.* Detroit, Mich.: Motschall Company, First Edition, 1954.

KNITTLE, RHEA MANSFIELD. *Early American Glass.* Garden City, N.Y.: Garden City Publishing Company, Inc., Reprint Edition, 1948.

LEE, RUTH WEBB. *Victorian Glass.* Northboro, Mass.: Published by the author, printed by the Ferris Printing Company, New York, Ninth Edition, 1944.

LEE, RUTH WEBB. *Early American Pressed Glass.* Enlarged and Revised. Northboro, Mass.: Published by the Author, Printed by the Ferris Printing Company, New York, Twenty-fifth Edition, 1946.

LEE, RUTH WEBB. *Sandwich Glass: The History of the Boston and Sandwich Glass Company.* Northborough, Mass.: Published by the author, Revised and Enlarged, The Ferris Printing Company, Sixth Edition, New York, 1947.

LEWIS, J. SIDNEY. *Old Glass and How to Collect It.* London: T. Werner Lourie, Ltd. (No Date Given).

LINDSEY, BESSIE M. *Lore of Our Land Pictured in Glass, Volume I.* Forsyth, Ill.: Published by the author, printed by Wagoner Printing Company, Galesburg, Ill., 1950.

LINDSEY, BESSIE M. *Lore of Our Land Pictured in Glass, Volume II.* Forsyth, Ill.: Published by the author, printed by Wagoner Printing Company, Galesburg, Ill., 1950.

LOGAN, HARLAN. *How Much Do You Know About Glass.* New York: Dodd, Mead & Company, 1951.

MARSH, TRACY H. *The American Story Recorded in Glass.* Published by the author, printed by Lund Press, Inc., Minneapolis, Minn., 1962.

McKEARIN, GEORGE S. AND HELEN. *American Glass.* New York: Crown Publishers, 7th Printing, 1946.

McKEARIN, HELEN A. *Early American Glass: The Collection of Alfred B. McClay.* New York: Anderson Galleries, Inc., Catalogue No. 4211, 1935.

METZ, ALICE HULETT. *Early American Pattern Glass.* Westfield, N.Y.: The Guide Publishing Company, March, 1958.

METZ, ALICE HULETT. *Much More Early American Pattern Glass.* Published by the author, printed by Spencer-Walker Press, Columbus, Ohio, 1965.

MILLARD, S. T. *Goblets.* Topeka, Kan.: The Central Press, Fifth Edition, 1947.

MILLARD, S. T. *Goblets II.* Holton, Kan.: Gossip Printers and Publishers, Second Edition, 1940.

MOORE, N. HUDSON. *Old Glass, European and American.* New York: Tudor Publishing Company, 1924.

NORTHEND, MARY HARROD. *American Glass.* New York: Tudor Publishing Company, Reprinted, 1947.

PETERSEN, ARTHUR G. *Salt and Salt Shakers.* Washington, D.C. : Washington College Press, 1960.

PETERSEN, ARTHUR G. *333 Glass Salt Shakers.* Takoma Park, Md.: Washington College Press, 1965.

PETERSEN, ARTHUR G. *400 Trademarks on Glass.* Takoma Park, Md.: Washington College Press, 1968.

PETERSEN, ARTHUR G. *Glass Patents and Patterns.* Sanford, Fla,: Celery City Printing Company, 1973.

PARKE-BERNET GALLERIES, INC. *Early American Glass Oriental Lowestaft: English Lusterware, The Superb Collection Formed by Mrs. Frederick S. Fish.* New York: Catalogue 159, 1940.

PARKE-BERNET GALLERIES, INC. *Early American Glass: The Renowned Private Collection of the Late Frederick K. Gaston.* New York: Catalogue 187, 1940.

PARKE-BERNET GALLERIES, INC. *Early American Glass: The Magnificent Collection Formed by the Late William T. H. Howe.* New York: Catalogue 227, 1940.

PARKE-BERNET GALLERIES, INC. *Early American Glass: The Magnificent Collection Formed by the Late William T. H. Howe*. New York: Part Two, Catalogue 273, 1941.

REVI, ALBERT CHRISTIAN. *Nineteenth Century Glass: Its Genesis and Development*. Edinburgh-New York-Toronto: Thomas Nelson and Sons, 1959.

REVI, ALBERT CHRISTIAN. *American Pressed Glass and Figure Bottles*. London-New York-Toronto: Thomas Nelson and Sons, 1964.

ROSE, JAMES H. *The Story of American Pressed Glass of the Lacy Period, 1825-1850*. Corning, N.Y.: The Corning Museum of Glass, Corning Glass Center, 1954.

WATKINS, LAURA WOODSIDE. *American Glass and Glassmaking*. New York: Chanticleer Press, 1950.

INDEX

Numbers in parentheses refer to the pattern number.
Italicized numbers refer to the page number of the illustration.

DATE DUE